The Great Refusal

The Great Refusal

Herbert Marcuse
and Contemporary Social Movements

Edited by Andrew T. Lamas, Todd Wolfson,
and Peter N. Funke

Foreword by Angela Y. Davis

TEMPLE UNIVERSITY PRESS
Philadelphia • *Rome* • *Tokyo*

TEMPLE UNIVERSITY PRESS
Philadelphia, Pennsylvania 19122
www.temple.edu/tempress

Library of Congress Cataloging-in-Publication Data

Names: Lamas, Andrew T. , 1954– editor.
Title: The great refusal : Herbert Marcuse and contemporary social
    movements / with a foreword by Angela Y. Davis ; edited by Andrew T.
    Lamas, Todd Wolfson, and Peter N. Funke.
Description: Philadelphia : Temple University Press, 2016. | Includes
    bibliographical references and index.
Identifiers: LCCN 2016022607| ISBN 9781439913031 (cloth : alk. paper) |
    ISBN 9781439913048 (paper : alk. paper) | ISBN 9781439913055 (ebk)
Subjects: LCSH: Marcuse, Herbert, 1898–1979. | Social movements—
    History—21st century.
Classification: LCC B945.M2984 G74 2016 | DDC 303.48/4—dc23
    LC record available at https://lccn.loc.gov/2016022607

Printed in the United States of America

9 8 7 6 5 4 3 2 1

Contents

Foreword: Abolition and Refusal • *Angela Y. Davis*   *vii*

Acknowledgments   *xiii*

1 Bouazizi's Refusal and Ours: Critical Reflections on the
   Great Refusal and Contemporary Social Movements
   • *Peter N. Funke, Andrew T. Lamas, and Todd Wolfson*   *1*

PART I MAPPING COORDINATES

2 Marcuse in the Crisis of Neoliberal Capitalism: Revisiting
   the Occupation • *Michael Forman*   *29*
3 Negating That Which Negates Us: Marcuse, Critical Theory,
   and the New Politics of Refusal • *Christian Garland*   *55*
4 Occupying and Refusing Radically: The Deprived and the
   Dissatisfied Transforming the World • *Peter Marcuse*   *66*

PART II LIBERATING RESISTANCE

5 Asia's Unknown Uprisings • *George Katsiaficas*   *83*
6 Chinese Workers in Global Production and Local Resistance
   • *Jenny Chan*   *98*
7 Queer Critique, Queer Refusal • *Heather Love*   *118*
8 Mic Check! The New Sensibility Speaks • *Imaculada Kangussu,
   Filip Kovacevic, and Andrew T. Lamas*   *132*

PART III PROTESTING VIOLENCE

9   The Work of Violence in the Age of Repressive Desublimation
     • *AK Thompson*   159

10   Neutrality and Refusal: Herbert Marcuse and Hélder Câmara
     on the Violence of Tolerance • *Sarah Lynn Kleeb*   176

11   Democracy by Day, Police State by Night: What the Eviction
     of Occupy Philadelphia Revealed about Policing in the
     United States • *Toorjo Ghose*   193

PART IV COMMUNICATING RESISTANCE

12   Insurrection 2011: Great Refusals from the Arab Uprisings
     through Occupy Everywhere • *Douglas Kellner*   211

13   Beyond One-Dimensionality • *Andrew Feenberg*   229

14   Herbert Marcuse and the Dialectics of Social Media
     • *Christian Fuchs*   241

15   Inklings of the Great Refusal: Echoes of Marcuse's
     Post-technological Rationality Today • *Marcelo Vieta*   258

PART V CONTESTING THEORIES

16   Hope and Catastrophe: Messianism in Erich Fromm and
     Herbert Marcuse • *Joan Braune*   283

17   The Dunayevskaya-Marcuse Correspondence: Crystallization
     of Two Marxist Traditions • *Russell Rockwell and*
     Kevin B. Anderson   299

18   The Existential Dimension of the Great Refusal: Marcuse,
     Fanon, Habermas • *Martin Beck Matuštík*   313

19   A Critical Praxis from the Americas: Thinking about
     the Zapatistas in Chiapas with Herbert Marcuse, Bolívar
     Echeverría, and Adolfo Sánchez Vázquez • *Stefan Gandler*   329

20   Where Is the Outrage? The State, Subjectivity, and Our
     Collective Future • *Stanley Aronowitz*   343

21   From Great Refusals to Wars of Position: Marcuse, Gramsci,
     and Social Mobilization • *Lauren Langman*   367

     Afterword: The Great Refusal in a One-Dimensional Society
     • *Arnold L. Farr and Andrew T. Lamas*   389

     Contributors   399

     Index   407

Foreword

Abolition and Refusal

Freedom is a constant struggle. The linkage between resistance and liberation is a central teaching of every freedom struggle. It is the central premise of this book, which critically examines Herbert Marcuse's concept of the "Great Refusal" and its relevance for understanding contemporary social movements.

The idea for this book was born in 2011, amid the Occupy movement, at the "Critical Refusals" conference in Philadelphia organized by the International Herbert Marcuse Society.[1] In my remarks at that conference, delivered from the same podium where my teacher Herbert Marcuse had spoken forty years earlier, I acknowledged what a great privilege it was then, and remains today, to have been his student and to have had him as my mentor.[2]

Today, nearly five years later, I write these words on the occasion of another amazing conference in Philadelphia—"Reclaiming Our Future: The Black Radical Tradition in Our Time."[3] At this very same moment, at the International Rosa Luxemburg conference in Berlin,[4] activists are launching

---

1. The conference was held October 27–29, 2011, at the University of Pennsylvania.

2. Angela Y. Davis, "Critical Refusals and Occupy," *Radical Philosophy Review* 16, no. 2 (2013): 425–439.

3. The conference was held January 8–10, 2016, at Temple University and two historic Black churches, Mother Bethel AME Church and Church of the Advocate. For more information, see the conference website, at http://www.theblackradicaltradition.org.

4. The twenty-first annual International Rosa Luxemburg conference, held January 9, 2016, in Berlin, was titled "Kein Gott, Kein Kaiser, Kein Tribun: Selber Tun!" (No God, No Emperor, No Tribune: Do It Yourself!). For more information, see the conference website, at http://www.rosa-luxemburg-konferenz.de.

a major campaign mobilizing people to flood Pennsylvania Governor Tom Wolf's office with postcards demanding freedom for Mumia Abu-Jamal, who addressed both conferences by telephone from prison.[5]

Marcuse's radical reworking of the Great Refusal concept was informed by a long life of radical engagements—beginning with Luxemburg's revolutionary theory, which he encountered as a member of a German soldiers' council that participated in the Spartacist uprising of 1919. In 1933, he introduced and developed an unknown dimension of radical humanist Marxism in the first major review of Marx's *Economic and Philosophical Manuscripts of 1844*. As a member of the Frankfurt School, he fused Freud and Marx in such a way that significantly highlighted the problems of consciousness and radical subjectivity. In the 1950s, 1960s, and 1970s, he was an indispensable theorist for all those around the world who sought liberation but confronted the domination of one-dimensional society. The questions he raised, the radical critical theory he developed, and his praxis of intellectual engagement remain relevant for our time and deserving of our critical attention.

What is clear to me is the deep connection between the Great Refusal and the abolitionist movements that have been and remain so important to freedom struggles in the Americas and elsewhere. We use the term *Black Radical Tradition* to associate the activist and scholarly work of the current moment with the anticapitalist analyses and radical demands of what progressive historians call the *Long Black Freedom Movement*. If the Great Refusal entails principled opposition to injustice and repression, then the Black Radical Tradition—a tradition that emanates from the theories and practices of Black liberation in the Americas—can certainly be described as a salient historical manifestation of the Great Refusal. This tradition has been embraced not only by people of African descent but also by those who eschew assimilation into oppressive structures and support the liberation of all people.

Marcuse must be acknowledged for reinterpreting Marxism in ways that embrace the liberation struggles of all those marginalized by oppression. In this regard, it would be productive to place his work in conversation with the insights of Cedric Robinson in works such as *Black Marxism: The Making of the Black Radical Tradition*.[6] Like Eric Williams and others,[7] Robinson

---

5. Mumia Abu-Jamal, a member of the Black Panther Party, journalist, activist, and author of many books, has been incarcerated for more than thirty years. See Mumia Abu-Jamal, *Writing on the Wall: Selected Prison Writings of Mumia Abu-Jamal*, ed. Johanna Fernández (San Francisco: City Lights, 2015).

6. Cedric J. Robinson, *Black Marxism: The Making of the Black Radical Tradition* (Chapel Hill: University of North Carolina Press, 1983). See also Robin D. G. Kelley's remarkable foreword to the second edition, published in 2000.

7. See, for example, Eric Williams, *Capitalism and Slavery* (New York: Russell and Russell, 1944); C.L.R. James, *The Black Jacobins: Toussaint L'Ouverture and the San Domingo Revolution* (New York: Dial, 1938); Walter Rodney, *How Europe Underdeveloped Africa*

insists that capitalism has been erected on the backs of Black people and people of color; thus, capitalism is racial capitalism.

Just as Marcuse took seriously the importance of feminist theories and practices in shaping the Great Refusal—the feminist movement was, he argued, "potentially the most radical movement that we have"[8]—Robin Kelley, author of *Freedom Dreams: The Black Radical Imagination*, also emphasizes the centrality of feminism. In the chapter titled "'This Battlefield Called Life': Black Feminist Dreams," Kelley points to the often unacknowledged role that Black Feminism has played in forging a truly radical Black Radical Tradition.[9] As Marcuse acknowledged Black art—Black music and literature (especially poetry)—as "revolutionary: it lends voice to a total rebellion which finds expression in the aesthetic form,"[10] Kelley points to the aesthetic dimension—music, poetry, and visual art—as simultaneous products and producers of the Black radical imagination.

In evoking the Black Radical Tradition, we also have to acknowledge the fact that Haiti was the historical forger of this tradition in the Americas. It was in Haiti that the world's first nonracial democracy—in other words, *the first democracy*—emerged. Democracy in the United States and in France was democracy of the elite—*elite democracy*—which the prevailing recognition of democracy failed to acknowledge as oxymoronic despite the irreconcilable opposition of the terms *elite* and *democracy*. In contrast, I want to point to the 1805 Constitution of Hayti (Haiti).

> Article 12. No whiteman of whatever nation he may be, shall put his foot on this territory with the title of master or proprietor. . . .
>
> Article 14. The Haytians [Haitians] shall hence forward be known only by the generic appellation of Blacks.[11]

Which is to say, everybody who is a citizen of Haiti—regardless of what might appear to be their racial affiliation—would be considered Black. That

---

(London: Bogle-L'Ouverture, 1972); Maryse Condé, *Segu*, trans. Barbara Bray (New York: Viking Penguin, 1987); and Maryse Condé, *I, Tituba, Black Witch of Salem*, trans. Richard Philcox (Charlottesville: University of Virginia Press, 1992).

8. Herbert Marcuse, "Marxism and Feminism," in *Collected Papers of Herbert Marcuse*, vol. 3, *The New Left and the 1960s*, ed. Douglas Kellner (London: Routledge, 2005), 165. This lecture was presented by Marcuse at Stanford University on March 7, 1974.

9. Robin D. G. Kelley, "'This Battlefield Called Life': Black Feminist Dreams," in *Freedom Dreams: The Black Radical Imagination* (Boston: Beacon, 2002), 135–156.

10. Herbert Marcuse, *Counterrevolution and Revolt* (Boston: Beacon, 1972), 127.

11. "The 1805 Constitution of Haiti," available at http://faculty.webster.edu/corbetre/haiti/history/earlyhaiti/1805-const.htm. I thank Siba Grovogui for bringing this aspect of the 1805 Haitian Constitution to my attention. See Siba N. Grovogui, "To the Orphaned, Dispossessed, and Illegitimate Children: Human Rights beyond Republican and Liberal Traditions," *Indiana Journal of Global Legal Studies* 18, no. 1 (2011): 41–63.

is to say, Black people, the lowest of the low, Black people who were not given their freedom but had to struggle for that freedom, Black people should be the measure of citizenship. Black people should be the measure of humanity.

If our freedom dreams can be enriched by this proposition, what happens if we imagine Black women as the measure of humanity? Racial hierarchies were temporarily overturned by the Haitian Revolution, establishing a goal toward which we continue to aspire today. If racial hierarchies need to be overturned, so, then, do gender hierarchies. Zora Neale Hurston reminded us that the Black woman is the mule of the world.[12] What if the mules of the world become the very height of humanity? This is the question that has been posed by the uprising of young people today. This is why Black Feminism is so central to the Black Radical Tradition.

So what does *radical* mean—aside from taking things at their root? It means opposition to racism—in the tradition of Ida B. Wells. It means anticapitalism—in the tradition of Claudia Jones and Paul Robeson. It means resistance to settler colonialism—in the tradition of Osceola. It means dedication to working-class struggles—in the tradition of Lucy Gonzalez Parsons, Henry Winston, and Hosea Hudson. It means linking art and struggle—in the tradition of Max Roach and Nina Simone. It means an integrative analysis—in the tradition of the Combahee River Collective and Audre Lorde. And since traditions are never only about the past, we can say that the Black Radical Tradition encompasses CeCe McDonald and the struggle for the rights of trans prisoners. It means acknowledging disability, challenging heteropatriarchy, and promoting gender diversity beyond the gender binary. The Black Radical Tradition encompasses the struggle for collective leadership, and I say *struggle* because we are just beginning to learn what *collective leadership* truly means. And the amazing organizations of young people today—Black Youth Project 100 (BYP 100), Dream Defenders, Black Lives Matter, and many others—are teaching us what that struggle is all about.

Herbert Marcuse, the philosopher of refusal and liberation, stood with his students, demonstrating the power of youth to transform the world. Fifty years ago, in his political preface to the 1966 edition of *Eros and Civilization*, Marcuse wrote about "the intellectual refusal . . . among youth in protest" as follows:

> It is their lives which are at stake and, if not their lives, their mental health and their capacity to function as unmutilated humans. Their protest will continue because it is a biological necessity. "By nature," the young are in the forefront of those who live and fight for Eros

---

12. Zora Neale Hurston, *Their Eyes Were Watching God* (Philadelphia: J. B. Lippincott, 1937).

against Death, and against a civilization which strives to shorten the "detour to death" while controlling the means for lengthening the detour. But in the administered society, the biological necessity does not immediately issue in action; organization demands counter-organization. Today the fight for life, the fight for Eros, is the *political fight*.[13]

The liberation of all people depends on our political struggle. This is why a reconsideration of Marcuse's concept of the Great Refusal is so important at this time.

---

13. Herbert Marcuse, *Eros and Civilization: A Philosophical Inquiry into Freud* (1955; repr., Boston: Beacon, 1966), xxv (emphasis in original).

Acknowledgments

This book has grown out of friendships and shared commitments. We are grateful to the many people who helped us bring this book into being.

Our project emerged from the "Critical Refusals" conference in Philadelphia that fortuitously occurred amid Occupy in October 2011. Meetings during the day, marching and occupying in the evening—there is no better circumstance for thinking about the unity of theory and practice and the limitations and possibilities of our situation. We thank the International Herbert Marcuse Society for organizing that conference and for hosting a series of panels on Marcuse and contemporary struggles. Participants on these and related panels include John Abromeit, Lorena Ambrosio, Finlay Allison, Heath Allen, Deborah Antunes, Stanley Aronowitz, Willie Baptist, Richard J. Bernstein, Sarah Bloom, Joan Braune, Nick Braune, Gabriella Callender, Alex Callinicos, Silvio Ricardo Gomes Carneiro, Michael X. Delli Carpini, Meghna Chandra, George Ciccariello-Maher, Angela Y. Davis, Mark Dudzic, Nick Dyer-Witheford, Nijmie Dzurinko, Julie Murphy Erfani, Arnold Farr, Andrew Feenberg, Michelle Fine, Edmund Fong, Michael Forman, Stefan Gandler, Christian Garland, Toorjo Ghose, Sam Gindin, Irving Goh, Lewis Gordon, Christopher Holman, Charles Howard, Jack Jacobs, Peter-Erwin Jansen, John Jarboe, Richard Kahn, Imaculada Kangussu, George Katsiaficas, Douglas Kellner, Dorothy Kidd, Sarah Lynn Kleeb, Filip Kovacevic, Deepa Kumar, Lauren Langman, Raffaele Laudani, Holly Lewis, Heather Love, Ania Loomba, Wolfgang Leo Maar, Bradley MacDonald, Nelson Maldonado, Peter Marcuse, Vanessa A. Massaro, Charles Mills, Emma Gaalaas Mullaney, Osha Neumann, Jeffery Nicholas, Vaimoana Litia Makakaufaki

Niumeitolu, Mark O'Brien, Robespierre de Oliveira, Lucius Outlaw, Leo Panitch, Clayton Pierce, Nina Power, Mark Purcell, Adolph Reed, Charles Reitz, David Roediger, Russell Rockwell, Adnan Selimović, Sally Scholz, Thiago Evandro Vieira da Silva, Eric Stanley, Janaina Stronzak, Gabriel Rockhill, Robert Tally, Annika Thiem, Nantina Vgontzas, and Zipporah Weisberg. We are grateful for the contributions that these and many other conference participants and occupiers made to this project.

The project was further nurtured by discussions at Marcuse Society conferences in 2013 at the University of Kentucky (organized by Arnold Farr) and in 2015 at Salisbury University (organized by Sarah Surak and Robert Kirsch). In 2014, throughout the fiftieth-anniversary year of the publication of Marcuse's *One-Dimensional Man*, an abundance of intellectual exchanges of consequence for our project occurred around the world in many universities and other institutions, including Columbia University; Brandeis University; Left Forum; Historical Materialism; Instituto de Filosofia, Artes e Cultura, Universidade Federal de Ouro Preto; Universidade Federal do Rio Grande do Norte; Universidade Federal do Espirito Santo; State University of Maringa; Pontificate Catholic University; Federal University of Santo Andre, Sao Bernardo e Sao Caetano; Frankfurter Institut für Sozialforschung; University of Heidelberg; Artes Liberarales Buchhandlung; Karl Marx Buchhandlung, Frankfurt; and Rosa-Luxemburg-Stiftung, Berlin.

This book would not have been possible without the continuing support and critical engagement of colleagues and students at our respective institutions—the School of Arts and Sciences' Urban Studies Program and the School of Social Policy and Practice at the University of Pennsylvania; the Department of Journalism and Media Studies at Rutgers University; the State University of New Jersey; and the School of Interdisciplinary Global Studies at the University of South Florida.

Valuable editorial contributions have been provided by Filip Kovacevic (University of Montenegro and University of San Francisco) and Parker Vanderslice-Lamas (University of Pennsylvania), and research assistance has been provided by the reference librarians and other staff at the University of Pennsylvania's Van Pelt Library, most notably Lauris Olson, John Pollack, David Toccafondi, and Anu Vedantham. For advice and guidance regarding translations, our appreciation is extended to Lisa Britton (University of Pennsylvania) regarding material in French, to Imaculada Kangussu (Universidade Federal de Ouro Preto) regarding material in Portuguese, to Stefan Gandler (Universidad Autónoma de Querétaro and Universidad Nacional Autónoma de México) regarding material in Spanish, and to the philosopher Charles Reitz regarding material in German. *Merci. Obrigado. Gracias. Danke.*

We extend our special appreciation to Temple University Press's wonderful staff, including Ann-Marie Anderson, Karen Baker, Kimberly Carolyn

Bluhm, Gary Kramer, Irene Imperio Kull, Marinanicole Dohrman Miller, Mary Rose Muccie, Kate Nichols, Joan Vidal, Kathryn Wertz, and Dave Wilson, and, in particular, to Aaron Javsicas, who provided invaluable support—and believed in the importance of this project—at every step along the way. We are grateful for the sharp, sensitive, and expert copyediting provided by Jonelle Seitz; the professional typesetting done by P. Manju; and other production services provided by Newgen—with a special appreciation to this book's wonderful project manager, Rebecca Logan. The anonymous reviewers who read our manuscript at various stages of its development provided critical and insightful comments that prompted us to make significant improvements to the book.

We are grateful to the Radical Philosophy Association, the *Radical Philosophy Review*, and the Philosophy Documentation Center for their ongoing support of scholarly work on Marcuse and radical theory and for their permission to reprint material by Christian Garland, Toorjo Ghose, and Heather Love.[1]

We have been inspired by the Media Mobilizing Project (whose work is setting the standard for the creative use of digital media tools in labor and community organizing campaigns) and the Bread and Roses Community Fund (still going strong, long after making its first grants back in 1971 to the Women's Liberation Center and to the Black Panther Party for its free breakfast program and liberation school for children at Philadelphia's Church of the Advocate). This book's royalties will be directed to these two progressive organizations in Philadelphia.

Kevin B. Anderson, Stanley Aronowitz, Joan Braune, Jenny Chan, Arnold L. Farr, Andrew Feenberg, Michael Forman, Christian Fuchs, Stefan Gandler, Christian Garland, Toorjo Ghose, Imaculada Kangussu, George Katsiaficas, Douglas Kellner, Sarah Lynn Kleeb, Filip Kovacevic, Lauren Langman, Heather Love, Peter Marcuse, Martin J. Beck Matuštík, Russell Rockwell, AK Thompson, and Marcelo Vieta joined us in writing chapters for this book. For their significant contributions, we profusely thank these authors, with whom we have formed, during the past few years, a global intellectual community—exchanging ideas, working together on manuscripts, and forming warm bonds. We are grateful to Jane McAdam Freud (the renowned sculptor and the great-granddaughter of Sigmund Freud) for gracing the cover of our book with an image of her profound sculpture,

---

1. Christian Garland, "Negating That Which Negates Us: Marcuse, Critical Theory, and the New Politics of Refusal," *Radical Philosophy Review* 16, no. 1 (2013): 375–385; Toorjo Ghose, "Democracy by Day, Police State by Night: What the Eviction of Occupy Philadelphia Revealed about Policing in the United States," *Radical Philosophy Review* 16, no. 2 (2013): 559–574; Heather Love, "Queer Critique, Queer Refusal," *Radical Philosophy Review* 16, no. 2 (2013): 443–457.

Sisyphus.[2] We are also especially honored to have Angela Y. Davis associated with this project through her foreword, "Abolition and Refusal," which, among other things, insightfully connects Marcuse's Great Refusal and the Black Radical Tradition.

We receive sustenance from close friends and family who helped in all phases and aspects of this project: Ginny, Jana, Parker, Ted, Themis, and Alex; Alison, Sebastian, and Rosa; and Hans Joachim, Ursula, Philipp, and Sebastian. We love them and thank them, once again, for loving us in the ways that they do.

To our readers, we urge you—in the dialectical spirit of becoming—to hold up your end, infusing this text with life by critically engaging with its ideas and by sending your own back out into the world for further engagement. *Let's connect!* We welcome dialogue with others committed to the development of critical theories for our time.

In the spring of 1845, Marx famously wrote his eleventh thesis on Feuerbach: "The philosophers have only interpreted the world, in various ways. The point, however, is to change it." Words and ideas matter, but living by them as we struggle—on behalf of one another and for a better world—matters even more. So, finally, we acknowledge and express our solidarity with the workers, farmers, students, activists, artists, organizers, intellectuals, and others that have been steadfastly committed to freedom struggles across the generations. Because of your long march and great refusals, we are able to imagine a better world. *Educate, agitate, organize!*

---

2. This sculpture, created in 2003, was on exhibition in Freud's midcareer retrospective at the Wooyang Contemporary Art Museum, in Gyeongju, South Korea, from December 15, 2015, through May 8, 2016. See the museum's website at http://www.wooyangmuseum.org/eng/html/.

I

Bouazizi's Refusal and Ours

Critical Reflections on the Great Refusal
and Contemporary Social Movements

PETER N. FUNKE, ANDREW T. LAMAS,
AND TODD WOLFSON

The Dignity Revolution: A Spark of Refusal

On December 17, 2010, in a small rural town in Tunisia, an interaction that happens a thousand times a day in our world—the encounter between repression's disrespect and humanity's dignity—became a flashpoint, igniting a global wave of resistance. On this particular day, a police officer confiscated the produce of twenty-six-year-old street vendor Mohamed Bouazizi and allegedly spit in his face and hit him. Humiliated and in search of self-respect, Bouazizi attempted to report the incident to the municipal government; however, he was refused an audience. Soon thereafter, Bouazizi doused himself in flammable liquid and set himself on fire.

Within hours of his self-immolation, protests started in Bouazizi's hometown of Sidi Bouzid and then steadily expanded across Tunisia. The protests gave way to labor strikes and, for a few weeks, Tunisians were unified in their demand for significant governmental reforms. During this heightened period of unrest, police and the military responded by violently clamping down on the protests, which led to multiple injuries and deaths. And as is often the case, state violence intensified the situation, resulting in mounting pressure on the government. The protests reached their apex on January 14, 2011, and Tunisian president Ben Ali fled the country, ending his twenty-three years of rule; however, the demonstrations continued until free elections were declared in March 2011.

Bouazizi's alienation, as well as his final act of refusal, became a trigger in Tunisia, because his circumstances reflected the life experience of so many in the age of neoliberal capitalism. Bouazizi lived in a place with few prospects, and he was immobilized by the weight of an unyielding economic system and a corrupt state, which sapped him of opportunity for security or self-realization. In this environment, Bouazizi never asked to be a martyr—in fact, one report states that his aspiration was simply to buy a pickup truck to make his work less burdensome[1]—but in the moment that he demanded dignity, he radiated the widespread feeling of refusal and thus ignited a wave of protests that engulfed North Africa and the Middle East. Following the demonstrations in Tunisia, protests and other forms of collective action developed in Egypt, Algeria, Libya, Syria, and Yemen, eventually spreading to all corners of the region and significantly redrawing the political map. The wave of protests was not confined to North Africa and the Middle East, however, as protests against austerity quickly emerged in southern Europe and then ignited the Occupy Wall Street movement that began in New York City and swept across the United States and eventually the world. In 2014, the United States became a flashpoint again, as protests erupted in Ferguson, Missouri, and then sporadically across the country as Blacks urgently demanded an end to police brutality, state violence, and systemic racism.

The Dignity Revolution, as the Tunisian uprising has since been named, was one of the first rebellions in a profound wave of struggle that emerged from the storm of the 2008 global economic crisis. As the ripple effects of this economic catastrophe confronted communities, people across the world responded to the escalation of poverty, inequality, state violence, and instability. In this moment, new radical forms of organizing and protest rekindled the emancipatory spirit. Communities as far flung as Cairo, London, Reykjavík, Quebec, Athens, Frankfurt, New York, Santiago, Hong Kong, Baltimore, and, of course, Tunis rose up to challenge exploitation, corruption, and oppression. In various forms, these struggles continue and new histories are being written as people say *no* to a system that—in the language of Occupy—burdens the 99 percent for the enrichment of the 1 percent, who, armed with weapons of capital and the state (e.g., law, market, ideology, police surveillance, military), are configured to defend and extend the privileges of power.

Of course, this is not the first time a wave of resistance dramatically shifted the balance of forces in society. At the height of the "long 1960s," Herbert Marcuse surveyed a world in revolt. In *An Essay on Liberation*, he wrote:

The Great Refusal takes a variety of forms. In Vietnam, in Cuba, in China a revolution is being defended and driven forward which

---

1. Rana Abouzeid, "Bouazizi: The Man Who Set Himself and Tunisia on Fire," *Time*, January 21, 2011, available at http://content.time.com/time/magazine/article/0,9171,2044723,00.html.

struggles to eschew the bureaucratic administration of socialism. The guerilla forces in Latin America seem to be animated by the same subversive impulse: Liberation. . . . The ghetto populations may well be the first basis of revolt (though not of revolution). The student opposition is spreading in the old socialist as well as capitalist countries. . . . It would be irresponsible to overrate the present chances of these forces . . . but the facts are there, facts which are not only the symbols but also the embodiments of hope. They confront the critical theory of society with the task of reexamining the prospects for the emergence of a socialist society qualitatively different from existing society.[2]

Probing both the alienation and exploitation of the human condition in advanced industrial society, as well as the conditions and strategies necessary for creating a new world, Marcuse became known as a "guru" of the New Left.[3] In many ways his scholarship offered a counterpoint to the explosion of protests and fronts of struggle that emerged in the 1960s. Consequently, Marcuse influenced (and was influenced by) a generation of organizers and activists who were involved in a diversity of radical political projects.

In his writing during this period, Marcuse assessed the New Left and other radical formations, focusing on how many of the organizations and movements were able to unite an antiauthoritarian politics with liberatory aspirations. Throughout his writing, Marcuse examined the subjective conditions of radical social change, as well as the need to reimagine the concept of the revolutionary class, given his assessment that the working class had been effectively integrated into the capitalist system. Marcuse also criticized the New Left for lack of robust organizational forms, and he contended that while radicalized youth, Blacks, and other marginalized populations could be critical catalysts for social change, ultimately, profound social transformation must be rooted in the mass of the industrial working class.

If we jump forward to the current wave of resistance, it is striking to compare the core attributes of contemporary movements to the New Left, as they share many characteristics despite radical transformations in capitalism, the state, and technology. In parallel fashion to Marcuse's broad analysis of the New Left, it is clear that certain dynamics have come to govern the current wave of struggle, constituting what scholars have begun to identify as the dominant logic of resistance of our time.[4] These characteristics include

---

2. Herbert Marcuse, *An Essay on Liberation* (Boston: Beacon, 1969), vii–ix.

3. See, for example, "One-Dimensional Philosopher," *Time* 91, no. 2 (1968): 38.

4. See Jeffrey Juris, *Networking Futures: The Movements against Corporate Globalization* (Durham, NC: Duke University Press, 2008); Todd Wolfson, *Digital Rebellion: The Birth of the Cyber Left* (Champaign: University of Illinois Press, 2014); and Peter N. Funke and Todd Wolfson, "Nervous Systems: Neoliberal Capitalism and the Cultural Logic of Resistance," in

an embrace of a diversity of actors and fronts of struggles, a commitment to leaderless and prefigurative forms of organizing, and a participatory governance process based in grassroots democracy and consensus decision making. Moreover, much of today's activism displays a distrust of existing institutions, a critique of elite financial power, the physical and virtual occupation of space, and a strategy of change, grounded in voluntarism and spontaneous uprisings rather than resilient movement building. Analysis of the wave of protest in the 1960s and 1970s reveals critical similarities to today's movement politics, along the lines just mentioned, and thus calls for a revisiting of Marcuse's engaged critical theory, in order to carefully tease out insights from the struggles he witnessed, participated in, and reflected on. Moreover, this excavation of Marcuse's frameworks may help scholars and activists identify the strengths and shortcomings of contemporary theory and practice of resistance.

Recent Research on Contemporary Social Movements

With the recent surge in political protest, scholars have responded with efforts to map different aspects of contemporary struggle. At the broadest level, scholars have investigated the impact that neoliberal capitalism has on the nature of resistance,[5] on democratic alternatives,[6] and on transnational formations in the global justice movement.[7] Analysts are engaging questions regarding the forms of movement networking,[8] democratic practices,[9] and political futures.[10] Jeffrey Juris, for example, argues that models of organizing have changed and hierarchical forms are giving way to largely unstructured,

---

Culture, Catastrophe, and Rhetoric: The Texture of Political Action, ed. Ralph Cintron and Robert Hariman (New York: Berghahn, 2015), 106–121.

5. Michael Hardt and Antonio Negri, *Multitude: War and Democracy in the Age of Empire* (New York: Penguin, 2004); Michael Hardt and Antonio Negri, *Commonwealth* (Cambridge, MA: Belknap, 2009).

6. Juris, *Networking Futures*.

7. Janet Conway, *Identity, Place, Knowledge: Social Movements Contesting Globalization* (Halifax, Canada: Fernwood, 2004); Janet Conway, *Edges of Modernity: The World Social Forum and Its "Others"* (New York: Routledge, 2013); Ruth Reitan, *Global Activism* (London: Routledge, 2007); Ruth Reitan and Shannon Gibson, "Climate Change or Social Change? Environmental and Leftist Praxis and Participatory Action Research," *Globalizations* 9, no. 3 (2012): 395–410; Peter N. Funke, "Building Rhizomatic Social Movements: Movement Building Relays during the Current Epoch of Contention," *Studies in Social Justice* 8, no. 1 (2014): 27–44.

8. Wolfson, *Digital Rebellion*; Juris, *Networking Futures*.

9. David Graeber, *Direct Action: An Ethnography* (Oakland, CA: AK Press, 2009).

10. Alex Khasnabish, *Zapatismo beyond Borders: New Imaginations of Political Possibility* (Toronto: University of Toronto Press, 2008).

fluid networks of resistance. Similarly, Arturo Escobar suggests a network-ing model that stresses self-organization and nonhierarchical, complex, adaptive behavioral systems.[11] Geoffrey Pleyers and Alain Touraine examine the ways in which the alterglobalization movement writ large asserts itself as a globalized actor against neoliberalism.[12] Todd Gitlin and Manuel Castells map the new cycle of protest as it intersects with capitalism, communication tools, and networking technology.[13] Along these lines, Paul Mason looks at Egypt, Great Britain, Greece, and elsewhere to argue that we are witnessing the expanding power of the individual, which enables new, dramatic politi-cal alternatives.[14] Likewise, Paolo Gerbaudo studies Egypt, Spain, and New York to argue for the increasing hybridity in social protest between online and offline worlds.[15]

While this scholarship has been both rich and insightful in uncover-ing some of the core practices and underlying ideologies of contemporary struggle, we see two tendencies that this volume aims to critically address. The first is an inattention to history and, therefore, to the relationship be-tween the contemporary cycle of struggle and previous periods as well as to the particular mode of the shifting capitalist political economy. Second, while some scholars, such as Gerbaudo, are critical of some aspects of con-temporary resistance, most scholarship tends toward a celebratory embrace of current movement practice. An intended contribution of our book is the application of a historically contextualized and renewed critical theory—as informed by Marcuse's radical legacy—for the study of contemporary social movements in the current cycle of resistance.

Summary of the Book

This book features analysis of contemporary social movements with par-ticular reference to Marcuse's revolutionary concept of the Great Refusal. In 2005, during the height of the global justice movement, Douglas Kellner maintained the continued importance of Marcuse.

---

11. Arturo Escobar, "Other Worlds Are (Already) Possible," in *World Social Forum: Challenging Empires*, 2nd ed., ed. Jai Sen and Peter Waterman (Montreal: Black Rose, 2009), 393–404. See also Arturo Escobar, *Territories of Difference: Place, Movements, Life, Redes* (Durham, NC: Duke University Press, 2008).

12. Geoffrey Pleyers and Alain Touraine, *Alter-globalization: Becoming Actors in a Global Age* (London: Polity, 2011).

13. Todd Gitlin, *Occupy Nation: The Roots, the Spirit, and the Promise of Occupy Wall Street* (New York: HarperCollins, 2012); Manuel Castells, *Networks of Outrage and Hope: Social Movements in the Internet Age* (London: Polity, 2013).

14. Paul Mason, *Why It's Kicking Off Everywhere: The New Global Revolutions* (London: Verso, 2012).

15. Paolo Gerbaudo, *Tweets and the Streets: Social Media and Contemporary Activism* (London: Pluto, 2012).

I would argue that in the present conjuncture of global economic crisis, terrorism and a resurgence of U.S. militarism, and growing global movements against corporate capitalism and war, Marcuse's political and activist version of critical theory is highly relevant to the challenges of the contemporary moment. Marcuse is especially useful for developing global perspectives on domination and resistance, radically criticizing the existing system of domination, valorizing movements of resistance, and projecting radical alternatives to the current organization of society and mode of life.[16]

A decade later, following a new wave of resistance, we join in recognizing the ongoing significance of Marcuse for understanding the strategy and sociopolitical horizons of contemporary struggle. The acknowledgement of Marcuse's continued relevance for critically analyzing both contemporary forms of domination and the possibilities for resistance frames this book, in which we revisit the Marcusean tradition as we survey the current moment of crisis and change. Oriented around Marcuse's concept of the "Great Refusal—the protest against that which is,"[17] this book maps the underlying logic of this new figure of resistance as it has materialized across the globe.

The chapters in this book analyze different elements and locations of the contemporary wave of struggle, drawing on the work and vision of Marcuse in order to reveal, with a historical perspective, the present moment of resistance. The chapters utilize and invoke various Marcusean concepts, insights, and claims, including those related to the catalyzing role of students and the materially oppressed, the state's use of repressive tolerance, the far-reaching dynamics of advanced capitalism, Eros, revolutionary subjectivity, repressive desublimation, and the liberation of consciousness. While embedding recent uprisings in their respective historical contexts, the book highlights the novel and common dimensions of the contemporary protest wave—tracing it from the 1960s to the Zapatistas, the East Asian uprisings of the 1980s and 1990s, the global justice movement of the 1990s and 2000s, and more recent mobilizations, including the Arab Spring, Occupy, Black Lives Matter, anti-austerity protests in Europe and the Americas, and rural migrant labor resistance in China.

While, of course, this book is not the first effort to critically assess contemporary social movements or to revitalize Left theory and practice in the twenty-first century, it does seek to understand recent uprisings by making use of Marcuse's powerful conceptual apparatus and, in the process, to

---

16. Douglas Kellner, "Introduction," in *Collected Papers of Herbert Marcuse*, vol. 3, *The New Left and the 1960s*, ed. Douglas Kellner (London: Routledge, 2005), 3.

17. Herbert Marcuse, *One-Dimensional Man: Studies in the Ideology of Advanced Industrial Society*, 2nd. ed. (Boston: Beacon, 1991), 63. Originally published in 1964.

critically assess, extend, and rework Marcuse's philosophical contributions in light of these developments. This volume is not a hagiography. As with the work of all theorists, Marcuse's frameworks and concepts must be reread and understood—with due respect but without nostalgia—as a product of their time and thus revisited for their validity and adapted, where appropriate, to the present condition.

The Great Refusal Contextualized

Herbert Marcuse (1898–1979) was born in Berlin. As a young soldier in 1918, Marcuse was "deeply influenced" by the wave of mass strikes and uprisings in Germany and the launch of the workers' councils movement, in which he became involved, and he "sympathized" with the radical Spartacus program of Rosa Luxemburg and Karl Liebknecht.[18] He received his Ph.D. in 1922, studied philosophy with Edmund Husserl and Martin Heidegger, wrote his second dissertation in 1932,[19] and became a member of the Institute for Social Research, or the Frankfurt School, in 1933. With the rise of Adolf Hitler, Marcuse—along with many scholars affiliated with the Institute—immigrated to the United States in 1934. He supported the United States in the fight against fascism during the Second World War, and after the war, he began his academic career in earnest, first at Columbia University and Harvard University, then at Brandeis University, and finally at the University of California–San Diego. Marcuse attained international renown during the 1960s as "the philosopher of the student revolts." His many books—all still in wide circulation, including *Reason and Revolution*,[20] *Eros and Civilization*,[21] *One-Dimensional Man*,[22] *Counterrevolution and Revolt*,[23] and *An Essay on Liberation*[24]—resonated deeply within the social movements then underway against the war in Vietnam and in response to consumerism, conformity, profitable waste, and poverty in the United States. He showed how various forms of repression within democracy—such as race- and gender-based inequality and the manipulation of bodily pleasures—integrated individuals into the destructive political economy of capitalism. Today, given the

---

18. See Douglas Kellner, *Herbert Marcuse and the Crisis of Marxism* (Berkeley: University of California Press, 1984), 14–15.

19. Herbert Marcuse, *Hegel's Ontology and the Theory of Historicity*, trans. Seyla Benhabib (1932; repr., Cambridge, MA: MIT Press, 1987).

20. Herbert Marcuse, *Reason and Revolution: Hegel and the Rise of Social Theory* (Boston: Beacon, 1941).

21. Herbert Marcuse, *Eros and Civilization: A Philosophical Inquiry into Freud* (Boston: Beacon, 1955).

22. Marcuse, *One-Dimensional Man.*

23. Herbert Marcuse, *Counterrevolution and Revolt* (Boston: Beacon, 1972).

24. Marcuse, *An Essay on Liberation.*

intensification of inequalities worldwide, his critical theory and humanist socialism are arguably more relevant than ever.

In the broadest sense, Marcuse's work and the project of the Frankfurt School more generally started out as a reaction to the perceived "crisis of Marxism," stemming from the absence of revolution and the bureaucratization of the Soviet experiences as well as the cooptation of the working class and the apparent stabilization of capitalism.[25] Broadly aligning with a Marxist humanism (as against the positivist dimension of a then ossified version of Marxism with its diminishment of conscious, human agency), Marcuse's response to this crisis consisted of restoring Marx's dialectic and focusing on the subjective factors that were the basis of radical social change. Hence, his oeuvre "can be seen as an attempt to rescue radical, socially transformative subjectivity."[26] In this light, the Great Refusal takes on a special significance as a hallmark of Marcuse's revolutionary project. As Douglas Kellner has written:

> Marcuse . . . constantly advocated the "Great Refusal" as the proper political response to any form of irrational repression, and indeed this seems to be at least the starting point for political activism in the contemporary era: refusal of all forms of oppression and domination, relentless criticism of all policies that impact negatively on working people and progressive social programs, and militant opposition to any and all acts of aggression against Third World countries. Indeed, in an era of "positive thinking," conformity, and Yuppies who "go for it," it seems that Marcuse's emphasis on negative thinking, refusal, and opposition provides at least a starting point and part of a renewal of radical politics in the contemporary era.[27]

Marcuse wrote during the "golden age" of capitalism, when "a comfortable, smooth, reasonable, democratic unfreedom prevail[ed] in advanced industrial civilization."[28] The historical conjuncture in which he wrote had a deep impact on Marcuse's scholarship, as he, like many scholars of that period, believed that struggles over material needs were receding as capital was increasingly able to fulfill the basic needs of everyone in society. With

25. See Kellner, *Herbert Marcuse and the Crisis of Marxism*, esp. 363–375.

26. Arnold L. Farr, "Herbert Marcuse," in *The Stanford Encyclopedia of Philosophy*, Fall 2014 ed., ed. Edward N. Zalta, available at http://plato.stanford.edu/archives/fall2014/entries/marcuse/. Farr also writes, "Indeed, Marcuse's entire project can be viewed as a quest for a new subjectivity." Arnold L. Farr, *Critical Theory and Democratic Vision: Herbert Marcuse and Recent Liberation Philosophies* (Lanham, MD: Lexington, 2009), 8.

27. Douglas Kellner, "From *1984* to *One-Dimensional Man*: Reflections on Orwell and Marcuse," *Current Perspectives in Social Theory* 10 (1990): 223–252.

28. Marcuse, *One-Dimensional Man*, 1.

capital's alleged increasing ability to meet the basic needs of society, Marcuse saw that Marx's revolutionary subject, the industrial proletariat, had become integrated into a stabilized capitalist system within a one-dimensional society, "conforming to existing thought and behavior and lacking a critical dimension and a dimension of potentialities that transcend the existing society."[29]

In this environment, where consumerist affluence and technological rationality replace freedom and authentic individuality, Marcuse became discouraged about the revolutionary potential of the working class. Because so many misinterpret Marcuse on this point, it is important to emphasize that Marcuse does not give up on the working class as *central* to the success of emancipation; rather, in the historical period of capitalism in which he was writing, he regards the working class as in need of a catalyst for realizing its own revolutionary role. Marcuse located the catalyst in those sectors of society that stood at society's margins, excluded from or discontented with the relative affluence and deathly stillness of the 1960s. When the student protests erupted, Marcuse saw this catalyst—in the same way that he would later turn to the women's movement—as a spearhead of emancipatory politics. It was the excluded and the discontented, because of their exclusion and discontentment, who made the Great Refusal and, with it, a radical new subjectivity possible.

In hindsight, while the movements of the New Left made great progress, the result was not a full-scale revolution, as some expected. As Marcuse himself notes, the movements of the period were not able to transcend problems of strategy and historical circumstance. State repression against Black radicals and others also played a significant role in explaining the demise of liberation movements in the United States.[30] While extremely valuable, Marcuse's work must also be interrogated to determine whether it carries intended or unintended implications that limit its strategic power. Many of the strategic and organizational problems of the New Left are mirrored in today's epoch of contention, and thus we caution against too celebratory an embrace of the New Left's protest logic of the 1960s, and, correspondingly, the unrefined adoption of Marcusean frameworks for contemporary struggle.

Marcuse's Insights

Here we point to a few critical dimensions where Marcuse's thought converges with the contemporary wave of resistance or where the radicality of his thought has not been sufficiently explored by activists or scholars.

---

29. Douglas Kellner, "Introduction to the Second Edition," in Marcuse, *One-Dimensional Man*, xxvii.

30. "Black militants pay with their lives: Malcolm X, Martin Luther King, Fred Hampton, George Jackson." Marcuse, *Counterrevolution and Revolt*, 1.

Specifically, in this section, we address Marcuse's reflections on the subjective dynamics of class formation, the necessity of Eros in movement politics, and his dialectical approach to social transformation that "understands the critical tension between 'is' and 'ought.'"[31] These critical dimensions of his thought have a great deal to offer contemporary political praxis. In the next section, "The Deep Grammar of Marcusean Politics," we confront some critical questions and possible shortcomings, arguably of relevance to a consideration of the New Left and contemporary uprisings. So, then, the goal in this section and the next is to examine, in broad strokes, the strengths and limitations of Marcusean political praxis.

Subjectivity

Marcuse's work emphasizes the subjective element of revolutionary agency. Radical subjectivity is vital for advancing emancipatory struggles—for understanding, theorizing, and furthering the critical processes of identity formation in general and class formation in particular. From a Marxist perspective, while people's structurally determined objective conditions (e.g., contemporary neoliberal capitalism) are key to creating a set of shared social circumstances (e.g., precarious working situations, burdensome debt, inadequate public schools, racial segregation, mass surveillance), it is through a set of collectivizing processes that classes of people recognize these common conditions. Put differently, "class in itself" exists on the objective basis of the capitalist structures of production, whereas the same working class only becomes a "class for itself" through developments that include processes of self-making within these given structures.[32] The focus on the subjective elements of radical consciousness was critical in the era of mass society, as Marcuse convincingly illustrates, and, arguably, is equally apt in the era of neoliberal capitalism. Struggles around subjective consciousness in general and class identity in particular remain a critical dimension of contemporary struggle. Occupy exemplified this outlook with the slogan "We are the 99 percent," which sought to frame a common class identity across a diversity of participants; note the slogan's declaration of a shared economic situation vis-à-vis the 1 percent. While Marcuse is not the only scholar to emphasize the subjective dimension of identity formation within struggle,[33] he clearly

---

31. Marcuse, *One-Dimensional Man*, 133.

32. Georg Lukács, a significant influence on Marcuse, uses Marx's concepts of "class in itself" and "class for itself" to elaborate his notion of class consciousness. See Georg Lukács, *History and Class Consciousness: Studies in Marxist Dialectics*, trans. Rodney Livingstone (Cambridge, MA: MIT Press, 1968). Originally published in 1923.

33. See E. P. Thompson, *The Making of the English Working Class* (New York: Vintage, 1963).

centers this discussion for the New Left, and it remains an ongoing theme that contemporary social movements must consider.

Eros

Deeply entwined with the subjective dynamics of class formation is Marcuse's critique of overemphasizing reason (Logos) at the expense of desire (Eros). Drawing on Freud, Marcuse's work fruitfully understands the role of Eros as a motivating force when analyzing and theorizing mobilizations, protests, and class formation.[34] Developing shared identities and solidarity, realizing the just struggle, and empathizing with others, Marcuse suggests, is not a process guided by mere rationality. It is not enough to analytically understand what is right and wrong or why resistance is necessary. Marcuse's discussion of Eros highlights the destructiveness of instrumental, domination-supporting reason and emphasizes the cultivation of imagination and new sensibilities, through, among other things, aesthetic education. Fantasy and art can be important for liberation, as they refuse "to accept as final the limitations imposed upon freedom and happiness by the reality principle."[35] Art for Marcuse practices the "Great Refusal," incarnating the emancipatory contents of memory, fantasy, and the imagination by producing images of happiness, by protesting "against unnecessary repression," and by struggling "for the ultimate form of freedom"—a life "without anxiety."[36] In Marcuse's view, fantasies and hopes embody the eruption of desires for increased freedom and gratification; hence, they can serve as resources for political engagement to create a better world. Marcuse's work on Eros brings back into the center of political analysis and action dimensions of political struggle—and, more broadly, of the human condition—that have been sidelined for the past few decades with the positivist turn in dominant research on social movements. Marcuse reminds us that emotional aspects are vital for understanding and acting on the political. Building on this legacy, the radical scholar George Katsiaficas (who was Marcuse's student and also has a chapter in this book) develops—through substantial research across the globe on the genesis of mass social movements—a theory of the "eros effect."[37] In addition, other scholars, such as Jeff Goodwin, James M. Jasper,

---

34. See Stanley Aronowitz, "Marcuse's Conception of Eros," *Radical Philosophy Review* 16, no. 1 (2013): 31–47.

35. Marcuse, *Eros and Civilization*, 149.

36. Ibid., 149–150.

37. See George Katsiaficas, *The Imagination of the New Left: A Global Analysis of 1968* (Boston: South End, 1999).

and Francesca Polletta reintroduce passion more generally into the analysis of social movement politics.[38]

Dialectics

As Marcuse details in *One-Dimensional Man*, the inability to think dialectically—to imagine "what ought to be" as against "what is"—is the foremost problem for radical social change in advanced industrial society. The acceptance of the given state of society as stable and fixed offers no vantage for imagining a better world within the contours of the actually existing world. Thus, without the dialectical imagination, structural transformation, in Marcuse's assessment, is impossible. Kellner amplifies this point, arguing that "critical and dialectical social theory should analyze containment and stabilization as well as contestation and struggle" and "*One-Dimensional Man* showed that the problems confronting the emerging radical movements were not simply the Vietnam War, racism or inequality, but the system itself, and that solving a wide range of social problems required fundamental social restructuring."[39]

The practice of seeing the limits of contemporary society, and thus the outlines of a new world within the present, is a continuing challenge for the working class and radical social movements. In fact, Margaret Thatcher gave form to the ever-increasing one-dimensionality of society when she uttered the now famous phrase "There is no alternative."[40] The belief that we have reached "the end of history,"[41] and, consequently, that there is no alternative to the rule of neoliberal capital, has forged a smooth and seemingly impregnable wall, making it difficult for social-movement organizers and activists, or artists and scholars for that matter, to penetrate society with a new logic that challenges the organization of society at its root. The call for organizers, activists, scholars, artists, and organic intellectuals to think and act dialectically, is arguably one of Marcuse's most important contributions to radical political praxis. In the past few decades of struggle, we have wit-

---

38. Jeff Goodwin, James M. Jasper, and Francesca Polletta, eds., *Passionate Politics: Emotions and Social Movements* (Chicago: University of Chicago Press, 2001).

39. Kellner, "Introduction to the Second Edition," xxxiv, xxxv.

40. The Conservative Party politician and the U.K.'s prime minister from 1979 to 1990, Margaret Thatcher reportedly often used the phrase "There is no alternative," which may be traced to the Victorian-era political theorist Herbert Spencer. See Margaret Thatcher, "Press Conference for American Correspondents in London," June 25, 1980, Margaret Thatcher Foundation, available at http://www.margaretthatcher.org/document/104389.

41. See Francis Fukuyama, *The End of History and the Last Man* (New York: Free Press, 1992). This book expands on an earlier essay, Francis Fukuyama, "The End of History," *National Interest* 16 (Summer 1989): 3–18.

nessed the dialectical commitment—from the World Social Forum's narrative that "another world is possible"[42] to the prefigurative, nonhierarchical politics on display in protest movements like Occupy, in economic justice initiatives such as the worker-recuperated enterprises in Argentina,[43] and in the continuing struggle in the past two decades not only for regime change but for deep forms of democracy in the revolutions across Latin America and elsewhere. While these narratives and practices—aiming to imagine what ought to be in the shadow of what is—may be incomplete and at times deeply flawed (and subject to backlash and counterrevolutionary politics), they are illustrative of what contemporary movement activists have implicitly or explicitly learned from (or, perhaps more likely, how they are in sync with) Marcuse's critical theory.

The Deep Grammar of Marcusean Politics

In this section, we sketch some of the possible challenges to and limitations of Marcusean thinking for our time. More specifically, we argue that Marcuse's assessment regarding the stability or durability of the capitalist political economy and the affluence it generates needs to be questioned and updated or extended to account for the increasing fragility and crisis-prone nature of capitalism as well as the growing impoverishment and alienation of widening swaths of society. We then also question some of the central implications of his writings, which may have—intentionally or not—motivated or validated a particular approach to resistance, struggle, and movement politics based on anarchist principles broadly understood. Or, perhaps, this political tendency arises not from Marcuse's work per se but rather independently and from misreading, misinterpretation, and misapplication. In any case, in a time of its ascendance on the Left, questions should also be raised about whether the anarchist approach to movement politics imposes limitations on sustained organizing, movement building, resilience, and, ultimately, movement success.

We are not suggesting that Marcuse, who updated Marxism for his time and considered himself a Marxist, necessarily advocated for a voluntarist, nonorganizational movement praxis. Rather, we want to ask questions about his understanding of the nature of capitalism and its relevance for the

---

42. See, for example, William F. Fisher and Thomas Ponniah, eds., *Another World Is Possible: Popular Alternatives to Globalization at the World Social Forum* (London: Zed, 2003).

43. Maurizio Atzeni and Marcelo Vieta, "Between Class and the Market: Self-Management in Theory and in the Practice of Worker-Recuperated Enterprises in Argentina," in *The Routledge Companion to Alternative Organization*, ed. Martin Parker, George Cheney, Valérie Fournier, and Chris Land (London: Routledge, 2014), 47–63; Marina A. Sitrin, *Everyday Revolutions: Horizontalism and Autonomy in Argentina* (London: Zed, 2012).

contemporary period, about the appearance of an affluent society, and about the allegedly regressive character of the working class. Arguably, Marcuse's work, and in particular the matters on which he focused his analytic apparatus, generated a spirit and thus cultivated possible lines of interpretation, some of which may have legitimated a particular and, in some ways, problematic approach to social movement theory and practice.

Capitalism

At the most fundamental level, Marcuse's understanding of the exigencies of social change emerges directly out of his analysis of the condition of capitalism in general and advanced industrial society in particular. This analysis plays a determining role in his consequent understanding of the working class and the possibility of mass, organized revolution. That is, Marcuse's penetrating analysis of one-dimensionality within advanced industrial societies sets the stage for a series of analytic insights—from capitalism's ability and interest in meeting basic needs and the consequent cooptation of the working class to the critical importance of students and other discontented groupings, the centrality of subjectivity, and what some might view as a nod to voluntarism and spontaneity. Do these findings and positions, which are products of a particular historical conjuncture, offer insight into the current conditions of neoliberal capitalism? Mobilizations during the six-year period—from the 2011 uprisings that spread from Tunis and Cairo to Madrid, Athens, Madison (Wisconsin), New York, and throughout the world to France's Nuit Debout in 2016[44]—were triggered by the volatility of capitalism and decades of neoliberal policies, which have impoverished increasing sectors of society around the globe. At least since the Great Recession of 2007–2009, but arguably much earlier, a crisis-prone capitalism has taken hold. If one understands Marcuse as highlighting the *stability* of capitalism, then his analysis of capitalism's condition seems problematic and anachronistic; however, if one reads Marcuse as highlighting the *durability* of capitalism, then his analysis seems useful, even prescient. In other words, does the transition from Marcuse's "advanced industrial society" to our neoliberal capitalism confirm or deny Marcuse's conceptual apparatus? Put another way, has one-dimensionality intensified or dissipated in the transition to neoliberalism? Did this transition require a lessening or a "deepening of what Marcuse called forms of repressive desublimation"?[45]

---

44. Angelique Chrisafis, "Nuit Debout Protesters Occupy French Cities in Revolutionary Call for Change," *The Guardian*, April 8, 2016, available at http://www.theguardian.com/world/2016/apr/08/nuit-debout-protesters-occupy-french-cities-in-a-revolutionary-call-for-change.

45. Douglas Kellner and Clayton Pierce, "Introduction: Marcuse's Adventures in Marxism," in *Collected Papers of Herbert Marcuse*, vol. 6, *Marxism, Revolution and Utopia*, ed.

On the important question of labor and radical subjectivity, Marcuse's analysis is also tested by the times. The working class around the globe has begun to emerge—but not without a backlash from the Right—as a vital actor in resisting and mobilizing in recent decades. Do these developments call into question Marcuse's notion of labor's complicity in the stabilization of capital, or do they confirm his key insights about the durability of capitalism, its ability to generate the goods for those it needs to produce and consume them, and the significance of the marginalized—even within the labor movement—for catalyzing change?

Movement Strategy

Out of this necessity to historicize capitalism and the recognition of changes from the period of Marcuse's advanced industrial society to the neoliberal capitalism of our era, we then also need to interrogate the Marcusean-inspired approach to movement politics as it finds expression in his conception (and in the popular reception) of the Great Refusal. First, does Marcuse privilege the discontented and alienated over the deprived and exploited as the core actors of emancipatory change? Amid historically racialized capitalism, such analysis may require a more explicit embrace and articulation of the critical framework developed by W.E.B. Du Bois.[46] Second, does Marcuse understand voluntarism and spontaneity as central to societal transformation? Third, following from the stress on spontaneity, is Marcuse's theory of social change undertheorized, lacking focus on what it takes to build resilient movement organizations and to move beyond the refusal and toward the collective demand? Arguably, the Great Refusal—or what sociologist John Holloway later called "the scream"[47]—too often has been seen as an end in itself rather than as an initial negation that is ultimately part of a broader process of social transformation. Is Marcuse's plea for the Great Refusal only

---

Douglas Kellner and Clayton Pierce (London: Routledge, 2014), 4. Douglas Kellner and Clayton Pierce observe in neoliberalism an intensification "of repressive desublimation—with the individuals' whole being integrated within the instrumental rationality of capitalist systems of domination and control, in which pleasures become intensified into forms of domination, such as addictive consumer sprees or obsession with media, sports, or other leisure activities. In short, shaping a subject's identity has become one of the most important targets of neoliberal governing strategies because human life itself has become a site of investment/disinvestment for corporations, governments, and institutions interested in extracting the most possible value from populations and the natural world." Ibid.

46. See W.E.B. Du Bois, *Black Reconstruction: An Essay toward a History of the Part Which Black Folk Played in the Attempt to Reconstruct Democracy in America, 1860–1880* (New York: Russell and Russell, 1935).

47. John Holloway, *Change the World without Taking Power: The Meaning of Revolution Today* (London: Pluto, 2002), 1.

a reactive "no," or does it also affirm building organizational capacity to transform refusal into collective demand for a new world?

Marcuse himself acknowledged some of these problems in a talk in 1975, which later became an essay, "The Failure of the New Left?"[48] In this piece, Marcuse argued that the New Left in part "destroyed itself by failing to develop any adequate organizational forms and by allowing internal splits to grow and spread, a phenomenon that was linked to anti-intellectualism, to a politically powerless anarchism and a narcissistic arrogance."[49] While Marcuse localizes the problem in the logic of the New Left, one might argue that for some the spirit of the Marcusean framework provokes or palliates—intentionally or not—this particular movement logic, which, arguably, is also embedded in the current wave of struggle. Similar to some groups and movements of the 1960s and 1970s, Occupy, for example, was mostly composed of the discontented and alienated, rarely engaging in a meaningful way with the poor and working class. Moreover, Occupy—though clearly historically significant as a movement of resistance—displayed a degree of distrust in movement building and relied on voluntarism and spontaneity and was, therefore, unable to develop what Marcuse marked as "adequate organizational forms." Finally, akin to sections of the New Left, Occupy was generally unable to move beyond the refusal and toward the collective demand. These dimensions may be relevant for understanding the short-lived nature of protest formations such as Occupy and force us to ask questions about the dominant logic of contemporary struggle.

Notwithstanding the timeliness and continuing relevance of Marcuse's oeuvre, it must be encountered critically with an eye for not only its insights but also its limitations. Though united in struggle, this volume's editors disagree on the answers to some of the questions above, and we welcome further critical engagement on these issues, given their significance for contemporary social movements. For further provocation and reflection, the authors of the following chapters offer scholars, activists, artists, and organic

---

48. Herbert Marcuse, "The Failure of the New Left?," in *Collected Papers of Herbert Marcuse*, vol. 3, *The New Left and the 1960s*, ed. Douglas Kellner (London: Routledge, 2005), 183–191. As Kellner indicates (191n1), "The Failure of the New Left?" provides an expanded version of a 1975 lecture given at the University of California–Irvine. It was published in German in 1975 in *Zeit-Messungen* and in *New German Critique* 18 (Fall 1979): 3–11, translated by Biddy Martin. But see Wini Breines's classic work, originally published in 1982, on Students for a Democratic Society and other New Left movement organizations, in which she writes eloquently and provocatively about the successes of efforts "to create participatory, non-hierarchical, and communal organizational forms." Her analysis of "prefigurative politics" is invaluable for those committed to the creation of democratic movements for social change. Wini Breines, *Community and Organization in the New Left, 1962–1968: The Great Refusal* (New Brunswick, NJ: Rutgers University Press, 1989), xxii, 46–52.
49. Marcuse, "The Failure of the New Left?," 185.

intellectuals critical frameworks for revisiting the contributions of Herbert Marcuse, a revolutionary philosopher.

Highlighting Critical Contributions, Chapter by Chapter

Marcuse's relationship to radical social movements of the 1960s and 1970s, not to mention his enduring relevance to many engaged intellectuals and activists in such movements today, may strike some as perplexing. If those earlier revolts were said to represent, among other things, a challenge to an older generation's understanding of oppression and resistance, and if "don't trust anyone over thirty" was a popularization of the expression of this purported generational divide, then the embrace by young, radical intellectuals of Marcuse—an old German émigré—appeared (and may continue to seem) remarkable to many observers.

What matters, though, is not our age but rather our commitments. The contributors to this book range widely in age—from those in their eighties to those more than fifty years younger. Such an intergenerational and otherwise diverse assembly of editors and authors—from four continents—can arguably be counted as a source of strength and hope for engaged, radical scholarship. It is just this sort of dialogue and comradery—without erasing difference—that characterized Marcuse's relationship to the youth revolt, the Black struggle, the women's movement, the environmental movement, Third World anticolonialism, and other social, political, economic, and cultural expressions of resistance in the 1960s and 1970s.

Angela Y. Davis—Distinguished Professor Emerita in the History of Consciousness and Feminist Studies Departments at the University of California–Santa Cruz—studied philosophy in the early 1960s at Brandeis University, where Herbert Marcuse was then teaching, and she subsequently pursued postgraduate study in philosophy under his supervision at the University of California–San Diego. In reflecting on his mentorship, she stated, "Herbert Marcuse taught me that it was possible to be an academic and an activist, a scholar and a revolutionary."[50] In turn, Marcuse explained what he learned about the philosophy of liberation from Davis's writings on Immanuel Kant, Georg Wilhelm Friedrich Hegel, and Frederick Douglass.[51] Such respect and engaged cooperation—such recognition, mutuality, and reciprocity—has been central to the intellectual work reflected in these pages.

---

50. *Herbert's Hippopotamus: A Story about Revolution in Paradise*, directed by Paul Alexander Juutilainen (Los Angeles: De Facto Fiction Films, 1996).

51. See the letter from Herbert Marcuse to Angela Davis, "Dear Angela," *Ramparts* 9 (February 1971): 22, reprinted in Herbert Marcuse, "Dear Angela," in *Collected Papers of Herbert Marcuse*, vol. 3, *The New Left and the 1960s*, ed. Douglas Kellner (New York: Routledge, 2005), 49–50.

This book presents twenty-one chapters, organized into five parts, which are briefly summarized below.[52] The chapters are preceded by a brilliantly provocative foreword in which Angela Davis associates Marcuse's Great Refusal with the long, historically potent Black Radical Tradition. The book closes with an afterword in which Arnold Farr and Andrew Lamas suggest a dialogue between Marcuse's concept of refusal and Martin Luther King Jr.'s concept of the dream—revealing a symmetry and unity between the two thinkers and their respective, interrelated radical traditions.

Part I: Mapping Coordinates

Following this introductory chapter, we turn to Chapter 2, "Marcuse in the Crisis of Neoliberal Capitalism: Revisiting the Occupation," in which Michael Forman, while concluding that Marcuse's work retains its relevance in the twenty-first century, nonetheless argues that if one-dimensional society persists, it is different from the world Marcuse addressed more than half a century ago, because the regime of capitalist accumulation Marcuse took for granted is no longer present. "Consequently," argues Forman, "any analysis that will appropriate the tools Marcuse bequeathed must, much as he would have done, do so with due consideration for the important elements that have reconstituted not only the practices of accumulation but also the ideologies that obscure the true nature of capitalist society and systematically undermine efforts at leveling a critique." Forman believes that addressing this challenge remains a problem for contemporary social movements, which, on one hand, continue to offer much promise but, on the other, have had difficulty elaborating a systematic analysis of, and a sustained practice against, the structural conditions they seek to transform. Still, Forman maintains that Occupiers, Indignados, Arab revolutionaries, and many others have given hope a new life and reminded both system administrators and their opponents that history has not come to an end.

In Chapter 3, "Negating That Which Negates Us: Marcuse, Critical Theory, and the New Politics of Refusal," Christian Garland argues that Marcuse's thought is significant for the renewal of a critical theory with a basis in radical praxis or what can be defined as a politics of refusal: the negation of that which negates us. For Garland, who speaks of an ontology of negativity, refusal and resistance should not be mistaken as simply passive withdrawal or retreat; rather, they are the active forms of radically different modes of being and doing—what Garland understands as Marcuse's definition of the Great Refusal.

---

52. These chapter summaries draw in part on abstracts developed in cooperation with the respective authors, to whom the editors extend their sincere appreciation.

In Chapter 4, "Occupying and Refusing Radically: The Deprived and the Dissatisfied Transforming the World," Peter Marcuse addresses two central questions of theory and praxis: *What is the Great Refusal?* and *What is the Long March through the Institutions?* It would contradict the critical method of radical inquiry—so central to the Marxist tradition—to seek to answer these two questions ahistorically. Grounding his analysis in what he refers to as the nonrevolutionary, historical situation of the contemporary moment, Peter Marcuse reconceptualizes his father's framework as follows: the Great Refusal might be seen as a bold refusal to accept the dominant wisdom and the dominant practices in one situation after another, while joined in a radical long march—composed of a diversity of struggles—through the dominant institutions, toward the common destination of a democratic, liberatory socialism.

Part II: Liberating Resistance

In this section of the book, we are reminded of Marcuse's declaration in his "Political Preface" to the 1966 reissue of *Eros and Civilization*: "But in the administered society, the biological necessity does not immediately issue in action; organization demands counter-organization. Today the fight for life, the fight for Eros, is the *political* fight."[53]

In Chapter 5, "Asia's Unknown Uprisings," George Katsiaficas identifies the international character and connections of contemporary social movements, with a particular focus on the Asian Wave of insurgencies. Katsiaficas maintains that, since 1968, the global movement's mobilizations have changed from being spontaneous and unconscious to evidencing a form of "conscious spontaneity" in which grassroots activists around the world synchronize protests with common aspirations. These Asian uprisings demonstrate the capacities of popular insurgencies to learn from and expand on prior mobilizations—adopting and adapting vocabulary, actions, and aspirations from various popular movements—without the need for a "conscious element" (or revolutionary party). Katsiaficas terms this new phenomenon—of popular movements emerging in their own right as hundreds of thousands of ordinary people take history into their hands—the "eros effect," a means of rescuing the revolutionary value of spontaneity, a way to stimulate a reevaluation of the unconscious. Rather than portraying emotions as linked to reaction, the notion of the eros effect brings them into the realm of positive revolutionary resources whose mobilization can result in significant social transformation.

---

53. Herbert Marcuse, "Political Preface," in *Eros and Civilization: A Philosophical Inquiry into Freud*, 2nd ed. (Boston: Beacon, 1966), xxv (emphasis in original).

In Chapter 6, "Chinese Workers in Global Production and Local Resistance," Jenny Chan documents the Great Refusal amid rural migrant workers in China's factories and urban spaces. With a shift in manufacturing from the developed countries of North America, Europe, and East Asia to China and other developing countries, not only has China become "the workshop of the world," but signs show that it is also becoming the epicenter of world labor unrest amid the processes of privatization, global outsourcing, and transnational manufacturing. Drawing on fieldwork in major Chinese industrial cities between 2010 and 2014 and supplemented with scholarly studies and government surveys, Chan's chapter analyzes the precarity and the individual and collective struggles of a new generation of factory workers. Chan also assesses the significance of the growing number of legal and extralegal actions taken by workers within a framework that highlights the deep contradictions among labor, capital, and the Chinese state. Finally, Chan looks into the effect of demographic changes and geographic shifts of population and production on the growth of working-class power in the workplace and the marketplace.

In Chapter 7, "Queer Critique, Queer Refusal," Heather Love maintains that in a moment of widespread assimilation of lesbians and gays, there are also continuing exclusions—of poor queers, queers of color, undocumented queers, disabled queers, nonmonogamous queers, transgender people, and others. Love maintains that Marcuse's reflections on sexuality, freedom, and negation are helpful in articulating a strategy and an ethics for a renewed queer criticism—one alive to both new inclusions and ongoing exclusions. Focusing on Marcuse's concept of the Great Refusal, Love's chapter considers the marginalization of gender and sexual outsiders as a political resource, the basis for a project of difference without limits.

In Chapter 8, "Mic Check! The New Sensibility Speaks," Imaculada Kangussu, Filip Kovacevic, and Andrew Lamas wrestle with the question of how one can find and develop the authentic freedom that, for Marcuse, is "the condition of liberation." In their critical reflections on Occupy, the authors consider the praxis of mic check as an expression of the "new sensibility," whose task is to gather and organize, to motivate and direct the rebellious forces of the future.

Part III: Protesting Violence

For the radical and the revolutionary, questions regarding toleration, dissent, resistance, protest, occupation, policing, incarceration, militarization, and violence are significant and perennial.

In Chapter 9, "The Work of Violence in the Age of Repressive Desublimation," AK Thompson observes that the black bloc has become "equal parts wish image and *bête noire*" since breaking onto the scene during the

1999 protests against the World Trade Organization (WTO) in Seattle. Thompson asks, "How are we to understand the new receptivity to violence among American activists, and how are we to understand the intense animosity that the black bloc has provoked?" By foregrounding the Great Refusal, Marcuse made clear that revolution starts not with the affirmation of the possible but rather with a condemnation of the present's inadequacy. For Marcuse, such a refusal amounted to a "protest against that which is."[54] Through acts of negation aimed at confronting the lack inherent in existing reality (regardless of what that reality might be), people discover "modes of refuting, breaking, and recreating their factual existence."[55] For Thompson, only with the erection of the barricade—the expression of the "gut hatred" that Marcuse held to be indispensable to the cultural revolution—does "the gesture of love" emancipate itself from the plastic confines of its contemporary repressive desublimation. In this way, explains Thompson, it becomes evident that the animosity generated by the black bloc connects to its capacity to highlight the extent of people's ongoing identification with a fraudulent reality.

In Chapter 10, "Neutrality and Refusal: Herbert Marcuse and Hélder Câmara on the Violence of Tolerance," Sarah Lynn Kleeb considers Marcuse's 1965 essay "Repressive Tolerance," in which he critiques the advocacy of toleration as something inherently and inevitably benevolent, seeing in this ideal the potential for passivity in the face of oppression, or even tacit support of oppressive conditions. Rather than encouraging citizens to challenge social structures that foster suffering and injustice, Marcuse suggests that modern notions of tolerance instead facilitate the maintenance of an often violent status quo, establishing a pattern of willingness to accept norms and policies that hamper the struggle for social justice and liberation. Kleeb notes that the liberation theologian Hélder Câmara—with similar intentions to Marcuse—denounces a passive tolerance that manifests as neutrality in the face of state-sanctioned violence. Reactionary violence on the part of those who are oppressed is generally condemned under the rubric of tolerance; however, the violence of the state in fostering the conditions for such reactionary violence, and in the repression of that reactionary violence once it is unleashed, are often passively tolerated or willingly applauded. Bringing these two insights together enables Kleeb to generate a critical evaluation of the aftermath of the now-infamous Toronto G20 protests in 2010. The widespread toleration of violent police suppression of peaceful protesters, as a tolerance that serves the cause of oppression, fostering violence rather than rejecting the

---

54. Marcuse, *One-Dimensional Man*, 63.
55. Ibid.

conditions that spawn it, illustrates the compatibility and continued relevance of Marcuse and Câmara.

In Chapter 11, "Democracy by Day, Police State by Night: What the Eviction of Occupy Philadelphia Revealed about Policing in the United States," Toorjo Ghose examines the eviction of Occupy Philadelphia from city hall on November 30, 2011, and analyzes police tactics to address public protests in the United States. He highlights three aspects of the police strategy deployed during the eviction: (1) a preconceived plan to manage protests, (2) the use of militarized tactics to implement this management plan, and (3) the imposition of a state of dissociative meditation triggered by the incarceration that followed the eviction. For Ghose, the strategy of management, militarization, and meditation (or the 3M strategy) demonstrates the Marcusean notion of repressive tolerance and characterizes the police response to public dissent.

Part IV: Communicating Resistance

Marcuse's critical theory of technology has become increasingly meaningful at a time when digital media and other new technologies have become so important in the work of contemporary social movements.

In Chapter 12, "Insurrection 2011: From the Arab Uprisings through Occupy Everywhere," Douglas Kellner discusses how, in 2011, political insurrections emerged as media spectacles. Demonstrating the relevance of Guy Debord, Michael Hardt and Antonio Negri, Slavoj Žižek, and other neo-Marxian theorists to this contemporary moment of resistance, Kellner shows the particular usefulness of Marcuse's theory of revolution—as a totality of upheaval—and the Great Refusal.

In Chapter 13, "Beyond One-Dimensionality," Andrew Feenberg explains Marcuse's conception of a new technology of liberation and how it can be extended to inform our understanding of contemporary movements that contest the technical arrangements that underlie our society. Feenberg focuses primarily on how Marcuse—who formulated a philosophical critique of the dystopian capitalism of our time while holding open the possibility of resistance and imagining a free society—reworked Heidegger to formulate the utopian aspect of his theory of technology.

In Chapter 14, "Herbert Marcuse and the Dialectics of Social Media," Christian Fuchs discusses the relevance of Marcuse's Hegelian-inspired dialectics for understanding contemporary social media and the Internet. With a focus on strengthening public and alternative media, Fuchs considers radical-reformist political demands with the potential to dialectically mediate the Great Refusal and the long march.

In Chapter 15, "Inklings of the Great Refusal: Echoes of Marcuse's Post-technological Rationality Today," Marcelo Vieta claims that Marcuse's affirmations of hope for a rerationalized technological inheritance—a "post-technological rationality"—still contain evocative theoretical and practical possibilities for contemporary radical social movements seeking alternative socioeconomic organization. The first part of the chapter briefly maps out key elements of Marcuse's politics of refusal. The second part illustrates contemporary echoes, or illustrative inklings, of Marcuse's politics of refusal via three moments of alternative social and economic arrangements that are emerging from the crises and contradictions of neoliberalism: (1) alternative community economies, (2) radical education initiatives, and (3) recuperated spaces of production.

Part V: Contesting Theories

Marcuse's own work is often best understood—and perhaps made most useful—when placed in critical dialogue with significant contributions of other theorists, such as Erich Fromm, Raya Dunayevskaya, Frantz Fanon, Jürgen Habermas, Bolívar Echeverría, Adolfo Sánchez Vázquez, and Antonio Gramsci.

In Chapter 16, "Hope and Catastrophe: Messianism in Erich Fromm and Herbert Marcuse," Joan Braune maintains that Marcuse's and Fromm's thinking about social transformation differ significantly in their understanding of history and the future, yielding distinct conceptions of the way that the past, present, and future ought to be theorized in relation to revolution. Braune shows how Fromm and Marcuse were influenced by the messianism debates among left-wing German Jewish intellectuals in Weimar Germany. She argues that key differences between Fromm and Marcuse in the 1950s and 1960s can be explained by considering the differing messianisms to which each thinker was attracted—prophetic messianism for Fromm and catastrophic messianism for Marcuse. For Braune, Fromm's critique of Marcuse's "despair" and of Marcuse's lack of "concern for the future" need to be situated in the context of the two thinkers' differing messianisms in order to be understood as stemming from a legitimate intellectual disagreement rather than a mere personal feud. Braune's argument offers important insights for how one might interpret Marcuse's Great Refusal as well as the movements that are informed by it.

In Chapter 17, "The Dunayevskaya-Marcuse Correspondence: Crystallization of Two Marxist Traditions," Russell Rockwell and Kevin B. Anderson maintain that any study of the development of radical philosophy since the mid-twentieth century—particularly as it relates to Marxist theories of opposition, refusal, and revolution—would be enriched by a close examination of the significant correspondence between Raya Dunayevskaya and Marcuse. Rockwell and Anderson argue that both Dunayevskaya and Marcuse, albeit in different ways, sought to create a Marxism for their time, an effort that involved reconceptualizing the dialectic, connecting Marx's *Grundrisse* to his early work and to *Capital*, and conceptualizing new forces of opposition and revolution.

In Chapter 18, "The Existential Dimension of the Great Refusal: Marcuse, Fanon, Habermas," Martin Beck Matuštík suggests a refiguration of Marcuse's refusals through Frantz Fanon's existential inventions in order to generate a concrete critical theory of liberation that gathers refusing voices from multiple margins and that envisions democracy as morally and sociopolitically anti-colonial and ethically postcolonial. Matuštík also presents Jürgen Habermas's reading of Marcuse in order to demonstrate, on one hand, how a Marcusean variant of critical theory deploys "existential" categories from the vantage point of social movements rooted in dissensus and, on the other hand, how Marcuse's concepts of radical subjectivity, new sensibility, and the Great Refusal immigrate into Habermas's ethical, moral, and democratic deliberations.

In Chapter 19, "A Critical Praxis for the Americas: Thinking about the Zapatistas with Herbert Marcuse, Bolívar Echeverría, and Adolfo Sánchez Vázquez," Stefan Gandler—in his project of developing a non-Eurocentric critical theory—seeks to articulate a radical social theory beyond the conventional Left dualism of reform and revolution. In focusing on the Zapatista rebellion in Mexico, Gandler juxtaposes the critical, liberatory theories of Marcuse, Echeverría, and Sánchez Vázquez and finds alternative ways of theorizing anticapitalist struggle.

In Chapter 20, "Where Is the Outrage? The State, Subjectivity, and Our Collective Future," Stanley Aronowitz examines the collapse of the so-called American dream and the decline in the working and living conditions of the great majority of those living in the United States, particularly Blacks and Latinos. He maintains that while large sections of the population are uneasy with neoliberalism, resistance remains weak: even where protests are manifest, as with Occupy, they constitute "signs without organization." Aronowitz diagnoses two problems in the history of the Left and in contemporary social movements in the United States—one relating to the enormity of the state and the second relating to subjectivity. While agreeing that the critical analysis of the political economy of capitalism is necessary, he argues that the Left must not fail to analyze everyday life and unconscious desire if it ever hopes to address the problem of radical subjectivity. A rekindling of radical imagination requires not only political economy but also psychoanalysis. In support of his Marcusean argument, Aronowitz proceeds in dialogue with Karl Polanyi, C. Wright Mills, Michel Foucault, Louis Althusser, Jürgen Habermas, and Robert McChesney, with a special focus on Wilhelm Reich's *The Mass Psychology of Fascism*.

In Chapter 21, "From Great Refusals to Wars of Position: Marcuse, Gramsci, and Social Mobilization," Lauren Langman argues that the progressive social movements of 2011, followed by the rise of Syriza in Greece and Podemos in Spain, can be best understood as Marcuse's Great Refusal—rejections and contestations of domination reflecting a variety of grievances stemming from the multiple legitimation crises of neoliberal capitalism. While explaining Jürgen Habermas's argument that the multiple legitimation crises of the capitalist system migrate to the lifeworlds—the realms of subjectivity and motivation that evoke strong emotions such as anger, anxiety, and indignation that dispose social mobilizations[56]—Langman notes that what is especially evident as a goal of contemporary social movements is the quest for dignity as rooted in an emancipatory philosophical anthropological critique of alienation, domination, and suffering pioneered by the Frankfurt School, which is quite cogently argued in Marcuse's critique of Marx's *Economic and Philosophical Manuscripts of 1844*.[57] But, as Langman explains, grievances and emotions alone do not lead to social movements; there must be recruitment, organization, organization building, leadership, tactics, and a vision. The chapter's central argument is that the Frankfurt School's critique of domination can be complemented by Antonio Gramsci's theory of hegemony in which "organic intellectuals" understand how the system operates and the salience of the cultural barriers to change, yet they proffer counterhegemonic narratives, organize subalterns, and initiate "wars of position." Langman appropriately ends his chapter by maintaining that a critical perspective on social movements provides a politically informed critique with visions of utopian possibility, in which membership in communities of meaning that are democratic and egalitarian, and grant and recognize identity, fosters solidarity, agency, creative self-realization, and the dignity of all.

The many contributors to this book take seriously the critical, historical legacy of Marcuse as a philosopher of resistance and liberation who was so significantly engaged with earlier generations of activists and intellectuals. Marcuse demonstrated what theory looks like when it is consciously political and in sync with the refusals and demands of the time. His was a theory of praxis that simultaneously led and followed. As the witticism goes about Marcuse in relation to his students, "They are my followers, so I must follow them." Amid the current cycle of resistance and repression, as the present generation of radicals stands at the crossroads of exhaustion and renewal, we, too, look to each other for sparks of refusal and ways forward.

---

56. See Jürgen Habermas, *Legitimation Crisis* (Boston: Beacon, 1975); and Jürgen Habermas, *The Theory of Communicative Action: Lifeworld and System* (Boston: Beacon, 1985).

57. Herbert Marcuse, "The Foundations of Historical Materialism," in *The Essential Marcuse: Selected Writings of Philosopher and Social Critic Herbert Marcuse*, ed. Andrew Feenberg and William Leiss (Boston: Beacon, 2007), 72–114. Essay originally published in 1932.

Part I

Mapping Coordinates

2

Marcuse in the Crisis
of Neoliberal Capitalism

Revisiting the Occupation

Michael Forman

F or a while, back in 2011, a new and potentially radical movement appeared to haunt a capitalist world mired in a crisis of accumulation.
While revolution was not on the horizon, the very word was once again pronounced outside the arena of commercial advertisement, where it had taken residence since the collapse of state socialism in Europe. At any rate, after Mohamed Bouazizi, a Tunisian street vendor, immolated himself on December 17, 2010, political revolutions shook the Arab world and, in effect, ushered in a new zeitgeist, one defined by demands for meaningful democracy, rational debate, a better life for most, and, for the first time in decades, a call for radical change that resonated with a vast audience. This phenomenon then hopped across the Mediterranean, particularly to Greece and Spain, from where it crossed the Atlantic and spread around the world.[1]

It is easy to imagine Herbert Marcuse addressing the crowds at Puerta del Sol or Zuccotti Park; yet the historical situation was, and remains, much different from what it was in the post–World War II era and what informed most of his work. It is far from clear, for example, that Indignados and Occupiers would understand Marcuse's calls for liberation from the affluent society. All of this has important implications for our assessment of Marcuse's work and its ability to illuminate both the current era and the praxis of these

---

I thank Jennifer A. Driscoll for her research assistance and Douglas Kellner, Nancy Hartsock, and Andrew Lamas for their helpful comments on this chapter.

1. See, for example, "Occuper Wall Street" [To occupy Wall Street], *Le Monde Diplomatique* [The Diplomatic World], October 13, 2011, available at http://www.monde-diploma tique.fr/carnet/2011-10-13-Occuper-Wall-Street.

new oppositional movements. To the degree that Marcuse holds onto Marxian political economy, the specificity of the regime of accumulation (i.e., the changing practices through which capital appropriates the surplus) plays a crucial role in the claims of critical theory.

Indeed, Marcuse framed his work in response to the unprecedented prosperity of the "golden age" of capitalism and sought to understand how true human emancipation might ensue. At least in the countries at the center of capitalist modernity, this period, in good measure defined by the Keynesian regime of accumulation, could credibly promise widespread prosperity and secure the consensus of the traditional working class, which was both victim and beneficiary. It is in this context that Marcuse's claim that "economic freedom would mean freedom *from* the economy"[2] appealed to rebels whose main concerns were normative, cultural, and spiritual, because they, too, generally could believe that material prosperity was a near certainty for most.

The so-called golden age, however, has been gone for almost four decades, replaced by a neoliberalism that has yielded high degrees of personal economic uncertainty alongside spectacular concentrations of wealth and degrees of inequality not seen since the eve of World War I.[3] If Marcuse's assertion about freedom is to resonate during the heyday of the neoliberal regime of accumulation, it has to speak not to people certain of improving material conditions but to those struggling to maintain or increase their material standards in an age of insecurity and growing disparities. Consequently, once the neoliberal regime of accumulation entered a generalized crisis, Marcuse's claims about economic, political, and intellectual freedom would have to take on new meaning. It is from this point of view that I begin by exploring how assumptions associated with the Keynesian era shape Marcuse's claims in order to examine how the practices of the neoliberal era might be incorporated into Marcuse's critical theory. My goal is to make some suggestions about how Marcusean categories might inform our understanding of the current conjuncture and of the social movements that sprung to life during 2011 and have since been severely repressed—but not before they had a significant impact on the popular imagination, the political discourse, and the lives of tens of thousands of activists. Much as Marcuse sought to reconstruct Marxism to address changing historical conditions,[4] I want to reconstruct the background of Marcuse's analysis to address new

---

2. Herbert Marcuse, *One-Dimensional Man: Studies in the Ideology of Advanced Industrial Society* (Boston: Beacon, 1964), 4 (emphasis in original).

3. Thomas Piketty and his collaborators have collected impressive distributional data on various measures of inequality. See Thomas Piketty, *Capital in the Twenty-First Century*, trans. Arthur Goldhammer (Cambridge, MA: Harvard University Press, 2014), 271–303.

4. Douglas Kellner, *Herbert Marcuse and the Crisis of Marxism* (Berkeley: University of California Press, 1984), esp. 363–375.

conditions and the possibilities for emancipation that they offer as the zeit-geist of rebellion ebbs and flows across the land.

The Social Pact and One-Dimensional Society

The so-called golden age of capitalism stretched from roughly the end of World War II to the mid-1970s. At least in the Global North, states were largely autochthonous, and the working class had been integrated through the mechanisms of the Keynesian welfare state, Fordist production, liberal democracy, and technological rationality. This arrangement had been structured, more or less explicitly, through a "social pact" between the state, capital, and the organizations (e.g., unions and parties) of the working class. While the specific shape of the pact differed among advanced capitalist societies, the general result was a widespread sense that the system delivered the goods and made up the best of all possible worlds precisely because it did deliver the goods—though the need for them was itself the product of manipulation—and because the only visible alternatives, the terrorist regimes of state socialism, were clearly less desirable.[5] This was the affluent society that mainstream social science would celebrate and Marcuse would criticize.

In retrospect, Marcuse's understanding of this epoch paralleled those of his mainstream contemporaries in some important ways. Like John Kenneth Galbraith, who heralded "the affluent society,"[6] Marcuse thought that the crisis tendencies of the process of capitalist accumulation had been largely contained, if not resolved, leading him to suggest that, barring a catastrophe such as nuclear war, capitalism "would continue to be capable of maintaining and even increasing the standard of living for an increasing part of the population"[7] and to propose that "we have to be liberated from a relatively well-functioning, rich, powerful society."[8] Thus—and perhaps because he mostly overlooked the fact that the arrangements underpinning one-dimensional society were themselves but a temporary truce in the class struggle, which the bourgeoisie would someday break—Marcuse also

---

5. See, for example, Stephen A. Marglin and Juliet B. Schor, eds., *The Golden Age of Capitalism: Reinterpreting the Postwar Experience* (New York: Oxford, 2000); and Eric Hobsbawm, *The Age of Extremes: A History of the World, 1914–1991* (New York: Vintage, 1996), 225–372. Contrast Leo Panitch and Sam Gindin, *The Making of Global Capitalism: The Political Economy of American Empire* (London: Verso, 2012), 80–85, 96–107, 133–145.

6. John Kenneth Galbraith, *The Affluent Society* (Boston: Houghton Mifflin, 1958). Of course, not everyone was included in this prosperity. See Michael Harrington, *The Other America: Poverty in the United States* (New York: Macmillan, 1962).

7. Marcuse, *One-Dimensional Man*, 25.

8. Herbert Marcuse, "Liberation from the Affluent Society," in *The Dialectics of Liberation*, ed. David G. Cooper (Harmondsworth, UK: Penguin, 1968), 175–192, available at http://www.marcuse.org/herbert/pubs/60spubs/67dialecticlib/67LibFromAfflSociety.htm.

seemed to think that Keynesian welfare capitalism had resolved the economic crisis tendencies of the system.

Similarly, and again much like his mainstream contemporaries, Marcuse saw a flat political landscape. Mainstream political scientists and sociologists, especially in the United States and the United Kingdom, the countries of the paradigmatic cases, attested to a widespread political complacency and optimism, which they termed "the civic culture." Its development, for example, in the United Kingdom could be understood "as a series of encounters between modernization and traditionalism—encounters sharp enough to effect significant change, but not so sharp or so concentrated in time as to create disintegration or polarization."[9] At its core, this civic culture embodied a broad acceptance of the legitimacy of bourgeois society, trust in its institutions and elites, and a sense of "political effectiveness" accompanied by a low-level emotional commitment to political ideas. Interestingly, however, the proponents of the civic-culture thesis barely considered the affluence associated with the world they described—an affluence that their less "civic" cases, Italy and Mexico, did not share—to be a factor; moreover, they did not foresee at all the broad civil unrest that was already brewing in the form of the Black liberation and Free Speech movements. While Marcuse, at least in *Eros and Civilization* (1955), did not predict this unrest either, he did suggest that tensions within the system made it possible.

If the so-called civic culture and the affluent society were characteristics of liberal democracies such as the United Kingdom and the United States, Marcuse did not give them the same valuation as his contemporaries did. He saw them as elements of a "one-dimensional society," one that "takes care of the need for liberation by satisfying the needs which make servitude palatable and perhaps even unnoticeable."[10] Just about everything functioned effectively to contain the transformative potential of the working class. In particular, Marcuse proposed that four factors associated with the production process were crucial. First, the mechanization of this process reduced physical effort and subsumed the worker in a routine that did not require much of the worker's attention. Second, increasing occupational stratification amounted to the decline of directly productive labor, the growth of administrative labor, and the assimilation of these two forms of activity so they might become largely indistinguishable. Third, through consumption patterns and the roles of the culture industry and the welfare state, the working class became ideologically integrated, its aspirations contained within

---

9. Gabriel A. Almond and Sydney Verba, *The Civic Culture: Political Attitudes and Democracy in Five Nations* (1963; repr., Newbury Park, CA: Sage, 1989), 5. See also Daniel Bell, *The End of Ideology: On the Exhaustion of Political Ideas in the Fifties* (New York: Free Press, 1962).

10. Marcuse, *One-Dimensional Man*, 24.

the parameters of what the system could deliver. Finally, the substitution of technical administration for direct domination in the labor process made the social relations of production ever less transparent: the capitalist became nearly invisible. The welfare/warfare state also played a crucial role in the stabilization of the whole system because this state "seem[ed] capable of raising the standard of *administered* living" by elaborating a system of total regulation of time, needs, and even consciousness.[11] This system, Marcuse believed, was well on its way to destroying the liberties achieved since the eighteenth century by subsuming the contending forces under the appearance of pluralism. Further, the constantly fueled fear of communism, the permanent enemy, functioned as a "cohesive power" to unite opposing forces into a patriotic whole.[12] Also, alongside the processes of political integration, Marcuse identified similar developments at the level of culture, where the yearnings for emancipation—associated with what he would later call the "aesthetic dimension"—would be managed and satisfied via the culture industry and mass consumption. Finally, the very universe of discourse would be closed by the prevalence of the language of administration, which would reduce reason to its instrumental aspects, define its goals in terms of the system that delivered the goods, and translate value concepts such as freedom into operational terms, "a translation which has the effect of reducing the tension between thought and reality by weakening the negative power of thought."[13] In short, the affluent society was a "totally administered society" in which the violence it did to its members went largely unperceived.

This analysis led Marcuse to conclude that the social force that had been at the center of disruption since the industrial revolution, the working class, had lost its capacity to initiate social transformation. In fact, he would soon argue that the processes that constituted the one-dimensional society had penetrated so deeply that they had, in a certain sense, become instinctive:

> The so-called consumer economy and the politics of corporate capitalism have created a second nature of man [one-dimensional man] which ties him libidinally and aggressively to the commodity form. The need for possessing, consuming, handling, and constantly renewing the gadgets . . . offered to and imposed upon the people . . . has become . . . "biological." . . . The needs generated by this system are thus eminently stabilizing, conservative needs: the counterrevolution anchored in the instinctual structure.[14]

---

11. Ibid., 48 (emphasis in original).
12. Ibid., 51.
13. Ibid., 104.
14. Herbert Marcuse, *An Essay on Liberation* (Boston: Beacon, 1969), 11. Michel Foucault's notion of "biopolitics" captures some of the same developments, but it misses the importance of class struggle in their production and containment. See, for example, Michel

While Marcuse would never abandon the notion of the strategic centrality of the working class to the success of any project of human emancipation,
this analysis led him to conclude that a catalyst was needed. This catalytic
force would have to reject the very sensibilities of late capitalist society, so it
could only be made up of those who, in one way or another, were excluded
from the core elements of the affluent society (e.g., students, women, marginalized minorities). Because of their very exclusion, the life experiences of
these groups made the "Great Refusal—the protest against that which is"—
possible for them.[15] What was needed was "a political practice which [would
reach] into the roots of containment and contentment in the infrastructure
of man, a political practice of methodical disengagement from and refusal
of the Establishment, aiming at a radical transvaluation of values."[16] It was
very much these excluded elements that rose in rebellion during the 1960s.
If they did not, in the end, bring about human emancipation, the revolution,
they did have important and in some ways defining consequences for the
subsequent restructuring of capitalist society, not only as it came to reconstitute itself once the Keynesian regime of accumulation hit new barriers to
continued capitalist growth but also as the integration of some elements of
previously excluded groups became an aspect of this reorganization of capitalism. To these changes I now turn.

The Neoliberal Counterrevolution

The revolt of the 1960s had significant positive effects, but the Great Refusal
never materialized. Much as Marcuse feared, the revolts of the 1960s were
followed by a preemptive counterrevolution.[17] In the end, the terms by which
the working class is integrated and social change contained shifted in important ways. Many old expectations no longer hold, the mix of cooptation
and repression has been altered, and instrumental rationality triumphs in
an uneasy alliance with the revolt against reason itself by the most reactionary representatives of the establishment.[18] In the event, this counterrevolution responded to two sets of factors whose interrelations were surely more
complex than I can account for here: the crisis of the Keynesian regime of
accumulation, resulting from the accrual of contradictions rooted in the
social pact and the cultural crisis that ensued from the revolts of the 1960s.
I turn first to the crisis of accumulation because its resolution strikes at the

---

Foucault, *The Birth of Biopolitics: Lectures at the Collège de France, 1978–1979*, ed. Michel
Senellart, trans. Graham Burchell (New York: Picador, 2010).

    15. Marcuse, *One-Dimensional Man*, 63.

    16. Marcuse, *An Essay on Liberation*, 6.

    17. Herbert Marcuse, *Counterrevolution and Revolt* (Boston: Beacon, 1972).

    18. Ibid., 129.

heart of some of Marcuse's central assumptions about the containment of conflict in one-dimensional society.

The economic crisis of the mid- to late 1970s was precipitated by problems with labor supply rooted in the social pact. In effect, the Global North experienced relative scarcities of labor because workers there were well organized and could make demands that tested the boundaries of the social pact itself. This placed limits on the adoption of new technologies and on the liberalization of international product markets. Furthermore, labor militancy—for example, in the form of wildcat strikes—had been growing since the early 1970s, not only in Europe and North America but also at the periphery of the capitalist world, in places such as Argentina and Chile. Along with increasing limits on natural resources and factors such as constraints on the mobility of capital and greater openness by official parties in the West to claims for business regulation, these elements led to declining profit and growth rates by the end of the period.[19] Intellectuals associated with the leading sectors of capital came to see these problems as related to the social uprisings of the 1960s, which were still fresh in their memory.[20] In the lively debate that ensued, the economic theories of Friedrich von Hayek and Milton Friedman ceased to be marginal; new demands for economic liberalization accompanied calls for the elimination of the welfare state. In the end, neoliberalism triumphed because, whatever its virtues, it would reduce both the organizational capacity of the working class and its members' ability to avail themselves of the state for protection.

Since Marcuse's day, then, neoliberal globalization and the rise of the financial sector to a hegemonic position have produced quite different conditions from those that prevailed during the golden age. Production processes have become global, and the working class itself has become more diverse as peoples from the Global South, and especially women,[21] have come to participate across borders, thereby increasing capital's ability to undermine hard-built solidarities and to maneuver against workers everywhere.[22] As a result, the condition of workers in most countries and at all levels, even among the most skilled strata in the information and health-care sectors, has grown increasingly insecure. Across the Global North, significant

---

19. David Harvey, *Enigma of Capital and the Crisis of Capitalism* (New York: Oxford, 2010), 12; Panitch and Gindin, *The Making of Global Capitalism*, 135–144.

20. The situation came to be seen as a "democratic surplus." Michel Crozier, Samuel P. Huntington, and Joji Watanuki, *The Crisis of Democracy: Report on the Governability of Democracies to the Trilateral Commission* (New York: New York University Press, 1975).

21. Nancy Hartsock, "Globalization and Primitive Accumulation: The Contributions of David Harvey's Dialectical Marxism," in *David Harvey: A Critical Reader*, ed. Noel Castree and Derek Gregory (Oxford: Blackwell, 2006), 167–190.

22. Kim Moody, *Workers in a Lean World: Unions in the International Economy* (London: Verso, 1997).

numbers of workers, many but by no means all women, migrants, and members of historically excluded minorities, have fallen into the so-called precariat. They hold part-time jobs, they are "independent contractors," they are underemployed. They do not expect job security or a career path, and they often do not want it. Amounting to as much as one-fourth of the adult population, the precariat do not partake of the "forms of labour-related security . . . that social democrats, labour parties and trade unions pursued as their 'industrial citizenship' agenda after the Second World War."[23]

While the system has continued to deliver the goods, the bases on which it has done so have changed markedly. From the United Kingdom to France to the United States, labor unions have declined to near irrelevancy, while parties associated with labor have turned to neoliberalism. The wage incomes of much of the population have become insufficient to absorb the surplus resulting from vastly increased productivity; much to the benefit of the financial and real-estate sectors, the gap has been filled with easy and expensive credit. Similarly, where the postwar years witnessed a tendency toward an increasingly egalitarian distribution of income, this trend has been reversed. In the United States, where the trend is most pronounced, the share of national income of the top decile has increased dramatically, while that of the bottom 60 percent has dropped; further, the top 1 percent, which took about 10 percent of national income in 1980, accounted for 20 percent in 2010 (down from 24 percent in 2007).[24] The affluent societies are much more affluent in the aggregate, but the material conditions of the working class, however defined, do not guarantee access to this affluence in the same ways. Even in "good times," insecurity, debt, and political disorganization prevail.

It is also important to note that the movements of the 1960s had deep cultural and ideological effects in the Global North and beyond, and that these effects are related to the advent of neoliberal capitalism. To a significant extent, the rebels of the 1960s succeeded in morally delegitimizing, ideologically if not in practice, the hierarchies based on gender, race, and sexual orientation. Women, Blacks, and other historically excluded groups now encounter different conditions from those of the 1950s. Activists of the 1960s also introduced concern about the human impact on the natural environment. Through their critique of social norms and practices, these movements helped to undermine the complacency of the "civic culture." At the same time, their partial success may have contributed to the victory of the

23. The term "precariat" is a compound of "precarity" and "proletariat." Coined by academics in the 1980s, there is some evidence that those to whom it pertains have embraced it. Guy Standing, "The Precariat," in *The Precariat: The New Dangerous Class* (London: Bloomsbury Academic, 2011), 1–25.

24. Looking at income from labor and capital during the last two centuries, Thomas Piketty shows that the period from 1950 to 1980 was anomalous. Piketty, *Capital in the Twenty-First Century*, 300–302.

neoliberal project because what Marcuse termed "the misplaced radicalism" of the "cultural revolution"[25] opened the door to a cult of atomistic individualism readily coopted into reified norms that equate market outcomes with justice. Thus, while the public distrusts the state, corporate elites, technological rationality, and labor organizations, it celebrates the entrepreneur as a folk hero who defies the establishment, and it placidly accepts market solutions to just about every problem. The dangling carrot of entrepreneurial success has replaced the expectation of rising wages. In effect, the performance principle once associated with labor has come to be associated with success in markets. Furthermore, this distrust of institutions and elites is even true of the so-called conservative public. In effect, claims about the duplicitousness of the system and demands for true individual freedom and self-expression were integrated as cynicism—a widespread cynicism about the system—which has become one of the characteristics of one-dimensional man. If the one-dimensional man of the 1950s believed all was well, the twenty-first-century one-dimensional man and woman believe there is no alternative to the privatization of everything.

Associated with these processes has been a significant change in the structure of state institutions as they seek to accommodate globalization. The state has certainly not withered away, for globalization is "intimately connected with legislative and administrative changes to deepen and extend market competition, including extensive treaties and coordination among states."[26] Yet even in the Global North, the contemporary capitalist state is quite different in capabilities and reach than it was in Marcuse's day. In the case of the United States, the abandonment of aspects of sovereignty results directly from state policy in the service of capital, especially financial capital. Still, a series of developments make for a qualitative change in the form of the state. While elements of the U.S. state have enhanced their capability to handle crises and manage the juridical infrastructures for capital accumulation, other states in the Global North have gone so far as to abandon their currencies in the effort to integrate into global capitalism. All states in the Global North have abandoned important functions and reduced the scope for popular input into these. Perhaps most significantly, and bucking a five-hundred-year-old trend, states (and especially the United States) have moved toward what might be called market feudalism, the parcelization of crucial elements of sovereign power.[27] Here I have in mind the privatization of aspects of states' educational, social-welfare, and even internal coercive functions, such as prisons and policing, as well as the outsourcing of war-making

---

25. Marcuse, *Counterrevolution and Revolt*, 129.

26. Panitch and Gindin, *The Making of Global Capitalism*, 223.

27. Sovereignty has never been as absolute as the models suggested. See John Agnew, *Globalization and Sovereignty* (Lanham, MD: Rowman and Littlefield, 2009), 47–96.

activities to corporate mercenaries. These practices have not only contributed to the profitability of capital; they have also involved it directly in traditional state functions and given particular firms a greater pecuniary stake in these functions, just as the population has been subjected to heightened surveillance and repression.[28] In effect, the neoliberal regime incorporates the working class through a shift in the balance between cooptation and coercion in favor of the latter.

Relatedly, states in the Global North and beyond have also changed in another significant way. Communism, as the permanent enemy, is gone. Mostly, the states which once proclaimed it are now integrated into the empire of global capitalism. Communism has been replaced with two better enemies: terrorism and crime—better because they do not pose an existential threat to states and societies in the Global North, better because they are truly permanent as they are not associated with any specific entity or state, and better because they do not offer a vision, however distorted, of a future that might hold any kind of appeal to significant numbers of their citizens. The result since 2001 has been both a new magnet for ideological cohesion (which justifies the increase in state surveillance and policing) and specialized military powers (themselves a direct attack on human rights and on long-established standards of humanitarian law and human rights). Who, after all, can argue against states protecting their citizens from real and unpredictable dangers? Given the indeterminate quality of the notion of terrorism and the purported pervasiveness of crime, these measures could easily be applied to opposition movements and dissenters, with broad support not only from the population at large but also from important liberal intellectuals because, as Michael Ignatieff has put it, "a constitution is not a suicide pact: rights cannot so limit the exercise of authority as to make decisive action impossible."[29] Furthermore, as has been the case with the wars in Afghanistan and Iraq, the new permanent enemy can also support the military-industrial complex while providing handy justification for imperial adventures and geopolitical maneuvering. Justifying the carceral state and general fear, the new permanent enemies effectively replace solidarity with fear.

---

28. Nina Bernstein, "Companies Use Immigration Crackdown to Turn a Profit," *New York Times*, September 28, 2011, available at http://www.nytimes.com/2011/09/29/world/asia/getting-tough-on-immigrants-to-turn-a-profit.html.

29. Michael Ignatieff, *The Lesser Evil: Political Ethics in an Age of Terror* (Princeton, NJ: Princeton University Press, 2004), 9. See Michael Forman, review of *The Lesser Evil*, by Michael Ignatieff, *Political Theory* 34, no. 4 (2006): 529–531. Ignatieff, an important figure in the Liberal Party of Canada, was director of the Carr Center for Human Rights Policy at Harvard University's Kennedy School when he wrote *The Lesser Evil*.

Finally, new developments at the level of technical rationality and what Marcuse called "positive thinking"[30] have also had a significant effect on one-dimensional consciousness. While the changes are arguably incremental, two aspects of them are worth mentioning. One of these has been the improvement of managerial knowledge. One widespread example of this is the practice of performance assessment reviews to which highly skilled workers (including college professors and medical doctors) are increasingly subjected. The practice is for employees to participate actively in the process by regularly and repeatedly formulating goals and then reporting on their own performance in relation to these goals. The intended effect is to raise both relative and absolute surplus value by increasing work effort and, in the case of salaried workers, lengthening the workday.[31] After all, who, when presented with the question "What are your new goals for the next year?," will say, "The same"? Not incidentally, this deployment of what Marcuse termed the "performance principle: the prevailing historical form of the reality principle,"[32] serves also to enhance the apparent rationality and morality of the system by psychologically integrating these workers into the managerial practice itself. In short, we are witnessing a clear example of technological domination of subjectivity through the introjection of the performance principle in ever expanding areas of life.

The second important development at the level of rationality and positive thinking has occurred in the realm of digital technologies themselves. The new media and technologies have dramatically enhanced the ability of capital to create needs by gathering vast amounts of information, which can then be used to manage desire and deny individuals the opportunity for critical reflection. Thus, for example, Facebook's revenues result from the selling of information about its "members" to marketers who can then target these users directly. It is even possible that participation in these commercial forms of surveillance makes people more tolerant of state surveillance. At any rate, these very same technologies also supply the state with a previously unmatched capability for surveillance that it can deploy at any time to regulate and govern the population, a development that is particularly worrisome given the already mentioned weakening of the kinds of protections associated with liberal constitutionalism.

---

30. By this, Marcuse means forms of analysis that permit the consideration, and even the experience, of "facts" only within the constraint of existing conditions, thereby foreclosing any potential for contestation; see Marcuse, *One-Dimensional Man*, chap. 7.

31. One consequence has been prolongation of labor time. For an analysis partly built on Marcusean notions, see Nichole Shippen, *Decolonizing Time: Work, Leisure, and Freedom* (New York: Palgrave Macmillan, 2014).

32. Herbert Marcuse, *Eros and Civilization: A Philosophical Inquiry into Freud* (Boston: Beacon, 1955), 35.

In sum, half a century after the publication of *One-Dimensional Man*, the system of total administration by which "the belief that the real is rational and the system delivers the goods"[33] still prevails and continues to make servitude unnoticeable. This society continues to contain the transformative potential of the working class, but with significant differences. First, while the mechanization of the production process continues to expand, it now subsumes workers in routines that, especially in the Global North, increasingly involve the supervision of robotic technologies. Second, if growing occupational stratification continues, the displacement of much directly productive labor to the periphery amounts to an even greater expansion of administrative labor, thereby blurring the distinctions between labor and management. At the same time, both productive and administrative labor become increasingly precarious, adding a new sense of insecurity to the experience of large portions of the population. Third, the repressive satisfaction of needs through mass consumption is fueled by an even greater penetration of the culture industry into everyday life, one that inures the subject to manipulation by state and capital. Today, furthermore, mass consumption needs are, in good measure, met through debt and increasing dependence and insecurity, which help contain aspirations within the limits of what the system can deliver. Finally, highly enhanced managerial methods and means of technical administration further conceal the relations of production and the role of capital by enlisting workers into their own management. In the regime of neoliberal global capitalism, raising the standard of administered living leads to deepening insecurity ("flexibility") and the return of wild swings in the business cycle. Adding the growing ideological importance of crime and terrorism, one-dimensional society perseveres by subsuming the contending forces under the appearance of pluralism while subjecting the population to increasing levels of coercion and administered fear.

Administered insecurity and fear are most important. Coercion and fear were certainly a part of the processes of one-dimensional society as Marcuse analyzed them. Although the fear of nuclear war was never far off, what prevailed, at least in the countries at the center of global capitalism and especially in the United States, was a sense of well-being and security in everyday life. This is gone. Employment practices bespeak of insecurity and precariousness. More important, perhaps, is the regime of outright fear: fear of crime, fear of terrorism, and fear for our children on the streets. Along with this regime of fear comes a sense of mutual distrust, which undermines solidarity and justifies rising levels of state violence expressed in the repression of opposition movements, mass surveillance, and mass incarceration. If the system still delivers the goods, there is no longer the expectation that

---

33. Marcuse, *One-Dimensional Man*, 84.

it will continue to do so. If the happy consciousness persists, it now fears that unhappiness will result from any effort at even the mildest of reforms.

At the same time, however, these economic, political, and technological developments also present new possibilities for organizing and constructing an oppositional politics. Crises of accumulation are not solved but shifted across space. A growing awareness of planetary political, social, and economic integration has been at the core of a slowly developing alterglobalization movement that seeks to reframe economic goals and substitute new sensibilities for those of the prevailing market-oriented societies.[34] Furthermore, in the midst of the neoliberal regime of accumulation, new social movements of still unrealized and even unformed potential have taken the world stage, in part by using the new media and technologies to disseminate information and coordinate action. It is to one of these movements that I now turn.

Crisis and Protest

The Occupy movement, which flourished in the autumn of 2011 and continues on a much more modest scale today, represents the most visible challenge to the one-dimensional society in recent times.[35] This is not to say that the movement ever articulated the Great Refusal, but it did raise significant and long-dormant grievances in the public sphere, and it did, if only for a while, articulate the possibility of another—better—world. In the remainder of this essay, I examine the Occupy movement in view of Marcusean categories and Marcuse's own claims in view of Occupy and the very different—as compared to those of the 1960s—circumstances it faced.[36]

The Occupy movement has as its immediate background the crisis of the neoliberal regime of accumulation in the so-called Great Recession, the latest in a series of crises that have afflicted global capitalism since the 1980s. The economic contraction began in the United States in 2007 and lasted into late 2009. Peculiar to this crisis was the fact that, unlike earlier ones that struck at particular regions and specific industries, it nearly brought

34. Manfred B. Steger, *The Rise of the Global Imaginary: Political Ideologies from the French Revolution to the Global War on Terror* (New York: Oxford University Press, 2008), 170–212.

35. In late 2014, the participants in the uprisings in Hong Kong embraced the terminology and approaches of Occupy. Occupy Central, one of their groups, spoke of "an outcry for freedom [that] will be heard far and wide." See Amy Wu, "An Outcry for Freedom Will Be Heard Far and Wide," *South China Morning Post*, October 6, 2014, available at http://www.scmp.com/comment/article/1610576/outcry-freedom-will-be-heard-far-and-wide.

36. My discussion is partly informed by my observations and notes of the broad sweep of events and of the specific forms I witnessed at Occupy Seattle, mainly between late September 2011 and December of that year, when the police finally evicted the Occupiers from their second encampment.

down the financial sector at the center of global capitalism. While neoliberal orthodoxy temporarily lost some of its appeal, it continued to have a hold on political elites and significant elements of the bourgeoisie. Thus, despite promising "real change," U.S. president Barack Obama, once in office, appointed figures long associated with neoliberal theory and with the financial sector to key economic positions, a trend that has continued into his second term in office. While his policies may have diverged from the neoliberal doctrine when it came to rescuing major firms, especially in the financial sector, this should not be seen as true heresy: leading elites have always sought and received exceptions from the rules of the game. Meanwhile, the population at large has been the object of austerity policies well in keeping with the still ideologically dominant neoliberal economic model. Aided by austerity policies, unemployment rates have remained high, especially in southern Europe. With the notable exception of Iceland, orthodoxy has been embraced even more enthusiastically in the Eurozone. Across the Global North, states cut social programs, sought to reduce public debt, and refused to intervene directly in the operations of capital, even against the advice of Nobel Prize–winning economists such as Joseph Stiglitz and Paul Krugman, who continue to find themselves excluded from official circles.

It is not surprising that under these circumstances public unrest would emerge. The most notable early rumblings in this regard were to be heard in the United Kingdom, where students and elements of the precariat, organized as the network UK Uncut, rose to protest tuition hikes and public-assistance cuts; similarly, in Greece, students and public employees have protested against austerity since at least the end of 2010. In the United States, there were some protests against tuition hikes, mainly in California in late 2009. Toward early 2011, groups such as New Yorkers against Budget Cuts (NYABC) would come to the fore. Much more visible was the response to Wisconsin Governor Scott Walker's attack on public-employee unions. There were large public demonstrations and a sit-in at the state capitol in Madison; Democratic Party state senators fled to Illinois in order to deny Republicans a quorum and thus block passage of the budget bills under question. In the event, the Wisconsin protests attracted major media attention for at least three reasons. First, Walker, a rising star in the Republican Party, sought the publicity to build his conservative credentials. He publicly declared his aim of undermining public-employee unions, a significant move as the public sector has been one of the few areas of union growth since the 1980s.[37] Second, the protests occurred simultaneously with those at Tahrir Square, and both Wisconsinites and Egyptians drew the connections. Finally, the

37. Scott Walker defended his actions in an editorial in the *Wall Street Journal*. See Scott Walker, "Why I'm Fighting in Wisconsin," *Wall Street Journal*, March 10, 2011, available at http://online.wsj.com/news/articles/SB10001424052748704132204576190260787805984.

imagery associated with schoolteachers, nurses, and firefighters taking a stand, along with the curious spectacle of state legislators on the run, caught the public imagination. In the end, protesters were evicted from the public space, the budget measures proposed by the governor passed, and a later effort to recall Walker failed.[38]

Still, for some time to come, the events in the United Kingdom, southern Europe, and the Middle East looked to have little resonance in North America. The Wisconsin protesters appeared defeated. Discontent and disillusionment spread, but protest and public disruption remained minimal, at least from the Left. On the Right, the Tea Party, financed by ultrareactionary elements, raised a populist outcry against the bank bailouts, but it did so in the name of "free markets." It seemed as though there still were no alternatives; yet something new was brewing.

Amplified by the media and social networks, two sets of events were to foster a spirit of liberation and revive hope in a hopeless situation around the world. First came the revolutions in North Africa and the Middle East. While these were largely presented in a positive manner by news media and elites who saw them as Lockean uprisings and likened them to a sanitized version of the Prague Spring, many found in them what the participants saw: expressions of solidarity, of Eros, of a yearning for true liberation. The courage and nonviolently defiant methods deployed, particularly in Tunisia and at Tahrir Square, soon seized public imagination of the Left in the West. Probably the first to import and adapt these methods were the Spanish Indignados, who, in a movement known as *movimiento 15 de mayo* or 15-M, occupied public squares to protest against austerity policies, unemployment, and hopelessness during the summer of 2011. Media coverage of 15-M was much less positive.

It is not clear that the Indignados directly inspired the Occupy Wall Street actions that began a few months later in mid-September.[39] There is also some dispute about the significance of the mid-July statement by the Canadian-based journal *Adbusters*: "Are you ready for a Tahrir moment? On September 17th flood into lower Manhattan, set up tents, kitchen, peaceful barricades and occupy Wall Street."[40] Still, on September 17, a group of protesters, mostly people associated with NYABC but also students and some

---

38. John Nichols, *Uprising: How Wisconsin Renewed the Politics of Protest, from Madison to Wall Street* (New York: Nation, 2012).

39. James K. Rowe and Myles Carroll suggest that as early as July, members of NYABC sought to emulate the Spanish model of the General Assembly. They do not, however, produce evidence that the Spanish events had much resonance beyond a narrow segment of the U.S. Left. See James K. Rowe and Myles Carroll, "Reform or Radicalism: Left Social Movements from the Battle of Seattle to Occupy Wall Street," *New Politics* 36 (June 2014): 162.

40. Quoted in Manuel Castells, *Networks of Outrage and Hope: Social Movements in the Internet Age* (Cambridge: Polity, 2012), 159.

labor figures, took up residence in Zuccotti Park, a private space open to public use.[41] The Occupy Wall Street movement had been born. The forcefulness
of the New York Police Department's response—including the mass arrest of
some seven hundred demonstrators on October 1 and the images of police
pepper-spraying obviously nonthreatening protesters, which spread widely
via social media—and the resoluteness of the demonstrators' commitment
to nonviolence only served to fuel anger and inspire those sympathetic to
Occupy. By October 15, a worldwide protest under the Occupy banner raised
the visibility of, and connections among, the various local movements.
Tens of thousands—in some cases hundreds of thousands—sought to occupy streets, parks, and public squares around the world, thereby giving
the movement, if not an internationalist position, at least a cosmopolitan
flavor. Slogans, manifestos, and video testimonies quickly spread and were
embraced through social media. It was a plaint: the happy consciousness was
much less happy, more willing to refuse to accept the proposition that all was
well. It was a reveille for the radical imagination.

Although in most cases, the numbers remained comparatively small and
the disruptions mostly inconsequential, it is clear that the Occupy movement
had an impact on the public consciousness. The very choice of the term "occupy" was significant. Since the early 1980s, capital and the state have been
privatizing public space or treating it as a commodity; however, the movement's protesters presented themselves as the champions of the public forum. They fought for a space where the common enterprise of politics could
be discussed, challenged, and perhaps transformed. The term "occupy" came
to denote an action aimed at recapturing territory on behalf of the vast majority and for the common good. More immediately, the political discourse
shifted to questions of distributive justice that remained in the public eye
through the electoral season in the United States a year later.[42]

Among the indications of the significance of the Occupy movement, one
stood out: the severity of the police repression applied against it. Since the
1980s, a well-established script had largely prevailed in the United States:
protesters engaged in acts of civil disobedience, police arrested them and
charged them with misdemeanors, and courts released them. While there
had always been a measure of police harassment and violence against demonstrators, especially Black protesters, the reactions against Occupy would
be more reminiscent of police reactions in Chicago in 1968 and at the

41. Writers for the 99%, *Occupying Wall Street: The Inside Story of an Action That Changed America* (New York: Haymarket, 2012), 5–23.
42. By October 2011, a CBS News/*New York Times* poll suggested that 43 percent of Americans agreed with the views of the Occupy Wall Street movement. Brian Montopoli, "Poll: 43 Percent Agree with Views of 'Occupy Wall Street,'" *CBS News*, October 26, 2011, available at http://www.cbsnews.com/8301-503544_162-20125515-503544/poll-43-percent-agree-with-views-of-occupy-wall-street/.

protests against the World Trade Organization (WTO) in 1999 than of reactions to, for example, reproductive rights marches. Indeed, in almost every city, including those governed by "progressive" mayors, such as Oakland and Seattle, the police used the pretext of "public health" to put on major shows of force, to subject protesters to pepper spray (oleoresin capsicum) and beatings, and ultimately to evict them from the public square. If nothing else, the widespread state violence with which Occupy was greeted suggests that the movement struck a negative cord with political elites. They seemed to see Occupy as a significant source of disruption, particularly when it acted in conjunction with labor groups and across regions, such as when Occupy protesters attempted to shut down West Coast ports (December 13, 2011) in a show of solidarity with port workers who were then in the midst of contract negotiations. In these cases, police forces deployed every available resource, exercised little self-restraint, and made numerous arrests.[43] In the event, the courts would later dismiss most of the charges against arrested protesters, but the system had made its point: it would not concede an inch of territory. Police tactics may, in some ways, have enhanced solidarity among radical protesters and their more moderate supporters, but, as Manuel Castells points out, the general slant of reporting, not to mention the fact that cameras were almost always behind police lines, served to drive a wedge "between the movement's actions and the perception of a majority of people whose life is dominated by fear."[44] It is thus not surprising that, while Occupy's plaints would transform the public discourse, this same public would recoil in fear from the movement. While the various elements of Occupy were highly visible, they remained largely isolated from their societies. The containment strategies worked.

Revolt in the Totally Administered Society

At any rate, much as Marcuse might have expected, in the Global North, in the Middle East, and in South America, the Occupy movement was largely built on relatively well-educated, yet disenfranchised, young people, those not fully integrated into the system of total administration; however, there was little sense that participants saw themselves as members of the affluent society. If anything, particularly in the United States, the initial motivation did not appear to be a rejection of the establishment and its core norms beyond neoliberalism. Rather, and not surprisingly because young people, women, and people of color have borne the brunt of the consequences of the

---

43. "Occupy Seattle Protests at Port Lead to Skirmish, Arrests," *Seattle PI*, December 13, 2011, available at http://www.seattlepi.com/local/transportation/article/Police-disperse -Occupy-2398699.php.

44. Castells, *Networks of Outrage and Hope*, 191.

economic crisis, the initial demands and slogans were reminiscent of the more traditional plaints of populism throughout U.S. history and of the redistributive politics of the classic labor movement of the New Deal era. They were the grievances of the precariat and of those who were being denied access to the American dream. Thus, in many localities, Democratic Party politicians sought to present themselves as being in agreement with the Occupiers, or at least with their demands for jobs and their critiques of austerity policies and structures of taxation that largely favor the very wealthy, the "1 percent." Still, these same politicians and liberal pundits attempted to make the demands "reasonable," acceptable to the capitalist order, by reducing them to a call for jobs and perhaps a mild restructuring of the tax code alongside an increase in the minimum wage.

Much more importantly, and very much unlike what Marcuse had observed, a much-weakened U.S. labor movement acted in solidarity with Occupy. This is a significant development because during the golden age, the U.S. labor movement, which at the time included about 36 percent of the workforce, largely rejected the New Left, supporting the U.S. war in Vietnam and other imperial projects and shamefully opposing first the Black liberation movement and then the women's movement. Still, a number of factors—including the collapse of the old permanent enemy; perhaps the presence of former New Left radicals in the organizing sections of labor; and, most importantly, the abrogation of the social pact by capital and the state—have produced a political shift among the labor unions, which now represent barely one-tenth of the workforce. Thus, in the neoliberal age, the U.S. labor movement joined protests for social justice for a short period beginning with the anti-WTO protests of 1999 and coming to an end with 9/11 (in 2001).[45] The labor movement led protests in response to an ambitious and sweeping antiunion legislation campaign in Wisconsin in early 2011. Today, we can speak of a loose alliance between the reform and the radical elements of the Left, of "an increasing ideological convergence on the Left," a convergence that can be traced back to the alterglobalization movement.[46]

This convergence constitutes a new development in post–World War II activism, which might be thought of as both a return to the reformist politics of the traditional labor movement and a demand for a society that responds to deeper needs for liberation, perhaps even to a call for a society that sees economic progress as a prerequisite for freedom. From this perspective, Occupy and related movements might prefigure a historically new development.

---

45. For a discussion of the alliance of the labor and social-justice movements in this period, see Michael Forman, "Social Rights or Social Capital? The Labor Movement and the Language of Capital," in *Social Capital: Critical Perspectives on Community and "Bowling Alone,"* ed. Scott L. McLean, David A. Schultz, and Manfred B. Steger (New York: New York University Press, 2002), 239–259.

46. Rowe and Carroll, "Reform or Radicalism," 161.

It is significant that Occupy included some important developments that arguably originated in the transformed sensibilities that arose during the 1960s. One clear element of these protests was a broad rejection of formal organization and leadership. "There is," Marcuse observed of 1960s radicals, "a strong element of spontaneity, even anarchism, in this rebellion, [perhaps] expression of the new sensibility, sensitivity against domination."[47] This was true of the 2011 radicals as well. Much as the Indignados before them, Occupiers quickly adopted an institutional form that, despite its apparent newness, had roots in nineteenth-century anarchism: the general assembly, "an extraordinary nightly display of consensual democracy in action."[48]

As an organizational form, the general assembly represents both a return to the past and a new development, which, if nothing else, bears an important utopian element. The practice of decision making by consensus, in small groups, can be thought of as avoiding the coercion inherent in majoritarian voting systems. It has been part of the anarchist repertoire at least since the Paris Commune of 1871, and Pierre-Joseph Proudhon had advocated something similar for countries as a whole. Many groups adopted this model during the 1960s, particularly in North America. More recently, it was embraced by direct-action activists during the 1999 Seattle protests and, on a much wider scale, by Argentine workers and activists. The Argentines, facing the threat of capital flight during the crisis of the early 2000s, demanded, "Que se vayan todos!" (Make them all go!). Across the country, workers and neighbors took over abandoned enterprises and communities and then sought to show they could manage them without hierarchies, through structures encouraging participation and learning. For this, they organized into group meetings in which issues were discussed and the role of facilitator was rotated regularly. The Argentines termed their organizational mode *horizontalidad* (horizontalism), to stress its egalitarian ethos. This same model emerged again among the Indignados. Not surprisingly, because anarchism, with its utopian individualism, has long attracted the U.S. Left (and the libertarian Right), the general-assembly model was also adopted by Occupy Wall Street. It guided the protests and administered an encampment that would feed, shelter, and educate several hundred people during the weeks of the occupation of Zuccotti Park.[49]

Horizontalism was adopted by most Occupy encampments. There were numerous variants on the model, but they all shared a rejection of formal leadership. Occupy Seattle, for example, held a general assembly daily, at

---

47. Marcuse, *An Essay on Liberation*, 89.
48. Writers for the 99%, *Occupying Wall Street*, 25.
49. Marina Sitrin, "One No, Many Yesses," in *Occupy! Scenes from Occupied America*, ed. Astra Taylor, Keith Gessen, and editors from *n+1*, *Dissent*, *Triple Canopy*, and *New Inquiry* (London: Verso, 2011), 8–11. See also Marina Sitrin, *Horizontalism: Voices of Popular Power in Argentina* (Oakland, CA: AK Press, 2006).

approximately 5:30 or 6:00 p.m. to make it possible for employed people to attend. For the most part, the Assembly claimed broad participation and aimed to make decisions by consensus. For some time, Occupy Seattle also made it possible for people to participate via its website. Over time (although it was a short time), the exchanges grew more sophisticated and informed as the participants tested and exchanged ideas and information. Like most of the larger occupations, Occupy Seattle established a library, developed learning groups that fostered discussions and invited speakers, and sought to make space for the arts. Furthermore, the group tried to include a variety of participants and sought the support of, for example, local tribes (and, by all appearances, such support was forthcoming). It was also generally welcoming of homeless people, and it was very clear that homeless youth regularly participated and spoke in assemblies and rallies. Less clear, however, was the occupation's success in attracting people of color, particularly Blacks, or its ability to hear some of their concerns. Some members of Occupy Seattle supported and many others opposed the effort to change the occupation's name to Decolonize/Occupy Seattle, revealing political arguments among groups within the occupation.

Another important element in the strategies of the Occupy movement was its absolute commitment to nonviolence. This is another utopian element, in the best of senses. It foreshadows the triumph of Eros over the destructive impulse, the pacification of existence in the service of human freedom and progress. Nonviolence, as an idea, also has deep roots in the traditions of protest in the United States, roots going back at least to Henry David Thoreau's writings about his opposition to slavery and the U.S.-Mexican war in the 1840s. In the wake of the heroic practices associated with the Black liberation movement and Martin Luther King Jr., nonviolence has acquired an almost doctrinal status among the Left in the United States. Thus, much like the alterglobalization movement before it, Occupy adopted nonviolence as a matter of principle. While there may have been conflicts over this issue with anarchist groups such as the black bloc, even these groups restricted their "violence" to the occasional destruction of property. This, it is worth pointing out, is in distinction to the traditional U.S. labor movement which, until the 1970s, would, on occasion, respond to violence with violence. It was not so with Occupy, which, by and large everywhere, resisted the temptation and provocation. In the words of Rebecca Solnit, "Violence is what police use. It's what the state uses. If we want a revolution, it's because we want a better world, because we think we have a better imagination, a more beautiful vision. So we're nonviolent; we're not like them in crucial ways."[50] Marcuse would have appreciated the spirit, if not always the conclusions.

50. Rebecca Solnit, "Throwing Out the Master's Tools and Building a Better House," in Taylor et al., *Occupy!*, 147.

Yet if the Occupiers were agreed on the question of nonviolence and methods, they did not seem to agree on goals and analysis. At Zuccotti Square, for example, differences were deep enough to produce a spatial segmentation of the Occupation into "neighborhoods" divided by political proclivities, ethnicity, and "class."[51] The ongoing discussions in a variety of fora may have helped forge common positions and raise deeper barriers among the participants. Initially, as both liberal sympathizers and, a little later, conservative detractors liked to point out, the statements coming out of the Occupation seemed inchoate. But this is not entirely fair. There is a difference between demands and a program: movements produce demands; parties produce programs. By the end of September, Occupy Wall Street had produced a sweeping statement of its positions and demands, which it translated into five languages. Drawing on national traditions dating back to the Declaration of Independence, Occupy Wall Street proclaimed its position in the language of rights and abuses of them; it avowed its solidarity with the lowly and oppressed everywhere, and it asserted a human right to express these positions.[52] Rather than inchoate, then, Occupy Wall Street's pronouncements raised demands for a truly free society while also exemplifying the difficulty of casting such demands within the dominant liberal and neoliberal discourses. The pattern in Seattle was similar, and the group placed a set of positions up for consideration by a broad audience via its website. While largely taking Occupy Wall Street's manifesto as their own, the Seattleites adopted a specific list of demands that were mostly consistent with the policies of the more advanced capitalist democracies of the golden age; in addition, their demands extended to environmentalist claims (the most popular entry) and demands for human rights around the world—thus projecting an emancipatory sensibility, if not a theory of liberation.[53] Indeed, if anything was to be missing, it was a theory of liberation and an analysis of capitalism. In other words, "the institutions of free speech and freedom of thought did not hamper the mental coordination with the established reality": the core of the dominant ideology was not brought into question.[54]

51. Writers for the 99%, *Occupying Wall Street*, 61–67.

52. See, for example, NYC General Assembly, "Declaration of the Occupation of New York City," September 29, 2011, available at http://www.nycga.net/resources/declaration/. The Indignados maintained web pages in various languages, including Catalan, Galician, French, and English. They also sought to present themselves as Europeans whose concerns reached well beyond the continent. See the ¡Democracia Real YA! website at http://www.democraciarealya.es/.

53. Occupy Seattle, "Demands," available at https://web.archive.org/web/20111013195733/http://occupyseattle.org/demands.

54. Marcuse, *One-Dimensional Man*, 104.

There was, indeed, little analysis of capitalism, its structures, contradictions, and ultimate irrationality. For example, on the rare occasions I witnessed the articulation of more radical formulations in Occupy Seattle fora, these came under fire, often being labeled as unrealistic or rejected with the same kind of anti-intellectualism Marcuse noted in the New Left of the 1960s. This was a general pattern among the Occupy movement. As a result, positions and grievances were articulated through vague and abstract categories such as "the middle class" and "the corporations." This certainly had the benefit that, in the United States at least, many people would more readily take the pronouncements of Occupy seriously because they could not be associated with socialism or communism. Unfortunately, in so doing, the Occupy discourse also failed to avail itself of analytical categories that would be helpful in shedding light on the deep-seated structural conditions at the origin of the current crisis, conditions which bespeak of the fundamental irrationality of capitalist society and which cannot be confronted in the absence of a critical theory capable of articulating them.

The absence of theoretically informed perspectives on capitalist crisis and, more generally, on bourgeois society posed a potentially more serious problem. Many of the grievances of the Occupy movement, for example, centered on the financial sector, the banks. This focus was accurate, but limited, because the critique was often uninformed and easily drifted into conspiracy theories associated with right-wing populism. One line of reasoning that gained much traction involved the U.S. Federal Reserve System (the Fed), long the bête noire of the populist Right. Here, too, the criticism was justified inasmuch as the Fed, as an institution, was designed to be largely shielded from the controls of popular sovereignty; however, the discourse presented the Fed not as the product of a system that had accepted the principle of popular sovereignty only under duress but as the product of highjacking by obscure and barely visible forces of an imagined authentic democracy that had once existed. One video clip, "How the Banks and the Government Are Stealing from You," that is still making the rounds advances this claim and proclaims that the state has no power at all over the Fed and its Board of Governors, which is not true (as they are appointed by the U.S. president and confirmed by the Senate). More worrisome, this same clip places its account of the Fed in a longer "history" of money and banking originating in the Middle Ages, when characters who look vaguely like Italian Renaissance depictions of Jews trick average people into their interest trap.[55] The point here is that without a

---

55. This video has been reposted a number of times on the Internet by "niknak72." It appears under the title "The Federal Reserve" on YouTube at http://www.youtube.com/watch?v=Sjagaad7AnY.

critical theory, the movement could be captured by the counterrevolutionary right-wing elements that have also gained new strength in the current
historical junction.

Furthermore, Occupy's rejection of formal leadership and organization made the movement difficult to revive after it was forcefully evicted
from visible public spaces. As a result, the movement was marginalized,
its claims co-opted into the dominant discourse, and its members isolated.
This also occurred in the Arab revolutions, especially in Egypt and Tunisia. There, young and relatively secular people, an unprecedented number of them women, provided the mass base for the demonstrations that
brought down the dictatorships. Yet as governments have been reconstituted, well-organized fundamentalist groups and, in Egypt, the military,
have seized control. In the United States, while revolution was unlikely,
lack of organization made the Occupation particularly vulnerable to cooptation, especially during the electoral cycle. Here, in keeping with a long
tradition of espousing elements of popular protest and transforming them
into sanitized electoral agendas, establishment elites co-opted some of the
demands of the Occupy movement while ultimately excluding it from the
process.

Despite all of this, it is clear that the recent revival of popular protest has
had a significant effect on the political environment. An analysis of Marcuse's contributions to social theory is especially helpful in understanding
the scope of these events. The protests opened up the discourse to highlight
the irrationalities of the system, but they failed to articulate a practice capable of transforming it. To this failure I now turn.

Marcuse in the Crisis of Neoliberalism

I look at my new device. It is sleek, modern, powerful. In a busy world where
human interaction is difficult to sustain, it allows me to keep in touch with
friends and family, to hear their voices, to share photographs and comments.
It helps me coordinate protest and revolt. Upon further thought, however,
I realize that the device is nothing more than a customer delivery conduit
with built-in obsolescence. It is the product of underpaid laborers in an authoritarian country that claims itself communist yet is a crucial player in
global capitalism. Its components, rich in rare earth metals, contribute to the
despoliation of the planet. It permits the state to know where I am at every
moment, what I believe, to whom I speak, what I like to eat and read. I am
aware of the fact that by keeping me constantly in touch, it also prolongs my
workday, but there is really no other way it could have come into being. Sharing my thoughts with state and capital is not really a big deal: Why would
they care anyway? Despite the negatives, has life ever been demonstrably

better? "The tension between appearance and reality melts away and both merge in one rather pleasant feeling."[56]

Marcuse offered similarly trivial examples (a new car, a walk in the park, a ride in the subway) as instances of "the happy marriage of the positive and the negative—the *objective* ambiguity which adheres to the data of experience" whose interrelation must be comprehended to burst "the harmonizing consciousness and its false realism."[57] This is a well-functioning society that conceals its irrationality behind the rationality of its technology and that conceals the precariousness of the existence of so many of its members behind its formal freedoms. Indeed, it doesn't so much hide its contradictions as present them, with irony, as unsolvable paradoxes. These contradictions are powerful enough to obscure the very inkling of the possibility of an alternative employment of this society's accomplishments to ensure the pacification of existence and the opening of human life to inner growth and to new experiences for their own sake. Theory, philosophy, can help us comprehend these facts, but "an insight into necessity . . . will not suffice when the accomplishments of science and the level of productivity have eliminated the utopian features of the alternatives."[58] Revolt in the public square highlights the negativity of the system and raises, for a while, the plaints of its victims, but it ultimately can be contained. Sometimes, it leads to concessions. However, for the refusal to be complete, practice must go beyond traditional protest because this has grown ineffective. At best, protest is capable of preserving the illusion of popular sovereignty in an administered society. Consequently, bridging the gap between an uncertain future of promise and a present with no alternatives will require that, by chance, "the most advanced consciousness of humanity, and its most exploited force" meet anew.[59]

So it was, with a note of forced optimism, that Marcuse closed his most important work, *One-Dimensional Man*. I end my reassessment of this classic enduring work in the same mood.

In this chapter, I seek to show that Marcuse's analysis of capitalist society is remarkably current but also that it is in some ways dated. It is current inasmuch as existing conditions grew out of those under which Marcuse wrote. The system of total administration of life and consciousness still prevails; the situation facing us is still that of a totally administered society in which technology and science continue to be deployed in the interest of domination. It is dated inasmuch as Marcuse elaborated in response to the conditions of the golden age of capitalism, conditions that no longer apply: the affluent society has grown stingier about sharing the goods, and the placid acceptance of

56. Marcuse, *One-Dimensional Man*, 226.
57. Ibid., 227.
58. Ibid., 254.
59. Ibid., 257.

the system has grown cynical and fearful as the proportions in the mix of cooptation with fear have changed. As both the reception of Occupy by the general public and Occupy's own anti-intellectualism suggest, the processes Marcuse attributed to one-dimensional society function to prevent critical rationality by presenting the irrational as rational and the rational need for radical transformation as fundamentally irrational; yet the mechanisms of this administration are different, and, in some important ways, their crisis is such that their inadequacy has become apparent. This has given rise to new social movements such as Occupy. Others will follow, continuing to demonstrate the potential to fuel a broad campaign for a significant social transformation and the barriers to doing so.

The new movements have their base among those not fully integrated into the system: the disenfranchised and the young, as well as a new category of outsiders, the precariat, contingent workers of various skills whose employment is unstable and often, but not always, ill-remunerated. Women have also played a newly significant role, particularly in the Middle East and in Latin America. In North America, there have been links to immigrant groups, First Nations, and other long-excluded elements of society. Unlike in the 1960s, and particularly in the United States, the Occupy movement helped to revive working-class activism, though it is really too soon to refer to it as militancy. While, in a sense, the Occupy movement and the Indignados—with their search for new forms of self-organization and their effort to link claims for social justice with concerns about, for example, ecological sustainability and a rejection of consumerism—appeared to embrace the elements for a broad call for true emancipation, they were unable to articulate a critique of capitalism itself. Occupy, in particular, largely restricted itself to populist accounts whose critique suggested a malfunctioning system rather than a set of social relations that structure a society fundamentally at odds with true human needs. Demands for good jobs, housing, security, and a more transparent political system are worthy, but "possession and procurement of the necessities of life are the prerequisite, rather than the content, of a free society."[60]

So, then, Marcuse's work retains relevance into the twenty-first century; yet if one-dimensional society persists, it is different from the world he addressed nearly half a century ago because the regime of capitalist accumulation he took for granted is, in fact, no longer with us. Consequently, any analysis that will appropriate the tools Marcuse bequeathed must, much as he would have done, do so with due consideration for the important elements that have reconstituted not only the practices of accumulation but also the ideologies that obscure the true nature of capitalist society and systematically undermine efforts at leveling a critique. This, as I have sought

---

60. Marcuse, *Eros and Civilization*, 195.

to show, remains a problem even in the face of a new era of protest, which, on one hand, continues to offer much promise but, on the other, has had trouble elaborating a systematic analysis of, and a sustained practice against, the structural conditions it seeks to transform. Still, Occupiers, Indignados, Arab revolutionaries, and many others gave hope a new life and reminded both system administrators and their opponents that history has not come to an end.

3

Negating That Which Negates Us

Marcuse, Critical Theory, and the New Politics of Refusal

CHRISTIAN GARLAND

> Dialectical theory . . . cannot offer the remedy. It cannot be
> positive. To be sure, the dialectical concept, in comprehending the
> given facts, transcends the given facts. This is the very token of its
> truth. It defines the historical possibilities, even necessities; but
> their realization can only be in the practice which responds to the
> theory.
> —HERBERT MARCUSE, *One-Dimensional Man*[1]

> Perspectives must be fashioned that displace and estrange the
> world, reveal it to be, with its rifts and crevices, as indigent and
> distorted as it will one day appear in the messianic light.
> —THEODOR ADORNO, *Minima Moralia*[2]

arcuse's thought is of key significance to the renewal of a critical
theory with its basis in radical praxis, or what can be defined as a
politics of refusal: the negation of that which negates us. To be sure,
refusal and *resistance* should not be mistaken as simply passive withdrawal
or retreat; rather, they are the active forms of a radically different mode of being and mode of doing, which Marcuse himself would identify as "the Great
Refusal." It is thus possible to speak of an ontology of negativity, for in spite
of everything, as Adorno said, "We are still alive."[3] Ontology, understood as

---

A version of this chapter was previously published as Christian Garland, "Negating That
Which Negates Us: Marcuse, Critical Theory, and the New Politics of Refusal," *Radical Philosophy Review* 16, no. 1 (2013): 375–385.

1. Herbert Marcuse, *One-Dimensional Man: Studies in the Ideology of Advanced Industrial Society* (Boston: Beacon, 1991), 253.

2. Theodor Adorno, *Minima Moralia: Reflections from Damaged Life* (London: Verso,
2005), 247.

3. "We only have any chance at all of withstanding the experiences of recent decades if
we do not forget for a moment the paradox that despite everything we are still alive." Theodor
Adorno, "Wird Spengler recht behalten?" [Will Spengler turn out to be right?], in *Gesammelte
Schriften in 20 Bänden* [Collected works in 20 volumes], vol. 20.1, ed. Rolf Tiedemann, with
the assistance of Gretel Adorno, Susan Buck-Morss, and Klaus Schultz (Frankfurt-am-Main:

being-in-the-world, can be said to describe material existence as the factual observation of social reality as it is. In recognizing that this same social reality is itself not given but the result of a very specific material ordering of society, one riven by antagonism and contradiction, human beings become aware of this fact by the nature of their (precarious) material existence and, in so doing, run up against the reified and deadening social relations of a world that is not their own and that they did not choose. However, in refusing as far as possible to reproduce the relations of capitalism, we assert our own negative and resistant subjectivity, something of which Marcuse was well aware and which he developed and sought to advance further in the entirety of his work.

It is contended here that this ontology of negativity can be defined starting simply from being-in-the-world—that is, by existence against things as they are. For to simply exist, *to be*, is not recognized by capital, which recognizes only the reproduction of value and the extraction of profit; human beings exist only as instrumental means to that end. A politically charged critical theory, such as the one outlined here, instead starts from an ontology of negativity, finding in the imperfection of thought the problem of working against a positive or spuriously objective standpoint that defines the negative in the moment of truth it uncovers, and vice versa. This negative project finds a tentative mode of praxis in a radical—one might say revolutionary—politics of refusal in which a social subjectivity takes hold of the existent, the accepted, the given in its own hands and begins the process of historical rupture and transformative promise that underlies such a mode of thought.

The aim here is to develop a critical theory of praxis that makes extensive reference to the critical theory of Marcuse. It is a critique of ideology protective of the state of things as they are as much as of positive modes of thought that severely limit the capabilities of opposition and critique. It seeks to contribute to the mapping of a collective escape plan from the "open-air prison"[4] in which we are presently confined.

Defining Negativity: Toward the Given, the Existent, and That Which Is

Defining what is meant by *negativity* is an important clarification, particularly when much contemporary Marxian theorizing tends to discard the concept altogether.[5] Indeed, the positivity of such thought, what Benjamin

---

Surhkamp, 1986), 309, quoted in Detlev Claussen, *Adorno: One Last Genius* (Cambridge, MA: Harvard University Press, 2008), 11–12.

4. Theodor Adorno, "Cultural Criticism and Society," in *Prisms*, trans. Samuel M. Weber and Shierry Weber Nicholsen (Cambridge, MA: MIT Press, 1997), 34.

5. The specific thinkers meant here are primarily Michael Hardt and Antonio Negri, Paolo Virno, and Franco "Bifo" Berardi. Hardt and Negri's thought is of immense importance

Noys calls *affirmationism*,[6] insists that negation is a futile form of critique; Marcuse's thought, by contrast, is rich with the power of the negative. Starting, then, from a negative ontology—a negative concept of being-in-the-world—it is thus possible to define a turn *against* it, for to exist *in spite of* capital and its imperatives and against the infernal continuum of the history it has made and would make for the future is merely *to be* and thus the negation of that which negates us. Marcuse saw the present nonlife of one-dimensional man and woman as essentially impossible to sustain, both in material and existential terms, despite the sometimes-mistaken view that the temporary relative integration of the working class as working class would mean the indefinite prolongation of this state of nonexistence. For Marcuse's critique of this society—advanced late capitalism—saw also that an apparent temporary dimming of class contradictions by the neon glare of the trinkets and baubles of consumerism would remain always that: temporary. In brutish terms, the "fight for the crude and material things without which no refined and spiritual things could exist"[7] is, in our era, becoming more and more apparent, and Marcuse himself was well aware of this: "The established system preserves itself only through the global destruction of resources, of nature, of human life, and the *objective* conditions for making an end to it."[8]

The arrest of these objective, material conditions—capable of finally abolishing poverty (globally), the overcoming of material necessity, and the end to the competitive struggle for existence—are *reimposed* by capital as the condition of its own reproduction, even as this conceptualization very realistically confronts human beings and all other forms of life with their own extinction. Therefore, the need to rupture, to break with the all-but-total unfreedom of the present, is the condition of a resistant subjectivity existing in and against the same world it seeks to break with, and the urgency of this need to break with the present is felt all the more the longer we are forced to exist within it. Thus, it is possible to speak here again of a negative ontology, recognizing that subjectivity exists within and against the deadening, reified relation of objects that is the status of human beings buying and selling themselves in the market. Subjective refusal—both individually and collectively—recognizes in its insubordination and refusal the negation of

---

and is itself a very significant contribution to reworking and reenergizing critical and revolutionary theory, but it is not without major flaws. For a nuanced and qualified critique *from the same side*, see John Holloway, Fernando Matamoros, and Sergio Tischler, eds., *Negativity and Revolution: Adorno and Political Activism* (London: Pluto, 2009).

6. Benjamin Noys, *The Persistence of the Negative: A Critique of Contemporary Continental Theory* (Edinburgh: Edinburgh University Press, 2010).

7. Walter Benjamin, "Theses on the Philosophy of History," in *Illuminations*, ed. Hannah Arendt, trans. Harry Zorn (London: Pimlico, 1999), 246.

8. Herbert Marcuse, *Counterrevolution and Revolt* (Boston: Beacon, 1972), 7 (emphasis in original).

this nonstatus, in which objectively we exist only for capital, insofar as it requires our labor. When labor can be exploited by capital, it is always crushed by this same dead weight of abstraction, the laws of surplus value, and the extraction of profit; however, the contradiction at work is the resistance and refusal of this same relation of objectification and exploitative abstract labor: the class struggle—for as a Filipina domestic worker said in relation to her own contestation of the relations of exploitation, "We will fight; we will get stronger. . . . *We exist in this world.*"[9]

Marcuse's critical theory of the changes wrought to the objective situation of the proletariat by the hyperdevelopment of capitalism, from the middle to late twentieth century on, made—and still makes—for discomforting reading for those who viewed and continue to view the proletariat in mock-heroic terms as struggling salt of the earth, in particular as blue-collar (male) factory workers, as if this objective and arbitrary category created and imposed by capital had some inherent and lasting value of its own that should be defended and preserved. The positive affirmation of labor—specifically manual labor—is completely foreign to Marxism and its definition of the proletariat as social negativity. Similarly, the mainstream of sociology, and Marcuse's other hostile critics, have taken this historical development to mean that capitalism itself has moved beyond class society, that it is no longer structured according to the capital-labor relation—the class relation—merely because the nature of labor has moved away from the factory and plant, once again only in the West, where the underside of consumerism is exposed by the brute reality of production in what has been called the *Third World*, itself a disputed and dubious term. That the products that must be consumed in the West—iPods and laptops, for example, sold and purchased as a mark of these countries' economic strength—are manufactured through slave conditions of sweatshop labor is the bad conscience of hi-tech capitalist society and the continuous reminder that, in Benjamin's phrase, "there is no document of civilization that is not simultaneously a document of barbarism."[10] Indeed, we are enmeshed in social relations of alienation and domination we did not choose or wish for, and yet we are compelled to reproduce them every day as a matter of survival. The turn against these same arbitrary relations is the Great Refusal, a different way of doing, a different mode of being. John Holloway writes:

> The argument is simple. We make capitalism: we must stop making it and do something else. This means setting doing against abstract labour: this we must, can and already do. . . .

---

9. "Britain's Secret Slaves," *Dispatches*, directed by Joe Ward and Andrew Smith, aired August 30, 2010, *Channel 4* (emphasis added).

10. Benjamin, "Theses on the Philosophy of History," 248.

Labour imprisons our bodies in an obvious way: it shuts them up in factories or offices or schools for a large part of our waking life, or binds them to computers or mobile phones. But, in a less obvious way, the abstraction involved in capitalist labour also creates an equally profound prison, a prison that encloses our minds—the way we think, the concepts we use. There is a tearing-apart at the core of our existence, the separation of ourselves from the determination of what we do, and this tearing-apart affects every aspect of our lives.[11]

Radical praxis—what has here been defined as *the new politics of refusal*—breaks open this false closure, this conquest of the unhappy consciousness that knows only the given, things as they are, and the ideology that says they must remain so. The material conflicts at work all the time in such a society find theoretical expression in critical theory, can be seen in recurrent forms across history—the resistance and refusal of exploitation, domination, and oppression—and find their most radical form in the class struggle. Class struggle is not just the motor of history but also the accelerator; we exist in and against the present and, in so doing, break open the linear narrative of exploitation and domination that remains.

Acts of refusal can be observed in groups of workers going on strike to oppose austerity measures, resisting a demanded speed-up in productivity aimed at restoring the rate of profit, or refusing to accept cuts in order to "pay off the deficit" from massive state intervention to rescue capitalist enterprises, which are themselves the victims of a crisis of profitability, of capital's valorization. Other examples include the 2010 United Kingdom's mass student protests refusing the burden of debt from education, which is becoming an unaffordable privilege even as it is being restructured into an instrumental production line for the social factory; the 2011–2012 spread of protest occupations across the Americas, Europe, and elsewhere, which for all their inchoate uncertainty were authentic expressions of protest and resistance; and the 2016 Nuit Debout mobilizations against, among other things, neoliberal labor law reforms in France. Indeed, the feeling-in-the-dark nature of such spontaneous movements may be seen as a mark of their authenticity. As with earlier resistant antagonistic subjectivities in Marcuse's time (e.g., in France in May 1968; in Italy in the "Hot Autumn" of the following year, no less than the movement of *autonomia operaismo*, which reached its high point in 1977; and in the United States, the anti–Vietnam War protests and campus protests of the 1960s and 1970s), it is possible to see the attempt at becoming, at self-creation in and against the objective world of capital and instrumental reason.

---

11. John Holloway, *Crack Capitalism* (London: Pluto, 2010), 109.

The class struggle can thus be seen as the struggle to refuse being objectified and reduced to the category of a proletarian; to refuse alienated, reified labor; and to refuse the categorization and identity imposed by capitalism. One does not need to privilege a social subject to see a negative universality at work in the commonalities and linkages of multiple antagonistic subjectivities that unify into a cohesive collective negativity—that of the revolutionary social subject. For just as we reproduce capital in everyday social relations, so too can we cease to do so in the refusal of relations of hierarchy and domination. Capital is, after all, a social relation that we (are compelled to) reproduce every day. As John Holloway has argued in *Crack Capitalism*, a different way of doing, of being-in-the-world—this world we exist in but are also against—is possible and everywhere present, frequently in small, daily acts, which just by their doing, by their very existence, are antagonistic to capital and hierarchical power. To treat others as autonomous human subjects—existing in and of themselves, not as simple instruments serving capital enmeshed in bureaucratic networks of power or through an identity-oriented label, whether *positive* or the older, cruder identifiers of racism, sexism, and exclusion of the other or contesting and refusing such labels—is to assert a *resistant subjectivity* that recognizes itself in reciprocal human relations of community and freedom, which are also the material negation of those imposed and reproduced by late capitalism.

Indeed, there is a different kind of doing, remaking the world in accordance with one worthy of human beings, one that is not based on objectified, abstract labor that enmeshes men and women in an alien and hostile struggle for material (and mental and emotional) survival. For it is the twofold nature of labor in which doing—the capacity of men and women to consciously remake the world—is made into the onerous and dead weight of abstract labor productive of value: such is the nature of the capital-labor relation. This negativity, against capitalism and all of its social relations of exploitation, hierarchy, and domination, may be seen as a negative dialectic, the collective social subject refusing and breaking—or at least seeking to break—the class relation and all other social relations of domination and oppression by which it remains objectified. Therefore, any reconciliation with the given reality of the present is rendered impossible but no less than this material negation of the existent. It embodies contradiction, rupture, antagonism, and refusal, opposing the false assurances of reconciliation and closure promised by positive identity-thinking—the synthetic totality of closure that is capitalism.

Marx's own recognition that a species-being (*Gattungswesen*) or creative human essence is what distinguishes human beings from every other species alive is also a defining foundational basis for Marcuse's thought and indeed critical theory. We have the power to consciously remake both the form and content of the world, and yet we are prisoners of it. Thus, in existing *in spite* of this and choosing to do what we consider necessary or desirable, and also in refusing as far as possible to reproduce the relations of capitalism, we assert our own negative and resistant subjectivity.

Moments of Insubordination, Subversion, and Hope

"No emancipation without that of society,"[12] as Adorno noted, and to this we might add that any politics based on an exclusive identity, such as gender or sexuality, which excludes the wider nature of society, is at best doomed to fail and at worst already comfortably on its way to being accommodated within it. For capitalism is based on an inherent antagonism and struggle between diametrically opposed material forces. The *class struggle* is this self-same process; indeed, it is the disruption and nonreproduction of capitalist social relations, their refusal and potential rupture, in which the future becomes truly unwritten, and a glimpse of a mode of life qualitatively beyond the form it presently takes as it is *not lived*.[13] For a social subjectivity must refuse—and does refuse—the objective subsumption of life under conditions of the class relation, and, indeed, the same can be said of other objectifying social relations based on gender or ethnicity and their concomitant material factors.

Class struggle is the recurrent social antagonism, the material contestation of the capitalist mode of production itself, because simply by existing within but also against this world of the present, the proletariat—the revolutionary social subject—becomes the inimical contradiction and contravention of what is imposed and demanded by the class relation, the objective necessity and prerequisite for the functioning and reproduction of capital and thus its own dissolution, which for all its apparent, opaque abstraction is in fact a very real, actually existing, material relation.

Resistant subjectivity can be seen in the negation of identity-thinking and the spurious naturalization of fixed social roles, such as gender divisions and the reduction of sexuality to genital sex-as-procreation. Put another way, there is sexual desire, or the erotic—Marcuse's pleasure principle—a uniquely rich process of life lived for its own sake, as an end in itself, which does not fulfill any functional instrumentality; thus, this desire can be viewed as a significant and inherently subversive activity, making noticeable the system's cracks. Indeed, it is possible to observe in the history of the domestication of sexuality and the construction of male-female roles an example of abstract labor produced against human beings, by human beings, just as we can see in the repressive desublimation of the market an obvious

---

12. Adorno, *Minima Moralia*, 173.
13. This is a paraphrase of a quotation by Ferdinand Kürnberger—"Life does not live"—which Adorno uses at the beginning of his *Minima Moralia* (19).

flipside to straightforward sexual repression embodied in traditional bourgeois social values and attitudes. In this flipside to traditional morality (as with monogamy, marriage, and the toleration of homosexuality only insofar as it tries to replicate the heterosexual couple), there is, of course, the commercial repository of unlimited, unlicensed alienation, from scantily clad celebrities on magazine covers to the equally consumable products of pornography and prostitution. Anything you want is yours, as long as you are willing to pay for it.

As convincingly explored by Marcuse in *Eros and Civilization*[14] and subsequent works, romantic love is an immeasurable, nonquantifiable form of happiness but one that, like everything else under late capitalism, is mutilated and distorted by instrumental reason. Love becomes an aggregate of calculating, mutual self-interest, from the legalistic nature of marriage (backed up by prenuptial agreements) to the permissive nature of the market that allows anything as long as it can be bought and sold. Love and sexuality are degraded into a barely recognizable imitation of themselves. The reassertion of Eros is the libidinous and Dionysian force of life against death, of desire, and of the erotic against the objectification and exploitation embodied in sexual and social repression and also the repressive desublimation of the market. Marcuse writes:

> Human freedom is thus rooted in the human *sensibility*: the senses do not only "receive" what is given to them, in the form in which it appears, they do not "delegate" the transformation of the given to another faculty (the understanding); rather, they discover or *can* discover by themselves, in their "practice," new (more gratifying) possibilities and capabilities, forms and qualities of things, and can urge and guide their realization. The emancipation of the senses would make freedom what it is not yet: a sensuous need, an objective of the Life Instincts (*Eros*).[15]

Marcuse was well aware of what has been further developed recently by Holloway: "When we say that doing exists as 'resentment-of, tension-against, rebellion-against abstract labour, as menace, as potential,' we are speaking of our internal antagonism: we exist as resentment-of, tension-against, rebellion-against ourselves, as menace, as potential."[16] It is in this continual subversion and rebellion that we become truly ourselves, rediscover our subjectivity against the objectification, the thingification of market relations. In

---

14. Herbert Marcuse, *Eros and Civilization: A Philosophical Inquiry into Freud* (Boston: Beacon, 1955).

15. Marcuse, *Counterrevolution and Revolt*, 71 (emphasis in original).

16. Holloway, *Crack Capitalism*, 221.

this sense, the materiality of doing is observable in struggles against the imperatives of capital, which manifest in multiple instances as opposition and resistance toward the imposition of the law of value and, indeed, the capital-labor relation, whether this be directly or indirectly mediated through political and institutional structures and restructuring (e.g., cuts to university funding, increased tuition fees, wage cuts, redundancies, and welfare-to-work programs, in spite of there being no actual work to be had). Critical theory, radical thought, of the kind developed by Marcuse, can also be seen as the negation of ideological identity-thinking, of spurious positivity and instrumental rationality; thought is, after all, itself a mode of doing, the attempt to critically think about the conditions of our time. The Great Refusal might be defined as what Holloway has called an "anti-power" or a "power-to"—that is, the capacity of human beings to remake the world in accordance with their needs and desires. Such a power challenges and negates existing top-down power structures that impose their own repressive "power-over" the human subject; material force must after all—and does—meet material force.[17]

When such an anti-power becomes widespread and operates against and in spite of the imperatives of capitalism—which includes, of course, the imperative of each-against-all and treating others as a means to an end—there can be seen the first manifestations of an alternative, different way of doing and of a qualitatively different form of life. As Marcuse argues in *Counterrevolution and Revolt*, in describing revolutionary social change in the hyperdeveloped countries—think here, for example, of the United States, the United Kingdom, and the European Union—"the revolution would be *qualitatively* different from its abortive precursors,"[18] "a qualitatively different *totality*."[19] This argument is very instructive in gaining perspective on what is actually at stake: literally, everything, for it is no longer possible to envisage partial or small-scale changes to a system rapidly running humanity into the ground and, quite likely, playing with her extinction. The use of the concept *totality* also needs to become a much more accepted and widely used one among those who would hope to contribute to a convincing social commentary and critique of the world as it is, and it is also useful in making a sharp separation between radical critics and the far-from-radical voices of institutionalized, liberal, identity politics, for whom such an unashamedly totalizing theory smacks of a tyrannizing *grand narrative*.

---

17. John Holloway, *Change the World without Taking Power: The Meaning of Revolution Today*, 2nd ed. (London: Pluto, 2005), 36.

18. Marcuse, *Counterrevolution and Revolt*, 2 (emphasis in original).

19. Ibid., 3 (emphasis in original).

Instead of a Conclusion

In his critical assessment that a significant portion of the population was seemingly contented, having been integrated into one-dimensional, capitalist society in the middle to late twentieth century, Marcuse was not (any more than Marx before him) pretending to make a conclusive, final diagnosis of the society he critiqued or attempting to predict the course of its likely future. To do so would be ahistorical and suggest a thoroughly un-Marxian misunderstanding of history. The class struggle is about contestation, after all, and is frequently manifested in nonrevolutionary forms, but the inherent antagonism and contradiction between capital and labor never goes away, because capital needs labor to exist.[20]

At the time *One-Dimensional Man* was published (1964), the now hidden, now open fight of class struggle merely appeared more hidden than previously. The next five decades would encompass the project of capital's restructuring and recomposition, leaving one side—that is, the side of labor—dispersed, disorganized, and demoralized. It may be contended that class struggle is once more becoming much more explicitly an open fight and has never gone away; the relative integration of labor in the middle to late twentieth century was only ever a passing, short-term phenomenon, and in the long-gone world of unionized full employment, class conflict persisted, just in a more hidden form. Now, more than a half century later, capital is much more defined by naked exploitation and the dispersal and recomposition of labor, as well as such supporting measures as wage cuts, mass redundancies, and, of course, the oversupply of labor. In the long-term project of capital recomposition, the social relation that is capital throws off far more labor than it needs. The resulting precarity amounts to chronic underemployment: a limited number of paid working hours, as observed most notoriously in "zero-hours contracts," in which there are no guaranteed paid work hours from week to week, and bogus self-employment, which further individualizes the terms of "work" even as it becomes ever scarcer and more insecure. Such "work" becomes the primary means of social reproduction in advanced capitalist society.

Of its particular time, Marcuse's observation that "the increasing satisfaction of needs even beyond subsistence needs also changes the features of the revolutionary alternative"[21] could, in fact, be reversed in our present epoch, which is one of capital in crisis. This reversal would be rendered as the increasing failure to satisfy needs, even those of subsistence, in what is an

---

20. "Capital is dead labour, which, vampire-like, lives only by sucking living labour, and lives the more, the more labour it sucks." Karl Marx, *Capital: A Critique of Political Economy*, vol. 1, trans. Ben Fowkes, (1976; repr., London: Penguin Classics, 1992), 342.

21. Marcuse, *Counterrevolution and Revolt*, 9.

era of crisis with austerity imposed on the great majority in a frantic effort to shift the cost of the system's failure back onto the general population—though it needs to be remembered that the system remains one of exploitation and domination and is a failure even when it is "working." The fact that the great majority, the proletariat, has changed completely in character—at least in the hyperdeveloped countries—even since Marcuse's time[22] does not, however, mean that the essential features of the capital-labor relation have changed at all but merely that they have been altered, something Marcuse critically observed and theorized well. Marcuse, like those who can be said to practice a new politics of refusal, asserts in thought and practice the reappropriation of doing, a different mode of being, as much as manifesting the resistant subjectivity outlined here. What can be theorized and indeed observed at work in this persistence of the negative is the inveterate antagonism toward the relations of capital—objectification, thingification of human beings, and alienation of human doing—no less than the refusal of capital's imperatives that we can see in its material and immediate manifestations as contestation of these instrumental, "inevitable" imperatives. A different way of doing, a politics of refusal, can be seen as offensive action against the logic of capital as it manifests in any number of immediate and practical material examples—resistance to austerity measures, cuts, and redundancies being just some of them. Similarly, this different way of doing can be seen as the refusal of hierarchical and bureaucratic systems and structures as much as the conscious effort toward their elimination. Indeed, the negative dialectical method employed by Marcuse aims at an immanent critique of the social world but also of all its ideological presuppositions. Recognizing the power of the negative in antagonism and refusal—for the negative dialectical moment breaks open what had previously been seen as given, immutable, and inevitable—and materially articulating this as critical theory and praxis remains the project and task of our time.

---

22. "The base of exploitation is thus enlarged beyond the factories and shops, and far beyond the blue collar working class." Marcuse, *Counterrevolution and Revolt*, 10.

4

Occupying and Refusing Radically

The Deprived and the Dissatisfied
Transforming the World

PETER MARCUSE

R eading my father's published and hitherto unpublished papers from the 1960s and early 1970s provides a strange mixture of déjà vu and astonishment: déjà vu because the context and the political forces and debates taking place then seem, *mutatis mutandis*, so similar to much of what is happening today, and astonishment because what is in them could have been written today and is still, almost half a century later, at the leading edge of debates about today's crises, their causes, and what can be done to change things. The world has not stood still since then, but the underlying forces that became apparent in the 1960s and 1970s are now again appearing in force, and Herbert Marcuse's analysis from that time is still strikingly relevant and, I believe, much needed today.[1] Political and theoretical approaches developed by the Left in the earlier period merit serious review and reconsideration today.

This chapter is a substantially revised and expanded version of Peter Marcuse, "Occupy Consciousness: Reading the 1960s and Occupy Wall Street with Herbert Marcuse," *Radical Philosophy Review* 16, no. 2 (2013): 481–489. I am indebted for help and provocation to Andrew Lamas. Appreciation is also extended for many discussions with members of the International Herbert Marcuse Society at its biennial conferences. For earlier and continuing reflections on the issues explored in this essay, see *Peter Marcuse's Blog: Critical Planning and Other Thoughts*, at http://pmarcuse.wordpress.com.

1. See, for example, Douglas Kellner, ed., *Collected Papers of Herbert Marcuse*, vol. 6, *Marxism, Revolution and Utopia* (London: Routledge, 2014).

Radical Subjectivity in a Nonrevolutionary Situation

The talk Marcuse gave before an overflow audience at Berlin's Free University in July of 1967 is a good place to start.[2] It was delivered at the height of the militancy of the student movement in Europe, shortly after a young student had been killed in a demonstration on the streets of that city, and the outrage in the audience was still apparent. Marcuse was seen as the guru of the New Left, an iconic figure in the protests, and he was asked to speak on the future potentials and limits of the student movement.

Change "students" to "occupiers," and you need change little else to make the talk a direct confrontation with what militant protestors and their allies are debating today. In what follows, I want to analogize the students of the 1960s with the occupiers and protestors of the recent period of uprisings.[3] The working class or proletariat of the 1960s is essentially unchanged, although weakened, today, and the excluded, those "outside the system" in the 1960s, are largely similar to those militantly claiming the right to the city in the Right to the City Alliance today. The historical setting is also, in long-range terms, I believe, analogous.

Marcuse's analysis begins with the realization of the gross disparity between what the conditions of everyday life around the world are and *what they could be*—a disparity that hits emotionally, even at the instinctual level, as the realization deepens. This is what Marcuse meant when he labeled his Berlin talk "The End of Utopia."[4] "Utopias," for the first time, are not necessarily "nowhere," not necessarily in the afterlife in heaven, but are realizable today, on earth, if all the technological advances capitalism has bred were used for the benefit of all—with an end of exploitation, a conversion from destructive to creative humane purposes, and a relief from unnecessary repression of feelings and desires.[5] The Occupy Wall Street movement was largely, if somewhat less explicitly, based on the same feelings: not that everything is bad today, but that things could be so much better, that war, discrimination, repression, inequality, all exist in ways that could be abolished with a major transformation of the system itself.

---

2. This talk was first published in English in Herbert Marcuse, "The End of Utopia," in *Five Lectures: Psychoanalysis, Politics, and Utopia*, trans. Jeremy J. Shapiro and Shierry M. Weber (Boston: Beacon, 1970), 62–82.

3. Occupy Wall Street, which began in September 2011 in New York City and spread globally, was inspired by and followed by other uprisings around the world—in northern Africa, southern Europe, Latin America, and elsewhere.

4. See note 2.

5. Regarding the repression of feelings and desires, see, of course, Herbert Marcuse, *Eros and Civilization: A Philosophical Inquiry into Freud* (Boston: Beacon, 1955).

But radical transformation of the entire system, Marcuse pointed out, was not on the table in the 1960s or indeed in the period of advanced capitalism. Nor is it today, and for the same reason it was not then. The system as it is "produces the goods." It satisfies basic needs enough to avoid movements for change that are radical out of material desperation (with the exception of a minority in the industrially developed world and a majority in the Third World, more on this below). The system further creates new, artificial "needs" whose allure can be satisfied quite within the system, "needs" whose satisfaction, or the possibility of such satisfaction, keeps the majority of the population from a level of discontent that would threaten the system.[6] So, it was clear to Marcuse—but not to many who were more idealistic and prominent in the movements at the time—that we were not then in a revolutionary situation. The reality of the situation is, however, pretty well clear to almost all today; indeed, one might formulate the task today—as Marcuse saw it then—as follows: *we must figure out what to do when a revolution is objectively indicated but subjective conditions (e.g., the readiness of the necessary actors) do not make it possible.* The objective reality was and is the lack of subjective readiness to take revolutionary action, the lack of agents of change in a position to make a revolution. It is objectively the fact that, as Arundhati Roy phrased it, "We be many and they be few. They need us more than we need them."[7] But if the need for and feasibility of achieving basic change is not in the consciousness of the many, there will not be fundamental change.

Where, then, are the agents of change for those transformations seen as necessary? Here Marcuse trod on sensitive ground within the oppositional movements of the 1960s. This question is still sensitive for the same reasons within analogous groups today. It has to do with the role of intellectuals and with the importance of theory—not regarding the same issue, but related issues. In the old Left, it had always been material deprivation that would be the motor of dramatic change, and their banner had been resistance to material exploitation; however, for the New Left, and for those in Occupy and other contemporary social movements (particularly in the countries of advanced capitalism), the background conditions are differently understood. Intolerable physical want is generally limited, under control, and does not result in such immediate distress as to produce massive social upheaval. Dissatisfaction is rather with what further could be obtained and what more—beyond satisfaction of brute physical needs—could be had. Such dissatisfaction is most likely articulated by intellectuals, in a relatively privileged position materially compared with the deprived, and it is elaborated in theoretical formulations sometimes seen as abstract and politically not

---

6. This, of course, is the main thesis developed in Herbert Marcuse, *One-Dimensional Man: Studies in the Ideology of Advanced Industrial Society* (Boston: Beacon, 1964).

7. Arundhati Roy, *War Talk* (Cambridge, MA: South End, 2003), 112.

helpful by the immediately deprived. A tension thus often appears, both in the 1960s and today, between the dissatisfied and the deprived—appearing in practice in a tension between intellectuals and grassroots activists. The relations were and are often touchy and seldom directly confronted. On this subject Marcuse made a number of points, all of direct relevance today.

One is that the motor of resistance to the existing system is no longer primarily the drive for the satisfaction of immediate material needs by the many but, rather, the subjective realization that satisfaction is not equally shared by all—that the system as a whole is unjust, environmentally destructive, repressive, and inhumane, depriving the many of the ability to achieve a full and satisfying life in many different ways. It is a shift in the source of dissatisfaction and resistance from primary concern with meeting the material necessities of life to a concern with the quality of life in the system as a whole.

In a striking response, during the post-lecture question period, to a remark by a member of his largely student audience in Berlin in 1967, Marcuse said:

> I should like to ask you all a question. If I really radically exclude humanitarian arguments, on what basis can I work against the system of advanced capitalism? If you only operate within the framework of technical rationality and from the start exclude theoretically transcendent concepts, that is, negations of the system—for the system is not humane, and humanitarian ideas belong to the negation of the system—then you continually find yourself in the situation of being asked, and not being able to answer, the question: What is really so terrible about this system, which continually expands social wealth so that strata of the population that previously lived in the greatest poverty and misery today have automobiles, television sets, and one-family houses? What is so bad about this system that we dare take the tremendous risk of preaching its overthrow? If you content yourself with material arguments and exclude all other arguments you will not get anywhere. . . . Humanitarian and moral arguments are not merely deceitful ideology. Rather, they can and must become central social forces. If we exclude them from our argumentation at the start, we impoverish ourselves and disarm ourselves in the face of the strongest arguments of the defenders of the status quo.[8]

---

8. Herbert Marcuse, "The Problem of Violence and the Radical Opposition," in *Five Lectures: Psychoanalysis, Politics, and Utopia*, trans. Jeremy J. Shapiro and Shierry M. Weber (Boston: Beacon, 1970), 96. The audience member's remark reads as follows: "The student opposition knows how difficult it is to get popular support in the advanced capitalist countries. In discussions with workers, students have repeatedly heard the answer: 'I don't know what you are talking about—I have got it good, much better than before.' And what does

It is a remarkable passage, coming from an intellectual with impeccable credentials but far from an "organic intellectual" in Antonio Gramsci's sense, addressed to students largely on their way to a similar career. Marcuse thus raised and took a firm position on a delicate question: *To what extent did the leadership of the resistance have to be in the hands of those themselves suffering most from its ill effects?* Marcuse's position was explicitly linked to a defense of theory as a necessary ingredient of strategy, in a way often spoken of as appropriate but less often put into practice in the parallel movements of today.

Raising these points leads inevitably to two central questions in the discussion of transformative change today:

Who and how? *Who wants to and who is in a position to bring about transformative change, and how can they best do it?*

Marcuse had comments on both questions. He made it quite clear that, despite the critical catalytic role of the students, they were not the ones likely to transform the system; indeed, forces leading to radical transformation were difficult to discern. In a passage that is eerily applicable to our recent situation in 2011—try substituting "Occupy Wall Street" for "students" and perhaps "Arab Spring" for "national liberation movements"—Marcuse wrote:

> I never said that the student opposition today is by itself a revolutionary force. . . . Only the national liberation fronts of the developing countries are today in a revolutionary struggle. But even they do not by themselves constitute an effective revolutionary threat to the system of advanced capitalism. All forces of opposition today are working at preparation and only at preparation—but toward necessary preparation for a possible crisis of the system. And precisely the national liberation fronts and the ghetto rebellion contribute to this crisis. . . . Perhaps the working class, too, can be politically radicalized.[9]

Earlier he had dealt explicitly with those traditionally considered in the forefront of resistance to the system, those under the heading of "the underprivileged." He puts their position in the context of the discussion of the subjective and objective factors challenging the system: subjectively the underprivileged, the deprived, are motivated to be critical of the system that holds them down, as the students and the occupiers, the dissatisfied,

---

this worker care about the terror in Vietnam? Humanitarian arguments wouldn't do, since humanity itself gave rise to terror." Ibid., 95. Note that the post-lecture questions and remarks, in abridged form, and Marcuse's complete responses are printed in *Five Lectures* as accompaniments to his "The End of Utopia" and "The Problem of Violence and the Radical Opposition" talks.

9. Marcuse, "The Problem of Violence and the Radical Opposition," 93.

are subjectively motivated by humanitarian instincts to challenge it. But, as Marcuse explains, "They [the deprived] are mostly groups that do not occupy a decisive place in the productive process and for this reason cannot be considered potentially revolutionary forces from the viewpoint of Marxian theory—at least not without allies."[10] This is precisely the point that the Republican Party's candidate Mitt Romney was making in his off-the-record talk to rich contributors in the 2012 U.S. presidential election campaign, when he wrote off 47 percent of the electorate as "victims" who were not worth trying to get into the Republican fold. They did not have the power to disrupt; they could be ignored. Welfare recipients, the unemployed, the disabled, the elderly, those without healthcare and unable to pay for it— Romney's assessment of the deprived certainly varies from Marcuse's, but the point is the same. Members of these groups are neither necessary for production—that is, the production of profit—nor feared as threatening its peaceful pursuit; thus, Romney sees them as not to be feared and, therefore, of no concern. Marcuse sees them as indeed of central concern but as needing allies to effectively produce change.

This is the concept of allies, discussed so widely in the Right to the City Alliance and the Occupy movement among those not themselves objectively deprived or dispossessed, but who, though privileged, are dissatisfied and have subjective reason to be critical. Marcuse divides the privileged into two groups:

> [One, the deprived, is the] new working class . . . consist[ing] of technicians, engineers, specialists, scientists, etc., who are engaged in the productive process, albeit in a special position. Owing to their key position this group really seems to represent the nucleus of an objective revolutionary force, but at the same time it is a favorite child of the established system.[11]

Thus, the hope, which may have powered the hopes placed on the Great Refusal—in which those who despite the benefits they garnered from the system realized its negatives well enough to refuse to go along and, by their absence, helped undermine the system—is very much realistically diluted here. The other group of the privileged who might be an effective opposition is "the student opposition in its widest sense,"[12] which I take the liberty of interpreting to include many academics as well.

10. Ibid., 85.
11. Ibid.
12. Ibid.

The Problem of Violence

Marcuse then segues into a discussion of the forms of opposition that these privileged but dissatisfied critics of the system may undertake and addresses another thorny issue of *the how of radical change*. Inherent within that issue is the question of violence. As a theoretical question, it lingers far in the background: Will any regime of power ever surrender that power voluntarily, or will violence ultimately be necessary to achieve real, systemic, transformative change? Most in the Marxist tradition would undoubtedly agree with Frederick Douglass's famous answer to that question.[13]

Yet in a much narrower sense, the question of violence today also bedevils many within contemporary social movements when confronted with accusations of engaging in violence, and it is one that they need to deal with when some within their ranks espouse and periodically practice it.[14] The idea of leaving the form of opposition to each group's own determination under the broad banner of the movement (whether it be, for example, Occupy, the global justice movement, or anti-austerity), the acceptance of a "diversity of tactics" position, may not work to draw in a larger mass of the population, as experience has shown; the entire movement is often held responsible for the very visible actions of even a small number of its members.

Here Marcuse takes a complex but clear position.[15] He makes several distinctions. A simple and obvious one is between violence against persons and violence against property. A second and less frequently considered one is the distinction between the different functions violence serves.

---

13. "If there is no struggle there is no progress. . . . Power concedes nothing without a demand. It never did and it never will." Frederick Douglass, *Two Speeches by Frederick Douglass: One on West India Emancipation, Delivered at Canandaigua, Aug. 4th, and the Other on the Dred Scott Decision, Delivered in New York, on the Occasion of the Anniversary of the American Abolition Society, May, 1857* (Rochester, NY: C. P. Dewey, 1857), 22, available at https://www.loc.gov/resource/mfd.21039/?sp=22.

14. See, for example, the position of CrimethInc. Ex-Workers' Collective, "Global Battle for the Soul of Humanity," *Adbusters*, September 28, 2013, available at http://www.adbusters .org/article/global-battle-for-the-soul-of-humanity/. Adbusters, a media group, played a pivotal role in encouraging Occupy Wall Street in New York City. The advocates of the effective use of violence are commonly referred to as "the black bloc" and are largely anarchist.

15. Marcuse wrote extensively on the role of violence in social change. See, for example, Herbert Marcuse, "Reflections on Calley," in *Collected Papers of Herbert Marcuse*, vol. 3, *The New Left and the 1960s*, ed. Douglas Kellner (London: Routledge, 2005), 50–53; and Herbert Marcuse, "Murder Is Not a Political Weapon," in Kellner, *Collected Papers of Herbert Marcuse*, 3:177–179. For Marcuse's response to the Weatherman faction, see Douglas Kellner, "Introduction: Radical Politics, Marcuse, and the New Left," in Kellner, *Collected Papers of Herbert Marcuse*, esp. 3:36. For an interview in which Marcuse critiques the terrorism of Baader-Meinhof, see Myriam Miedzian Malinovich, "Herbert Marcuse in 1978: An Interview," *Social Research* 48, no. 2 (1981), available at http://www.myriammiedzian .com/#!summer81-herbert-marcuse/cj98.

There are many different kinds of violence employed in defense and in aggression. For example, the violence of the policeman who overpowers a murderer is very different, not only externally but in its instinctual structure, its substance, from the violence of a policeman who clubs a demonstrator. Both are acts of violence, but they have completely different functions.[16] And note not only differences in individual instinctual structure and function but also differences in the functions violence serves in the broad social and legal structure of society.

> The establishment has a legal monopoly of violence. . . . In contrast, the recognition and exercise of a higher right and the duty of resistance, of civil disobedience, is a motive force in the historical development of freedom, a potentially liberating violence. . . . The concept of violence covers two different forms: the institutionalized violence of the established system and the violence of resistance, which is necessarily illegal in relation to positive law.[17]

A further, but critical, distinction is that between private and public (or governmental) violence.

> In relation to this totality [of public violence] the right of liberation is in its immediate appearance a particular right. Thus the conflict of violence appears as a clash between general and particular or public and private violence, and in this clash the private violence will be defeated until it can confront the existing public power as a new general interest.
>
> As long as the opposition does not have the social force of a new general interest the problem of violence is primarily a problem of tactics.[18]

Marcuse goes on to explore in which situations violence against government power might nevertheless be a useful tactic, in a very nuanced discussion. But the general point might well be applied to the developments in the Arab Spring revolts, about which the decisive question could be formulated as whether the oppositional forces in fact reflect "the social force of a new general interest"[19] or, thus far, only a collection of competing private interests. Marcuse's conclusion seems a sound one today and might help shift the debate from a generalized pro- or contra-violence argument to a more

---

16. Marcuse, "The Problem of Violence and Radical Opposition," 103.
17. Ibid., 89–90.
18. Ibid., 90.
19. Ibid.

concrete one examining the historical and immediate political context of the disputed actions.

Radical Subjects and Revolutionary Mobilization

If neither the student opposition nor its privileged allies are in a position to achieve systemic change because they have neither the power to disrupt the system's functioning nor the power to overcome it by violence, *who*, then, might the critical agents of change be?

In response, Marcuse adopts a classically materialist position: essentially, that agents of change might be those who have the greatest and most pressing interest in such a change, whom he variously speaks of as the deprived and as including the underprivileged, ghetto residents, those oppressed by colonialism, and those in national liberation movements.

> But even they do not by themselves constitute an effective revolutionary threat to the system of advanced capitalism. All forces of opposition today are working at preparation and only at preparation—but toward necessary preparation for a possible crisis of the system. . . . For the preparation and eventuality of such a crisis perhaps the working class, too, can be politically radicalized. But we must not conceal from ourselves that in this situation the question whether such radicalization will be to the left or the right is an open one.[20]

Is Marcuse anticipating the Tea Party as we see it today in the United States? In any case, what is clear is that radically progressive or revolutionary forces of opposition do not have today a "mass basis in the developed countries of advanced capitalism."[21] It is a situation whose realism needs to be urgently recognized.

So, what is to be done? What advice could one glean from Marcuse's analysis of more than fifty years ago that might be useful for theorists of and activists in contemporary social movements? Posing the question in relation to Occupy in 2011, for example, indicates the possible contemporary relevance of Marcuse's position.[22]

> We cannot let ourselves think that the success of the student [read: Occupy] opposition would push the situation to a stage from which

---

20. Ibid., 93.

21. Ibid., 93.

22. Perhaps this question could also be posed in relation to the Left section in the campaign of the democratic socialist Bernie Sanders, who sought the Democratic Party's nomination in the 2016 U.S. presidential race.

we can ask about the construction of a free society. If the student [read: Occupy] opposition remains isolated and does not succeed in breaking out of its own limited sphere, if it does not succeed in mobilizing social strata that really will play a decisive role . . . on account of their position in the social process of production, then the student [read: Occupy] opposition can play only an accessory role . . . as the nucleus of a revolution, but if we have only a nucleus, then we don't have a revolution. The student [read: Occupy] opposition has many possibilities of breaking out of the narrow framework within which it is enclosed today and changing the intelligentsia, the "bourgeois" intelligentsia, from a term of abuse into a *parole d'honneur*. But that would mean breaking out of or extending the framework to the point where it included quite different forces that could materially and intellectually work for a revolution.[23]

Marcuse's Long View of Human History

Reading today, in the post-Occupy world of enduring crises, the recently discovered transcripts of the lectures Marcuse gave in Paris in 1974 is something of a shock.[24] Not because his words are in any way less valid today than they were then but, rather, because his message has moved from déjà vu to *perdu de vue*, from something as true today as it was then to something now barely noticed or forgotten. The written transcripts of the lectures give a feel for the situation in which they were delivered that the carefully printed texts of the present published material can only suggest—an emotional sense of change, of hope, of eagerness to understand, of optimism. The word "revolution" was still in the air, at least among the French students but also internationally, among Third World anticolonialists and among radicals in the arts, the Black liberation movement, the women's and gay rights movements, and some parts of the working class. The epochal development that justified the optimism, which was at the center of Marcuse's long view of human history, was that humankind had finally arrived at the point that scarcity had been overcome, that the realm of necessity had been reduced to manageable

---

23. Ibid., 97. And remember that when Marcuse speaks of "revolution," he is using the term not in its conventional sense but rather as shorthand for "fundamental system change." In reflecting on his experiences in Paris in May 1968, he wrote, "The traditional idea of the revolution and the traditional strategy of the revolution are outdated; they are simply surpassed by the development of our society." Herbert Marcuse, "Reflections on the French Revolution," in Kellner, *Collected Papers of Herbert Marcuse*, 3:45.

24. See Herbert Marcuse, *The 1974 Paris Lectures at Vincennes University*, ed. Peter-Erwin Jansen and Charles Reitz (Kansas City, KS: Jansen/Reitz, 2015). The original materials on which this self-published book is based are available at the Marcuse archive in the J. C. Senckenberg Universitätsbibliothek at the Johann Wolfgang Goethe-Universität Frankfurt am Main in Frankfurt, Germany.

proportions, and that the realm of freedom had opened up as a realizable utopia worth fighting for.

In the 1950s, 1960s, and 1970s, Marcuse understood the Great Refusal as the reaction to a new historical situation in which the possibilities of a different kind of life—freed from want, from the need for alienated labor, from oppression and injustice—not only existed but had become visible, had an increasing subjective force, and made refusal not merely an internal psychological reaction but a viable political, social, economic force.

In most of the second half of the twentieth century, that hopeful view of the historical situation was still widespread. From the heady visions of a different world after the defeat of fascism in the Second World War to the militant labor movements and liberation movements of the Third World and civil-rights movements and social welfare policies of the industrialized world, the thread can be traced. The Occupy movement is its most recent manifestation in the United States.

But two things have happened that have gone in the opposite direction. There is no room here to go into details, but the basic facts seem clear, and they are linked. The first is that the dominant forces within the existing system, the holders of power and wealth in the economy and in the state, have been strong enough to make any radical opposition seem hopeless. On the one hand, the system has really "produced the goods," as Marcuse was wont to say, and the sharp tooth of poverty constitutes no egregious threat to stability. Marcuse already saw the effect of that development, highlighting the instrumental role of technology in producing it, and he understood its subjective as well as objective consequences. He thus saw the cutting edge of radical change, ultimately the possibility of revolution, lying not in the increasing immiseration of the masses but rather in its exact opposite: the increasing adequacy of the development of the productive forces of society to overcome poverty and, even much further, to overcome the necessity of alienated labor, of work merely to survive and to make a living. That realization, he argued, would increase, become overwhelming, and lead to a subjective refusal to go along with a system that demanded work unwillingly done, that stifled creativity, and that limited freedom. Refusal would be effective under those circumstances; it would inevitably undermine the taken-for-granted nature of a system that alienated human beings from the work they spent most of their lives doing. In 2015, the *New York Times* prominently featured a piece headlined "A Toxic Work World," which begins,

> For many Americans, life has become all competition all the time. Workers across the socioeconomic spectrum, from hotel house-keepers to surgeons, have stories about toiling 12- to 16-hour days (often without overtime pay) and experiencing anxiety attacks and

exhaustion. Public health experts have begun talking about stress as an epidemic.[25]

The analysis blames this toxicity on the lack of "flexibility" by employers in arranging for work hours; it bemoans the fact that simple caring for children at home is undervalued, without once examining the nature of contemporary work, what about it is so toxic, why work must be competitive rather than mutually supporting, enriching, and creative—a part of life, not its master. The stage is set for resistance, but the enemy is not identified, the cause is concealed and made to appear simply a fact of life. The concept of alienation, so widely discussed just a few decades ago, has simply disappeared. The concept of "creative work" has replaced it—"creative" being defined to include what Wall Street's hedge-fund managers and merger specialists do.

In Marcuse's early work, and that of the Frankfurt School in Germany and then the United States, the problem of toxic work was a central concern, as alienated labor was seen as a central problem of society, and the lack of truly creative work was seen as a direct source of social unrest and, ultimately, deep social change. But that change was not seen as predetermined in direction. Today, the possibility of a shift to the Right, rather than to the Left, is an ascending hallmark of the scene internationally. Proposals approaching the fascist have once again become very visible, alternate possibilities for "handling" the problem. In the 1960s and 1970s, the Right's influence was reduced in many arenas by challenges from powerful social movements. Today, hostility to immigrants, unyielding racism, growth of a massive carceral system, and reduction of social welfare expenditures—all in the name of austerity, security, and nativism—represent a reversal of direction since the time of Marcuse's key writings. By 2016, in the U.S. presidential election campaign, Donald Trump—with his slogan "Make America Great Again!"— showed strong fascist tendencies, while elections in Austria, France, Venezuela, Brazil, Ecuador, Germany, and elsewhere revealed strong tendencies toward fascism. Oppressive and exploitative relationships underlying these events are not fundamentally different today from what they were fifty years ago; if anything, they have been growing more visible and harsh. But the public reaction in the United States and elsewhere is bifurcated. In 2015 and 2016, in the U.S. presidential primary campaigns, heated pressure for change came (among the voting population) from both the deprived and the dissatisfied, but this time in dangerously different directions perhaps harking

25. Anne-Marie Slaughter, "A Toxic Work World," *New York Times*, September 18, 2015, available at http://www.nytimes.com/2015/09/20/opinion/sunday/a-toxic-work-world.html. Anne-Marie Slaughter, the president of New America, a think tank, is the author of *Unfinished Business: Women Men Work Family* (New York: Random House, 2015), from which this essay is adapted.

back to the 1920s and 1930s: the deprived largely going Right in the Trump movement in the Republican Party and the dissatisfied largely pushing Left within the movement supporting the democratic socialist Bernie Sanders in the Democratic Party. Sanders drew enthusiastic crowds at political rallies, and even the words "revolution" and "socialism" became printable in the mainstream media without quotation marks, even if rather emptied of their meaning. But Trump's crowds were larger, and his rigidity, rhetoric of violence and racism, and dumbing down of the ideological discourse were in plain view and amplified by the mainstream media.

Granted that these events fall short of reestablishing fascism in its formal meaning; nonetheless, they represent a shift in economic and political relationships, and in ideological trends nationally and internationally, that further reverses a progressive, optimistic trend of which Marcuse's work had been a part in the 1960s.

Transformative Actions toward the Alternative Dimension of Utopia

In the 1960s, the possibility of revolutionary change appeared to be very much on the table. Revolution was seen as a holistic concept brought about by changed men and women and creating changed men and women. Revolution seemed to be a virtuous circle, with Marcuse's Great Refusal as a central approach, essentially assuming a weakening of existing structures of power and rendering them vulnerable to overthrow, while at the same time teaching practitioners how to live an alternative life, as in alternative communes and alternative relationships. But events were not supporting that assumption, and the difficulty was recognized even among those most strongly encouraging basic change, resulting in pessimism of the intellect and optimism of the will. The "Long March through the Institutions," the formulation of Rudi Dutschke in Germany characterizing the hopeful aspirations of rebellious students and their allies in Berlin, was in effect calling for immediately practical steps—if over time (hence "the Long March")—in the direction of revolution, recognizing revolution as on the future agenda but not the immediate agenda of history. With this different understanding of revolution, Dutschke and the students hoped to link immediately practicable changes in specific key institutions with an overall vision of what a new and very different society might be like: an approach to bringing out the utopian dimension lying alongside and within the one-dimensional realm of existing reality.

Many efforts in this direction already exist today; they need their common relationship to the existing system to be constantly highlighted, with the name of that system—the presently dominating one of capitalism—kept in the forefront. The time could never be riper for the explicit critique of capitalism. No single, abrupt, and comprehensive movement from the one dimension of reality to an alternative dimension approaching the utopian is likely; however, activities in the here and now—in this one-dimensional reality of our contemporary situation—can be transformative in moving toward an alternative future that is closer to the utopian.

The Liberation of Consciousness

What is needed, Marcuse concludes, in a trenchant phrase, is the "liberation of consciousness."

> Now the liberation of consciousness . . . means more than discussion. It means . . . demonstrations, in the literal sense. The whole person must demonstrate his participation and his will to live, that is, his will to live in a pacified, human world. [It is] harmful . . . to preach defeatism and quietism, which can only play into the hands of those that run the system. . . . We must resist if we still want to live as human beings, to work and be happy.[26]

"The liberation of consciousness" is not a bad slogan for an ideological campaign to return the direction of social action to that which it seemed to be taking at the high point of Marcuse's engagement. But, Marcuse points out, an ideological campaign alone will, of course, not do it. There are very practical issues of power, organizing, planning, and, yes, negotiating and compromising that must be undertaken along the way. But along the way and in the end, the liberation of consciousness must be a vital ingredient in any serious personal and social transformation in the direction of a new and better world.

---

26. Marcuse, "The Problem of Violence and Radical Opposition," 94.

Part II

Liberating Resistance

5

Asia's Unknown Uprisings

GEORGE KATSIAFICAS

We have all heard of the Arab Spring of 2010–2011, but who among us knows anything about the Asian Wave of 1986–1992? Despite its lack of recognition, this chain reaction of uprisings against oppressive regimes transformed the region's political landscape, overthrowing eight dictatorships in nine countries during six years.

East Asia's regional string of uprisings had a huge political impact. Almost overnight (and for decades thereafter), "People Power" became activists' common global identity—cutting across religious, national, and economic divides as uprisings unfolded in the Philippines (1986), South Korea (1987), Burma (1988), Tibet (1989), China (1989), Taiwan (1990), Nepal (1990), Bangladesh (1990), and Thailand (1992). These grassroots uprisings overthrew eight entrenched local dictatorships: Philippine dictator Ferdinand Marcos was forced into exile; South Korea's Chun Doo-hwan was disgraced and compelled to grant direct presidential elections before being imprisoned; Taiwan's forty-year martial-law regime was overturned; Burma's mobilized citizenry overthrew two dictators only to see their successors massacre thousands; Nepal's monarchy was made constitutional; military ruler Hussain Muhammad Ershad in Bangladesh was forced to step down and eventually sent to prison; and Army Commander Suchinda Kraprayoon in Thailand was forced to vacate the office of prime minister.

Leading up to the 1980s, East Asian dictatorships had been in power for decades and seemed unshakable, yet the wave of revolts transmogrified the region. These insurgencies threw to the wind the common notion that Asians are happier with authoritarian governments than democracy, that "Asian despotism" continues to define regimes there. They ushered in greater liberties and new opportunities for citizen participation—as well as for international capital.

The Asian Wave of insurgencies was rendered invisible to popular understanding, but it is not the only global episode of insurgency that remains unrecognized. For decades after 1968, activists and analysts believed that their own country's movement comprised the center of protests. Today, the international character and connections of movements in 1968 is evident. As planetary integration accelerates, human beings are rapidly becoming self-conscious as a species. World history opens new possibilities, but we must assimilate properly the recent past if we are to proceed effectively into the future. National histories today are unable to do justice to the global freedom movement, to comprehend the simultaneous emergence of freedom struggles in many places. When conceptualized solely within national boundaries, accurate representations of contemporary uprisings become implausible, and future strategy is blurred.

Since 1968, the global movement's mobilizations have changed from being unconsciously spontaneous to having a form of "conscious spontaneity" in which grassroots activists around the world synchronize protests with common aspirations. Asian uprisings again show the capacities of popular insurgencies to expand on preceding examples and to borrow each other's vocabulary, actions, and aspirations. Popular movements assimilate lessons from previous protest episodes, and people improvise tactics and targets from their own assessments of past accomplishments and failures.

The 1989 revolutions in Eastern Europe against Soviet regimes are well known, yet Eurocentric bias often diminishes the significance and inspiration provided by their Asian precursors, rendering them invisible. The accomplishments of Asian uprisings are noteworthy and their character significantly more grassroots than contemporaneous turmoil in Eastern Europe (where Mikhail Gorbachev's willingness to abandon Russia's buffer states triggered the movements), but they remain uncelebrated, even within the region where they transpired. Alongside Eurocentric biases (such as the oft-repeated notions that "civil society" and the "autonomous individual" do not exist in Asia), several other factors account for the failure to comprehend the Asian Wave: overt information suppression by governments, Asian modesty, the mass media's fragmentation of history, and the region's religious diversity. While the fourteen countries affected by the Arab Spring almost entirely represent predominantly Muslim societies, the Asian Wave included Buddhists, Hindus, Christians, Muslims, and Confucians.

The Eros Effect

Cycles of revolt develop in relation to each other. From the global eruption of 1968 to the string of Asian uprisings, from Eastern Europe in 1989 to the alterglobalization confrontations of elite summits, ordinary people glean the lessons of history. Today, not only is there global motion from the grassroots, but the grammar of insurgency is similar everywhere. Since World War II, humanity's increasing awareness of our own power and strategic capacities has become manifest in sudden and simultaneous contestation of power by hundreds of thousands of people, a significant new tactic in the arsenal of popular movements that I have named the eros effect.[1]

During moments of the eros effect, universal interests become generalized at the same time as dominant values of society (national chauvinism, hierarchy, and domination) are negated. As Herbert Marcuse so clearly formulated it, humans have an instinctual need for freedom—something that we grasp intuitively—and it is this instinctual need that is sublimated into a collective phenomenon during moments of the eros effect.[2] Dimensions of the eros effect include the sudden and synchronous emergence of hundreds of thousands of people occupying public space; the simultaneous appearance of revolts in many places; the intuitive identification of hundreds of thousands of people with each other; their common belief in new values; and suspension of normal daily routines like competitive business practices, criminal behavior, and acquisitiveness. People's intuition and self-organization—not the dictates of any party—are key to the emergence of such moments. Actualized in the actions of millions of people in 1968, the eros effect continues to be a weapon of enormous future potential.

The eros effect is not simply a general strike, armed insurrection, or massive mobilization. Rather, it can be all of these and more. It is not an act of mind; nor can it be willed by a "conscious element" (or revolutionary party). It involves popular movements emerging in their own right as ordinary people take history into their hands. The concept of the eros effect is a means of rescuing the revolutionary value of spontaneity, a way to stimulate a reevaluation of the unconscious. Rather than portraying emotions as linked to reaction, the notion of the eros effect seeks to bring them into the realm of positive revolutionary resources whose mobilization can result in significant social transformation. As Marcuse understood, nature is an ally

---

1. See George Katsiaficas, "Eros and Revolution," *Radical Philosophy Review* 16, no. 2 (2013): 491–505. For an earlier theoretical formulation of the eros effect, see George Katsiaficas, "The Eros Effect" (paper prepared for presentation at American Sociological Association national meeting, San Francisco, CA, 1989), available at http://www.eroseffect.com/articles/eroseffectpaper.PDF. See also George Katsiaficas, *The Imagination of the New Left: A Global Analysis of 1968* (Boston: South End, 1987), in which the concept of the eros effect is developed from its historical emergence.

2. For Marcuse's formulation, see Herbert Marcuse, *An Essay on Liberation* (Boston: Beacon, 1969).

in the revolutionary process, including internal, human nature.[3] This point is earlier elaborated in *Eros and Civilization: A Philosophical Inquiry into Freud*, in which Marcuse writes, the "Great Refusal is the protest against unnecessary repression, the struggle for the ultimate form of freedom—'to live without anxiety.'"[4] Later, in *One-Dimensional Man*, Marcuse also indicates, as Douglas Kellner explains, that

> the Great Refusal is fundamentally political, a refusal of repression and injustice, a saying no, an elemental oppositional to a system of oppression, a noncompliance with the rules of a rigged game, a form of radical resistance and struggle. In both cases, the Great Refusal is based on a subjectivity that is not able to tolerate injustice and that engages in resistance and opposition to all forms of domination, instinctual and political.[5]

Uprisings are terrible, beautiful events. No one relishes the task of recounting the dead and wounded, of remembering the brutality of militaries and blood in the streets. Those who participate have difficulty overcoming the guilt they feel for injuries and deaths, while people who do not rise to the occasion cannot easily overcome the shame they feel for staying home (or fleeing). Nevertheless, far more than we realize, the world we live in has been created by revolutionary insurgencies—from the American Revolution in 1776 to the Russian Revolution in 1917 and from the Gwangju Uprising in 1980 to the Arab Spring.

The oft-repeated phrase "The people make history" cannot be comprehended without focusing on popular uprisings, when the actions of very large numbers of people—sometimes hundreds of thousands or more—speak for themselves and portray freedom's meaning in history. Contemporary instances of the simultaneous appearance of movements without regard for national borders involve a process of mutual amplification and synergy. In the period after 1968, as the global movement's capacity for decentralized international coordination developed, five other waves of international insurgencies can be discerned:

1. The disarmament movement of the early 1980s
2. The wave of Asian uprisings from 1986–1992

---

3. Herbert Marcuse, "Nature and Revolution," in *Counterrevolution and Revolt* (Boston: Beacon, 1972), 59–78.

4. Herbert Marcuse, *Eros and Civilization: A Philosophical Inquiry into Freud* (Boston: Beacon, 1955), 149–150.

5. Douglas Kellner, "Marcuse and the Quest for Radical Subjectivity," *Social Thought and Research* 22, nos. 1–2 (1999): 14.

3. The revolts against Soviet regimes in Eastern Europe[6]
4. The alterglobalization wave from Seattle in 1999 to antiwar mobilizations on February 15, 2003
5. The Arab Spring, the Greek rebellion, and the Occupy movement in 2011

In my view, such globally synchronized waves of protest are significant precursors of future events.

Dialectic of Uprisings

Uprisings may be powerful vehicles for overthrowing entrenched dictatorships, but they are also useful to global elites whose interests transcend nations. The eros effect is clearly effective in overthrowing existing governments, but the system has become adept at riding the wave of uprisings to insert new regimes to stabilize its operations. The wave of People Power uprisings helped incorporate more of the world into the orbit of Japanese and U.S. banks. The South Korean working class's heroic struggles for union rights became useful to neoliberal economic penetration of the country.[7] In democratic South Korea and Taiwan, as in the Philippines after Marcos and elsewhere, newly elected administrations accelerated neoliberal programs that permitted foreign investors to penetrate previously closed markets and to discipline workforces of millions of people in order to extract greater profits. The system's capacity to use the energy of insurgencies to reform archaic social relations and adapt to new technologies should never be underestimated—nor should the strength of the forces of Thanatos.

The twentieth century will be remembered for horrific wars, mass starvation, and revolutions—as well as for humanity's technological progress and prosperity. It will be known as a time when human beings began a struggle to transform the entire capitalist world system. Uprisings at that century's end reveal that from the grassroots, millions of people around the world constituted a protracted people's struggle against capitalism and war.

---

6. Those who disregard the popular character of the Eastern European wave around 1989 would do well to remember Rosa Luxemburg's admonition: "Let's speak plainly. Historically, the errors committed by a truly revolutionary movement are infinitely more fruitful than the infallibility of the cleverest Central Committee." Rosa Luxemburg, "Organizational Questions of the Russian Social Democracy," in *Rosa Luxemburg Speaks*, ed. Mary-Alice Waters (New York: Pathfinder, 1970), 169. For historical context and background information on this pamphlet written in response to Lenin by Luxemburg in 1904, see Waters, ed., *Rosa Luxemburg Speaks*, 152–175.

7. See Loren Goldner, "The Korean Working Class: From Mass Strike to Casualization and Retreat, 1987–2007," *libcom.org*, January 9, 2008, available at http://libcom.org/history/korean-working-class-mass-strike-casualization-retreat-1987-2007.

Without anyone telling people to do so, millions in the alterglobalization movement confronted elite meetings of those who govern the world economic system. No central organization dictated this focus. Rather, millions of people *autonomously* acted according to their own consciousness.

In the twenty-first century, as society's velocity of change accelerates, so too do people's capacities to assimilate tactics of recent struggles and to adapt new technologies to changing circumstances. Without the management consultants needed by the corporate elite, people adapted new technologies far faster and more robustly than did their rulers. During the Arab Spring, the increasing sophistication of protesters' use of social media (e.g., Facebook, Twitter, YouTube) and the cross-border speed with which the revolt spread offer a glimpse of People Power's potential. What some have called Uprising 2.0 refers to people's use of the Internet to quickly propagate news from one part of the world to another, to coordinate actions in real time, and to directly have a global voice.

Humanity's unending need for freedom constitutes the planet's most powerful natural resource. In the struggle to create free human beings, political movements play paramount roles. Uprisings accelerate social transformation, change governments, and revolutionize individual consciousness and social relationships. Lifelong friendships are formed amid new values for everyday life. Even among nonparticipants, bonds are created through powerful erotic energies unleashed in these exhilarating moments. These instances of what Marcuse called "political eros" are profoundly important in rekindling imaginations and nurturing hope.[8]

Most popular insurgencies result in expanded liberties for millions of people; when people are brutally repressed, the regime's days are numbered. The enormous energies of uprisings transform people's everyday existence and continue to resonate long past their peaks. Post-uprising surges in the Philippines, South Korea, Taiwan, Nepal, Bangladesh, and Thailand revealed phenomenal activation of civil society and outbreaks of working-class strikes.[9] Autonomous media and grassroots organizations mushroomed, feminism strengthened, and subaltern groups and minorities mobilized to win greater rights and more dignity.

Not only do uprisings heighten ongoing struggles and build insurgent organizations, they also construct longitudinal integration of past episodes into future actions. In the 1960s, Latin American activists fought U.S. imperialism while minorities in the United States led a mobilization against racism. Many people, especially German and American activists, fought against the Vietnam War. In the 1970s, localized uprisings against the International

---

8. Herbert Marcuse, *The Aesthetic Dimension: Toward a Critique of Marxist Aesthetics* (Boston: Beacon, 1972), 64.

9. See George Katsiaficas, *Asia's Unknown Uprisings*, 2 vols. (Oakland, CA: PM, 2012).

Monetary Fund (IMF) occurred in dozens of Third World countries. In the 1980s, Asians mobilized against local dictatorships. More recently, as the global movement has become increasingly aware of its own power, its strategy and impact have become focused on the transformation of the global capitalist system.

Growing Grassroots Intelligence

The 1980 Gwangju People's Uprising in South Korea is a significant indication of the capacity of people to govern themselves far more wisely than military dictatorships, corporate elites, or "democratically" sanctioned governments. People's global capacity for direct self-government (as well as the deadly absurdity of elite rule) is plainly evident in the wake of Gwangju. In 1980, Human Rights Watch estimated that three thousand people had been killed; yet the people's "community of love" brought hundreds of thousands of people closer together than ever. Solidarity sustained their struggle for seventeen years until finally the dictator Chun Doo-hwan was convicted and sent to prison. Gwangju is a shining example of people's contemporary capacity to live together with Eros at their side while death stands at their doorstep.

Empirical analysis of the concrete emergence of the Gwangju Uprising provides a glimpse of humanity's evolving collective wisdom. Like the 1871 Paris Commune, the people of Gwangju in 1980 spontaneously rose up against the overwhelming forces arrayed against them. In both cities, an unarmed citizenry, in opposition to their own governments, effectively gained control of urban space. Hundreds of thousands of people created popular organs of political power that effectively and efficiently replaced traditional forms of government; crime rates plummeted during the period of liberation, and people embraced new forms of kinship with each other.

A significant difference, however, is that in Gwangju, no preexisting insurgent armed force like the Parisian National Guard led the assault on power. Gwangju was liberated without the government's defeat by a foreign power or planning by political parties; rather, a spontaneous process of resistance to the brutality of thousands of paratroopers threw forward men and women who rose to the occasion. At the decisive moment in the armed struggle, the city's transportation workers heroically assembled a column of buses and more than one hundred taxis that led a victorious assault by more than one hundred thousand people against flamethrowers and machine guns. Many key activists in this struggle had no previous political experience.

Not only did people rise up against horrendous violence and defeat thousands of elite paratroopers pulled off the front lines with North Korea (with U.S. approval); the citizenry then governed the liberated city through daily direct-democratic rallies. There was no internecine violence or any looting or crime in what became known as the "absolute community."[10]

To illustrate people's superior capacity for self-government at the end of the twentieth century, we can compare the republican democracy of the Paris Commune (its election of leaders) with Gwangju's direct democracy (where daily meetings of hundreds of thousands of people were its highest governing body). We can contemplate the enormous difference between the events of March 18, 1871, (when the uniformed, armed Parisian National Guard seized power amid drum rolls) with those of May 18, 1980, (when Gwangju's people began their heroic resistance to more than fifty thousand South Korean paratroopers and elite soldiers). We can observe the difference between the internal discipline imposed from above on Parisians (posters called for "Death to Looters") and Gwangju's absolute community.

Eurocentric Views of Civil Society

For decades, social scientists have sought to locate specific variables and relationships that could predict the occurrence of social insurgencies, an elusive goal that continues to animate many researchers in the social-movement field. Filling abstract hypotheses with empirical data, investigators produce administrative social research useful to the control center; yet because their hypothetical-deductive methodology subsumes the unique character of social reality beneath the rubric of a standardized formula, they often obscure rather than enlighten. Caught within dominant ideological assumptions, the system's analysts fail to anticipate emergent forces. György Lukács maintained that bourgeois ideology blinds those immersed in it, obscuring emergent factors: "A radical change in outlook is not feasible on the soil of bourgeois society."[11] Lukács's insight might help explain why mainstream theorists failed to comprehend the existence of the Asian Wave.

Neither their partisans nor their enemies can predict when uprisings will erupt. In January 1917, Lenin declared, "We of the older generation may not live to see the decisive battles of this coming revolution."[12] In 1984, Samuel Huntington surmised, "The likelihood of democratic development in Eastern Europe is virtually nil," and "with a few exceptions, the limits of

---

10. See Choi Jungwoon, *The Gwangju Uprising: The Pivotal Democratic Movement That Changed the History of Modern Korea* (Paramus: Homa and Sekey, 2006), 85, 131.

11. György Lukács, "Reification and the Consciousness of the Proletariat," in *History and Class Consciousness: Studies in Marxist Dialectics*, trans. Rodney Livingstone (London: Merlin, 1971), 109–110.

12. V. I. Lenin, "Lecture on the 1905 Revolution," in *V. I. Lenin: Collected Works*, vol. 23, ed. M. S. Levin, trans. M. S. Levin and Joe Fineberg (Moscow: Progress, 1964), 253. The lecture was first published in *Pravda*, no. 18, on January 22, 1925.

democratic development in the world may well have been reached."[13] Five years later, Huntington's perspective was proven to be specious.

Similar examples of other theories' inability to clarify uprisings can be found in mainstream understandings of social movements. No previously formulated sociological variable proves robust in explaining the emergence of the Asian Wave. Neither Seymour Martin Lipset's "democratic threshold"[14] nor James Davies's "J-curve"[15] provides us with an adequate understanding of the emergence of this wave. Quantitative measurements of repression and nationally specific political or economic variables offer little more help.[16] There is no single explanatory dimension to which we can point—except the influence of one uprising on another.

The eros effect, arising as it does from the unconscious, cannot be verified scientifically, since it involves an unconscious process of identification. Interviews of key activists in every one of the countries involved indicated that great inspiration and energy crossed borders and taught lessons. If the Asian movements had erupted within months of each other rather than years, as did the 2011 Arab Spring, no doubt more recognition would have been given to their meaningful coincidence.

Another reason that the Asian Wave is unknown can be found in Westerners' mistaken belief that civil society did not exist before Euro-American penetration. Idealizing European social history as their only model, Eurocentrists do not find replicas of the indigenous emergence of a bourgeoisie and the individual in Asia. They conclude that "civil society" there is nonexistent, or at best insignificant. John Keane notes that "in early modern usages, 'civil society' was typically contrasted with the 'Asiatic' region, in which, or so it was said, civil societies had manifestly failed to appear."[17] Instead of locating Asia's heritage of values and relations as a resource, observers point to the dearth of American-style voluntary groups and conclude that there is no civil society.[18]

---

13. Samuel Huntington, "Will More Countries Become Democratic?," *Political Science Quarterly* 99, no. 2 (1984): 217–218.

14. Seymour Martin Lipset, "Some Social Requisites of Democracy: Economic Development and Political Legitimacy," *American Political Science Review* 53, no. 1 (1959): 69–105.

15. James C. Davies, "Toward a Theory of Revolution," *American Sociological Review* 27, no. 1 (1962): 5–19.

16. George Katsiaficas, "Uprisings in Comparative Perspective," in *Asia's Unknown Uprisings*, vol. 2, *People Power in the Philippines, Burma, Tibet, China, Taiwan, Bangladesh, Nepal, Thailand, and Indonesia, 1947–2009*, 2nd ed. (Oakland, CA: PM, 2013), 438–454.

17. John Keane, *Global Civil Society?* (Cambridge: Cambridge University Press, 2003), 31. On the next page, Keane demonstrates that Alexis de Tocqueville believed that civil society was not possible in Muslim society.

18. See George Katsiaficas, *Asia's Unknown Uprisings*, vol. 1, *South Korean Social Movements in the 20th Century* (Oakland, CA: PM, 2012), in which the case of Korea is discussed at length. Also see Gregory Henderson, *Korea: The Politics of the Vortex* (Cambridge, MA:

Autonomous secularism in Western Europe helped to create a space in which citizens could assert their rights and capitalism could develop. This outcome of Western Europe's historical development has been hypostatized as the model that all societies must take in order for "civil society" to exist. Jürgen Habermas, in particular, has posited a long list of requirements in order for "genuine" civil society to be said to exist: a free press and literacy, individual rights, civility, and sites for collective deliberation.[19] For Habermas, as for many other theorists, Western European privacy and atomization stand in sharp contrast to Asia and the East, where they believe the bourgeois individual did not develop. The question of alternative forms of the "autonomous individual" is seldom asked.[20] Privacy and individual rights in the West are considered fundamentally different than in Asia's densely packed cities. In Habermas's view, coffee houses in eighteenth-century Europe contributed greatly to the public sphere and civil society. Following in his footsteps, many people have asked whether Asia's teahouses might be considered similar domains. For those who hold European society in high regard, the answer is no.[21]

Habermas's bias severs the possibility of uncovering in history the telos of his own theories: "ideal speech situations." During daily sessions of deliberation by tens of thousands of people in the Gwangju Uprising—to say nothing of other such insurgent moments, differences were not only tolerated but painstakingly discussed. Each individual was free to speak his or her mind, while collective will formation was an urgent necessity. Language analysis of discourse in emergent communes might find them to be moments of communicative competence, opening a possible link to Habermas's utopian speculation.

Harvard University Press, 1968), 4, in which Henderson finds "amorphousness and isolation in social relations."

19. See William A. Callahan, "Comparing the Discourse of Popular Politics in Korea and China: From Civil Society to Social Movements," *Korea Journal* 38, no. 1 (1998): 281–282; and William A. Callahan, *Cultural Governance and Resistance in Pacific Asia* (New York: Routledge, 2006), 14, in which Callahan claims that Michel Foucault "understands China in an Orientalist fashion as the 'exotic East' that is the opposite of the modern West."

20. For my discussion of individual and group in Islamic societies, see George Katsiaficas, "Individual and Group: Comparative Cultural Observations with a Focus on Ibn Khaldun," *Journal of Biosciences* 39, no. 1 (2014): 1–6.

21. See Susanne H. Rudolf and Lloyd I. Rudolf, "The Coffee House and the Ashram: Gandhi, Civil Society and Public Spheres," in *Civil Society and Democracy*, ed. Carolyn M. Elliott (Oxford: Oxford University Press, 2003), 377–404. Even in regard to Asian teahouses, the argument is made elsewhere that the nature of discussions does not reach the lofty height of individual autonomy attained in European cafes. From my experiences, many teahouses and even street corners in Asia might be more of a civil space than the interiors of Europe's finest cafes. Neighbors in Asia often have more long-lasting and cooperative roles in each other's lives than in the United States, where people often do not know members of their community at all.

A similar pro-European bias can be located in the work of conservative commentator Lucian Pye, who posited Protestantism as an ideal basis for civic culture and suggested Asia's lack of it might mean it would be the last continent to democratize.[22] Where only a few decades ago Confucian values were blamed for lack of business acumen and the ease with which Western businesspeople could take advantage of polite "Orientals," today Confucian culture is positively correlated with wealth.[23] As Asia's economies grew rapidly in the 1970s and 1980s, Singapore's Lee Kuan Yew and Malaysia's Mahathir bin Mohamad embraced "Asian values" as a reason for their success. They believed that unlike the West, Asians prize family above individual, social order above individual freedom, and hard work above leisure. Seeing these values as rooted in Asian philosophers like Lao-tzu, Mencius, and Confucius, Kim Dae Jung persuasively postulated Asia's cultural traditions as possibly providing a base from which new "global democracy" could be constructed.[24]

For all the talk of "Asian" values, the continent is incredibly diverse, embracing lands from Palestine to Korea, Siberia to Sri Lanka. Even if we limit ourselves to East Asia, diversity is much greater than many people appreciate. Among the ten Asian countries I have researched, there were five major religions: Islam (Bangladesh and Indonesia), Hinduism (Nepal), Confucianism (China, Taiwan, and South Korea), Catholicism (Philippines), and Buddhism (Thailand, Burma, and South Korea). South Korea also has many Protestants and Catholics, who make up possibly more than one-third of its population.

To be sure, vibrant forms of civil society existed in Asia. No less than a hundred disparate women's newspapers were published in Beijing between 1905 and 1949, and Chinese chambers of commerce in market towns were said to number at least two thousand in 1912, with about two hundred thousand merchant members, and an additional 871 associations in larger cities.[25] Eurocentrists have formulated democracy as a European (Greek) invention, yet research has revealed republican forms of government in ancient Sumerian cities.[26] In India, republics arose in the Ganges plain with elected

---

22. Lucian Pye, *Asian Power and Politics: The Cultural Dimensions of Authority* (Cambridge, MA: Belknap, 1985).

23. See Larry Diamond, ed., *Political Culture and Democracy in Developing Countries* (Boulder, CO: Lynne Rienner, 1993).

24. Kim Dae Jung, "Is Culture Destiny? The Myth of Asia's Anti-democratic Values," *Foreign Affairs* 73, no. 6 (1994): 189–194.

25. Gordon White, Jude Howell, and Shang Xiaoyuan, "Market Reforms and the Emergent Constellation of Civil Society in China," in *Civil Society and Democracy*, ed. Carolyn M. Elliott (Oxford: Oxford University Press, 2003), 266–267.

26. See Thorkild Jacobsen, "Primitive Democracy in Ancient Mesopotamia," *Journal of Near Eastern Studies* 2, no. 3 (1943): 159–172.

leaders and assemblies, which gave rise to egalitarian breakaways from the Hindu caste system such as Jainism and Buddhism.[27]

Asia's traditional civil society, so different from the West's, has been a great source of strength for social movements. From the tree and the drum that Korean villagers could use to announce grievances and find consensual means of resolving them to the Chinese people's traditional right to petition for redress of grievances and the Nepalese understanding of the *dharma*'s meaning that kings should rule justly, such longstanding cultural traditions—however dated and old-fashioned—continue to be operative means of rallying opposition against ruling powers.

Civil institutions were of tremendous importance during the Gwangju Uprising, including the YMCA, YWCA, Namdong Catholic Cathedral, Women's Pure Pine Tree Society, Nok Du Bookstore, Wildfire Night School, Clown Theater Group, and the Artists' Council. Nonetheless, leading American Koreanists insist that civil society did not reawaken until the National Assembly elections of 1985.[28] In Gwangju, activists reminded me that even under the harsh terms of the military dictatorship, they spread word of movements by taking food to neighbors' homes—a longstanding tradition in Korea, especially when fresh *kimchi* is made—in order to whisper news and organize events.

Conservative American anticommunists obscured the existence of civil society in Eastern Europe by insisting that "totalitarian" states had swallowed all autonomous elements of society. As the cunning of history invalidated Cold War propaganda on both sides, the political practice of *Solidarność* (Solidarity) in Poland caused Polish dissidents to talk of "the rebellion of civil society against the state."[29] Today, there seems to be general agreement that uprisings in Poland at the end of the twentieth century emanated from civil society.

Since many Western theorists believe civil society is a function of economic development, they expect the trajectory of the West and its kind of civil society to be the future of "less developed" countries. In actuality, changing dynamics at the end of the twentieth century might reverse the political truism that "the country which is more developed industrially only

---

27. Romila Thapar, *A History of India* (Harmondsworth, UK: Penguin, 1966), 53; Jack Goody, "Civil Society in an Extra-European Perspective," in *Civil Society: History and Possibilities*, ed. Sudipta Kaviraj and Sunil Khilnani (Cambridge: Cambridge University Press, 2001), 156.

28. Bruce Cumings, "Civil Society in West and East," in *Korean Society: Civil Society, Democracy and the State*, ed. Charles Armstrong (London: Routledge, 2002), 24.

29. See John Ehrenberg, "Civil Society," *New Dictionary of the History of Ideas* (New York: Scribner's, 2004).

shows, to the less developed, the image of its own future."[30] The 1997 IMF crisis in Asia was followed a decade later by the global economic meltdown that began in the United States. As infrastructure deteriorates and the central government seizes more powers, predictions that the United States is becoming a Third World country appear increasingly accurate. Rather than the West showing the East its future, the opposite may be occurring.

Civil society is the locus of significant strengths for movements, and it is also an important target for the long-term transformation of values needed for a genuine revolution—for "socialism worthy of the name." Marcuse indicated clearly that the kind of changes needed were "not merely a question of changing the institutions but rather, and this is more important, of totally changing human beings in their attitudes, their instincts, their goals, and their values."[31]

Contemporary Emergence of Species-Being

Cultural, religious, ethnic, and national differences, while appearing to constitute tremendous discrepancies among various social movements, obscure the essential similarities of movements all over the world today. The forging of a global culture of resistance to corporate capitalism since 1968 is nothing less than a world-historical force that is elevating humanity from nationalities, races, and religions into a species-being that includes all humans. Whatever their specific identity today, people increasingly recognize that their ties to each other in insurgent movements are far more important than their ties to the rulers of their societies. More than at any other time in modern history, people reject the world capitalist system and seek to replace it with direct-democratic forms of self-government that respect all human life and protect the planet from predatory corporations and militarized nation-states.[32]

Wherever we look today, from Taksim to Tahrir Squares, from Indignados to Occupy, people seize public space where they can speak freely, they challenge their government's policies, and they build forms of organization based on direct democracy. Creatively synthesizing direct-democratic forms of decision making and militant popular resistance, people's movements will continue to develop along the historical lines revealed in previous global waves: within a grammar of autonomy, "conscious spontaneity," and the

---

30. Karl Marx, "Preface to the First German Edition," in *Capital: A Critique of Political Economy* (New York: International, 1967), 8–9.

31. Herbert Marcuse, "Marcuse Defines His New Left Line," in *Collected Papers of Herbert Marcuse*, vol. 3, *The New Left and the 1960s*, ed. Douglas Kellner (New York: Routledge, 2005), 101.

32. See Naomi Klein, *This Changes Everything: Capitalism vs. the Climate* (New York: Simon and Schuster, 2014).

eros effect. This global grammar of insurgency includes rejection of control by political parties in favor of autonomous modes of decision making. These three qualities—autonomy, eros (international solidarity), and direct democracy—globally tie together movements that appear to be vastly different on the surface. This grammar of insurgency reaches beneath and above insurgencies' specific demands, aims, and ideologies.

A global revolution with pluralist and decentralized forms is underway. Visible in global waves of uprisings, ordinary citizens' aspirations for people power and more democracy continue to emerge everywhere. While now seemingly marginalized, the international movement today involves more activists opposing global capitalism than at any other point in the history of our species. While the airwaves broadcast a version of history that emphasizes the need for central authorities and social conformity, beneath the radar, people's understanding and self-guided actions constitute a powerful undercurrent. As we become increasingly aware of our own power and strategic capacities, our future impact can become more focused and synchronized. One tendency we can project into the future is the continual activation of a global eros effect of synchronous actions unifying people around the world.

Simultaneously today, men and women in all cultures yearn for love and freedom—and they actualize the struggle in their daily lives. Our erotic passions for freedom and justice are sublimated into political movements that unite us. These passions grow from the tender feeling for ourselves and the extension of that kindness to the partners of our unconscious in others. The life-forces within us bring us together and make us strong. To the extent that we are fond of others—including other species—even when they appear more and more different from us, we grow freer.

The real axis of evil—the IMF, the World Bank, and the World Trade Organization, abetted by nation-states bristling with weapons of mass destruction in the service of two hundred billionaires—will not willingly relinquish their grip on humanity's vast wealth. Globally synchronized struggles by hundreds of millions of people are needed to transform the global system. As Immanuel Wallerstein has long insisted, the system is undermining itself as it condemns a billion people at its periphery to semi-starvation and ravages our planet, while compelling all of us to work harder for more years with less money and diminished security. While Wallerstein points to a long transition similar to the centuries it took to supplant feudalism, uprisings help accelerate the end of capital's rule, simultaneously creating free women and men capable of living in a world of cooperation and solidarity.

Recent Asian insurgencies will help inform future uprisings—which, however reluctantly undertaken, will be necessitated by the systematic crisis tendencies of the existing world system. Sad and joyous, full of suffering while bringing forth tears of happiness, uprisings are moments of extreme desperation, during which human hearts act according to people's fondest dreams. By understanding these dreams and remaining true to them, we become more capable of a future of freedom.

6

Chinese Workers in Global Production and Local Resistance

JENNY CHAN

With a shift in manufacturing from the developed countries of North America, Europe, and East Asia to the emerging economies, China has become not only the workshop of the world but also the epicenter of labor unrest. Given China's preeminence as the twenty-first century's largest economy and its continued integration into, and transformation of, the global capitalist system, victories by and defeats of working people in China are of world historical significance. It has been suggested that elements of a Marcusean approach to industrial capitalist society—particularly the concept of the Great Refusal as transformational resistance from the margins of society—may be useful to scholars and activists developing today's critical theory of the Chinese situation.[1] Herbert

My gratitude, first and foremost, goes to Andy Lamas. I immensely benefited from his theoretical insights and passionate engagement with Herbert Marcuse's arguments. He enriches our understanding of the politics of labor in globalized China and in the world. I also thank Ngai Pun and Mark Selden, who have guided me through my graduate studies and academic career development in Hong Kong and England.

1. "Marcuse's concept of the Great Refusal may prove useful for understanding widespread resistance in contemporary China. Given that this resistance is so often generated by those who are among the most marginalized and precariously situated of China's working class, namely, rural migrant workers, Marcuse's observations about resistance from the margins of a totally administered society seem relevant and prescient." Andrew T. Lamas, "Accumulation of Crises, Abundance of Refusals," *Radical Philosophy Review* 19, no. 1 (2016): 4. For Marcuse's use of the Great Refusal concept, see Herbert Marcuse, *Eros and Civilization: A Philosophical Inquiry into Freud* (Boston: Beacon, 1955); Herbert Marcuse, *One-Dimensional Man: Studies in the Ideology of Advanced Industrial Society* (Boston: Beacon, 1964); and Herbert Marcuse, *An Essay on Liberation* (Boston: Beacon, 1969).

Marcuse did not write extensively about China, though he did offer percep-tive critique. In an April 1978 interview, in which he discussed the potential of Cuba and China to develop "the foundations for a free and just society," Marcuse said that "as far as both are concerned, especially China, it seems to me we see there the same we have seen so many times, namely the prior-ity of repressive modernization over liberating socialization: a technocratic authoritarian trend, at the expense of socialism."[2] With the turn toward what was officially termed "socialist modernization" and the development of a capitalist-oriented market economy—engineered (after the death of Mao Zedong in 1976) by Hua Guofeng, Zhao Ziyang, Deng Xiaoping, and other Chinese leaders—evidence for Marcuse's evaluation of "repressive modern-ization" continues to be manifest in the country's widespread workplace re-sistance.

Yet even as the size and complexity of China's working class grows, class contradictions sharpen, and social protest proliferates, the language of class has largely disappeared from Chinese discourse.[3] As Ching Kwan Lee and Yuan Shen demonstrate, under dual pressure from the state and academic institutions, many scholars who study workers in post–Cultural Revolution China "shun class analysis and define away labor issues as those of mobility, migration, and stratification."[4] For them the word *class* connotes antagonism and confrontation in the Marxist sense, eliciting dark memories of violent social struggles throughout China in the mid-1960s to the early 1970s. It is an image that is out of step with the "harmonious society" and the "Chi-nese dream" that contemporary China's leaders proclaim.[5] Policy makers

---

2. Herbert Marcuse and Gianguido Piani, "An Interview with Herbert Marcuse by Gianguido Piani," in *Collected Papers of Herbert Marcuse*, vol. 6, *Marxism, Revolution, and Utopia*, ed. Douglas Kellner and Clayton Pierce (New York: Routledge, 2014), 366.

3. Beverly J. Silver, *Forces of Labor: Workers' Movements and Globalization since 1870* (Cambridge: Cambridge University Press, 2003); Ho-fung Hung, ed., *China and the Transfor-mation of Global Capitalism* (Baltimore: Johns Hopkins University Press, 2009); Ching Kwan Lee and Mark Selden, "Inequality and Its Enemies in Revolutionary and Reform China," *Economic and Political Weekly* 43, no. 52 (2008): 27–36; Ann Anagnost, "From 'Class' to 'Social Strata': Grasping the Social Totality in Reform-Era China," *Third World Quarterly* 29, no. 3 (2008): 497–519; Joel Andreas, "Industrial Restructuring and Class Transformation in China," in *China's Peasants and Workers: Changing Class Identities*, ed. Beatriz Carrillo and David S. G. Goodman (Cheltenham, UK: Edward Elgar, 2012), 102–123; Alvin Y. So, *Class and Class Conflict in Post-socialist China* (Singapore: World Scientific, 2013); David S. G. Goodman, *Class in Contemporary China* (Cambridge, UK: Polity, 2014).

4. Ching Kwan Lee and Yuan Shen, "China: The Paradox and Possibility of a Public So-ciology of Labor," *Work and Occupations* 36, no. 2 (2009): 110.

5. Xi Jinping, who became China's president in 2013, is associated with the phrase "Chi-nese dream," while his predecessor Hu Jintao is associated with the concept of a "harmonious society," though it is an ancient idea in Chinese culture. For a discussion of Hu's conception of the "harmonious society," see You-tien Hsing and Ching Kwan Lee, eds., *Reclaiming Chi-nese Society: The New Social Activism* (London: Routledge, 2010); and Maureen Fan, "China's

and academics working in a social stratification paradigm analyze data on household income distribution, educational attainment, and occupational rankings to document the rise of a middle class, or various middle-class strata, while downplaying durable and deepening structures of class inequality. In this context, this chapter discusses the Chinese rural migrant workers, particularly their collective struggles within a framework that highlights the intensification of contradictions among labor, capital, and the state.

With the influx of foreign direct investment and the relaxation of state restrictions on rural-to-urban migration since the 1980s, successive cohorts of internal migrant workers have become the core of China's new working class in transnational manufacturing. By 2013, some 268 million Chinese rural migrants were drawn into industrialization and urbanization, an increase of 44 million from 2008, when the National Bureau of Statistics began to monitor the work and employment conditions of the rural migrant labor force in the wake of the global financial crisis.[6] China's economy was hit hard, as exports had comprised one-third of gross domestic product (GDP) in value, but it recovered quickly in the latter half of 2009 following the rollout of a fiscal stimulus of 4 trillion yuan over twenty-seven months—jointly funded by the government and state and nonstate enterprises—which was "equal to three times the size of the United States effort."[7] In 2014, by purchasing power parity, China surpassed the United States to become the world's largest economy.[8] While its extraordinary growth rates have begun to slow, China's trade, investment, and construction now have significant regional and even global influence.

Party Leadership Declares New Priority: 'Harmonious Society,'" *Washington Post*, October 12, 2006, available at http://www.washingtonpost.com/wp-dyn/content/article/2006/10/11/AR2006101101610.html. For more on the concept of the "Chinese dream," see Xi Jinping, *Xi Jinping: The Governance of China* (Beijing: Foreign Languages, 2014); Clarissa Sebag-Montefiore, "The Chinese Dream," *New York Times*, May 3, 2013, available at http://latitude.blogs.nytimes.com/2013/05/03/whats-xi-jinpings-chinese-dream/; "China's Future: Xi Jinping and the Chinese Dream," *The Economist*, May 2, 2013, available at http://www.economist.com/news/leaders/21577070-vision-chinas-new-president-should-serve-his-people-not-nationalist-state-xi-jinping; Robert Lawrence Kuhn, "Xi Jinping's Chinese Dream," *New York Times*, June 4, 2013, available at http://www.nytimes.com/2013/06/05/opinion/global/xi-jinpings-chinese-dream.html; and Martin Patience, "What Does Xi Jinping's China Dream Mean?," *BBC News*, June 6, 2013, available at http://www.bbc.com/news/world-asia-china-22726375.

6. National Bureau of Statistics, "Investigative Report on the Monitoring of Chinese Rural Migrant Workers in 2013" [in Chinese], May 12, 2014, available at http://www.stats.gov.cn/tjsj/zxfb/201405/t20140512_551585.html.

7. Christine Wong, "The Fiscal Stimulus Programme and Public Governance Issues in China," *OECD Journal on Budgeting* 2011, no. 3, (2011): 2–3, available at http://www.oecd.org/gov/budgeting/49633058.pdf.

8. International Monetary Fund, *World Economic Outlook Database*, available at http://www.imf.org/external/pubs/ft/weo/2014/02/weodata/index.aspx.

Supplementing the official statistics with field-research data, this chapter examines the role of local governments in drawing in businesses and investments, as well as the specific conditions of Chinese rural migrant workers' production and reproduction in the contemporary political economy. I document the ways in which aggrieved workers, at times of labor crises, have organized to take legal and extralegal actions to defend their rights and interests autonomously, without the leadership or mobilization of trade unions. What, then, are the prospects for Chinese labor to strengthen its associational power against the backdrop of privatization of state enterprises and the emergence of rural migrant workers at the marginalized center of a new working class? The answer hinges not only on the evolving consciousness and praxis of working people amid changing labor-capital relations but also on the ways in which the state prioritizes worker interests relative to those of international and domestic capital. Provincial governments such as that of Guangdong were compelled to enforce new collective-bargaining regulations to regulate industrial relations, precisely when an increasing number of workers leveraged their power to disrupt production to demand higher pay and better conditions within the tight delivery deadlines. In addition to discussing the significance of workplace-based structural power at key nodes of the global supply base, I conclude by outlining the impact of Chinese demographic changes on the growth of workers' bargaining power in the marketplace.

Chinese Rural Migrant Workers

With China's structural transformation over the past four decades, economic growth has spurred dreams of success from all walks of life. "Wage work in the city," comments Sally Sargeson, "became the means for self-actualization [of women peasant-migrants] in family and village."[9] For nearly all, however, it was transient; many among the first generation of rural migrants drawn to the urban labor market in the 1990s returned to their villages to marry, settle in, and raise children.[10] The returned migrants and their families have access

---

9. Sally Sargeson, *Reworking China's Proletariat* (Houndmills, UK: Macmillan, 1999), 219.

10. Ching Kwan Lee, *Gender and the South China Miracle: Two Worlds of Factory Women* (Berkeley: University of California Press, 1998); You-tien Hsing, *Making Capitalism in China: The Taiwan Connection* (New York: Oxford University Press, 1998); Delia Davin, *Internal Migration in Contemporary China* (Houndmills, UK: Macmillan, 1999); Dorothy J. Solinger, *Contesting Citizenship in Urban China: Peasant Migrants, the State, and the Logic of the Market* (Berkeley: University of California Press, 1999); Lisa Rofel, *Other Modernities: Gendered Yearnings in China after Socialism* (Berkeley: University of California Press, 1999); Ngai Pun, *Made in China: Women Factory Workers in a Global Workplace* (Durham, NC: Duke University Press, 2005); Tamara Jacka, *Rural Women in Urban China: Gender, Migration, and Social Change* (Armonk, NY: M. E. Sharpe, 2006); Jaesok Kim, *Chinese Labor in a Korean*

to village-allocated subsistence plots of land. The Rural Land Contracting Law, revised and implemented in March 2003, upholds the "thirty-year no-change rule" to household-contracted farmland for rural people, including those who migrated to work before the law went into effect.

For rural migrants, agricultural land tenure is a form of insurance in the event of layoffs or return to the home village and a basis for subsistence for returned migrants whose access to welfare and retirement benefits remain limited.[11] Sporadic efforts toward cooperative rural construction and alternative-development initiatives aside, sustainable farming and lucrative nonfarm work opportunities in the remote countryside are scarce. Following China's accession to the World Trade Organization in 2001, villagers and farm workers experienced ever more intense market pressures, one of the factors accelerating migration. Despite the elimination of agricultural taxes in 2005 and the extension of local insurance schemes, much of the countryside has remained stagnant, as youth have left en masse for the cities and jobs in industry, construction, and services. Some villagers, including rural migrants, have leased or transferred their land-use rights to boost income. Others, as a result of rural land grabs involving state-capital collusion, have no choice but to search for nonfarm jobs, resulting in windfall profits for cadres and loss of land rights for those who had tilled the land throughout their lives.[12] They become new proletarians in the socialist market economy.

Still, the majority of Chinese rural migrants have experienced "incomplete proletarianization," in that they possess agricultural land-use rights as a birthright while working for wages as hired laborers to make ends meet.[13] Poverty-alleviation officials and the All-China Women's Federation, for example, facilitated labor out-migration in accord with paramount leader Deng Xiaoping's 1992 call to "let some people get rich first."[14] The goal was to obtain remittances and assure the development of marketable skills in young migrants while jumpstarting China's export-oriented industrialization. Rural surplus labor has been channeled to urbanizing

---

Factory: Class, Ethnicity, and Productivity on the Shop Floor in Globalizing China (Stanford, CA: Stanford University Press, 2013).

11. Shaohua Zhan and Lingli Huang, "Rural Roots of Current Migrant Labor Shortage in China: Development and Labor Empowerment in a Situation of Incomplete Proletarianization," *Studies in Comparative International Development* 48 (2013): 81–111; An Chen, "How Has the Abolition of Agricultural Taxes Transformed Village Governance in China? Evidence from Agricultural Regions," *China Quarterly* 219 (2014): 715–735.

12. Julia Chuang, "China's Rural Land Politics: Bureaucratic Absorption and the Muting of Rightful Resistance," *China Quarterly* 219 (2014): 649–669.

13. Ngai Pun and Huilin Lu, "Unfinished Proletarianization: Self, Anger, and Class Action of the Second Generation of Peasant-Workers in Reform China," *Modern China* 36, no. 5 (2010): 493–519.

14. "Income Distribution in China: To Each According to His Abilities," *The Economist*, May 31, 2001, available at http://www.economist.com/node/639652.

areas through social networks and government development paths. As a Communist Party secretary put it, "We consider migrant labor to be a kind of cooperation between eastern and western parts of the country."[15] At the turn of the millennium, Beijing leaders attempted to rebalance the economy by initiating the Go West campaign, through which financial and human resources were channeled to underdeveloped central and western provinces.[16] This cohort of migrant workers includes tens of millions who were born, and even have spent their entire lives, in and around cities yet retain "rural household registration" in perpetuity while being denied equal citizenship rights.[17]

As market reforms accelerated in the decade of the 1990s and thereafter, the fragmentation of labor and the diversification of ownership in the hands of Chinese and international capital profoundly challenged both workers and trade unions.[18] Many small and medium-sized state firms went bankrupt, were privatized, or were restructured, throwing an estimated thirty-five to sixty million urban workers out of work.[19] The "iron rice bowl" of lifelong job security and accompanying welfare was shattered as state firms reoriented to make profits and cut costs in intensified market competition.[20] In recent years, with the consolidation of profit-making state-owned enterprises, China's industrial system has divided into three segments "consisting of

15. Solinger, *Contesting Citizenship in Urban China*, 71.

16. David S. G. Goodman, "The Campaign to 'Open Up the West': National, Provincial-Level and Local Perspectives," *China Quarterly* 178 (2004): 317–334; Andrew Ross, *Fast Boat to China: Corporate Flight and the Consequences of Free Trade—Lessons from Shanghai* (New York: Pantheon, 2006).

17. For an overview of China's rural and urban household registration (*hukou*) policy and its recent reform, see Martin King Whyte, ed., *One Country, Two Societies: Rural-Urban Inequality in Contemporary China* (Cambridge, MA: Harvard University Press, 2010); and Kam Wing Chan, "Achieving Comprehensive *Hukou* Reform in China," Paulson Institute, December 16, 2014, available at http://www.paulsoninstitute.org/think-tank/2014/12/16/achieving-comprehensive-hukou-reform-in-china/.

18. Mary E. Gallagher, *Contagious Capitalism: Globalization and the Politics of Labor in China* (Princeton, NJ: Princeton University Press, 2005); Tim Pringle, *Trade Unions in China: The Challenge of Labor Unrest* (Abingdon, UK: Routledge, 2011); Eli Friedman, *Insurgency Trap: Labor Politics in Postsocialist China* (Ithaca, NY: Cornell University Press, 2014); Eli Friedman and Sarosh Kuruvilla, "Experimentation and Decentralization in China's Labor Relations," *Human Relations* 68, no. 2 (2015): 181–195.

19. Ching Kwan Lee, *Against the Law: Labor Protests in China's Rustbelt and Sunbelt* (Berkeley: University of California Press, 2007); Dorothy J. Solinger, *States' Gains, Labor's Losses: China, France, and Mexico Choose Global Liaisons, 1980–2000* (Ithaca, NY: Cornell University Press, 2009); William Hurst, *The Chinese Worker after Socialism* (Cambridge: Cambridge University Press, 2009); Lu Zhang, *Inside China's Automobile Factories: The Politics of Labor and Worker Resistance* (New York: Cambridge University Press, 2015).

20. Sarosh Kuruvilla, Ching Kwan Lee, and Mary E. Gallagher, eds., *From Iron Rice Bowl to Informalization: Markets, Workers, and the State in a Changing China* (Ithaca, NY: Cornell University Press, 2011).

large, central-government firms; hybrid local and foreign firms; and small-scale capitalism,"[21] to which we may add the dominance of gigantic foreign-invested manufacturers that have access to cheap land, labor, and numerous privileges from local governments across China. Corporate management has prioritized labor controls with an emphasis on profit, organizational flexibility, and production efficiency, reconfiguring Chinese industrial relations in the global economy.

The 2013 government survey data clearly showed that China's east coast was still the primary destination for rural migrant workers nationwide but that the most rapid increase in investment and GDP was in the west. As enterprises have built new factories in the hinterland in accord with national policy, the gap in employment has narrowed in central and western China: 162 million rural migrants worked in the eastern region, 57 million in the central region, and 50 million in the western region.[22] The young people express a desire to broaden their horizons and experience a modern life and cosmopolitan consumption in megacities such as Shenzhen, Shanghai, and Beijing, as well as in other fast-developing cities in inland provinces. In their own words, we can hear the aspirations of this new generation; however, we can also hear evidence of what Marcuse defined as "repressive desublimation," as heartfelt impulses and authentic longings for a "free and pacified existence" are deformed and repressively molded into the reified categories of a one-dimensional consumerist discourse.[23] For instance, a woman migrant worker in Beijing commented, "If I had to live the life that my mother has lived, I would choose suicide."[24] Growing corn and wheat on tiny parcels of land and keeping a few pigs and chickens may not leave her hungry, but getting ahead and moving upward is nearly impossible if one seeks to eke out a living on the small family plot. The young generations have their eyes firmly on the cities. "Birds, don't be silly, no one cares whether you're tired from flying, people only care how high you fly," mused a nineteen-year-old migrant working girl.[25] Coming from a village in central China, she hoped to secure a better life for her mother and herself in Shanghai. While large companies are manufacturing rosy dreams

21. Barry Naughton, "China's Distinctive System: Can It Be a Model for Others?" *Journal of Contemporary China* 19, no. 65 (2010): 441.

22. National Bureau of Statistics, "A Graphical Illustration of the Chinese Rural Migrant Workers in 2013" [in Chinese], May 12, 2014, available at http://www.stats.gov.cn/tjsj/zxfb/201405/t20140512_551634.html.

23. Herbert Marcuse, "The Conquest of the Unhappy Consciousness: Repressive Desublimation," in Marcuse, *One-Dimensional Man*, 56–83; Herbert Marcuse, "The Catastrophe of Liberation," in Marcuse, *One-Dimensional Man*, 231.

24. Hairong Yan, *New Masters, New Servants: Migration, Development, and Women Workers in China* (Durham, NC: Duke University Press, 2008), 25.

25. Jenny Chan, "Who Speaks for China's Workers?," *Labor Notes*, May 29, 2013, available at http://www.labornotes.org/blogs/2013/05/who-speaks-china%E2%80%99s-workers.

of entrepreneurial success for the dreamers, low-wage migrant workers face a reality of unjust conditions in the workplace and acute problems in a society characterized by soaring income gaps;[26] environmental degradation; and the commodification of social services, housing, education, and medical care.[27]

The Chinese State, Labor, and Capital

The government recognizes the only official union organization, the All-China Federation of Trade Unions (ACFTU), and its branches across all levels. In the three years from 1997 to 2000 alone, the union bureaucracy, whose strength had been centered in state-owned enterprises, lost at least seventeen million members in the wave of privatization or corporate restructuring.[28] Many newly founded enterprises ignored official guidelines to establish unions. In response, the ACFTU has targeted large foreign-invested companies such as Foxconn[29] and Walmart to unionize. As of December 2009, "unions had been set up in 92 percent of the Fortune 500 companies

---

26. The latest data for 2013 indicate that China's Gini is 0.47 (internationally, a Gini coefficient of 0.4 or above is considered high)—a level comparable to that of Nigeria and slightly higher than that of the United States (0.45), where income inequality has also risen steadily over decades. "Inequality: Gini Out of the Bottle," *The Economist*, January 26, 2013, available at http://www.economist.com/news/china/21570749-gini-out-bottle.

27. Deborah S. Davis and Wang Feng, eds., *Creating Wealth and Poverty in Postsocialist China* (Stanford, CA: Stanford University Press, 2009); Martin King Whyte, "Soaring Income Gaps: China in Comparative Perspective," *Daedalus: the Journal of the American Academy of Arts and Sciences* 143, no. 2 (2014): 39–52; Shi Li and Terry Sicular, "The Distribution of Household Income in China: Inequality, Poverty and Policies," *China Quarterly* 217 (2014): 1–41; John Knight, "Inequality in China: An Overview," *World Bank Research Observer* 29, no. 1 (2014): 1–19.

28. Rudolf Traub-Merz, "All China Federation of Trade Unions: Structure, Functions and the Challenge of Collective Bargaining," in *Industrial Democracy in China: With Additional Studies on Germany, South-Korea and Vietnam*, ed. Rudolf Traub-Merz and Kinglun Ngok (Beijing: China Social Sciences Press, 2012), 11–51, available at http://library.fes.de/pdf-files/bueros/china/09128/09128-english%20version.pdf.

29. Foxconn Technology Group (a.k.a. Hon Hai Precision Industry Company) was founded in Taipei, Taiwan, in 1974 and incorporated in Shenzhen, China, in 1988. By 2004, Foxconn had become China's largest employer, and it currently has more than one million employees. Adam Pick, "Foxconn Takes Number-One Rank in EMS," *EMS Now*, May 30, 2006, available at http://www.emsnow.com/npps/story.cfm?ID=19523; IHS Technology, "Foxconn Rides Partnership with Apple to Take 50 Percent of EMS [Electronics Manufacturing Services] Market in 2011," July 27, 2010, available at http://www.isuppli.com/Manufacturing-and-Pricing/News/Pages/Foxconn-Rides-Partnership-with-Apple-to-Take-50-Percent-of-EMS-Market-in-2011.aspx. "Foxconn is China's largest private-sector employer, and its activities have turned the coastal town of Shenzhen into the electronics workshop of the world." Juliette Garside, "Apple's Factories in China Are Breaking Employment Laws, Audit Finds," *The Guardian*, March 29, 2012, available at https://www.theguardian.com/technology/2012/mar/30/apple-factories-china-foxconn-audit.

operating in China," and this trend has continued since.[30] By 2012, the centralized Chinese trade-union organization claimed a total membership of 258 million nationwide[31]—surpassing the International Trade Union Confederation global membership of 176 million workers in 161 countries and territories excluding China. Among Chinese union members, 36 percent (94 million) were rural migrant workers, the fastest growing segment of the union and the labor force since the early 2000s.[32] The number of union members is impressive, but from the purpose of serving worker interests, we may ask: To what end?

Fieldwork has generated information about the response of Foxconn Trade Union—China's largest industrial union, with more than one million members—to the tragedy of employee suicides. Foxconn shocked the world when the "twelve leaps," the suicides of young rural migrant workers who leaped from factory dormitories in Shenzhen city, took place during the first five months of 2010.[33] Foxconn union chairwoman Chen Peng, special assistant to CEO Terry Gou, not only failed to investigate the workplace factors responsible for worker depression but also made insensitive public comments, including "Suicide is foolish, irresponsible and meaningless and should be avoided."[34] Here, dominant capital reacted precisely as theorized by Marcuse: "In terms of the establishment and in terms of the rationality of the establishment, such behavior would and must appear as foolish, childish and irrational."[35] Not unlike their peers in other workplaces, and perhaps in an extreme form, the million-strong Foxconn workers are not collectively represented in a meaningful way.

---

30. Mingwei Liu, "'Where There Are Workers, There Should Be Trade Unions': Union Organizing in the Era of Growing Informal Employment," in Kuruvilla, Lee, and Gallagher, *From Iron Rice Bowl to Informalization*, 157.

31. *China Labor Statistical Yearbook 2012* [in Chinese] (Beijing: China Statistics Press, 2013), 405–406.

32. "20% of Chinese Join Trade Unions," *China Daily*, January 7, 2012, available at http://www.chinadaily.com.cn/china/2012-01/07/content_14400312.htm.

33. Jenny Chan and Ngai Pun, "Suicide as Protest for the New Generation of Chinese Migrant Workers: Foxconn, Global Capital, and the State," *Asia-Pacific Journal*, September 13, 2010, available at http://japanfocus.org/-Jenny-Chan/3408; Ngai Pun and Jenny Chan, "Global Capital, the State, and Chinese Workers: The Foxconn Experience," *Modern China* 38, no. 4 (2012): 383–410; Ngai Pun and Jenny Chan, "The Spatial Politics of Labor in China: Life, Labor, and a New Generation of Migrant Workers," *South Atlantic Quarterly* 112, no. 1 (2013): 179–190; Jenny Chan, "A Suicide Survivor: The Life of a Chinese Worker," *New Technology, Worker and Employment* 28, no. 2 (2013): 84–99; Ngai Pun, Yuan Shen, Yuhua Guo, Huilin Lu, Jenny Chan, and Mark Selden, "Worker-Intellectual Unity: Trans-border Sociological Intervention in Foxconn," *Current Sociology* 62, no. 2 (2014): 209–222.

34. Jia Xu, "Foxconn Rallies to End Suicides by Workers," *China Daily*, August 19, 2010.

35. Herbert Marcuse, "On the New Left," in *Collected Papers of Herbert Marcuse*, vol. 3, *The New Left and the 1960s*, ed. Douglas Kellner (New York: Routledge, 2004), 125.

The dependence of the unions on management, as well as the limits on their activity posed by the party-state, severely undermines the capacity of enterprise unions to represent the workers.[36] In the words of Anita Chan, the unions are "an integral part of factory management" and "worse than weak."[37] Five years on, in February 2015, ACFTU legal department head Guo Jun criticized Foxconn, among other companies, for imposing illegal overtime of "more than ten hours every day" on workers, in some cases resulting in "deaths and suicides."[38] But the practice of compulsory, excessive overtime work on this scale was well known to government leaders throughout the years. If the central-level union staff were really interested in building harmonious labor relations, they failed to reform the management-dominated unions at Foxconn,[39] Walmart,[40] and other firms.

In the face of rising labor protests, China's leaders have sought to legitimize governance and to stabilize production by initiating a series of legal reforms. Between 1978 and 1995, forty-nine labor laws and regulations were enacted, including the national Labor Law, which came into force on January 1, 1995.[41] The provisions of a written employment contract, minimum wages, overtime premiums, rest days, occupational health and safety, and social benefits—under the promotion of the "rule of law"—have inspired citizens to file claims through fast-expanding labor-dispute arbitration committees and courts.[42] As the state seeks to channel labor conflict away from the street, Ching Kwan Lee observes that "the law has become the pivotal

36. Feng Chen, "Union Power in China: Source, Operation, and Constraints," *Modern China* 35, no. 6 (2009): 662–689.

37. Anita Chan, "Strikes in China's Export Industries in Comparative Perspective," *China Journal* 65 (2011): 42.

38. Zhang Xiang, "Foxconn's Long Hours Causing Workers' Deaths: Union," *China Daily*, February 3, 2015, available at http://www.chinadaily.com.cn/china/2015-02/03/content _19477082.htm.

39. Nicki Lisa Cole and Jenny Chan, "Despite Claims of Progress, Labor and Environmental Violations Continue to Plague Apple," *Truthout*, February 19, 2015, available at http://truth -out.org/news/item/29180-despite-claims-of-progress-labor-violations-and-environmental -atrocities-continue-to-plague-apple-s-supply-chain.

40. Anita Chan, ed., *Walmart in China* (Ithaca, NY: Cornell University Press, 2011).

41. Isabelle Thireau and Linshan Hua, "The Moral Universe of Aggrieved Chinese Workers: Workers' Appeals to Arbitration Committees and Letters and Visits Offices," *China Journal* 50 (2003): 83–103.

42. Neil J. Diamant, Stanley B. Lubman, and Kevin J. O'Brien, eds., *Engaging the Law in China: State, Society, and Possibilities for Justice* (Stanford, CA: Stanford University Press, 2005); Kinglun Ngok, "The Changes of Chinese Labor Policy and Labor Legislation in the Context of Market Transition," *International Labor and Working-Class History* 73 (2008): 45–64; Margaret Y. K. Woo and Mary E. Gallagher, eds., *Chinese Justice: Civil Dispute Resolution in Contemporary China* (Cambridge: Cambridge University Press, 2011).

terrain of labor politics."[43] Aggrieved workers "mobilize the law" by quoting specific clauses of legal protection when their rights are violated.

Arbitration committees are grassroots state organizations that bring together labor and management to resolve labor conflicts. In 1993, China's State Council promulgated Regulations on the Handling of Enterprise Labor Disputes, enabling employees of all kinds of enterprises to raise complaints to local labor dispute arbitration committees. The significance was that while the 1987 Provisional Regulations on the Handling of Enterprise Labor Disputes in State Enterprises stipulated the rights to arbitration by state employees only, the 1993 regulations for the first time granted workers in private and foreign-invested firms, the majority of whom are rural migrants, equal access to arbitration.[44] Effective May 1, 2008, the Labor Dispute Mediation and Arbitration Law made arbitration free of charge for all parties and extended the statute of limitations for filing cases from sixty days to one year, thereby encouraging workers to bring their cases to arbitration. Unpaid workers were the greatest beneficiaries of extending the time limit for filing claims.[45] But not all incidents of labor disputes fall within the domain of arbitration and the courts. Workers know that government arbitrators do not accept demands such as those for wage increases above the legal minimum.

Labor disputes submitted for arbitration and litigation have spiraled since the mid-1990s, paralleling the rising number of worker protests. Official statistics for 1996 show that 48,121 labor disputes were accepted for arbitration, and the total increased to 120,191 in 1999, involving more than 470,000 laborers in the context of massive layoffs of state sector workers. The upward trend continued from the year 2000, reflecting widespread incidences of rights violations as the nonstate and restructured state sector expanded. Labor cases further skyrocketed to 693,465, involving more than 1.2 million laborers nationwide in the economic crisis of 2008. Following the economic recovery and government intervention, newly accepted arbitration cases fell to 600,865 in 2010 and further to 589,244 in 2011. In 2012, however, the total number of labor-dispute cases rebounded (641,202), despite greater

43. Ching Kwan Lee, "Pathways of Labor Activism," in *Chinese Society: Change, Conflict and Resistance*, ed. Elizabeth J. Perry and Mark Selden (London: Routledge, 2010), 76.

44. Virginia E. Harper Ho, *Labor Dispute Resolution in China: Implications for Labor Rights and Legal Reform* (Berkeley, CA: Institute of East Asian Studies, 2003).

45. Jenny Chan, "Meaningful Progress or Illusory Reform? Analysing China's Labor Contract Law," *New Labor Forum* 18, no. 2 (2009): 43–51; Mary E. Gallagher, John Giles, Albert Park, and Meiyan Wang, "China's 2008 Labor Contract Law: Implementation and Implications for China's Workers," *Human Relations* 68, no. 2 (2015): 197–235.

responsiveness on the part of the government and its trade union offices to resolve conflicts.[46]

Research in 2009–2011 found that disgruntled workers again and again rejected arbitration decisions and appealed to higher courts when they perceived arbitrators' awards to be significantly below what they believed the labor law guaranteed them.[47] Within fifteen days of an arbitration ruling, workers have a right to apply for a trial of the original dispute. Such appeals have become increasingly common. If either side is dissatisfied with the verdict, it can appeal to a higher court, where a second trial is final.

Notwithstanding important legal reforms, the state-capital nexus is powerful even as specific worker grievances surface in lawsuits. Chinese governments at all levels have fostered a "flexible" labor regime wherein rules and regulations are bent to the investors' advantage. It is observed that employers systematically "ignored the law with impunity because of the lack of effective implementation and enforcement by local regulatory or supervisory organizations, including the trade union, the local labor bureau and the courts."[48] China, in furthering its integration into the capitalist global economy, has chosen to accumulate wealth and pursue high-speed growth at the expense of socialist goals, notably the quest for social equality and shared prosperity. The nature of the Chinese state has radically changed, with officials and elites turning a blind eye to violations of law, as if labor abuses are inevitable (if not always acceptable at all times) in the course of economic transformation.[49] While progressive reforms of national laws and related legal institutions are necessary in basic labor protection, huge discrepancies exist between workers' employment rights in formal law and the actual enforcement of these rights. Negotiations over wages and benefits, for example, remain contested and fraught.

Outside of state-sanctioned dispute-resolution paths, Chinese workers have also taken direct action to advance their rights and interests. The oscillation between legal and extralegal avenues has fueled activism by some, but others have become depressed and embittered. Such a wide range of responses and dispositions is arguably typical of any long-term struggle against hegemonic power; however, the key point is that continued resistance

---

46. *China Labor Statistical Yearbook 2013* [in Chinese] (Beijing: China Statistics Press, 2014), 348–349.

47. Feng Chen and Xin Xu, "'Active Judiciary': Judicial Dismantling of Workers' Collective Action in China," *China Journal* 67 (2012): 87–107.

48. Mary Gallagher and Baohua Dong, "Legislating Harmony: Labor Law Reform in Contemporary China," in Kuruvilla, Lee, and Gallagher, *From Iron Rice Bowl to Informalization*, 44.

49. Dorothy J. Solinger, *States' Gains, Labor's Losses: China, France, and Mexico Choose Global Liaisons, 1980–2000* (Ithaca, NY: Cornell University Press, 2009).

by workers may inspire and catalyze new forms of consciousness and organization, opening possibilities for social and economic alternatives.

Challenges, Reforms, and Worker Resistance

Laborers' right to strike was recognized in China's constitution in 1975 and 1978, only to be revoked in 1982 and in subsequent constitutions. But this legislative change has not stopped workers from going on strike. Labor unrest has been growing, fueled in part by a younger and better-educated cohort of workers[50] who are less tolerant of injustice and highly motivated to demand higher wages and better benefits.[51] They understand that they stand at a strategically key node of production, with the integration of large manufacturers heavily dependent on transnational supply chains, just-in-time production strategies, and tight delivery schedules for consumer products precisely timed to holiday seasons and new product launch dates. This awareness potentially enhances their bargaining power and increasingly empowers workers to schedule concerted actions at times for maximum impact and leverage.[52]

In these times of crisis and the upsurge of "emergent sentiments of collective identity,"[53] when discontents are shared and articulated, workers have undertaken joint actions to secure their rights and interests. These acts of refusal have taken many forms, including the following:

- Strikes
- Slowdowns while on the job
- Coordinated absenteeism
- Protests and demonstrations (including sit-ins and rallies)

---

50. As of 2013, 46.6 percent of those classified as rural migrant workers were born after 1980, and the majority (60.6 percent) of these young people had completed nine years of formal education. An additional 20.5 percent are high-school graduates. National Bureau of Statistics, "Investigative Report."

51. Jeffrey Becker, *Social Ties, Resources, and Migrant Labor Contention in Contemporary China: From Peasants to Protestors* (Lanham, MD: Lexington, 2014); Manfred Elfstrom and Sarosh Kuruvilla, "The Changing Nature of Labor Unrest in China," *ILR Review* 67, no. 2 (2014): 453–480; Daniel Y. Zipp and Marc Blecher, "Migrants and Mobilization: Sectoral Patterns in China, 2010–2013," *Global Labour Journal* 6, no. 1 (2015): 116–126, available at https://escarpmentpress.org/globallabour/article/view/2293/2356.

52. Jenny Chan, Ngai Pun, and Mark Selden, "The Politics of Global Production: Apple, Foxconn, and China's New Working Class," *New Technology, Work and Employment* 28, no. 2 (2013): 100–115; Jenny Chan, Ngai Pun, and Mark Selden, "Apple's iPad City: Subcontracting Exploitation to China," in *Handbook of the International Political Economy of Production*, ed. Kees van der Pijl (Cheltenham, UK: Edward Elgar, 2015), 76–97.

53. Michael Mann, *Consciousness and Action among the Western Working Class* (London: Macmillan, 1973), 50.

- Blockage of highways or main bridges (to pressure local officials to mediate disputes on the scene—turning "streets into courtrooms")
- Riots (burning police cars, damaging targeted government buildings or factory properties)
- Petitions to government offices (again, to pressure officials to speed up settlement, instead of going through time-consuming bureaucratic procedures such as filing individual or collective lawsuits with arbitration committees)
- Social-media campaigns to disseminate open letters, to garner support, and to tweet in emergency situations
- Suicides (including threats of mass suicides)
- Murder (killing factory bosses in revenge, particularly in cases of severe industrial injuries and nonpayment of wages)
- Other kinds of violence (physical assault and abuses)

Many such actions to date have been short-lived and mostly confined to single workplaces, without workers forming broader alliances across geographical regions; however, a significant feature of such resistance is that workers have acquired organizing and communication skills in and through successive struggles. Interestingly, Marcuse stressed the emancipatory potential of a resistance that is "diffused, concentrated in small groups and around local activities, [as] small groups . . . are highly flexible and autonomous."[54] Two workplace-based protests in South China are evidence of how workers, management, and the local state have reacted to explosive moments of class tensions.

Under Chinese labor law, employers are legally required to provide five types of social insurance—old-age pensions, medical insurance, work-injury insurance, unemployment benefits, and maternity insurance—but the vast majority of workers classified as rural migrants lack rudimentary coverage of such benefits. According to the latest statistics, in 2013, the government estimated that only 28.5 percent of 166 million rural migrant workers were covered by work-injury insurance, 17.6 percent had medical insurance, 15.7 percent had old-age pensions, 9.1 percent had unemployment benefits, and 6.6 percent had maternity insurance.[55] A significant example of worker protest erupted in spring 2014, involving more than forty thousand workers from all production departments at the world's largest footwear supplier, the Taiwanese-owned Yue Yuen Industrial (Holdings) Ltd. in Dongguan, Guangdong Province, whose sneakers are sold to Nike, Adidas, Timberland,

---

54. Marcuse, "On the New Left," 126.
55. National Bureau of Statistics, "Investigative Report."

and other global brands.[56] Workers demanded employment benefits that the company had denied them. When worker-management negotiations broke down, a factory-wide strike closed the plant between April 14 and 25, compelling government officials to mediate the disputes onsite. On May 1, Yue Yuen corporate executives—under pressure from stability-obsessed, higher-level officials—promised to provide insurance premiums in accordance with the workers' current wages. The company refused, however, to pay the "historical debts"—that is, the unpaid welfare benefits owed to employees for previous work. In the absence of strong pro-labor government support for the full set of demands, workers accepted the partial victory and returned to work.

If large-scale strikes such as that at Yue Yuen sometimes win victories, the question remains whether workers in smaller workshops can secure the fundamental rights to collective bargaining and effective representation in the face of unified action by capital, the company unions, and the local state. In Marcusean terms, the workers struggle against the combined forces of the "one-dimensional" universe.

In May and early June 2010, 1,800 workers at Honda, including "student interns," participated in an on-and-off factory-wide strike to demand an 800-yuan-per-month pay raise in Nanhai District, Guangdong. Companies are increasingly facing pressure to raise wages and improve conditions to retain workers, particularly a young cohort, who frequently change jobs in an attempt to get higher pay and benefits.[57] The Honda worker representatives also insisted on reforming their union.[58] Bargaining by workers' direct actions, in the form of strikes or otherwise, has been and remains a viable way to address workers' shared grievances. The official slogan of the ACFTU is "When there's trouble, seek the trade union." Worker leaders, again and again, only found company unions unresponsive to their plight. In August 2010, Kong Xianghong, vice-chair of the Guangdong Federation of Trade Unions, presided over the direct election of shop-floor union representatives and subsequent collective wage bargaining in 2011. Many workers were disappointed, however, that the discredited factory union chair was permitted

56. Jenny Chan and Mark Selden, "China's Rural Migrant Workers, the State, and Labor Politics," *Critical Asian Studies* 46, no. 4 (2014): 599–620.

57. Equally important, state efforts to boost incomes between 2008 and 2012 led to average annual increases in statutory minimum wages of 12.6 percent. "China Initiates New Round of Minimum Wage Increases," *China Briefing*, January 4, 2013, available at http://www.china-briefing.com/news/2013/01/04/china-initiates-new-round-of-minimum-wage-increases.html.

58. Florian Butollo and Tobias ten Brink, "Challenging the Atomization of Discontent: Patterns of Migrant-Worker Protest in China During the Series of Strikes in 2010," *Critical Asian Studies* 44, no. 3 (2012): 419–440; Dave Lyddon, Xuebing Cao, Quan Meng, and Jun Lu, "A Strike of 'Unorganised' Workers in a Chinese Car Factory: The Nanhai Honda Events of 2010," *Industrial Relations Journal* 46, no. 2 (2015): 134–152.

to remain as head of a partially reformed union and the two "elected" vice-chairs were top-level managers, reflecting continued managerial control. Moreover, while the company was forced to yield on the important wage issue (namely, it agreed to an overall increase of 500 yuan for workers and underpaid student interns) under pressure from the provincial trade union to restore industrial and political peace, it was able to ignore all other worker demands, including those for women's rights and improved welfare benefits (paid maternity leave and a one-hour meal break among them). As a result, the union committee quickly lost the confidence of rank-and-file workers.

Worker solidarity frequently dissipated when leaders were intimidated, arrested, or bought off or when state-brokered settlements provided workers with limited gains while leaving the power structure and fundamental patterns of inequity and injustice intact.[59] Tim Pringle, in assessing the future of Chinese union reforms in light of growing labor challenges, stresses the need not only for "more accountable enterprise-level union chairpersons and committees" but "more supportive, interactive and, at times, directive relationships between the higher trade unions and their enterprise-level subordinates."[60] To maintain governance legitimacy, the state continues to search for mechanisms for resolving labor conflicts and managing social discontents while simultaneously embracing development policies that subject the society to the deep structural problems of global capitalism.

Toward Radical Subjectivity and Institutional Change?

In opposing their factory bosses and management-controlled unions, worker consciousness is being heightened, possibly constituting (together with other developments) preconditions for the formation of radical subjectivity, with which workers can build power to seek significant social, political, and economic changes. Utilizing Marcuse's perspective, one might see in these refusals the "disintegration of [a repressive] work morality" that "threatens to become a material force which endangers the smooth functioning of the system."[61] At present, however, workers face numerous obstacles in building their movements. Under decentralization, regional competition to secure and hold foreign investment in their domains—across the coastal provinces and between the interior regions—is very intense. The state-society relationships are contentious, requiring ever more legislative efforts, media advocacy, and direct involvement in labor management by government officials.

---

59. Xi Chen, *Social Protest and Contentious Authoritarianism in China* (New York: Cambridge University Press, 2012).

60. Tim Pringle, *Trade Unions in China* (Abingdon, UK: Routledge, 2011), 162.

61. Herbert Marcuse, "A Conversation with Hans Magnus Enzensberger," in *Collected Papers of Herbert Marcuse*, vol. 3, *The New Left and the 1960s*, ed. Douglas Kellner (New York: Routledge, 2004), 141.

In October 2013, the Guangdong Provincial People's Congress released for public discussion its "Regulations on Enterprise Collective Consultations and Collective Contracts (Revised Draft)."[62] The goal was to establish an effective negotiation system that would harmonize labor relations or, to put it directly, reduce the incidence of strikes. This document also suggests the possibility that a directly elected union leadership could emerge within a party-state-led model of dispute mediation and unionization in the workplace.[63] In response to strong opposition from major business associations, the provincial government weakened the critical provisions and on September 25, 2014, passed Regulations on Enterprise Collective Contracts in Guangdong, effective January 1, 2015. Article 18 stipulates that over 50 percent of the workforce must endorse the formal call for compulsory talks to take place, a formidable obstacle to worker actions. Even if negotiations do happen, Article 24 prohibits workers from engaging in a work stoppage or slowdown.[64] Under such circumstances, as Marcuse points out, state directives constitute an orchestrated attempt to contain workers' dissatisfaction within the repressive institutions of the status quo. In actual labor-capital-state contests, the long-term effect of the regulations on workers' power is to be carefully observed.[65]

Above all, Mary Gallagher characterizes "the activist state" in which the Chinese government "has struggled to maintain its labor system through more direct management of labor disputes."[66] Time and again, settlement of high-profile worker protests through direct government mediation is undertaken to quickly restore "social stability."[67] Indeed, officials have skillfully developed a wide array of "protest absorption" techniques to resolve labor disputes at the scene with the goal to maintain sociopolitical stability, such as redefining workers' "realistic expectation" and thereby lowering their

---

62. Standing Committee of Guangdong Provincial People's Congress, "Regulations on Enterprise Collective Consultations and Collective Contracts in Guangdong (Revised Draft)" [in Chinese], October 11, 2013, available at http://www.rd.gd.cn/rdgzxgnr/flcazjyj/201310/t20131011_136865.html.

63. Chris King-chi Chan and Elaine Sio-ieng Hui, "The Development of Collective Bargaining in China: From 'Collective Bargaining by Riot' to 'Party State-Led Wage Bargaining,'" *China Quarterly* 217 (2014): 221–242.

64. Standing Committee of Guangdong Provincial People's Congress, "Regulations on Enterprise Collective Contracts in Guangdong" [in Chinese], September 28, 2014, available at http://www.gdrd.cn/gdrdfb/ggtz/201409/t20140928_142698.html.

65. For an early bleak assessment of the Guangdong regulations, see Aaron Halegua, "China's New Collective Bargaining Rule Is Too Weak to Ease Labour Conflicts," *South China Morning Post*, February 25, 2015, available at http://www.scmp.com/comment/insight-opinion/article/1723213/chinas-new-collective-bargaining-rule-too-weak-ease-labour.

66. Mary E. Gallagher, "China's Workers Movement and the End of the Rapid-Growth Era," *Daedalus: The Journal of the American Academy of Arts and Sciences* 143, no. 2 (2014): 87.

67. Benjamin L. Liebman, "Legal Reform: China's Law-Stability Paradox," *Daedalus: The Journal of the American Academy of Arts and Sciences* 143, no. 2 (2014): 97.

claims to lawful compensation. At the same time, government representatives move to pressure management to grant some economic concessions to the most adversely affected workers and simultaneously manipulate workers' familial and social relations to silence the resistance.[68] The immediate result is that in many cases, workers' individual grievances are partially addressed and collective actions broken up. As China's officials make extensive use of their discretionary power, and spent as much as 769.1 billion yuan on "stability maintenance" in 2013 (which exceeded the total annual military budget),[69] rather than enabling workers to exercise their fundamental rights to freedom of association, it is unclear how long this government interventionist strategy will remain viable, particularly when workers' basic rights and interests are routinely violated.

Workplace suicide is understood as one extreme form of labor protest chosen by some to expose an intolerable and oppressive production regime in which rural migrant workers are deprived of dignified work and life, but many are organizing autonomous groups—bypassing the company trade unions—to engage in a wide range of protests and other refusals. Such bypassing mirrors the processes Marcuse observed in the United States in the late 1960s and early 1970s when he noted "the resistance of the rank and file workers to the union misleaders."[70] In recent years, union revitalization and labor insurgency in the Americas and in the Global South, however limited their successes, has increasingly drawn scholarly attention.[71] In today's China, at the heart of the world's factory, young workers seek redress of immediate grievances but also wide-ranging changes of policy and practice

68. Yang Su and Xin He, "Street as Courtroom: State Accommodation of Labor Protest in South China," *Law and Society Review* 44, no. 1 (2010): 157–184; Yanhua Deng and Kevin J. O'Brien, "Relational Repression in China: Using Social Ties to Demobilize Protesters," *China Quarterly* 215 (2013): 533–552; Ching Kwan Lee and Yonghong Zhang, "The Power of Instability: Unraveling the Microfoundations of Bargained Authoritarianism in China," *American Journal of Sociology* 118, no. 6 (2013): 1475–1508; Ching Kwan Lee, "State and Social Protest," *Daedalus: The Journal of the American Academy of Arts and Sciences* 143, no. 2 (2014): 124–134.

69. Michael Martina, "China Withholds Full Domestic-Security Spending Figure," *Reuters*, March 4, 2014, available at http://www.reuters.com/article/2014/03/05/us-china-parliament-security-idUSBREA240B720140305. For the 2015 annual sessions of the National People's Congress (NPC) and National Committee of the Chinese People's Political Consultative Conference (CPPCC), see http://www.xinhuanet.com/english/special/2015lh/.

70. Herbert Marcuse, "Correspondence with Rudi Dutschke," in *Collected Papers of Herbert Marcuse*, vol. 6, *Marxism, Revolution and Utopia*, ed. Douglas Kellner and Clayton Pierce (New York: Routledge, 2014), 335.

71. Abigail Cooke, Taekyoon Lim, Peter Norlander, Elena Shih, and Chris Tilly, "Introduction to the Special Issue: Labor in the Global South—a Search for Solutions," *Journal of Workplace Rights* 15, nos. 3–4 (2011): 293–301; Rina Agarwala, Jenny Chan, Alexander Gallas, and Ben Scully, "Editors' Introduction," *Global Labour Journal* 6, no. 1 (2015): 1–3, available at https://escarpmentpress.org/globallabour/article/view/2480/2347.

by industry and government amid the deep tensions being played out in global production. In unprecedented ways, tens of thousands of workers have participated in collective refusals as China further integrates into the global capitalist system.

Conclusion

China's rise could not have occurred without the painstaking efforts and hard labor of rural migrant workers. They have built new Chinese industrial cities and made the products demanded in global markets. In the process, these workers have enriched capital and the state; however, through their common experience of exploitation and with new technological and social knowledge, they have fought back for fair treatment, dignity, and a better life. With much at stake for working people, capital, and the state, struggles—from below and above—are likely to continue amid rapidly changing contexts.

Demographic changes have slowed the growth of the working-age population at a time of general aging,[72] and all indicators suggest a reduction in the labor supply in coming decades, potentially increasing the marketplace bargaining power of workers.[73] As economic activities are expanding outside of China's coastal cities, a substantial workforce is now being recruited within inland regions, and many migrant workers are being sent back from urban centers to their home provinces, in some cases close to their hometowns, where they may draw on local social networks for support—not only for daily life but perhaps also in renewed struggles for fairness and justice with profit-maximizing corporations, the official trade-union establishment, and a powerful state apparatus. With a greater sense of entitlement associated with belonging to a place, and perhaps greater social resources to bring to the fight for their interests (regarding wages, reduced work time for family

---

72. Two sets of demographic data are particularly relevant. First, Chinese fertility is presently 1.6 children per woman, down from more than 6 children in the 1950s and 2.5 in the 1980s. The number of laborers aged twenty to twenty-four is projected to decline from 125 million in 2010 to approximately 80 million in 2020. Baochang Gu and Yong Cai, "Fertility Prospects in China," United Nations Population Division Expert Paper No. 2011/14, 2011, available at http://www.un.org/esa/population/publications/expertpapers/2011-14_Gu&Cai _Expert-paper.pdf. Second, China's 2010 Population Census, moreover, showed that the zero-to-fourteen age group comprised 16.6 percent of total population, down 6.3 percent compared with the 2000 census data. National Bureau of Statistics, "Press Release on Major Figures of the 2010 National Population Census," April 28, 2011, available at http://www.stats .gov.cn/english/NewsEvents/201104/t20110428_26448.html.

73. Karen Eggleston, Jean C. Oi, Scott Rozelle, Ang Sun, Andrew Walder, and Xueguang Zhou, "Will Demographic Change Slow China's Rise?," *Journal of Asian Studies* 72, no. 3 (2013): 505–518; Deborah S. Davis, "Demographic Challenges for a Rising China," *Daedalus: The Journal of the American Academy of Arts and Sciences* 143, no. 2 (2014): 26–38.

and a balanced life, benefits, working conditions, job tenure and security, public health, environmental quality, housing, education, and the full range of citizenship rights in the places where they live *and* work), the result may be enhanced working-class power in factories and local communities.[74]

We observe that young workers (women and men) have expectations regarding consumption that make them vulnerable to co-optation by a capital-state alliance diversifying its economy to generate and meet rising consumer demands. "Realize the great Chinese dream, build a harmonious society," reads a government banner. The definition of that dream and the determination of who may claim it are at stake in the contemporary struggles of rural migrant workers. Will the current period of protest in localized sites of resistance across China develop further through alliances across class lines and across the urban-rural divide into a more broadly based social movement, against the backdrop of rapid industrialization and capital relocation? Will the demands and visions of discontented workers—and the responses and initiatives of capital and the state—generate revolutionary, reformist, or reactionary conditions? To a significant extent, the answers—and the future of China and global capitalism—depend on the evolving consciousness and praxis of the new generation of rural migrant workers.

---

74. Eli Friedman, "China in Revolt," *Jacobin*, nos. 7–8 (2012), available at https://www
.jacobinmag.com/2012/08/china-in-revolt/.

7

Queer Critique, Queer Refusal

HEATHER LOVE

The Great Refusal takes a variety of forms.
—HERBERT MARCUSE, *An Essay on Liberation*[1]

What is the relation between queer theory and critical theory? There is a tendency to cordon off the politics of sex, gender, and sexuality from the proper sphere of politics: the redistribution of wealth, decolonization, political economy, and racial justice. In contrast with these insistently material and large-scale social forces, sexuality and gender expression are often seen as private and volitional, a matter of preference rather than justice, pleasure rather than politics. The long-standing association of women with the private sphere and of homosexuality with immaturity and self-indulgence has made articulating the stakes of feminist and queer politics even more of a struggle. The queer politics of antinormativity have come under fire as individualist and out of touch with material realities—lifestyle choices dressed up as revolutionary action.

These associations have been challenged in recent work that articulates links between sexual nonnormativity and political economy as well as wider struggles for economic justice and social transformation. The work of activist organizations like Queers for Economic Justice and the Sylvia Rivera Law Project that make questions of homelessness, poverty, and economic and racial justice central has drawn critical attention to these intersections, as has the work of scholars doing queer materialist and queer-of-color analyses. Building on the deep links between socialism and LGBT rights, as well as on pioneering work by Third World and Marxist feminists, scholars such as Lisa

---

A version of this chapter was previously published as Heather Love, "Queer Critique, Queer Refusal," *Radical Philosophy Review* 16, no. 2 (2013): 443–458.
1. Herbert Marcuse, *An Essay on Liberation* (Boston: Beacon, 1969), vii.

Duggan, Jasbir Puar, Miranda Joseph, Kevin Floyd, David Eng, Rosemary Hennessy, Roderick Ferguson, Grace Kyungwon Hong, Robert McRuer, Dean Spade, Amber Hollibaugh, and Chandan Reddy have considered the intersections between gender and sexual domination and economic hierarchy and state power as well as the effects of race, ethnicity, nation, religion, language, and ability.[2]

Questions remain, however, about how to translate between queer analytics and those that aim to address other forms of domination. How does sexuality articulate with political economy, and what kinds of translations or comparisons are involved in thinking them together? What sites or objects of knowledge are best suited to analyze these articulations? How can we mediate between the small scale of sexual desire and the large scale of global political transformation? What is the relevance of developments in communities of sexual and gender dissidence to other forms of antinormativity? How do we account for the relation between hierarchies of sexuality and gender and other forms of social power? If parsing the relation between sexual revolution and economic revolution seems a somewhat dated task—given a lack of collective faith in revolutionary politics—we might ask more modestly: What energies do queer politics and queer thought have to contribute to broader projects of social transformation? What is the relation between the queer struggle and other struggles for freedom? What claim, if any, can still be made on behalf of the homosexual as a revolutionary agent, or as the harbinger of a new era, in a moment when gays and lesbians are being rapidly integrated into the state, capital, the military, and the family?

Scholarship that addresses the links between materiality and sexuality has taken on new urgency in a moment of the widespread integration of difference into a neoliberal world economic order. Critics of homonormativity (Duggan), homonationalism (Puar), and queer liberalism (Eng) have argued that LGBT identity politics does not recognize the complicity of contemporary sexual politics with global domination. Activists who have condemned

---

2. See, for instance, Lisa Duggan, *The Twilight of Equality? Neoliberalism, Cultural Politics, and the Attack on Democracy* (Boston: Beacon, 2003); Chandan Reddy, *Freedom with Violence: Race, Sexuality, and the US State* (Durham, NC: Duke University Press, 2011); Jasbir Puar, *Terrorist Assemblages: Homonationalism in Queer Times* (Durham, NC: Duke University Press, 2007); David L. Eng, *The Feeling of Kinship: Queer Liberalism and the Racialization of Intimacy* (Durham, NC: Duke University Press, 2010); David L. Eng, Judith Halberstam, and José Esteban Muñoz, editors' introduction to "What's Queer about Queer Studies Now?," special issue, *Social Text* 23, nos. 3–4/84–85 (2005): 1–17; Kevin P. Murphy, Jason Ruiz, and David Serlin, editors' introduction to "Queer Futures," special issue, *Radical History Review* 100 (Winter 2008): 1–9; and Jordana Rosenberg and Amy Villarejo, "Queerness, Norms, Utopia," editors' introduction to "Queer Studies and the Crises of Capitalism," special issue, *GLQ: A Journal of Lesbian and Gay Studies* 18, no. 1 (2012): 1–18. Critical prison studies and transgender studies come together in Eric A. Stanley and Nat Smith, eds., *Captive Genders: Trans Embodiment and the Prison Industrial Complex* (Oakland, CA: AK Press, 2011).

the "pinkwashing"[3] tactics of self-justification by the Israeli state as well as the "No Homonationalism" campaign[4] in the Netherlands (and other such campaigns across Europe) have also made it clear that antihomophobic projects can be folded into oppressive national and transnational regimes. In the contemporary moment, a coalitional politics of social justice cannot be assumed, since there is increasing evidence of the complicity of LGBT politics with projects of state power and economic and racial domination.

Queer studies is founded on a political vision of a nonidentitarian coalition of social outsiders and has committed itself to the project of "antihomophobic inquiry" ever since.[5] But that project has been subject to continual revision and critique in response both to the shifting conditions of LGBT politics and existence and to the changing facts of institutionalization on the ground. In their editors' introduction to "What's Queer about Queer Studies Now?," David Eng, Judith (Jack) Halberstam, and José Esteban Muñoz emphasize the need to apply pressure to the political significance of queer knowledge projects:

> The contemporary mainstreaming of gay and lesbian identity—as a mass-mediated lifestyle and embattled legal category—demands a renewed queer studies ever vigilant to the fact that sexuality is intersectional, not extraneous to other modes of difference, and calibrated to a firm understanding of queer as a political metaphor without fixed referent. A renewed queer studies, moreover, insists on a broadened consideration of the late-twentieth-century global crises that have configured historical relations among political economies, the geopolitics of war and terror, and national manifestations of sexual, racial, and gendered hierarchies.[6]

Eng, Halberstam, and Muñoz note that the contradictions of the present moment have provoked a crisis in the field of queer studies, one that requires a renewal of queer studies. The field of queer studies is perhaps unique in having been constantly subject to such calls since the moment of its inception.

---

3. For more on pinkwashing, see Sarah Schulman, "Israel and 'Pinkwashing,'" *New York Times*, November 22, 2011, available at http://www.nytimes.com/2011/11/23/opinion/pinkwashing-and-israels-use-of-gays-as-a-messaging-tool.html. Extensive coverage of anti-pinkwashing activism can also be found on the website *Electronic Intifada*, available at http://electronicintifada.net/.

4. See the campaign's blog at http://nohomonationalism.blogspot.com/.

5. On the coalitional politics of marginality, see Michael Warner, introduction to *Fear of a Queer Planet: Queer Politics and Social Theory*, ed. Michael Warner (Minneapolis: University of Minnesota Press, 1993), vii–xxxi. For a discussion of "antihomophobic inquiry" as a critical praxis that does not depend on a positive notion of identity, see Eve Kosofsky Sedgwick, *Epistemology of the Closet* (Berkeley: University of California Press, 1990), 27.

6. Eng, Halberstam, and Muñoz, "What's Queer about Queer Studies Now?," 1.

In the inaugural issue of *GLQ*, the premier journal in the field, Judith Butler warned that the term *queer*, in order to maintain political efficacy, would "have to remain that which is, in the present, never fully owned, but always and only redeployed, twisted, queered from a prior usage and in the direction of urgent and expanding political purposes."[7] If *queer* tends to be magnetized toward a fixed referent—gay and lesbian—key figures in the field repeatedly wrench it away again. Invoking Butler, the editors Eng, Halberstam, and Muñoz identify openness to "a continuing critique of its exclusionary operations" as "one of the field's key theoretical and political promises."[8] At the same time, they firmly wrench it away from sexuality, suggesting a broader set of concerns as the proper object of the field in the era of queer liberalism. The editors ask, "What does queer studies have to say about empire, globalization, neoliberalism, sovereignty, and terrorism? What does queer studies tell us about immigration, citizenship, prisons, welfare, mourning, and human rights?"[9] The essays in the special issue exemplify the renewal of queer studies by

> insist[ing] that considerations of empire, race, migration, geography, subaltern communities, activism, and class are central to the continuing critique of queerness, sexuality, sexual subcultures, desire, and recognition. At the same time, these essays also suggest that some of the most innovative and risky work on globalization, neoliberalism, cultural politics, subjectivity, identity, family, and kinship is happening in the realm of queer studies.[10]

The crisis of the field of queer studies is evident here in the editors' repeated turn to a broad social field that does not insist on—and even at times seems to exclude—sexuality as an object. *Sexuality studies* hardly seems the right term to describe this mode of inquiry, which sets "subaltern communities" and "sexual subcultures" in opposition (even though these terms might be understood in many contexts to refer to the same thing).

The contemporary moment is marked by the widespread but uneven integration of LGBT people into the state, capital networks, the military, and the family. This situation represents a crisis for the field of queer studies, which is divided between its commitment to antihomophobic inquiry and its commitment to an antinormative, anti-identitarian, anticapitalist, and antistate politics. As queerness appears to converge in some contexts, with the workings of capital, state-sanctioned identity politics, and empire,

---

7. Judith Butler, "Critically Queer," *GLQ: A Journal of Lesbian and Gay Studies* 1, no. 1 (1993): 19.

8. Eng, Halberstam, and Muñoz, "What's Queer about Queer Studies Now?," 3.

9. Ibid., 2.

10. Ibid.

scholars in the field are not sure whether to work to forward the thriving
of gender and sexual minorities or to subject them to queer critique. The
tension between universalizing and minoritizing models of sexuality—between the anti-identity platform of queer theory and its inescapable links
to nonnormative gender and sexual identities—has structured the field
from the start.[11] In the current moment, this defining tension has tipped
into crisis, since the two agendas that follow from these views—widespread
antinormativity and attention to the specific challenges of gender and sexual minorities—no longer easily dovetail but can actually be seen to be in
conflict. There are, of course, important distinctions to be made between
dominant and nondominant positions within the field of sexual and gender difference. One might argue that what we are seeing is a parting of the
ways, a widening gap between those who have made it and those for whom
it does not get better.[12] Some queers will never be citizens, will never be at
home in the nuclear family, will never be good agents of capital or bearers of
rights. To account for the ongoing exclusion of these subjects—poor queers,
queers of color, undocumented queers, disabled queers, nonmonogamous
queers, and others—while continuing to offer a critical account of ongoing
and rapidly expanding assimilation is, I believe, the central challenge facing
contemporary critics. It requires insisting on domination in the field of sexuality and gender as material and consequential—contra the longstanding
trivialization of queer experience and in the face of a new LGBT consensus.
Herbert Marcuse's reflections on sexuality, freedom, and negation are helpful in articulating a strategy and an ethics for a renewed queer criticism—
one alive to both new inclusions and ongoing exclusions.

I n *The Freudian Left*, Paul A. Robinson notes the importance of "the perversions" for Marcuse. "Only the resexualized body, the polymorphously
perverse body, resisted transformation into an instrument of labor."[13] For
this reason, writes Robinson, Marcuse understood the "social function of
the homosexual" as "analogous to that of the critical philosopher."[14] Despite
his persistent attention to homosexuality as a form of resistance to capitalist

---

11. Sedgwick defines "universalizing" and "minoritizing" understandings of sexuality in
Sedgwick, *Epistemology of the Closet*, 1, 82–86.

12. I am referring to the It Gets Better Project, an online campaign that seeks to address high rates of queer youth suicide. See the project's website at http://itgetsbetter.org. The
project has been widely critiqued for its racial and class exclusions. See, for instance, Jasbir
K. Puar, "Coda: The Cost of Getting Better," *GLQ: A Journal of Gay and Lesbian Studies* 18,
no. 1 (2012): 149–158; and "Queer Suicide: A Teach-In," *Social Text*, 2010, available at http://
socialtextjournal.org/periscope_topic/queer_suicide_a_teach-in.

13. Paul A. Robinson, *The Freudian Left: Wilhelm Reich, Geza Roheim, Herbert Marcuse*
(New York: Harper and Row, 1969), 207.

14. Ibid., 208.

dominion over the body, and despite his significance to the New Left more broadly, Marcuse's work was not taken up widely in the gay liberation movement. Nor has it been taken up in the contemporary field of queer studies, which has understood his work as out of step with a form of queer politics invested in resistance rather than liberation. However, Marcuse's reflections on nonnormative sexuality as an engine of freedom offer an important model for thinking through the relation between queer desires, communities, and ways of life and more general struggles for social transformation. In *Eros and Civilization*, Marcuse refused the instrumental incorporation of sexuality into a modern capitalist order intent on productivity and endless expansion. In *One-Dimensional Man*, he offered a critical account of "repressive desublimation" as an apparent liberation of sexuality that was in fact a reinscription of the dominant order.[15] Marcuse gave us many tools to regard the apparent triviality of erotic experience as a political resource, a potential site of resistance to capitalism and to instrumental reason.

More than any other recent critic, Kevin Floyd has brought Marcuse into conversation with contemporary queer studies, in part by resituating his work in the history of gay liberation. As Floyd argues, the place of sexuality in Marcuse's work has been understood primarily through his account of "repressive desublimation" in *One-Dimensional Man*. Shifting attention to Marcuse's earlier account of "surplus repression" in *Eros and Civilization* offers a different and more positive view of the place of sexuality in revolutionary politics. Focusing on the figures of Orpheus and Narcissus in *Eros and Civilization* and their close ties to same-sex desire, Floyd emphasizes Marcuse's investment in "the power of a critical, utopian articulation of regression with homoeroticism to negate the historically specific subject-object dynamic that obtains under the regime of instrumental reason."[16] More specifically, Floyd invests in the possibilities for queer liberation in Marcuse's account of reification by suggesting that the perversions offer an image of the reification of the entire body that might counter the reification of genital sexuality in the bourgeois sexual order.[17] But if Floyd is the contemporary critic most invested in the potential of Marcuse's work for queer studies and queer politics, he is also highly attentive to the problems that attend this alliance. Despite Marcuse's interest in the political potential of perversion, Floyd argues, "*Eros and Civilization* ultimately represents homosexual liberation and proletarian revolution as wholly incommensurate, if not contradictory,

---

15. Herbert Marcuse, *One-Dimensional Man: Studies in the Ideology of Advanced Industrial Society* (Boston: Beacon, 1964), 56–83.

16. Kevin Floyd, "Rethinking Reification: Marcuse, Psychoanalysis, and Gay Liberation," *Social Text* 66, vol. 19, no. 1 (2001): 110.

17. Ibid., 111–113.

political imperatives."[18] Finally, according to Floyd, "Marcuse is more interested in utopian figures of perversion than he is in real perverts."[19]

Marcuse's lack of engagement with "real perverts" and with the real social movements undertaken by perverts themselves no doubt contributed to
his dismissal by later queer critics. But this dismissal can also be understood
as a result of the influence of Michel Foucault's influential critique of liberation as a version of the "repressive hypothesis." *The History of Sexuality: An
Introduction* includes no direct mention of Marcuse—the name of Wilhelm
Reich stands in for a version of sexual liberation as a break with repression—
although Foucault alludes to Marcuse in his account of the "strictly relational character of power relationships."[20] In arguing that "where there is
power, there is resistance, and yet, or rather consequently, this resistance is
never in a position of exteriority,"[21] Foucault considers both power and resistance as dispersed across the social field. He writes, "These points of resistance are present everywhere in the power network. Hence there is no single
locus of great Refusal, no soul of revolt, source of all rebellions, or pure law
of the revolutionary."[22] Foucault's glancing invocation of Marcuse's concept
of the Great Refusal, elaborated across his work from *Eros and Civilization*
to *One-Dimensional Man* to *An Essay on Liberation*, does not, as many have
noted, do justice to the complexity of Marcuse's thought or the concept of refusal in his work.[23] Furthermore, this dismissal of the Great Refusal does not
acknowledge the extent to which refusal—both queers' refusal of dominant
norms of gender, sexuality, and intimacy and society's refusal of queers—has
been a historical reality for gender and sexual outsiders.

Marcuse's understanding of refusal not just as a positive form of revolt
but also as the radical potential in a history of social exclusion emerges in his
1974 address at Stanford University, "Marxism and Feminism." Articulating
a relation between the specific liberation of women and a general challenge

---

18. Ibid., 114.

19. Ibid.

20. Michel Foucault, *The History of Sexuality: An Introduction*, vol. 1, trans. Robert Hur-
ley (New York: Vintage, 1978), 95.

21. Ibid.

22. Ibid., 95–96.

23. See, for instance, Jonathan Dollimore's discussion of this moment in *Death, Desire,
and Loss in Western Culture*. Dollimore notes that "by the 1980s, *Eros and Civilization* was
being disregarded, often mentioned only in passing as a foil to Foucault's influential anti-
essentialist account of power and resistance to it." He continues, "Since [this mention of
Refusal] was taken to refer to Marcuse's irredeemable essentialism—at least by those who
had not read him—it is instructive to recall how Marcuse endorses the way in which psychoanalysis necessarily dissolves the individual. . . . It is also worth noting that Marcuse's notion
of 'repressive desublimation' anticipates Foucault's own account of the relationship between
sexuality and power." Jonathan Dollimore, *Death, Desire, and Loss in Western Culture* (New
York: Routledge, 1998), 346n6.

to the capitalist order, Marcuse begins the address by suggesting that the "Women's Movement is perhaps the most important and the most radical political movement that we have."[24] He points to the resources that women can bring to bear in contesting social repression and the domination of the Performance Principle.[25] Feminism's potential to transform society at large is not only a result of the progressive liberation of women, which Marcuse traces; it is also a result of the fact that in patriarchal society woman "came to be regarded as inferior, as weaker, mainly as the support for, or as the adjunct to man, as sexual object, as tool of reproduction."[26] Marcuse looks forward to the moment when *"specifically feminine* characteristics"[27]—"receptivity, sensitivity, non-violence, tenderness and so on"[28]—would be generalized and come to infuse a renewed socialism, a feminist socialism that would help build a *"qualitatively* different society."[29] This form of socialism would aim "for making life an end in itself, for the development of the sense and the intellect for the pacification of aggressiveness, the enjoyment of being, for the emancipation of the sense and of the intellect from the rationality of domination: creative receptivity versus repressive productivity."[30]

Marcuse's comments on the contributions of the feminist movement to a generalized freedom can be extended to a consideration of the role that homosexual liberation might play in a broader social transformation. The radical potential of feminist socialism for Marcuse depends not on the natural capacities of women—for the "feminine" characteristics that would help transform the world are not natural but rather have become "second nature" through "thousands of years of social conditioning."[31] The deep link between a history of social exclusion and the disruptive power of refusal is clear in "Marxism and Feminism." That argument is not elaborated in Marcuse's work on sexuality and the perversions, in part because Marcuse did not (as Floyd points out) discuss the gay liberation movement in the same concrete terms through which he engaged the women's movement. But it is also the case that Marcuse's reflections on sexuality tended to focus on the individual body rather than on collective experience, large-scale structures of oppression, or processes of socialization. As a consequence, for Marcuse, the pervert remains a figure of revolution rather than a member of a revolutionary class. Nonetheless, by reading Marcuse's later reflections back into his account of the perversions, we can see how a specifically queer

24. Herbert Marcuse, "Marxism and Feminism," *Women's Studies* 2 (1974): 279.
25. Ibid., 282.
26. Ibid., 283.
27. Ibid., 282 (emphasis in original).
28. Ibid., 283.
29. Ibid., 282 (emphasis in original).
30. Ibid., 286.
31. Ibid., 280.

refusal might figure not only as a romantic protest—the "soul of revolt," in Foucault's terms—but as a historical resource produced by the exclusion of gender and sexual outsiders.

Marcuse reflects on the revolutionary potential of sexual nonnormativity most extensively in *Eros and Civilization*. While in "Marxism and Feminism" it is the collective history of women that gives the feminist movement the power to resist the Performance Principle, in *Eros and Civilization* this power of refusal is associated with the figures of Orpheus and Narcissus. These figures are inassimilable to any concrete struggle for sexual rights: they are, for starters, mythological heroes rather than human individuals, and they are associated not with the fixed social identities of the modern sexual order but with diffuse erotic energies and the aesthetic. Nonetheless, these emblems of the Great Refusal are associated with male-male erotics, and in that sense, they can be understood as queer figures for Marcuse. Associated with the power of negativity, Orpheus and Narcissus represent "the redemption of pleasure, the halt of time, the absorption of death; silence, sleep, night, paradise—the Nirvana principle not as death but as life."[32] In this sense, they refuse the order of genital sexuality and procreation as well as the principle of production that it reflects and reproduces.

In my book *Feeling Backward: Loss and the Politics of Queer History*, I draw on Marcuse's account of refusal to trace a tradition of queer negativity across the twentieth century. Focusing on the history of queer exclusion from the family as well as from public life, I trace a genealogy of backward figures, acts of negation, and aesthetic practices of refusal. Beginning with the figure of Lot's Wife, whose disobedience to God takes the form of an excessive attachment to a perverse and difficult past, and drawing connections among queer isolates, I argue for the need to develop a queer politics that incorporates rather than disavows the damage it seeks to repair.[33] I argue that the history and persistence in the present of queer refusal—or, really, society's refusal of queers—has led to the development of a queer art of refusal.

Marcuse's account of Orpheus and Narcissus in *Eros and Civilization* offers another powerful account of figures that belong to this backward queer genealogy. Associated with the aesthetic and with death, Orpheus and Narcissus figure refusal of the dominant order by activating a set of tropes closely associated with same-sex desire and with the "impossible" existence of gender and sexual outsiders. Marcuse writes:

32. Herbert Marcuse, *Eros and Civilization: A Philosophical Inquiry into Freud* (Boston: Beacon, 1955), 164.
33. Heather Love, *Feeling Backward: Loss and the Politics of Queer History* (Cambridge, MA: Harvard University Press, 2007), 150–151.

In contrast to the images of the Promethean culture-heroes, those of the Orphic and Narcissistic world are essentially unreal and unrealistic. They designate an "impossible" attitude and existence. The deeds of the culture-heroes also are "impossible," in that they are miraculous, incredible, superhuman. However, their objective and their "meaning" are not alien to the reality; on the contrary, they are useful. They promote and strengthen this reality; they do not explode it. But the Orphic-Narcissistic images do explode it; they do not convey a "mode of living"; they are committed to the underworld and to death. At best, they are poetic, something for the soul and the heart. But they do not teach any "message"—except perhaps the negative one that one cannot defeat death.[34]

By living "an impossible existence"—of being excluded from central sites of social inclusion and reproduction (the family and the couple)—queers have developed resources of negativity. Marcuse conjures this history by activating some very old and, some would say, ideological understandings of same-sex eroticism, linking queerness to death and impossibility. And yet in claiming these aspects of queerness in the name of the Great Refusal, he situates them as a crucial ingredient of Left politics. Such a claim, deriving as it does from a history of social exclusion and nonrecognition, cannot be understood simply as a brief for bodily pleasure or aesthetic experience. Only refusal is positive for Marcuse; the Orphic-Narcissistic order can emerge only through the negation of what exists.

An association of contemporary LGBT people with refusal, let alone with the underworld, may seem far-fetched at best and politically retrograde at worst. At a time when gender and sexual outsiders are losing their relation to the shadowy margins of society, the utility of such associations is not at all evident. Yet I insist, perhaps paradoxically, on the continuing importance of queer refusal. The historical exclusion of queers from normative definitions of intimacy, the family, reproduction, and basic human thriving has resulted in the production of a crucial resource, a resistance to the world as it is given. The ongoing marginalization and denigration of queer subjects—which persist in spite of new inclusions—make evident the value of refusal, negativity, and engagement with difference as a project without a limit. Of course, there is no program that lays out how to harness and use the power of negativity, and it can be hard to accept the power of refusal, because it is linked to a long and painful history of social exile. Yet despite these difficulties, Marcuse's account of the Great Refusal suggests the potential of considering refusal as a resource.

---

34. Marcuse, *Eros and Civilization*, 165.

Emphasizing the power of the negative in queer history has particular urgency at a moment of increasing social inclusion of gays and lesbians. Marcuse's account of the Great Refusal can help now to remind us of the value of queer culture at a time when it is being liquidated through assimilation. At the same time, it reminds us of all those who are still left out of the new consensus. Full inclusion is a reality for very few people. Most LGBT people are still suffering on the outside of gender and sexual norms— suffering violence, discrimination, hostility in private and public, suffering the dismissal and marginalization of their intimate lives. At a time when gays and lesbians are coming in from the cold, being transformed into husbands and wives, parents, soldiers, heroes, and dignified citizens contributing to the productivity and the security of the nation, we need to remember how much this world is still wanting.

To address the unevenness of this new landscape—new inclusions and ongoing exclusion, stigmatization, and violence—we need an account of sexual and gender difference as an axis of domination as well as attention to the diverse social locations of queers, who are situated as both dominant and subordinate in relation to many different forms of power. Queer politics was developed as an attempt to forge a coalition of nonnormative and antinormative others; it is clear that a blanket outsider status does not attach to all LGBT people in the present. Still, the contemporary account of homonormativity may misrepresent this moment, given the extremely various ways in which queers are positioned in relation to dominant institutions and norms. I think we can find a model for a site-specific account of queerness that is sensitive to power hierarchies in Cathy J. Cohen's influential 1997 essay, "Punks, Bulldaggers, and Welfare Queens: The Radical Potential of Queer Politics?" Cohen addresses the racial and class exclusions of canonical queer theory. But rather than getting rid of *queer*, she develops a renewed vision of *queer* that would privilege "one's relation to power, and not some homogenized identity, in determining one's political comrades."[35] Cohen focuses on the significance of sexual stigma, considering figures marked by sexual, economic, gender, and racial marginalization. By imagining a politics that would make "the nonnormative and marginal positions of punks, bulldaggers, and welfare queens . . . the basis for progressive transformation coalition work,"[36] she offers a model that is flexible and critical enough to account for our contemporary reality.

---

35. Cathy J. Cohen, "Punks, Bulldaggers, and Welfare Queens: The Radical Potential of Queer Politics?," in *Black Queer Studies: A Critical Anthology*, ed. E. Patrick Johnson and Mae G. Henderson (Durham, NC: Duke University Press, 2005), 22.

36. Ibid.

At the end of *One-Dimensional Man*, Marcuse considers the apparent foreclosure of revolutionary possibilities in the administered society, when "the administered life becomes the good life of the whole."[37] He writes:

> This is the pure form of domination. Conversely, its negation appears to be the pure form of negation. All content seems reduced to the one abstract demand for the end of domination—the only true revolutionary exigency, and the event that would validate the achievements of industrial civilization. In the face of its efficient denial by the established system, this negation appears in the politically impotent form of the "absolute refusal"—a refusal which seems the more unreasonable the more the established system develops its productivity and alleviates the burden of life.[38]

Instead of the search for absolute refusal, Marcuse searches for the "concrete ground for refusal" in a moment when "'the people,' previously the ferment of social change, have 'moved up' to become the ferment of social cohesion."[39]

Although this new cohesion can be a cause for political despair, Marcuse draws attention to what is concealed by the "conservative popular base": "the substratum of the outcasts and outsiders, the exploited and persecuted of other races and other colors, the unemployed and the unemployable."[40] These excluded subjects have little hope of social integration; Marcuse positions them as the victims of society rather than as its constituents. Radical protest is undertaken in the name of these outsiders, but the transformation of society that extreme opposition suggests is anything but guaranteed.

> The economic and technical capabilities of the established societies are sufficiently vast to allow for adjustments and concessions to the underdog, and their armed forces sufficiently trained and equipped to take care of emergency situations. However, the spectre is there again.[41]

Though the politics of the underdog presents "nothing but a chance,"[42] it is a chance that, Marcuse insists, must be taken again and again. He writes:

> The critical theory of society possesses no concepts which could bridge the gap between the present and its future; holding no promise

---

37. Marcuse, *One-Dimensional Man*, 255.
38. Ibid.
39. Ibid., 256.
40. Ibid.
41. Ibid., 257.
42. Ibid.

and showing no success, it remains negative. Thus it wants to remain loyal to those who, without hope, have given and give their life to the Great Refusal.[43]

What would it mean in the contemporary moment to remain loyal to those "who have given and give their life to the Great Refusal"? I want to suggest that rather than assenting to the convergence of queerness with liberal capital, we need to insist on the ongoing exclusion of queers from the social world—to look for the substratum "below" the rising cohesion. If this cohesion were really cohesive, there would be no need to protest—but the fact is that social exclusion still affects the majority of queer and transgender people. We need an account of social exclusion that is not focused on absolute domination or absolute negation but that is calibrated to notice the forms of domination and negation that take place at a smaller scale.

During her "Critical Refusals" conference keynote, Angela Davis emphasized the difference between contemporary movement politics and the movements of the 1960s.[44] This struggle, she suggested, is not about separate struggles on behalf of individual groups fighting their own battles but about a general movement united around shared goals, dispositions, and refusals. Therefore, instead of the creaky engineering of coalition across already-given differences, activists today are building a movement that expresses unity from the start. The Occupy movement is radically inclusive—it expresses a new understanding that all struggles for social justice and for the fuller expression of human capacities are interrelated, and that we cannot think about the struggle against economic oppression apart from the struggles against racism, xenophobia, sexism, homophobia, transphobia, ableism, and all the hatreds and inequalities that structure our world. Davis celebrated the unity of this new movement, but she also issued a reminder and a directive, arguing that unity must be a *complex* unity—"a complicated unity that does not erase difference."[45] So we must not forget the differences that make up this unity—nor should we fail to recognize the creative and political power of our differences. We must remember the fact that it was the power of these polarities that sparked and fed these movements in the first place, and we

---

43. Ibid.

44. Angela Y. Davis's keynote address, "Critical Refusals and Occupy," was delivered on October 28, 2011, at "Critical Refusals," the fourth biennial conference of the International Herbert Marcuse Society held at the University of Pennsylvania, Philadelphia, October 27–29, 2011. See Angela Y. Davis, "Critical Refusals and Occupy," in "Critical Refusals," ed. Arnold L. Farr, Douglas Kellner, Andrew T. Lamas, and Charles Reitz, special issue, *Radical Philosophy Review* 16, no. 2 (2013): 425–439.

45. Ibid.

must not hope to legislate them out of existence or resolve them into smooth unity.

I emphasize this call to remember difference and the complexity of unity—and to consider it in relation to the force of queer negativity. What would this mean? It is an argument I am in part hesitant to make, since the recent history of Left activism has been marked by a powerful longing for unity and by confusion about how to generate both the wide participation and the energy that have marked the Occupy movement to date. I do not discount that, but I do register some ambivalence about the articulation of the movement under the banner of "the 99 percent." Several speakers at the "Critical Refusals" conference described their discomfort with the rhetoric of "occupation";[46] I register my discomfort with the language of statistical majority. My perspective comes out of my formation in a queer activist and academic context and from my attachment to an understanding of political organizing that is based in the notion of shared marginality. From that point of view, the overwhelming majority of 99 percent—just one percentage point shy of unanimity—makes me nervous. At the same time, I am grateful for its inclusiveness and its power and happy to be able to say, "I am the 99 percent." But I can't help thinking: What new exclusions does this create? Who is abjected or queered in this new movement?

The questioning of unity has been blamed for the fragmentation of the Left, and Occupy was the cause of massive relief and joy for many about the possibility of a new progressive majority. My purpose is not to undermine that unity but simply to issue a caution and a reminder about the limits of inclusion. As we come together under the banner of the 99 percent, we need to remember the differences that are ignored in the move to unity. We need to continue to argue for the significance of difference, tension, and disagreement as the animating spirit of politics rather than as something we will get past or get over as we achieve our goals. True inclusion does not aim to overcome difference and conflict—rather, it *is* difference. To incorporate all those outsiders and "losers" and social others who first dreamed the dream of inclusion, difference and conflict must remain central to the movement. What would it mean to pursue a powerful, broad-based movement in the name of negativity, refusal, marginality, and stigma? Could we organize on the basis of stigma or social exclusion? This sounds difficult, and it is. But the way to avoid creating a one-dimensional movement is not by adding in some dimensions but rather by installing difficulty and difference and refusal at the heart of the movement.

---

46. "Critical Refusals" (the fourth biennial conference of the International Herbert Marcuse Society, University of Pennsylvania, Philadelphia, October 27–29, 2011).

8

Mic Check!

The New Sensibility Speaks

IMACULADA KANGUSSU, FILIP KOVACEVIC,
AND ANDREW T. LAMAS

You can cut all the flowers but you cannot keep spring from
coming.
—Attributed to PABLO NERUDA

On Freedom and Liberation

Nature and labor are the two sources of value. So any reflection on freedom and liberation—or on the forces that repress their realization—must address the question of value. In 1964, Herbert Marcuse observed that the expanding conquest of nature (including human nature) and the increasing productivity of labor (enabled by significant technological developments) made possible the internal political stability of advanced industrial society, with the emergence of "a comfortable, smooth, reasonable, democratic unfreedom."[1] But there was a problem: under these conditions, any nonconformist behavior or rebellion against the system not only seemed "socially useless" but could also be subject to severe retaliation by the forces of the status quo.[2] On the one hand, the majority of people appeared to accept the prevailing values and norms as the system seemed able to deliver material goods. On the other, the popular understanding of freedom of thought, speech, and assembly came increasingly to be redefined as the freedom of buyers and sellers to gather for the business of consumption in the capitalist marketplace of exchange. In the face-off with the Soviet Union, this freedom was further informed by Cold War ideology of free enterprise, free markets, free trade, and free people. This all meant that the ceaseless exploitation of nature and labor was conveniently swept under the rug.

---

1. Herbert Marcuse, *One-Dimensional Man: Studies in the Ideology of Advanced Industrial Society* (Boston: Beacon, 1964), 1.
2. Ibid., 2.

Marcuse rejected the notion that the freedom of capitalist profit making represents the embodiment of freedom. He thought that capitalism meant thankless labor, insecurity, injury, and even premature death for the vast majority of people and that it also imposed on the individual "alien needs."³ Marcuse envisioned an alternative society geared toward the satisfaction of vital human needs, which would radically redefine what was understood as economic and political freedom under capitalism. The freedom from the market, the freedom from corrupt oligarchic political process, the freedom from the propagandistic mass media, and the freedom for autonomous individual artistic, cognitive, and spiritual pursuits would all have a chance in this alternative society. However utopian such an alternative vision might have seemed from the perspective of the 1964 status quo, Marcuse believed that the chances for its realization in practice were not nil. He argues that what makes it seem utopian is not its impossibility but rather the purposeful "implanting of material and intellectual needs" that ground, strengthen, and affirm the functioning of the capitalist status quo.⁴

In the tradition of humanist Marxism, Marcuse claims that all human needs, including the biological, are defined according to the interests of the ruling class of any given society. What is considered human is essentially that which is desirable by the masters to be considered as such. The basic needs of individuals are understood as the needs of the status quo and of the powers that administer it. As Marcuse writes, "No matter how much [an individual] identifies [oneself with one's needs] and finds [oneself] in their satisfaction, they continue to be what they were from the beginning—products of a society whose dominant interest demands repression."⁵ From Marcuse's perspective, this state of affairs is neither just nor tolerable. In contrast to those who believed in the power of gradual modifications gained through the electoral process and of the evolutionary development of more progressive social norms, Marcuse rejected such frameworks because he deemed them relatively powerless to affect the deep structures of the psyche. Only a revolutionary process would be able to push the individual out of the generationally installed psychological repression and facilitate the emergence of the burning "consciousness of servitude," which is the precondition of liberation.⁶

It is clear, however, that the so-called affluent Western societies generate mechanisms that tend to suppress the traces of such consciousness and to obscure authentic choices by providing those with money the opportunity to make a multitude of superficial consumerist decisions: This brand or that

---

3. Ibid.
4. Ibid., 4.
5. Ibid., 5.
6. Ibid., 7.

brand of toothpaste, of mobile phone, of cereal? As Marcuse points out, these choices could hardly signify freedom because they do not help us overcome our essential alienation—"free election of masters does not abolish the masters or the slaves."[7] We are still unfree and will remain so until "the decisions over life and death, over personal and national security" are no longer made without our knowledge and beyond our control.[8]

In recent years, Slavoj Žižek has discussed Marcuse's claim that authentic freedom is "the condition of liberation,"[9] for which, most likely, Marcuse found inspiration in Hegel's statement from *Philosophy of Right*[10]—"freedom wills freedom."[11] The key question is how one can come to acquire and exercise this authentic freedom. How does one become free enough to desire liberation? This question is clearly central to radical organizing, critical pedagogy, and all transformative, consciousness-raising projects. In his early book *Reason and Revolution*, Marcuse's answer to this question was typically Hegelian: "the laborious process of education through history."[12]

The first step in this long-term historical process is, according to Marcuse, the experience of inner freedom. Marcuse approvingly quotes Hegel's claim that the "ground of the existence of freedom is the subjectivity of the will."[13] This subjectivity of the will, which is the core of the individual ego, is the primary substance of freedom because it finds itself negatively affected by the immensity of the whole.[14] It strives to preserve its difference and, in doing so, it increasingly discovers the superficiality of its inner freedom in confrontation with its actual subordination to the whole. And it is here that the spark of rebellion is born. This experience creates what Marcuse called the "real specter of liberation" and may provide the psychological grounding for the commitment to qualitative social and political change.[15]

Advanced industrial societies dull this impulse for authentic social transformation by providing individuals with the promise of an ever more comfortable lifestyle while limiting the scope of their imaginations through increasingly sophisticated production and targeted delivery of images and

---

7. Ibid.

8. Ibid., 32.

9. Slavoj Žižek, *Living in the End Times* (London: Verso, 2010), 290. Žižek has stated this before, in *First as Tragedy, Then as Farce* (London: Verso, 2009), 143.

10. G.W.F. Hegel, *Elements of the Philosophy of Right*, ed. Allen W. Wood, trans. Hugh Barr Nisbet (Cambridge: Cambridge University Press, 1991). Originally published in 1820.

11. Herbert Marcuse, *Reason and Revolution: Hegel and the Rise of Social Theory* (London: Humanities, 1991).

12. Ibid., 189.

13. Hegel, *Elements of the Philosophy of Right*, quoted in Marcuse, *Reason and Revolution*, 200.

14. Marcuse, *Reason and Revolution*, 188.

15. Marcuse, *One-Dimensional Man*, 52.

desires. Techniques for consumer surveillance and mass customization now far surpass what was technologically possible in the 1960s.

Beyond the carrot is the stick. Marcuse believes that the horizon of possibility is further sharply defined by the repressive political and moral authorities and that those who try to rebel are "kept in line by a brutality, which revives medieval and early modern practices."[16] In this way, advanced industrial societies develop their own brand of totalitarianism. They come to determine almost everything in the individual's existence—his or her emotions, attitudes, needs, aspirations, and dreams. There is no space that is not invaded and taken over by social demands. The individual is forced to identify with society even in the utmost recesses of his or her soul. According to Marcuse, "the 'inner' dimension of the mind in which opposition to the status quo can take root is whittled down."[17] Such one-dimensional existence threatens to swallow up the individual who becomes a mere cog in the gigantic machine that churns out material goods at the price of cognitive devastation.[18] In a certain sense, the distinction between ideology and reality becomes blurred, and individuals in their daily lives come to identify with the social functions they are assigned by the system. They may even become willing accomplices in their own subjugation and react negatively, sometimes even violently, to anybody advocating the possibility of a qualitatively different order. This is the Procrustean bed in which the authoritarian personality is born.

Marcuse's reflections on the repressive structure of advanced industrial societies retain their contemporary relevance and perhaps have even greater import today, as the economic backdrop has shifted from what Marcuse (and some other public intellectuals of the time, such as John Kenneth Galbraith[19]) then viewed as a condition of growing affluence to what is today more commonly experienced as anxiety, precarity, and rising inequality. The absence of "representative institutions in which . . . individuals work for themselves and speak for themselves"[20] is as glaring today as in the 1960s; however, it is also true that in the historical record oppression has always met resistance. Despite the drive toward the totally administered society, Marcuse nonetheless hopes (perhaps without optimism) that there is some

---

16. Ibid., 23.

17. Ibid., 10.

18. For a brilliant, fictional account of this phenomenon in relation to an assembly-line worker's body and consciousness, see the critical masterpiece *Modern Times*, directed by Charlie Chaplin (Beverly Hills, CA: United Artists, 2003), DVD. The film was originally released in 1936.

19. John Kenneth Galbraith, *The Affluent Society* (Boston: Houghton Mifflin, 1958); cf. Michael Harrington, *The Other America: Poverty in the United States* (New York: Macmillan, 1962).

20. Marcuse, *One-Dimensional Man*, 206.

basis for the development of "a new sensibility" qualitatively different from the one-dimensional subjectivity normalized in modern capitalist society. As Douglas Kellner summarizes, "Marcuse was engaged in a life-long search for a revolutionary subjectivity, for a sensibility that would revolt against the existing society and attempt to create a new one."[21]

Traces of Hope, through Negation

There are signs, and then there are signs.

> As I went walking I saw a sign there
> And on the sign it said "No Trespassing."
> But on the other side it didn't say nothing,
> That side was made for you and me.[22]

In the one-dimensional society described by Marcuse, individuals are situated within the consumerist ideological apparatus that preconditions their needs, dreams, and aspirations and thereby erases the difference between false and true consciousness. Subjectively, they may feel free, and yet they are more overtly surveilled and subtly influenced, manipulated, or controlled than at any other time in recorded human history.

One-dimensional society, like any social structure, relies for its stability on the circulation and normalization of ordered signifiers.[23] These signifiers form a schema that determines how the world is perceived. In Kantian terms, schema is the product and procedure of imagination: it links phenomena and concepts and, in this way, constitutes a human world. The manner, the mode, and the frame through which the phenomena are synthesized and integrated by the individual are given a priori. According to Kant, the integrating synthesis (the act of the mind) precedes the phenomena: it constitutes and shapes them and, in doing so, "designs" the world we live in. In other words, our world is the product of a schema created by human imagination. The media scholar Stephen Duncombe put it well when he wrote,

---

21. Douglas Kellner, "Marcuse and the Quest for Radical Subjectivity," *Social Thought and Research* 22, nos. 1–2 (1999): 3.

22. Woody Guthrie, "This Land Is Your Land," on *This Land Is Your Land: The Asch Recordings*, vol. 1, Smithsonian Folkways Recordings, 1997, CD. Words and music by Woody Guthrie. WGP/TRO © Copyright 1956, 1958, 1970, and 1972 (copyrights renewed) Woody Guthrie Publications, Inc., and Ludlow Music, Inc., New York, NY. Administered by Ludlow Music, Inc. Used by permission. In a telling and sadly ironic sign of the times, payment of a fee was required for the right to publish these four lines!

23. See AK Thompson, *Black Bloc, White Riot: Anti-globalization and the Genealogy of Dissent* (Oakland, CA: AK Press, 2010), 50.

"Reality is always refracted through imagination, and it is through imagination that we live our lives."[24]

Marcuse modified Kant by grounding the *a priori* not in the so-called "transcendental apperception" but in the empirical context that, among other things, includes "the supra-individual experiences, ideas [and] aspirations of particular social groups."[25] In this way, Marcuse highlighted the importance of history in the construction of our experience of the world. The horizon of the existing society—akin to what the philosopher of science Thomas Kuhn called a paradigm—frames our perceptions.[26] Still, according to Marcuse, it is possible to make a distinction between true and false consciousness. The former reflects "as fully and adequately as possible, the given society and the given facts," while the latter is selective and expresses only the point of view of the dominant social and political forces.[27] The same conclusion is reached many years later by Slavoj Žižek, who describes false consciousness as a "deranged scenario [that] throws out of joint the 'proper order of things': it distorts our approach to the world by violently imposing upon it a certain partial perspective."[28]

In *One-Dimensional Man* and across his oeuvre, Marcuse searches beyond the repressive social frame to document the sources of the dominant ideology and its construction of one-dimensionality, along the way finding traces of hope in the hidden, unexpurgated content of certain fundamental social concepts. Marcuse's approach is to use these concepts as critical instruments to uncover the "limits, suppression, and denials" of the status quo.[29] This is possible because the concept in its essence transcends the given facts and makes it possible to distinguish what a thing potentially is (and can be) from its contingent function in the established reality: these two dimensions can be perceived in terms of the tension between *is* and *ought to be*.

For example, "Woman is free" is a proposition that aims to define reality while affirming a truth that has not yet become true in actuality. In this case, "the copula 'is' states an 'ought,' a desideratum."[30] The statement turns into an ethical imperative, and the epistemological question becomes the moral one. In the light of a conceptual truth, which the status quo denies, the

---

24. Stephen Duncombe, *Dream: Re-imagining Progressive Politics in an Age of Fantasy* (New York: New Press, 2007), 18.

25. Marcuse, *One-Dimensional Man*, 208.

26. See Thomas Kuhn, *The Structure of Scientific Revolutions* (Chicago: University of Chicago Press, 1962).

27. Marcuse, *One-Dimensional Man*, 208.

28. Slavoj Žižek, *The Fragile Absolute; or, Why is the Christian Legacy Worth Fighting For?* (London: Verso, 2000), 85.

29. Marcuse, *One-Dimensional Man*, 215.

30. Ibid., 133.

statement appears false. This produces a pervasive tension and a potentially fruitful conflict between what is revealed—in expression, speech, acts, behavior—and what is not expressed and must stay off the stage, as "negatively present" or as present only in the form of the "repelled material."[31] For example, amid Occupy and in its immediate aftermath, the conventional media, mainstream foundations and think tanks, and elected officials began issuing statements and reports on inequality—not just income inequality but also wealth inequality—and sometimes even linked this inequality to discussions of class and class conflict.[32] The sudden appearance of such matters in dominant mainstream arenas of discourse—called forth, of course, by the financial crisis and Occupy's intervention—demonstrates the "negative presence" of certain questions (e.g., the economy's production of gross class inequalities) *in the prior period of things-as-usual.* So Occupy's mic check in 2011 was an opening to a new linguistic event. Particularly in its more radical expressions, Occupy attempted to crack open the shell of appearance to reveal the hidden core, the negative essence of capitalism—namely the class struggle. Once this is perceived—which is why it is an impermissible topic of study in polite society—questions can be raised about whether a different way of organizing society on behalf of the "99 percent" might be possible.

The slogan "Another world is possible," most often associated with the first World Social Forum meeting, in Porto Alegre, Brazil, in 2001, succinctly frames the idea asserted by Marcuse that every society is confronted with the possibility of a different historical project, of another possible frame that can radically transform the established reality. In a recent work, Žižek voices his agreement and points to the history of philosophy from Kierkegaard and Nietzsche to Wittgenstein, which defines the core of being human as "*a concrete practico-ethical engagement and/or choice which precedes (and grounds)*

---

31. Ibid., 209.

32. See, for example, this analysis by Todd Gitlin: "It's a cliché, a true one, that the Occupy movements of 2011–12 changed the conversation. Reform mayors like New York City's Bill De Blasio (theme: 'a tale of two cities') were elected. On talk shows, best-seller lists and the business sections of newspapers—even, yes, in university economics departments—inequality is all the rage. At the time of writing, Thomas Piketty's *Capital in the 21st Century* ranks #4 among all books on US Amazon, and #15 in Britain. In the US, this subversive little theme has infiltrated the rhetoric of the Democratic Party and even right-wing populists among the Republicans, including the libertarian David Brat, who up-ended House majority leader Eric Cantor in a Virginia primary on 10 June, declaring: 'All the investment banks in the New York and [Washington] DC—those guys should have gone to jail. Instead of going to jail, they went on Eric's Rolodex, and they are sending him big cheques.'" Todd Gitlin, "Where Are All the Occupy Protestors Now?," *The Guardian*, June 17, 2014, available at http://www.theguard ian.com/cities/2014/jun/17/where-occupy-protesters-now-social-media.

every 'theory.'"[33] In a certain sense, Kant is vindicated: theory precedes any possible knowledge.[34]

When the potentialities of society outgrow its existing institutions, the established rationality reveals its inherent irrationality and the urgency of different projects becomes palpable. Marcuse stressed that the alternative must be grounded in the "attained level of the material and intellectual culture," hence demonstrating "its own higher rationality."[35] The alternative begins its historical existence by refusing and negating the given. As with the dialectic, this is central to the Great Refusal, which involves "consciousness: the recognition and seizure of liberating possibilities."[36]

> It involves freedom. To the degree to which consciousness is determined by the exigencies and interests of the established society, it is "unfree"; to the degree to which the established society is irrational, the consciousness becomes free for the higher historical rationality only in struggle against the established society. The truth and the freedom of negative thinking have their ground and reason in this struggle.[37]

In the Great Refusal, negative thinking is at work within and against the established reality. For Marcuse, the key aspect of this process is that it "proceeds on empirical grounds" and that its "truth" will also be decided on these grounds.[38] Marcuse warned that the "truth" of an alternative historical project should not be confused with its "success"—that is, its acceptance by the status quo. He pointed out that "Galilean science was true while it was still condemned; Marxian theory was already true at the time of *Communist Manifesto*; fascism remains false even if it is in ascent on an international scale."[39] In other words, external durability and apparent strength must never be taken as "the sole criterion of the truth of a content."[40] This is

---

33. Slavoj Žižek, *The Parallax View* (Cambridge, MA: MIT Press, 2006), 75 (emphasis in original).

34. The same has also occurred in hard sciences: Heisenberg wrote that Einstein convinced him that it was not the empirical observation that gave rise to theory but that, on the contrary, it was theory that shaped the empirical world by deciding what to focus on. See Werner Heisenberg, "The Quantum Mechanics and a Conversation with Einstein," in *Physics and Beyond: Encounters and Conversations*, ed. Ruth Nanda Anshen (New York: Harper Collins, 1971).

35. Marcuse, *One-Dimensional Man*, 220.

36. Ibid., 222.

37. Ibid.

38. Ibid., 223.

39. Ibid.

40. Marcuse, *Reason and Revolution*, 131.

necessary consolation for those—in Tahrir Square to Zuccotti Park to Syntagma Square—who are beaten back and removed, as they find other ways back into the arena of struggle.

In any given society, no matter how repressive and one-dimensional, one can still discern those forces that, in the here and now, embody alternative, qualitatively different values. Ordinary people's capacity to self-organize for governance, defense, sustenance, care, education, and the creative arts has been demonstrated again and again—from the Paris Commune in 1871 to the Gwangju Uprising in South Korea in 1980.[41] In 2011, during the massive campaign of nonviolent resistance in Tahrir Square, protestors occupied a Kentucky Fried Chicken fast-food restaurant and turned it into the "KFC Clinic," providing medical care for the sick and injured.[42]

In the concluding pages of *One-Dimensional Man*, Marcuse writes of the marginalized, the rejected, the condemned, "the substratum of the outcasts and outsiders, the persecuted of other races and colors, the unemployed and unemployable."[43] It is their plight that unmasks all the lies and deceptions of the status quo. The state of their existence reveals the existing sociopolitical structures as deeply discriminatory and unjust. Their daily life is spent in desperation, and their very existence—*their refusal of nonexistence*—is a harsh indictment of the comforts and progress of the so-called affluent society. Still, the brute force of their suffering is not enough. What has always been required for rebellion and for the construction of an alternative political future is the development of critical consciousness, appropriate resources, and solidarity. Again and again, organic intellectuals have arisen to facilitate this development through radical pedagogy, alternative culture, and counterhegemonic organizations.[44] The Zapatistas in Mexico are a notable example of sustained resistance, but they are primarily concentrated in the Lacandon Jungle in Chiapas, Mexico's southernmost state. Such resistance in urban areas has been more difficult to sustain. Black liberation movements in modern U.S. history have been concentrated, for the most part, in urban areas, and they have been met with powerful state repression.

---

41. George Katsiaficas, "The Commune: Freedom's Phenomenological Form," *Asia's Unknown Uprisings*, vol. 2, *People Power in the Philippines, Burma, Tibet, China, Taiwan, Bangladesh, Nepal, Thailand, and Indonesia, 1947–2009* (Oakland, CA: PM, 2013), 380–399.

42. "Egypt Unrest," *BBC News*, February 11, 2011, available at http://www.bbc.co.uk/news/world-12434787.

43. Marcuse, *One-Dimensional Man*, 256.

44. See Antonio Gramsci, *Selections from the Prison Notebooks*, ed. Quinton Hoare and Geoffrey Nowell Smith (New York: International, 1971); Franz Fanon, *The Wretched of the Earth*, trans. Constance Farrington (New York: Grove, 1963); Gustavo Gutierrez, *A Theology of Liberation: History, Politics, and Salvation*, ed. and trans. Sister Caridad Inda and John Eagleson (Maryknoll, NY: Orbis, 1973); James H. Cone, *Black Theology and Black Power* (New York: Seabury, 1969).

The Black Lives Matter movement (in its liberal and radical manifestations), which began growing in 2013, primarily in the United States, has theoretically linked together the dehumanization of Black people with issues of state violence, racialized poverty and inequality, patriarchy, mass incarceration, White supremacy, and structural racism—all taboo conceptualizations in normal times. Black Lives Matter uses a combination of grassroots organizing, sophisticated digital-media campaigns, and mass action in the streets to protest police brutality, mourn its victims, and address other linked issues. Like Black liberation movements of the past, this one is lifting voices and raising hopes for a transformed society; however, during the 2016 U.S. presidential election season, Black Lives Matter was also scapegoated to mobilize sections of the White voting population.[45]

In the past fifty years, since the publication of Marcuse's *One-Dimensional Man* in 1964, new forms of nonviolent struggle and armed resistance have emerged throughout the world. Demonstrations, protests, occupations, and resistance of all sorts have challenged hierarchies of power and even, at times, capitalist hegemony. Meanwhile, the neoliberal logic of this phase of capitalist development has continued to spread and generated financial crises and fierce competition among capitals, with labor and nature paying the steep price. It is true that, in light of the tremendous repressive power of the status quo, the demands of the protesters and occupiers may appear as mere "fantasy."[46] But what if, as Marcuse argues, in terms of the authentic truth of human existence, phantasy is more "real" than reality?

On Phantasy, Art, and Rebellion

Marcuse's philosophical examination of the concepts of Freud's psychoanalysis in *Eros and Civilization* revealed that Freud came to the same conclusion as Hegel, albeit using a completely different intellectual framework. Freud introduced the concept of the unconscious into which he "relegated . . . those mental forces opposed to the reality principle"[47] and stressed the importance of the act of phantasy making, which is "kept free from reality testing and

---

45. See Glen Ford, "Bill Clinton Insults Blacks in Order to Build Hillary's 'Big Tent' Party," *Black Agenda Report*, April 13, 2016, available at http://www.blackagendareport.com/bill_clinton_insults_blacks.

46. Imaculada Kangussu writes, "The use of the term 'phantasy,' which preserves its Greek roots (*phantasia*) and its identification with imagination in classical philosophy . . . disappears with the term 'fantasy,' which is much more common in English." Imaculada Kangussu, "Marcuse on Phantasy," *Radical Philosophy Review* 16, no. 1 (2013): 389. We use the term *phantasy* throughout the rest of the chapter to preserve the connections and reflect Marcuse's usage.

47. Herbert Marcuse, *Eros and Civilization: A Philosophical Inquiry into Freud* (Boston: Beacon, 1974), 140.

remain[s] subordinated to the pleasure principle alone."[48] Phantasy making therefore retains a high degree of freedom even in the consciousness of
adults; however, this commitment to the free play of pleasure and gratification comes at a price. From the standpoint of the reality principle, phantasy
appears "useless, untrue—a mere play, daydreaming."[49] Still, it provides a
demonstrable link to the possibility of another, qualitatively different type
of psychological functioning.

In *Eros and Civilization*, Marcuse uses the terms *phantasy* and *imagination* in such a way that indicates that, for his purposes, the two should be
treated synonymously and interchangeably. In other words, he integrates
the Freudian concept of phantasy into the traditional philosophical concept of imagination. In fact, already in the pre–World War II essay titled
"Philosophy and Critical Theory," Marcuse explains the crucial connections
between the concept of phantasy/imagination and the struggle to realize a
free society.

> The abyss between rational and present reality cannot be bridged
> by conceptual thought. In order to retain what is not yet present as
> a goal in the present, phantasy is required. The essential connection
> of phantasy with philosophy is evident from the function attributed
> to it by philosophers, especially Aristotle and Kant, under the title
> of "imagination." Owing to its unique capacity to "intuit" an object
> though the latter be not present and to create something new out of
> the given material of cognition, imagination denotes a considerable
> degree of independence from the given, of freedom amid a world of
> unfreedom.[50]

Marcuse emphasized that Freud saw phantasy as playing a decisive role
in the functioning of the psyche because his psychoanalytic practice convinced him of its capacity to preserve the remembrances of images prior
to the individuation process. In other words, phantasy acted as the repository of the "archetypes of the genus, the perpetual but repressed ideas of

---

48. Sigmund Freud, "Formulations on the Two Principles of Mental Functioning," in *The Standard Edition of the Complete Psychological Works of Sigmund Freud*, trans. and ed. James Strachey (London: Hogarth Press and the Institute of Psycho-analysis, 1958), 12:222. See also Marcuse, *Eros and Civilization*, 140.

49. Marcuse, *Eros and Civilization*, 142.

50. Herbert Marcuse, "Philosophy and Critical Theory," in *Negations: Essays in Critical Theory*, trans. Jeremy Shapiro (Boston: Beacon, 1968), 154. Another passage on phantasy and society reads, "When Freud emphasized the fundamental fact that phantasy (imagination) retains a truth that is incompatible with reason, he was following in a long historical tradi-tion." Marcuse, *Eros and Civilization*, 160.

the collective and individual memory, the tabooed images of freedom."[51] According to Freud, these archaic elements, which shaped the protohistory of humanity, continue to exert a powerful influence in the individual unconscious.[52] They provide the "image of an immediate union between the universal and the particular under the rule of the pleasure principle," in comparison with which all later historical developments, and even the civilization itself, appear as degradations.[53]

This, in fact, presents a serious contradiction, which is well detected by Freud. For civilization to develop at all, this image must be repressed by the emerging powers of rationality; it must "remain buried in the unconscious, [while] imagination [which rescues it from oblivion] must be made into a mere fantasy, child's play, daydreaming."[54] This is why emancipation from the repressive reality principle may at first glance seem like "retrogression."[55]

However, Marcuse insists that imagination contains not only the backward-looking but also the forward-looking dimension. This dimension is manifested by the imagination's refusal to "accept as final the limitations imposed upon freedom . . . [and] forget what can be."[56] The critical theorist Fredric Jameson elaborates on the sociopolitical significance of this insight. He postulates that even the "energy of revolutionary activities" is likely to be derived from this inexhaustible, unconscious source.[57]

Following Freud's lead, Marcuse writes that the images of phantasy are sublimated and externalized as works of art. Works of art preserve the truths of imagination and mold them into "a subjective and at the same time objective universe."[58] This universe is at loggerheads with the established reality. This is why Marcuse refers to artistic practices as embodying the "Great Refusal," the term originally coined by the mathematician and philosopher Alfred North Whitehead.[59]

---

51. Marcuse, *Eros and Civilization*, 140–141.

52. The historian and philosopher Martin Jay claims that the key insight of Freud was that "humanity, in general and in its individuals, is still dominated by 'archaic' powers." Martin Jay, "Reflections on Marcuse's Theory of Remembrance," in *Marcuse: Critical Theory and the Promise of Utopia*, ed. Robert Pippin, Andrew Feenberg, and Charles P. Webel (South Hadley, MA: Bergin and Garvey, 1988), 36.

53. Marcuse, *Eros and Civilization*, 142.

54. Ibid., 147.

55. Ibid.

56. Ibid., 149.

57. Fredric Jameson, *Marxism and Form* (Princeton, NJ: Princeton University Press, 1971), 113.

58. Marcuse, *Eros and Civilization*, 143–144.

59. Alfred North Whitehead wrote, "The truth that some proposition respecting an actual occasion is untrue may express the vital truth as to the aesthetic achievement. It expresses the 'great refusal' which is its primary characteristic." Alfred North Whitehead, *Science and the Modern World* (New York: Macmillan, 1926), 228, quoted in Marcuse, *Eros and Civilization*, 149. For his understanding and radical deployment of the Great Refusal

The capacity of art to speak truth to power comes at the price of alienation within the repressive society. On the one hand, art goes a long way toward transcending the condition of alienated existence, while, on the other, it is forced to accept certain rules of the game and therefore remains "with all its truth, a privilege and an illusion."[60] According to Marcuse, the gap that traditionally divides the aesthetic dimension from the practices of everyday life can be bridged by the explicit emphasis on radical political change. In *An Essay on Liberation*, he writes of the new rebels who desire to "see, hear, feel new things in a new way," who want to "dissolve the world of ordinary and orderly perception."[61]

Using humor and satire as a weapon against dominant power is an ancient practice. In recent years, rebellious efforts to destroy existing cultural paradigms, to invent new languages, have featured street theater, performance art, marching bands, pink princesses, and dancing clowns at important sites of resistance (e.g., meetings of the World Bank and the International Monetary Fund). Such nonviolent, aesthetic interventions represent a potential threat to the functioning of hegemonic power. How so? They interrupt the normalized narrative that is in mass circulation. They refuse the monopolization, by corporate and military-industrial networks, of the definition of what is real. Alongside such tactics as blockades, destruction of corporate property, and fighting with the police, these aesthetic interventions are also in accordance with the libertarian tradition of direct action.[62]

If fighting the powers that be, according to their own logic, is a fight already lost, then activists may innovate and improvise by incorporating the aesthetic dimension into their activities. The alterglobalization movement of the 1990s and 2000s made widespread use of a form of protest called tactical frivolity. For instance, when protesting against the deportation of immigrants, activists blockaded the Frankfurt Airport with an orchestra. In David Graeber's words, in this way, the act of blockading became "an art form."[63] Protestors have also been creative with their attire in attempts to disarm state resistance and draw wider public interest. The Pink Block made effective use of "extravagant pink carnival costumes, and cheerleaders and

---

concept, Marcuse relies more on André Breton's surrealism than on Whitehead's aesthetics. See Douglas Kellner, *Herbert Marcuse and the Crisis of Marxism* (Berkeley: University of California Press, 1984), 279.

60. Marcuse, *One-Dimensional Man*, 63.

61. Herbert Marcuse, *An Essay on Liberation* (Boston: Beacon, 1969), 37.

62. David Graeber, "The New Anarchists," *New Left Review* 13 (January–February 2002): 62. In *Direct Action* (1912), Voltairine de Cleyre establishes the difference between "direct action," when people act by themselves without following a leader or being represented by somebody, and "indirect action," which involves voting for politicians to represent them: she suggests that indirect action annuls individual rebellion and creates dependency. See Voltairine de Cleyre, *The Voltairine de Cleyre Reader* (Oakland, CA: AK Press, 2004), 59.

63. Graeber, "The New Anarchists," 67.

samba bands."[64] Protesters in Prague dressed as fairies.[65] In the United States, activists of the Revolutionary Anarchist Clown Bloc protested while wearing colorful wigs and riding high bicycles, and the group Billionaires for Bush, dressed in tuxedos and evening gowns, placed fake money into the pockets of police officers, thanking them for repressing the dissent. In Quebec, the Deconstructionist Institute for Surreal Topology built an enormous catapult that launched teddy bears at the Free Trade Area of the Americas (FTAA) Summit. In Mexico, the Zapatistas made hundreds of paper airplanes out of letters written to ask soldiers to put down their weapons. In an interview with the Nobel Prize novelist Gabriel García Márquez, the Zapatista leader Subcomandante Marcos, a masked personage allegedly impersonated by different persons, proclaimed that *Don Quixote* was "the best book of political theory."[66]

The aim of these activities is to "expose, delegitimize, and dismantle mechanisms of [repressive] rule" in order to expand the spaces of autonomy and self-governance rather than to take over the levers of state power.[67] Marcuse was one of the first to discern this change of political orientation on the part of radical activists. He wrote about the events of May 1968 in France:

> The radical protest tends to become antinomian, anarchist, and even non-political. Here is another reason why the rebellion often takes

---

64. Marta Kolářová, "Fairies and Fighters: Gendered Tactics of the Alter-Globalization Movement in Prague (2000) and Genoa (2001)," *Feminist Review*, no. 92 (2009): 100. "The colour dimension is important here; pink is associated with girls from childhood, but is also a symbol for queer and transgender. It signifies love and peace, and activists build on it strategically; they say it has the power to calm down police and aggressive activists in confrontation." Ibid., 100.

65. Ibid.

66. Subcomandante Marcos, "The Hourglass of the Zapatistas," in *A Movement of Movements: Is Another World Really Possible?*, ed. Tom Mertes (London: Verso, 2004), 14. The constructed character is now known as Subcomandante Galeano. As one source describes the persona, "Marcos un día tenía los ojos azules, otro día los tenía verdes, o cafés, o miel, o negros, todo dependiendo de quién hiciera la entrevista y tomara la foto. Así fue reserva en equipos de futbol profesional, empleado en tiendas departamentales, chofer, filósofo, cineasta, y los etcéteras. . . . Había un Marcos para cada ocasión, es decir, para cada entrevista. Y no fue fácil, créanme, no había entonces *wikipedia*." (One day Marcos had blue eyes, another day green, or brown, or honey, or black, it all depended on who was doing the interview and who was taking the photograph. Whether booking for professional soccer teams, an employee of department stores, chauffer, philosopher, film director, or any other etcetera to be found. . . . There was a Marcos for every occasion—that is, for every interview. And it wasn't easy, believe me, there was no *Wikipedia* back then.) "El Subcomandante Marcos anuncia su desaparicion" [Subcomandante Marcos announces his disappearance], *Otramérica*, May 25, 2014, available at http://otramerica.com/personajes/el-subcomandante-marcos-anuncia -desaparicion/3204 (translated by Veronica Brownstone and Andrew Lamas).

67. Graeber, "The New Anarchists," 68. See also John Holloway, "Beyond Power?," in *Change the World without Taking Power: The Meaning of Revolution Today* (London: Pluto, 2002).

on the weird and clownish forms which get on the nerves of the Establishment. In the face of the gruesomely serious totality of institutionalized politics, satire, irony, and laughing provocation become a necessary dimension of the new politics. . . . The rebels revive the desperate laughter and the cynical defiance of the fool as means for unmasking the deeds of the serious ones who govern the whole.[68]

There is nothing frivolous in this fight, no matter how "light-hearted" the means might appear. As Marcuse explains, the activists know full well that what is at stake is "simply their life, the life of human beings which has become a play thing in the hands of politicians and managers and generals."[69] The contemporary anarchist writer AK Thompson echoes Marcuse's insight: "For the kids . . . there is only one struggle. It is the fight for our lives."[70]

Checking the Mic

I Can't Hear You

Mic check is Occupy's spoken word. Mic check is what happens to poetry when people are desperate to speak, to be heard, to listen, and to debate about things that matter out in the open, no longer afraid, or even if they are still afraid. Mic check is a kind of spoken word poetry writ large in the sky, over what once was the commons but now—at least for a moment—is reclaimed from forces of commodification and privatization. Mic check is a *commoning praxis* in which people no longer have common songs of resistance but nonetheless want to speak in unison with their voices in an effort to create solidarity for a new world. "Poetry can repair no loss, but it defies the space which separates. And it does this by its continual labour of reassembling what has been scattered."[71]

Mic check was widely popularized by Occupy and is one of its novel features; however, mic check has also been used as a tactic by other groups and dates back at least to antinuclear demonstrations and global justice protests

---

68. Marcuse, *An Essay on Liberation*, 63–64.
69. Ibid., x.
70. Thompson, *Black Bloc, White Riot*, 28.
71. "What is the labour of poetry? By this I do not mean the work involved in writing the poem, but the work of the written poem itself. Every authentic poem contributes to the labour of poetry. And the task of this unceasing labour is to bring together what life has separated or violence has torn apart. Physical pain can usually be lessened or stopped by action. All other human pain, however, is caused by one form or another of separation. And here the act of assuagement is less direct. Poetry can repair no loss, but it defies the space which separates. And it does this by its continual labour of reassembling what has been scattered." John Berger, "The Hour of Poetry," in *The Sense of Sight: Writings by John Berger*, ed. Lloyd Spencer (New York: Pantheon, 1985), 249.

toward the end of the twentieth century. Mic check is not a classic call and response, though it does borrow from that social art of Black liberation. It is more a call followed by responsive repetitions of the call. In practice, mic check involves the repeating of words by the speaker. Those in proximity to the speaker listen to and then loudly and in unison repeat the words or phrases of the speaker to confirm that they have heard but also so that others more remotely situated may have the opportunity to hear, as well. In large public gatherings, mic check produces an experience of successive aural waves—in hearing and repeating—of the original speaker's remarks. It can be thrilling to hear public speech that moves you and then immediately becomes voiced as your own; it can be uncomfortable and even disconcerting to repeat words with which you disagree, and that might never have crossed your lips, so that others may—in the spirit of democratic exchange—have the opportunity to hear and judge for themselves what is being said.

For some, mic check is the call to prayer, an invocation of beloved community. Mic check gavels to order the congregation of Occupiers: draw near to hear the spoken word, and let it resound far and wide so that those others farther back may also hear and join in our assembly. For others, mic check is a defiant call of a community in resistance, assembling for struggle. For others, it creates a space of ever-expanding democratic assembly where we say the words of others, where we offer our own testimony, where we create community by our common assembly of embodied democratic voices. For others, it is the symbol for a rising wave of horizontalism—"us[ing] direct democracy to create horizontal, nonhierarchical social relationships that would allow participants to openly engage with each other."[72] For others, it is just a means for amplifying the voice in a large crowd. For others, it is "mic checking"—a technique for interrupting electronically amplified speech, a kind of political heckling of a speaker with whose views one is in disagreement.[73] For some, it is exhilaratingly transgressive, like the best performance art; in a sense, unsanctioned performance art is a kind of transgressive and aesthetic occupation of space, and it says "something is happening here that is not supposed to be happening here, but we are doing it anyway." For

---

72. Marina Sitrin, "Horizontalism and the Occupy Movements," *Dissent* 59, no. 2 (2012): 74–75.

73. See Luke Smith, "The Human Mic: Not Just for Occupy," *Mother Jones*, November 21, 2011, available at http://www.motherjones.com/mojo/2011/11/human-mic-occupy-bachmann-scott-walker; Teamster Power, "Occupy Atlanta Mic Checks Home Depot for Union Busting," *Teamster Nation Blog*, November 19, 2011, available at http://teamster nation.blogspot.com/2011/11/occupy-atlanta-mic-checks-home-depot.html; Sunny Moraine, "'Mic Check!': #Occupy, Technology and the Amplified Voice," *Cyborgology* (blog), October 6, 2011, available at http://thesocietypages.org/cyborgology/2011/10/06/mic-check-occupy-technology-the-amplified-voice/; and Carrie Kahn, "Battle Cry: Occupy's Messaging Tactics Catch On," *National Public Radio*, December 6, 2011, available at http://www.npr.org/2011/12/06/142999617/battle-cry-occupys-messaging-tactics-catch-on.

others, mic check is an initiation ritual: I know I have become a part of Occupy once I participate in mic check. Mic check is a rite of passage, passage
of a message from one to all who listen, repeat, and then perhaps speak their
own words of grievance, protest, and demand, sharing their own visions for
freedom and a better world.

Mic check—the human microphone, the people's microphone—is the
embodiment of an invention, a critique, and a claim. It is a social invention
designed to enable amplification when legal restrictions prohibit the use of
electronic amplification devices (as was the case in Zuccotti Park, the site
of Occupy Wall Street); it is also a political invention for public speech in
the privatized, commodified, state-regulated territory of contemporary everyday life. It is a critique of intolerance of dissent and of the closing off of
space, typically urban space, for free and genuine democratic deliberation by
the people on matters of significance. It is a critique of the state and the elite
class, which increasingly views members of the public as either consumers
or criminals—both of which are dehumanizing conceptualizations. It is a
critique of rising inequality and wealth accumulation. Finally, it is a claim
for a fair share of power and for meaningful participation in the governance
of society. It is a claim for humanity respected, dignified and free, and for
an earth whose renewing bounty must be protected for future generations. It
is a reclaiming of what was once for the people but now has been privatized
by the 1 percent. Occupy represents a reclaiming on behalf of the majority
of that which has been taken for the few. It is a reclaiming of the commonwealth for the common good. It is heartening to note that for some time
Occupy captured the interest and approval of a substantial portion of the
U.S. public.[74]

Nobody Says "Mic Check"

We can say that the mic check is a performative speech act, as defined by the
linguist John Langshaw Austin in his classic *How to Do Things with Words*.[75]
According to Austin, a sentence may have a "constative" function—when
something is affirmed or described, as in "the book is on the table." Or, it
may have a "performative" function—when it realizes an act, as when somebody says, "I declare the session is open." For our purposes here, the performative function is more important since it goes beyond mere enunciation

---

74. By October 2011, a CBS News/*New York Times* poll reported that 43 percent of Americans agreed with the views of the Occupy Wall Street movement. Brian Montopoli, "Poll: 43
Percent Agree with Views of 'Occupy Wall Street,'" *CBS News*, October 26, 2011, available
at http://www.cbsnews.com/8301-503544_162-20125515-503544/poll-43-percent-agree-with
-views-of-occupy-wall-street/.

75. John Langshaw Austin, *How to Do Things with Words* (Cambridge, MA: Harvard
University Press, 1962).

and presupposes a covenant or agreement. It implies the existence of a collectivity willing to act.

This is why when somebody says—actually, nobody ever *says* "mic check"—when somebody *yells* "mic check," we have a pragmatic act of will, an act of collective choice. Participation, not justification, is brought forth. The mic check *interaction*—relational, political, and democratic—involves all those present in the act of creation, in the opening up of the horizons of possibility. It creates a microphone, but without distancing the one who speaks from those who listen; rather, it links the speaker and the audience in the constitution of an alternative sociopolitical reality. Those who listen *must* speak, or those who speak *cannot be heard.*

This alternative sociopolitical reality unmasks the Achilles' heel of capitalism—the class struggle. In fact, class struggle (as discussed earlier) is the hidden core of politics in capitalist societies. It is a sign of the pervasiveness of the economic over the political. Indeed, one can go so far as Žižek and claim that politics in capitalism is nothing else but "the distance of the economy from itself."[76] In addition, we can paraphrase Lukács and say that, in capitalist societies, politics is the supporter of class "unconsciousness."[77] In other words, it often happens that certain policies are implemented, which may mitigate short-term suffering, while the economic structure that produces the suffering and violence is left intact and even justified, sustaining the functioning of the unjust global system.

The Occupy Wall Street movement, which popularized the practice of mic check, can itself be seen as one collective performative act against the capitalist status quo. Many critics have called the movement amorphous, fuzzy, vague, and romantic and attacked it for not formulating a specific political project and for not having a political program—not even a list of demands! Some have called its activities a hysterical acting-out, and perhaps it may have seemed so at times. Still, one should keep in mind Žižek's claim (influenced by the psychoanalytic theories of Jacques Lacan) that any free act implies "a hole" in the given reality. It implies the intervention of "another dimension" that cannot be explained in terms of the status quo.[78] In a very important sense, freedom means the ability to choose that which frames the frame, that which is outside the picture and yet determines the meaning of its content.

In the case of the Occupy movement, we are also confronted with what Žižek terms as Hegel's "positing of presuppositions," the idea that meaning

---

76. Slavoj Žižek, *The Year of Dreaming Dangerously* (London: Verso, 2012), 27.

77. Georg Lukács, *History and Class Consciousness: Studies in Marxist Dialectics*, trans. Rodney Livingstone (Cambridge, MA: MIT Press, 1971), 52, 133. Originally published in 1923.

78. Slavoj Žižek, *Absolute Recoil: Towards a New Foundation of Dialectical Materialism* (London: Verso, 2014), 20.

is always created retroactively.[79] In other words, the success or failure of Occupy's choices and performative acts can only be determined by their effects, and those effects may take a long time to materialize. As pointed out by the French philosopher Alain Badiou, in this respect, the classic example is that of Christianity.[80] Nobody today can dispute its "success," and yet it took centuries for its effects to become the constitutive components of the established reality. Or, as Marcuse puts it (as referenced earlier), "The truth of a historical project is not validated *ex post* through success, that is to say, by the fact that it is accepted and realized by the society."[81]

Necessity and Contingency

In his book on Hegel's practical philosophy, the contemporary philosopher Robert Pippin defines what Hegel called the "spirit" as the product of the "natural beings' . . . sublating relation to nature."[82] In other words, the spirit is neither an immaterial substance nor a divine mind; it is not the commander of human agents according to its own purposes but rather a "form of individual and collective mindedness, institutionally embodied in the recognizable relations."[83] From this perspective, being an agent is "an achieved social status such as, let us say, being a citizen or being a professor, a product or result of the mutually recognitive attitudes."[84] As applied to contemporary social movements such as the Occupy, this means that the meaning of its acts emerges from their social impact and not from the conscious intentions of the actors—that is, the Occupy activists.

In every emergence of meaning, there is a certain degree of contingency. By retroactively positing the reasons of the action, the effects of the action create, or fail to create, the event. According to Žižek, the autonomous act is not grounded in instrumental reason or strategic calculation. It does not

---

79. Ibid., 6, 31. "It is quite true what philosophy says: that life must be understood backwards. But then one forgets the other principle: that it must be lived forwards." Søren Kierkegaard, journal entry IV A 164 (1843), in *Søren Kierkegaard: Papers and Journals*, ed. and trans. Alastair Hannay (London: Penguin, 1996), 161.

80. For Badiou, Paul founds Christianity, and he does so by militantly organizing around a simple (but impossibly possible) truth claim: *Christ is risen!* This powerful reframing of time, reality, and possibility becomes politically instructive. "I am not the first to risk the comparison that makes of [Paul] a Lenin for whom Christ will have been the equivocal Marx." Alain Badiou, *Saint Paul: The Foundation of Universalism*, trans. Ray Brassier (Stanford, CA: Stanford University Press, 2003), 2.

81. Marcuse, *One-Dimensional Man*, 223.

82. Robert B. Pippin, *Hegel's Practical Philosophy: Rational Agency as Ethical Life* (Cambridge: Cambridge University Press, 2008), 53.

83. Ibid., 51.

84. Ibid., 52.

"apply a preexisting norm, but creates a norm in the very act of applying it."[85] In this way, the "microphone" in the mic check is created by the free will of the activists and brought forth by their desire, and it transforms their performative gesture in the truth of the situation. According to Charles Reitz, "Mic check fuses a sensual, visceral, and intellectual experience: listening, learning, and acting in vocal solidarity in a gesture of group identity-building in defiance of an oppressive order. So, I do see it as a manifestation of Marcusean refusal."[86]

For Marcuse, the source of the autonomous act—the "soil for revolution"—is found in "a highly developed consciousness and imagination" rather than in the material conditions of impoverishment, misery, and despair.[87] There is no automatic transition from the existing squalor to qualitatively different values. The situation is, of course, complicated by the fact that corporate capitalism uses all means at its disposal to suffocate the emergence of the rebellious consciousness and imagination. As already pointed out, it seeks to coordinate and control the cognitive and instinctual needs of the vast majority and turn them into willing accomplices in their own enslavement. As one of the most dramatic results of this repressive process, the working class, which Marx and Friedrich Engels extolled as the revolutionary subject of history, has become quite conservative in advanced industrial societies. It no longer can be considered the carrier of radical political and social change.

This is why, according to Marcuse, orthodox Marxist theory must be revised, and its scope must be extended into "a dimension of the human existence hardly considered in Marxian theory."[88] This is the rationale of Marcuse's engagement with Freud's ideas in *Eros and Civilization*. A different society presupposes different subjects, with different vital needs, drives, and cognitive and emotional frameworks. In both *Reason and Revolution* and *Eros and Civilization*, Marcuse seeks to demonstrate that, in human beings, there is an inexhaustible freedom of the drives that cannot be eliminated, only distorted and repressed.

In *Reason and Revolution*, Marcuse concerns himself with the question of essence. He argues that Hegel's claim that essence, as the truth of being, is "held by thought" was a contradiction.[89] According to Marcuse, "essence" reveals itself only in the dynamic process of transition when something

85. Žižek, *Absolute Recoil*, 21.

86. Charles Reitz, e-mail message to Andrew Lamas, August 14, 2015. Also see Charles Reitz, *Art, Alienation, and the Humanities: A Critical Engagement with Herbert Marcuse* (Albany: State University of New York Press, 2000); and Charles Reitz, ed., *Crisis and Commonwealth: Marx, Marcuse, McLaren* (Lanham, MD: Lexington, 2013).

87. Marcuse, *An Essay on Liberation*, 15.

88. Ibid., 16.

89. Marcuse, *Reason and Revolution*, 149.

"turns into its opposite."[90] The resolution of the contradiction occurs only when essence passes into existence, when it stops being a mere thought and becomes embodied. We could say that mic check speaks as a metaphor for this central teaching of *Reason and Revolution*, as the protester's thought—a declaration of refusal and imagination—becomes embodied by the full participation of the people's assembly, each member of which, through the collective act of democratic listening and speaking in solidarity but with differences, *embodies the thought* and circulates it throughout the body politic of resistance and occupation. Marcuse stresses that this process of resolution is the source of all social and political transformations. "The essence can 'achieve' its existence when the potentialities of things have ripened in and through the conditions of reality."[91]

According to Hegel, the established reality itself is the result of the antagonistic process between what is and what could be. He posits the existence of the dialectical relationship between the real and the possible. In Marcuse's interpretation, this metaphysical framework acquired sociopolitical significance. In the existing capitalist reality, Marcuse recognizes "the seed of its transformation into a new form" and conceptualizes this transformation as "a 'process of necessity' . . . not determined from outside by external forces but, in a strict sense, a self-development."[92] In this way, the necessity of overcoming capitalism is encoded in the historical process itself. Reitz, suggesting that we read Hegel's master-slave dialectic alongside Marcuse's oeuvre on this matter, concludes, "The master is prone to delusions of grandeur and obstinate defense of the status quo, [while] the slave [is] forced by necessity to see the world as it really is: its ugliness and hypocrisy, yet also attainable emancipatory alternatives. Mic check is an instrument of emancipation from the irrational to the rational."[93]

Such Stuff as Dreams

Dreams are not only demands. Like the mic check, they can be a call to attention, to awareness, to other voices, to other ways of seeing, to fairness, to more just ways of structuring community, to critical consciousness, to new sensibility.

Demands—particularly universal demands—are also more than they appear. Demands for recognition, respect, and dignity of all persons and all creation; demands for universal health care, housing, and education; demands for tools for communication, production, and play; demands for socially useful

90. Ibid., 148.
91. Ibid., 149.
92. Ibid., 153–154.
93. Reitz, e-mail message to Lamas.

labor free from toil and domination; demands for free time to be with family and friends and in community with others; demands for clean air, clean water, and healthy food; demands for free expression, for well-being and self-determination; demands for international solidarity and the free movement of people across borders; demands for justice, freedom, peace, and love—all of these demands and many others are, in a sense, more than petitions to governments. They are also expressions of deep yearnings in the human psyche.

Written in the form of a letter addressed to Occupy Wall Street activists, the pamphlet by the anarchist collective CrimethInc. reads, in part, as follows:

> The important thing is not just to make demands upon our rulers, but to build up the power to realize our demands ourselves. If we do this effectively, the powerful will have to take our demands seriously, if only in order to try to keep our attention and allegiance. We attain leverage by developing our own strength.
>
> Likewise, countless past movements learned the hard way that establishing their own bureaucracy, however "democratic," only undermined their original goals. We shouldn't invest new leaders with authority, nor even new decision-making structures; we should find ways to defend and extend our freedom, while abolishing the inequalities that have been forced on us.
>
> *The occupations will thrive on the actions we take.* We're not just here to "speak truth to power"—when we *only* speak, the powerful turn a deaf ear to us. Let's make space for autonomous initiatives and organize direct action that confronts the source of social inequalities and injustices.
>
> Thanks for reading and scheming and acting. May your every dream come true.[94]

In rereading the first sentence, we see articulated a position that acknowledges the necessity (at least in this historical moment) of making demands on the state but also the insufficiency of such politics. In emphasizing this insufficiency, the CrimethInc. collective seeks to persuade certain elements of Occupy to think beyond petition-the-state reformism and to enter more boldly into the tradition of radical freedom movements: to "imagine a new society"[95] (as Robin D. G. Kelley describes it) and to "start refusing

---

94. CrimethInc., "Dear Occupiers: A Letter from Anarchists," October 7, 2011, available at http://www.crimethinc.com/blog/2011/10/07/dear-occupiers-a-letter-from-anarchists (emphasis in original).

95. Robin D. G. Kelley, *Freedom Dreams: The Black Radical Imagination* (Boston: Beacon, 2002), 9. As Blondie sings, "Dreaming is free." Blondie [Debbie Harry and Chris Stein], "Dreaming," on *Eat to the Beat*, Chrysalis, 1979, LP.

to play the game"[96] (as Marcuse writes in the concluding pages of *One-Dimensional Man*). This is the long-standing radical tradition of collective self-reliance, resistance, and self-determination, from the occupation of London by armed peasants in the antifeudal revolt of 1381 to the global freedom struggles in the 1960s and the Zapatistas' anticapitalist uprising in Chiapas in 1994. In every case, resistance is nourished by the imagination of a new society (sometimes as a total break with the oppressive past and other times as a reconstruction of that which has been lost or as a restoration of that which is endangered). Inspiration may also be found, as for the surrealists, in the hidden truths of human existence frequently revealed in phantasies and dreams: "Cannot the dream also be applied as the solution of the fundamental problems of life?"[97]

Dreams may not be able to directly transform the world, but they have the potential to transform the individuals who can change the world. Indeed, in this context, one might recall the famous "I Have a Dream" speech delivered in 1963 by Martin Luther King Jr.[98] It reveals that King knows what Frederick Douglass knows: "Power concedes nothing without a demand."[99] A great dream is like a great demand in that it issues a bold confrontation, a negation of a negation. But it is more than this. For King, the dream is a demand but also a declaration of the existence in the here and now of the alternative future that we will construct together. In a political situation that seems both unbearable and impossible to change, the first step toward justice and freedom is to dream of the "beloved community."[100] We come together in love, first in our dreams and then with locked arms on the Edmund Pettus

---

96. Marcuse, *One-Dimensional Man*, 257.

97. André Breton, *Les Manifestes du Surréalisme* (Paris: Editions du Sagittaire, 1946), 26, quoted in Marcuse, *Eros and Civilization*, 149. In 1924, in the *Manifesto of Surrealism*, Breton writes, "I believe in the future resolution of those two seemingly contradictory states, dream and reality, into a sort of absolute reality, of surreality, so to speak." André Breton, *What Is Surrealism? Selected Writings*, ed. Franklin Rosemont (New York: Pathfinder, 1978), 377.

98. Martin Luther King Jr., "I Have a Dream," in *A Testament of Hope: The Essential Writings and Speeches of Martin Luther King, Jr.*, ed. James M. Washington (New York: HarperOne, 2003), 217–220. This speech, delivered on August 28, 1963, at the March on Washington for Jobs and Freedom, synthesized portions of King's previous sermons and speeches with selected statements by other prominent public figures.

99. Frederick Douglass, "West India Emancipation," in Frederick Douglass, *Two Speeches by Frederick Douglass: One on West India Emancipation, Delivered at Canandaigua, Aug. 4th, and the Other on the Dred Scott Decision, Delivered in New York, on the Occasion of the Anniversary of the American Abolition Society, May 1857* (Rochester, NY: C. P. Dewey, 1857), 22, available at https://www.loc.gov/resource/mfd.21039/?sp=22.

100. Martin Luther King Jr., "Facing the Challenge of a New Age," in *The Papers of Martin Luther King, Jr.*, vol. 3, *Birth of a New Age, December 1955–December 1956*, ed. Clayborne Carson, Stewart Burns, Susan Carson, Dana Powell, and Peter Holloran (Berkeley: University of California Press, 1997), 458.

Bridge in Selma.[101] When we come together in love, in acknowledgement of our common humanity and shared destiny, we find the strength in ourselves and in others to refuse what diminishes us, to struggle for what is right, to care for one another, to create a new and better society. In a movement for liberation, we are the stuff of our dreams.

So, then, a wonderful dream is not only like a powerful demand. It is like a Great Refusal. This is where King's Dream and Marcuse's Great Refusal meet: love and Eros are the grounds on which we meet to think together beyond the apparent limitations of the present order and to unite in struggle for freedom. But, of course, such talk of dreams, love, and resistance can seem inconsequential and naively utopian, given the strength of the forces arrayed in opposition, both within and from without ourselves. As the argument goes, the Paris Commune and its progeny are always impossible projects; however, Badiou responds by reminding us that "emancipatory politics always consists in making seem possible precisely that which, from within the situation, is declared to be impossible."[102] *Demand the impossible!*

But resist with what effect? The capitalist order stands strong, even as it has been challenged in various ways by a vigorous global justice movement, the Occupy movement, and major anti-austerity mobilizations, as well as by major electoral victories by the Left in Latin America and southern Europe. The system seems to have weathered every threat—even the potentially delegitimizing Great Recession of 2007–2009—with renewed force and vigor; many corporations and their shareholders have even enhanced their wealth positions in the wake of the financial crisis. One may legitimately ask, *a crisis for whom?*

Do the protests and refusals directed toward attaining greater space for autonomy, democracy, and freedom leave an impact, even if nothing structural appears to have changed? Stephen Duncombe would respond in the affirmative: "The experience of doing something different, whether it is acting out a new form of democracy in a meeting or taking over a street for a dance party, is a transformative experience in itself."[103] But, the Marxist geographer David Harvey points out, "to succeed, the movement has to reach out to the 99 percent. This it can do and is doing step by step."[104] "To

---

101. Hundreds of civil-rights marchers, in peaceful protest, on the Selma-to-Montgomery March for voting rights were viciously attacked—by local and Alabama state police—while marching out of Selma across the Edmund Pettus Bridge. This incident became known as "Bloody Sunday." Under the leadership of Martin Luther King Jr. and others, two other large marches across the bridge followed, and within less than five months, President Lyndon B. Johnson signed the Voting Rights Act of 1965.

102. Alain Badiou, *Ethics* (London: Verso, 2001), 121.

103. Duncombe, *Dream*, 172.

104. David Harvey, "The Party of Wall Street Meets Its Nemesis," *Verso* (blog), October 28, 2011, available at http://www.versobooks.com/blogs/777-david-harvey-the-party-of-wall-street-meets-its-nemesis.

change everything, we need everyone"[105] was the rallying cry of the People's Climate March that took place on September 21, 2014, in more than 2,000 cities in almost 150 countries. This movement and others represent efforts at building up the network of global solidarity that can channel and amplify the desire to construct a qualitatively different world. For a chance at success, contemporary social movements must make themselves relevant to the daily concerns of all those who are marginalized, disrespected, and injured by the forces of corporate capitalism around the globe. They have the task of ushering the way to the constitution of "a new sensibility," as elaborated by Marcuse in *Eros and Civilization* and *An Essay on Liberation*. They open the possibility of influencing the yet unwritten future.

> *In the dark times*
> *Will there also be singing?*
> *Yes, there will also be singing*
> *About the dark times.*[106]

This, then, is the task of the "new sensitivity"—to gather and organize, to motivate and direct the rebellious forces of the future. Those who know how to sing should sing, those who know how to dance should dance, those who know how to write should write—until the world wakes up. The struggle is in the streets—but not only there. Educate, agitate, organize! All of this is impossible, but silence is not an option. Will you join us? Can we join with you?
Mic check! Mic check!

---

105. Wen Stephenson, Naomi Klein, and Avi Lewis, "What Will It Take to Force a Real Conversation about Climate Change?," *The Nation*, October 26, 2015, available at http://www.thenation.com/article/what-will-it-take-to-force-a-real-conversation-about-climate-change/. See also Melissa Davey, Adam Vaughan, and Amanda Holpuch, "People's Climate March: Thousands Demand Action around the World," *The Guardian*, September 21, 2014, available at http://www.theguardian.com/environment/live/2014/sep/21/peoples-climate-march-live; Lisa W. Foderaro, "Taking a Call for Climate Change to the Streets," *New York Times*, September 21, 2014, available at http://www.nytimes.com/2014/09/22/nyregion/new-york-city-climate-change-march.html#; and Darren Mara, "Mass Global Rallies Call for Climate Action," *SBS News*, September 22, 2014, available at http://www.sbs.com.au/news/article/2014/09/22/mass-global-rallies-call-climate-action.
106. Bertolt Brecht, "Motto to the 'Svendborg Poems,'" trans. John Willett, in *Poems, 1913–1956*, ed. John Willett and Ralph Manheim (London: Eyre Methuen, 1976), 320.

Part III

Protesting Violence

9

The Work of Violence in the Age of Repressive Desublimation

AK THOMPSON

Law and order are always and everywhere the law and order which
protect the established hierarchy; it is nonsensical to invoke the
absolute authority of this law and this order against those who
suffer from it and struggle against it—not for personal advantages
and revenge, but for their share of humanity. There is no other
judge over them than the constituted authorities, the police, and
their own conscience. If they use violence, they do not start a
new chain of violence but try to break an established one. Since
they will be punished, they know the risk, and when they are
willing to take it, no third person, and least of all the educator and
intellectual, has the right to preach them abstention.
—HERBERT MARCUSE, "Repressive Tolerance"[1]

Sublime Ambivalence

Recounting the feudal origins of high bourgeois culture, in *One-Dimensional Man* Herbert Marcuse notes how people's historic inability to reconcile form and content, heart and mind, "is" and "ought," tended to prompt generative encounters with alienation. By stimulating what amounted either to recollections or anticipations of yet-to-be realized happiness, these sublime agonies supplemented the positivist instrumentality of official bourgeois culture even as they stood against it. At their logical conclusion, they compelled the aesthetic (in both of its overlapping but distinct senses) to indict the world as it was given.[2]

This feudal inheritance, Marcuse noted, was "an outdated and surpassed culture" that could only be recaptured through "dreams and childlike regressions." Nevertheless, he did not hesitate in noting that—precisely by

---

1. Herbert Marcuse, "Repressive Tolerance," in *A Critique of Pure Tolerance*, by Robert Paul Wolff, Barrington Moore Jr., and Herbert Marcuse (Boston: Beacon, 1965), 116–117.

2. The arguments rehearsed here coincide with those advanced in AK Thompson, "The Resonance of Romanticism: Activist Art and the Bourgeois Horizon," in *Cultural Activism: Practices, Dilemmas, and Possibilities*, ed. Begüm Özden Firat and Aylin Kuryel (Amsterdam: Rodopi, 2011).

virtue of its nonresolution—this culture was, at the same time, an intoxicating vision of a "*post*-technological" and reconciled future. Indeed, for Marcuse, feudal society's "most advanced images and positions seem to survive their absorption into administered comforts and stimuli; they continue to haunt the consciousness with the possibility of their rebirth in the consummation of technical progress."[3]

Confronting these passages half a century after they were penned cannot help but yield an uncanny effect. It is not easy, for instance, to overlook the degree to which what was once true of the bourgeoisie's encounter with feudal culture seems to apply equally well to our own encounter with Marcuse today. On first blush, the intellectual figurehead of the New Left in the United States confronts us as an endearing anachronism, a source of wishful stimuli that (like a latter-day Walt Whitman ready to "charge [us] full with the charge of the Soul"[4]) cannot help but swaddle us in childlike innocence. Great Refusal! Eros! Abolition of the performance principle!

Almost immediately, however, the pleasure of this initial response is troubled by the realization that it has been a long time since we have been innocent. Extending the Marcuse-Whitman analogy, we might even deduce that there is no way for the body electric to escape. Like the rest, it is (we are) plugged into—and thus drained by—this society's erotic economy. As with feudal culture for the bourgeoisie, the initial promise of infantile regression we find in Marcuse gives way to a renewed sublime agony. Correspondingly, the encounter with innocence reveals itself to be ambivalent—as does the childlike regression itself, which in one moment underscores (and even seems to justify) postmodernism's fêted man-child before suggesting a hazardous course toward the realization of an unfulfilled promise. Nowhere does this tension become more evident than in Marcuse's discussion of political violence.

On one hand, Marcuse cries out in opposition to the prosaic horrors that turn violence into workaday "aggressiveness" (those forms of antisocial social cohesion that enact a calculated regression from the deepest chambers of technorational society's windup heart).[5] On the other hand, regressions of this sort prompt a desire for consequential action that cannot be contained by repressive desublimation's proxy resolutions. By following these desires through to their logical conclusion, actors might reconnect to (and thus assume ownership over and responsibility for) the capacity for violence that

---

3. Herbert Marcuse, *One-Dimensional Man: Studies in the Ideology of Advanced Industrial Society* (Boston: Beacon, 1964), 59 (emphasis in original).
4. Walt Whitman, "I Sing the Body Electric," in *The Portable Walt Whitman*, ed. Mark van Doren (New York: Viking, 1972), 158.
5. Marcuse, *One-Dimensional Man*, 70.

stands as a precondition to genuine human being.[6] Through its unbearable nonresolution, the sublime ransacks the past to devise viable images of a future happiness. In Marcuse, this ambivalence finds its most acute expression in his treatment of violence, which he disavows on account of the inadequacies of its proxy before finally embracing it as a profane, political-ontological inevitability.

Stagnant Hope

In John Cameron Mitchell's 2006 cult classic film *Shortbus*,[7] the owner of a postmodern, post-9/11 sex club lovingly describes his creation by noting how "it's just like the sixties, only with less hope." For more than twenty years, Fredric Jameson has alerted us to the fact that the postmodern condition is inseparable from such nostalgic echoes.[8] And, following Walter Benjamin, we might envision that echoes of this sort could be of use when guiding our desires toward desirable resolutions.[9] But while such echoes indicate a superficial continuity between two moments, it is necessary to acknowledge (as the sex-club owner did) that, today, the search for resolutions to human desires is more fruitfully pursued by abandoning hope.

To be sure, the resolutions to the feeling of constitutive lack available in the 1960s tended to be much further from the hopeful cultivation of a new sensibility than adherents often held them to be.[10] Nevertheless, the counterculture remained valuable precisely on account of its ability to constitute an antithetical "we" (a mode of existence capable of repolarizing one-dimensional society in order to bring it—regardless of whether it had been

---

6. For a discussion of the relationship between political violence and what it means to be human, see AK Thompson, *Black Bloc, White Riot: Anti-globalization and the Genealogy of Dissent* (Oakland, CA: AK Press, 2010), esp. 7–9, 22–25.

7. *Shortbus*, directed by John Cameron Mitchell (New York: THINKFilm, 2006).

8. Fredric Jameson, *Postmodernism; or, The Cultural Logic of Late Capitalism* (Durham, NC: Duke University Press, 1991), 16–20.

9. Walter Benjamin, "Paris, Capital of the Nineteenth Century," in *Reflections: Essays, Aphorisms, Autobiographical Writings* (New York: Schocken, 1978), 148.

10. Marveling at the counterculture, for instance, Marcuse could not help but note how music could "move the body, thereby drawing nature into rebellion." Furthermore, he thought that such "Life music" found its authentic basis in "black music," which he took to be "the cry and song of the slaves and the ghettos." Succumbing to what now strikes us as an unnerving Romanticism, Marcuse noted how, "in this music, the very life and death of black men and women are lived again. The music is body; the aesthetic form is the 'gesture' of pain, sorrow, indictment." As a result of this powerful assault on mediation, Marcuse found it self-evident that such music would also appeal to White radicals entrapped by one-dimensionality's "pleasant unfreedom." Nevertheless, even here, and "with the takeover by the whites, a significant change occurs: white 'rock' is what its black paradigm is *not*, namely, *performance*." Herbert Marcuse, *Counterrevolution and Revolt* (Boston: Beacon, 1972), 114 (emphasis in original).

the counterculture's intention—to the brink of civil war). From this vantage, the promise lay not in the counterculture's positive, affirming content but rather in its capacity to muster a Great Refusal—to produce a moment of pure negation capable of liberating humanity's productive capacities and setting them along a different course.

The counterculture betrayed its moment. By focusing inward on the cultivation of positive content rather than determining what would be required to move from self-affirming rebellion to the self-abolition required by revolution, the counterculture's degeneration echoed the limitations that Jean-Paul Sartre had noted in Charles Baudelaire's sublime tantrums a generation earlier.[11] In this way, it assured that it would be reabsorbed by the status quo—and that its energies would serve to revitalize (rather than to abolish) it.[12] What was true of the counterculture also holds for Marcuse, who played a central role in revitalizing Left politics by binding movement activities to the resolution of libidinal desires. Reading his texts, one cannot help but note how he enveloped critical theory's negative dimensions[13] in a positive normative vision in which human biology itself abetted revolution.[14] Although Marcuse sometimes acknowledged this ambivalence explicitly, one cannot help but be left with the impression that it was surely the positive vision (that Whitmanesque stroll through some new Eden) and not the powerful negative thrust of his critical theory that drew the movement to him.

Today's new cycle of struggle seems to cry out for Marcuse's return. The enthusiasm in the streets and squares since 2010–2011 has signaled a kind of resurgence of political optimism that, with few exceptions, has not been witnessed since the 1960s. Nevertheless, closer investigation reveals that this renewal is inflected with a different temperament—one that might lead us to conclude that it, too, is "just like the sixties, only with less hope." As can

---

11. Jean-Paul Sartre, *Baudelaire* (New York: New Directions, 1950), 51–52.

12. This dynamic has been recounted extensively by commentators reviewing the legacy of the New Left and, in particular, the tragic *denouement* of May 1968. To get a sense of the degree to which this dynamic now saturates our culture (and even our counterculture), it suffices to consider how, in *Shortbus*, the protagonist's experience of lack—that is, sexual frustration—is depicted as being enough to knock the power out in Manhattan (presented in maquette, a cardboard stand-in for itself). By finally attaining sexual ecstasy, however, the scene is once again illuminated. For those prone to historical recollection, lights going out in Manhattan cannot help but evoke the 1987 blackout; however, in this case, the pursuit of a purely personal libidinal resolution is enough to dissuade mass violence and looting. In this way, erotic stimulation becomes social regulation. Correspondingly (though it was probably not the director's intention), the city is correctly presented as running on sexual energy (eros), which, in vampiric fashion, is channeled directly into its rational and calculating infrastructure.

13. As Horkheimer noted, such theory was grounded in "a concept of man as in conflict with himself" until all social contradictions were resolved. Max Horkheimer, "Traditional and Critical Theory," in *Critical Theory: Selected Essays* (New York: Continuum, 1968), 210.

14. Herbert Marcuse, *An Essay on Liberation* (Boston: Beacon, 1969).

be attested by the now-regular devolution of bacchanalian exuberance into protracted civil war (e.g., Tahrir Square, Taksim Square), this ambivalence is political; however, it is ontological, too. Whether tacitly acknowledged or explicitly embraced, the disavowal of hope by contemporary social-movement actors must be seen as a move away from deferred gratification and proxy resolutions and toward concrete reckoning.

Meanwhile, the echoes persist. Many of the ideas that Marcuse put forward as cautionary tales in *One-Dimensional Man* had become the profane features of everyday life by the time Jameson published his groundbreaking book on postmodernism.[15] Indeed, it is impossible to read many of Marcuse's observations without being struck by the feeling that they are prescient first drafts, thematic sketches destined to find their way to center stage a generation later. Consider, for instance, how retrospectively *avant la lettre* Marcuse can sound in a passage such as this: "The good urge to *épater le bourgeois*," he writes, "no longer attains its aim because the traditional 'bourgeois' no longer exists, and no 'obscenity' or madness can shock a society which has made a blooming business with 'obscenity.'"[16] To be clear, Marcuse's point was that the traditional bourgeois "no longer exists" because one-dimensional society obliterated the sublime culture it had inherited from the feudal era through a process of radical social dispersion. Recounting the desublimated sexuality that found pervasive expression in the literature of his time, for instance, Marcuse reports that it had become "part and parcel of the society in which it happens, but nowhere [could it be said to constitute] its negation," as might have previously been the case with the sublimated sexuality of the Romantics. "What happens" in this literature, he concludes, "is surely wild and obscene, virile and tasty, quite immoral—and, precisely because of that, perfectly harmless."[17] To get a sense of this dismal blossoming's contemporary manifestations, it suffices to recall how, in *Postmodernism*, Jameson observes that the "offensive features" of contemporary aesthetic production "no longer scandalize anyone and are not only received with the greatest complacency but have themselves become institutionalized." Indeed, they are "at one with the official or public culture of Western society."[18]

Alternately, and following Marcuse, we might recall how one salient feature of high modernist art was that it tended to respond "to the total character of repression . . . with total alienation."[19] For Marcuse, expressions of this sublime tendency could still be found in the work of figures like John Cage. "But," he wonders, "has this effort already reached . . . the point where

15. Jameson, *Postmodernism*.
16. Marcuse, *One-Dimensional Man*, 50.
17. Ibid., 77.
18. Jameson, *Postmodernism*, 4.
19. Herbert Marcuse, *Counterrevolution and Revolt* (Boston: Beacon, 1972), 116.

the oeuvre drops out of the dimension of alienation . . . and turns into a sound-game, language-game—harmless and without commitment, shock which no longer shocks, and thus succumbing?"[20] As clear anticipations of Jameson, such comments alert us to the prescience and enduring value of Marcuse's insights; however, they also underscore the profound inadequacy of a purely representational approach to the problems we now confront. At their threshold, these problems take the form of an intractable tension between complicit aggression and a potentially liberating violence that always seems just out of reach.

Siren Song

Revolutionary at its inception, the regime of representational politics that came into being through bourgeois victory in the late eighteenth century has degenerated into a form of repressive desublimation. Politics, a thing with grave consequences and previously unavailable to the masses (politics as a form of productive activity, always and necessarily entailing a violence before which the sovereign must stand unflinchingly as final arbiter), is now widely disseminated through representation. This "resolution" to the problem of genuine being, which gives access to the thing without demanding responsibility for its consequences, allows us to feel the satisfaction of participation (of acting out, of acting as if) without having to deal with the substance to which it refers. Meanwhile, the productive violence of politics itself continues to be hoarded by the state, which claims a monopoly on the legitimate right to use it.

Through the course of the twentieth century, however, it became clear that this proxy would never satisfy the desire for the Real (that *thing* which escapes symbolization, and which cannot be represented) that it inadvertently stimulates. In response to our growing impatience, we are now placated with unending opportunities for what Marcuse called "aggressiveness"—forms of violence that are primarily representational, cathartic, and complicit in the reproduction of a highly managed labor force.[21] Like the commodity sphere they subtend, however, these satisfactions are prone to wearing thin. Meanwhile, the violent transformation of social reality brought about by a state politics at war with our interests enjoins us to muster a response.

Since the advent of the bourgeois public sphere, this response has occasionally found expression in the activities and campaigns of modern social movements. An effective means of exploiting the contradictions between what Marx called "the substance" and "the phrase" of the bourgeois

---

20. Ibid.
21. Marcuse, *One-Dimensional Man*, 76–78.

revolution,[22] these movements tallied significant victories over the course of the nineteenth and twentieth centuries. Nevertheless, because they were conceived as demand-based formations that sought greater recognition from constituted power and because, consequently, they staked their claim in the public sphere,[23] they have tended to become complicit in the reproduction of the bourgeoisie's representational paradigm.[24] This schizoid position has been a source of tremendous anxiety, and the wholesale erosion of the public sphere (a "structural transformation" that began more than a century ago[25] but that ended with a whimper under neoliberalism's shadow) has only exacerbated the problem.

In response, forces committed to social justice but antagonistic toward the established social-movement repertoire have struggled to devise means of contesting state power that are not contingent on its recognition. Inevitably, these have involved a scramble to reconnect with violence—that force now known primarily by way of repressive desublimation (through which the state supposedly enacts the will of those it represents) or through the proxy of aggression (which remains indexed to the perpetuation of the status quo). Recounting the death of politics under such conditions, the anonymous French insurrectionists in the collective Tiqqun stated it thus: "Violence is what has been taken away from us."[26] To be sure, the efforts of groups like Tiqqun to reconnect with violence have thus far remained tactically inconclusive.[27] Nevertheless, they have proven to be extremely important from the standpoint of political pedagogy.

This has certainly been the case with respect to state responses, which have consistently sought to reiterate the representational fiction through which bourgeois authority first found legitimation; however, it has also been true for social movement participants themselves. Here, on the one hand, we

---

22. Karl Marx, *The Eighteenth Brumaire of Louis Bonaparte* (New York: Mondial, 2005), 3.

23. For more on the relationship between social movements and the advent of the public sphere, see Charles Tilly, *Social Movements, 1768–2004* (Boulder, CO: Paradigm, 2004), esp. 35–37; and Sidney Tarrow, *Power in Movement: Social Movements and Contentious Politics*, 2nd ed. (Cambridge: Cambridge University Press, 1998), esp. 54–56.

24. This is one of the guiding contentions of "the social movement society" thesis. See David S. Meyer and Sidney Tarrow, eds., *The Social Movement Society: Contentious Politics for a New Century* (Lanham, MD: Rowman and Littlefield, 1998).

25. Jürgen Habermas, *The Structural Transformation of the Public Sphere: An Inquiry into a Category of Bourgeois Society* (Cambridge, MA: MIT Press, 1981).

26. Tiqqun, *Introduction to Civil War*, trans. Alexander R. Galloway and Jason E. Smith (Los Angeles: Semiotext(e), 2010), 34.

27. Tiqqun has been associated with the Invisible Committee and, in turn, the Tarnac Nine, a group—classified by the French government as a "terrorist enterprise"—predominantly composed of graduate students charged in 2008 with using sabotage to disrupt train traffic throughout France.

find those who are seduced by the promise of a politics beyond representation, a politics freed from the aggressive distortions of repressive desublimation. In the United States, this tendency has been nurtured by CrimethInc., which has argued that "a small group that behaves confidently as if they are living in a different world can call into question things everyone else takes for granted; if they take their departure far enough at the right time, they can make the impossible possible by persuading others that it is so on the strength of their own conviction."[28] On the other hand, we find those whose psychic structure has been fundamentally reordered by the representational paradigm. Instead of a Great Refusal, these forces respond to movement violence by entrenching themselves all the more deeply into the existing regime—despite the fact that, through the contemporary normalization of naked force, this regime no longer seeks to legitimate itself through reference to once-sacred, self-evident truths.

As symptoms of the cultural logic of late capitalism, these two tendencies echo those noted by Marcuse in his introduction to *One-Dimensional Man*, written more than fifty years ago. In that text, Marcuse recounts how the triumph of industrial society was such that it could manage qualitative transformations for the foreseeable future even as it appeared to be riven by forces that heralded its dissolution.[29] As was true for Marcuse in his own time, it is too soon to know which of these tendencies will prevail. Will social movements continue along a path of incremental tinkering that ends by legitimating the opposition (our enemy, constituted power), or will they resolve their contradictory stance by disavowing representational seductions and embracing the properly martial elements that continue like hollow devotions to find expression in even the most staid mobilization (e.g., the march, the drum, the banner, the blockade)?

Although the answer cannot be known in advance, recent events are enough to suggest that the latter option alone points to liberation.[30] For it to be realized, however, it is necessary to first highlight and then foster those pedagogical moments when protest turns violent and when violence tears at the representational screen that envelops us all. Through these tears, it is sometimes possible to glimpse another politics and, in turn, another world.

---

28. CrimethInc., "Crowd Dynamics and the Mass Psychology of Possibility: An Account of Spatial Movement, an Allegory of Social Movement," *Harbinger* 5 (2002), available at http://www.crimethinc.com/tools/downloads/pdfs/harbinger5.pdf.

29. Marcuse, *One-Dimensional Man*, xv.

30. The advent of the Black Lives Matter movement and the riots that have erupted in the wake of recent police shootings of unarmed Black people have yielded more indictments of police and transformations of the state's violent practices than have years of petitions and peaceful protests. See Ret Marut, "Next Time It Explodes," *CrimethInc. Ex-Workers' Collective* (blog), August 13, 2015, available at http://www.crimethinc.com/blog/2015/08/13/since-the-ferguson-uprising/.

Such visions make clear that our enemies are twofold. On the one hand, we confront the ambassadors of constituted power, the purveyors of representation, and the peddlers of repressive desublimation. On the other, we face erstwhile allies committed to social justice but seduced by representation's siren song. Of these two enemies, the former is inestimably more important; however, we shall not muster the force to confront them effectively until the latter is first addressed.

In what follows, I draw on Marcuse's observations about repressive desublimation, social movements, and violence to understand the tremendous hostility that frequently accompanies violent eruptions at contemporary political demonstrations. In particular, I am interested in what social-democratic and labor-bureaucratic responses to black bloc violence reveal about the aggrieved parties. Through a consideration of such erstwhile-ally responses to black bloc street fighting during protests against the G20 in Toronto during the summer of 2010 and in the subsequent actions of Occupy demonstrators in Oakland, I propose that black bloc violence can play an important pedagogical role in clarifying the meaning of politics in an era stricken by repressive desublimation.

To understand why, it is necessary to consider three interrelated dynamics. First, black bloc actions make a direct claim on the productive character of violence while simultaneously undermining its repressively desublimated aggression-based proxies (though they are always, tellingly, denounced as having more in common with the latter). Second, they are seductive to those who feel that their desire for real life and real consequences is not being (and cannot be) met by current, repressively desublimated, arrangements. Finally, they expose the ineffectual fiction that underwrites the social-democratic identification with representational politics. To be sure, the black bloc poses these problems (stimulates these promises) without being able to resolve them through the means to which it currently lays claim. Nevertheless, by its ability to point out *the possibility* of an outside to this "comfortable, smooth, reasonable, democratic unfreedom,"[31] it has already proven felicitous.

Violent Response

I concede that, in light of the recent riots ignited by police violence against Black people throughout the United States, my choice of case studies may now seem anachronistic. And, to be sure, the insights I glean from them could no doubt be harvested from more recent events. Still, I feel compelled to focus my attention as I have for three important reasons. The first is that, although the Toronto G20 protests in June 2010 generated a considerable amount of immediate commentary, they have not received the more careful

---

31. Marcuse, *One-Dimensional Man*, 1.

retrospective consideration they deserve. Second, while riots like those that took place in Baltimore in April 2015 inevitably challenge the legitimacy of representational politics, black bloc actions add an important dimension both to street dynamics and to the analysis thereof. Since there was no black bloc in Baltimore, it is best to treat the case separately and on terms more suited to it. Finally, and more personally, because the Toronto riot is of biographical importance to me, recounting my observations helps implicitly to explain how and why I have come to read both Marcuse and social movements as I now do.

I should begin by noting that, unlike in previous mobilizations against global summits, I mostly had to sit out the G20 in Toronto. Along with being in the final throes of dissertation writing at the time, I was also preoccupied with arranging details for the promotion of *Black Bloc, White Riot*, which was scheduled for release later that summer.[32] These considerations, however, did not prevent my roommates from assuming prominent roles in the Toronto Community Mobilization Network, the main organizing body for the protests. In the lead-up to the actions, I did what I could to share the materials and lessons I had amassed from similar mobilizations in the past; mostly, however, I stayed out of their way.

That was how things stood until the early morning of June 26, when I received a phone call from my roommates, who had just learned that there was a warrant out for their arrest on charges of conspiracy. All of a sudden, I was in the midst of a "Miami model" moment, and my roommates were calling on me to help them work through it.[33] Since, miraculously, cops had yet to show up at our door, I urged my roommates to make their way home so that they could prepare to enter police custody on the best possible terms. By the end of the morning, they—along with more than a dozen others—had been picked up and branded as ringleaders, part of the "main conspiracy group."[34]

The events that unfolded subsequently made clear that whatever conspiracy may have existed could be set into motion without my roommates or any of their co-accused being present. That afternoon, Toronto was thrown into tumult. And though they numbered in the thousands, the police lost control

32. AK Thompson, *Black Bloc, White Riot: Anti-globalization and the Genealogy of Dissent* (Oakland, CA: AK Press, 2010).

33. The "Miami model" is a repressive police strategy involving preemptive arrest, strategic incapacitation, and overwhelming force first devised by John Timoney to deal with protests against summit meetings of the Free Trade Area of the Americas (FTAA) in Miami in 2003. See Kris Hermes, *Crashing the Party: Legacies and Lessons from the RNC 2000* (Oakland, CA: PM, 2015), 308n89.

34. For more information about the "main conspiracy group" and the context in which they were charged, see "Toronto G20 Main Conspiracy Group: The Charges and How They Came to Be," *Infoshop*, October 19, 2014, available at http://www.infoshop.org/toronto-g20 -conspiracy.

of the streets. A black bloc broke into the financial district and set cop cars on fire. Through their agitation, they opened a path through police lines that allowed other demonstrators to approach a fortified summit site additionally protected by the exceptional suspension of the rule of law.[35] With my room-mates in detention along with hundreds of others at some sketchy East End warehouse that the cops had turned into a dungeon, I began keeping track of responses to the events that had unfolded.

Writing in *Canadian Dimension*, Adam Davidson-Harden critiqued the black bloc by claiming that it had helped legitimate the state's security efforts. Moreover, by suppressing discussion of protestor grievances, it ultimately provided cover for the G20 and its agenda. "The black-clad mob . . . has left a lot of people not only in the general public but in the wider nonviolent so-cial/global justice movements in Canada feeling disgusted, demoralized and dispirited," he wrote. In his view, this was "just the result you want if your goal is to marginalize and stifle dissent."

> While the more numerous non-violent voices were indeed heard on the streets and at Queen's Park (25,000 in the main march!), they weren't "heard" in the more meaningful, mass sense as loudly as the same reels of destruction overplayed in the media, and the same accounts of destruction and violence witnessed to on the ground by journalists, activists and citizens. The blocistes . . . take the dis-cursive space away from the broader movements, inviting and in-deed compelling the public (through the media, of course) to only focus on the violence of smashing, burning, destroying, throw-ing, hitting . . . which are all pointless, repulsive, destructive, and frightening.[36]

This assessment would be reiterated by Sid Ryan of the Ontario Federa-tion of Labour (OFL) who, in a *Toronto Star* article titled "Thousands Stood Up for Humanity," asserted that despite the fact that the message on June 26 had been "clear," it was tarnished by the black bloc, whose actions violated democratic norms. In contrast, Ryan noted, the OFL worked explicitly to maintain such norms. In practical terms, this meant working

> diligently to ensure that our democratic right to lawful assembly would be respected, and that citizens could participate in a safe and

---

35. For a full account of the action of that afternoon, see "Behind the Mask: Violence and Representational Politics," *Upping the Anti*, no. 11 (November 2010), available at http://up pingtheanti.org/journal/article/11-behind-the-mask-violence-and-representational-politics.

36. Adam Davidson-Harden, "How the 'Black Bloc' Protected the G20," *Canadian Di-mension*, June 29, 2010, available at https://canadiandimension.com/articles/view/web -exclusive-how-the-black-bloc-protected-the-g20.

peaceful event. To this end, we liaised with the Toronto Police and cooperated at every turn. On the day, hundreds of volunteer marshals facilitated what was an extraordinarily successful event, given the tension that had pervaded the city in the days before. Shamefully, a small number of hooligans used the cloak of our peaceful and lawful demonstration to commit petty acts of vandalism in the streets of Toronto.

According to Ryan, "Despite their stated goal of challenging the anti-democratic nature of the G20, these actions actually undermined democracy." As a result, "the weeks and months of effort to educate and activate ordinary people on issues of social, environmental, and economic justice . . . went up in flames."[37] This position was further elaborated in a media statement by Canadian Labour Congress (CLC) president Ken Georgetti: the CLC "abhors the behaviour of a small group of people who have committed vandalism and destroyed property." Noting that the CLC worked in conjunction with others to organize "a peaceful demonstration," he insisted:

> We cooperated with police . . . and had hundreds of parade marshals to maintain order. . . . Our rally and march were entirely peaceful from start to finish. It appears that a small group of anarchists, who are unknown to us, became involved in some violent and destructive activities as the day progressed.

In conclusion, Georgetti issued the following resolute declaration: "We condemn these actions and we will continue to exercise our democratic right to free expression in a peaceful manner at all times."[38] Finally, Canadian Union of Public Employees (CUPE Ontario) president Fred Hahn and secretary-treasurer Candace Rennick added their voices to this chorus when, in an official statement, they decried the events as amounting to

> nothing short of the abandonment of the rule of law, both by a small group who took part in the protests, and by a massive and heavily armed police force who were charged with overseeing them. Due process, civil liberties and the right to peaceful protest have been the

---

37. Sid Ryan, "Thousands Stood Up for Humanity: Anti-summit Marchers Braved Hooligans, Police and Even the Weather to Push a People's Agenda," *Toronto Star*, June 29, 2010, available at http://www.thestar.com/opinion/editorialopinion/2010/06/29/thousands_stood_up_for_humanity.html.

38. Canadian Labour Congress, "Statement by Ken Georgetti, President of the Canadian Labour Congress on Vandalism Surrounding Toronto G20 Meeting," *Marketwired*, June 26, 2010, available at http://www.marketwired.com/press-release/statement-ken-georgetti -president-canadian-labour-congress-on-vandalism-surrounding-1282103.htm.

victim. . . . And it's a sad day when some of those, who feel powerless to change the direction of their elected leaders, find in that feeling of powerlessness an excuse to break the law and vandalize the property of their fellow citizens and who, in so doing, silence the legitimate voices of so many others whose commitment to protest and dissent is matched by their rejection of violence and vandalism.[39]

This line of reasoning was not restricted to social democratic and labor leaders, however. In a blog post filed on June 28, 2010, Milan Ilnyckyj (who became a Ph.D. student at the University of Toronto in 2012) complained that the black bloc had come to "dominate the news coverage" and obscure "legitimate messages from activist groups." Moreover, these actions seemed doomed "to justify the expense and intrusion of the heavy-handed security that now accompanies these events." Summing up his position, he noted that the black bloc "just distracts from serious discussions" by acting out its "incoherent rage." As a result, and "given how effectively the violent minority drowns out important messages," the task befalling sensible people involved "finding some way to keep a lid on them."[40]

For scholars and activists who have followed the debates surrounding the black bloc since its emergence on the streets of Seattle in 1999, perspectives like those recounted here will no doubt sound familiar. Indeed, they reflect positions that are widely held by social-movement commentators and participants. Moreover, they rely on a series of well-established rhetorical conventions. To get a sense of how pervasive this narrative and conceptual coherence has become, it suffices to briefly revisit some of the commentary that erupted around black bloc participation in the Occupy movement. Here, alongside journalist Chris Hedges's widely cited and vitriolic denunciation (in which he likened the black bloc to a "cancer"[41]), one finds comments like those by John Blackstone of CBS News, who wondered whether the black bloc might be "hijacking Occupy Oakland." In a report published on November 4, 2011, he noted that "by destroying property and challenging police," the black bloc (despite its small numbers) might "hijack the message of otherwise peaceful protests." The consequences, for Blackstone, were

---

39. Fred Hahn and Candace Rennick, "Statement on G20 Protests and Aftermath by CUPE Ontario," *CUPE/SCFP Ontario*, June 30, 2010, available at http://cupe.on.ca/archivedoc 1168/; also quoted in Krystalline Kraus, "G8/G20 Communique: Is the Left Abandoning the Movement When Solidarity Is Needed Most?," *Rabble.ca Blogs*, July 20, 2010, available at http://rabble.ca/blogs/bloggers/statica/2010/07/g8g20-communiqué-left-abandoning-movement-when-solidarity-needed-most.

40. Milan Ilnyckyj, "Black Blocheads," *A Sibilant Intake of Breath* (blog), June 28, 2010, available at https://www.sindark.com/2010/06/28/black-blocheads/.

41. Chris Hedges, "The Cancer in Occupy," *Truthdig*, February 6, 2012, available at http://www.truthdig.com/report/item/the_cancer_of_occupy_20120206.

clear: "Those intent on violence may be on the fringes, but once the trouble begins, they often get the spotlight. In Oakland, city officials have warned that more violence could bring another order to close down the Occupy encampment."[42]

One day later, Sheila Musaji filed a story with the *American Muslim* in which she declared without equivocation that the black bloc and its tactics were definitely "hurting the Occupy Movement."[43] Quoting from personal correspondence with San Francisco Bay–area blogger Rashid Patch, Musaji helped cultivate the impression that the black bloc was composed primarily of "angry, uncaring, sadly damaged" youth. By Patch's account, participants in the black bloc "were never socialized, perhaps barely housebroken. Often seriously abused as children, they are responding in kind to the world." But while "these are the kind of people who turn into Charlie Mansons—or followers of the Charlie Mansons," Patch nevertheless found some of them to be "astonishingly intelligent, brilliantly creative, and terribly, terribly bitter about every aspect of life."

> They are a symptom of society's madness and violence. Some of them take on that role consciously, and argue with great fervor that their vandalism is a logical political response to the conditions of their life—that violence is the only rational response to a pathological society.[44]

Always Repolarize!

What are we to make of such comments? Clearly they raise both strategic and tactical questions that cannot be ignored. After all (and even according to the accounts of its participants), the black bloc actions in Toronto were improvisational at best.[45] In addition to these concerns, however, the statements cited above also give symptomatic expression to a peculiar conception of the political and to the anxious social-democratic allegiance that underwrites it. Even though it is asserted in defiance to the status quo, this conception accords with the bourgeois logic of representation. In the end, I argue, it amounts to a form of repressive desublimation. When considered from this vantage, it becomes clear that at least part of the hostility directed

---

42. John Blackstone, "Is 'Black Bloc' Hijacking Occupy Oakland?," *CBS News*, November 4, 2011, available at http://www.cbsnews.com/news/is-black-bloc-hijacking-occupy-oakland/.

43. Sheila Musaji, "The 'Black Bloc's' Tactics Are Hurting the Occupy Movement," *American Muslim*, November 5, 2011, available at http://theamericanmuslim.org/tam.php/features/articles/the-black-bloc/0018863.

44. Patch, quoted in ibid.

45. See, for instance, Zig Zag, "Fire and Flames! A Militant Report on Toronto Anti-G20 Resistance," July 2010, http://www.kersplebedeb.com/blog/torontog20_fireandflames.pdf.

toward the black bloc arises from the fact that, through its actions, it brings this complicity to light.

To substantiate these claims, it is useful to review Marcuse's comments on repressive desublimation to confirm that the dynamics he describes coincide with those underlying bourgeois representational politics and the social-movement commitment thereto. In Marcuse's account, by opening up previously inaccessible fields of potential self-resolution, repressive desublimation amounts to a "liquidation of two-dimensional culture." However, "this liquidation . . . takes place not through the denial and rejection of the 'cultural values'" that organized the bourgeoisie's ascent to class dominance (values that explicitly made use of the aesthetic as a field for the cultivation of sublime and transformative experiences of alienation) but rather through their "wholesale incorporation into the established order, through their reproduction and display on a massive scale."[46] While sublimation helps highlight the inadequacy of the world, desublimation works to provide the desired object without the accompanying resolution. When applied to politics, repressive desublimation turns a dynamic founded on antagonism[47] into a perverse form of inclusion. To give but one example, one might highlight (as Marcuse himself did) how bourgeois representational politics produces situations where opposition to the system becomes evidence that the system itself is working. As Marcuse notes in "Repressive Tolerance":

> The exercise of political rights (such as voting, letter-writing to the press, to Senators, etc., protest demonstrations with a priori renunciation of counterviolence) in a society of total administration serves to strengthen this administration by testifying to the existence of democratic liberties which, in reality, have changed their content and lost their effectiveness. In such a case, freedom (of opinion, of assembly, of speech) becomes an instrument for absolving servitude.[48]

Meanwhile, the profound distrust expressed by those who have aligned themselves with representational politics toward those who enact the Great Refusal by embracing violence (and, hence, Being itself) directly alerts us to the significance of those political actors and their acts. This significance owes not to tactical efficacy (which is always debatable) but rather to the fact

---

46. Marcuse, *One-Dimensional Man*, 57.

47. Although it is not universally accepted as an accurate assessment of the defining features of political life, Carl Schmitt's friend-enemy distinction has regained currency in the neoliberal era. Although critical of his account in some respects (especially concerning the mythological basis of his purely national conception of discrete "modes of existence"), I find it to be a useful reference point for the discussion at hand. See Carl Schmitt, *The Concept of the Political* (Chicago: University of Chicago Press, 1996).

48. Marcuse, "Repressive Tolerance," 84.

that the act itself repolarizes the political universe, calls the self-evidence of one-dimensionality into question, and forces those who would abide by representational politics' repressively desublimated stipulations to account for the inevitable contradictions arising from their claim to secure political freedom through unfree means. "Under a system of constitutionally guaranteed . . . civil rights and liberties," Marcuse notes, "opposition and dissent are tolerated unless they issue in violence."

> The underlying assumption is that the established society is free, and that any improvement, even a change in the social structure and social values, would come about in the normal course of events, prepared, defined, and tested in free and equal discussion, on the open marketplace of ideas and goods.[49]

The violence that sometimes takes place at demonstrations calls these presumptions into question. And though the melee may come to be representationally contained, the fact of the rupture produces pedagogical and therapeutic effects that cannot be ignored. The ensuing nervousness arises not from the chaos per se (indeed, the chaos might be quite minimal) but from the fact that such violence reveals that the commitment to representational politics is as likely to lead to liberation as are the forms of self-expression opened by repressive desublimation.

This is the pedagogical value of the Great Refusal. For Marcuse, such a refusal amounted—in its pure negativity—to a "protest against that which is."[50] Through acts of negation aimed at repolarizing the political universe while confronting the lack inherent in existing reality, people discover "modes of refuting, breaking, and recreating their factual existence."[51] The sequence of events described in this passage is far from arbitrary; carried out at the conceptual level and involving the objectification and reparsing of the material world, the act of refuting must come first. Indeed, it accords with the role assigned by Marx to "imagination" in his discussion of the human labor process in chapter 7 of *Capital*.[52] Refutation is then followed by the act of "breaking"—the necessarily negative political-productive act required to prepare the way for subsequent acts of creation and recreation, the transformative reconfiguration of the reality.

---

49. Ibid., 92.

50. Marcuse, *One-Dimensional Man*, 63.

51. Ibid.

52. Karl Marx, *Capital: Critique of Political Economy*, vol. 1 (Moscow: Progress, 1977). Originally published in 1867.

However, only with the erection of the barricade (the polarizing two-dimensional expression of the "gut hatred"[53] or "biological hatred"[54] that Marcuse held to be indispensable to the cultural revolution) does "the gesture . . . of love"[55] underlying efforts to productively transform society emancipate itself from the plastic confines of its contemporary repressive desublimation. Considered from this perspective, it becomes evident that the animosity generated by the black bloc owes to its capacity to highlight the extent of people's ongoing identification with a fraudulent reality. "To discuss tolerance in such a society," writes Marcuse, "means to re-examine the issue of violence."

> Even in the advanced centers of civilization, violence actually prevails: it is practiced by the police, in the prisons and mental institutions, in the fight against racial minorities. . . . This violence indeed breeds violence. But to refrain from violence in the face of vastly superior violence is one thing, to renounce a priori violence against violence, on ethical or psychological grounds (because it may antagonize sympathizers) is another.[56]

Reviewing Marcuse's comments makes clear that, whatever his misgivings about "aggressiveness" as an outgrowth of repressive desublimation, he was open to considering violence a productive social force. Indeed, he maintained that this force needed to be protected from bourgeois ethics and representational politics. In the hands of constituted power, violence becomes the means by which the status quo is endlessly reproduced. By seizing hold of violence in a moment of Great Refusal, insurgent forces signal the possibility that another production is possible. Society is repolarized, and one-dimensionality dissolves. In contrast, "with respect to historical violence emanating from among ruling classes, no such relation to progress seems to obtain."[57]

---

53. Marcuse, *Counterrevolution and Revolt*, 130.
54. Herbert Marcuse, *Eros and Civilization: A Philosophical Inquiry into Freud* (Boston: Beacon, 1966), xix.
55. Marcuse, *Counterrevolution and Revolt*, 130.
56. Marcuse, "Repressive Tolerance," 102.
57. Ibid., 108.

Neutrality and Refusal

Herbert Marcuse and Hélder Câmara
on the Violence of Tolerance

Sarah Lynn Kleeb

The notion of tolerance lies at the heart of modern democratic society. The question of what a citizenry will or will not put up with, and the mechanisms by which that putting up with are justified, defended, or denied, are ubiquitous and defining components of both contemporary discourse and activism with regard to social justice. In his incisive and prescient essay "Repressive Tolerance" (1965), Herbert Marcuse identifies a more sinister element at work in the relentless advocacy of toleration as something inherently and inevitably benevolent, an ideal toward which all must aspire. As the title of his essay suggests, tolerance, for Marcuse, is not always liberatory; it is rarely extended in favor of those who demand absolute and radical justice. Rather, it frequently serves to condition citizens to tolerate that which ought to be intolerable: social and structural oppression, economic impoverishment, the quashing of dissent, and the (social, economic, political) mechanisms that maintain the conviction that each of these is unavoidable.

The call to neutrality or nonviolence, particularly as manifest in condemnations of oppressed persons who protest outside of the "tolerable" limits of the law—that is, those who actively disrupt the status quo rather than merely voicing dissatisfaction with it—makes visible the tension surrounding tolerance as a peaceful and benign concept. In the name of an oppressive peace, we are frequently urged to neither tolerate nor facilitate protest that extends beyond certain "acceptable" limits. Likewise, when palpable, immediate, and acute violence is used against those participating in such protests, as in the brutal force of militarized police in riot gear, this action is not likewise condemned; it is merely portrayed as the reestablishment of a tenuous equilibrium.[1] The violence of this act, and of the passive (or active) approval of such an act as an acceptable norm, is minimized, hidden beneath the rhetoric of what will and will not be tolerated.

Defining Tolerance

It goes without saying that the concept of tolerance is touted as a central defining component of contemporary democracy. In many nations, legislation is firmly in place to encourage citizens to treat as equals those who believe differently than they do (e.g., religiously, ideologically) and to acknowledge the potential validity of a variety of often competing truth claims. Various freedoms—of speech, of religion, of assembly—are particularly oriented to foster this kind of putting up with the divergent beliefs of fellow citizens. While advocating pluralism may be a laudable practice (as opposed to, say, the extermination of those who espouse claims contrary to the dictates of the state), Marcuse suggests, in "Repressive Tolerance," that this construction of compliance ultimately conditions those who abide to similarly comply with repressive norms that serve only to maintain an unjust status quo. Citizens are urged to acknowledge validity even in positions they might find morally abhorrent, and, for Marcuse, the most troubling are those that restrict, rather than enhance, freedom and liberation; this, in turn, fosters a climate of agreeableness to a variety of similarly offending thoughts or actions.

> Within the framework of such a social structure, tolerance can be safely practiced and proclaimed. It is of two kinds: (1) the passive toleration of entrenched and established attitudes and ideas even if their damaging effect on man and nature is evident, and (2) the active, official tolerance granted to the Right as well as to the Left, to movements of aggression as well as to movements of peace, to the party of hate as well as to that of humanity. I call this non-partisan tolerance "abstract" or "pure" inasmuch as it refrains from taking sides—but in doing so it actually protects the already established machinery of discrimination.[2]

In this light, tolerance prepares citizens to acknowledge as potentially valid a variety of social structures and governmental policies that ultimately foster extreme social and economic inequality, a condition of lived violence

---

1. At the end of April 2015, we saw this clearly played out in much of the public reaction to the Baltimore Uprising (the protests that emerged from the death of Freddie Gray in Baltimore, Maryland, while in police custody).

2. Herbert Marcuse, "Repressive Tolerance," in *A Critique of Pure Tolerance*, by Robert Paul Wolff, Barrington Moore Jr., and Herbert Marcuse (Boston: Beacon, 1969), 85.

as a daily reality for many. As we abide even the most reprehensible behaviors and public voices, those with a "damaging effect on man and nature," we become habituated to accepting the *intolerance* of others in the name of tolerance itself. This tolerance may develop into a default condition, often devolving into passive acceptance rather than active engagement and continued negotiation of the delineation of moral and social norms, particularly with regard to affairs of the state.[3] In such instances, we do not practice tolerance; we submit to it.

When experienced as praxis, as an active process in democratic societies, tolerance can indeed be a useful tool, directed toward ensuring a plurality of views, negotiating space for dissenting voices, and maintaining equal representation. As Marcuse notes:

> Impartiality to the utmost, equal treatment of competing and conflicting issues is indeed a basic requirement for decision-making in the democratic process—it is an equally basic requirement for defining the limits of tolerance. But in a democracy with totalitarian organization, objectivity may fulfill a very different function, namely, to foster a mental attitude which tends to obliterate the difference between true and false, information and indoctrination, right and wrong. In fact, the decision between opposed opinions has been made before the presentation and discussion get under way—made, not by a conspiracy or a sponsor or a publisher, not by any dictatorship, but rather by the "normal course of events," which is the course of administered events, and by the mentality shaped in this course.[4]

When peaceful assembly is met with a militarized police force, for example, citizen observers frequently extend their compliance in a way that suggests that this kind of sanctioned violent response is a *necessary exchange* for the maintenance of the aforementioned freedoms we (ideally) enjoy in democratic societies.[5] Thus, says Marcuse, tolerance

---

3. Examples of such affairs include the continued use by the United States of the Guantanamo Bay detention facility, the ongoing deployment of indiscriminate drone strikes by the United States in the Middle East, the ease with which reports by major media outlets of hundreds of thousands of dead civilians—victims of the invasion of Iraq—are swallowed and then washed down.

4. Marcuse, "Repressive Tolerance," 97.

5. Such was the case with the 2010 Toronto G20 protests, discussed later in this chapter. Recent events in the United States—the seemingly ubiquitous slaughter of Black men by police officers, which triggered the protests, and the police response to these protests, in Ferguson, Missouri; Baltimore, Maryland; Boston, Massachusetts; and many other U.S. cities—act as unfortunate reminders of the immediate and continued relevance of such observations.

is made compulsory behavior with respect to established policies. Tolerance is turned from an active into a passive state, from practice to non-practice: laissez-faire the constituted authorities. It is the people who tolerate the government, which in turn tolerates opposition within the framework determined by the constituted authorities.[6]

The tolerance of these authorities has a limit: it will only put up with so much and such kinds of resistance. Those living under these authorities, on the other hand, are acclimatized to the idea and practice of excusing that which they find reprehensible and are encouraged to accommodate even intense forms of physical violence in the name of repressing dissent and upholding social structures mired in inequality and oppression. Recourse to such violence on the part of law enforcement is ultimately established as the accepted—and expected—norm.

Moreover, for Marcuse, contemporary forms of tolerance are in and of themselves repressive, fostering injustice as a fundamental character of their existence. When we abide the words and practices of hate groups, when we ignore structural inequality, when we claim neutrality in the face of political divides, we passively foster the violence of the state merely by our inaction. This is tolerance in its abstract, "passive state."[7] Rather than advocating our own positions, we *refrain from* decrying positions that foster suffering and inequality. As our tolerance leads us to capitulate before the status quo, according to Marcuse, we ultimately tolerate the intolerable.

> As deterrents against nuclear war, as police action against subversion, as technical aid in the fight against imperialism and communism, as methods of pacification in neo-colonial massacres, violence and suppression are promulgated, practiced, and defended by democratic and authoritarian governments alike, and the people subjected to these governments are educated to sustain such practices as necessary for the preservation of the status quo. Tolerance is extended to policies, conditions, and modes of behavior which should not be tolerated because they are impeding, if not destroying, the chances of creating an existence without fear and misery.[8]

As we become ever more accustomed to brutality, to violence of the state, to the maintenance of an economic structure that builds wealth on ever-intensifying human suffering, we accept the unacceptable. The very freedoms upheld by the call to tolerance are simultaneously destabilized by that

---

6. Marcuse, "Repressive Tolerance," 82–83.

7. Ibid., 82.

8. Ibid.

very tolerance itself, when it functions to render citizens placid in the face
of inequality. As a pacifying tool of the authoritarian state, this tolerance,
which passively fosters immense suffering, can itself be a form of violence.
"What is proclaimed and practiced as tolerance today, is in many of its most
effective manifestations serving the cause of oppression."[9] One example of
this tolerance manifesting as violence can be found in the popular response
to the security state erected in Toronto, Ontario, Canada, during the 2010
G20 summit, a response that will be discussed in some detail shortly. In the
actions of officers, and in the response of many in the general public to those
actions, we find one instance in which the social condition of tolerance did,
in fact, serve "the cause of oppression."

Defining Violence

Marcuse's critique of tolerance, and the present project of connecting such
tolerance with violence, is likewise echoed in the works of many liberation
theologians. In particular, liberation theologian Dom Hélder Câmara (1909–
1999), former archbishop of Olinda and Recife in Brazil, emphasizes a more
nuanced understanding of violence and the complicity of the status quo in
maintaining various forms of violence against those who live in material
poverty. As detailed later in this section, Marcuse insists on a delineation
between violence used in the interest of sustaining ultimately oppressive conditions and violence used as a reactionary tactic by those attempting to transform present social conditions in a way that is liberatory for those who suffer
from inequality. This insistence is likewise evident in the works of Câmara
particularly and in liberation theology generally. Alongside what is typically
understood as "violence" (e.g., physical violence, psychological violence), liberation theologians like Câmara posit the idea of "institutional violence," an
often implicit violence inherent in the very structures of existing societies.[10]
Institutional violence is the violence that inevitably occurs in the most basic
preservation of existing norms, in which one person's gain necessitates another's suffering, and where tolerance is merely expressed as an extension
of the norms that sustain such a system. Citizens of the system often unwit-
tingly participate in such inequality merely by existing and conforming to
general norms in their society and by upholding the seemingly innocuous
ideal of tolerance. This meticulous investigation of violence as something
more than mere outward aggression—as something obscured, abstract, and
present regardless of intention—is a key connection between Marcuse, critical theory more generally, and many types of liberation theology.

---

9. Ibid., 81.
10. See, for example, Gustavo Gutiérrez, "Notes for a Theology of Liberation," *Theological Studies* 31, no. 2 (1970): 251.

In his short tract *Spiral of Violence* (1971), Câmara parses the very notion of violence in revolutionary movements mounted against oppressive (and, for Câmara, particularly economic) conditions. In this context, all forms of violence are not equivalent: revolutionary violence erupts as a *symptom of a preexisting violent social condition*, and the claim of neutrality in terms of violence as such is bound up with that initial violent state. Câmara offers a tripartite conception of violence: the First Violence—the preexisting, structural, and oppressive violence within a society; the Second Violence—the reactionary violence of the oppressed who protest and resist the First Violence; and the Third Violence—the ruthless intervention of representatives of authority quashing the dissent of the masses as they rebel.[11] Delineated in this way, any violence that may occur as dissident parties protest the conditions of an oppressive social structure is wholly dependent on the initial violence of that very oppression. Rather than condemning those who resist, Câmara insists on the initial and foundational culpability of those *who maintain a situation worthy of resisting.* Because the conditions for protest are necessary precursors to that protest itself, those enacting the Second Violence are doing so solely in response to those who perpetuate the First Violence. Thus, the Third Violence, which attempts to reestablish an unjust status quo that proclaims oppressive conditions as the norm to be tolerated, is likewise dependent on the First Violence of that state itself. In short, for Câmara, violence that occurs in the name of a liberatory vision of social justice cannot be evaluated by the same rubric used to condemn the violence of oppression (First Violence) and repression (Third Violence). The Second Violence is purely reactionary, merely mediating the First and the Third.

It is crucial to emphasize that Câmara's First Violence is explicitly and directly made manifest in oppressive tendencies within and between societies; it is linked entirely to systemic social inequality. Whether oppression is explicitly supported or implicitly socially sanctioned, those who live in poverty are ultimately reduced "to a subhuman condition."[12] What he calls "the heritage of poverty"—that is, the fruits of institutionalized structures sustained by material inequality that are passed down through generations as children become adults in a situation of extreme poverty—"does more than just kill, it leads to physical deformity . . . to psychological deformity . . . and to moral deformity."[13] This last category is intended to highlight a kind of "fatalism" Câmara identifies in "those who, through a situation of slavery, hidden but nonetheless real, are living without prospects and without hope."[14] Not only does such inequality foster immeasurable physical, psychological,

---

11. Hélder Câmara, *Spiral of Violence* (London: Sheed and Ward, 1971), 30–37.
12. Ibid., 25.
13. Ibid., 26.
14. Ibid.

and emotional damage, but it renders this condition potentially fixed: deter-mining and delimiting an individual's agency and maintaining a situation in which hope borders on delusion is an implicit and passive form of violence. By constructing an image of reality that leaves little room for hope, this fatal-ism portrays an individual's future as static, stationary, predetermined, and bound endlessly to the "heritage" of poverty.

When individuals are able to exercise resistance against the First Vio-lence of the oppressive state, when communities of dissent are formed and oriented toward action that destabilizes the status quo, they reject the vio-lence done by the (sometimes passive) tolerance of oppression. They (re)-claim their agency, wrested from those who would maintain such condi-tions, and exercise their capacity for moral choice in their rejection of such conditions of poverty. One of the central tenets of many Central and South American liberation theologies is the construction of liberation as a specifi-cally historical process that is acted out in the material realm and that car-ries a goal of active—substantive—change.[15] This change, however, as acted out in history, often manifests various forms of violence of its own. This is Câmara's Second Violence, predicated in all cases by the First Violence of oppression: "Established violence, this violence No. 1, attracts violence No. 2, revolt, either of the oppressed themselves or of youth, firmly resolved to battle for a more just and human world."[16] These two forms of violence—the active and passive violence that destroy life, hope, and autonomy and the dissident violence of those who resist—are not at all equivalent for Câmara; nor are they equivalent for many liberation theologians (or critical theorists like Marcuse). By making such distinctions, liberation theologians have of-ten been condemned for supposedly advocating violent resistance, when in actuality they were developing a careful theory of violence that identified the hypocrisy by which state-sanctioned violence remains the accepted norm, particularly when used to crush uprisings that constitute the Second Vio-lence illustrated by Câmara.

The Violence of Tolerance

As Gustavo Gutiérrez, one of the founding theologians of liberation theol-ogy, clearly states in his seminal work *A Theology of Liberation*, one of the

---

15. Clearly, this is a perspective shared by Marcuse and the broader school of critical theory, rooted in Marx's famous eleventh thesis on Feuerbach: "The philosophers have only *interpreted* the world in various ways; the point is to *change* it." Karl Marx, "Theses on Feuer-bach," in *Collected Works of Karl Marx and Friedrich Engels, 1845–47*, vol. 5, *"Theses on Feuer-bach," "The German Ideology" and Related Manuscripts*, by Karl Marx and Friedrich Engels (New York: International, 1976), 5 (emphasis in original).

16. Câmara, *Spiral of Violence*, 30.

landmark texts of Central and South American liberation theology, there exists

> a double standard which assumes that violence is acceptable when the oppressor uses it to maintain "order" and bad when the oppressed invoke it to change this "order." Institutionalized violence violates fundamental rights so patently that the Latin American bishops warn that "one should not abuse the patience of a people that for years has borne a situation that would not be acceptable to anyone with any degree of awareness of human rights." An important part of the Latin American clergy request, moreover, that "in considering the problem of violence in Latin America, let us by all means avoid equating the *unjust violence* of the oppressors (who maintain this despicable system) with the *just violence* of the oppressed (who feel obliged to use it to achieve their liberation)."[17]

Here we begin to see clear lines of commonality between the kind of theory represented by liberation theologians and that of Marcuse himself. Marcuse, too, identifies the distinction between the potential violence of revolution (Câmara's Second Violence) and the established violence of the system, which perpetuates suffering and alienation (Câmara's First Violence). In "Repressive Tolerance," Marcuse observes that, traditionally, both are seen as violating ethical standards, but "since when is history made in accordance with ethical standards? To start applying them at the point where the oppressed rebel against the oppressors, the have-nots against the haves is serving the cause of actual violence by weakening the protest against it."[18] As well, the demarcation between these two forms of violence is often negotiated and distributed by those maintaining the established order and thus is systematically tailored to suit the needs of those in power. It is precisely here that Marcuse's theory of "repressive tolerance" becomes quite clear. He states:

> To discuss tolerance in such a society means to re-examine the issue of violence and the traditional distinction between violent and non-violent action. The discussion should not, from the beginning, be clouded by ideologies which serve the perpetuation of violence. Even in the advanced centers of civilization, violence actually prevails: it is

---

17. Gustavo Gutiérrez, *A Theology of Liberation: History, Politics, and Salvation*, 2nd ed. (Maryknoll, NY: Orbis, 1988), 64. This work by Gutiérrez is considered by many as the common foundation of all liberation theology in this region. The original edition, issued in 1974, inspired (and continues to inspire) generations of liberationist thinkers, both within and outside theological institutions.

18. Marcuse, "Repressive Tolerance," 103.

practiced by the police, in the prisons and mental institutions, in the fight against racial minorities; it is carried, by the defenders of metropolitan freedom, into the backward countries. This violence indeed breeds violence. But to refrain from violence in the face of vastly superior violence is one thing, to renounce a priori violence against violence, on ethical or psychological grounds (because it may antagonize sympathizers) is another. Non-violence is normally not only preached to but exacted from the weak—it is a necessity rather than a virtue, and normally it does not seriously harm the case of the strong.[19]

In a situation of "pure" (i.e., passive) tolerance, which maintains approval of violence on the part of the state in upholding the status quo, and which denies in every instance the validity of reactionary or revolutionary violence on the part of those oppressed by this status quo, discussing violence becomes necessary to discussing tolerance, and vice versa. The two are intimately bound to one another. Passive tolerance can in itself be institutional or structural violence; it perpetuates a condition of suffering by refraining from challenging oppressive social conditions and by acquiescing to the repression of those who would speak out against such conditions. By exalting tolerance as one of the highest virtues of modern democracy, such acquiescence is not only seen as valid; it carries with it the validation of the actor as *the person who tolerates*. Upholding ideals is cast as virtuous, and this obscures the violence done when these ideals are enacted in very different ways among oppressors and oppressed. In such a context, to "do" tolerance is to "do" violence.

The idea of a tolerance that can itself be a form of violence emerges from this comparative engagement with Marcuse and Câmara. The acceptance of a hegemonic set of norms, which either actively fosters or passively acquiesces to a kind of toleration that poses fundamentally different questions to representatives of the state and to those who would challenge the oppressive machinery of such a state, shares a common narrative with the demonization of those who attempt to disrupt the workings of such machinery via direct action. The outline of this narrative may be described as follows:

1. Violence is to be tolerated when enacted by authorized parties or when such violence is a structural component of a given society.
2. Violence is to be decried when used as a tool of resistance.
3. These are maintained as absolute and mutually reinforcing mechanisms.

Additionally, expanding the idea of what, exactly, constitutes "violence" facilitates a nuanced critique that not only outlines the basic duplicity of

---

19. Ibid., 102.

such a situation but also suggests that the preconditioned position of tolerance carries a more insidious, less visible form of violence on its own. If, for example, we follow the thought of Walter Benjamin, it may be suggested that violence exists in any condition that robs the individual of the opportunity for moral choice—that uncomfortable but necessary occasion for wrestling with oneself, engaging in an inner mediation of what one considers acceptable or unacceptable, living out the murky nights of solitude laboring in the act of sorting out our judgments against ourselves.[20] Tolerance as a default requisite enables acquiescence to that which should not be tolerated (or, at least, to that which *ought to be discursively negotiated as tolerable or intolerable*). This, then, is the condition that obscures the opportunity for moral reflection, evaluation, and acceptance or rejection among citizens who ought to have the opportunity to decide whether such things might or might not be (morally) abided. Thus, this coerced enactment of tolerance functions as an expression of the complex Benjaminian notion of violence.

In considering the idea of violence enabled through even abstract concepts such as ideals or norms, we can simultaneously investigate whether these very ideals or norms can themselves function as tools of a more invisible, covert kind of violence all their own. The brutal physicality of typical violence can simultaneously embody these alternate or additional forms, particularly when even our highest virtues turn out to be merely at the service of such systemic violence. When Marcuse says, "Tolerance is extended to policies, conditions, and modes of behavior which should not be tolerated because they are impeding, if not destroying, the chances of creating an existence without fear and misery," he is pointing to this idea of tolerance as a kind of violence that takes root as a given, that is positioned as "neutral," and that facilitates an environment of acceptance even toward the abhorrent.[21] That is, while there may be little immediate harm in making social space for those with varying, or even opposing, worldviews, the precondition of tolerance within a fundamentally unequal society establishes a *pattern*, a condition of acclimatization to injustices done in the name of the ideals of the contemporary democratic state.[22] This pattern can easily be abused by

---

20. Walter Benjamin, "Critique of Violence," in *Selected Writings*, vol. 1 (Boston: Belknap, 1999), 277–300; cf. Tim Finney, "Potentiality and Reconciliation: A Consideration of Benjamin's 'Critique of Violence' and Adorno's 'Progress,'" *Colloquy* 16 (December 2008): 97–109.

21. Marcuse, "Repressive Tolerance," 82.

22. I have in mind examples such as the U.S. Supreme Court decision to allow a local Missouri chapter of the Ku Klux Klan (KKK) to participate in the Adopt-a-Highway program in the late 1990s, setting the precedent for this and other, similar groups (such as the American Nazi Party) to continue with such civic activities. Here, an active and legally recognized hate group is validated as a social organization, its dedication to fostering racial oppression considered inconsequential as a function of tolerance and equal representation in the public sphere. In a lovely twist, it is worth noting, the state of Missouri did rename the highway in question the Rosa Parks Highway in November 2000, shortly after the group's approved

authorities and is frequently used to encourage citizens to tolerate the existence of social structures that are constructed on a foundation composed of vast social and economic disparity. By expanding our understanding of what violence is and how it manifests, and by connecting this knowledge to the contemporary enforcement of a tolerance that seeks not to include dissenting voices that critique the status quo but to exclude and effectively quash such voices, we arrive at a novel and necessary rubric for evaluating the usefulness (or lack thereof) of the rhetoric of nonviolence, neutrality, and toleration.

Violence, Tolerance, and the Toronto G20

In 2010, the city of Toronto, Ontario, hosted the annual G20 summit. In preparation for this event, the downtown core was placed under lockdown, a literal fence stretched for miles around the city center, and a temporary detention facility, later dubbed "Torontonomo Bay," was erected on Eastern Avenue for confining protesters who were deemed unlawful. A small number of protesters committed generally expected and commonplace acts of vandalism against private property; yet 1,100 protesters were arrested during the summit, the largest mass arrest in Canadian history. Between stark and inhumane conditions in the detention center and the brutality enacted by militarized police whose nametags were frequently removed to avoid recognition,[23] there can be little doubt of the physical violence of the event.[24] Immediately following the G20 summit in 2010, a local poll showed that a disturbing 73 percent of Torontonians believed that the actions of the police were justified. At a year's distance, the same poll was taken; this time, 41 percent still maintained that police actions were justified. While this is a remarkable shift that ought to be applauded, such applause must not overshadow the fact that nearly half of Torontonians polled still considered the physical and psychological abuse of peaceful protesters to be contextually tolerable.

---

adoption of that particular stretch of road. Unfortunately, such admittedly satisfying irony does little to actually undermine the (political and social) validity granted to the KKK by this action, and perhaps makes its accommodation go down all the more smoothly.

23. On one occasion, an officer even provided a badge number belonging to a Quebec police officer who was neither present nor assigned to the G20 summit. Adrian Morrow, "Ontario Police Watchdog Reopens G20 'Nobody' Arrest Investigation," *Globe and Mail*, November 30, 2010, available at http://www.theglobeandmail.com/news/toronto/ontario -police-watchdog-reopens-g20-nobody-arrest-investigation/article1316308.

24. This brutality includes physical beatings, as well as "kettling" a large number of peaceful protesters. For a detailed account of Toronto G20 conditions and the actions of the police in engaging protesters, see Sarah Lynn Kleeb, "The Violence of Tolerance: At the Intersection of Critical Theory and Liberation Theology," *Radical Philosophy Review* 16, no. 2 (2013): 549–558.

Those who were unlawfully beaten and arrested during the Toronto G20 protests were taken to the aforementioned detention center, which has been described in testimonials as "'cold' with 'barely any food or water' and 'no place in the cages to even sit,' and 'tantamount to torture.' Other allegations included harassment, lack of medical care, verbal abuse, and strip searches of females by male officers."[25] This has prompted years of investigations following the events of the G20, some conducted internally by the police and many others issued and advanced by watchdog groups and civil- and human-rights associations. Amnesty International has accused police of brutality and violation of civil liberties,[26] and the Canadian Civil Liberties Association has claimed that many of the arrests "occurred without 'reasonable grounds to believe that everyone they detained had committed a crime.'"[27] Stemming from such investigations, thirty-two officers have been charged with "discreditable conduct" in their engagements with protesters at the summit; only two of these have been found guilty, and fourteen have been "dismissed, withdrawn or stayed."[28] Constable Babak Andalib-Goortani was found guilty in his role in the infamous and brutal beating of Adam Nobody.[29] Convicted of excessive force and assault with a weapon, Andalib-Goortani was originally sentenced to forty-five days imprisonment, but this penalty was overturned.[30] He was ultimately suspended without pay from December 2013 until February 2015, when he returned to "administrative duties" with the Toronto Police force, given an ultimate sentence of "one year of probation and seventy-five hours of community service."[31] Superintendent David Mark Fenton, the most senior official to be charged, was responsible for

---

25. Lulu Maxwell, "'I Will Not Forget What They Have Done to Me,'" *Toronto Star*, June 28, 2010 available at http://www.thestar.com/news/gta/g20/2010/06/28/i_will_not_forget_what_they_have_done_to_me.html.

26. "Amnesty Calls for Summit Security Review," *CBC News*, June 28, 2010, available at http://www.cbc.ca/news/canada/amnesty-calls-for-summit-security-review-1.910004.

27. Jill Mahoney and Ann Hui, "G20-Related Mass Arrests Unique in Canadian History," *Globe and Mail*, June 28, 2010, available at http://www.theglobeandmail.com/news/world/g8-g20/news/g20-related-mass-arrests-unique-in-canadian-history/article1621198/.

28. "Senior Toronto Cop Set to Face G20 'Kettling,' Mass Arrest Hearing," *Toronto Star*, November 16, 2014, available at http://www.thestar.com/news/gta/2014/11/16/senior_toronto_cop_set_to_face_g20_kettling_mass_arrest_hearing.html.

29. Joe Friesen, "How a Man Named Nobody Became the Battered Face of G20 Protests," *Globe and Mail*, November 30, 2010, available at http://www.theglobeandmail.com/news/toronto/how-a-man-named-nobody-became-the-battered-face-of-g20-protests/article1320838/.

30. Alyshah Hasham, "No Jail for Toronto Police Officer Convicted of G20 Assault," *Toronto Star*, January 29, 2015, available at http://www.thestar.com/news/crime/2015/01/29/no-jail-for-toronto-police-officer-convicted-of-g20-assault.html.

31. "Babak Andalib-Goortani Back at Work on Toronto Police Force," *CBC News*, February 18, 2015, available at http://www.cbc.ca/news/canada/toronto/babak-andalib-goortani-back-at-work-on-toronto-police-force-1.2962582.

giving the order to "kettle" the protesters, whom he reportedly referred to as "terrorists."[32] In August 2015, Fenton was found guilty of two counts of "discreditable conduct" and one count of "unnecessary exercise of authority" for his actions.[33] Despite this conviction, Fenton remained in charge of his division during his trial and sentencing. While prosecutors pushed for a one-year demotion as punishment for Fenton, his lawyer suggested that the "personally and professionally devastating" results of the trial and conviction themselves were sufficient reprimands for his client's actions, further noting that "Fenton has become the focus of the failings in the G20. . . . If he fell into error, [his superiors] were similarly in error and had more experience than he had."[34] Not only have there been shockingly few consequences for officers whose actions were not merely reported but often caught on video;[35] the Toronto G20 protests have been downright profitable for senior officers, who have been allowed a total of $387,000 of overtime pay, allocated by the federal government.[36]

As quoted earlier, Marcuse asserts in "Repressive Tolerance" that "what is proclaimed and practiced as tolerance today, is in many of its most effective manifestations serving the cause of oppression."[37] The tolerance of the 41 percent of Torontonians who accepted G20 police actions as acceptable is made clear in the overall lack of serious disciplinary action taken against such officers. It is obvious in the defense of accused officers by former chief of police Bill Blair, who launched largely fruitless internal investigations of the summit, despite the overwhelming evidence of brutality and violations of Canada's Charter of Rights and Freedoms.[38] Such tolerance clearly does little but "[serve] the cause of oppression." As protesters responded to the First Violence (that of the very existence of the G20), militarized and adrenalized officers enacted the Third Violence (literally beating peaceful pro-

---

32. Daniel Otis, "Officer in G20 Disciplinary Hearing Says He Only Sought Public Safety against 'Anarchists,'" *Toronto Star*, January 16, 2015, available at http://www.thestar.com/news/crime/2015/01/16/officer-in-g20-disciplinary-hearing-says-he-only-sought-public-safety-against-anarchists.html.

33. "Mark Fenton, G20 Officer Who Ordered Mass Arrests, to Get Sentencing Hearing," *CBC News*, April 12, 2016, available at http://www.cbc.ca/news/canada/toronto/g20-officer-sentencing-1.3532708.

34. Ibid.

35. The aforementioned removal of nametags has made identifying officers recorded in low-quality cell-phone videos difficult, particularly as fellow officers have repeatedly refused to identify their coworkers, instead maintaining the so-called thin blue line of police solidarity.

36. Emily Jackson, "Senior Toronto Police Officers to Get G20 Overtime Pay After All," *Toronto Star*, March 26, 2012, available at http://www.thestar.com/news/gta/2012/03/26/senior_toronto_police_officers_to_get_g20_overtime_pay_after_all.html.

37. Marcuse, "Repressive Tolerance," 81.

38. The Canadian Charter of Rights and Freedoms is akin to the Bill of Rights in the United States.

testers into submission). Bringing together Marcuse and Câmara allows for the assertion that the preconditioning of tolerance to the intolerable makes acceptance and approval of the First and Third Violence all the more palatable. When tolerance is encouraged toward the workings of the state itself, and discouraged toward those who protest in the interest of revolutionary progress toward justice and liberation, the repressive nature of that tolerance becomes hauntingly evident. The very notion of moral choice becomes problematic or questionable within a system of conditioning that invariably praises those who uphold the status quo, even by reprehensible means, and demonizes those who resist, even if their goals are liberatory.

Toleration as a benevolent default standard is dependent on social freedom if it is not to be used as a tool for validating an unjust state; tolerance and liberation are conditional on, and intimately bound to, one another. "Universal toleration," Marcuse states, "becomes questionable when its rationale no longer prevails, when tolerance is administered to manipulated and indoctrinated individuals who parrot, as their own, the opinions of their masters, for whom heteronomy has become autonomy."[39] As long as we live in a world in which Câmara's First and Third Violence are considered not just acceptable but necessary, as long as citizens are encouraged to tolerate both active and passive violence on the part of the state, and as long as horrifyingly large minorities of people (41 percent) validate brutalization of peaceful protesters, such universal toleration remains suspect, worthy of the ruthless critique offered by those like Marcuse and Câmara. The call for tolerance, envisioned by most as a positive aspiration, has fostered the construction of an illusory freedom. What is imagined as an expression of moral choice is often no choice at all; it is no coincidence that considerable swaths of North American citizens accept, or even applaud, the direct violence of police against protesters—and this is visible from the events of 2010 in Toronto to the support shown for officers whose actions have propelled the Black Lives Matter movement in the United States. In the present context, tolerance is never "just" tolerance; it is always already laden with acquiescence in the interest of maintaining violent structures and institutions. Marcuse notes:

> Tolerance is an end in itself only when it is truly universal, practiced by the rulers as well as by the ruled, by the lords as well as by the peasants, by the sheriffs as well as by their victims. And such universal tolerance is possible only when no real or alleged enemy requires in the national interest the education and training of people in military violence and destruction. As long as these conditions do not prevail, the conditions of tolerance are "loaded": they are determined

---

39. Marcuse, "Repressive Tolerance," 90.

and defined by the institutionalized inequality . . . i.e., by the class
structure of society. In such a society, tolerance is *de facto* limited on
the dual ground of legalized violence or suppression (police, armed
forces, guards of all sorts), and of the privileged position held by the
predominant interests and their "connections."[40]

In terms of the legacy of the G20 in Toronto, this "loaded" tolerance
that supports "legalized violence or suppression" is glaringly evident at the
present moment. Despite numerous calls to resign in the years since 2010,
former chief of police Bill Blair maintained his position until retiring on
April 25, 2015. The next day, Blair announced his intention to run for federal
office as a Member of Parliament (MP) in Canada's Liberal Party.[41] His announcement has garnered the support of many members of the Liberal Party
in the general population, as well as Liberal Party leader Justin Trudeau.
When pressed on the issue of the G20 at a recent appearance with Trudeau,
Blair justified the actions of officers, saying, "We had a very, very truncated
period of time in which to prepare. There was very little time to train our
officers and put them through various scenarios, but we did our best. And
I acknowledge that we faced some very significant challenges, particularly
when violence began to occur and the destruction of property."[42] The word-
ing here is noteworthy, beyond even the absolute deflection of responsibility. The final phrase—"when violence began to occur and the destruction of
property"—is ambiguous. By distinguishing but still connecting these two, it
seems the intended interpretation would be something like, "when violence
and destruction of property began, on the part of the protesters," blaming
the "significant challenges" on the Second Violence of those who engaged in
acts of resistance, the vast majority of which were peaceful. This is certainly
the opinion of many who parrot the narrative Blair has maintained. Yet
perhaps a bit of culpability subliminally seeps through in the separation of
"violence" that "began to occur" and "destruction of property," the latter of
the two being the only instance of physical violence on the part of a minority of protesters. It was not protesters who beat others with clubs, who broke

---

40. Ibid., 85.

41. As is frequently the case in North American politics, "Liberal" here is something of
a misnomer. This party tends to fall on the center-left side of the political spectrum (comparable, for example, to the generally loose usage of the term in U.S. politics). While osten-
sibly "liberal" in comparison to Canada's Tories, or Conservative Party, the actually leftist
(socialist or social democratic) political parties in Canada are the New Democratic Party (a
representative of which held the seat for which Blair ran) and the Green Party. It is worth noting that Blair was ultimately successful in his run for MP, being elected to the Scarborough
Southwest riding in October 2015.

42. Laura Payton, "Justin Trudeau, Bill Blair Defend Record over Handling of G20 Protest," *CBC News*, April 27, 2015, available at http://www.cbc.ca/news/politics/justin-trudeau
-bill-blair-defend-record-over-handling-of-g20-protest-1.3044577.

bones, who deprived prisoners; nor were they responsible for celebrating and defending the institutional violence of the modern world, represented in this instance by the very existence of the G20.

Interpreted this way, the precarious position of tolerance in the present context is made plainly evident. The active negotiation of norms and conditions, oriented toward a liberatory progression that moves ever away from injustice, from the First Violence, is unquestionably a worthy pursuit. Whether such a pursuit is possible within a context where the terms of toleration are "loaded," as Marcuse says, is an entirely different—and vitally important—question. Here, the ideal is also its own negation; in accepting tolerance as a worthy ideal, we simultaneously, unknowingly, and passively authorize its utilization against that very same ideal: that of an inclusionary tolerance that advances toward a more just society. In their actions, the Toronto G20 protesters (as so many protesters worldwide before and after them) enacted a Marcusean Great Refusal: a refusal to validate, support, or tolerate the measures of institutionalized violence manifest within the G20 itself, a refusal played out in vandalism by some but peacefully by the overwhelming majority. Dissidents asserted their moral choice to reject the ideology of a global system that thrives on palpable suffering. They enacted a refusal to tolerate both the conditions from which reactionary and revolutionary violence originates (the First Violence) and *the requisite precondition of a tolerance that maintains acceptance and legitimation of those who construct and uphold such conditions.* It is this act of rejection, however, the resolute "no" that in and of itself subverts and refuses to tolerate the First Violence, that was interpreted as Second Violence by the Toronto Integrated Security Unit,[43] who met it with an excessively forceful Third Violence. This is the intolerance borne of a tolerance shaped over time into its own opposite, a tolerance wielded such that it "protects the already established machinery of discrimination."[44]

The intersections of violence and tolerance in contemporary society—both in terms of how that society is maintained and how that society is resisted—are multiple and manifold. Tolerance is one of the most elevated ideals of modern democracy, and violent actions and reactions are outwardly shunned; however, the line of distinction between these may not be as clear as is often assumed. The present analysis has suggested that these are not mutually exclusive but possibly mutually constitutive, when wielded in the ways discussed here. The way out of such a labyrinthine structure where the

43. This was the title given to the assemblage of more than twenty thousand officers that descended on Toronto, brought in from the Royal Canadian Mounted Police, Toronto Police Department, the Armed Forces of Canada, and several other provincial and regional defensive bodies.
44. Marcuse, "Repressive Tolerance," 85.

ideal is its own negation is not entirely clear, even decades after Marcuse and Câmara were writing. Perhaps peculiar to the (broadly defined) tradition of critical theory is that the noblest aspiration for a critical theorist is to become *irrelevant*. Where much scholarly work is driven by a desire to be correct, the desire of the critical theorist is to use insights to create a world in which such insights are no longer applicable; here, a society in which tolerance is not constructed in such a way that it is "serving the cause of oppression," fostering violence rather than rejecting the conditions that spawn it. The haunting resiliency of the astoundingly compatible messages of Marcuse and Câmara highlights not only their capacity for insightful, necessary, and powerful analysis but also the stagnant nature of the forms of oppression that seem to appear again and again and again, each time further fortified and entrenched in our very social-institutional structures. The current positive appraisal of the insights of such thinkers, decades after their work was written, speaks to their prescience and continued relevance. Their continued relevance, however, may not be something to celebrate. In showing how forward-thinking they are, we simultaneously discover just how sluggishly progress toward liberation has been made, how entrenched violence is in the very basic structures of our world, how "loaded" the conditions of tolerance remain.

11

Democracy by Day, Police State by Night

*What the Eviction of Occupy Philadelphia
Revealed about Policing in the United States*

Tolerance is extended to policies, conditions, and modes of
behavior which should not be tolerated because they are impeding,
if not destroying, the chances of creating an existence without fear
and misery.
—HERBERT MARCUSE, "Repressive Tolerance"[1]

n the early hours of the morning of November 30, 2011, Occupy Philadelphia was evicted from the Dilworth Park Plaza at city hall by the Philadelphia Police Department. The eviction brought to an end one of the
largest and longest occupations in the Occupy movement. Commencing on
October 6, 2011, hundreds of Occupiers lived in more than three hundred
tents on the doorstep of the offices of Philadelphia's city council and government. Approximately one month after Angela Davis led a march from
the Marcuse conference[2] at the University of Pennsylvania to Occupy Philadelphia, we witnessed—during the eviction—elements of the police state
that she talked about in her keynote address. While there has been some
scholarship about the Occupy movement,[3] very little has been written about
the police tactics used on Occupiers, especially during the evictions. How
did the police go about evicting an encampment that had enjoyed considerable support in the city and had hosted notable speakers like Angela Davis,
David Harvey, Frances Fox Piven, Jesse Jackson, and Ray Lewis, a former

A version of this chapter was previously published as Toorjo Ghose, "Democracy by Day,
Police State by Night: What the Eviction of Occupy Philadelphia Revealed about Policing in
the United States," *Radical Philosophy Review* 16, no. 2 (2013): 559–574.

1. Herbert Marcuse, "Repressive Tolerance," in *A Critique of Pure Tolerance*, by Robert
Paul Wolff, Barrington Moore Jr., and Herbert Marcuse (Boston: Beacon, 1965), 82.

2. "Critical Refusals," the fourth biennial conference of the International Herbert Marcuse Society, was held October 27–29, 2011, at the University of Pennsylvania in Philadelphia.
The march to Philadelphia's city hall followed the keynote address by Angela Davis on the
evening of October 28, 2011.

3. Janet Byrne, ed., *The Occupy Handbook* (New York: Back Bay, 2012).

Philadelphia police captain? What do these police tactics tell us about the strategies used to address demonstrations and protests in public spaces in this country? How does a movement like Occupy respond to these tactics and strategies? These are some of the questions I grapple with in this chapter.

As an Occupier, I had camped at Dilworth Plaza, participated in actions, conducted workshops, and held some of my social-work classes there. I was present at the time of the occupation, and I was part of the first group to get arrested that night of the mass eviction. As a participant observer, I documented the eviction as it unfolded that night. In this chapter, I draw on my notes and experiences to examine the way the police engaged with demonstrators and the manner in which the latter responded. I proceed by describing the conceptual lens through which I analyze the events of the eviction night. I then describe the results of my analysis and conclude with a discussion of their implications.

Conceptual Framework

Herbert Marcuse notes that tolerance can be an instrument of repression when it allows free rein to the unleashing of discriminatory and oppressive practices on marginalized communities.[4] Critiquing tolerance that fails to distinguish between progressive and oppressive practices, he advocates for discriminatory tolerance, whereby it is extended to the former and withdrawn from the latter. He notes, for example, that even though tolerance is touted as a crucial element of democratic processes, tolerating the repressive practices of the state undermines, rather than advances, democracy.[5] Extending an analysis of tolerance to the context of conditions in postcolonial societies such as India, scholars note that in an era of heightened democratic sensibilities, a forced tolerance of marginalized communities pushes the state to manage their basic survival needs.[6] However, in doing so, initiatives for larger structural change are undermined, thus ensuring the continued segregation of these communities from civil society. These notions of tolerance suggest that the state might justify intolerant practices targeting marginalized communities and those engaged in dissent by (1) embedding these practices in a discourse of tolerance (as is done in the case of segregationist management practices in postcolonial conditions) and (2) by arguing, as Marcuse warns, that the rightness or wrongness of practices is a matter of opinion and that a democratic society would tolerate these opinions as well

---

4. Marcuse, "Repressive Tolerance," 102, 110.

5. Ibid., 81, 84.

6. Partha Chatterjee, "Democracy and Economic Transformations in India," *Economic and Political Weekly* 43 (2008): 53–62; Kalyan Sanyal, *Rethinking Capitalist Development: Primitive Accumulation, Governmentality and Post-colonial Capitalism* (New Delhi: Routledge, 2007).

as all practices. I argue that both notions of tolerance support repressive state practices and examine the way they informed police tactics used in the eviction of Occupy Philadelphia from city hall.

Results

My analysis highlights three aspects of the police strategy deployed during the eviction: (1) a preconceived plan to manage protests and demonstrations, (2) the use of militarized tactics to implement this management plan, and (3) the imposition of a state of dissociative meditation brought about by the incarceration that followed the eviction. I argue that the strategy of management, militarization, and meditation (the 3M strategy) demonstrates the Marcusean and postcolonial notions of repressive tolerance and is crucial to understanding the way the police address dissent in the United States.

Management

Weeks before the eviction of Dilworth Plaza, Jean Quan, mayor of Oakland, California, admitted what we in the Occupy movement had suspected for some time—namely, that she had been in communication with mayors of eighteen cities to coordinate efforts to deal with occupations all over the country.[7] Ten days before the eviction in Philadelphia, in response to White House Press Secretary Jay Carney's denial that the federal government was involved in scripting a coordinated response to the Occupy movement, the *San Francisco Bay Guardian* published a story documenting the manner in which a nationally coordinated response was indeed being scripted by a little-known think tank, the Police Executive Research Forum (PERF).[8] Calling itself an independent research organization, PERF nevertheless counts among its members top-ranking police officials holding high-ranking public offices in Canadian, British, and U.S. cities.[9] In a conversation with Amy Goodman on *Democracy Now!* on November 17, 2011, Chuck Wexler, PERF's executive director, noted that PERF had participated in a phone conference on November 10, 2011, with police chiefs in several cities in order to guide

7. Amy Goodman, "Former Seattle Police Chief Norm Stamper on Paramilitary Policing from WTO to Occupy Wall Street," *Democracy Now!*, November 17, 2011, available at http://www.democracynow.org/2011/11/17/paramilitary_policing_of_occupy_wall_street.

8. Shawn Gaynor, "The Cop Group Coordinating the Occupy Crackdowns," *San Francisco Bay Guardian*, November 18, 2011, available at https://www.indybay.org/newsitems/2015/12/10/18780854.php.

9. Police Executive Research Forum, "About PERF," available at http://www.policeforum.org/about-perf (accessed June 16, 2016). See also "Police Executive Research Forum," *Wikipedia*, June 15, 2016, available at https://en.wikipedia.org/wiki/Police_Executive_Research_Forum (accessed June 16, 2016).

them on their response to the Occupy protests.[10] It is perhaps not a coincidence that this event was followed immediately by a spate of Occupy evictions across the country, many of which were marked by brutal police tactics.

I call attention to two important points about PERF that are critical to understanding the events that unfolded at Dilworth Plaza in the early hours of November 30, 2011. First, PERF's story is intricately tied to a history of violent police action targeting public demonstrations, both in Philadelphia and in other cities. The president of PERF's board of directors is Philadelphia's police commissioner, Charles Ramsey, while his predecessor in PERF was John Timoney, Philadelphia's former police commissioner and former chief of the Miami Police Department. As the chief of the Metropolitan Police Department in the District of Columbia (Washington, D.C.) before taking over the reins in Philadelphia, Ramsey's hard-line approach to demonstrators protesting the Iraq war and gatherings of international banking institutions such as the International Monetary Fund and the World Bank led to arrests that were eventually thrown out by the courts as unconstitutional.[11] Similarly, Timoney gained notoriety during the 2000 Republican National Convention in Philadelphia with a brutal crackdown on protestors that resulted in injuries and arrests that were overturned in the courts.[12] He went on to replicate this model in Miami during the Free Trade Area of the Americas protest, noting at the time that it was the first trial run for Homeland Security measures.[13] Ramsey and Timoney are part of a membership list that Shawn Gaynor, in his investigative piece in the *San Francisco Bay Guardian*, notes "reads as a who's who of police chiefs involved in crackdowns on anti-globalization and political convention protesters resulting in thousands of arrests, hundreds of injuries, and millions of dollars paid out in police brutality and wrongful arrest lawsuits."[14] Clearing the streets quickly, effectively, and with force if necessary, is a tactic that marks PERF's strategies in managing protests.

The second aspect to highlight about PERF is the way it justifies the use of force to clear the streets, an orientation that was enunciated by Wexler in the earlier-referenced conversation on *Democracy Now!*. Norm Stamper, who had been chief of the Seattle Police Department during the crackdown on demonstrators protesting the gathering of the World Trade Organization in 1999, had just acknowledged the egregiousness of his decision to use

10. Goodman, "Former Seattle Police Chief."

11. Paul Fain, "A Fine Mess," *Washington City Paper*, December 7, 2001, available at http://www.washingtoncitypaper.com/articles/22904/a-fine-mess/.

12. David Rovics, "John Timoney's Bloody Journey," *Counterpunch*, December 2, 2011, available at http://www.counterpunch.org/2011/12/02/john-timoneys-bloody-journey/.

13. Jeremy Scahill, "The Miami Model," *Information Clearing House*, November 24, 2011, available at http://www.informationclearinghouse.info/article5286.htm.

14. Gaynor, "The Cop Group."

chemical weapons on civilian protestors during that protest when Wexler put forward the argument that while the majority of protestors had been nonviolent, Stamper's actions had been justified given the propensity of a group of protestors to engage in violence and vandalism. Wexler notes:

> Norm, what you had in Seattle is you had this group of anarchists that somehow was able to cause such disturbances that it forced a reaction. . . . And today, you know, the police struggle between these two extremes, between people who go to exercise their First Amendment rights and then people who are there to cause, you know, damage and destruction.[15]

Wexler goes on to state that the police were reluctant actors in these protests, attempting to keep the peace by building relationships with protestors and being forced to move in when the small band of "anarchists" invariably turned violent. As the Occupy movement spread across the United States, PERF authored a document detailing this strategy of engagement with protestors.[16] Marked by methods of identifying "anarchists" to pull them from the protests, utilizing undercover police officers to infiltrate protests, and mapping the movement through Facebook and other social media, this was a comprehensive plan to execute the clearance strategy.

This strand of protest management—characterized by the bipolar strategy of building relationships with demonstrators while simultaneously clearing them from the streets—was in evidence in Occupy sites across the country. In Los Angeles, Antonio Villaraigosa, the city's first Latino mayor, initially sided with the Occupiers, occasionally bringing them food and water. Yet on the night of November 30, even as we were being cleared from Dilworth Plaza, the police in Los Angeles evicted Occupiers from the city hall premises, utilizing strategies eerily similar to what we were witnessing in Philadelphia.

We had witnessed this bipolar strategy in Occupy Philadelphia. There was a constant presence in the encampment, of officers sporting red armbands identifying themselves as part of the civil affairs unit of the police force. They talked with us—debating points, clearing traffic for licensed demonstrations, and building the kind of relationships warranted by the clearance strategy. Police Commissioner Ramsey and PERF executive director

---

15. Goodman, "Former Seattle Police Chief."

16. Gaynor, "The Cop Group"; Tony Narr, Jessica Toliver, Jerry Murphy, Malcolm McFarland, and Joshua Ederheimer, *Police Management of Mass Demonstrations: Identifying Issues and Successful Approaches* (Washington, DC: Police Executive Research Forum, 2006), available at http://www.policeforum.org/assets/docs/Critical_Issues_Series/police%20manage ment%20of%20mass%20demonstrations%20-%20identifying%20issues%20and%20success ful%20approaches%202006.pdf.

Wexler walked through the Occupy Philadelphia encampment at one point, noting its quick response to events through social media.[17] The iron fist was never too hidden, though. I heard police officers warning us that they would target us when the crackdown came. I saw members of the civil affairs unit march into the encampment one day and drag away two African American teenagers who had become emboldened enough to say something sarcastic to them. It was only when some of us interceded on their behalf, pointing out that verbally engaging officers who were lounging about our encampment did not constitute a criminal offense, that they "rediscovered" their roles as community liaisons and released the teenagers. I read the incendiary posts that one of the officers left on the Occupy Philly website warning Occupiers of impending reprisals.

The hollowness of the city administration's tolerance of us was revealed when Occupiers accepted an offer by the mayor to move to a plaza next to city hall in order to allow a proposed construction project at Dilworth Plaza to proceed. Occupy Philadelphia voted to move in order to support the labor unions involved in the construction and started packing up one night to relocate across the street. The police response was breathtakingly swift. In a matter of minutes, a large contingent of them in riot gear cordoned off the new site and pushed those walking across back to the original occupation site. Apparently the mayor had not expected to be taken up on an offer that was made merely to position him as the reasonable party in our negotiations. For the city and its police force, as might have been anticipated given the city police's connections to PERF, clearance had always been the only option, cloaked all the while in a discourse of reasonable engagement and tolerance.

Militarization

On the night of November 29, I had decided to catch up on some sleep at home. We had spent two sleepless nights on alert, waiting for the eviction after the city's deadline to leave had expired. We knew that across the country, Occupy Los Angeles was on high alert, too, and some of us had anticipated that the evictions would happen in concert. I live a few minutes from city hall and thought that I would be able to make it back if required. I was responsible for documenting the names of anyone who got arrested and making sure that they would have the bail money and legal support they needed. Just as I got into bed around midnight, I heard the helicopters and realized that the eviction had officially started. Attempting to get back, I ran into police barricades that had been thrown up all around the block of

---

17. Larry Miller, "Police Reviewing Social Media," *Philadelphia Tribune*, October 14, 2011, available at http://www.phillytrib.com/newsarticles/item/1034-police-reviewing -social-media.html.

streets surrounding Dilworth Plaza. Finding a small courtyard that led to the plaza still unblocked, I went through minutes before the police shut off that access point.

Stepping onto the main road facing the plaza was like walking onto the set of a bizarre postapocalyptic movie. Approximately fifty demonstrators stood on the street, facing down hundreds of police officers in riot gear who were blocking off Dilworth Plaza. I could see a larger contingent of fellow Occupiers marching away from the plaza, disappearing down a street, tailed by a large contingent of police. On the other side of the square in front of Dilworth Plaza, I saw more officers pour out of a school bus. I later learned that school buses might have been used to transport police officers to the scene in order to deflect attention away from the large show of force on display here at city hall.

Having grown up in Calcutta, India, one of the most populated cities in the world, I am used to being lost in crowds. Yet that day, I felt dwarfed by what was happening in front of Dilworth Plaza. I felt crowded in by the massive numbers of police all around us, forming fences with their bicycles held out as shields. I felt truly outnumbered for the first time in our occupation by the sheer number of police cars and vans that had been brought out in preparation to carry us away. I felt cut off from the eyes of the world as I looked up at the silent, darkened, and hulking office buildings of Center City that night, suddenly unsure about the advisability of occupying such a deserted landscape. My tenuous bonds with community and the safety that lay therein were further strained when I saw an entire phalanx of mounted police appear and line up behind us. I looked up and saw the lit, spread-eagled human form that is the symbol of Aramark, a Fortune 500 company headquartered in a building towering over us, which generates much of its $12.5 billion in annual revenues by supplying food and uniforms to state and federal penitentiaries. I realized what it must feel like to be part of communities targeted by the huge police force surrounding me. I looked around me at the place where I had slept, organized, taught, and made friends, and I realized that it had lost all semblance of safety for me: I was now in a militarized zone.

It was at this point that one of the demonstrators was able to establish a live feed on his laptop camera and broadcast to the Occupy Philadelphia website the events that were taking place around us. Suddenly, we had an audience. A hundred people logged on immediately, then two hundred, and within minutes we were being watched by an audience of more than a thousand. Words of encouragement and solidarity began streaming in from across the country. It broke the spell of being invisible and unheard, and energized us into action. We marched to the middle of the street even as the phalanx of officers moved up to form a line across from us. We chanted and raised banners. "Who do you protect? Who do you serve?" we asked the officers. The humor that has always marked Occupy chants reemerged. "You're sexy, you're cute, so please get out of your riot suit," invited one chant. Some officers smiled, despite themselves. I saw some others shaking their heads in disbelief. Perhaps the overwhelming show of force was not having its desired effect.

By now, the news cameras had started to congregate around us. We noticed the police closing down the last few access points to the plaza and the street where we had gathered. In an impromptu press conference right next to where we had gathered on the street, Police Commissioner Ramsey stated that the plaza had been cleared without any arrests and, pointing to us, noted that we were engaging in our right to free speech by chanting in the street. The strategy of expressing tolerance for our freedom of expression while simultaneously using a show of overwhelming force was being executed to the letter. A reporter commented that Occupy Los Angeles was being evicted at that same moment and asked Ramsey if it had been a coordinated action with the Philadelphia police. "No comment," replied the commissioner. Another asked him how long the police would remain there without arresting us. "As long as it takes," he answered. I shouted out to him then: "We'll be here because these are our public spaces, Commissioner." He turned to me and replied, "Then I guess we'll be here for some time."

True to the clearance agenda outlined above, "as long as it takes" turned out to be another forty-five minutes. As the police moved in on our encampment, tearing down tents and canopies, some demonstrators on the street resurrected a tent, hoisted it above their heads, and marched up and down the police line, chanting, "Is this what you're afraid of?" Planting the tent in front of the police lines, two protestors crawled in, telling the grim-faced officers in front of them, "We might as well get comfortable, Occupy-style." Reducing the encounter to farce had the effect of underlining the incongruousness of the show of force that we were being confronted with. It was also great television, and the news reporters were filming every second of it. Apparently, tolerance of free speech did not extend to humor. I saw William Fisher, a Philadelphia police captain from the civil affairs unit, gather some of his men together and give the order to clear the streets.

Things started happening quickly after that. Fisher issued the first of three warnings to us. Incongruously (or so it seemed at the time), we were surrounded by police officers dressed in shorts, using their bicycles as instruments to herd the crowd. Some protestors were pushed back onto the pavement. Those of us who stayed on the street were quickly surrounded by a fence of bicycles. We later realized that those bicycles represented the latest technology in militarized protest management. Later that night, and in days to come, the police would (1) ride bicycles through marching protestors, cutting off streets faster than any squad car was able to do, (2) raise bicycles as shields whose protrusions were infinitely more dangerous than an ordinary flat riot shield, and (3) use bicycles as effective clubs to brutally beat back demonstrators.

By the second warning, most of the protestors had been pushed back onto the pavement. I had been so busy averting the bikes in order to record the names of people in the circle that I had not noticed how effectively the police had cut us off from the demonstrators on the pavement. There were fewer than ten of us left, and most had never been arrested at a protest before. Talking to these people later, I realized that we all reached the same conclusion sometime between the second and third warnings: that we were going to hold our ground on that street because we believed that we were engaging in our right to free expression. "I do not like being bullied," said one of the remaining demonstrators, a high-ranking union official.

The third warning was issued, and we were formally arrested. As nonviolent protestors not resisting arrest, we should have been walked to the police van—pursuant to the established protocol and past practice; however, the new era of clearance and militarization brought new rules. We were handcuffed with plastic ties that were tight enough to cut off circulation. "Do we really warrant this, officer?" I asked, pointing out that we posed no threat to them. "You broke the law, and this is how we deal with criminals," I was informed. As we were having this exchange, I saw a group of mounted police advance slowly on my fellow demonstrators on the pavement. Suddenly, one horse broke loose and charged into the crowd. We all tensed as we saw a woman fall under its flailing hooves. I later learned that the woman's ankle had been broken, and had it not been for the quick reflexes of a fellow Occupier who had pulled her out from under the horse, her injuries would have been much more extensive.

Marcuse argues for the merits of discriminating tolerance (i.e., tolerance for progressive voices and practices coupled with intolerance for repressive ones) to allow marginalized stances to battle hegemonic structures on a more level playing field.[18] The manner in which the police extended tolerance to us initially, before withdrawing it when arresting us and violently squelching our voices, demonstrates how tolerance is always practiced in discriminatory ways by repressive agents. Repressive tolerance is thus predicated on conditional tolerance being extended by institutional agents, such as the police, to those engaged in questioning the status quo. The transformation of the city into a militarized zone that night revealed to us exactly what lay behind that veil of tolerance.

---

18. Marcuse, "Repressive Tolerance," 109–111.

Meditation

The third stage of our experience that night was marked by an imposed silence that started as soon as we entered the police van. We were kept there for almost three hours, the last hour in pitch darkness inside the bowels of the police station, with all the lights in the windowless vehicle switched off. Handcuffed tightly, with our arms becoming progressively more numb, conversation faltered. I started thinking about the marchers outside and the power of the state that they were confronting. I thought about the horses mowing down my friends and wondered if we were safer inside the van. Yet I could not help wondering about what lay ahead of us, now that all the rules had apparently changed. This was a state that I was not familiar with, and it made me extremely nervous. Later, in the dark, one of my fellow arrestees revealed that he suffered from anxiety and that he needed his medication soon. We rallied around him as best as we could.

Our collective anxiety increased when we were finally taken to the police station and booked. While filling out the paperwork, we watched a television news conference where the mayor announced that the eviction had taken place without any arrests. The police officers booking us laughed, and one of my fellow arrestees remarked that we did not seem to exist. It was easy to believe him. At that moment, we were in the dungeons of the "Roundhouse," the popular term for Philadelphia's central police station, which is built in the shape of a pair of handcuffs. We were realizing that courting arrest had forced the city to deviate from its management script of clearance while engaging in the discourse of tolerance. The mayor, though, was unwilling to acknowledge the deviation, and we felt cut off from the rest of the world.

That sense of isolation grew when we were confined three to a room, in cells that measured seven by seven feet. Each cell had a metal toilet that was dysfunctional and filthy. I squeezed into the corner of a metal cot shared by two others and discovered that the undulations on the beaten surface made it impossible to sit comfortably on it. The next fourteen hours were some of the most tedious I have ever spent. Sleeping was a failed endeavor, given my discomfort, so I stared at the wall and took stock of my situation. When would we be let out? Would it be easier to mark time by not focusing on its passage? Or should I engage in the game I usually play on long airplane flights, in which I try to guess when a quarter of an hour has gone by? What would happen if I needed to use the toilet? Would they provide us with toilet paper? Would I offend my cellmates? Were fifteen minutes up yet? Under the constant scrutiny of my cellmates, cameras, and passing guards, I was never more aware of the social codes that make it bearable for people to live in close proximity to each other. Yet as I became more dissociated from my surroundings with each passing hour, I could feel these codes becoming increasingly unimportant. Did it really matter what people thought as I went to the toilet? What was really the point of keeping track of time when I had no idea when we would be let out? Perhaps as a way to cope with being so exposed to the scrutiny of others, I started cutting them out of my thinking as my world shrunk down to my immediate physical surroundings. The hypervisibility of the cell made me feel as invisible as when I had first confronted the might of the police state at Dilworth Plaza. In a matter of a few hours, I had gone from being part of a vibrant body politic organizing for social change to being totally focused on bodily functions and the timing of the next meal of stale cheese and bread.

I refer to this process of extreme dissociation as the meditative state induced by imprisonment. I was experiencing, of course, only a fraction of what is visited on communities of color who make up the overwhelming majority in prisons in the United States. What the Occupy experience revealed, however, was that the meditative stage was a logical culmination of the strategy of management and militarization. It was through this process, which had commenced from the moment the police arrived at Dilworth Plaza, that we were shorn of the connection to community and reduced to primeval concerns about basic needs.

The sense of being constantly monitored in that cell was exacerbated a few hours into the experience when I saw a woman walk slowly down the corridor and stop in front of my cell. "Ghose?" she asked, as she consulted a list. She was an Immigration and Customs Enforcement (ICE) agent and told me that she needed to verify the legality of my status in the United States. Apparently, my last name had caught her attention. I was escorted to a small room where I was asked to provide another set of fingerprints that would now have to be checked against a separate federal database for verification. I told her that I was a citizen. "A naturalized one," she replied, "and illegal, since you haven't registered with the selective services." She told me that I was facing a five-year prison term for not registering.

This turned out to be the final piece of the state strategy aimed at stripping all sense of citizenship from those who had dared to question its machinery. I had no idea up until that point that ICE now routinely places agents in jails in order to check the status of those arrested who might have "foreign" last names. I had started the evening as a social-work professor who, in advocating for social change, was putting into practice what I constantly teach in my classroom. If the state were going to have its way, however, I would end it being branded an illegal noncitizen engaged in criminal acts. Along with the rest of my fellow dissenters, I was now being exposed to the repercussions of stepping beyond the limits that state tolerance had delineated for me. Not only was I a target of militarized action; I was also a monitored subversive in jail: citizenship and community were quite literally going to be stripped away from me.

I might not have shaken myself out of the stupor that is induced by the imposed meditation of imprisonment if I had not been a faculty member of a prestigious, Ivy League university. I was, however, invested with all of the social and institutional privileges associated with being one, and I was fully cognizant of my rights. I was also, finally, angry and ready to battle back from the dissociative state into which I had slipped. I told the ICE agent that she was wrong and that I was well above the age at which people needed to register. "Do not mess with me, sir," she said. "I am a federal agent." I told her then that I was a professor and that she was out of line for trying to intimidate me with incorrect information. That gave her pause, and she left the room in order to verify my credentials. When she returned, she shrugged and said, "You need to blame all those illegal Mexican immigrants that make this necessary." I was now furious and angrily told her to spare me her racist discourse. I also reminded her that the exchange had been recorded and that I would have access to it if I chose to take her to court.

When I returned to my cell, things had changed drastically. I had a new cellmate who happened to be a fellow Occupier. He told me that the police had finally cornered the marchers in a lane and arrested more than fifty of them. I saw them streaming in and being processed. One bled from his head where he had been clubbed with a police bicycle. Another in tattered clothes nursed an injured arm that had been twisted when he had been wrestled to the ground during his arrest. Putting all of us there, though, undermined the sense of isolation that had set in earlier. We started using the people's mic, an Occupy method to relay information by repeating it from one group to another, to exchange information and keep track of each other. Apparently, there was a large contingent of Occupiers gathered outside the Roundhouse, and David Harvey, the well-known radical geographer, was going to address the crowd. Someone started a chant, and the entire jail resounded with it as we beat on the cell bars in time. "This is what a police state looks like," we roared, as everyone—Occupiers and non-Occupiers—joined in. With one voice, we demanded food, toilet paper, and medication for those who needed it. For the first time that night, I saw the guards look at each other uncertainly. The volume of the chants kept increasing until they finally decided to give in. A cell at the end of the row was cleared out to be used as a restroom. One of the guards started handing out extra sandwiches. We were assured that the Occupier who suffered from anxiety would be given his medication. In the battle with the state to make the withdrawal of tolerance illuminate its limits for the other side, we had just landed a body blow.

Discussion

The events of Occupy Philadelphia's eviction night demonstrate important aspects of police tactics in dealing with demonstrations and public protests.

They also have implications for the formulation of protest strategies in the future.

Summarizing the 3M Strategy

An analysis of the eviction of Occupy Philadelphia indicates that the police engaged in a carefully orchestrated strategy marked by the management of protest marches, the militarization of its tactics, and an imposed meditation in the confines of strictly monitored jail cells. The strategy cleared the streets, even as city leaders engaged in a discourse of tolerance, converted public spaces into militarized zones, and sought to break the spirit of the movement by intimidating and incarcerating Occupiers. It is important to note that Occupy Philadelphia and Occupy Los Angeles were the last of the major city encampments to be evicted. The visible and documented brutality of the police response in the California cities of Berkeley, Davis, and Oakland—where Occupiers had been teargassed and beaten up and a veteran had been shot—was absent in this eviction. I argue that Oakland and Berkeley were early instances of the strategy later implemented in Philadelphia, where we were subjected to a refined and well-executed (but no less brutal) version of it.

The ideals of liberal democracy are unsullied, and perhaps even bolstered, by the execution of the 3M strategy. As in earlier crackdowns perpetrated by the PERF membership, every arrest that was contested was thrown out. Karen Simmons, the municipal court judge in the First Judicial District of Pennsylvania, responding to the prosecution's charge that we were impeding traffic in standing our ground on the streets, noted that "when weighing public expression against public inconvenience, public expression wins every time, at least in my court."[19] It was a rousing victory for us and one of a series of similar legal victories across the country for the movement.

The important point to note, however, is that the 3M strategy anticipates this legal loss, with cities even paying significant damages to those arrested in similar circumstances in the past. I argue that the strategy is predicated on giving ground in the courtroom, which becomes the price for the institutionalization of the use of unconstitutional means to stifle protest. Legal rulings like Judge Simmons's reassure us about the health of democracy and civil society in the United States by delivering a slap on the wrist of law enforcement. However, the ruling is just that: a slap on the wrist that will not undermine the 3M strategy in any way. Our courtroom victory, therefore, will not result in any deviation from this strategy, just as earlier losses in the

---

19. Judge Karen Simmons, Municipal Court, First Judicial District of Pennsylvania, Philadelphia, April 26, 2012, remarks from the bench as noted by the author.

courts did not dissuade Commissioner Ramsey from repeating the tactics with us.

Both the Marcusean and the postcolonial notions of repressive tolerance are at the heart of the 3M strategy. The clearance strategy was implemented even as police and city officials paid constant homage to our free-speech rights. Repression, therefore, was ensconced in a discourse of tolerance. Moreover, when the unconstitutionality of the strategy was revealed in court, its continuation was predicated on the assumption that society would tolerate what Marcuse refers to as "radical right" strategies, because the triumph in court meant that society was tolerant of Left strategies. Marcuse reminds us that this equivalence is a false one because the police serve the interests of those in power and are in a far more powerful position than those who dissent.[20]

Lessons Learned

There were moments during the eviction process when the 3M strategy was effectively resisted. When the police first moved into Dilworth Plaza, they were unprepared for the decision by Occupiers to split into two groups, one that marched through the city and another that stayed to rally in front of the plaza. This move thwarted the 3M strategy in several ways. The march through the streets of Philadelphia broke the police containment around city hall, undermining the goal of confronting and dealing with protestors in a nonresidential, deserted part of the city, away from the eyes of its residents. Moreover, the prolonged confrontation in front of the plaza and on the street corners of Philadelphia's Center City defeated the strategy to complete the operation expeditiously, allowing news reporters to arrive and broadcast in real time. The intention to clear the plaza quickly and declare "victory" was evident from the fact that Commissioner Ramsey arrived with a prepared statement declaring the end of the operation, an hour after the police moved in. Finally, the fact that some of us courted arrest early in front of the plaza, while others were arrested at different points during the night, undermined the city's narrative that the eviction had happened without arrests (as the mayor initially declared), as well as the alternative message, that the police had arrested only those Occupiers who had decided to stay in the encampment (as was referenced in Ramsey's press conference on the street). In effect, our decision to vacate the plaza but hold other public ground forced the police to make arrests when we were engaged in expressing opinion in public space rather than resisting police orders to vacate government property. This was a crucial point that was driven home by our lawyers and ultimately resulted in the arrests being vacated. More importantly, it revealed to us that

20. Marcuse, "Repressive Tolerance," 102.

the police were not interested in merely securing city hall for construction purposes, as they had been claiming, but sought to clear the streets of all demonstrators.

An important tactic started to emerge during the march that night and was later crystallized into an effective strategy in future marches. To thwart the militarized tactic of bicycle-mounted police encircling marchers and cutting off streets for the purpose of shutting down the march, demonstrators dispersed quickly when stopped, reassembling at another street corner to continue the march. Information about which corner to assemble on was passed around by word of mouth, and, at times, different strands of the march would split into different streets, rejoining at designated spots. This allowed the march to continue longer than the police intended. When they eventually did arrest a large group of demonstrators, the police had to do so by preventing marchers from dispersing, after the order to disperse had been given. This unconstitutional tactic enabled those arrested to win their freedom in court. The prolonged, nonviolent march caught the attention of the city and undermined the police strategy of preventing people from taking their message to the streets. These strategies need to inform future public action if activists are to successfully circumnavigate the barriers to public expression that 3M strategies seek to erect.

The solidarity that emerged in jail was a powerful mode of resistance to the imposed state of dissociative meditation that I have described earlier. It forged associational relationships among those jailed and gave birth to collective actions that undermined the power of our jailors over us. Various movements among the incarcerated community have underlined the importance of such solidarity. Occupy has continued to engage in jail and prison solidarity for all incarcerated people, not just Occupiers. Our experience that night highlights the salience of such efforts in targeting a crucial element of the 3M strategy and undermining the enduring sense of isolation that develops through incarceration.

Finally, the legal campaign to fight the arrests helped bring together a team of well-known civil-rights attorneys who volunteered to defend us pro bono. This has been the pattern in Occupy sites all over the country. Although I have argued that the overturning of the arrests by themselves will not undermine the 3M strategy in the long run, the victories won by this team were crucial for our personal well-being and for the future of the movement. Not only did they keep us out of prison, but given the cumulative and increasingly detrimental consequences of convictions, these legal victories allow us to confront the police state with less at stake if we are arrested again. The logical next step in this battle is to cobble together a legal strategy aimed at winning victories that serve as a deterrent for the implementation of the 3M strategy. This is a challenging prospect given the willingness of cities to pay large sums to those victimized by the use of disproportional force in police actions targeting demonstrations without actually curbing such action. What is at stake, however, is no less than the ability to gather freely in public spaces and voice dissent.

Conclusion

The 3M strategy described in this chapter represents a scripted police response to dissent. Embedded in the discourse of tolerance, it systematically delineates the boundaries of appropriate expression in the United States today. Perhaps one of the greatest gains of the Occupy movement has been to bring the 3M strategy into focus. This chapter highlights the manner in which the strategy was effectively negated at some points of the eviction night. Progressive movements in the future need to incorporate these successful tactics and address the 3M program if they are to succeed in dismantling the police state that is erected under the cover of tolerance across the country.

Part IV

Communicating Resistance

12

Insurrection 2011

Great Refusals from the Arab Uprisings
through Occupy Everywhere

DOUGLAS KELLNER

There are decades when nothing happens, and there are weeks
when decades happen.
—Attributed to VLADIMIR ILYICH LENIN

I n 2011, reports of the Arab Uprisings, the Libyan revolution, the U.K. Riots, the Occupy movements, and other political insurrections cascaded
through broadcasting, print, and digital media, seizing people's attention
and emotions and generating complex and multiple effects that may make
2011 as memorable—and, perhaps, as significant—in the history of social
upheaval as 1968. In 2011, once more, as in 1968, multiple insurrections generated discourses of revolution. Intransigent and growing economic crises
put global capitalism and its free-market ideology in question, and multiple
political uprisings against authoritarian and neoliberal rule made the year
2011 memorable and perhaps a turning point in history, in which popular
insurrections become a constant factor in local, national, and global politics.

In this chapter, I first discuss how in 2011 political insurrections emerged
as media spectacles, and I then engage some of the discourses of the political insurrections of the contemporary moment and carry out a brief study
of the Occupy movements to indicate how political insurrection as media
spectacle has played out in the United States and other Western and non-
Western societies. I suggest that global economic crisis and a new era of
political insurrection mean that once more, Marxian discourse is relevant
to contemporary political struggles and that theorists like Guy Debord, Herbert Marcuse, Michael Hardt and Antonio Negri, Slavoj Žižek, and other
neo-Marxian theorists can be used to describe the insurrections of the contemporary moment. In this chapter, I demonstrate how Marcuse's theory of
revolution and the Great Refusal is relevant to these discussions and then
discuss in more detail the movement from Occupy Wall Street to Occupy
Everywhere as a resurrection of the New Left for the twenty-first century.

Political Insurrection as Media Spectacle

> *The entire life of societies in which modern conditions of production reign announces itself as an immense accumulation of spectacles. Everything that was directly lived has moved away into a representation.*
> —GUY DEBORD, *Society of the Spectacle*[1]

In the past decades, media spectacle has become a dominant form in which news and information, politics, war, entertainment, sports, and scandals are presented to the public and circulated through the matrix of old and new media and technologies.[2] By "media spectacles," I mean media constructs that present events that disrupt ordinary and habitual flows of information and that become popular stories, capturing the attention of the media and the public and circulating through broadcasting networks, the Internet, social networking, cell phones, and other new media and communication technologies. In a global networked society, media spectacles proliferate instantaneously, become virtual and viral, and, in some cases, become tools of sociopolitical transformation, while other media spectacles become mere moments of media hype and tabloidized sensationalism.

Dramatic news and events are presented as media spectacles and dominate certain news cycles. Stories like the 9/11 terror attacks, Hurricane Katrina, and the rise of Barack Obama during the 2008 U.S. presidential election were produced and multiplied as media spectacles that were central events of their era. In retrospect, 2011 appears as a year of popular uprisings in an era of cascading media spectacle. Following the North African Arab uprisings, intense political struggles erupted across the Mediterranean in Greece, Italy, and Spain, all of which faced economic crises and cutbacks of social programs. In February and March 2011, workers and students in Madison, Wisconsin, occupied the state capitol building to protest and fight against cutbacks of their rights and livelihood when the right-wing Republican governor Scott Walker signed a bill to curtail union rights and reduce social programs, including student aid and healthcare; Egyptians declared

---

1. Guy Debord, *Society of the Spectacle* (Detroit, MI: Black and Red, 1970), 1, available at http://library.brown.edu/pdfs/1124975246668078.pdf (emphasis in original).

2. In this chapter, I build on and expand my concept of media spectacle as developed in a series of books, including Douglas Kellner, *The Persian Gulf TV War* (Boulder, CO: Westview, 1992); Douglas Kellner, *Grand Theft 2000: Media Spectacle and a Stolen Election*, (Lanham, MD: Rowman and Littlefield, 2001); Douglas Kellner, *From 9/11 to Terror War: The Dangers of the Bush Legacy* (Lanham, MD: Rowman and Littlefield, 2003); Douglas Kellner, *Media Spectacle and the Crisis of Democracy: Terrorism, War, and Election Battles* (Boulder, CO: Paradigm, 2005); Douglas Kellner, *Guys and Guns Amok: Domestic Terrorism and School Shootings from the Oklahoma City Bombing to the Virginia Tech Massacre* (Boulder, CO: Paradigm, 2008); and Douglas Kellner, *Media Spectacle and Insurrection, 2011: From the Arab Uprisings to Occupy Everywhere* (London: Continuum, 2012).

their solidarity with protestors in Madison and sent them pizzas. For weeks during the summer of 2011, there were also widespread demonstrations in Israel in which demonstrators, like in Tahrir Square in Cairo, occupied and set up a tent city in Tel Aviv to protest against declining living conditions and government policies in Israel.

In the face of the failures of neoliberalism and a global crisis of capitalism as well as tremendous economic deficits and debts in these countries, enabled and produced by unregulated neoliberal capitalism, there were calls by established political regimes to solve debt crises on the backs of working people by cutting back on government spending and social programs that help people rather than corporations. These struggles—intensifying as capitalist economic crises intensified—emerged globally with powerful protest movements against government austerity programs emerging in Spain, Italy, the United Kingdom, Greece, and other European countries. In many of these struggles, youth played an important role, as young people throughout the world were facing diminishing job possibilities and an uncertain future in an era of global economic crisis.

In spring 2011, with the North African Arab uprisings in Tunisia, Egypt, and Libya, we saw that political insurgencies and hoped-for revolutions unfolded as media spectacles that circulated images and discourses of revolt, insurrection, freedom, and democracy through global media. These insurrections, which erupted in December 2010 and January 2011 and have continued to shake the world and reconstitute the political landscape of North Africa and the Middle East, may be seen in retrospect as inaugurating a new epoch of history, in which political uprisings and insurrections radicalize entire regions of the world and drive out corrupt and entrenched dictatorships.

However, I should begin with some caveats and cautionary warnings. While Al Jazeera, CNN, and most U.S. media networks at first repeatedly used the term "revolution" to describe the events in Tunisia, Egypt, and Libya, it was unlikely that fundamental democratic transformations of these societies would take place, and, indeed, in the period from 2011 to 2016, there have been complex mixtures of progress, regression, intense struggles, and continual upheavals. Hence, I use in this chapter the more modest term "North African Arab uprisings" to describe the important media spectacles and political insurrections of the Arab Spring, which may yet be looked back on as world-historical and transformative events.[3]

---

3. After initially using the discourse of "revolution" to describe the overthrow of dictatorships in Tunisia and Egypt, Al Jazeera and other global networks then used terms like "Libya's uprising," "Egypt's new era," and "Tunisia in transition," as well as terms like "Arab Spring," "Arab Awakening," or "Arab uprising," to describe the events described in this chapter. Curiously, Wikipedia has its pages on the events under the rubric of "Tunisian Revolution," "Egyptian Revolution of 2011," and "Libyan Civil War (2011)." In this chapter, I follow Marcuse's concept of revolution as a rupture with and overthrow of the previous social order that

In the title of my recent book, *Media Spectacle and Insurrection, 2011: From the Arab Uprisings to Occupy Everywhere*, I use the term "insurrection" to describe the entire array of uprisings in 2011, from the North African Arab uprisings through the Occupy movements, since we did not know if these events and movements would produce a new and liberated social order.[4] Yet reflecting on the dramatic uprisings in North Africa in the Arab Spring, it is, to be sure, revolutionary to overthrow military regimes and corrupt dictators who have been oppressing their people for decades. It is revolutionary to put aside a government and political system and to construct (or to attempt to construct) another freer and more democratic one. It is tremendous that self-organizing people can produce a popular upheaval from below that, they hope, will fundamentally alter their political fate and future. These events are clearly astonishing examples of people's power, of the masses becoming a force in history, throwing off decades of oppression, and fundamentally altering the forces of sovereignty in specific societies.

Yet from the perspective of half a decade and intense years of struggle since the 2011 Arab Spring, it is clear that the North African Arab uprisings did not produce a revolution proper but rather new forms of military government in Egypt, involving the overthrow and arrest of Muslim Brotherhood leaders after they won an election in 2012, followed by repression of the Brotherhood's members and continued struggles against the military government. While Tunisia appeared to effect a popular democratic transformation, attacks on the country by radical Islamic forces in March and June of 2015 imperiled a prosperous democratic future, and Libya has undergone constant civil war and turmoil since the overthrow of the Gaddafi regime (and the killing of Muammar Gaddafi himself) in October 2011.

The rise of ISIS and Islamic radical groups throughout North Africa and the Middle East, in 2014–2016, further imperil a democratic future for the region. In any case, it is in retrospect premature to pronounce the "eighteen days that shook the world" in the North African Arab uprisings, or Arab Spring, a "revolution" at this time. And we cannot predict the form that the insurrections will ultimately take in Egypt, Tunisia, Libya, Yemen, Bahrain, Syria, and other Middle Eastern states that were challenged by their people in the Arab Spring, which, in 2011, blossomed into a year of insurrection.

---

develops new forms of economy, politics, culture, and social relations, involving a decisive rupture with the previous regime and an entirely different society with nonoppressive social relations and a new economy, polity, social institutions, culture, and subjectivities. For more on Marcuse's concept of revolution, see Douglas Kellner, *Herbert Marcuse and the Crisis of Marxism* (Berkeley: University of California Press, 1984); and Douglas Kellner and Clayton Pierce, eds., *Collected Papers of Herbert Marcuse*, vol. 6, *Marxism and Revolution* (London: Routledge, 2012).

4. Kellner, *Media Spectacle and Insurrection, 2011*.

To be sure, if the Egyptians were to throw out the corrupt leaders and functionaries of the past three decades, this would be remarkable; however, if the same people are governing in similar ways in Egypt, the word "revolution" wanes in significance—hence my use of the term "uprising." In addition, I advocate multicausal analysis, arguing that media spectacles such as presidential elections, wars, and political insurrections have multiple causes and are caught up in a complex matrix of events. For instance, there is not just one cause that generated the Bush-Cheney intervention into Iraq in 2003. While the official reason that the United States went to war in Iraq, to eliminate Saddam Hussein's "weapons of mass destruction," was obviously bogus, there were multiple hidden agendas that led the United States to invade and occupy Iraq.[5] These included control of Iraqi oil, establishment of bases in the Middle East for future interventions, the accumulation of tremendous amounts of money by war profiteers and military contractors (often closely related to the Bush-Cheney gang), and a wealth of geopolitical factors.

Indeed, the Bush-Cheney Iraq intervention was organized as a media spectacle that would present U.S. military power as dominant in the world and would facilitate the establishment of new U.S. military bases in the Middle East near the world's largest oil supplies. A successful intervention into Iraq would also aid in the reelection of the Bush-Cheney administration for a second term. Further, the Iraq (mis)adventure embodied the fantasies of U.S. president George W. Bush and a cabal of neocon ideologues who envisaged a New American Century and emergence of Western-style "democracies" throughout the region. George W. Bush imagined that he was battling the forces of "evil" and could succeed in destroying a force of evil that his father (the former U.S. president George H. W. Bush) had failed to eliminate. Thus, while the official justification of seizing Saddam Hussein's "weapons of mass destruction" was clearly a fake excuse, it would also be a mistake to see the Iraq invasion simply as a grab for oil or any other single primary cause.[6]

Major events like the Bush-Cheney administration's Iraq intervention and the North African Arab uprisings are thus overdetermined and have multiple causes. The dynamics in each specific country in the Arab insurrections are dissimilar, although there may be common goals, aspirations, and tactics of struggle. Thus, I do not want to argue that media spectacle is the primary cause of current events and world history today but rather to suggest that media spectacle is a form in which political insurrections and struggles are represented and circulated and that media spectacle can become a causal factor in an overdetermined matrix of events. For instance, the Tunisian uprising could have helped inspire the Egyptian uprising, which apparently

5. Kellner, *Media Spectacle and the Crisis of Democracy*, 39–76.
6. Ibid.

helped inspire uprisings in Libya and throughout the Middle East. In these cases, masses of people who had long been oppressed suddenly rose up and demanded radical change and democratic freedoms.

The North African uprisings thus constituted a break and rupture with their previous totalitarian governments and, in turn, inspired insurrections and a cycle of struggles throughout North Africa and the Middle East (and elsewhere). Media spectacle became the form of the uprisings that immediately circulated via Al Jazeera and other television networks, new media like Facebook and YouTube, and various social networking groups, as well as print media. In each case, there were unprecedentedly large demonstrations in oppressive societies that had not allowed freedom of speech and assembly. In response to these insurrections, state authoritarian governments fought back against the demonstrators, often killing many who henceforth became martyrs. In turn, demonstrations often erupted at the martyrs' funerals and continued to intensify with radical demands for the dictators and their regimes to open up new freedoms and democratic possibilities.

In many cases, participants in the struggles took their own videos, both of the insurrections and of state violence against the protestors. These videos were circulated via Twitter, Blackberries, cell phone networks, and the Internet, and in some cases through global cable television networks, which used YouTube and recirculated videos taken by participants in the insurrections. The people were thus participating in the creation of the spectacles of the Arab Awakening and uprising, not only in that their bodies were part of the democratic masses but in that they were documenting and articulating their own resistance. Thus, individuals within the masses found their own voices and helped construct the spectacle in part through their own do-it-yourself media artifacts sent to the Internet, circulated throughout social networks, and, in some cases, disseminated through global television networks like Al Jazeera.

Looking at the 2011 North African Arab uprisings globally and historically, I would suggest that they may be read as a set of interconnected spectacles with many parts, as were the anticommunist uprisings in 1989 that led to the collapse of the Berlin Wall and Soviet empire and then to the fall of the Soviet Union itself—world-historical events that provide an anticipatory parallel to the media spectacles of 2011. In the 1980s, demonstrations in Poland from the Solidarity movement were visible in Hungary via television and other media, which helped inspire demonstrations in that country, which, in turn, were visible in other Eastern bloc countries like East Germany (DDR) and Czechoslovakia. The powerful images of people uprising against the communist regimes, demanding freedom and a new society, produced a chain of movements, insurrections, and the overthrowing of communist regimes—much like the Arab uprisings—and the collapse of bureaucratic state communism.

In this complex historical matrix in the late 1980s, the then dominant broadcasting media of television circulated images and forms of struggle via television that were seen throughout the Soviet bloc countries, helping produce multiple uprisings and the delegitimation of autocratic communist regimes, leading to the collapse of the Soviet empire in eastern Europe and culminating in the fall of the Berlin Wall and in the Velvet Revolution in Czechoslovakia in 1989.[7] These dramatic events of 1989 eventually lead to the collapse of the Soviet regime in the USSR itself, driving some people to see 1989 as the beginning of a new epoch in history.[8]

Resonant and viral images of the spectacle of uprisings against repressive state communist governments spread through the global broadcasting and news networks and inspired people in neighboring Soviet bloc countries, helping to motivate people to hit the streets and demonstrate for change themselves. Hence, throughout the Eastern bloc state-communist nations, there were uprisings and struggles, with governments resigning or being overthrown. Democratic revolutions thus inspired a whole cycle of struggle in 1989—just as we witnessed in the North African Arab uprisings and Middle East in 2011.

---

7. To be sure, there were organized opposition movements to the Soviet regimes within the Eastern Central Europe Soviet bloc countries and within the Soviet Union itself for decades. These oppositional movements had long been producing critiques of the regime, sometimes clandestinely circulated, and had organized opposition to the Soviet system. On the other hand, certainly the cascading collapse of one communist regime after another, seen throughout Europe and the communist bloc on television, and discussed on radio, in newspapers, and via other media, helped mobilize massive crowds that led to the overthrow of the communist regimes. For a first-person witness of these events, see the narrative and concise analysis by Timothy Garton Ash, *The Magic Lantern: The Revolution of '89 Witnessed in Warsaw, Budapest, Berlin, and Prague* (New York: Random House, 1990), republished with a new afterword in 1999. Garton Ash describes, among other themes, the role of the media in making images of the oppositional movements visible to various publics and the struggle for media access by the oppositional movements. In a key summary judgment, Garton Ash writes, "In Europe at the end of the twentieth century all revolutions are telerevolutions." Timothy Garton Ash, *The Magic Lantern: The Revolution of '89 Witnessed in Warsaw, Budapest, Berlin, and Prague* (New York: Vintage, 1999), 94. About the Prague Velvet Revolution, Garton Ash writes that "television is now clearly opening up to report the revolution," signaling that Václav Havel and the oppositional movement had won the revolution. Garton Ash, *The Magic Lantern* (1999), 101.

8. Francis Fukuyama famously argued that the collapse of Soviet communism by the 1990s marked the triumph of Western ideas of freedom and democracy and thus the end of major political conflicts; see Francis Fukuyama, *The End of History and the Last Man* (New York: Free Press, 1992). With the 9/11 terror attacks on the United States and the resulting era of Terror War, Fukuyama's ideas were widely discredited. See Douglas Kellner, *From September 11 to Terror War: The Dangers of the Bush Legacy* (Lanham, MD: Rowman and Littlefield, 2003). To some extent, though, the Ideas of Freedom and Democracy are indeed part of the struggle in the North African Arab Uprisings, which revealed that many more enemies of a free society had to be eliminated before one could seriously argue that we had entered the realm of freedom dreamed of by liberals and by Karl Marx and Herbert Marcuse.

Such events are complex and overdetermined, and media spectacle alone is but one factor in the complex matrix of history; nonetheless, media spectacle is certainly a significant factor, even an increasingly important factor, as media spectacles proliferate globally through new media and social networking. Indeed, broadcasting and new media have become ubiquitous throughout the Middle East, as part of a new global media ecology.[9] In my book *Media Spectacle and Insurrection, 2011,* I discuss the role of Al Jazeera, new media and social networking, and media spectacle in the Arab Awakening and uprisings during the Arab Spring of 2011, but I am also concerned with providing contextual and multicausal analysis of these events, beginning with Tunisia and then turning to Egypt and Libya.[10] While my argument is that media spectacle is the form in which the Arab Awakening and uprising have circulated throughout North Africa and the Middle East, media spectacle itself is not the cause of the cascading insurrections, and each country needs to be addressed in terms of its own history, society, culture, and political regimes in order to provide contextual and multicausal analysis of the Arab uprisings and use multiple political discourses to describe the complexity of the events.

Impressively, the people of Egypt and Tunisia overthrew corrupt dictators and, through nonviolent demonstrations, expressed their will for change and yearnings for democracy, freedom, social justice, and dignity. As Žižek argues, the Egyptian (and arguably Tunisian) revolutions were secular, with demonstrators combining calls for democracy and freedom with demands for social justice.[11] The uprisings echoed the "people power" movements of the 1960s and exemplified the model of the "multitude" seizing power developed by Hardt and Negri. As they argue in a widely circulated article on the Arab uprisings:

One challenge facing observers of the uprisings spreading across North Africa and the Middle East is to read them as not so many repetitions of the past but as original experiments that open new political possibilities, relevant well beyond the region, for freedom and

9. For more on the new media ecology that the Internet and other new technologies have produced, see Mark Poster, *The Second Media Age* (Cambridge, MA: Blackwell, 1995); and Richard Kahn and Douglas Kellner, "Technopolitics, Blogs, and Emergent Media Ecologies: A Critical/Reconstructive Approach," in *Small Tech: The Culture of Digital Tools,* ed. Byron Hawk, David M. Rider, and Ollie Oviedo (Minneapolis: University of Minnesota Press, 2008), 22–37.

10. Kellner, *Media Spectacle and Insurrection, 2011.*

11. Slavoj Žižek, "For Egypt, This Is the Miracle of Tahrir Square," *The Guardian,* February 10, 2011, available at http://www.guardian.co.uk/global/2011/feb/10/egypt-miracle-tahrir-square/. See also Olivier Roy, "This Is Not an Islamic Revolution," *New Statesman,* February 15, 2011, available at http://www.newstatesman.com/religion/2011/02/egypt-arab-tunisia-islamic.

democracy. Indeed, our hope is that through this cycle of struggles the Arab world becomes for the next decade what Latin America was for the last—that is, a laboratory of political experimentation between powerful social movements and progressive governments from Argentina to Venezuela, and from Brazil to Bolivia.[12]

Hardt and Negri do not mention here the role of charismatic Latin American leaders with political parties who galvanized social movements to win state power in democratic elections. In his documentary film *South of the Border*, Oliver Stone focuses on several such figures who led movements to produce Left and center-left regimes.[13] While Stone arguably exaggerates the role of the charismatic Latin American leaders that he interviews in his film and downplays the role of social movements, it is likely that the Latin American Left evolved a progressive agenda because of a combination of charismatic leaders and progressive political parties aligned with social movements.

The Latin American insurrections have been described by Hardt and Negri and their followers in terms of revolutionary desires articulated in nonhierarchical, rhizomatic networks without central authority or leadership. Žižek, by contrast, calls for strong political movements with a specific program and goals, claiming that the self-organization of protest movements "is clearly not enough to impose a reorganisation of social life. To do that, one needs a strong body able to reach quick decisions and to implement them with all necessary harshness."[14] The question thus emerges from the Egyptian and Tunisian insurrections whether movements and masses without charismatic leaders and progressive parties can construct a genuinely democratic society, without producing oppressive institutions and violence. Their challenge is also to generate political leaders and groups who nurture democratic institutions and social relations without developing oppressive modes of power and reverting to old modes of authoritarian governance.[15]

In mediating between Hardt and Negri, who describe the political insurrections of 2011 in terms of networks of revolutionary desire and political

---

12. Michael Hardt and Antonio Negri, "Arabs Are Democracy's New Pioneers," *The Guardian*, February 24, 2011, available at http://www.guardian.co.uk/commentisfree/2011/feb/24/arabs-democracy-latin-america.

13. *South of the Border*, directed by Oliver Stone (Burbank, CA: Cinema Libre Studio, 2009).

14. Slavoj Žižek, "Shoplifters of the World Unite," *London Review of Books*, August 19, 2011, available at http://www.lrb.co.uk/2011/08/19/slavoj-zizek/shoplifters-of-the-world-unite.

15. The Occupy movements present other examples of leaderless movements, perhaps a defining feature of the uprisings of 2011 in the time of the spectacle, when anyone can participate and create—as they choose—their own parts in the spectacle and in the movement.

experiment, and Žižek, who calls for strong political organization and revolutionary political strategy, we might reflect on the use of Marcuse's concept of revolution and the Great Refusal in the contemporary moment. Like
Gilles Deleuze and Félix Guattari, and Hardt and Negri, Marcuse points to
the role of revolutionary desire and the body in motivating political insurrection but equally insists on the cultivation of critical subjectivity and critical theory to intelligently merge theory with practice. In addition, Marcuse
theorizes the destructive instincts, described in Sigmund Freud's concept of
Thanatos, that threaten that an unleashed subjectivity engaged in passionate
political insurrection can generate violence and destruction, a danger that a
critical political subjectivity needs to be constantly vigilant toward; Marcuse
argues for channeling destructive instincts into liberating actions and goals.

Marcuse's concept of the Great Refusal also provides an illuminating
perspective from which to view the insurrections of 2011 and the radical
struggles of the twenty-first century. In 1964, Marcuse perceived only a
slight chance that the most exploited and persecuted outsiders, in alliance
with an enlightened intelligentsia, might mark "the beginning of the end"
and signify some hope for social change:

> However, underneath the conservative popular base is the substra-
> tum of the outcasts and outsiders, the exploited and persecuted of
> other races and other colors, the unemployed and the unemploy-
> able. They exist outside the democratic process; their life is the most
> immediate and the most real need for ending intolerable conditions
> and institutions. Thus their opposition is revolutionary even if their
> consciousness is not. Their opposition hits the system from without
> and is therefore not deflected by the system; it is an elementary force,
> which violates the rules of the game and, in doing so, reveals it as
> a rigged game. When they get together and go out into the streets,
> without arms, without protection, in order to ask for the most primi-
> tive civil rights, they know that they face dogs, stones and bombs,
> jail, concentration camps, even death. Their force is behind every
> political demonstration for the victims of law and order. The fact that
> they start refusing to play the game may be the fact which marks the
> beginning of the end of a period.[16]

Marcuse's concept of revolution as a totality of upheaval is relevant to
the insurrections of 2011, with revolution conceptualized as a rupture with
and overthrow of the previous social order and development of new forms
of social relations in all spheres of life. For Marcuse, revolution involves a

---

16. Herbert Marcuse, *One-Dimensional Man: Studies in the Ideology of Advanced Industrial Society* (Boston: Beacon, 1964), 256–257.

decisive break with the previous regime and construction of an entirely different emancipated society with nonoppressive social relations and a new economy, polity, social institutions, culture, and subjectivities. Marcuse's concepts of revolution and the Great Refusal are useful in interpreting the insurrections of the contemporary era as they provide normative visions of a goal of total social transformation, aiming at social justice and emancipation. Hence, whereas the Arab uprisings can be seen as manifestations of the Great Refusal on a massive regional scale, it is unlikely that they will produce revolutions such as those that Marcuse envisaged.

Likewise, the Occupy movements of 2011 exemplify the Great Refusal but, in hindsight, do not constitute revolutions. In the next section, I discuss how the Occupy movements of 2011 embody key ideas of Hardt and Negri, Marcuse, and Debord and the Situationist International, but I argue as well that new political movements need new discourses and politics and that the Occupy movements provide anticipations of a new revolutionary political discourse and practice.

From Occupy Wall Street to Occupy Everywhere

We are the 99 percent.
—OCCUPY WALL STREET SLOGAN

In September 2011, the Occupy Wall Street movement emerged in New York as a variety of people began protesting the economic system in the United States, corruption on Wall Street, and a diverse range of other issues. The Occupy Wall Street project was proposed by *Adbusters* magazine on July 13, 2011, and on August 9, Occupy Wall Street supporters in New York held a meeting for "We, the 99%." On September 8, the *We are the 99 Percent* Tumblr was launched, and on September 17, Occupy Wall Street protesters began camping out and demonstrating at Zuccotti Park in downtown New York close to Wall Street, setting up a tent city that would be the epicenter of the Occupy movement for many months. Using social media, more and more people joined the demonstrations, which received widespread media attention when police attacked peaceful demonstrators, yielding pictures of young women being sprayed with pepper gas by police. Mainstream media attention and mobilizing through social media brought more people to demonstrate, and by the first weekend in October, there was a massive protest in lower Manhattan, with a march across the Brooklyn Bridge that blocked traffic and led to more than seven hundred arrests.

The idea caught on, as similar Occupy demonstrations soon broke out in San Francisco, Los Angeles, Chicago, Boston, Denver, Philadelphia, Washington, D.C., and several other cities. On October 5, in New York, major unions joined the protest in New York, and thousands marched from Foley

Square to the OccupyWallStreet encampment in Zuccotti Park. Celebrities, students and professors, and ordinary citizens joined the protest in support, and daily coverage of the movement was appearing in U.S. and global media.

As it has come to own all major political stories of 2011, the *Guardian* (the British national daily newspaper) was initially the place to go for coverage of Occupy Wall Street in the global media, with a live blog documenting news and actions related to the movement as well as a webpage collecting key stories and links to other stories.[17] As the Occupy movement came to London, the *Guardian* focused special attention on the local occupation, which involved dramatic clashes with the city of London when occupiers demonstrated and set up a camp outside the venerable St. Paul's Cathedral. Debates within the Church of England regarding how to deal with the occupation led a high-ranking official to resign.[18]

In the United States, police violence against the movement appeared to intensify support for Occupy Wall Street, and on October 5 Al Jazeera broadcast footage from demonstrators who recorded police beating up other demonstrators. This called attention to the fact that the participants were using media to organize, to document violence against them, and to circulate their message globally. Occupy Wall Street was traversing the globe as the major media spectacle of the moment.

During the weekend of October 8 and 9, large crowds gathered in Occupy sites throughout the country, and it appeared that new protest movements had emerged in the United States that articulated with the global struggles of 2011. Like the movements in the Arab uprising, the Occupy movements were using new media and social networking to organize their movement and specific actions, as well as to document police and government assaults on the movement—documentation used to recruit more members and to intensify the commitment and resolve of its participants.

Occupy Wall Street was focused against financial capitalism and the corruption of the political class in the United States, just as the 1990s anticorporate global capitalism movement focused on the World Trade Organization, World Bank, International Monetary Fund, and other instruments of global capital. In Greece, Spain, and Italy, people demonstrated against these same institutions of global capitalism, as well as against their own national governments. Like the Arab uprisings, Occupy Wall Street and other anticorporate movements were outside the domain of old-fashioned party

---

17. See the "Occupy Wall Street" page at http://www.guardian.co.uk/world/occupy-wall-street.

18. Stephen Bates, "Church of England Split over St. Paul's Handling of Occupy London Protest," *The Guardian*, October 27, 2011, available at http://www.theguardian.com/uk/2011/oct/27/church-st-pauls-occupy-london.

politics, as they embraced diversity and tended to be leaderless. After meeting with Egyptian and other militants, some members of Occupy Wall Street indicated that they were going to search for specific issues that could lead to particular actions, but no specific demands were made to define the movement as a whole, although specific actions were undertaken by some Occupy encampments.

The movement produced a great diversity of slogans, including humorous ones like "We demand sweeping, unspecified change!" and "One day the poor will have nothing to eat but the rich," as well as those such as "We are the 99 percent" and "Banks got bailed out; we got sold out," which, as critiques of economic inequality and greed, became characteristic of the movement. Momentum continued, the protests spread globally, and by mid-October there were more than one thousand Occupy sites in more than eighty countries. Activism in these movements was taking place simultaneously online and in the streets, and activists circulated information, planned events, and mobilized for action. Indeed, by mid-October, there were more than 1.2 million followers of the hundreds of Occupy Wall Street Facebook pages; during the global protests on October 15–16, 2011, the overall volume of Twitter doubled, as an analysis from Trendrr indicated.[19]

Interestingly, many of the tactics and goals of the Occupy movement— creating situations, demonstrating outside organized party or movement structures, and using slogans and art of different forms to raise consciousness and inspire revolutionary movements—replicated the politics and vision of Guy Debord and the Situationist International.[20] With eruptions of struggle, police and establishment brutality, and renewed protest and actions, 2011 was looking more and more like 1968. Yet new media and social

---

19. See Jennifer Preston, "Occupy Wall Street, and Its Global Chat," *New York Times*, October 17, 2011, available at http://query.nytimes.com/gst/fullpage.html?res=9F05E3D612 38F934A25753C1A9679D8B63.

20. First published in 1967 in France, Guy Debord's *The Society of the Spectacle* was published in translation in a pirate edition by Black and Red (Detroit, Michigan) in 1970; another edition appeared in 1983 and a new translation in 1994. The key texts of the Situationists and many interesting commentaries are found on various websites, producing a curious afterlife for Situationist ideas and practices. For further discussion of Debord and the Situationists, see Steven Best and Douglas Kellner, "From the Society of the Spectacle to the Realm of Simulation: Debord, Baudrillard, and Postmodernity," in *The Postmodern Turn* (New York: Guilford, 1997), chap. 3. For more on Debord's life and work, see also Vincent Kaufmann, *Guy Debord: Revolution in the Service of Poetry* (Minneapolis: University of Minnesota Press, 2006). For information on the complex and highly contested reception and effects of Guy Debord and the Situationist International, see Greil Marcus, *Lipstick Traces: A Secret History of the Twentieth Century* (Cambridge, MA: Harvard University Press, 1989); Tom McDonough, ed., *Guy Debord and the Situationist International* (Cambridge, MA: MIT Press, 2002); and McKenzie Wark, *50 Years of Recuperation of the Situationist International* (New York: Temple Hoyne Buell Center for the Study of American Architecture/Princeton Architectural Press, 2008).

networking created new terrains of struggle. In using new media and social networking, the Occupy movements had the same decentralized structure as the computer networks they were using, and the movement as a whole had a virtual dimension as well as people organized in specific spaces. Thus, even if people were not occupying the spaces where the organizing and living were taking place, they could participate virtually and mobilize to participate in specific actions. The Occupy movement also embodied the Great Refusal in its demands to break with politics of the past and generate new revolutionary politics and forms of struggle. Moreover, while the right-wing Tea Party movement, which had helped the Republicans win Congress in 2010 and block all progressive and even mildly ameliorative initiatives, were hierarchical and top-down, the Occupy movements were genuinely bottom-up. The Occupy movement exemplified Deweyan strong democracy and was highly participatory and experimental in its ideas, tactics, and strategies. While the Tea Party was financed by rich right-wing Republicans, like the Koch brothers, and had a national television network in Fox News to promote their goals and fortify their troops, the Occupy movements produced their own media, including their own websites, news media, videos, and live streams that broadcast live action taking place at Occupy sites.[21]

As Michael Greenberg points out, by the middle of October, polls indicated that more than half of Americans polled had a positive view of the movement. By mid-October, according to a Brookings Institution report of the Time/ABT SRBI survey, 54 percent of Americans held a favorable view of the protest.[22] Suddenly, or so it seemed, there was less talk of budget cuts that would limit, if not dismantle, social insurance programs such as Medicare while extending Bush's tax cuts and more talk about how to deal with economic inequality.

Several events pointed to an altered political climate. In New York, Governor Andrew Cuomo partially reversed his opposition to extending the so-called millionaire's tax, pushing through legislation for a higher tax rate for the wealthiest New Yorkers. Bank of America, Wells Fargo, and JPMorgan Chase abandoned plans to charge a monthly fee to use their debit cards after an outpouring of indignation from customers—a minor event in the larger picture but indicative of the public's rapidly shifting mood. More significantly, in Ohio, 61 percent of voters rejected a referendum favored by Repub-

---

21. See, e.g., the Occupy Solidarity Network's *Occupy Wall Street* site, at http://occupy wallst.org, and "Occupy Wall St NYC," *Livestream*, available at http://www.livestream.com/ occupywallstnyc (accessed January 3, 2012).

22. Michael Greenberg, "What Future for Occupy Wall Street?," *New York Review of Books*, February 9, 2012, available at http://www.nybooks.com/articles/archives/2012/feb/09/ what-future-occupy-wall-street; Elisabeth Jacobs, "Not So Demanding: Why Occupy Wall Street Need Not Make Demands (Yet)," Brookings Institution, November 3, 2011, available at http://www.brookings.edu/research/papers/2011/11/03-ows-jacobs.

lican governor John Kasich that would have severely restricted the collective bargaining rights of 360,000 public employees. In Osawatomie, Kansas, on December 6, President Obama gave a speech that echoed almost verbatim what I had been hearing from protesters in Zuccotti Park: he deplored "the breathtaking greed of a few" and called the aim to "restore fairness" the "defining issue of our time."[23]

By the end of October, establishment violence against the Occupy movements intensified, and on October 25, police brutality was used to forcefully remove Occupy Oakland militants, causing a concussion and hospitalization of Scott Olsen, a young Iraq war veteran. Olsen became a cause célèbre, and the Oakland movement organized a general strike on November 2 that closed down much of the inner city and first slowed and then shut down the Port of Oakland, the country's fifth biggest, as thousands of marchers descended on the port. The same day in New York, demonstrators ascended on the Lehman Brothers building, where George W. Bush was allegedly meeting, shouting, "Arrest George Bush" and calling for a citizen's arrest, which apparently kept Bush imprisoned in the building until he was spirited out in a limousine after the demonstrators left for other destinations. Henceforth, through social media, demonstrators could be assembled into flash mobs that could occupy any site at a moment's notice and submit corrupt businessmen, politicians, and others to the wrath of the people.

The Occupy movements had generated a new political discourse that focused on economic inequalities, greed and the corruption of Wall Street and financial institutions, and the need for people to organize and demonstrate to force government to meet their needs. As evidence that the Occupy movements presented a threat to the established system of power, in November 2011, police and city governments closed down some of the biggest Occupy encampments, sometimes violently. In the face of this repression, people continued to rally to the cause of the movement, and demonstrations, occupations, and actions continued through the year. The brutality used in closing down the Occupy Wall Street site in Zuccotti Park in December presented the frightening image of a fascist police state. Pictures surfaced of police beating up demonstrators, tearing apart and bulldozing their campsites, and throwing their possessions, including the Occupy Wall Street library that had collected more than five thousand books, into garbage trucks.

One of the main features of the Occupy movements was the use of media to document Occupy as well as the actions of police. The spectacle of police throughout the United States brutally tearing down Occupy camps made the United States look like the thug regimes overthrown in the Arab uprisings. The accumulated documentation of brutal police power provided material to radicalize new members and harden the resolve of experienced activists,

---

23. Greenberg, "What Future for Occupy Wall Street?"

which made possible a continuation of radical Occupy movements into the future.

After the political establishment shut down some of the major Occupy sites, including Occupy Wall Street in New York, members began taking specific actions, transforming public spaces into "temporary autonomous zones" occupied temporarily by flash mobs of protestors. As Michael Greenberg indicates:

> On December 1, for instance, protesters gathered in front of Lincoln Center to await the end of the final performance of Philip Glass's opera *Satyagraha*, about the life of Gandhi. The idea was to dramatize their affinity with Gandhi's method of nonviolent resistance. The following day, occupiers launched twenty-four hours of dance, "radical theater," and "creative resistance" near Times Square meant "to educate tourists and theater-goers about OWS [Occupy Wall Street]" and to demonstrate "a more colorful image of what our streets could look like." December 6 was the day to "reclaim" selected bank-owned vacant homes in poor neighborhoods, reinstalling a handful of willing families that had been foreclosed upon and evicted. On December 12 there was a march on Goldman Sachs's offices in Manhattan. On December 16 there was a rally at Fort Meade in Maryland where Private Bradley Manning, a hero to the movement, was standing trial for allegedly releasing classified government documents to WikiLeaks. The next day, more rallies were scheduled in New York and elsewhere, this time for immigrants' rights. And so on.[24]

On December 16, the three-month anniversary of the beginning of the Occupy Wall Street movement, happened to correspond to the first anniversary of the death of the vegetable vendor Mohamed Bouazizi in Tunisia, who had set himself on fire and burned to death in protest, a media spectacle that was frequently taken as the spark that ignited the Arab uprisings. As I argue above, the Occupy Wall Street and Occupy Everywhere movements were inspired by the Arab Spring, creating an American autumn and winter that guaranteed that 2011 would long be remembered in history books and popular memory as a time in which media spectacle took the forms of political resistance and insurrection.

As 2012 began to unfold, Occupy movements continued to undertake actions throughout the United States and the globe, and the movement morphed from being primarily located in tent cities and occupations of specific sites to groups focused on particular actions. The movement's base

---

24. Ibid.

expanded to include individuals who had not participated in the first wave of occupations and to make coalitions with various groups for targeted actions.

Occupy groups in the United States also began focusing on politicians, heckling candidates for the Republican presidential nomination in the primaries, which began in earnest in early 2012. Those affiliated with the Occupy movement demonstrated against various and sundry politicians of both parties and carried out protest actions at various politicians' offices in Washington or locally. How the Occupy movements would participate in the 2012 presidential election was of interest to both parties as well as those participating in or sympathizing with the movement. Indeed, it was the very nature of the multiplicity and complexity of the Occupy movements that they could not fit into standard political models and were thus spontaneous and unpredictable in nature.

The Occupy groups and their allies could point to specific victories in early 2012, to which their movements had partially contributed. On January 18, 2012, major Internet industry websites went black in a day of protest against two proposed congressional bills, the Stop Online Piracy Act (SOPA) and the Preventing Real Online Threats to Economic Creativity and Theft of Intellectual Property Act (PIPA), which, opponents claimed, could lead to online censorship and force some websites out of business. By midday, Google officials asserted that 4.5 million people had signed its petition against SOPA,[25] while Wikipedia claimed that 5.5 million people had accessed the site and clicked on a link that would put them in touch with local legislators to register their opposition to the legislation. Evidently, the action had an impact, as politicians who had been in favor of the bill suddenly indicated opposition to it, and the bill's sponsors withdrew it for further consideration. In other developments, on January 18, 2012, the Obama administration announced it would temporarily deny a permit for the building of the highly toxic Keystone XL pipeline, which would have transported extremely dirty oil from a vast oil deposit in Alberta, Canada, to refineries on the Texas Gulf Coast.[26] And on the same day, activists were celebrating

---

25. A variety of online petitions against SOPA were launched, including the ACLU's "Sign the Pledge: I Stand with the ACLU in Fighting SOPA," previously available at https://secure.aclu.org/site/SPageServer?pagename=sem_sopa&s_subsrc=SEM_Google_Search -SOPA_SOPA_sopa%20bill_p_10385864662 (accessed February 9, 2012), and Broadband for America's "Hands Off the Internet," available at http://www.broadbandforamerica.com/handsofftheinternet?gclid=COqHzpuska4CFQN8hwod0GBVew. The Edward Snowden revelations of intense government spying on U.S. citizens and allies, as well as on stated enemies, in 2014 renewed and intensified debates over individual privacy.

26. Multiple websites devoted to blocking the construction of the Keystone XL pipeline were created by environmental organizations, such as the Natural Resources Defense Council and 350.org. See, for example, 350.org's "Stop the Keystone XL Pipeline," at http://350.org/campaigns/stop-keystone-xl/. Major demonstrations were held in opposition to the highly contested pipeline. On November 6, 2015, the project of Keystone XL was rejected by the

in Wisconsin, having received more than one million signatures on petitions for a recall election to potentially unseat Governor Scott Walker, who
was financed with ultra-right-wing Tea Party movement money and had
attacked union bargaining rights in a highly publicized affair that led union
workers, students, activists, and their supporters to occupy the Wisconsin
state capitol in Madison in protest in May 2011.[27]

In summary, new politics and subjectivities emerged from specific sites
of the Occupy movement, which are both local and global in inspiration,
leading to a new era of global, national, and local political struggle with un-
foreseeable outcomes in an era in which insurrections are emerging in the
form of media spectacle. These movements were inspired and connected in
certain ways with the North African Arab uprisings that began an intense
year of struggle throughout the world in 2011, which unleashed turmoil in
the region that is still ongoing, with uncertain results. History and the future
are open and depend on the will, imagination, and resolve of the people to
create their own lives and societies rather than being passive objects of their
masters. Media spectacle is a contested terrain on which the key political
struggles of the day are fought, and 2011 was a year rich in examples of media spectacles as insurrections and Great Refusals on a global scale.

Obama administration after more than six years of review. Gregory Korte and David Jackson, "Obama Administration Rejects Keystone Pipeline," *USA Today*, November 6, 2015,
available at http://www.usatoday.com/story/news/politics/2015/11/06/obama-reject-keystone
-pipeline/75293270/.

27. There were many websites devoted to recalling Scott Walker, including one set up
by United Wisconsin. See Mary Bottari, "One Million Petition for the Recall of Wisconsin
Governor Scott Walker," *PR Watch*, January 17, 2012, available at http://www.prwatch.org/
news/2012/01/11246/one-million-petition-recall-wisconsin-governor-scott-walker. Walker
was not unseated in the recall, so he remained governor of the state and also became, for
a brief time in 2015, a Republican Party candidate in the 2016 U.S. presidential election
campaign.

13

Beyond One-Dimensionality

ANDREW FEENBERG

erbert Marcuse was uniquely able to join the tradition of the Frankfurt School to the political movements of his time. He recognized the oppositional potential of these movements and interpreted them both critically and generously. In recent years, as radical movements have reemerged after a long hiatus, there has been a revival of interest in Marcuse's thought. He formulated a philosophical critique of the dystopian capitalism of our time while holding open the possibility of resistance and imagining a free society. His relevance is proven by the fact that his key ideas appear unacknowledged in the writings of many contemporary social critics. But one of his most important contributions, his conception of a new technology of liberation, has failed to strike a chord. In this chapter, I explain this contribution and show how it can be extended to inform our understanding of contemporary movements that contest the technical arrangements underlying our society.

Marcuse's critique of technology has several sources. Like Max Horkheimer and Theodor Adorno, he interprets the modern "dialectic of enlightenment" politically. He distinguishes premodern "substantive" rationality, encompassing both means and ends, from the purely instrumental rationality of modern technological society. The incorporation of human beings into the technical system as deskilled producers and passive consumers suppresses resistance to social injustice and thus perpetuates a competitive and destructive social order. Common sense itself is corrupted as adjustment to the facts of life becomes conformity to the exploitative system that establishes those facts. The system not only prevails in the reified organization of society but is lived by the individuals as the necessary form of their own experience.[1]

György Lukács's early Marxist theory lies in the background of this Frankfurt School approach. In *History and Class Consciousness*, Lukács is sensitive to the dystopian threat of modernity, which he describes with the concept of reification, the transformation of human relations into law-governed, thing-like institutions and processes subject to technical manipulation.[2] But Lukács is not resigned to the triumph of a purely instrumental social logic; nor does he project an apocalyptic transcendence. Instead, he describes an immanent dialectic between reification and dereification, between capitalist forms and the resistant lives they organize but fail completely to contain. This dialectic would lead to a socialist revolution in which the reified rigidity of the institutions would be softened to allow a fluid interaction between social forms and human content.

Marcuse repeats this dualistic figure: reification versus dereification; law-governed, technically mediated institutions versus life; form versus content. The basic question, then, is how to conceive of the interaction between these antinomial opposites rather than forcing an impossible choice between them that would lead to either dystopia or regression behind the level of emancipation achieved by modernity.

Early in his career, Marcuse was also a student of Martin Heidegger, with whom he remained in a tacit critical relationship until at least *One-Dimensional Man*.[3] Heidegger's influence is present in Marcuse's interpretation of Greek philosophy and the concept of technological rationality. The latter influence converges with themes also present in the early Marxist work of Lukács. These themes are as follows:

---

1. Max Horkheimer, *Eclipse of Reason* (New York: Seabury, 1947). See also Theodor W. Adorno and Max Horkheimer, *Dialectic of Enlightenment*, trans. John Cumming (New York: Herder and Herder, 1972), which was originally published as *Philosophische Fragmente* (New York: Social Studies Association, 1944) and then revised as *Dialektik der Aufklärung* (Amsterdam: Querido Verlag, 1947). For a more recent translation, see Theodor W. Adorno and Max Horkheimer, *Dialectic of Enlightenment*, ed. Gunzelin Schmid Noerr, trans. Edmund Jephcott (Stanford, CA: Stanford University Press, 2002).

2. György Lukács, *History and Class Consciousness: Studies in Marxist Dialectics*, trans. Rodney Livingstone (Cambridge, MA: MIT Press, 1971). This book was originally published in 1923 as *Geschichte und Klassenbewußtsein: Studien über marxistische Dialektik*.

3. Herbert Marcuse, *One-Dimensional Man: Studies in the Ideology of Advanced Industrial Society* (Boston: Beacon, 1964). For more on Marcuse and Heidegger, see Herbert Marcuse, *Heideggerian Marxism*, ed. Richard Wolin and John Abromeit (Lincoln: University of Nebraska Press, 2005); Andrew Feenberg, *Heidegger and Marcuse: The Catastrophe and Redemption of History* (New York: Routledge, 2005); and Frederick Olafson, "Heidegger's Politics: An Interview with Herbert Marcuse," in *Marcuse: Critical Theory and the Promise of Utopia*, ed. Robert B. Pippin, Andrew Feenberg, and Charles Webel (South Hadley, MA: Bergin and Garvey, 1988), 95–104.

1. The emergence of scientific-technical rationality as a dominant cultural framework
2. The differentiation of this formalistic paradigm of rationality from meanings and values circulating in the lifeworld
3. The consequent loss of understanding of significant aspects of the world
4. The potential for catastrophe implicit in this limitation of the dominant culture to technical manipulation

In this chapter, I focus primarily on the relationship between Marcuse and Heidegger. I conclude by showing how Marcuse drew on Heidegger to formulate the utopian aspect of his theory of technology.

The Concept of Essence

The key common element in Heidegger's and Marcuse's critiques of modern technology is the eclipse of an earlier technical relation to reality, Greek *technē*. According to Heidegger, Aristotle's concept of essence is an ontological interpretation of the guiding knowledge associated with craft production. In *Being and Time*, this notion forms the background to the theory of worldhood.[4] In "The Question Concerning Technology," Aristotle's four causes are invoked to explain *technē* as a form of instrumentality different from modern technology.[5]

Marcuse followed Heidegger's Aristotle interpretation, not only in his early work but in *One-Dimensional Man* as well. But Marcuse shifted the emphasis toward one aspect of that interpretation, the normative aspect. He explained the concept of essence in terms of potentiality. Essences are the highest realization of what appears imperfectly in the world. Thus essences are, in some sense, ideals, but they are not, for that matter, merely subjective. Essences are *dynamis*, force or tendencies in the things themselves. Greek *technē* brings forth such preexisting essences and allows them to manifest themselves. This contrasts with modern technology, which operates without a notion of essential potentialities and instead imposes subjectively elaborated plans on a reality reduced to bare raw materials.

Modern thought dismisses the essences of antiquity as dogmatic obstacles to the free exercise of human powers. The rejection of the idea of essence is reflected in the methodology of the sciences and eventually of all

---

4. Martin Heidegger, *Being and Time*, trans. John Macquarrie and Edward Robinson (New York: Harper and Row, 1962); see especially "The Worldhood of the World," div. 1, pt. 3. The book was first published as *Sein und Zeit* in 1927.

5. Martin Heidegger, "The Question Concerning Technology," in *The Question Concerning Technology and Other Essays*, trans. William Lovitt (New York: Harper and Row, 1977), 3–35.

the academic and technical disciplines. Reality is analyzed exclusively under those empirical aspects that expose it to calculation and control. Once essence is expelled from science, nature is revealed as an object of technology and, along with nature, human beings, too, are incorporated into a smoothly functioning social machine. This is the basis of Marcuse's critique of what he calls "technological rationality," a form of rationality that grasps its objects on purely functional terms without presupposing any goal except its own application and extension.

In *One-Dimensional Man*, Marcuse argues that such "value-neutral" functionalism is uniquely compatible with capitalism.

> Theoretical reason, remaining pure and neutral, entered into the service of practical reason. The merger proved beneficial to both. Today, domination perpetuates and extends itself not only through technology but *as* technology, and the latter provides the great legitimation of the expanding political power, which absorbs all spheres of culture.
>
> This interpretation would tie the scientific project (method and theory), *prior* to all application and utilization, to a specific societal project, and would see the tie precisely in the inner form of scientific rationality. . . .
>
> It is precisely its neutral character which relates objectivity to a specific historical Subject—namely, to the consciousness that prevails in the society.[6]

Technological rationality only appears as "pure reason" when artificially separated from its social context. Considered in that context, science and technology are inherently biased precisely by their indifference to values. Neutrality is just the reverse side of control of objects, indifferent to their own inherent potentialities.

Traditional forms of knowledge are too closely integrated to the very lifeworld that capitalism must destroy in the course of its advance. They condense cognitive and valuative dimensions, function and meaning, in ways that block technological rationalization—for example, by limiting the exploitation of labor and the natural environment. Capitalism systematically reduces the role of cultural norms and politics in determining ends. Actions associated with artistic production, craft, the care of human beings, and the cultivation of nature aim only to realize the potentialities of their objects. They do not offer the prospect of full control, so they are dismissed as irrational and inefficient. Value neutrality overthrows all restraints on power:

---

6. Marcuse, *One-Dimensional Man*, 158, 159, 156 (emphasis in original).

essences no longer stand in the way, dictating right and wrong courses of action. Technology can be adapted to the ruthless pursuit of domination.

In this sense, the link between ends and means has never really been broken. Modern knowledge is both neutral and biased, breaking the chains of tradition only to enter the prison house of power. Heidegger seems to have willingly entered that prison house, believing that Nazism was the new *technē* rather than just another political technology, but this was a grave error of judgment, as he may have realized later. He then retreated to the hope in a "free relationship" to technology that would leave actual technology untouched and merely change the prevailing attitude toward it.[7]

Marcuse's program is more radical. Rejecting both modern empiricism and the traditional notion of essence, he calls for rejoining imagination and reason in the creation of a new technological base. Tradition cannot guide this development, and Marcuse does not suggest that we abandon modern science despite his critique of its cultural impact. The cognitive achievements made possible by the destruction of the traditional concept of essence are undeniable, but so is the danger of spiritual and material extermination represented by a technology unrestrained by any limits.

Instead of these conventional responses to the crisis, Marcuse argues for a reform of science and technology based on the emergence of an "aesthetic *Lebenswelt*," a new structure of experience encompassing aesthetic criteria.[8] Aestheticized perception would embrace functional aspects of objects in the larger framework of their essence, the second dimension. This is not the ancient concept of essence but rather the Hegelian concept, understood as the potentialities that emerge from the tensions in the objects' inner structure and connections. This concept was historicized by Marx and underlies his conception of socialism as the determinate negation of capitalism. But the proletariat no longer plays the role of historical agent that Marx assigned it. Today, these potentialities appear in artistic and political experience. Marcuse argues that the New Left offered an example of such a recovery of the critical force of experience.

Experience informed by the imagination and no longer dulled by conformity to the established "facts of life" gives access to "existential truths" that reflect intrinsic potentialities of things.[9] This mode of experience responds to norms of peace, harmony, and flourishing that have been preserved and developed by philosophy and art throughout history, even as the repressive structure of class society prevented their realization in reality. According to Marcuse, advanced societies are so rich and their technologies so powerful

---

7. Heidegger, "The Question Concerning Technology," 3.

8. Herbert Marcuse, *An Essay on Liberation* (Boston: Beacon, 1969), 31, 45.

9. Herbert Marcuse, "Nature and Revolution," in *Counterrevolution and Revolt* (Boston: Beacon, 1972), 69.

that they can at last realize the potentialities revealed in these experiences. Although the popular struggles of the New Left were weaker than the earlier proletarian movement, they held a radical promise of reconciling technology with meaning. Marcuse extrapolates this tendency into a socialist future in which technological rationality would incorporate values once again, but in a modern way; that is, on the basis of imaginative reflection on experience.

> Only if the vast capabilities of science and technology, of the scientific and artistic imagination direct the construction of a sensuous environment, only if the work world loses its alienating features and becomes a world of human relationships, only if productivity becomes creativity, are the roots of domination dried up in the individuals. No return to precapitalist, pre-industrial artisanship, but on the contrary, perfection of the new mutilated and distorted science and technology in the formation of the object world in accordance with "the laws of beauty." And "beauty" here defines an ontological condition—not of an *oeuvre d'art* isolated from real existence . . . but that harmony between man and his world which would shape the form of society.[10]

This would be the equivalent of the creation of a modern form of *technē*, and, in fact, Marcuse argues that the link between art and craft in antiquity can be restored in this new form. Already the wealth of advanced industrial society begins to liberate the aesthetic impulse, but capitalism limits the aestheticization of the object world to consumer goods. Under socialism, a technology can be devised that pursues idealizing strategies in the public domain similar to those of art. Misery, injustice, suffering, and disorder shall be not just stripped out of the artistic image of the beautiful but removed practically from existence by appropriate technological solutions to human problems.

Technical Politics

Unfortunately, Marcuse offers few and not very relevant examples to illustrate his program, which corresponds fairly closely with the way we usually think about technical professions such as medicine or architecture that subordinate function to an immanent goal. Marcuse appears to call for a professionalization of the whole technical realm. This has implications for design, since each technical discipline would, like medicine, have an overarching mission. Designs would embody the values implied in each mission rather

---

10. Herbert Marcuse, "Cultural Revolution," in *Collected Papers of Herbert Marcuse*, vol. 2, *Towards a Critical Theory of Society*, ed. Douglas Kellner (New York: Routledge, 2001), 138–139.

than be subject to the mere will to power of government and business. Values, Marcuse writes, would "operate in the project and in the construction of the machinery, and not only in its utilization."[11] In the case of medicine, this is obvious insofar as all the instruments of the profession are conceived in the light of health, the essential potentiality of the living organism. Architecture more nearly resembles other technical domains such as urban planning and engineering, in which the construction of essences is an imaginative act. The technical professional is confronted with materials that have potentials only a creative act of invention can bring forth. The guiding values and meanings in such cases can and should be drawn from a commitment to the flourishing of life.

This is how Marcuse interpreted the environmental movement, the beginnings of which he witnessed toward the end of his life. Design and development are no longer guided exclusively by the pursuit of profit and power but respond also to the "life instinct." Life exemplifies the idea of essence, unfolding its potentialities through growth in interaction with the environment. Recognition of life as a value can guide the transformation of technology in accordance with a renewed notion of essence.[12]

Marcuse avoids dystopian despair and the vacuity of an appeal to a mere spiritual change, as well as the regressive notion of a return to premodern craft. These positions imply that technology cannot be changed, only approached in a different spirit or abandoned. Marcuse's position is rare among radical critics of modernity in that he recognized the flexibility of technology, its potential for reconfiguration under different social conditions. His position is also original in posing the problem at the level of the historical form of rationality and its relation to experience. However, he has little to say about the concrete possibilities of change, no doubt because social movements around technical problems were few and far between in his time.

After a generation of political action in the technical sphere around such issues as environmental reform and innovation on the Internet, we can pursue his argument a step further and far more concretely. As Ulrich Beck has argued, the differentiations that make modernity possible have reached their limits.[13] Modern technology has such vast and threatening impacts that it can no longer conserve the degree of autonomy and specialization it formerly enjoyed. A new politics emerges as the public is drawn into technical controversies. This picture has two sides: a negative side and a positive side,

---

11. Marcuse, *One-Dimensional Man*, 232.

12. Herbert Marcuse, "Ecology and the Critique of Modern Society," *Capitalism, Nature, Socialism: A Journal of Socialist Ecology* 3, no. 3 (1992): 29–38. This article is the transcript of a talk given by Marcuse shortly before his death in 1979.

13. Ulrich Beck, *Risk Society: Towards a New Modernity*, trans. Mark Ritter (London: Sage, 1992). This book was originally published as *Risikogesellschaft: Auf dem Weg in eine andere Moderne* (Frankfurt am Main: Suhrkamp Verlag, 1986).

the one criticizing the flaws of the existing system and the other identifying its unrealized potential. I focus here on technological examples, although so intertwined are the various systems in modern societies that related struggles arise in relation to bureaucracy and markets.

The negative side is revealed by the environmental movement. The dominant technological rationality is based on a simplified understanding of its objects. Reduced to raw materials and disconnected from their natural background, the materials incorporated into the technical system have unanticipated side effects that become fatefully significant as the system develops. Eventually these side effects cause such destruction and disease that ordinary people are affected and protest. The protests influence legislation and regulation and eventually feed back into technological designs that reflect a more realistic understanding of nature's complexity. This overall dynamic leads to a weakening of the technocratic and deterministic ideologies that armor the prevailing hegemony against change. Technical politics in this form has become part of mainstream political life as these interventions proliferate.

The positive side of the new picture is at work in other domains, such as information technology. Systems introduced in the context of military and business enterprise have been transformed by users in pursuit of personal fulfillment. The communicative opportunities opened by the systems have a role parallel to that of environmental side effects, revealing complex potentials unsuspected by their original designers. These potentials are benign rather than threatening, and they are deserving of independent development. They enable new forms of sociability and multiply creative possibilities for ordinary people. The democratic implications of these technologies emerge as resistance grows to commercial exploitation and political suppression.[14]

These examples reveal a dialectic of function and meaning. As functional, technology responds to a causal logic and is explained in relatively differentiated and autonomous technical disciplines. As meaningful, technology belongs to a way of life and embraces not only a minimal significance directly related to its function but also a wide range of associations that constitutes the human world. The evolution of modern technology takes place increasingly through the interaction between these dimensions. Modern societies tend to separate them institutionally—for example, distinguishing engineering from everyday understanding, management from working life, and control from communication. But in practice there is constant

14. Andrew Feenberg, *The Philosophy of Praxis: Lukács, Marx, and the Frankfurt School* (London: Verso, 2014). This book, newly revised in 2014, was first published as *Lukács, Marx, and the Sources of Critical Theory* (Lanham, MD: Rowman and Littlefield, 1981) and then again as *Lukács, Marx, and the Sources of Critical Theory* (Oxford: Oxford University Press, 1986).

interchange between the differentiated dimensions. They interact and conflict not only institutionally but within the individuals as they respond in routine or innovative ways to the technical environment in which they live. The stripping down of complex social forms and meanings to functional residues coexists with other social processes tending in the opposite direction, toward a reconstruction of complex meaning systems.

The technical disciplines respond to these public interventions by gradually incorporating a broader range of concerns in their concept of the object and their practices. The meanings these concerns imply do not appear within the disciplines directly and immediately but indirectly through mediations that address side effects and opportunities identified in protest, hacking, and innovation. The results in such cases are improved technical disciplines and technologies as judged from both technical and normative standpoints. Feedback from "reality," as experienced by ordinary people, is thus not extraneous to the technical but essential to its successful development.

The difference between the practices involved in using technology and transforming it corresponds to reification and dereification in Lukács's sense. Technologies impose a reified form on the lifeworld that appears as their content. Where that lifeworldly content overflows the form, the relational aspect of technology is brought to consciousness in a process of dereification. Established designs are opened up to revisions responding to new values. This process of dereification is a signifying practice, a new disclosure. It grants a different meaning to the technically mediated social world.

Reification cannot be abolished once and for all by joining the heterogeneous fragments, but its effects can be mitigated by their interaction. The inherited technical system, based on technical codes elaborated at a time when resistant publics were systematically disempowered, is now contested on a widening scale. Struggle and dialogue between experts and lay actors, between formal and informal modes of thought, call into question the industrial heritage. A new configuration of industrial society is emerging from these struggles, against enormous resistance, to be sure.

In sum, neither technical nor everyday rationality are complete in themselves; they form halves of a fragmented whole that communicate through democratic processes.[15] The outcome fulfils Marcuse's demand for a new concept of reason in a manner he did not anticipate, not just through incorporating values into technical disciplines but through an enlarged social dialogue. This dialogue is not merely verbal, but it involves political struggle, and often its outcome is enforced by law or regulation rather than by a handshake. But in the long run, a tacit consensus is achieved as the world is

---

15. Brian Wynne, *Rationality and Ritual: Participation and Exclusion in Nuclear Decision-Making* (London: Earthscan, 2011).

continually reconstituted through intervention in technical disciplines and technology.

Conclusion: From Existential Marxism to Rebellious Subjectivity

Technical politics depends on a new form of politicization that is only slowly emerging as the older union-based militancy declines. Marcuse witnessed the earliest stages of this development in the years immediately following the publication of *One-Dimensional Man*. He was struck by the willingness of the new activists to break free from the established society and its rituals of competition and consumption. This was called "dropping out" in the 1960s, but for many of the "dropouts," and for many of those who sympathized with their goals, it was just as much about changing the society as about evading its pressures and limits. Marcuse was swept up by the movement that idolized him, but he was not uncritical. He argued for engagement with social problems and for a greater emphasis on theory and effective strategy. The argument is still relevant.

The "rebellious subjectivity" that animated the movement was not a mere matter of opinion. Marcuse explains it as an affirmation of Eros, the life instinct. He believed resistance emerged from the psychic depths, from a somatic reaction to a society bent on waste, death, and destruction. This quasi-Freudian account of the movement coexists in his late work with an earlier theme, the threat to individuality. Together, these themes suggest continuity with Marcuse's early existential Marxism. I want to briefly explore this continuity in conclusion, once again showing how a single conceptual framework unifies apparently disparate influences and stages in the development of Marcuse's thought.

On the terms of *Being and Time*, passive conformity to the reified technical environment would be a manifestation of *das Man*. Acting on the basis of a perceived conflict between human values and technical disciplines and designs requires a break with everyday certainties. Heidegger's notion of resolute authentic action was intended to explain such a break. He defined it as "precisely the disclosive projection of what is factically possible at the time."[16] The reference to facticity pointed beyond objective knowledge to the lived encounter of the individual with the potentialities made visible by his or her situation. Heidegger interpreted this proposition in terms of a vague notion of historical destiny, but it is available for other uses.

When Marcuse was working with Heidegger and very much still under his influence, he reinterpreted the concept of authenticity in terms of

---

16. Heidegger, *Being and Time*, 345.

revolutionary decision. He argued for the relevance of the concept to Marxist social theory. Such an existential interpretation of the revolutionary impulse had never been explored in the Marxist tradition. The usual interest-based explanations of class consciousness could hardly account for the passion for a new life expressed in the revolution.

In contemporary terms, we would say that traditional Marxism lacks a concept of revolutionary identity. This is precisely what Marcuse's social version of the Heideggerian concept of authenticity sets out to provide. Once the decisive action of the authentic individual is treated as resistance to capitalism, it offers an original account of the revolution as a dereifying practice. "What is factically possible at the time" can be reinterpreted as the potential for socialism disclosed by the lived experience of the contradictions of capitalism. In Marcuse's later work, the concept of individuality is substituted for the discredited Heideggerian concept of authenticity, but the structure of the early theory is retained.

We can apply this theory to contemporary struggles over technical systems and technology if we eliminate the revolutionary pathos. Then, authentic individuality suggests democratic political engagement with what Heidegger calls the "challenge" of technology, rather than socialist or nationalist revolution. That challenge is not, as Heidegger supposes, about favoring spirit over materialism, but it has to do with the reconstruction of the material basis in terms of life-affirming values.

In his later work, Marcuse formulates the challenge in terms of the second dimension of essence, which transcends the empirical particulars and functional prescriptions toward the new world contained potentially within the existing technical system. Recognition of that potential is an existential decision motivated by a critical sense of the absurdity of a way of life based on competition and violence in a society no longer dominated by real scarcity. This is Marcuse's interpretation of the New Left, which exemplified the Great Refusal of capitalism in its day. Toward the end of his life, Marcuse responded to the restabilization of capitalism with a call for a "long march through the institutions."[17] The prospects of revolution receded, but the task of individuality remained and was still connected to resistance. We now know that during a period of reaction, that resistance consists in the struggle for democratization of societal institutions that are based on technical rationality.

Obstacles to this struggle must be removed. Chief among these obstacles are private ownership of the means of production, irresponsible and secretive administration, and the deficiencies of the educational system. The first two obstacles armor the established social world against change from below, while the last disqualifies the citizenry from intervening. In all societies

17. Herbert Marcuse, *Counterrevolution and Revolt* (Boston: Beacon, 1972), 55–56.

today except for the most repressive modern states, pressure from below has, on occasion, defeated these obstacles, but democratic interventions are still regarded as questionable exercises. Democratic political theory has scarcely begun to reflect on their significance. Meanwhile, education for citizenship is increasingly replaced by job training.

The fruitful resistances and dialogues between lay and expert that have had such impacts on medicine, urban planning, the environment, the Internet, and many other technical fields do not yet guide thinking about the future. But promoting such interactions is one of the new tasks of the democratic process that has been unfolding in the modern world since the Enlightenment. It is not a substitute for the revolution Marcuse advocated but a necessary form of struggle in all modern societies, whether capitalist or socialist.

Herbert Marcuse and the Dialectics of Social Media

CHRISTIAN FUCHS

One methodological and epistemological principle that guided Herbert Marcuse's works throughout his life was the importance of dialectical thinking, as inspired by Georg Wilhelm Friedrich Hegel. This theme and approach can already be found in his earlier works, such as his great book on Hegel, *Reason and Revolution*,[1] as well as in his later, famous work, *One-Dimensional Man*.[2] In the latter book, Marcuse argues against positivist, administrative, and uncritical thinking in politics and ideology. He opposes such thought with dialectical thinking that is "two-dimensional" and operates with "transcendent, critical notions."[3] In his essay "The Concept of Essence," Marcuse writes, "The dialectical concepts transcend given social reality in the direction of another historical structure which is present as a tendency in the given reality."[4]

This chapter explores how dialectical thinking may be used for understanding the role of social media in society. Social media are World Wide Web–based platforms such as blogs (e.g., Blogger, Wordpress, Tumblr), social networking sites (e.g., Facebook, LinkedIn, VK, Renren), sites for sharing user-generated content (e.g., YouTube, Vimeo, Youku Tudou), microblogs

---

1. Herbert Marcuse, *Reason and Revolution: Hegel and the Rise of Social Theory* (London: Oxford University Press, 1941).

2. Herbert Marcuse, *One-Dimensional Man: Studies in the Ideology of Advanced Industrial Society* (Boston: Beacon, 1964).

3. Ibid., 85.

4. Herbert Marcuse, "The Concept of Essence," in *Negations: Essays in Critical Theory* (1968; repr., London: MayFlyBooks, 2009), 63. The essay was originally published as "Zum Begriff des Wesens," *Zeitschrift für Sozialforschung* 5, no. 1 (1936): 1–39.

(e.g., Twitter, Weibo), and wikis (e.g., Wikipedia). It is evident that all media are, to a certain extent, social because they reflect and transmogrify society in complex ways. The actual change that communication systems such as Facebook reflect is that the World Wide Web (WWW, W3), since 2005, has become more a system of cooperative work and community formation than it was before.[5] These media are social because they enable and are means of sharing, communication, community making, and collaboration. In the first of the following sections, I discuss the relevance of Marcusean-Hegelian dialectics for understanding social media. In the second section, I draw conclusions and reflect on the relevance of Marcuse's notion of the Great Refusal in the age of the Internet and social media.

Herbert Marcuse, Hegelian Dialectics, and Social Media

Stalinist, Maoist, and negative dialectics underestimate the role of human subjects in dialectical processes.[6] They reduce dialectics to a structuralist-functionalist schematism that dominates the will of humans who, as is argued by dogmatic dialecticians, cannot shape the dialectic. Marcuse writes, "Soviet Marxism subjugates the subjective to the objective factors in a manner which transforms the dialectical into a mechanistic process."[7] To avoid a deterministic dialectic, a conception based on the dialectic of subject and object, human actors and social structures, is needed. Such a conception can be found implicitly in the philosophical writings of Marx and was, in the twentieth century, explicitly formulated by Marcuse against deterministic interpretations of Marx. Structuralist dialectics tend to reduce human activity to structures that determine them. Marcuse opposes passive dialectics by active dialectics—that is, dialectics as the art of "not getting captured by the contradictions, but . . . translat[ing] them possibly into directed moving forces."[8]

Marcuse points out that for Marx, capitalist crisis is a negating moment for the economic structures by which capitalism develops itself. Crisis is an aspect of objective dialectics, by which Marx means that the contradictions

---

5. Christian Fuchs, *Social Media: A Critical Introduction* (London: Sage, 2014).

6. Christian Fuchs, *Foundations of Critical Media and Information Studies* (London: Routledge, 2011), 11–74.

7. Herbert Marcuse, "Dialectic and Logic since the War," in *Collected Papers of Herbert Marcuse*, vol. 6, *Marxism, Revolution and Utopia*, ed. Douglas Kellner and Clayton Pierce (London: Routledge, 2014), 89; see also Herbert Marcuse, *Soviet Marxism: A Critical Analysis* (New York: Columbia University Press, 1958).

8. Wolfgang Fritz Haug, "Zur Dialektik des Antikapitalismus" [On the Dialectics of Anticapitalism], *Das Argument* [The Argument] 269 (2007): 12 (author's translation).

that are immanent in capitalism again and again result in crises. Marcuse summarizes:

> Capitalist society is a union of contradictions. It gets freedom through exploitation, wealth through impoverishment, advance in production through restriction of consumption. The very structure of capitalism is a dialectical one: every form and institution of the economic process begets its determinate negation, and the crisis is the extreme form in which the contradictions are expressed.[9]

Marcuse considered private property and alienated labor to be objective contradictions of capitalism.

> Every fact is more than a mere fact; it is a negation and restriction of real possibilities. Wage labor is a fact, but at the same time it is a restraint on free work that might satisfy human needs. Private property is a fact, but at the same time it is a negation of man's collective appropriation of nature. . . . The negativity of capitalist society lies in its alienation of labor.[10]

He wanted to avoid deterministic dialectics and to bring about a transition from a structural-functionalist dialectic toward a human-centered dialectic. Therefore, he argues that capitalism is dialectical because of its objective antagonistic structures and that the negation of this negativity can only be achieved by human praxis.

> The negativity and its negation are two different phases of the same historical process, straddled by man's historical action. The "new" state is *the truth* of the old, but that truth does not steadily and automatically grow out of the earlier state; it can be set free only by an autonomous act on the part of men, that will cancel the whole of the existing negative state.[11]

Necessity happens "only through societal praxis."[12] Marcuse explains:

> In the Marxian dialectic, thought, subjectivity, remains the decisive factor of the dialectical process. . . . The result [of the development of

---

9. Marcuse, *Reason and Revolution*, 311–312.
10. Ibid., 282.
11. Ibid., 315 (emphasis in original).
12. Herbert Marcuse, "Zur Geschichte der Dialektik" [On the History of Dialectics], in *Schriften* [Writings], vol. 8 (Frankfurt, Germany: Suhrkamp, 1966), 224 (author's translation).

society] depends on the conditions of possibilities for struggle and
the consciousness that develops thereby. This includes that its bearers have understood their slavery and its causes, that they want their
own liberation and have seen ways of how to achieve this. . . . The
necessity of socialism depends on the societal situation of the proletariat and the development of class consciousness.[13]

The antagonisms of capitalism necessarily create crises and are founded
on class relations. The sublation of capitalism and the realization of human
essence can be achieved only based on necessity and the possibilities conditioned by necessity; it can be created only by the free activity of humans who
try to transform possibilities into concrete reality. The dialectic of society is
shaped by a dialectic of freedom and necessity.

Not the slightest natural necessity or automatic inevitability guarantees the transition from capitalism to socialism. . . . The revolution
requires the maturity of many forces, but the greatest among them
is the subjective force, namely, the revolutionary class itself. The realization of freedom and reason requires the free rationality of those
who achieve it. Marxian theory is, then, incompatible with fatalistic
determinism.[14]

Hegel points out, with his concept of the determinate negation, that
the negative is at the same time positive—that contradictions dissolve not
into nothingness but into the negation of the particular content. Negation
is "the negation of a specific subject matter."[15] The new contains the old and
more; therefore it is richer in content.[16] To stress the importance of human
subjects in the dialectic of society, Marcuse argues that determined negation is "determinate choice."[17] Marcuse does not, as incorrectly argued by
Hans Heinz Holz, refuse the notion of determinate negation,[18] but rather
he embeds this concept into subject-object dialectics. Also, Wolfgang Fritz
Haug mistakes Marcuse in claiming that he assumed that the ideology of

13. Ibid.
14. Marcuse, *Reason and Revolution*, 318–319.
15. Georg Wilhelm Friedrich Hegel, *Science and Logic* (London: Routledge, 2002), §62.
Originally published in 1812.
16. Ibid.
17. Marcuse, *One-Dimensional Man*, 221.
18. Hans Heinz Holz, *Weltentwurf und Reflexion: Versuch einer Grundlegung der Dialektik* [World Design and Reflection: An Attempt at the Foundation of the Dialectic] (Stuttgart,
Germany: J. B. Metzler, 2005), 109, 499.

capitalism outdated the determinate negation historically.[19] In the passage that Haug criticizes, the epilogue to *Reason and Revolution*, Marcuse does not, as claimed by Haug, say that determinate negation is impossible today; rather, he writes that repressive ideology enables capitalism "to absorb its negativity"[20] and that, at the same time, the "total mobilization of society against the ultimate liberation of the individual . . . indicates how real is the possibility of this liberation."[21] The determinate negation of capitalism would be objectively possible but would be forestalled subjectively; there would be no necessity.

Marcuse later worked out this dialectical hypothesis in more depth in *One-Dimensional Man*. It is far from any deterministic logic. The historical reality of fascism and world war curbed Marcuse's belief that revolution would take place soon, but he was never a pessimist or defeatist. In the late 1960s, the emergence of the student movement convinced Marcuse that late capitalist society had not only potentials for liberation but actual political forces that aim at and work for liberation.

For Marcuse, only specific contradictions that relate to material and mental resources and the degree of freedom in a societal situation are determined. These are objective aspects of dialectics, on which alternative possibilities for development are based. Humans make their own history based on given conditions. Freedom is a comprehended and apprehended necessity. Humans can shape society under given conditions if they have understood necessity and the possibilities that are inherent in society.

> The determinate negation of capitalism occurs *if* and *when* the proletariat has become conscious of itself and of the conditions and processes which make up its society. . . . None of the given alternatives is *by itself* determinate negation unless and until it is consciously seized in order to break the power of intolerable conditions and attain the more rational, more logical conditions rendered possible by the prevailing ones.[22]

Conscious human activity within existing conditions is, as a subjective factor, an important aspect of the dialectic of society. Marcuse understood that the concept of human practice is needed for conceiving dialectics in a nondeterministic form and that thereby the notion of freedom can be situated

---

19. Wolfgang Fritz Haug, "Dialektik" [Dialectic], in *Historisch-Kritisches Wörterbuch des Marxismus* [Historical-Critical Dictionary of Marxism], vol. 2 (Hamburg, Germany: Argument, 1995), 690.

20. Marcuse, *Reason and Revolution*, 437.

21. Ibid., 439.

22. Marcuse, *One-Dimensional Man*, 222–223 (emphasis in original).

in dialectical philosophy. It is a wrong claim that there is a tendency in Marcuse's works to "dissolve the objective contradiction into subjective disagreement" and that he neglects immanent contradictions of capitalism.[23] For Marcuse, objective contradictions condition, constrain, and enable subjective action, and objective reality is the result of human practices' realization of possibilities that are constitutive features of objective reality. Dialectics are, for Marcuse, based on the dialectics of subject/object and freedom/necessity. Dialectics are the unity of the subjective dialectic and the objective dialectic. By having elaborated such a metadialectic, Marcuse was able to work against the ideas and political practice of deterministic dialectics. Determinate negation can be forestalled by ideology or direct violence, which means that society becomes all-totalitarian and contradictions are suppressed. But there is always the possibility for determinate negation. If negating forces are forestalled, it becomes the task of political praxis to restore the conditions for protest by protesting.

Marcuse understood Hegelian dialectics as (a) the dialectic of the subject and the object, (b) the dialectic of the individual and society, (c) the dialectic of the subjective and the objective dialectic of capitalism, (d) the dialectic of chance and necessity, and (e) the dialectic of essence and existence. These dialectics can also be found in the realm of contemporary social media.

The Dialectic of the Subject and the Object

Human beings as subjects use social-media technologies for creating, sharing, and communicating information online and for engaging in collaborative work and the formation of communities. Through these subjective practices, they create and recreate an objective world: they objectify information that is stored (e.g., on computers, servers, cloud storage devices) and that is communicated to others, thereby bringing about new meanings and joint understandings and misunderstandings of the world. These objective changes of the world condition (i.e., enable, constrain, further) human practices that are organized offline, online, and in converging social spaces. Social media are based on a dialectic of human practices and on the social structures that these practices create and recreate, so that structures condition practices and practices produce structures.

---

23. Hans-Ernst Schiller, "Gehemmte Entwicklung: Über Sprache und Dialektik bei Herbert Marcuse" [Inhibited Development: About Language and Dialectic in Herbert Marcuse], in *An unsichtbarer Kette* [An Invisible Chain] (Lüneburg, Germany: Klampen, 1993), 115–116 (author's translation).

The Dialectic of the Individual and Society

In capitalism, individual use-value—that is, the satisfaction of human needs—can mainly be achieved by purchasing commodities, which necessitates exchange-value, money, and the selling of one's labor power. Individual satisfaction of needs can be achieved only by entering social relations of exchange and exploitation. Capitalism's antagonism between use-value and exchange-value is an antagonism between individual needs and social-class relations. On corporate social media, the relationship of the individual and the social is highly antagonistic: social media exist only through social relationships that enable sharing, communication, collaboration, and community. But these social relations are today at the heart of the realization of neoliberal performance principles that render social-media platforms the perfect tools for individual self-presentation, individualistic competition, and the individual accumulation of reputation and contacts. It is no accident that "social" media are called YouTube, MySpace, and Facebook and not OurTube, CollectiveSpace, and Groupbook. It is all about "you" and not "us" as a collective. The individualistic, private-property character of social media—the fact that user data is sold as a commodity to advertisers—is hidden behind social media's social appearance: you do not pay for accessing Twitter, Facebook, Google, or YouTube, and the obtained use-value seems to be the immediate social experience these platforms enable. The commodity character of personal data does not become immediately apparent because there is no exchange of money for use-values that one experiences. The commodity fetish thereby becomes inverted: the social seems the immediate positive experience on social media, whereas the individualistic logic of money and the commodity remains hidden from the users.

The Dialectic of the Subjective and the Objective Dialectic of Capitalism

Social media is embedded in the dialectic of capitalism's objective and subjective dialectics. It reflects capitalism's objective contradictions. One of these antagonisms is the one between real and fictitious value. Financialization can easily result in the divergence of stock-market values and profits. Such a divergence was at the heart of the crisis of the "new economy" in 2000. Financialization is a response to contradictions of capitalism that result in capitalists' attempts to achieve spatial (global outsourcing) and temporal (financialization) fixes to problems associated with overaccumulation, overproduction, underconsumption, falling profit rates, profit squeezes, and class struggles. The ideological hype of the emergence of a "web 2.0" and "social media" that communicated the existence of a radically new Internet was primarily aimed at restoring the confidence of venture capital to invest in the Internet economy. The rise of Google, Facebook, Twitter, Weibo, and related targeted advertising-based platforms created a new round of financialization of the Internet economy, with its own objective contradiction: in a situation of global capitalist crisis, corporate social media attract advertising investments because companies think targeted advertising is more secure and efficient than conventional advertising. Financial investors share these hopes and believe in social media's growing profits and dividends, which spurs their investments of financial capital in social-media corporations. The click-through rate (the share of ads that users click on in the total number of presented ads) is, however, on average, just 0.1 percent,[24] which means that only one out of one thousand targeted ads yields actual profits. And even in these cases, it is uncertain whether users will buy commodities on the pages to which the targeted ads direct them. The social-media economy involves high levels of uncertainty and risk. A social-media finance bubble is continuously building itself up. If a specific bankruptcy or other event triggers a downfall of the stock-market value of an important social-media company, the bubble could suddenly explode because investors may lose confidence in the business model, and this may quickly spread and intensify. Financial crises involve complex dialectics of objective contradictions and subjective behavior.

The Dialectic of Chance and Necessity

Capitalism's objective contradictions with necessity bring about crises. The exact causes and times of crises are, however, contingent and therefore not predetermined. This means for the capitalist Internet economy that its next crisis will come, but that the point of time and users' reactions to it are not predetermined. Marcuse's notion of determined negation as determinate choice is of particular importance in this respect: the next crisis of the Internet economy will result in new qualities of the Internet. We do, however, not know what these changes will look like. That depends on the choices that users collectively make in the situation of crisis. The future of the Internet is dependent on the outcomes of class struggles. If users let themselves be fooled by the ideologies advanced by marketing gurus, capitalists, the business press, neoliberal politicians, and scholars celebrating every new capitalist social-media hype, no alternatives to the capitalist Internet may be in sight during and after the next crisis of the Internet. But if they struggle for an alternative, noncommercial, noncapitalist, nonprofit, commons-based, and therefore truly social Internet, then alternatives may become possible.

---

24. Fuchs, *Social Media*, 116.

The Dialectic of Essence and Existence

For Hegel, essence is a universalistic concept. He argues, "The Absolute is *essence*."[25] Essence is the Ground of Existence. "The Ground is the unity of identity and distinction. . . . It is essence posited as *totality*. . . . Ground is ground only insofar as it grounds."[26] In Marx's philosophical writings, Hegelian essence is interpreted as sociality and cooperation. "The individual is the social being."[27] "By social we understand the co-operation of several individuals."[28] The logic and dialectic of essence had specific ethical and political importance for Marcuse. He stresses that essence is connected to possibilities and that a true society is one that realizes the possibilities that are enabled by structural aspects such as technological forces, economic productivity, political power relations, and worldviews. Essence in society is connected with what humans could be.[29] Marcuse builds his concept of essence on Marx's insight that the social is the most fundamental category in any society, that socialism is therefore the formation appropriate to humans, and that capitalism is a form of alienated, false, and reified existence. What is in essence possible in a society would, however, depend on and be conditioned by that which is.

> Here the concept of what could be, of inherent possibilities, acquires a precise meaning. What man can be in a given historical situation is determinable with regard to the following factors: the measure of control of natural and social productive factors, the level of the organization of labor, the development of needs in relation to possibilities for their fulfillment (especially the relation of what is necessary for the reproduction of life to the "free" needs for gratification and happiness, for the "good and the beautiful"), the availability, as material to be appropriated, of a wealth of cultural values in all areas of life.[30]

The ethico-political is connected to questions of what can and should be, because society *can* be based on the existing preconditions to reduce pain,

---

25. Georg Wilhelm Friedrich Hegel, *Encyclopaedia of the Philosophical Sciences: The Logic* (Oxford: Oxford University Press, 2010), §112 (emphasis in original). Originally published in 1830.

26. Ibid., §121 (emphasis in original).

27. Karl Marx, *Economic and Philosophic Manuscripts of 1844* (Mineola, NY: Dover, 2007), 105.

28. Karl Marx and Friedrich Engels, *The German Ideology* (New York: International, 1939), 50. Originally published in 1846.

29. Marcuse, "The Concept of Essence," 31–64.

30. Ibid., 53.

misery, and injustice; to use existing resources and capacities in ways that satisfy human needs in the best possible way; and to minimize hard labor.[31]

Media are tools for communication, and therefore they promise to realize human essence; however, capitalist media subsume this communicative use-value under the logic of exchange-value, so that the commodification of content, audiences, users, and access turns these tools into means for capital accumulation and the diffusion of ideologies. Media thereby becomes individual private property that enhances the wealth of the few by exploiting the labor of the many. Capitalist social media such as Twitter, Facebook, and YouTube promise a new level of sociality but, at the same time, literally commodify sociality, and they impose the logic of private property and commodities on online communications.

Noncommercial, commons-based, and public-service online media—such as Wikipedia, noncommercial free software, creative commons projects, sharing platforms that operate on gift logic, alternative online news media, and peer-to-peer sites—question and transcend the logic of online commodity and are expressions of human essence and the Internet's essence. The antagonism between the online commons and the online commodity form is complex because it involves not just users and capitalists but also artists, whose income partly depends on the profits of media companies who exploit them, so that the online "freeconomy" challenges not just capitalist profits but also online wage labor. Radical reforms are the only solution of this antagonism—namely, radical reforms that foster public funds so that alternative projects can employ workers. It is a mistake to take an immanent defensive political position that opposes transcendental projects with the argument that they destroy jobs of cultural workers. We need reforms and platforms that strengthen the alternative realities on the Internet so that the latter can increasingly realize its own essence.

The Great Refusal in the Age of the Internet and Social Media

For both Marx and Marcuse, the dialectic was not just an objective condition of capitalism expressing itself in crises but also a practical force that—conditioned by objective conditions—expresses itself in and conditions social struggles. Marcuse wrote *One-Dimensional Man* before the 1968 revolt, and he was much more pessimistic at this stage than he was in the late 1960s. He argued for a Great Refusal, the organized political rejection of capitalism, but he said it was a mere hope.

---

31. Marcuse, *One-Dimensional Man*, 44, 126, 222.

The second period of barbarism may well be the continued empire of civilization itself. But the chance is that, in this period, the historical extremes may meet again: the most advanced consciousness of humanity, and its most exploited force. It is nothing but a chance. The critical theory of society possesses no concepts which could bridge the gap between the present and its future; holding no promise and showing no success, it remains negative. Thus it wants to remain loyal to those who, without hope, have given and give their life to the Great Refusal.[32]

Under the impression of the rebellions of the late 1960s, Marcuse, who actively participated in the student movement, took up the notion of the Great Refusal again in *An Essay on Liberation*.

The Great Refusal takes a variety of forms. In Vietnam, in Cuba, in China, a revolution is being defended and driven forward which struggles to eschew the bureaucratic administration of socialism. The guerrilla forces in Latin America seem to be animated by that same subversive impulse: liberation. . . . The ghetto populations may well become the first mass basis of revolt. . . . The student opposition is spreading in the old socialist as well as capitalist countries. . . . None of these forces *is* the alternative. However, they outline, in very different dimensions, the limits of the established societies, of their power of containment. When these limits are reached, the Establishment may initiate a new order of totalitarian suppression. But beyond these limits, there is also the space, both physical and mental, for building a realm of freedom which is not that of the present: liberation also from the liberties of exploitative order—a liberation which must precede the construction of a free society, one which necessitates an historical break with the past and the present.[33]

After more than thirty years of neoliberal hegemony, movements and parties such as Occupy, 15-M and Podemos in Spain, the Indignant Citizens Movement and Syriza in Greece, the Left Bloc in Portugal, and the movements supporting Jeremy Corbyn in the United Kingdom and Bernie Sanders in the United States give us a glimmer of political hope for liberation from the exploitative order and for life beyond capitalism. But an even stronger tendency has been the strengthening of Far Right parties throughout the world, which somewhat tarnishes hope and has increasingly sharpened social and

---

32. Ibid., 257.
33. Herbert Marcuse, *An Essay on Liberation* (Boston: Beacon, 1969), viii.

political antagonisms. As a consequence, the situation may soon be that the only political option is the one between socialism and fascist barbarism. The new "Big Crisis" has brought about not just more austerity and an intensification of neoliberalism but also attempts at renewing the Left and the Great Refusal. The Great Refusal as a dialectical movement that combines the party and the social movement in order to try to abolish capitalism is back in force and has the potential to gain power and spread in a domino effect. A network of party and movement, government and civil society, is a power that can command resources and attention and use these resources to support one, two, or many radical networks in other countries. Furthermore, the success and growth of the Left in one country can give tremendous motivation to activists in other countries; it can result, among other things, in more public attention for the Left in these countries.

Writing in 1972, Marcuse feared a weakening of the New Left and therefore propagated Rudi Dutschke's "strategy of the *long march through the institutions*: working against them while working in them" and the "effort to build up counterinstitutions."[34] The notion of the "long march" has today become a swearword because it has led to phenomena such as the German Green Party taking power together with the Social Democratic Party in a government that fought wars in Kosovo in 1999 and Afghanistan in 2001 and exercised brutal neoliberal politics against the poor and the unemployed.

Andrew Feenberg has taken up Marcuse's concepts of the Great Refusal and the long march to suggest how we should think about the Internet.[35] He interprets the Great Refusal in the context of the Internet as a "dystopian critique of the Internet" that inspires "a similarly uncompromising refusal" and argues for a long march of Internet reforms, in which "the system as a whole is rarely the object of resistance" and change is "piecemeal."[36]

Feenberg interprets the Great Refusal and the long march in a dualistic and nondialectical manner, as "two different strategies," and argues for pure reformism.[37] Marcuse, however, was a much more revolutionary reformist and reformist revolutionary, who argued for working inside the institutions against the institutions in order to improve the conditions for revolution and for building counterinstitutions that transcend capitalist and dominative logics. Feenberg also ignores the negative effects of Dutschke's strategy. The Great Refusal requires attempts at institutional reforms that help build

34. Herbert Marcuse, *Counterrevolution and Revolt* (Boston: Beacon, 1972), 55 (emphasis in original).

35. Andrew Feenberg, "Great Refusal or Long March: How to Think about the Internet," in *Critique, Social Media and the Information Society*, ed. Christian Fuchs and Marisol Sandoval (New York: Routledge, 2014), 109–124.

36. Ibid., 122.

37. Ibid.

better conditions for revolutionary struggles. The long march risks becoming part of domination if it does not aim at fostering the revolution in the last instance. Feenberg's strategy resembles the social-democratic revisionism that Rosa Luxemburg fiercely criticized and that Marcuse always rejected: "Between social reforms and revolution there exists for the social democracy an indissoluble tie. The struggle for reforms is its means; the social revolution, its aim."[38]

Feenberg, for a critical theorist of technology, also has a remarkably dualist and therefore undialectical understanding of models of the Internet.[39] He distinguishes between a consumption model that is based on the logic of commerce, consumption, and commodities and a community model that he associates with reciprocity, democracy, online politics, and activism.[40] He overlooks the contemporary antagonistic dialectic of the Internet, where the logics of gift/commerce, individualism/sociality, labor/play, commodity/community often dialectically overgrasp (what Hegel terms "übergreifen") into each other.[41] There are alternative spaces beyond the commodity on the Internet, and social struggles combined with media reforms have the potential to expand them; however, they do not, as community Internet spaces, exist independent from the commodity Internet. In a capitalist society, the commodity Internet and the community Internet have to relate in the form of complex dialectical antagonisms to each other.

Feenberg reproduces the technodeterministic myth that the Facebook and Twitter revolutions are central and coconstitutive moments for the cycle of struggles that started in 2008. "The recent Arab revolts should be proof enough of the Internet's remarkable political potential."[42] In contrast, my own empirical studies of social media in protests, published in the book *OccupyMedia!*, show a much more dialectical picture.[43] The practices of Occupy and other contemporary protest movements are embedded into societies full of antagonisms. Societal antagonisms condition antagonisms when these movements use the Internet and social media: the antagonism between protest communication and communication control on social media, a dialectic of online and offline protest communication, the antagonism

---

38. Rosa Luxemburg, "Reform or Revolution," in *The Essential Rosa Luxemburg* (Chicago: Haymarket Books, 2008), 41. Essay originally published in 1899.

39. Feenberg, "Great Refusal or Long March."

40. Ibid., 117–122.

41. Christian Fuchs, *Internet and Society: Social Theory in the Information Age* (New York: Routledge, 2008); Fuchs, *Foundations of Critical Media and Information Studies*, 64, 114; Christian Fuchs, *OccupyMedia! The Occupy Movement and Social Media in Crisis Capitalism* (Winchester, UK: Zero, 2014); Christian Fuchs, *Social Media*; Christian Fuchs, *Culture and Economy in the Age of Social Media* (New York: Routledge, 2015).

42. Feenberg, "Great Refusal or Long March," 119.

43. Fuchs, *OccupyMedia!*, 70.

of alternative social media's critical voice and autonomy on the one hand and resource precarity on the other hand, the antagonism of for-profit and not-for-profit (social) media, the antagonism of voluntarism and vulnerability of social-media-donation models, the antagonism of state-funded stability and control of alternative social media, the antagonism of for-profit organization and loss of autonomy, and the antagonism of the stability of paid media activism and the logic of bureaucratization and commodification.[44]

Feenberg has little to say about how politics can try to manage and organize the media and society's antagonisms in such a way that the possibilities for radical change are enhanced. In a manner remindful of celebratory cultural studies that celebrates audiences as always resisting, he takes on the notion of interpretive flexibility from the social constructivism of technology and the concept of participatory design and, therefore, trusts that users always resist and subvert dominant uses of technology. Technology is always unfinished and open for change, but power, including communicative power, within stratified societies tends to be asymmetrically distributed, which puts alternative noncommercial uses and designs of technology within capitalist society at a disadvantage.

It is, therefore, a disservice for social movements and alternative media to celebrate their resistant potentials, to proclaim their democratic horizontalism and prefigurative politics without considering the limits posed for protest by capitalism and the resulting need for political strategy and organization.[45] Given the predominant antagonisms, the Left requires political organizations that take over the power of institutions in order to make radical reforms, such as channeling resources toward movements and groups that struggle for revolutionary change and establishing noncapitalist media.

Feenberg's "critical theory of technology" is idealist, distant from a concept of political organization, dualist, and undialectical. It is, therefore, no surprise that none of Feenberg's major books contain any single work by Hegel in the bibliography.[46] It does, then, also come as no surprise that Feenberg's revised and extended version of his 1981 book on Lukács contains only two all-too-brief references to Hegel's *Science of Logic* and no references at all to the *Encyclopaedia*, Hegel's magnum opus of systematic dialectical think-

---

44. Fuchs, *Culture and Economy in the Age of Social Media*, 343–378.

45. Todd Wolfson, *Digital Rebellion: The Birth of the Cyber Left* (Urbana: University of Illinois Press, 2014).

46. Andrew Feenberg, *Transforming Technology: A Critical Theory Revisited* (Oxford: Oxford University Press, 2002); Andrew Feenberg, *Alternative Modernity: The Technical Turn in Philosophy and Social Theory* (Berkeley: University of California Press, 1995); Andrew Feenberg, *Questioning Technology* (London: Routledge, 1999); Andrew Feenberg, *Heidegger and Marcuse: Catastrophe and Redemption of History* (New York: Routledge, 2005); Andrew Feenberg, *Between Reason and Experience: Essays in Technology and Modernity* (Cambridge, MA: MIT Press, 2010).

ing that develops the totality.[47] Given that Lukács and Marcuse were two of the greatest dialectical philosophers of the twentieth century, one wonders how Feenberg's Lukácsean and Marcusean "critical theory of technology" is possible without a thorough engagement with and understanding of Hegel's works on dialectical logic. The result is what can best be characterized as a dualist theory of technology.

A critical theory of the media, communication, culture, technology, and the Internet requires a dialectical-philosophical foundation and, therefore, a renewed engagement not just with Marx, Marcuse, and Lukács but also with Hegel.[48] Hegel understands the dialectic in the *Science of Logic* as a process, in which a posited reflection-in-itself *externalizes itself into a negative other so that there is what Hegel calls external reflection.* The determining reflection is "the unity of *positing* and *external* reflection."[49] The sublation of the contradiction between one thing and another thing determines the emergence of what Hegel terms "*Gesetzsein*"[50]—the "*posited.*"[51] Positedness is a reflection in and for itself: "It is *positedness*—negation which has however deflected the reference to another into itself, and negation which, equal to itself, is the unity of itself and its other, and only through this is an *essentiality*. It is, therefore, positedness, negation, but as reflection into itself it is at the same time the sublatedness of this positedness, infinite reference to itself."[52] But for Hegel, the sublation that is positedness repels itself in an absolute recoil so that it posits its own presuppositions and starts the dialectical process all over again.[53] For Hegel, the world is dialectical and, therefore, dynamic and unfinished.

Marcuse, in his own magnum opus, *Reason and Revolution*, shows how to best dialectically interpret Hegel's dialectical laws of reflection in order to posit the dialectic of reflection-in-itself, reflection-in-another, and positedness as the dialectic of the subjective dialectic and the objective dialectic, in

47. Andrew Feenberg, *The Philosophy of Praxis: Marx, Lukács and the Frankfurt School* (London: Verso, 2014).

48. Christian Fuchs, "The Dialectic: Not Just the Absolute Recoil, but the World's Living Fire That Extinguishes and Kindles Itself; Reflections on Slavoj Žižek's Version of Dialectical Philosophy in *Absolute Recoil: Towards a New Foundation of Dialectical Materialism*," *tripleC: Communication, Capitalism and Critique* 12, no. 2 (2014): 848–875.

49. Georg Wilhelm Friedrich Hegel, *Science of Logic*, trans. A. V. Miller (New York: Humanities, 1969), 405 (emphasis in original). Originally published in 1812–1816.

50. Georg Wilhelm Friedrich Hegel, *Wissenschaft der Logik* [Science of Logic], vol. 2 (Frankfurt, Germany: Suhrkamp, 1969), 189–190.

51. Georg Wilhelm Friedrich Hegel, *The Science of Logic*, ed. and trans. George Di Giovanni (Cambridge: Cambridge University Press, 2010), 351–353 (emphasis in original).

52. Ibid., 353 (emphasis in original).

53. Fuchs, "The Dialectic," 848–853.

which "the negativity and its negation are two different phases of the same historical process, straddled by man's historical action."[54]

In a communication process, whether it takes place online or offline, an individual posits his or her own identity by relating in and through symbolic process to another person, who, in return, posits his or her identity by communicatively responding. So identity as the individual reflection-in-itself is only possible as the communicative reflection-into-another. This communicative negation is negated in situations—where the communicative process is sublated—either by a rupture that causes a breakdown in the social relationship (e.g., a quarrel between friends that ends the relationship, death) or the emergence of a positive new quality (e.g., an occasional acquaintance turns into a friendship). Such a sublation in a social relationship is a communicative reflection in and for itself. It, however, does not stop but exists only in and through further communication between humans, so that the sublation of a social relation to a new quality in an absolute recoil goes back to the start and is posited as a new dialectic of the communicative reflection-in-itself and the reflection-into-another, and so on. The result of communication in an absolute recoil becomes the starting point for further communication. Communication posits its own presuppositions so that the communicative social relations between humans develop in and through communication.

The dialectic is not a teleological process because humans make their own history based on the conditions they are posited in and that they posit. The Internet in capitalism is an antagonistic dialectical system, in which the individual, property, capital, the commodity, and the market are reflected into the social, the commons, labor, the gift, and the community; they reflect themselves into their others so that there is an antagonistic recoil of mutual positing of opposites. The resulting antagonisms constitute the Internet's actuality, development, and potentiality, which face power asymmetries. Given these asymmetries, only politics of radical reformism can make a socialist sublation more likely. We need the Marcusean dialectic of the Great Refusal and the long march. The communist and the capitalist Internet are both realities with asymmetric powers that are contained in each other as the capitalism of the communist Internet and the communism of the capitalist Internet.

The twenty-first century's New Left, as presently symbolized by democratic-socialist forces such as Syriza, Podemos, the German Left Party, the United Socialist Party of Venezuela, and the Bolivian Movement for Socialism, has the potential to do radical-reformist media politics that strengthen an alternative, democratic-socialist media and Internet landscape, as well as the potential for transcending capitalism by democratic socialism. These parties have the opportunity, for example, to introduce a citizens' media

54. Marcuse, *Reason and Revolution*, 315.

check (or voucher) that is based on a combination of the taxation of capital and the use of participatory budgeting for the distribution of this tax revenue to households with the obligation that they donate the amount to noncommercial media organizations.[55] The participatory media fee is one of the possible reforms that could strengthen public and alternative media.[56] It is a typical radical-reformist political demand that has the potential to dialectically mediate the Great Refusal and the long march.

The future is determined by the antagonisms, crises, conditions, and struggles of the present. We will experience a humane future with media and an Internet that correspond to society's essence only if the strategy of fostering a dialectic of left-wing governments and social struggles succeeds. A socialist future requires a Marcusean media moment, a dialectical critical theory of the media and technology that informs revolutionary-reformist, left-wing media politics.

---

55. Fuchs, *Culture and Economy in the Age of Social Media*, 380.
56. Ibid.

15

Inklings of the Great Refusal

Echoes of Marcuse's Post-technological Rationality Today

MARCELO VIETA

For Herbert Marcuse, the technological inheritance of late modernity was double-sided: while it was true that "technological rationality" had captured and alienated life by privileging the instrumental and the exchangeable, technology could still be redeployed under the auspices of other forms of reason for the project of liberation from toil, scarcity, and necessity. "If the completion of the technological project involves a break with the prevailing technological rationality," writes Marcuse, "the break in turn depends on the continued existence of the technical base."[1]

For Marcuse, the possibilities of a "post-technological rationality"—a "technological rationality . . . stripped of its exploitative features" and legislated by different means and ends—meant that we could bootstrap onto the technological base and reappropriate it so that the "total automation" of toil would be the optimum and "concrete alternatives," "cooperation," "self-determination," and "tenderness toward each other" the potential.[2] His affirmations of hope for a rerationalized technological inheritance still contain evocative theoretical and practical possibilities for today's movements

---

1. Herbert Marcuse, *One-Dimensional Man: Studies in the Ideology of Advanced Industrial Society* (Boston: Beacon, 1964), 231.

2. Ibid., 238, 251; Herbert Marcuse, *An Essay on Liberation* (Boston: Beacon, 1969), 86, 88–92. As I address elsewhere, this double-sidedness in Marcuse's conceptualizations of technology makes his critical theory unique among substantivist philosophers of technology such as Martin Heidegger (his doctoral supervisor) and his Frankfurt School contemporaries Theodor Adorno and Max Horkheimer. See Marcelo Vieta, "Marcuse's 'Transcendent Project' at 50: Post-technological Rationality for Our Times," *Radical Philosophy Review* 19, no. 1 (2016): 143–172.

that struggle for alternative organizational arrangements against the current form of technological and economic rationality: neoliberalism.

To incite "the break" from prevailing technological rationalities and mediations, Marcuse called for an ethico-political commitment of *refusing* the continuation of misery, toil, and injustice. This call was to be a standpoint of negation of established existence and would also strive for new technological realities, new social relations, and new ways of engaging with nature. Indeed, Marcuse's ultimate plea for liberation—the Great Refusal—was to begin with the "administered individuals . . . who have made their mutilation into their own liberties and satisfactions" within contemporary advanced industrial society.[3]

Marcuse did not offer a clear blueprint for what seems upon first reading a paradox: How can those whose minds and bodies are captured within a one-dimensional, technologically rationalized reality strive to liberate themselves from this total administration? The answer, for Marcuse, scattered throughout his mature writings, was to be found in *the determinate negation of the status quo* in acts of "solidarity" and "autonomy,"[4] in "the [prefigurative] ingression of the future into the present" via actions of "spontaneity,"[5] and in the negation of the profit and performance principle more generally via the privileging of imagination, fantasy, and play rather than positivist reason, seriousness, and commodified life.[6] In sum, the struggle for an alternative reality had to be lived through and experimented with via actions and logics that themselves were alternatives to the status quo. For Marcuse, this liberation from technological rationality most fundamentally required a "new radicalism"[7] grounded in a negative dialectical mode of engagement and within *a politics of refusal*.

The politics of refusal—the new radicalism—was to be a socioeconomic, sociopolitical, and sociocultural revolt catalyzed by a new aesthetically and sensuously driven subject.[8] This new subject would embody a "radical consciousness"[9] who "decides that it is enough, and that it is time to enjoy";[10] who, possessed by a "freedom of thought"[11] for a "new Form of life,"[12] would be able to think and do otherwise. This new subject, however, was to also

---

3. Marcuse, *One-Dimensional Man*, 250.

4. Marcuse, *An Essay on Liberation*, 88.

5. Ibid., 89.

6. Marcuse, *Eros and Civilization: A Philosophical Inquiry into Freud* (Boston: Beacon, 1955), 193.

7. Marcuse, *An Essay on Liberation*, 88.

8. Vieta, "Marcuse's 'Transcendent Project' at 50."

9. Herbert Marcuse, *Counterrevolution and Revolt* (Boston: Beacon, 1972), 54.

10. Marcuse, *An Essay on Liberation*, 90.

11. Marcuse, *One-Dimensional Man*, 253.

12. Marcuse, *An Essay on Liberation*, 90.

be savvy enough to neither seek exodus from modern life in an idealized premodern existence nor place hopes for freedom on the overthrow of the technological inheritance *tout court*. Rather, the politics of refusal guiding the new radical subject first takes up a resolute commitment of "refusing to play the game,"[13] a game that is always already rigged against true freedom. Second, it seeks to reorganize the technological inheritance in order to liberate us as much as possible from the realm of necessity in order to free "human energy and time"[14] so as to maximize the "development of the realm of freedom."[15] That is, a politics of refusal intends to critically realize, via the force of determinate negation and the prefiguration of the ethical and social transformations being struggled over, "the actual human condition in the given society" *and* "the 'given' possibilities to transcend this condition, to enlarge the realm of freedom."[16] In what I show to be his prefigurative disposition, Marcuse continues, "In this sense, negative thinking is by virtue of its own internal concepts 'positive': oriented toward, and comprehending a future which is 'contained' in the present. And in this containment . . . the future appears as possible liberation."[17]

The politics of refusal realizes that the real problems of late modernity rest with the stubborn entrenchment of alienated work, or what Marcuse termed (from Freud) "the Performance Principle."[18] For the "construction of a free society," in turn, the politics of refusal is a striving to "create new incentives for work" driven by the "Pleasure Principle" and the affirmation of life rather than "exploitative repression."[19] In sum, a politics of refusal that struggles against "repressive" forms of labor while continuing to recognize the continued need for some form of work would (1) try to render to the technological inheritance as much toil as possible while (2) striving to redirect its most antihuman and antienvironmental means by (3) aiming for the proliferation of solidarity-based work under the auspices of a new, libidinal work instinct. Work and technology would thus be placed in the service of "the creation of a sensuous environment," of "cooperation" rather than competition, of a solidary reality that would unleash work into an "elemental, instinctual, creative force."[20]

My principal aim in this chapter is to reclaim Marcuse's vision for a politics of refusal and social transformation for contemporary radical Left practices seeking alternative socioeconomic and organizational realities. In

---

13. Marcuse, *One-Dimensional Man*, 257.
14. Marcuse, *An Essay on Liberation*, 90.
15. Ibid., 91.
16. Ibid., 87.
17. Ibid.; see also Marcuse, *Counterrevolution and Revolt*, 49.
18. Marcuse, *Eros and Civilization*, 35.
19. Marcuse, *An Essay on Liberation*, 91.
20. Ibid., 88–91.

the process, I suggest the efficaciousness of Marcuse's critical theory of technology for radical alternatives that struggle against an ocean of neoliberal values and practices while forging new islands of another technological and social reality. The first part of the chapter briefly maps out what I view to be key elements of Marcuse's politics of refusal. In the second part, I illustrate a few contemporary echoes of Marcuse's politics of refusal via three moments of alternative social and economic arrangements that have emerged from the crises and contradictions of neoliberalism: (1) alternative community economies, (2) radical education initiatives, and (3) recuperated spaces of production. They are illustrative inklings, I ultimately suggest, of Marcuse's Great Refusal today.

The Great Refusal and Prefiguring Liberation

Inspired by radical rereadings of Walter Benjamin, Theodor Adorno, Maurice Blanchot, Alfred North Whitehead, André Breton, Karl Marx, Friedrich Nietzsche, Sigmund Freud, and others, and particularly by the proposals and struggles of the New Left of his time, Marcuse's Great Refusal was not a call for a vanguardist-led revolution or a return to a pretechnological past.[21] Rather, the Great Refusal was to be an instinctual revolt at the level of the individual and a political and cultural struggle at the social level that would begin by saying *no* to the one-dimensional society that had seized our every thought, habit, and act. For guidance, Marcuse drew on the determinately negative aesthetic practices of the avant-garde artists of the early twentieth century, the cultural and organizational practices of the marginalized, and movements that merged sensual and aesthetic sensibilities with resistance to the status quo, such as the commune and student movements of late 1960s. These aesthetic expressions, protests of the marginalized, and alternative living experiments were to be vaunted and imitated because their deeply imaginative, instinctual, and sensual practices already offered an "absolute refusal,"[22] or a "determinate negation,"[23] of one-dimensional society. They engaged in a new radicalism via spontaneity and anarchistic tendencies that drew out a new sensibility against domination and a "feeling" and "awareness" that "the joy of freedom and the need to be free must precede liberation."[24]

---

21. Vanguardist revolutions were, for Marcuse, rendered bankrupt by the inhumanness of actual existing communism that in ways proved equally alienating and exploitative in practice. At the same time, calls for Heideggerian-like returns to the land and an idealized past were conservative reactions of hopelessness that acquiesced undeserved power to the technological inheritance.

22. Marcuse, *One-Dimensional Man*, 255.

23. Ibid., 228. See also Vieta, "Marcuse's 'Transcendent Project' at 50," 147, 163–166.

24. Marcuse, *An Essay on Liberation*, 89.

These already existing marginal groups offered new ways of thinking and acting that articulated a "transcendent project" of refusal beyond one-dimensional reality.[25] Embodying a politics of refusal, the projects and values of marginalized groups articulated for Marcuse ways of, simultaneously refusing to engage in the established reality, critiquing it in practice, and proposing new ways of thinking and acting that mapped out, in the present, a less repressive, less alienating world.

Quoting Adorno, Marcuse explicitly articulated his politics of refusal in *Eros and Civilization*: "This Great Refusal is the protest against unnecessary repression, the struggle for the ultimate form of freedom—'to live without anxiety.'"[26] A politics of refusal thus continued the Marxist critique of alienation and exploitation but also moved beyond its more orthodox strands by explicitly calling on the elimination of *all* painful forms of labor. The Great Refusal, then, is ultimately a political standpoint that charts aspects of a postcapitalist, post-one-dimensional world by interlacing resistance and alternatives with the ethics, values, and practices that are desired and struggled over. It was, for instance, not to be a demand for "abundance for all" at the same unsustainable levels as in contemporary industrial society.[27] Rather, it was to aim first for "a non-oppressive distribution of scarcity" and second for "a rational organization of fully developed industrial society," but one "*without toil*—that is, without the rule of alienated labor over the human existence" by the "general automatization of labor." Instead, Marcuse called for the "reduction of labor time to a minimum."[28]

For Marcuse, it was the very struggling and desiring for another world that made the refusal itself the negative critique of the established reality, foreshadowing the new, nonrepressive reality by peeling away the contingency of the established reality and exposing its contradictions. Thus, refusal of a technological rationality that upholds one-dimensional life also charts the beginnings of the new world inside of the shell of the old.[29] In this sense, the Great Refusal is an ideal. Rather than a finite, fully developed destination, it is a desire and an objective that seizes on the Western philosophical tradition's yearning for freedom rooted in the potentiality of Being to be other than how it appears. But it is also an ethico-political commitment to this yearning that puts into practice the struggle for another form

---

25. Marcuse, *One-Dimensional Man*, 220. See also Vieta, "Marcuse's 'Transcendent Project' at 50."

26. Marcuse, *Eros and Civilization*, 149–150.

27. Ibid., 151.

28. Ibid., 151–152 (emphasis in original).

29. Carl Boggs Jr., "Revolutionary Process, Political Strategy, and the Dilemma of Power," *Theory and Society* 4, no. 3 (1977): 359–393; Benjamin Franks, *Rebel Alliances: The Means and Ends of Contemporary British Anarchisms* (Edinburgh: AK Press, 2006).

of existence. It is a striving that begins with seemingly utopian imaginaries that prefigure another world in the now.[30] It retains the hope that a refusal to play the game and a commitment to thinking and acting otherwise will gradually build and proliferate the other world from out of the margins and into real alternatives to one-dimensional reality. This, as I show shortly, has many sympathies with some of today's prefigurative social movements and alternative socioeconomic experiments against and beyond neoliberalism.[31]

For Marcuse, one way that a politics of refusal could be provoked was via the openings for alternatives that may arise from out of the merger of the inherent human desire for freedom, the socioeconomic practices of the marginalized, and the inevitable crises of the established system.[32] For him, other potentialities for life could come to fruition via both the fractures and crises that the status-quo system is susceptible to—its "internal contradictions"[33]—*and* the spontaneous, decentralized, and diffuse nature of bottom-up struggle from the "subversive grass roots."[34] In *An Essay on Liberation*, Marcuse writes:

> The change itself could then occur in a general, unstructured, un-organized, and diffused process of disintegration. This process may be sparked by a *crisis of the system* which would activate the resistance not only against the political but also against the mental repression imposed by the society. Its insane features, expression of the ever more blatant contradiction between the available resources for liberation and their use for the perpetuation of servitude, would

---

30. Again, note Marcuse's phrasing: "this ingression of the future in the present." Marcuse, *An Essay on Liberation*, 89.

31. For Marcuse, as I further articulate in this chapter, prefigurative standpoints manifested in actual practices of autonomous and diffuse groups on the margins. See Marcuse, *An Essay on Liberation*, 90. The concept of prefiguration (rooted in his notion of potentiality) was present, for him, in the possibilities inherent in existing alternative socialist and anarchistic practices of "autonomy" and "solidarity" (88). As Harry Cleaver writes in unintended synchrony with Marcuse, utopian prefiguration is about "the search for the future in the present, and the identification of already existing activities which embody new, alternative forms of social cooperation and ways of being." Quoted in Richard J. F. Day, *Gramsci Is Dead: Anarchist Currents in the Newest Social Movements* (London: Pluto, 2005), 156. For contemporary theories of prefiguration in today's newest alterglobalization social movements, see Marina Sitrin and Dario Azzellini, *They Can't Represent Us! Reinventing Democracy from Greece to Occupy* (London: Verso, 2014); David Graeber, *Direct Action: An Ethnography* (Oakland, CA: AK Press, 2009); John Holloway, *Change the World without Taking Power: The Meaning of Revolution Today* (London: Pluto, 2002); and Day, *Gramsci Is Dead*.

32. Vieta, "Marcuse's 'Transcendent Project' at 50."

33. Marcuse, *Counterrevolution and Revolt*, 56.

34. Ibid., 42.

undermine the daily routine, the repressive conformity, and rationality required for the continued functioning of the [established]
society.[35]

Crisis moments, then, are both threatening instances of disorganization for
the status quo's socioeconomic order and opportunities of reorganization
for alternatives to this status quo. In turn, these inherent moments of crisis
could lead to the unraveling and eventual disintegration of "the internal
structure and cohesion of the capitalist system,"[36] as breakdown in one place
could ignite spontaneous and inventive forms of social expressions "from
below" at vulnerable points across the system. Assessing the strength of the
status quo, Marcuse continues:

> Now it is the strength of [the system's] moral fiber, of the operational
> values . . . , which is likely to wear off under the impact of the grow
> ing contradictions within the society. The result would be . . . resis
> tance to work, refusal to perform, negligence, indifference—factors
> of dysfunction which would hit a highly centralized and coordinated
> apparatus, where breakdown at one point may easily affect large sec
> tions of the whole.[37]

These contradictions of the system could thus subsequently stimulate a
"contagion"[38] and contribute to broader liberational movements of workers'
control, cooperatives, and more benign and humane uses of technology.[39]
The potential Marcuse saw for the reorganization of life and work emerging
immanently out of contradiction, crisis, and contagion is in close affinity
to what autonomist Marxists have called people's continued capacities for
the "refusal" of and "exodus" from alienating and oppressive social structures and exploitative forms of labor.[40] Similarly, contradiction, crisis, and

---

35. Marcuse, *An Essay on Liberation*, 83 (emphasis added).

36. Ibid., 82.

37. Ibid., 84.

38. Marcuse, *Counterrevolution and Revolt*, 42.

39. Ibid., 43–47.

40. Autonomist Marxist conceptualizations of "refusal" and "exodus" (or exit) are capacities always already present with living labor. They prefigure "potential mode[s] of life that
[challenge] the mode of life now defined by [capitalist] work." Kathi Weeks, "The Refusal
of Work as Demand and Desire," in *The Philosophy of Antonio Negri*, vol. 1, *Resistance in
Practice*, ed. Timothy S. Murphy and Abdul-Karim Mustapha (London: Pluto, 2005), 121.
Moreover, for autonomist Marxists, as with Marcuse, acts of refusal and exodus from the
capital-labor relation can emerge from out of desires that "rebel against the present system of
work and work values" and as "creative practice[s] . . . that seek to reappropriate and reconfigure existing forms of production and reproduction" (122).

contagion, for Marcuse, were pregnant with a politics of refusal, holding the DNA of the potential Great Refusal.

Hints of the Great Refusal in Our Times

Marcuse's assessment of the possible forms that a post-technologically rationalized life could take echoes many of today's contemporary experiments with horizontalized, recommunalized, and anticapitalist forms of social and economic reorganization. Indeed, Marcuse's own words could be used to accurately describe contemporary movements of alternative socioeconomic arrangements: in Marcuse's *Counterrevolution and Revolt*, written in 1972, we see him provisionally theorizing practices such as directly democratic social experiments[41] (as political but perhaps not necessarily economic power from below) and workers' control (as economic but perhaps not necessarily political power from below).[42] From his earlier *An Essay on Liberation*, published a year after the events of May 1968, we read of his hopes for practices of "solidarity and cooperation," "autonomy," and "self-determination" that must suffuse "relationships of production [as] a new way of life, a new Form of life," in which, prefiguratively, "their existential quality must show forth, anticipated and demonstrated, in the fight for their realization."[43] And in 1955's *Eros and Civilization*, we see evidence of how people can aspire toward the refusal of the "Profit and Performance Principle" more generally[44] via the automatization of labor and the privileging of imagination, fantasy, and play over alienated work and toil.[45] Ultimately, for Marcuse, the "performance principle" (alienated labor) can be libidinally reconstituted into a nonsurplus-repressive, Eros-laden, and life-affirming "reality principle" in which play and work would themselves be reconciled and fused under a new order not subject to "administration" by "rational routine" or the "mastery instinct."[46]

In what remains, I offer three examples of radical social experiments of reorganization unfolding today, experiments that echo Marcuse's transcendent project of a post-technological rationality that holds the germs of a Great Refusal. These movements do not outwardly espouse Marcusean values, but Marcuse's critical theory helps us understand them in nonessentialist and nonsubstantivist ways. They, at the same time, critique the established order of neoliberal capitalism, emerge from its cycles of crises, *and* experiment with—prefiguratively—new social, cultural, economic, and

---

41. Marcuse, *Counterrevolution and Revolt*, 45.
42. Ibid., 43.
43. Marcuse, *An Essay on Liberation*, 88.
44. Marcuse, *Eros and Civilization*, 83–90.
45. Ibid., 193.
46. Ibid., 218–219.

technological realities. These experiments are seeing today's marginalized and grassroots groups revalorizing and reorganizing land, property, productive technologies, work, housing, education, and other spaces for meeting life's needs and for play and artistic expression. Some of these experiments include community and neighborhood groups from seemingly depleted urban corners, the poor in the Global North and South, the precariously employed, the chronically unemployed, the landless, the dispossessed, and indigenous groups of all kinds. In the process, they are reappropriating the technological inheritance, reinventing new technological mediations, and reorganizing life itself—from the margins—in ways that subvert and refuse the ideologies of private property, individualism, managerialism, and growth at all costs. They favor—rather than the unsustainable offerings of neoliberal capital—socialized wealth, communal ownership, cooperation, participatory democracy, subsidiarity, care of the environment, mutual aid, new modes of social production, and, in some cases, the refusal of the wage-based system of work itself. And throughout, these alternatives are under-girded by new forms of radicalized rationalities and subjectivities.

From Crisis to the Refusal of Capitalist Economic Activity: Reappropriating Community Economies

There has been renewed talk since the early 2000s in contemporary critical theory and radical social activism that the "global society of control" can be successfully resisted via "refusal" by "desertion, exodus . . . nomadism . . . subtraction and defection."[47] Indeed, myriad "community economies" have long exemplified such forms of refusals of defections from neoliberal capital. Community economies, according to J. K. Gibson-Graham, reflect both the capacities, assets, and practices already in place in localities that reach beyond capitalist wage-based work, privately owned enterprises, and competitive markets. They do so in their diverse forms of noncapitalist and collective labor; cooperative and communal organization; and gifting, sharing, householding, reciprocal, and redistributive forms of transactions. Moreover, community economies, while not completely unproblematic in their sometimes gendered, racialized, and patriarchal biases, are often, at their most self-conscious and critical moments, prefigurative of another reality *and* transformative in the "here and now" despite the continued presence of global capital.[48] Moved to action by the soaring rate of personal debt,

---

47. Michael Hardt and Antonio Negri, *Empire* (Cambridge, MA: Harvard University Press, 2000), 212.

48. J. K. Gibson-Graham, *The End of Capitalism (as We Knew It): A Feminist Critique of Political Economy* (Minneapolis: University of Minnesota Press, 2006); J. K. Gibson-Graham, "Enabling Ethical Economies: Cooperativism and Class," *Critical Sociology* 29, no. 2 (2003):

the precariousness of our world's ecology, the North's overconsumption, and the ultimate emptiness of our acquisitive lifestyles, many communities throughout the world today have chosen to exit the consumerist and productivist maelstrom by reigniting purposeful and intentional ways of living that integrate local assets and practices with "both inner and outer aspects of life into an organic and purposeful whole."[49] For the people already practicing these alternative economic initiatives, outlets of "subtraction"[50] also form part of a greater "revolution in fairness"[51] that strives to break the cycle of personal dissatisfactions with wage labor, inequality, and environmental decay.

Latin America's new community economies and cultural expressions from the grassroots, rooted in local practices and direct responses to the sociopolitical and socioeconomic collapse of its neoliberal regimes, are recent examples of economic reinventions emerging out of moments of crises. This was especially witnessed during the years spanning the turn of the millennium.[52] Illustrative of these social upheavals in Latin America were the new social compositions that emerged in Argentina around the financial and political crisis of late 2001 and early 2002. With the temporary collapse of its neoliberal model at the time, countless local social groups that had been emerging since the mid-1990s had by then blanketed Argentina's urban centers and public spaces, creating alternative social institutions organized by directly democratic decision-making structures that filled the void left by systemic breakdown and a crumbling, impotent nation-state. By the turn of the millennium, Argentina's increasing class divisions crystallized into the strident radicalization of local people and marginalized groups. Throughout these years, a contagion of bottom-up popular resistance spread across all popular sectors, seen most vividly in the widespread direct-action tactics of property occupations and squatting; the now-famous road blockages of the *piquetero* (the unemployed workers' movement); and myriad other spontaneous community mobilizations, such as the mushrooming of *clubes de*

123–161; J. K. Gibson-Graham, "Surplus Possibilities: Postdevelopment and Community Economies," *Singapore Journal of Tropical Geography* 26, no. 1 (2005): 4–26.

49. Duane Elgin, "Voluntary Simplicity and the New Global Challenge," in *The Consumer Society Reader*, ed. Juliet Schor (New York: New Press, 2000), 397.

50. Hardt and Negri, *Empire*, 212.

51. Elgin, "Voluntary Simplicity," 406.

52. Maristella Svampa and Sebastián Pereyra, *Entre la ruta y el barrio: La experiencia de las organizaciones piqueteras* [Between the road and the neighborhood: The experience of the piquetera organizations] (Buenos Aires: Biblos, 2003); Maurizio Atzeni and Marcelo Vieta, "Between Class and the Market: Self-Management in Theory and in the Practice of Worker-Recuperated Enterprises in Argentina," in *The Routledge Companion to Alternative Organization*, ed. Martin Parker, George Cheney, Valérie Fournier, and Chris Land (London: Routledge, 2014), 47–63; Marina A. Sitrin, *Everyday Revolutions: Horizontalism and Autonomy in Argentina* (London: Zed, 2012).

trueque (barter clubs), *asambleas barriales* (neighborhood assemblies), and locally based food security and provisioning projects.[53] Other specific micropolitical and microeconomic forms sprouting up from below and spurred on by crisis at the time included squatters' initiatives and property occupations that served to immediately resolve the dearth of affordable and safe housing; worker-recuperated businesses that surged in light of sharply rising unemployment rates and business closures (which I review in the next section); and the emergence of free and cooperatively run popular schools, free community health clinics, neighborhood cultural clubs, alternative money schemes, and radical community radio, television, and Internet-based projects.

What spilled over—contagiously—into all forms of popular struggle in the country at the time was a renewed sense of collective purpose against a callous, exploitative, and socially alienating system; a growing ethos of self-organization and direct participatory democracy "from below" via extremely flat—or "horizontal"—organizing structures;[54] and a massive "reactivation" of "communitarian social experience."[55] As Marcuse envisioned, such resistances and bottom-up struggle created new possibilities for life for Argentina's marginalized who began to articulate themselves in the rupture of "work discipline" and, subsequently, "slowdown, spread of disobedience to rules and regulations, wildcat strikes, boycotts, sabotage, [and] gratuitous acts of noncompliance."[56] This resistance also resonates with autonomist Marxist interpretations of Argentina's spontaneous struggles. Antonio Negri, for instance, observed during this period that the responses by groups such as the *piqueteros*, *asambleas barriales*, and *clubes de trueque* to neoliberal enclosure and crisis bore witness to a new "energy . . . [of] conviction, and . . . egalitarian social recomposition"[57] that emerged from the urban *barrios* and industrialized towns of the country at the time—the areas that most deeply felt the callousness of neoliberalism and its moment of collapse. These experiments that served to at least temporarily reconstruct the social,

---

53. Ana Dinerstein, "The Battle of Buenos Aires: Crisis, Insurrection and the Reinvention of Politics in Argentina," *Historical Materialism* 10, no. 4 (2002): 5–38; Sitrin, *Everyday Revolutions*; Svampa and Pereyra, *Entre la ruta y el barrio*.

54. Colectivo Situaciones, "Asambleas, cacerolas y piquetes (sobre las nuevas formas de protagonismo social)" [Assemblies, pots and pickets (on new forms of social activism)], *Borradores de Investigación* [Research Drafts], no. 3 (2002), available at htti://www.nodo50.org/colectivosituaciones/borradores_03.html; Colectivo Situaciones, "Causes and Happenstance (Dilemmas of Argentina's New Social Protagonism)," *The Commoner* 8 (Autumn–Winter 2004): 1–15; Sitrin, *Everyday Revolutions*.

55. Svampa and Pereyra, *Entre la ruta y el barrio*, 233.

56. Marcuse, *An Essay on Liberation*, 83.

57. Antonio Negri, "The Ballad of Buenos Aires: A Critique of the Italian Edition of the Book *19 and 20: Notes for the New Social Protagonism* by Colectivo Situaciones," *Generation Online*, 2003, available at http://www.generation-online.org/t/sitcol.htm.

cultural, and economic fabric of Argentina grew spontaneously and contagiously as the system experienced, as Marcuse seemed to predict, disruption and cracks in key places, leading to "contradictions of the system"[58] coming to the surface and a general "dysfunctioning of the whole"[59] of Argentina.

Given these cracks and openings in the system that expanded via crisis and contagion, neighbors, unemployed and precarious workers, and the poor reorganized everyday life, production, and work, as well as the provisioning and acquisition of food and other necessities, around rematerialized values and practices of mutual aid and nonmonetary exchange. These community-based groups came together to fill a void left by an increasingly dysfunctional system in breakdown. In the process, they began to refute the neoliberal order that had relegated them to the margins *and* to create new economic and productive spaces for themselves.[60] These alternative, community-based spaces can also be seen as contemporary versions of Marcuse's notions of new technological reasoning (i.e., post-technological rationality) and co-operative and nonhierarchical economic reorganization budding from out of a politics of refusal promulgated by need and crisis. Moreover, they are self-determining and self-managed experiments by radicalized subjectivities attuned to notions of solidarity, the plight of their immediate surroundings, and the needs of each community member.

Similar recent rerationalizations of life that hint at a Marcusean politics of refusal and a "transcendent project" stimulated by system-wide contradiction, crises, dysfunction, and breakdown have emerged in recent years in other parts of the world. What comes immediately to mind are the countless actions of alternative community economies and communal ownership by the marginalized, indigenous groups, and the dispossessed, as well as by growing portions of the so-called middle class exhausted by the psychic, social, and environmental effects of acquisitiveness, competition, and environmental degradation. Among many others, these actions include:

- Squatter and intentional community movements learning to live collectively with less, and in more sustainable ways, such as the global slums movement,[61] the Copenhagen Squatters' Movement,[62]

---

58. Marcuse, *Essay on Liberation*, 84.

59. Marcuse, *Counterrevolution and Revolt*, 43.

60. Marcelo Vieta, "Learning in Struggle: Argentina's New Worker Cooperatives as Transformative Learning Organizations," *Relations Industrielles/Industrial Relations* 69, no. 1 (2014): 186–218; Atzeni and Vieta, "Between Class and the Market."

61. See "Naked Cities: Struggle in the Global Slums," *Mute* 2, no. 3 (2006), available at http://www.metamute.org/editorial/magazine/mute-vol-2-no.-3-%E2%88%92-naked-cities-struggle-global-slums.

62. See Michael Scølardt, "A Short History of the Copenhagen Squatters Movement," *Indymedia Ireland*, September 3, 2006, available at http://www.indymedia.ie/article/78192.

New York City's Squat!net autonomous infrastructures initiative,[63]
Barcelona's Can Masdeu occupied and self-managed intentional
community,[64] and the broader ecovillages movement[65]

- Brazil's landless workers' and peasants' movement that has been
  taking over and reviving fallow land since the 1980s[66]
- The Zapatistas' indigenous movements' horizontally controlled
  economic systems[67]
- The embrace of the Quechua concept of *sumak kawsay* (*buen vivir*, or good living) by indigenous communities throughout Latin
  America[68]
- Europe's myriad grassroots and autonomous social centers, such
  as Italy's Centri Sociali Autogestiti[69]
- Local, asset-based community development, such as Kerala's women's textile cooperatives and Italy's social cooperatives that consistently counter economic downturns in the rest of the economy and
  the pulling back of the neoliberal state's social services[70]

---

63. See "About," *Squat!net*, available at https://en.squat.net/about/ (accessed July 2, 2015).

64. See Vall de Can Masdeu, "Who Are We," available at http://www.canmasdeu.net/who-are-we/?lang=en (accessed June 23, 2016).

65. See T. Baker, "Ecovillages and Capitalism: Creating Sustainable Communities within an Unsustainable Context," in *Environmental Anthropology Engaging Ecotopia: Bioregionalism, Permaculture, and Ecovillages*, ed. Joshua Lockyer and James R. Veteto (New York: Berghahn, 2013), 285–300; and Lisa Mychajluk, "Building Capacity to Live and Work Together at an Ecovillage in Support of Sustainable Community: A Case Study" (master's thesis, Ontario Institute for Studies in Education, University of Toronto, 2014).

66. See Friends of the MST, "What Is the MST?," available at http://www.mstbrazil.org/content/what-mst (accessed July 15, 2015); and Ethan Miller, "Solidarity Economics: Strategies for Building New Economies from the Bottom-Up and the Inside-Out," Grassroots Economic Organizing Collective, June 2005, available at http://www.geo.coop/archives/SolidarityEconomicsEthanMiller.htm.

67. See Raúl Zibechi, "The Art of Building a New World: Freedom According to the Zapatistas," September 9, 2013, available at http://www.schoolsforchiapas.org/wp-content/uploads/2014/07/Freedom-According-to-the-Zapatistas.pdf.

68. See Michela Giovannini, "Indigenous Community Enterprises in Chiapas: A Vehicle for Buen Vivir?," *Community Development Journal* 50, no. 1 (2014): 71–87; Eduardo Gudynas, "Buen Vivir: Today's Tomorrow," *Development* 54, no. 4 (2011): 441–447; and Bob Thomson, "Pachakuti: Indigenous Perspectives, *Buen Vivir, Sumaq Kawsay* and Degrowth," *Development* 54, no. 4 (2011): 448–454.

69. See Andre Pusey, "Social Centres and the New Cooperativism of the Common," *Affinities: A Journal of Radical Theory, Culture, and Action* 4, no. 1 (2010): 176–198.

70. See Sonia George, "Enabling Subjectivities: Economic and Cultural Negotiations—a Gendered Reading of the Handloom Sector and the Special Economic Zone of Kerala," *Indian Journal of Gender Studies* 20, no. 2 (2013): 305–334; and Vanna Gonzales, "Italian Social Cooperatives and the Development of Civic Capacity: A Case of Cooperative Renewal?," *Affinities: A Journal of Radical Theory, Culture, and Action* 4, no. 1 (2010): 225–251.

- Bartering and local currency exchanges that have taken hold in both the Global South and North, such as the *clubes de trueque* in Argentina and the Local Exchange Trading Systems (LETs) across Europe and North America[71]
- Environmentally sound practices of the community-sustained agricultural (CSA) movement, neighborhood food co-ops and markets, the community gardens movement, and Cuba's cooperatively run *organopónicos*[72]
- The degrowth,[73] do-it-yourself (DIY), and radical simplicity movements[74]

These experiments of refusal and community-based sociotechnical reinvention are leading to compelling and transformative proposals for alternative community economies. Their reorganizations of socioeconomic life—via myriad forms of alternative economies, networks of solidarity, and self-determined forms of production and provisioning—have been springing up across the world over the past decades, embracing what has also been termed "the social and solidarity economy."[75] They offer rich contemporary examples of rerationalized technological reorderings constructed around decommodified principles of cooperation, self-determination, and economies of solidarity. In their praxis, such experiments immanently critique capitalism's "sacrosanct" pillars of private property, profit, self-interest, and competition by replacing them with common ownership, mutual aid, and cooperation.

---

71. See Peter North, "Complementary Currencies," in *The Routledge Companion to Alternative Organization*, ed. Martin Parker, George Cheney, Valérie Fournier, and Chris Land (London: Routledge, 2014), 182–194.

72. See Miguel A. Altieri and Fernando R. Funes-Monzote, "The Paradox of Cuban Agriculture," *Monthly Review* 63, no. 8 (2012), available at http://monthlyreview.org/2012/01/01/the-paradox-of-cuban-agriculture/; Michela Giovannini and Marcelo Vieta, "Cooperatives in Latin America," in *Handbook of Cooperative and Mutual Businesses*, ed. Jonathan Michie, Joseph Blasi, and Carlo Borzaga (Oxford: Oxford University Press, forthcoming); and Steven McFadden, "The History of Community Supported Agriculture," Rodale Institute, available at http://www.newfarm.org/features/0104/csa-history/part1.shtml (accessed April 6, 2016).

73. See Research and Degrowth, "Short History," available at http://www.degrowth.org/short-history (accessed July 3, 2015).

74. See Trapeze Collective, ed., *Do It Yourself: A Handbook for Changing Our World* (London: Pluto, 2007); and Jim Merkel, *Radical Simplicity: Small Footprints on a Finite Earth* (Gabriola Island, BC: New Society, 2003).

75. Ash Amin, *The Social Economy: International Perspectives on Economic Solidarity* (London: Zed, 2009); José Luis Coraggio, "La economía social como vía para otro desarollo social" [The social economy as a way to another kind of social development], *Urbared*, no. 1 (2002), available at http://www.coraggioeconomia.org/jlc/archivos%20para%20descargar/La%20Economia%20Social%20como%20alternativa%20estructural%204.pdf.

Training for the Politics of Refusal: Radical Education Initiatives

Today, throughout the Global North and South, we can also find a surge of popular education projects contesting the hegemony of increasingly commodified primary schools and postsecondary institutions.[76] These alternative educational spaces are akin to Marcuse's "areas of withdrawal" to think collectively and away from the hullabaloo of the society of speed in order to reflect and learn about the "redistribution of socially necessary labor (time)"[77] into free time (i.e., Marx's "real wealth") and the path to true freedom and self-actualization. They are examples of Marcuse's vision for the creation of "independent schools and 'free universities'" to facilitate the emergence of radicalized forms of social actors and for learning about solidarity-based work and a new libidinal work instinct.[78] That is, they can be seen as providing training for the new, radical subject's politics of refusal.

The Toronto Freeskool[79] and the Anarchist Free University (AFU)[80] are two examples of critical education projects that aspire to create new, nonoppressive, and nonalienating realities out of the status quo. In the case of the now dormant AFU, "an open, volunteer-run, non-hierarchical collective," throughout the 2000s it offered "a variety of courses on arts and sciences" for the building of "a vibrant and productive community free from the struggles for power, profit and prestige that are the consequences of existing social and economic structures."[81] The AFU's nonhierarchical, community-led courses explored subjects such as alternative economic practices, DIY projects, gender and LGBTQ issues, and community gardening, among many others. The Toronto School of Creativity and Inquiry (TSCI), active between 2004 and 2010,[82] and New York City's 16 Beaver Group,[83] active since 1999, have held radical artist event series and reading groups and have been involved

---

76. The Edu-Factory Collective, *Toward a Global Autonomous University: Cognitive Labor, the Production of Knowledge, and Exodus from the Education Factory* (New York: Autonomedia, 2009).

77. Marcuse, *An Essay on Liberation*, 90.

78. Marcuse, *Counterrevolution and Revolt*, 54–56.

79. See Toronto Freeskool, "Toronto Freeskool Manifesto and Core Values," https://torontofreeskool.wordpress.com/about/ (accessed April 16, 2015).

80. See Megan Kinch, "Toronto's Free Schools: It Takes Community," *Toronto Media Co-op*, January 30, 2013, available at http://toronto.mediacoop.ca/story/torontos-free -schools/16025.

81. Anarchist Free University, "Mission Statement," available at https://freeskoolsproject .wikispaces.com/anarchist+free+u (accessed April 6, 2016).

82. See Rob Shields, "Entangled Territories: Toronto School of Creativity and Inquiry," *Space and Culture*, February 24, 2009, available at http://www.spaceandculture .org/2009/02/24/entangled-territories-toronto-school-of-creativity-inquiry/.

83. See 16 Beaver Group, "About 16 Beaver," available at http://16beavergroup.org/about/ (accessed July 5, 2016).

in counterhegemonic community interventions, offering yet more promising examples of critical community education initiatives with deep affinities to the politics of refusal. In the case of TSCI, a project which I was a part of,[84] its radical community interventions and critical pedagogy initiatives included counterhegemonic cartography exhibits, proposals for locally rooted alternative economic arrangements, radical art interventions and noncapitalist transformations of the city, and myriad projects looking at ways of moving beyond the neoliberal enclosures of life. Critical U's community-led and postsecondary for-credit course offerings, active in Vancouver, British Columbia, between the late 1990s and early 2000s, were rooted in the concept of "utopian pedagogy," contesting the status quo in collaborative learning sessions with those who could not afford formal postsecondary education and the broader community.[85] And Argentina's Universidad Trashumante is a team of activist educators traveling in a reconfigured bus throughout the country's hinterland, offering critical pedagogical and community educational opportunities to marginalized communities.[86]

These exemplary popular and community-based education experiments—and there are innumerable others around the world today—show how collectivities are critically pausing from the din of consumerist life, rupturing the cult of technologically mediated distraction, and using their time to reflect on human beings' continued capacities to forge alternative, noncapitalist communities. They are organized outside of the confines of the traditional university and distinguished by their horizontal modes of organizing and their willingness to collectively conceptualize more utopian modes of social and productive existence. And they are educational experiments that encourage participants to critically reflect on, seek out, create, and share—proactively, cooperatively, and prefiguratively—how to act on revelations of critical thought and social change for moving beyond crises and institutional and technological domination. They are forging new, noncommodified educational spaces from which to conceive new presents and different futures from within and beyond the vantage point of our current globalized neoliberal enclosures. In the critical theoretical language of Marcuse, they do not maximize capitalist productive time but, rather, something resembling Marx's "disposable time"—the so-called unproductive time with regard to capital, or the time set apart from the processes of valorizing commodities for the self-development of individuals and communities. At the same time, they are helping to create a new commons for learning the

---

84. Others involved with TSCI included Greig de Peuter, Adrian Blackwell, Christine Shaw, and Enda Brophy.

85. Mark Coté, Richard J. F. Day, and Greig de Peuter, eds., *Utopian Pedagogy: Radical Experiments against Neoliberal Globalization* (Toronto: University of Toronto Press, 2007).

86. See the organization's blog site, at http://universidadtrashumante.blogspot.com/.

politics of refusal and alternative forms of living outside the marketplace. Furthermore, their collective education practices are, again, rooted in notions of mutual aid, noncommercialized interactions, and affinity groupings.

Recuperating Spaces of Production

Yet another vivid example of creative reappropriation of technology that deserves further reflection from a Marcusean politics of refusal is Latin America's *empresas recuperadas por sus trabajadores* (worker-recuperated enterprises, or ERTs). Emerging out of the already mentioned neoliberal crises in Latin America around the turn of the millennium and in its subsequent widespread turn to the Left (the so-called pink tide), ERTs are new enterprises formed by workers who take over and recuperate the troubled capitalist firms that had employed them, subsequently converting them into worker cooperatives.[87] Created directly as workers' bottom-up responses to the worst effects of neoliberal policies, practices, and crises, this new and simultaneously workers' and cooperative movement has been contagiously spawning new cases of workplace takeovers and technological, economic, social, and productive innovations over the past two decades. They have been spreading in more recent years into a growing worldwide movement of ERTs in other national settings and localities facing austerity and socioeconomic downturns, such as across southern Europe (Spain, Italy, France, and Greece), in South Korea and South Africa, and even in the United States.[88]

87. Henrique T. Novaes, *O fetiche da tecnologia: A experiência das fábricas recuperadas* [The fetish of technology: The experience of the recovered factories] (São Paolo, Brazil: Expressão Popular, 2007); Marie Trigona, "Workplace Resistance and Self-Management: Strategic Lessons from Latin America," *ZNet*, July 21, 2009, available at https://zcomm.org/znetarticle/workplace-resistance-and-self-management-by-marie-trigona/; Marcelo Vieta and Andrés Ruggeri, "Worker-Recovered Enterprises as Workers' Co-operatives: The Conjunctures, Challenges, and Innovations of Self-Management in Argentina and Latin America," in *Co-operatives in a Global Economy: The Challenges of Co-operation across Borders*, ed. Darryl Reed and J. J. McMurtry (Newcastle upon Tyne, UK: Cambridge Scholars, 2009), 178–225; Marcelo Vieta, "The Social Innovations of Autogestión in Argentina's Worker-Recuperated Enterprises: Cooperatively Organizing Productive Life in Hard Times," *Labor Studies Journal* 35, no. 3 (2010): 295–321; Marcelo Vieta, "From Managed Employees to Self-Managed Workers: The Transformations of Labour at Argentina's Worker-Recuperated Enterprises," in *Alternative Work Organisations*, ed. Maurizio Atzeni (Houndmills, UK: Palgrave Macmillan, 2012), 129–156; Marcelo Vieta, "Learning in Struggle: Argentina's New Worker Cooperatives as Transformative Learning Organizations," *Relations Industrielles/Industrial Relations* 69, no. 1 (2014): 186–218.

88. Marcelo Vieta, "The Emergence of the Empresas Recuperadas por Sus Trabajadores: A Political and Sociological Appraisal of Two Decades of Self-Management in Argentina," Euricse Working Paper no. 55/13, May 20, 2013, available at http://papers.ssrn.com/sol3/papers.cfm?abstract_id=2267357; Vieta, "Learning in Struggle"; Marcelo Vieta, Sara Depedri, and Antonella Carrano, *The Italian Road to Recuperating Enterprises: The Legge Marcora*

Greig de Peuter and Nick Dyer-Witheford have called the socialized redistribution of surpluses and labor processes by workers themselves in these recuperated worker cooperatives a type of "labour commons" that reflect practices of "commoning."[89] As a labor commons, worker co-ops fundamentally return surpluses back to the business's producer-members—its workers—for them to choose how to use and redistribute. This, in fact, is the distinguishing characteristic of most worker cooperatives as social(ized) businesses; at a worker cooperative, it is labor—the direct producers—that *hires* capital, not the other way around, as in capitalist businesses.[90] Progressive social and economic researchers have also shown that worker cooperatives have many positive outcomes (i.e., "positive externalities") for their communities because workers are more committed to the survival of their firms and localities when compared to distant shareholders and external investors. Such positive outcomes include better health for workers who self-manage their enterprises[91] and the protection of entire communities from economic downturns, because worker co-ops tend support their worker-members and surrounding communities in ways that investor-owned firms do not.[92] Such is the case with Latin America's worker-recuperated firms.

Present in almost all sectors of Argentina's urban economy, as well as throughout the economies of Uruguay, Brazil, and, to a lesser extent, Venezuela, Mexico, Colombia, Paraguay, Bolivia, and Peru, the phenomenon of ERTs today includes approximately forty thousand or more workers that have taken over and reorganized upwards of five hundred once-capitalist firms that went bankrupt or shut down because of the implosion of these countries' national economies in the 1990s and early 2000s.[93] As most sectors of their national economies found it increasingly difficult to compete with goods produced by multinational firms that had encroached into their

---

Workers' Buyouts; A Euricse Report on Italian Workers' Buyouts in Times of Crisis (Trento, Italy: European Research Institute on Cooperatives and Social Enterprises, 2015).

89. Greig de Peuter and Nick Dyer-Witheford, "Commons and Cooperatives," *Affinities: A Journal of Radical Theory, Culture, and Action* 4, no. 1 (2010): 37–39.

90. John G. Craig, *The Nature of Co-operation* (Montréal: Black Rose, 1993), 94.

91. David Erdal, *Beyond the Corporation: Humanity Working* (London: Bodley Head, 2011); Richard Wilkinson and Kate Picket, *The Spirit Level: Why Greater Equality Makes Societies Stronger* (New York: Bloomsbury, 2010).

92. Saul Estrin, "Workers' Co-operatives: Their Merits and Their Limitations," in *Market Socialism*, ed. Julian Le Grand and Saul Estrin (Oxford: Clarendon, 1989), 165–192; Avner Ben-Ner, "On the Stability of the Cooperative Type of Organization," *Journal of Comparative Economics* 8, no. 3 (1984): 247–260; Sonja Novkovic, "Defining the Co-operative Difference," *Journal of Socio-Economics* 37, no. 6 (2008): 2168–2177.

93. Trigona, "Workplace Resistance and Self-Management"; Atzeni and Vieta, "Between Class and the Market"; Vieta, "The Emergence of Empresas Recuperadas por Sus Trabajadores"; Andrés Ruggeri and Marcelo Vieta, "Argentina's Worker-Recuperated Enterprises, 2010–2013: A Synthesis of Recent Empirical Findings," *Journal of Entrepreneurial and Organizational Diversity* 4, no. 1 (2015): 75–103.

local economies, a rising tide of small- and medium-sized businesses went bankrupt throughout the region starting in the early 1990s.[94] More than two decades after the first recuperations in the region emerged, these worker-run cooperatives show, in particular, how a redirected technological apparatus of production can be redeployed to serve ends that are less capitalist and more locally focused. Moreover, Latin America's worker-recuperated enterprises, in their emergence from out of capitalist workplaces in economic decline, and in their mere existence within a sea of continued capitalist values, directly critique the most revered of modern institutions, the private investor-owned business.[95] Besides saving jobs and reappropriating the machineries of capitalist production for cooperative production, these worker-recuperated enterprises experiment with new forms of social production and the sharing of social wealth in ways that are akin to Marcuse's call to proliferate solidarity, workers' control, and cooperation.[96]

In the largest ERT movement in the world today, almost fourteen thousand Argentinean workers now self-manage more than three hundred ERTs.[97] Social researchers and progressive journalists have placed much weight on how many ERTs tend to tightly engrain themselves in the communities and neighborhoods that surround them.[98] As workers give back to the community groups, friends, families, and neighbors that assisted them in their most harrowing days of occupation and resistance,[99] and as they learn cooperative values and solidarity "in struggle,"[100] ERTs create and return social wealth to their communities in myriad ways. In Argentina, in particular, ERTs are also known as *la fábrica abierta* (the open factory), as many of them double as cultural and educational centers and even community dining rooms and free medical clinics run by workers, neighbors, or volunteers. And some of these new worker co-ops redirect significant portions of their

94. Alejandro Portes and Kelly Hoffman, "Latin American Class Structures: Their Composition and Change during the Neoliberal Era," *Latin American Research Review* 38, no. 1 (2003): 41–82.

95. Atzeni and Vieta, "Between Class and the Market"; Vieta, "From Managed Employees to Self-Managed Workers."

96. Marcuse, *An Essay on Liberation*, 88; see also Marcuse, *Counterrevolution and Revolt*.

97. Andrés Ruggeri, *Informe del IV relevamiento de empresas recuperadas en la Argentina, 2014: Las empresas recuperadas en el periodo 2010–2013* [IV survey report of recovered companies in Argentina, 2014: Businesses recovered in 2010–2013] (Buenos Aires: Cooperativa Chilavert Artes Gráficas, 2014), available at http://base.socioeco.org/docs/_informe_iv_relevamiento_2014.pdf.

98. Marcelo Vieta, "The Social Innovations of *Autogestión* in Argentina's Worker-Recuperated Enterprises: Cooperatively Organizing Productive Life in Hard Times," *Labor Studies Journal* 35, no. 3 (2010): 295–321; Vieta, "Learning in Struggle."

99. Vieta, "The Social Innovations of *Autogestión*."

100. Griff Foley, *Learning in Social Action: A Contribution to Understanding Informal Education* (London: Zed, 1999); Vieta, "Learning in Struggle."

revenues to community-development projects, such as building affordable housing for marginalized neighbors, contributing to youth sports and popular education initiatives, establishing alternative media spaces, spearheading recycling initiatives, involving themselves in the struggles of other social justice groups, and even hiring unemployed neighbors.[101]

The members of these worker co-ops have also fundamentally reorganized their labor processes into flattened organizational structures they call *horizontalidad* (horizontality).[102] ERTs are managed by recallable workers' councils and ad hoc decision-making groups on shop floors, and many of them belong to broader federations of ERTs and worker cooperatives that collaborate in their productive and political activities. In these horizontalized workplaces, production decisions are now made collectively and in directly democratic ways. They also hold regular workers' assemblies on shop floors to debate bigger issues that affect the entire collective, such as when to take on new members, when to purchase new machinery, and when to engage in solidarity networks with other ERTs and community and labor struggles.[103]

In the words of ERT protagonists, these new social relations within and beyond the walls of these "workspaces without bosses" tend to be framed by values of *compañerismo* (camaraderie) and are pierced by "an ethics of the other" that its workers describe as "Esto es de todos" (This belongs to all of us). They broadly express this solidarity with the plight of other workers in the phrase "Si nos tocan a uno, nos tocan a todos" (If they touch one of us, they touch us all).[104]

And perhaps most evocatively for reconfiguring the very notion of work, ERT workers make it a point of eating and playing together regularly (e.g., daily communal lunches and weekly soccer games or barbeques) and take many breaks throughout the day (e.g., regular *mate* tea breaks). Refusing contracts and projects when the work proves to be too onerous, sharing production processes with other ERTs and cooperatives, and allowing workers regular time off to attend to personal matters are other ways that capitalist notions of work are revalued and redesigned.

ERTs thus show ways of beginning to create what Marcuse called "work as free play," or the merger of work and play.[105] ERT protagonists do so in order to rehumanize their work and as a reminder of what they could not regularly do when they were employees working for a boss. These seemingly

101. Vieta, "The Social Innovations of *Autogestión*"; Vieta, "From Managed Employees to Self-Managed Workers"; Vieta, "Learning in Struggle."

102. Sitrin, *Everyday Revolutions.*

103. Vieta, "Learning in Struggle."

104. Vieta, "The Emergence of Empresas Recuperadas por Sus Trabajadores"; Vieta, "Learning in Struggle."

105. Marcuse, *Eros and Civilization*, 218.

modest reconfigurations of work time have infinitely beneficial effects for workers, helping ease the tensions and stresses that come with working for a living. Indeed, these reconfigurations of a workspace and the rhythms of work would be unheard of in capitalist firms with other conceptualizations of work, with other ideas regarding "productive" and "nonproductive" time, and with their focus on maximizing profits rather than on worker and community well-being.[106] They are, I argue, actual prefigurations of the reconciliation of the pleasure and reality principles; they are Marcuse's "first prerequisite for freedom"—"the reduction of the working day."[107]

Transforming and reorganizing previously capitalist spaces of production into other forms of economic, social, and cultural production and, in the process, redirecting the technological inheritance to noncapitalist ends, ERTs are examples of how workers themselves *can* indeed run their own affairs and reappropriate technologies once used solely for capitalist purposes. In Marcusean terms, they operate with a different technological rationality under the rubric of more libidinally infused conceptualizations of work, time, and collaboratively guided projects of social production.

From Sketches of the Great Refusal to Real Alternatives

It can be argued that alternative socioeconomic experiences and practices such as those I map out in this chapter are still comparatively small in scale and too fragmented to truly contest the stubbornly entrenched and planetary nature of the established neoliberal capitalist system. Today's alternative socioeconomic and technological experiments, some may counter, lack the fully formulated expressions of the *total* reworking of the technological base and the *total* transformation of society that Marcuse ultimately seemed to desire. Indeed, contrary to Marcuse's ultimate vision, perhaps we must question whether such "total" transformations of the system can ever be achieved lest we be reseduced back into hegemonic and oppressive forms of vanguardist, *etatist*, or universalist thought and practice. Contemporary alternative socioeconomic practices that have, for the past two decades, taken up the slogan of "another world is possible" nevertheless do have within them at least the germ of a Great Refusal.

---

106. For more details on these themes, see Vieta, "The Social Innovations of *Autogestión*"; Atzeni and Vieta, "Between Class and the Market"; Vieta, "The Emergence of Empresas Recuperadas por Sus Trabajadores"; and Vieta, "Learning in Struggle."

107. "Since the length of the working day is itself one of the principal repressive factors imposed upon the pleasure principle by the reality principle, the reduction of the working day to a point where the mere quantum of labor time no longer arrests human development is the first prerequisite of freedom [to self-actualize]." Marcuse, *Eros and Civilization*, 152.

The promise of the worldwide alterglobalization movements and the existing alternative economic arrangements that have emerged spontaneously in recent decades is to provide living examples of possible alternatives. They provide us with evidence of how Marcusean modes of post-technological rationality and life can emerge from neoliberal capture and its myriad moments of crisis. The bottom-up responses to these crises can be seen as upholding similar rematerialized values of pleasure, solidarity, and practices of cooperation and direct democracy that parallel Marcuse's transcendent project. For us today, they serve as models for immanently countering neoliberal enclosures and, at the same time, reinventing present social relations and institutions from below. In turn, they prefigure and project the potentiality for another world. In short, these real-world experiments offer nascent but nevertheless promising viable alternatives to, and communal freedom from, oppression, alienation, and exclusion. These are all visions of the other world that Marcuse might have been anticipating.

This chapter offers sketches of the Great Refusal via myriad forms of alternative reorganizations of the socioeconomic and cultural dimensions of life taking hold around the world today. The contemporary examples of the politics of refusal considered in this chapter not only highlight the continued relevance of Marcuse's praxical thought for today's radical social movements for change; they, more importantly, embody the concrete possibilities and hopes that Marcuse's critical theory offers projects aspiring to creatively appropriate the technologies and organizations of late modernity for new life-affirming means and ends. They serve as poignant contemporary instances of real alternatives emerging from capitalism's (dis)orders and (dis)organizations. They are, I believe, examples of what Marcuse might have had in mind for a post-technological rationality. In Latin America's worker-recuperated enterprises, critical educational projects, and other forms of alternative and locally rooted community economies, there is a prefigurative tendency in these social and economic experiments that point to another kind of technologically mediated world grounded in more horizontalized, deindividualized, recommunalized, and anticapitalist forms of collective expressions, economics, production, and values. Not surprisingly, they are, in the process of their technological reappropriations and inventiveness, rediscovering life-affirming ways of unleashing more human-centered and ecologically sensitive potentialities. They are clearing the way for reengaging with the world, for satisfying our social and cultural desires, and for meeting our economic needs in less competitive and more communal ways. They show how to (re)organize our lives along values of solidarity and community rather than competition and individualism.

The irresistibility for more and more people around the world of not only reactively resisting global capital and neoliberal enclosure but also proactively seeking out and reinventing alternative forms of technologically mediated life can be seen as modeling Marcuse's Nietzschean call for aspiring to a "different experience of the world,"[108] attainable via "will and joy . . . the logic of gratification"[109] and "being-as-end-in-itself—as joy (*Lust*) and enjoyment."[110] Moreover, a growing number of us are engraining our alternative technological spaces, practices, ethics, and politics with "attractive labor," a new form of work that flows from "pleasurable co-operation" and the "release" of creative and "libidinal forces."[111] Indeed, the experiments that I review in this chapter are undergirded by a politics of refusal grounded in an alternative technology of liberation rather than the logic of domination.

---

108. Marcuse, *Eros and Civilization*, 216.
109. Ibid., 124.
110. Ibid., 121–122.
111. Ibid., 217.

Part V

Contesting Theories

16

Hope and Catastrophe

Messianism in Erich Fromm
and Herbert Marcuse

JOAN BRAUNE

erbert Marcuse's Great Refusal suggests a rupture and dramatic break
from that which is. Although a total break with the past, especially
in the midst of a crisis, might seem to be how anyone would describe
a revolution, Erich Fromm rejects Marcuse's Great Refusal in favor of a different perspective on the nature of revolutionary transformation. While every bit as radical as Marcuse, Fromm is wary of what could be considered
Marcuse's "catastrophic messianism."[1] I argue that Herbert Marcuse's and
Erich Fromm's thinking about social transformation locates them in different categories in their understanding of the relationship between past, present, and future and in their understanding of revolution. A useful paradigm
for understanding this difference between Fromm and Marcuse lies in their
differing messianisms.

The influence of Jewish and Marxist messianism on the Frankfurt School
and on Marxism broadly is receiving growing acknowledgment and has
been rediscovered by thinkers from Jürgen Habermas to Jacques Derrida.[2] A
partially secularized version of the traditional Jewish hope and enthusiasm

---

1. Erich Fromm, *You Shall Be as Gods: A Radical Interpretation of the Old Testament and
Its Tradition* (New York: Holt, Rinehart, and Winston, 1996), 133.

2. See, for example, Eduardo Mendieta, *Global Fragments: Globalizations, Latinameri-
canisms, and Critical Theory* (Albany: State University of New York Press, 2007); Michael
Löwy, *Redemption and Utopia: Jewish Libertarian Thought in Central Europe: A Study in
Elective Affinity*, trans. Hope Heaney (Stanford, CA: Stanford University Press, 1992); Jürgen
Habermas, *Religion and Rationality: Essays on Reason, Religion, and Modernity*, ed. Eduardo
Mendieta (Cambridge, MA: MIT Press, 2002); Richard Wolin, *Labyrinths: Explorations in the
Critical Theory of Ideas* (Amherst: University of Massachusetts Press, 1995); Jacques Derrida,

for the coming of the messianic age of justice and peace, messianism arose as a topic of passionate debate in German Jewish intellectual circles in the years shortly before World War I. The messianism debate was inherently political—specifically, it was about finding a lens for theorizing social change in its relationship to the past, present, and future. Walter Benjamin, Gershom Scholem, Franz Rosenzweig, Ernst Bloch, Martin Buber, and many others in Jewish intellectual circles of the period, and somewhat across the political spectrum, laid claim to messianism in varying degrees and interpreted their projects in relation to it. Both Fromm's and Marcuse's ways of thinking were influenced by the messianism debates. Fromm used the term "messianism" more frequently, returning to the topic and responding to the Weimar messianism debates in his work from the 1950s through the 1970s. In this chapter, I articulate Fromm's distinction between two kinds of messianism, prophetic and catastrophic, and I explain how Fromm's concern about Marcuse's approach to revolutionary change is tied to Fromm's concern about catastrophic messianism and "forcing the Messiah,"[3] a critique to which he thinks Marcuse's philosophy is subject.

Prophetic and Catastrophic Messianism

Fromm's and Marcuse's messianisms share some common sources, not least of them Marx's *Economic and Philosophical Manuscripts of 1844* (commonly known as the *Paris Manuscripts*), which can themselves be seen as part of the wider trajectory of messianism broadly construed. In the *Paris Manuscripts*, communism is the fulfillment of history and human striving; the "resurrection of nature"; and the resolution of fundamental antagonisms between humanity and nature, theory and practice, private and public. In addition to Marx's influence, both Fromm and Marcuse were Jewish and were influenced by Jewish tradition to varying degrees. Although many have underplayed the influence of Judaism on the Frankfurt School, this is beginning to be rectified, especially through growing interest in Benjamin's messianism. Jack Jacobs's book, *The Frankfurt School, Jewish Lives, and Antisemitism*, is also an important contribution.[4] At the same time, it is important to note that classifying Marcuse or Fromm as somehow "messianic" is not to interpret their work as surreptitiously religious or their Marxism as somehow lacking in "materialism." Fromm describes the Enlightenment itself (not

---

Specters of Marx: The State of the Debt, the Work of Mourning, and the New International, trans. Peggy Kamuf (New York: Routledge, 1994).

   3. Erich Fromm, *The Revolution of Hope: Toward a Humanized Technology* (New York: Harper and Row, 1968), 8.

   4. See Jack Jacobs, *The Frankfurt School, Jewish Lives, and Antisemitism* (New York: Cambridge University Press, 2015).

known for its piety) as messianic, and he sees "atheists" Baruch Spinoza and Marx as among the foremost proponents of prophetic messianism.

Although messianism transcends its theological origins, it is useful to contextualize this discussion within Marcuse's and Fromm's own connections with Judaism. For Marcuse and his affinities with Judaism, I mainly refer the reader to Jacobs's new book, but briefly: although Marcuse was not brought up with much religious practice, his parents did belong to a synagogue and attended services at least yearly, and if Jacobs is right that Martin Heidegger blocked Marcuse's dissertation because Marcuse was Jewish, that would surely have influenced Marcuse's sense of Jewishness.[5] Jeremy Popkin remembers from his childhood that Marcuse attended a Passover Seder at his childhood home and made a toast to the first successful slave revolution, the Jewish slaves' escape from Pharaoh.[6]

The influence of Judaism on Fromm was admittedly far greater than on Marcuse and has been much commented on and studied. Fromm grew up in an Orthodox Jewish home and, when in his early twenties, studied almost daily with a Talmud teacher, the influential socialist Russian exile Salman Rabinkov. Fromm was one of the founders of the Frankfurt Freies Jüdisches Lehrhaus, an influential center of left-wing German Jewish intellectual life in which Gershom Scholem, Franz Rosenzweig, Abraham Joshua Heschel, and many others participated. Fromm also briefly participated in the Zionist movement in his early twenties, and he soon came to see Zionism as just another of the pernicious nationalisms to which he was opposed.[7] (In an interesting twist that deserves further study, as Jack Jacobs points out, Fromm had the greatest exposure to Judaism of any member of the Frankfurt School of his generation but was also the most ardently anti-Zionist.) Fromm's sociology dissertation was on the Jewish law, and he helped found and lead the psychoanalytic therapeutic commune, or "Therapeuticum," which was so permeated with Jewish religiosity that it was jokingly nicknamed the "Torah-peuticum." In short, Fromm was deeply formed by Jewish culture, religion, and intellectual life, and the influence of the Jewish intellectual tradition on his work is always clearly apparent, long after his formal break from Jewish religious life and theistic belief in his late twenties.

Despite their commonalities—a Marxist background and some level of identification with Judaism—Marcuse's and Fromm's messianisms had differing historical and philosophical affinities, and the two thinkers were moving in somewhat different directions in the 1950s and 1960s. It was in

---

5. Ibid., 112–114.

6. Jeremy Popkin, "Herbert Marcuse's Years at UC San Diego: An Interview with Richard H. Popkin" (lecture delivered at the conference of the International Herbert Marcuse Society, University of Kentucky, Lexington, November 7, 2013).

7. Rainer Funk, *Erich Fromm: His Life and Ideas: An Illustrated Biography* (New York: Continuum, 2000), 40.

large part because of their differing messianisms, although the debate was
never explicitly over that term, that Marcuse and Fromm critiqued and cari-
catured one another in the way that they did, beginning with their public
exchange in the 1950s in the pages of *Dissent* magazine and in *Eros and
Civilization* and *The Art of Loving*. Marcuse portrayed Fromm as a preachy,
head-in-the-clouds idealist, naive about the distortion of concepts and values by capitalism and administered society, who perpetuated the mistakes
of the past through praise of old-fashioned, conservative virtues like asceticism. Fromm, for his part, portrayed Marcuse as a nihilistic, despairing intellectual, lacking a vision of hope for the future and substituting immature
rebellion for revolutionary strategy while being consumed by a desire for
regression to early, childhood forms of sexual expression (the state of the
"satiated baby"[8]). Of course, neither thinker's characterization of the other
is entirely charitable or accurate. However, their disagreements arise from a
fundamentally different way of looking at revolution and its relationship to
history and time. Understanding these different outlooks requires returning
to the messianism debates of the early twentieth century. In the remainder of
this section, I articulate Fromm's account of the shift from a prophetic to a
catastrophic messianic paradigm in Germany in the early twentieth century,
and then I explore how Fromm's critique of catastrophic messianism and his
differences with Marcuse are related.

Fromm believes that the betrayals of socialism in 1914 by the Social
Democratic Party, the malaise and despair resulting from the senseless car-
nage of World War I, and the subsequent assassinations of socialist revolutionary Rosa Luxemburg and anarchist revolutionary Gustav Landauer were
a near deathblow to the revolutionary spirit of prophetic messianism.[9] In
the wake of this deadly blow, in Fromm's view, a new messianism emerged,
which he calls "catastrophic messianism," and which he opposes. "Prophetic" messianism, according to Fromm, is humanistic and open to Enlightenment ideals, looking forward to—"actively" hoping for—a future that
can be conceived, imagined, and partially constructed within the present.
Prophetic messianism is a "horizontal" longing, a longing for this-worldly,
human-made progress.[10] "Catastrophic" messianism, by contrast, is apocalyptic and eschatological in outlook, seeing revolutionary change not as a
result of progress but a "catastrophic" break with preceding time, leading to
a future that cannot be accurately described under present conditions. For
the catastrophic messianist, the messianic event enters history from outside;
it is a force majeure, not an outcome of human activity. Catastrophic messianism is consequently a "vertical" longing for external or transcendent

8. Fromm, *The Revolution of Hope*, 8.
9. Erich Fromm, *The Sane Society* (New York: Rinehart, 1955), 239.
10. Fromm, *You Shall Be as Gods*, 133.

intervention, entering history in a time of collapse to save a corrupted humanity from itself.[11]

Fromm's prophetic messianism has much in common with the messianism of neo-Kantian socialist and Jewish thinker Hermann Cohen, whom Fromm cites as one of his influences on the question.[12] In the early 1900s, Jewish thinkers in the Enlightenment tradition, like Cohen and Leo Baeck, had theorized Judaism in Kantian terms as the "religion of reason." According to Cohen, humanity as a whole would bring about the messianic age, making history truly global for the first time and universalizing socialism.[13] The arrival of the messianic age depended on humanity becoming the subject and object of its own knowledge and love.[14] Universalist (anti-Zionist and antinationalist), humanist, socialist, and calmly rational, Cohen's messianism influenced a generation of German Jewish intellectuals. In *The Religion of Reason*, Cohen seems to agree with Marx that human nature (species-being, *Gattungswesen*) is yet to be fulfilled.[15] Because he holds that humanity evolves through knowledge and love, Cohen rejects any equation of Jewish messianism with any mere return, whether to a pagan mythological Golden Age or a Rousseauian state of nature; the messianic age is "a new heaven and a new earth."[16] Intervening between prehistoric Eden (interpreted allegorically to refer to a harmony between humanity and nature) and the present is the irreversible birth of human knowledge and culture, and the messianic future does not relinquish these achievements.[17] The messianic age redeems humanity through the universalization of knowledge, through a more equitable distribution of intellectual life.[18] Cohen's messianism stood in sharp contrast to the messianism that rose to popularity among some German Jewish intellectuals and others following World War I. Cohen came to represent a mainstay of Enlightenment optimism and Kantian rationalism that some young radicals repudiated as outmoded. Certainly Cohen's endorsement, with the majority Social Democratic Party, of World War I at the end of his life was a leading reason why many young Jewish socialists and anarchists shifted and were unwilling to be identified with Cohen or his philosophy. Nevertheless, the rejection of Cohen's style of messianism was also related to a rejection of Enlightenment values and to despair about

---

11. Ibid.

12. Erich Fromm, *On Being Human* (New York: Continuum, 1994), 143.

13. Andrea Poma, *The Critical Philosophy of Hermann Cohen*, trans. John Denton (Albany: State University of New York Press, 1997), 236.

14. Ibid., 236–237.

15. Ibid., 237.

16. Hermann Cohen, *Religion of Reason: Out of the Sources of Judaism*, trans. Simon Kaplan (Atlanta: Scholars, 1995), 248, 250.

17. Ibid., 130–131, 248.

18. Ibid., 248, 232.

the possibility of a revolution based on the education and mobilization of the masses of workers. Cohen's optimism and hopefulness about the future became inseparable from reformism in the minds of some radical critics.

Following the near-death of Cohen's style of rationalistic messianism, a new messianism emerged. Romantic, nihilistic, anarchic, and yearning for an apocalyptic, catastrophic event, this new messianism envisioned a future that would be totally other and wholly new, arriving not as an outcome of human progress or planning but suddenly, in a time of disorder and despair, through a dramatic "rupture" with all prior history. Benjamin, Scholem, and others identified themselves with this new messianism, which Michael Löwy, Anson Rabinbach, and others have described in detail.[19] Fromm stands, sometimes isolated, as a prominent Marxist theorist who condemned the betrayal of the Social Democratic Party and who honored Luxemburg and Landauer but who also continued to defend the prewar, universalistic messianism, seeing it as true to Marx's vision. Fromm critiqued the new messianism under the label of catastrophic or apocalyptic messianism.[20]

Marcuse's Messianism and Fromm's Critique of "Forcing the Messiah"

Marcuse's affinities with catastrophic messianism are apparent in a number of places in *Eros and Civilization* and *One-Dimensional Man*. In *Eros and Civilization*, Marcuse conceives revolution, the messianic event, as a dramatic rupture with all prior history. Just as the French revolutionists fired shots at the Paris clocks (Marcuse cites Benjamin's discussion of this), the revolution fights and vanquishes time.[21] The continual flux of time leads people to relinquish utopian hopes, Marcuse argues, since through the experience of time's passing, people are taught that all pleasures are fleeting (even life itself, which ends in death).[22] In the fight against time's dominion, Marcuse's revolution has two chief weapons at its disposal: expectation of the future and remembrance of the primal past. By a dramatic break with history, Marcuse's messianic age simultaneously restores and redeems something that existed prior to history and human consciousness. (One of the

---

19. For some very useful intellectual historical work on catastrophic messianism, see Michael Löwy, *Redemption and Utopia: Jewish Libertarian Thought in Central Europe: A Study in Elective Affinity*, trans. Hope Heaney (Stanford, CA: Stanford University Press, 1992); and Anson Rabinbach, *In the Shadow of Catastrophe: German Intellectuals between Apocalypse and Enlightenment* (Berkeley: University of California Press, 1997).

20. Fromm, *On Being Human*, 141.

21. Herbert Marcuse, *Eros and Civilization: A Philosophical Inquiry into Freud* (Boston: Beacon, 1955), 233.

22. Ibid., 231.

popular slogans of the new messianism that arose in rebellion against Cohen's rationalist messianism was Vienna journalist Karl Kraus's line, "Origin
is the goal," expressing this view that the future would restore and redeem
the ancient past.[23])

In Marcuse's *Eros and Civilization*, this primal past can be understood
from a collective or an individual standpoint. It can be recovered not only
through remembrance of a nonrepressive collective past but also through
remembrance of a period of time within each individual's life, in infancy, in
which the individual, not yet initiated into repression, existed in a state of
undifferentiated identity with the world and of nonrepressive sexual enjoyment. Caught between the desire to recover a long-lost past and the desire
to inaugurate a future that is totally other, Marcuse's philosophy may be
subject to Fromm's critique of "forcing the Messiah." Fromm argues that
since *prophetic* messianism views the messianic age as the outcome of human progress, it encourages productive and revolutionary action, while
catastrophic messianism is linked to a loss of hope and a loss of confidence
in the potential of humans to effect revolutionary change. Catastrophic messianism's hopelessness leads to inactivity and passivity at best or, at its worst,
to attempts to "force the Messiah"—that is, to instigate or prolong crises to
force a revolution on a populace that is not yet supportive of one. According
to Fromm, neither passive, inactive waiting nor mere wishing (even with
very intense desire) is sufficient to qualify as hope, although both waiting
and wishing can often give the false appearance of hopefulness. Another
kind of false hope, "forcing the Messiah,"[24] according to the Talmudic tradition in which Fromm was so extensively trained, was the attempt to calculate
the date of the Messiah's arrival or the false announcement of the Messiah's
arrival.[25] Fromm observed an attempt to "force the Messiah" in fascism's
deification of leaders, but he also held that "forcing the Messiah" was a problem on the Left in various ways.[26]

In *You Shall Be as Gods: A Radical Interpretation of the Old Testament
and Its Tradition*, Fromm offers a brief account of the various false Messiahs
that arose throughout Jewish history, including seventeenth-century messianic figure Sabbatai Zevi and his followers. The Sabbateans, whom Jewish
orthodoxy would charge with "forcing the Messiah," preached a peculiar
doctrine of "redemption through sin," according to which the messianic age
would be ushered in by the ritualistic negation or violation of various previous religious laws and social mores.[27] Like Georges Sorel ("general strike"),

23. Rabinbach, *In the Shadow of Catastrophe*, 31.
24. Fromm, *The Revolution of Hope*, 8.
25. Fromm, *You Shall Be as Gods*, 153.
26. Fromm, *The Revolution of Hope*, 8.
27. Rudolf Siebert, *The Critical Theory of Religion: The Frankfurt School from Universal
Pragmatic to Political Theology* (Berlin: Walter de Gruyter, 1985), 311.

Carl Schmitt ("state of exception"), and Walter Benjamin ("divine violence") three centuries later, the Sabbateans lauded the ability of a law-breaking praxis to create new law.[28] Shades of this perspective can be seen in Marcuse, for example, when he writes, "If the guilt accumulated by the civilized domination of man by man can ever be redeemed by freedom, then the 'original sin' must be committed again: 'We must eat from the tree of knowledge in order to fall back into the state of innocence.'"[29] Marcuse is quoting from German writer Heinrich von Kleist's "On the Marionette Theater," a kind of antihumanist parable, in which it is suggested that an unconscious puppet is a better dancer than a human, and a trained bear, a better sword fighter. In a mythologized account of human nature, the short story describes a fallen humanity wandering in search of lost innocence and lost unity with nature, and then it suggests, "The gates of Eden are barred against us and the angel drives us on. We must make a journey round the world and see whether we can perhaps find another place to creep in at."[30] The story concludes with the following dialogue:

> "You mean . . . that we must eat again from the tree of knowledge in order to relapse into the state of Innocence?"
>
> "Certainly," he replied. "That is the last chapter of the history of the world."[31]

According to Kleist's mythos of return, humanity's *telos* is the return to innocence. God and nonconscious matter are alike in their innocence, while the fallen human soul is on a journey of return: origin is the goal. The quasi-Romantic yearning for return through transgression of the status quo and cultural conventions was a thread running through Weimar culture. Marcuse's quotation from Kleist is situated in a discussion of the need to return to a precivilizational situation and fresh starting point in order to jettison surplus repression. According to Marcuse, liberation from surplus repression will necessarily appear to be a regression.[32] The return to innocence is possible only through a transgression of the present order that must appear as "barbarism" from the standpoint of that order.[33] The suggestion, quoted by Marcuse in *Eros and Civilization*, that humanity must eat again from the tree of knowledge—salvation through disobedience and creeping back into the garden, in Kleist's phrasing—also resembles Marcuse's remark in *One-Dimensional Man* that art is radical because of its potential

---

28. Löwy, *Redemption and Utopia*, 101.
29. Marcuse, *Eros and Civilization*, 198.
30. Heinrich von Kleist, "Puppet Theatre," in *Salmagundi* 33–34 (1976): 85.
31. Ibid., 88.
32. Marcuse, *Eros and Civilization*, 199.
33. Ibid., 198.

for "transgression."[34] "The decisive distinction is not the psychological one between art created in joy and art created in sorrow, between sanity and neurosis"—here he may be digging at Fromm, although Fromm most probably has no objection to art created in sorrow—"but that between the artistic and the societal reality. The rupture with the latter, the magic or rational transgression, is an essential quality of even the most affirmative art. . . . Whether ritualized or not, art contains the rationality of negation. In its advanced positions, it is the Great Refusal—the protest against that which is."[35]

Fromm would not object to the Kleist narrative's exultation of revolt; in fact, Fromm frequently uses the disobedience of Adam and Eve as a positive symbol for revolutionary sentiment and psychological maturity. Rather, the difficulties center on the impossibility of *return* to a lost Eden and of the fundamental impossibility of encountering the world from a standpoint abstracted from human history. As Marx famously wrote in the 1844 *Paris Manuscripts*, humanity "is no abstract being squatting outside the world."[36] Precisely because we are human beings attempting to know, we can have no concept of life before attempts to explain the world through reason, myth, faith, or similar means. (Max Horkheimer and Theodor Adorno, of course, also wrestled with this problem in their *Dialectic of Enlightenment*.) A return to primordial innocence lies beyond our powers of conceptualization and outside of all our categories. We are asked by Marcuse to create a future that is necessarily impossible to describe. There can be no blueprints or utopian models. It is hard to see how there could even be a transitional program, and Marcuse noticeably never attempts to write one, unlike Fromm, who wrote a proposed program for the Socialist Party–Social Democratic Federation (SP-SDF), for example. Marcuse's messianic event is unlikely to be a product of strategizing and movement building, at least for Marcuse in the period of *Eros and Civilization* and *One-Dimensional Man*, before he became more fully radicalized by the New Left. One wonders if Marcuse's eventual embrace of Third World revolutionism—in a 1968 Paris interview, he stated that a revolution in the United States would be impossible—is related to a desire for the intervention of what lies outside.[37]

For his part, Fromm probably saw the doctrine of "redemption through sin" of Sabbatai Zevi's followers as connected to catastrophic messianism. Fromm would have known that Scholem, scholar of Jewish mysticism and

---

34. Herbert Marcuse, *One-Dimensional Man: Studies in the Ideology of Advanced Industrial Society* (Boston: Beacon, 1991), 63.

35. Ibid.

36. Karl Marx, *Early Writings*, ed. and trans. T. B. Bottomore (New York: McGraw-Hill, 1965), 43.

37. Herbert Marcuse, "Marcuse Defines His New Left Line," in *Collected Papers of Herbert Marcuse*, vol. 3, *The New Left and the 1960s*, ed. Douglas Kellner (London: Routledge, 2005), 106.

longtime friend of Benjamin, had written the definitive biography on Zevi, and Fromm considered Scholem a catastrophic messianist.[38] Fromm also would have known that the new messianic enthusiasm, which had swept through left-wing German Jewish intellectual circles around the time of World War I, had included some lively enthusiasm about Zevi.[39] Since catastrophic messianism held that the messianic age could not be brought about through constructive action, the advent of the messianic age could be speeded only by disruption of the status quo. For the catastrophic messianist, as for the Sabbateans, the messianic age could be brought about not through building the institutions and structures of a new society—not through the establishment of alternative presses, free schools, free clinics, or communes; not through building "dual power" (as Antonio Gramsci suggested); not through the attempt to organize workers' councils, alternative political parties, clubs, or study groups on a grand scale to reach the masses—but *only* through a rupture with history and a generalized refusal to follow the standards of the past. This refusal would leave an empty and traumatic void where the status quo once stood and in which something new could be constructed. Contrast this, for example, with Fromm's attempt to model some organizing on the "Bellamy Clubs," his role in founding the the antinuclear-weapons organization SANE (National Committee for a Sane Nuclear Policy), and his service on the national committee of the Socialist Party (SP-SDF), for which he wrote his own "manifesto and program." By contrast, catastrophic messianism, like "forcing the Messiah," depends on the occurrence or production of crisis and puts the activist in the paradoxical position of "hoping" for disaster.

In *The Revolution of Hope*, Fromm writes that the hopelessness that leads to false Messiahs is characterized in the political arena by "phrase making and adventurism," "nihilism," and "disregard for reality."[40] Fromm worried that such hopelessness was rapidly becoming characteristic of some of the young activists of his time.[41] Of these youth, he wrote, "They are appealing in their boldness and dedication but they are unconvincing by their lack of realism, sense of strategy, and, in some, by [their] lack of love for life."[42] It was not long after Fromm's worry to this effect that there was an upsurge of groups, such as the Weather Underground in the United States and the Baader-Meinhof Group in Germany, that attempted to "force" a revolution without first building a mass movement. To some extent, the tendency toward small-group sabotage (which Marxists have tended to condemn

---

38. Fromm, *On Being Human*, 142.
39. Löwy, *Redemption and Utopia*, 147.
40. Fromm, *The Revolution of Hope*, 8.
41. Ibid.
42. Ibid.

under the name of Blanquism) has always been a temptation influencing some on the Left, and it seems to emerge when hope is in decline and desperation on the rise. As the authors of *Catastrophism: The Apocalyptic Politics of Collapse and Rebirth* argue, the Left as a whole has a worrying tendency to yearn for crises—for an economic crisis, for example, or a military draft—in the despairing view that only a dramatic crisis can lead to revolt.[43] Yet history seems to demonstrate that the Left's yearning for crises is unwarranted. In fact, in times of crisis, the masses often become more reactionary, for example, by blaming a persecuted minority for the crisis instead of seeing the problem as systemic.

Fromm held that Marcuse, in the period of *Eros and Civilization* and *One-Dimensional Man*, had fallen prey to the reality-disregarding false hope that attempts to "force the Messiah." He writes in a footnote in *The Revolution of Hope* that "hopelessness shines through Herbert Marcuse's *Eros and Civilization* and *One-Dimensional Man*."[44] He quotes from Marcuse's conclusion to *One-Dimensional Man*:

> The critical theory of society possesses no concepts which could bridge the gap between the present and its future; holding no promise and showing no success, it remains negative. Thus it wants to remain loyal to those who, without hope, have given and give their life to the Great Refusal.[45]

Fromm concludes:

> These quotations show how wrong those are who attack or admire Marcuse as a revolutionary leader; for revolution was never based on hopelessness, nor can it ever be. But Marcuse is not even concerned with politics; for if one is not concerned with steps between the present and the future, one does not deal with politics, radical or otherwise. Marcuse is essentially an example of an alienated intellectual, who presents his personal despair as a theory of radicalism. . . . This

---

43. Sasha Lilley, David McNally, Eddie Yuen, and James Davis, *Catastrophism: The Apocalyptic Politics of Collapse and Rebirth* (Oakland, CA: PM, 2012).

44. Fromm, *Revolution of Hope*, 8.

45. Ibid., quoting Marcuse, *One-Dimensional Man*, 257. Perhaps strangely, Fromm leaves out the Walter Benjamin quotation with which Marcuse's book concludes: "It is only for the sake of those without hope that hope is given to us." Marcuse, *One-Dimensional Man*, 257. Fromm, for his part, never openly criticized Benjamin, which is puzzling, since it seems that Fromm's critique of catastrophic messianism applies equally to Benjamin. This absence may be due to the fact that Fromm's second wife accompanied Benjamin on his final trek before his suicide, but it could also have to do with the lack of wide public reception of Benjamin's writings until after Fromm's death; work on Benjamin would have been of interest primarily to a circle of critical theorists and others "in the know."

is not the place to show in detail that it is a naive, cerebral daydream, essentially irrational, unrealistic, and lacking love for life.[46]

These statements are rude, no doubt, but are not irrelevant. First, Fromm's perception of Marcuse as a despairing, catastrophic messianist is linked to a disagreement—a disagreement with Marcuse about the *conceivability* or *imaginability* of the socialist future and of socialist humanity. Fromm always tries to reach beyond mere opposition (first negation) to present an image of the time to come. Even in his psychoanalytic work, Fromm views his major contribution to psychoanalysis as an attempt to offer an account of psychological health as latently visible, rather than merely describing pathologies. Beneath the surface of the pathologies prevalent under capitalism, there are signs of yearning for healthy, fulfilled relationships. Although most members of the Frankfurt School tended to concentrate on providing critiques of existing society, Fromm additionally described a positive goal for which to strive: the productive or revolutionary character and the flourishing, humanistic society. No critical theorist of his generation—not even Marcuse, with his frequent openness to "utopia"—tries to say as much as Fromm does about what a socialist society and a socialist person would be like, and Fromm defends our ability to make such assertions.

Fromm's insistence on positive descriptions does not, as Marcuse might think, place Fromm in with the Dale Carnegies and Norman Vincent Peales of his own time or, in contemporary terms, with the Joel Osteens and Oprah Winfreys of today. Always dialectical, Fromm's point is never that we should be more cheerful and optimistic but rather that we must push beyond mere negation to the "negation of the negation." Unlike Hegel's owl of Minerva, however, which only spreads its wings at dusk, Fromm's messianic hope places the subject of history into a kind of relationship with the future in such a way that the contours of the potential socialist future are not entirely hidden from the rational student of present conditions.

According to Fromm, the messianic future can be conceptualized to a rather large extent from the standpoint of present-day capitalism. For example, we can legitimately say that the socialist future would be one of "love," and we have a pretty good idea about what we mean when we say this. In this vein, Fromm writes (in response to Marcuse):

---

46. Fromm, *Revolution of Hope*, 8–9. Fromm notes in his correspondence with Raya Dunayevskaya that he curtailed this critique significantly, relegating it to a small footnote instead of a full chapter in *Revolution of Hope*, in light of the red-baiting of Marcuse going on in the media at that time. See letter from Erich Fromm to Raya Dunayevskaya, July 31, 1968, in *The Dunayevskaya-Marcuse-Fromm Correspondence, 1954–1978: Dialogues on Hegel, Marx, and Critical Theory*, ed. Kevin B. Anderson and Russell Rockwell (Lanham, MD: Lexington, 2012), 158.

> [Some people] share the opinion of the basic incompatibility between love and normal secular life within our society. They arrive at the result that to speak of love today means only to participate in the general fraud; they claim that only a martyr or a mad person can love in the world of today, hence that all discussion of love is nothing but preaching. [In their exchange in *Dissent* magazine, Marcuse had accused Fromm of "preaching."[47]] This very respectable viewpoint lends itself readily to a rationalization of cynicism. . . . This "radicalism" results in moral nihilism.[48]

Fromm continues, defending his view that love is not inconceivable or impossible under capitalism:

> I am of the conviction that the answer to the absolute incompatibility of love and "normal" life is correct only in an abstract sense. The *principle* underlying capitalistic society and the *principle* of love are incompatible. But modern society seen concretely is a complex phenomenon. . . . "Capitalism" is in itself a complex and constantly changing structure which still permits a good deal of non-conformity and of personal latitude.[49]

Although capitalism is alienating by its nature, nonalienated experiences are not entirely impossible within it. Capitalism must be vanquished not because it makes our ideals and concepts meaningless but precisely because the meaningful ideals and concepts that humanistic, life-loving people struggle to actualize stand in contradiction with the system in which they live. Fromm certainly believed that capitalism makes it harder, for example, to love or to find joy in creativity and productiveness.[50] It is precisely because we continue to experience love and joy, to a limited and often distorted extent, that we are able to anticipate a society in which they would be given fuller expression. Consequently, concepts like love are in fact revolutionary, according to Fromm, as they assist in socialist planning and constitute a bridge between the present and the future.

---

47. Herbert Marcuse, "The Social Implications of Freudian 'Revisionism,'" *Dissent* 2, no. 3 (1955): 233.

48. Erich Fromm, *The Art of Loving* (New York: Harper and Row, 1956), 131.

49. Ibid., 131–132 (emphasis in original).

50. Fromm's concept of productiveness or activeness should not be misunderstood as any sort of capitalist worker productivity (or "performance principle"). The revolutionary and the biophilic (life-loving rather than death-loving) personalities are active and productive, but this activeness and productiveness may not equate to busyness or "getting a lot done"; philosophical thought, for example, is included as a kind of activeness or productiveness.

It must be noted that in Marcuse's thought, the caesura between present and future is not consistently absolute. Like Fromm,[51] Marcuse saw potential in the utopian imagination (as is certainly evidenced in *Eros and Civilization* and *The Aesthetic Dimension*, if not as much in *One-Dimensional Man*). In the era of *Eros and Civilization* and *One-Dimensional Man*, it seems that the mediation between present and future is not primarily conceptual but rather aesthetic and libidinal. This differs from Marcuse's earlier *Reason and Revolution* (a book Fromm praised and respected)[52] and the later period of his *An Essay on Liberation* (which Fromm sees as a recuperation of Marcuse's earlier hopefulness). While Fromm rather unabashedly makes extensive use of terms with historical baggage such as *humanism, love, hope, faith, progress, utopia*, and *reason*, Marcuse holds that revolutionary strategy and discourse must break from concepts present under capitalism, creating an opening into which something entirely new can enter. The final chapter of *One-Dimensional Man* takes up Benjamin's conception of catastrophe, worrying that now that technology has brought our imagined horrors and utopian dreams into reality, "archetypes of horror as well as of joy, of war as well as of peace *lose their catastrophic character*."[53] For Marcuse, this loss of catastrophic power means that the revolutionary potential of utopian visions and terms like *hope* and *love* has been severely inhibited. The view that capitalism has so broadly poisoned concepts leads to a narrow circumscription of the arena of revolutionary activity. The following passage, in which Marcuse seems to propose sabotaging the mainstream media, is worth quoting at length:

> To take an (unfortunately fantastic) example: the mere absence of all advertising and of all indoctrinating media of information and entertainment would plunge the individual into a traumatic void where he would have the chance to wonder and to think, to know himself (or rather the negative of himself) and his society. Deprived of his false fathers, leaders, friends, and representatives, he would have to earn his ABC's again. But the words and sentences which he would form might come out very differently, and so might his aspirations and fears.
>
> To be sure, such a situation would be an unbearable nightmare. While the people can support the continuous creation of nuclear

51. Fromm wrote a foreword to Edward Bellamy's *Looking Backward* and an afterword to George Orwell's *1984*, pointing out in both the need for utopian thought. See Erich Fromm, foreword to *Looking Backward*, by Edward Bellamy (New York: New American Library, 1960), v–xx; and Erich Fromm, afterword to *1984*, by George Orwell (New York: Signet Classics, 1961), 313–326.
52. Erich Fromm, *Marx's Concept of Man* (London: Continuum, 2004), 60–61.
53. Marcuse, *One-Dimensional Man*, 248 (emphasis added).

weapons, radioactive fallout, and questionable foodstuffs, they cannot (for this very reason!) tolerate being deprived of the entertainment and education which make them capable of reproducing the arrangements for their defense and/or destruction. The nonfunctioning of television and the allied media might thus begin to achieve what the inherent contradictions of capitalism did not achieve—the disintegration of the system.[54]

Marcuse is surely right that many people would experience trauma if faced with the sudden absence of television (or the Internet). But Fromm would object that the tactic Marcuse half-jokingly proposes here—and Marcuse's Great Refusal broadly—rests on mere destructiveness rather than on a healthy "productive character" or "revolutionary character" (Fromm's terms for the psychologically healthy individual). For Fromm, true revolution is motivated by a radical kind of productivity, in the sense of Marx's species-being (*Gattungswesen*)—that is, of human nature as productive. Although Fromm would have to admit that revolution involves certain destructive actions, he would point out that Marcuse's approach to revolution is limited by its emphasis on the gap between present and future. For example, Marcuse in the period of *One-Dimensional Man* cannot suggest sparking revolution through building an alternative media; such a media would be forced to employ the distorted language of capitalism. Rather, for Marcuse, revolution must be sparked by an *absence* of what has become commonplace and by an ensuing crisis. While Fromm attempts to identify contradictions within and build on the present, Marcuse's approach seems to depend more on sweeping away the present and returning society to an unblemished blank slate. Fromm would worry that such a revolutionary strategy would lead to a reactionary or oppressive outcome, regardless of its emancipatory intent.

Just as revolution is supposed for Marcuse to arise from a crisis and a subsequent rebuilding of society from the rubble, it seems that for Marcuse the individual must renounce the bonds that bind her, make a clean break with the status quo, and then rebuild herself. While Fromm would argue that the worker under capitalism, such as a doctor, a teacher, or a factory worker working with a "complicated machine"—he is less optimistic about salespeople[55]—may find a certain degree of happiness and fulfillment, Marcuse holds in *Eros and Civilization* that *any* "socially useful" activity that does not result in the destruction of the present order plays into the hands of the

---

54. Ibid., 245–246.
55. This is evident from his work on the "marketing orientation," but see also Fromm's interview with Mike Wallace. Erich Fromm, interview by Mike Wallace, *Mike Wallace Show*, ABC, aired May 25, 1958, available at http://www.hrc.utexas.edu/multimedia/video/2008/wallace/fromm_erich_t.html.

administrators.[56] The tailor or hairdresser who feels satisfaction in her work does so merely in anticipation of payment or in the form of repressive satisfaction at having fulfilled her role in the system.[57] Unlike Fromm, Marcuse fundamentally rejects the possibility of theorizing the sane individual from within the concepts of bureaucratized, technologically advanced capitalism.

As Naomi Klein's book *The Shock Doctrine: The Rise of Disaster Capitalism* demonstrates at length, approaches to societal change and to psychotherapy that attempt to create crises and a subsequent blank slate on which a new society or new personality can be imprinted leave societies or individuals submissive to authorities and easily susceptible to influence.[58] Although Klein lodges her critique against the neoconservative Chicago School, not against the Left, the attempt to instigate change through the creation of blank spaces can have an antidemocratic side and can undermine the agency of workers.

The last two decades have seen an important revival of scholarship on the work of Fromm and Marcuse. No longer "forgotten intellectuals,"[59] Fromm and Marcuse are being rediscovered as among the most insightful critics of the administered, bureaucratized, instrumentally rational society; of the authoritarian personality; and of the power of administered society to distort the consciousness of workers and others. In spite of Fromm's and Marcuse's important similarities, Fromm's distinction between prophetic and catastrophic messianism helps us to see the differing affinities of each thinker and the differing practical implications of their thought in the 1950s and 1960s. Fromm's trenchant critique and his examination of the "messianic" options available to the radical Left may help us to further interrogate Marcuse's Great Refusal and to be less wary of using the concepts of the present to describe the transfigured future. Fromm's discussion of catastrophic messianism and "forcing the Messiah" continues to issue a resounding warning for our times, as we seek an approach to revolutionary change and to the uncertainty of the future that is hopeful, rational, and active.

---

56. Marcuse, *Eros and Civilization*, 208.

57. Ibid., 220–221.

58. Naomi Klein, *The Shock Doctrine: The Rise of Disaster Capitalism* (New York: Henry Holt, 2007).

59. See Neil McLaughlin, "How to Become a Forgotten Intellectual: Intellectual Movements and the Rise and Fall of Erich Fromm," *Sociological Forum* 13 (June 1998): 215–246. (McLaughlin's term for Fromm could perhaps be applied to Marcuse as well.)

The Dunayevskaya-Marcuse Correspondence

Crystallization of Two Marxist Traditions

RUSSELL ROCKWELL AND KEVIN B. ANDERSON

R aya Dunayevskaya, the Marxist-Humanist philosopher and activist, initiated a correspondence in 1954 with Herbert Marcuse, the noted member of the Frankfurt School of Critical Theory, which continued at various levels of intensity for nearly a quarter of a century.[1] Here, we focus on the years 1956–1957, during which Dunayevskaya completed *Marxism and Freedom*,[2] to which Marcuse contributed an important preface. This key dialogue was followed by a nearly three-year hiatus, broken by Marcuse's resumption of the correspondence in 1960, as he embarked on research for his most well-known work, *One-Dimensional Man*.[3] This second, briefer phase of the correspondence was characterized by an intensive exchange on automation and working-class subjectivity, as well as by both Dunayevskaya's and Marcuse's analyses and concretizations of a then largely unnoticed work by Karl Marx, the *Grundrisse*. Any study of the development of radical philosophy since the mid-twentieth century—particularly as it relates to Marxist theories of opposition, refusal, and revolution—would be enriched by a close examination of the significant correspondence between Dunayevskaya and Marcuse.

---

1. Kevin B. Anderson and Russell Rockwell, eds., *The Dunayevskaya-Marcuse-Fromm Correspondence, 1954–1978: Dialogues on Hegel, Marx, and Critical Theory* (Lanham, MD: Lexington, 2012).

2. Raya Dunayevskaya, *Marxism and Freedom: From 1776 until Today* (1958; repr., Amherst, NY: Humanity, 2000).

3. Herbert Marcuse, *One-Dimensional Man: Studies in the Ideology of Advanced Industrial Society* (Boston: Beacon, 1964).

Biographical and Philosophical Background: Dunayevskaya

A U.S. Marxist of Ukrainian Jewish origin, Dunayevskaya began her correspondence with Marcuse in December 1954. Previously, she had served as a Russian-language secretary to Leon Trotsky in Mexico. Dunayevskaya soon became a well-known critic—from the Left—of the USSR, developing these critiques as part of the Johnson-Forest Tendency, a left-wing Trotskyist tendency that included the noted Afro-Caribbean Marxist C.L.R. James and the Chinese American philosopher and activist Grace Lee Boggs. In 1939, in the wake of the Hitler-Stalin Pact, James and Dunayevskaya broke with Trotsky, disagreeing with his position that despite the pact, the Soviet Union must still be defended as a workers' state, albeit a degenerate one.

As World War II raged, Dunayevskaya embarked on a diagnosis of the economic structure of the USSR, which she and James now described, contrary to orthodox Trotskyism, as a state-capitalist society. Official Soviet theorists and their supporters abroad continued to argue that its state represented a postcapitalist society in which Marx's concept of socialism had begun to be realized. In 1944, Dunayevskaya translated from the Russian for the flagship journal *American Economic Review* an article on Marxist pedagogy in the Soviet Union,[4] along with a brief commentary on it;[5] the article had originally appeared in the USSR's most prominent theoretical journal. The article argues that Marx's law of value and surplus value—a law endorsed in previous Marxist theory and official USSR doctrine as characteristic of capitalist society alone—indeed operated in the Soviet Union, which nonetheless was still officially held to be socialist. In arguing her case that capitalism was being restored in the Soviet Union, Dunayevskaya's commentary refers not only to this admission that the law of value operated in the USSR but also to Marx's concept of alienated labor from the *Economic and Philosophical Manuscripts of 1844.*[6]

Dunayevskaya's aim in translating and publishing the article in the *American Economic Review* was to reveal the counterrevolutionary trajectory of Russian society and to put forth her alternative view of the USSR as a state-capitalist society, part of a new stage of global state capitalism.[7] It was seen as a step beyond the stage of monopoly capitalism as theorized by

---

4. "Teaching of Economics in the Soviet Union," trans. Raya Dunayevskaya, *American Economic Review* 34, no. 3 (1944): 501–530. This article was unsigned when it originally appeared in *Pod Znamenem Marxizma* [Under the Banner of Marxism].

5. Raya Dunayevskaya, "A New Revision of Marxian Economics," *American Economic Review* 34, no. 3 (1944): 531–537.

6. Ibid.

7. Besides the long discussion in *Marxism and Freedom* and the *American Economic Review* pieces themselves, Dunayevskaya's relevant writings on state-capitalism are collected

Vladimir Lenin and others, a new stage of capitalism that comprised not only other authoritarian forms like Nazism but also more liberal versions like the Popular Front government in France and the New Deal in the United States. Dunayevskaya's translation and critique of the Russian article provoked a controversy that hit the front page of the *New York Times*.[8] During the next year, several prominent Marxist economists, among them Paul Baran,[9] weighed in with criticisms of Dunayevskaya. Dunayevskaya's rejoinder closed the debate, again making an argument for the theory of state capitalism.[10]

During this period, the Johnson-Forest Tendency also theorized workers' resistance to alienated labor and authoritarian management, lauding the wartime wildcat strikes that violated the Roosevelt-inspired, no-strike pledge between the large trade unions and capital. They also wrote on Georg Wilhelm Friedrich Hegel and the young Marx while elaborating a pluralistic concept of revolutionary subjectivity that included not only rank-and-file labor (in opposition to the burgeoning labor bureaucracy) but also Blacks, women, and youth as independent collective subjects not necessarily linked to labor in a direct fashion.[11] But by the time Dunayevskaya initiated her correspondence with Marcuse in late 1954, her thirteen-year collaboration with James was ending. And although the basis had been laid beforehand, her dialogues with Marcuse would be crucial to her subsequent development as a dialectician.

Biographical and Philosophical Background: Marcuse

More than a decade senior to Dunayevskaya, the German-born Marcuse was a Marxist from his youth who also studied with the existentialist philosopher

---

in Raya Dunayevskaya, *The Marxist-Humanist Theory of State Capitalism: Selected Writings by Raya Dunayevskaya* (Chicago: News and Letters, 1992).

8. Will Lissner, "Soviet Economics Stirs Debate Here," *New York Times*, October 1, 1944, p. 30.

9. Paul Baran, "New Trends in Russian Economic Thinking?," *American Economic Review* 34, no. 4 (1944): 862–871. See also Oscar Lange, "Marxian Economics in the Soviet Union," *American Economic Review* 35, no. 1 (1945): 127–133; and Leo Rogin, "Marx and Engels on Distribution in a Socialist Society," *American Economic Review* 35, no. 1 (1945): 137–413.

10. Raya Dunayevskaya, "Revision of Reaffirmation of Marxism? A Rejoinder," *American Economic Review* 35, no. 4 (1945): 660–664.

11. For background, see Kevin B. Anderson and Russell Rockwell, introduction to Anderson and Rockwell, *The Dunayevskaya-Marcuse-Fromm Correspondence, 1954–1978: Dialogues on Hegel, Marx, and Critical Theory*; and Peter Hudis and Kevin B. Anderson, introduction to *The Power of Negativity: Selected Writings on the Dialectic in Hegel and Marx*, by Raya Dunayevskaya (Lanham, MD: Lexington, 2002).

Martin Heidegger in the 1920s. Of Jewish descent, Marcuse subsequently joined the Frankfurt School and left Germany after 1933, winding up in New York, where he became the principal philosopher of the group during its time at Columbia University. In Germany, he had published *Hegel's Ontology and the Theory of Historicity*,[12] a 1932 study often thought to have been predominately influenced by Heidegger's philosophy. More recent treatments have not shared that assessment and have shifted attention to the importance of Marcuse's distance from Heidegger and his close reading of Hegel's *Science of Logic*.[13]

No doubt Marcuse's encounter with Marx's just-published 1844 *Manuscripts*, also in 1932, and which he reviewed in a substantial article[14] a few months after publishing *Hegel's Ontology*, provided many of the elements he felt had been missing in Marxism, thus paving the way for his move from Heidegger to the Frankfurt School; however, it would be a mistake to draw a sharp divide between *Hegel's Ontology* and Marcuse's subsequent Marxist writings. Although Seyla Benhabib herself tends to play down any connection to Marx in her introduction to the English translation of *Hegel's Ontology*, she cites a postcard from Marcuse to Karl Löwith, dated July 28, 1931, wherein Marcuse summarizes his intentions in writing the work:

> It is true that a longer work of mine on Hegel will appear this fall: it is an interpretation of the [*Science of*] *Logic* and the *Phenomenology of Spirit* as foundations for a theory of historicity. The *Hegel-Marx* question is not explicitly addressed, although I hope this interpretation will throw some new light on this connection. Nor does this work contain a critical discussion of Heidegger nor is it intended to do so. Rather, the whole is a necessary preparation for articulating the fundamental nature of historical happening.[15]

Certainly Marcuse indicates here that the subject of his study is Hegel, including, at least implicitly, his relation to Marx, and that the work was not Heideggerian.

---

12. Herbert Marcuse, *Hegel's Ontology and the Theory of Historicity*, trans. Seyla Benhabib (Cambridge, MA: MIT Press, 1987).

13. Russell Rockwell, "Hegel and Critical Social Theory: New Perspectives from the Marcuse Archives," *Sociological Quarterly* 45, no. 1 (2004): 141–159; see also John Abromeit, "Herbert Marcuse's Critical Encounter with Martin Heidegger, 1927–1933," in *Herbert Marcuse: A Critical Reader*, ed. John Abromeit and W. Mark Cobb (New York: Routledge, 2004), 131–151.

14. Herbert Marcuse, "New Sources on the Foundation of Historical Materialism," in *Heideggerian Marxism*, ed. Richard Wolin and John Abromeit (Lincoln: University of Nebraska Press, 2005), 86–121.

15. Marcuse, *Hegel's Ontology and the Theory of Historicity*, xii (emphasis in original).

Reason and Revolution,[16] published in 1941, a decade after *Hegel's Ontology* and the review of the 1844 *Manuscripts*, is Marcuse's most important work on Hegel and Marx. It was the first book by a Marxist to provide a systematic analysis of all of Hegel's major works, as well as the first work in English to assess in some detail Marx's 1844 *Manuscripts*. Also in 1941, Marcuse published "Some Social Implications of Modern Technology," an article that drew from Marx's critique of alienated labor to take up new developments, among them the relatively conservative "labor bureaucracy" that, in his view, had by the 1920s come to dominate the large trade unions of Europe and the United States.[17] In this article, he also espouses an affirmative stance toward the possibilities of emancipation, in a world where "fascist barbarism" had polarized society: "The 'ideal' has become so concrete and universal that it grips the life of every human being, and the whole of mankind is drawn into the struggle for its realization."[18] Marcuse published these two works contemporaneously with Dunayevskaya's break with Trotsky and her ensuing analyses of the capitalist direction of the Russian economy and society.

Although there is no indication that Marcuse knew of Dunayevskaya's work at the time, *Reason and Revolution* had a strong influence on Dunayevskaya and her Johnson-Forest Tendency comrades.[19] Marcuse worked at research and intelligence agencies of the U.S. government during World War II and afterward, until 1950. However, recent work by Douglas Kellner demonstrates that Marcuse developed a sort of "underground" theorization of social change,[20] advocating that the Frankfurt School, which he hoped to see reconstituted, programmatically reflect that the post–World War II world was "dividing into Soviet and neo-fascist camps," a situation demanding that revolutionary theory "ruthlessly and openly criticize" both camps.[21] These analyses suggest that Dunayevskaya's work at that time would have been of special interest to him had he known of it.

Since much of what follows stresses key differences between Marcuse and Dunayevskaya, it behooves us to underline some of their similarities of

---

16. Herbert Marcuse, *Reason and Revolution: Hegel and the Rise of Social Theory* (1941; repr., Amherst, NY: Humanity, 1999). For interpretation and context, see Kevin Anderson, "On Hegel and the Rise of Social Theory: A Critical Appreciation of Herbert Marcuse's *Reason and Revolution*, Fifty Years Later," *Sociological Theory* 11, no. 3 (1993): 243–267.

17. Herbert Marcuse, "Some Social Implications of Modern Technology," in *The Essential Frankfurt School Reader*, ed. Andrew Arato and Eike Gebhardt (New York: Urizen, 1978), 149.

18. Ibid., 159.

19. Anderson and Rockwell, *The Marcuse-Dunayevskaya-Fromm Correspondence*, 232–235.

20. Douglas Kellner, "Introduction: Technology, War and Facism: Marcuse in the 1940s," in *Collected Papers of Herbert Marcuse*, vol. 1, *Technology, War and Fascism*, ed. Douglas Kellner (London: Routledge, 1998), 12–15.

21. Herbert Marcuse, "33 Theses," in *Collected Papers of Herbert Marcuse*, vol. 1, *Technology, War and Fascism*, ed. Douglas Kellner (London: Routledge, 1998), 217.

approach, which were strongest during the 1940s, before they were in contact. First, while Marcuse did not share Dunayevskaya's state-capitalist theory, he did stress that modern capitalism was not only driven by organized monopolistic tendencies but also by the growth of the modern militarized state. Second, from the 1940s onward, both were interested in the changing condition of the working classes under the influence of forms of technology that became known as *automation* by the 1950s. Third, both were largely in agreement concerning the relative conservatism of the labor bureaucracies of the developed capitalist countries, although Dunayevskaya—unlike Marcuse—was to maintain the notion that rank-and-file labor remained a revolutionary subject. In addition, both saw forces outside labor as key elements in future radicalization and revolutionary possibilities. Fourth, both sought explanations of why labor had not spearheaded a decisive revolution against capital, with Marcuse focusing on the effects of the culture industry and psychological factors like the authoritarian personality and Dunayevskaya emphasizing how White racism undermined class solidarity in the United States. Fifth, both shared a Hegelianized version of Marxism, and both espoused a more subject-centered approach that contrasted with more dominant versions of Marxism, especially official Soviet *diamat*, or dialectical materialism. Here Dunayevskaya was inspired by Lenin's new appreciation of the importance of human subjectivity in his Hegel Notebooks of 1914–1915, which she contrasted not only to the vulgar materialism of Stalin's *diamat* but also to Nikolai Bukharin's avowedly mechanical materialism. Marcuse was indebted to György Lukács's *History and Class Consciousness*, which he contrasted to the positivism of "normal" social science. In dialectical fashion, however, each of these areas of affinity also contained differences and contradictions, some of which we explore in the next section.

Inside the Development of Marxist Humanism and Critical Theory

The Dunayevskaya-Marcuse Correspondence I: Debate over Marxism and Freedom, *1956–1957*

This phase of the correspondence, 1956–1957, focused on Dunayevskaya's work toward achieving publication of her book *Marxism and Freedom*. In 1956, Marcuse commented on chapter drafts. In one important letter, he disagrees both with what he sees as Dunayevskaya's "non-dialectical" (i.e., too affirmative) stance on the revolutionary nature of the contemporary working class and with her position on Russia, because of the fundamental

distinctions she had drawn between Lenin and Stalin.[22] Overall, the year
includes four letters from Marcuse, which comment (often favorably) on
Dunayevskaya's draft chapters, provide news on potential publishers, and
offer valuable words of encouragement to push ahead with the work. Also in
this period, Dunayevskaya comments favorably on the publication of Marcuse's Freudian Marxist work, *Eros and Civilization*.[23] Finally, there is a letter in which Dunayevskaya describes Marcuse's response to her analysis of
Hegel's *Philosophy of Mind* in a letter on Hegel (written in 1953)[24] that she
had left with him at their first in-person meeting in early 1955.[25] In a letter
to her partner, John Dwyer,[26] Dunayevskaya writes of how Marcuse's "eyes
lit up as to the paragraph where Marx stopped in the *Philosophy of Mind* and
where my analysis began."[27] To add a little context, Dunayevskaya's analysis
in this 1953 letter took up Hegel's introduction to the *Philosophy of Mind*.
She commented on Hegel's dialectic of necessity and freedom (the subsec-
tion in Hegel's text before which Marx's analysis of Absolute Mind in his
1844 *Manuscripts* had stopped). She then continued beyond this point in
the text by examining the concluding syllogisms of the main text, where
Hegel's discussion of Absolute Mind or Spirit compressed the philosophical
presentation in the introduction: she attempted to identify the internal logic
and the movement to a new (postcapitalist) society in the work's final three
paragraphs.

In contrast to 1956, 1957 was a contentious year. Marcuse's preface to
Marxism and Freedom (which we discuss later in the chapter) and Dunayevskaya's characterization of the "American roots of Marxism" (both in the text
of the work and in prepublication publicity) were the centers of attention.[28]

The correspondence is enhanced when viewed in the light of crucial and
surprising developments around two of Marcuse's 1958 publications, his
preface to *Marxism and Freedom* and his book *Soviet Marxism*. In the preface to *Marxism and Freedom*, the main consideration is whether Marcuse is
correct in his apparent assumption that Dunayevskaya's and his own views
are in accord on their interpretations of the dialectic of necessity and freedom in the mature Marx texts, the *Grundrisse* and *Capital*.

---

22. Anderson and Rockwell, *The Dunayevskaya-Marcuse-Fromm Correspondence*, 26.

23. Ibid., 25; Herbert Marcuse, *Eros and Civilization: A Philosophical Inquiry into Freud*
(Boston: Beacon, 1955).

24. Dunayevskaya wrote this letter in May 1953 to Grace Lee Boggs. See Dunayevskaya,
The Power of Negativity, 15–32.

25. Anderson and Rockwell, *The Dunayevskaya-Marcuse-Fromm Correspondence*, 6.

26. Ibid., 28–29. John Dwyer (1912–1989) was Dunayevskaya's husband and political associate.

27. Ibid.

28. Ibid., 40–44.

Overall, in this preface, Marcuse sees Dunayevskaya's book as a major breakthrough, writing that with "some notable exceptions" like Lukács's *History and Class Consciousness*, Marxist theorists had failed to grasp Marx's dialectic at its core, which Marcuse credits Dunayevskaya with having done. Remarkably, this preface may also have been the first occasion when Marcuse himself, perhaps following Dunayevskaya's initial reference in her text, carried out a substantial discussion of Marx's *Grundrisse*, a work heretofore little known. Marcuse remarks that Marx's 1844 *Manuscripts*, after years of oblivion and neglect, had become the focus of attention as the "ground" of Marx's writings on economics and politics. Now adding the *Grundrisse* to the mix, Marcuse writes:

> The inner identity of the philosophical with the economic and political "stage" of Marxian theory was not elucidated (and perhaps could not be adequately elucidated because a most decisive link was still missing, namely, the *Grundrisse der Kritik der Politischen Oekonomie* of 1857–1858, first published in 1939 and 1941). Dunayevskaya's book goes beyond the previous interpretations. It shows not only that Marxian economics and politics are throughout philosophy, but that the latter is from the beginning economics and politics.[29]

Marcuse's preface then focuses on the section in *Marxism and Freedom* in which Dunayevskaya cites the *Grundrisse* at the conclusion of her analyses of all three volumes of Marx's *Capital*. First, she quotes from volume 3 of Marx's *Capital*:

> Freedom in this field [material production] can only consist in socialised man, the associated producers, rationally regulating their interchange with Nature, bringing it under their common control, instead of being ruled by it as by the blind forces of Nature; and achieving this with the least expenditure of energy and under conditions most favourable to, and worthy of, their human nature. But it nonetheless still remains a realm of necessity. Beyond it begins that development of human energy which is an end in itself, the true realm of freedom, which, however, can blossom forth only with this realm of necessity as its basis. The shortening of the working-day is its basic prerequisite.[30]

Then, she writes:

29. Herbert Marcuse, preface to Dunayevskaya, *Marxism and Freedom*, xxi.
30. Quoted in Dunayevskaya, *Marxism and Freedom*, 145.

The only force which can overcome this necessity therefore is freedom which in itself and for itself inseparably combines objective
conditions, subjective activity and purpose. In the *Grundrisse* Marx
said that once the productive process is "stripped of its antagonistic form," the "measure of wealth will then no longer be labor time,
but leisure time." The free time liberated from capitalist exploitation
would be for the development of the *individual's powers.*[31]

Dunayevskaya sees Marx's passage on freedom and necessity as his evoca-
tion of the "creative plan of the workers" leading toward the new society.[32]
In this, Dunayevskaya refers in a different form (as Marcuse put it, the inner identity of the philosophical with the economic and political "stage"
of Marxian theory) to the dialectic of necessity and freedom that she had
already described five years earlier in her writing on the "Philosophy" section of Hegel's introduction to *Philosophy of Mind.* This is at the point in
Hegel's text, as we discuss earlier, where Marx had stopped in 1844, more
than two decades prior to his return to these concepts in *Capital.*[33] Amaz-
ingly, at this point, in 1957, neither Dunayevskaya (in the text of *Marxism
and Freedom*) nor Marcuse (in his preface) explicitly linked *this* necessity-
and-freedom dialectic (of Hegel's *philosophy* and Marx's *social theory* of
overcoming capitalism).[34]

In his preface, Marcuse, apparently following Dunayevskaya's method
in *Marxism and Freedom*, combines a paraphrase of the above passage from
the third volume of *Capital* with a quotation from the *Grundrisse* meant to
elaborate it. He writes:

For Marx, it [a truly rational societal organization of labor] is to be
solved by a revolution which brings the productive process under
the collective control of the "immediate producers." But this is not
freedom. Freedom is living without toil, without anxiety: the play
of human faculties. The realization of freedom is a problem of *time*:
reduction of the working day to the minimum which turns quantity
into quality. A socialist society is a society in which free time, not
labor time is the social measure of wealth and the dimension of the
individual existence.[35]

---

31. Dunayevskaya, *Marxism and Freedom*, 145 (emphasis in original).
32. Ibid.
33. Anderson and Rockwell, *The Dunayevskaya-Marcuse-Fromm Correspondence*, 29.
34. In the 1953 letter on Hegel, Dunayevskaya mentions that she was reading the third
volume of *Capital* at the time she was studying *Philosophy of Mind*. See Dunayevskaya, *The
Power of Negativity*, 25.
35. Marcuse, preface to Dunayevskaya, *Marxism and Freedom*, xxiii (emphasis in
original).

Marcuse's quotation from the *Grundrisse*, which follows, reads in part:

> Saving of labor time is increase of free time, i.e., time for the full
> development of the individual. This is the greatest productive force,
> which in turn reacts upon the productivity of labor. . . . It is evident
> that labor time cannot remain in abstract opposition to free time—as
> it appears from the point of view of bourgeois economics. Labor can-
> not become play. . . . Free time—which is leisure time as well as time
> for higher activity—transforms its possessor into a different subject.[36]

Marcuse seems to imply that his position was in accord with that found
in Dunayevskaya's text, but his analyses of Marx's two texts—most directly
on the realm of necessity Marx theorizes in *Capital*—suggest that *no* freedom could be found in labor for the necessities of life (which Marcuse identifies with Marx's concept of the "realm of necessity").[37] In contrast, as we
show, in the text of *Marxism and Freedom*, Dunayevskaya issues the quotation from Marx's *Capital*, in which Marx explicitly discusses the *forms of
freedom* inherent in the realm of necessity.[38] Finally, in the last sentence of
the passage from Marx's *Grundrisse*, as Marcuse quotes it, actually concludes
with the clause, "*and he then enters into the direct production process* [realm
of necessity] *as this different subject,*"[39] which certainly reinforces Dunayevskaya's position concerning freedom in the realm of necessity.

In his preface, Marcuse delivers high praise indeed for Dunayevskaya's
work; nonetheless, Dunayevskaya's response to seeing what she regards as
his negative view of the revolutionary potential of American workers was
swift. She writes:

> Your Preface certainly points up some fundamental questions in
> dispute as well as illumination. I wouldn't think of discarding it. By
> pointing to what I have called the forever beating heart of Marxism,
> the workers who in their everyday life and struggles have given it a
> new life and dimension—you will certainly have stirred a polemic
> that should be going at full blast as soon as the book is published.
> Sharp disagreements have never disturbed me; monolithism has.[40]

This issue remained a key sticking point in their dialogue.

---

36. Ibid.

37. Marcuse, preface to Dunayevskaya, *Marxism and Freedom*, xxiii.

38. Dunayevskaya, *Marxism and Freedom*, 145.

39. Karl Marx, *Grundrisse: Foundations of the Critique of Political Economy (Rough
Draft)*, trans. Martin Nicolaus (London: Penguin, 1973), 712 (emphasis added).

40. Anderson and Rockwell, *The Marcuse-Dunayevskaya-Fromm Correspondence*, 39.

In the September 21, 1956, letter, in which Marcuse first disagrees with Dunayevskaya on the contemporary revolutionary potential of the working class, as well as on her analysis of the Soviet Union—that is, her "assumption of a complete break between Leninism and Stalinism"[41]—Marcuse also mentioned for the first time his forthcoming study of Soviet Marxism.[42] In the same letter, he also reported reading Dunayevskaya's chapter on volumes 2 and 3 of *Capital*, included in which were her original analyses of the *Grundrisse* and assessment of Marx's analysis of the dialectic of the realm of necessity and the realm of freedom in volume 3 of *Capital*. In the text of *Soviet Marxism*, then, Marcuse again places important emphasis on the *Grundrisse*.[43] He writes in a footnote, "This is the most important of Marx's manuscripts, which shows to what extent the humanist philosophy is fulfilled and formulated in the economic theory of *Capital*."[44] On the freedom and necessity dialectic, Marcuse writes, "The relation between necessity and freedom . . . is the key problem in the Hegelian as well as the Marxian dialectic."[45] Marcuse cites Hegel's *Smaller Logic* of the *Encyclopedia of the Philosophical Sciences*, in which Hegel terms the passage from necessity to freedom the "hardest" of all dialectical transitions.[46] Marcuse criticizes Soviet Marxism for following Friedrich Engels (rather than Marx) in viewing freedom as "recognized necessity" or, as Hegel put it, as "abstract negation" instead of "freedom concrete and positive."[47] But in view of the Dunayevskaya-Marcuse correspondence, it is equally interesting to follow Hegel's text one more step, to "what we may learn" (from "freedom concrete and positive" over "abstract negation")—that is, to Hegel's warning of "what a mistake it is to regard freedom and necessity as mutually exclusive."[48] For, sure enough, in the section of *Soviet Marxism* on "Principles of Commu-

---

41. Ibid., 26.

42. Ibid. This work was published as Herbert Marcuse, *Soviet Marxism: A Critical Analysis* (New York: Columbia University Press, 1958; repr., New York: Vintage, 1961). Citations refer to the Vintage edition.

43. It should be noted that even prior to Dunayevskaya's initiation of the correspondence with him, Marcuse recorded his appreciation of the importance of Marx's *Grundrisse*. Attached to the new 1954 epilogue to *Reason and Revolution* (published in New York by Humanities Press in 1954) was "A Supplement to the Bibliography," in which Marcuse wrote under the heading "Marx" the following: "Most important is the first publication of Marx's manuscript '*Grundrisse der Kritik der politischen Oekonomie*' written in 1857–1858. This is actually the first version, previously unknown, of *Das Kapital*. It is far more 'philosophical' than the final version and shows how Marx's mature economic theory grows out of his philosophical conceptions." Marcuse, *Reason and Revolution*, 440.

44. Marcuse, *Soviet Marxism*, 185n5.

45. Ibid., 135.

46. Ibid., 136.

47. Ibid.

48. G.W.F. Hegel, *Hegel's Logic: Being Part One of the Encyclopedia of the Philosophical Sciences (1830)*, trans. William Wallace (Oxford: Clarendon, 1975), 220.

nist Morality," Marcuse writes, "Man comes into his own *only* outside and 'beyond' the entire realm of material production for the mere necessities of life."[49]

The Dunayevskaya-Marcuse Correspondence II: *Toward* One-Dimensional Man, *1960–1961*

Following the tensions around the publication of Dunayevskaya's *Marxism and Freedom*, nearly three years passed since his last letter to Dunayevskaya before Marcuse renewed the correspondence, asking for her perspectives on themes he was developing for a work called *Studies in the Ideology of Advanced Industrial Societies* (later titled *One-Dimensional Man*), particularly, "a more affirmative attitude of the laborer not only towards the system as a whole but even to the organization of work in the more highly modernized plants."[50] Unfortunately, the short burst of correspondence that Marcuse's letter ignited, though interesting and providing new insights into their subsequent development, marked the end of a sustained and focused dialogue between the two of them.

Before considering the status of the dialogue through a look at this latest phase of the correspondence, it is helpful to point out that Marcuse sent his letter to Dunayevskaya, dated August 8, 1960, during the period of his new preface to *Reason and Revolution*, "A Note on Dialectic," dated March 1960. Although undoubtedly also influenced by Max Horkheimer and Theodor Adorno's melancholy *Dialectic of Enlightenment*, many of the points Marcuse developed in "A Note on Dialectic" could have been formulated as well-considered responses to the dialogue on dialectics he had engaged in with Dunayevskaya, especially in the first year of their correspondence, when he repeatedly asked for more time to respond properly to the points she raised on Hegel's dialectic.[51] Tracing back a little further, however, we can see in Marcuse's 1954 epilogue to *Reason and Revolution*, published right before the correspondence with Dunayevskaya began, the notion that by the turn of the twentieth century the "larger part of the laboring classes were made into a positive part of the established society."[52] He concludes the 1960 preface to *Reason and Revolution*, "A Note on Dialectic," with the notice, "I have omitted the Epilogue written for the second edition because it treated in a much

---

49. Marcuse, *Soviet Marxism*, 219 (emphasis added).
50. Anderson and Rockwell, *The Dunayevskaya-Marcuse-Fromm Correspondence*, 59. Marcuse was referring to research for the book that would be published as *One-Dimensional Man*.
51. Anderson and Rockwell, *The Dunayevskaya-Marcuse-Fromm Correspondence*, 3–15.
52. Marcuse, *Reason and Revolution*, 436.

condensed form developments which I discuss more fully in my forthcoming book, a study of advanced industrial society."[53]

While it is true that Marcuse opens the new phase of correspondence with Dunayevskaya on the "old" topic of the "integration of the working class," the new twist concerns the distinction he draws between the more than century-long process in which the working classes "were made into a positive part of the established society" and the "more affirmative attitude of the laborer to the organization of work."[54] Dunayevskaya responds with a brief description of a pamphlet "just off the press" from her News and Letters Committees, titled *Workers Battle Automation*, indicating that she would send it along to him.[55] Before also providing a very detailed annotated bibliography of economic and sociological work germane to the subject of Marcuse's book-in-progress, she points out that the workers writing in the pamphlet expressed various viewpoints on the topic of automation and work. In his response to Dunayevskaya, Marcuse expressed general agreement with most of what he had read in the pamphlet, in which Charles Denby, author of *Indignant Heart: A Black Worker's Journal*, and other worker-writers took up the increased alienation and unemployment resulting from automation in major industries like auto, coal, and steel; however, then Marcuse refers Dunayevskaya to the *Grundrisse* to support his argument that merely partial automation (the kind he said was experienced by the workers writing in *Workers Battle Automation*) "saves the capitalist system." He quickly adds that "consummated automation would inevitably explode it." Marcuse forcefully disagrees with one of the worker's views, arguing that the worker's view of the needed "humanization of labor" was mistaken, since Marx's theory suggested that "complete dehumanization" of the realm of necessity (total automation) was the prerequisite for the "realm of freedom."[56]

A new hypothesis evident in Marcuse's brief remarks is that not only is there an observable long-term trend in the integration of the working class, but this class and the capitalists share a powerful economic and social interest antithetical to Critical Theory—the arrest of automation. Moreover, Marcuse seems to imply that the different reasons behind these interests— for example, decline in the rate of profit for the capitalists and technological unemployment for the workers—are less significant than the conflict of the combined forces of workers and capitalists with the technological progress that automation represented.

These 1960 exchanges offered the clearest signs to date that the trajectory of Dunayevskaya's and Marcuse's theory development were in opposite

53. Herbert Marcuse, *Reason and Revolution* (Boston: Beacon, 1960), xiv.
54. Anderson and Rockwell, *The Dunayevskaya-Marcuse-Fromm Correspondence*, 59.
55. Ibid., 60.
56. Ibid., 66.

directions despite, or perhaps also as a result of, the long correspondence. This correspondence had to persevere under the impact of rapidly developing technology, especially automated production and intensive challenges to recreating the dialectic to the point where it could grasp and mold these trends in the direction of a postcapitalist society of freedom. Increasingly, Dunayevskaya's trajectory took the name "Marxist Humanism," while Marcuse recommitted to the original Critical Theory tradition.

Epilogue

In the published version of *One-Dimensional Man*, Marcuse famously formulated the concept of the Great Refusal, a form of radical opposition to the system that could be found not in the employed working class but in marginalized groups, such as the unemployed and bohemian artists. For her part, Dunayevskaya continued to evoke rank-and-file industrial labor (as against the labor bureaucracy), as well as what she termed new forces of revolution: Blacks, women, and youth. Both Marcuse and Dunayevskaya, albeit in different ways, sought to create a Marxism for their era, an effort that involved reconceptualizing the dialectic, connecting the *Grundrisse* to early Marx and to *Capital*, and conceptualizing new forces of opposition and revolution. Their correspondence, especially at the juncture we examine here, illuminates this process of dialectical creativity in a way that speaks not only to their era but to ours as well.

18

The Existential Dimension of the Great Refusal

Marcuse, Fanon, Habermas

Martin Beck Matuštík

erbert Marcuse analyzes domination, human development, language, and culture by theorizing actual liberation struggles. He introduces into critical social theory a dose of existentially material concretion, which he articulates under the category of the Great Refusal: the embodied performative politics from the margins, consisting of pluralized, humorous, and earnest dissent by oppressed outsiders. From Marcuse's use of Sigmund Freud's precritical anthropology, which Marcuse linked to Karl Marx, thinkers and activists can learn how to invent analogical moves for existentially material critical theory and praxis. What would it mean to link the existential categories of transgression with dissenting democratic agencies?

Marcuse insists that to launch the transgressive strategies of the Great Refusal against the rhetoric of an untrue one-dimensional whole (based on logocentric reason, patriarchy, racist epistemic evidence or validity, homogenizing identity logic, and contaminated grammar), oppositional humor, clowning, and sober refusals must be articulated with a new vigor. Ahead of such social movements as Occupy or the so-called Arab Spring, the Marcusean hope for change marks off an existential emancipatory dissent that offers attractive strategies for an otherwise dispersed activism or the naively dangerous transgressions that may reemerge with conservative postrevolutionary conservatism. Marcuse's conceptual apparatus has an advantage over them that, when harnessed practically, provides critical self-corrective tools for genuinely progressive social change.

This chapter combines, revises, and extends portions of Martin J. Beck Matuštík, *Specters of Liberation: Great Refusals in the New World Order* (Albany: State University of New York, 1998), and Martin Beck Matuštík, "Existence and the Communicatively Competent Self," *Philosophy and Social Criticism* 25, no. 3 (1999): 93–120.

This critical possibility of great refusal must be continually imagined, discovered, and theorized. Yet it also raises a problem for any earnest clown and refusenik in the present age: if domination becomes internalized via socialization, what are the available sources of irony, dissent, and liberation? What is it in virtue of that critical theory and social movements correct themselves from regressive blind alleys? Marcusean dissenting refusals embody hope for a radically democratic agency of personal and social change. That the new specters of liberating change are given for the sake of the wretched of the earth prompts one to imagine a world wholly other than our real, existing unjust worlds.

It is widely accepted in mainstream social theory that humans are individualized insofar as they are socialized. This insight is often mobilized against existential categories as if there were an inherent contradiction between existential refusals and social change. Marcuse's strategies for social change show the marginality of such theoretical suspicion. Given this basic insight, one must still explain how humans *do* adopt some critical distance from that culture in which they become knowers as well as responsible and linguistic subjects. To be a good American, is it sufficient to be just that—an American individualized through American socialization? Best common sense tells us that it is not. The obvious point calls for some explanation. Existential philosophy provides an answer to this issue by thematizing that there is a mode of inwardness that is incommensurable with conventional sociality.

It is in his concept of the Great Refusal that Marcuse retains the key insight of concrete existential thought and incorporates it into critical social theory. He finds resources of liberation in the cleavages within pure or binary notions of nature and culture. We are socialized into both notions; resources of irony, critique, and refusal are situated within the human capacity to adopt some distance from both. This harnessed competence empowers a performative, lived, or existential dialectic of critical individualization through socialization in the one-dimensional world.

According to Marcuse, the existing one-dimensional political and social universe incarnates "a false concreteness" and "misplaced abstractness." "The concreteness of the particular case which the translation achieves is the result of a series of abstractions from its *real* concreteness, which is in the universal character of the case." *Bad* materialism and empiricism affirm sinister facticity. *Bad* idealism and rationalism translate one-dimensional universality into a speculation or functionalism. Both pure transgressions and formal agency—adopted in one-dimensional situations—turn out to be tragic comedies of themselves (a travesty of clowns and *refuseniki*).[1]

---

1. Herbert Marcuse, *One-Dimensional Man: Studies in the Ideology of Advanced Industrial Society* (Boston: Beacon, 1964), 107, 108n26, 110 (emphasis in original).

If Marcuse is right, and ahead of similar postmodern insights, then just as the aporias of the inner and the outer, the inside and outside, present false problems, so must those of marginality and institutions. These are false binaries. Genuine promises of liberation confront certain one-dimensional particulars and certain one-dimensional universals. They confront each other in theory and practical politics.

This critical social theory is consistent with praxis of an existential either-or: either drift within the one-dimensional inner-outer or adopt a radically honest relation within the inner-outer; either celebrate the fragmentary transgressions and homogenizing agencies or affirm excluded difference and open identity; either be a dupe of disconnected marginality and abstract universality or empower the disenfranchised, who suffer in the margins, and establish emancipatory institutional coalitions as well as solidary communities; either promote diversity as a form of nominal gender, race, and class tokenism or strive for the concrete universal of a radical multicultural, multiracial, and multigendered democracy. *This* either-or, in contrast to the straw-man reading of the decisionist either-or logic attributed to existentialism in general, envisions a concrete singular universal by refusing the one-dimensional impostor.

The jargon of the status quo is the jargon of homogenizing reality. It valorizes the end of the Cold War as a victory for the canons of western culture, it interprets prodemocracy movements as the vindication of Western political interests, and its universal doctrine of free trade is locally partial to the global reign of the first-world multinationals. Celebrating multiculturalism, democratic pluralism, and open trade on terms of a globally regional pillage by the West is, by all commonsense standards, deceptive. Can a critical theory resist this outcome without theorizing in its praxis the standpoint of the immiserated? Marcuse searches for an anticolonial critical theory. He does not envision this as one of the many issues brought into our democratic discourse *after* we have established a procedural framework for *this* democracy. His quest marks the core of a radically democratic starting point for a true liberation theory and practice.[2]

Marcuse makes us aware that theorizing from the standpoint of Western, middle-class, existentialist (and deconstructionist) rebellions alone does not give us any right to speak for the wretched of the earth. A European de-centering of the "European idea" by European postmodernity suffices rather poorly in delivering the perspective of the colonial lifeworlds into those of the colonized. Striving for some reciprocal reversibility of such perspectives would be a tragic joke, because abstractly reversible positions may seem liberally radical but are only so in a conservative sense. Again, this insight provides us some tools for reading unattractive regressive outcomes of initially progressive revolutionary change (to give just a few examples: nationalist

2. Herbert Marcuse, *An Essay on Liberation* (Boston: Beacon, 1969), 6, 35, 46–48, 56, 66.

regression of the Yugoslav Praxis philosophy, the Iranian Revolution, and the Arab Spring). Marcuse defines as *radical* someone who or some movement that struggles for a historically material liberation of the immiserated. Radicals are not those who sketch textual or imaginary otherness (not every "Yes we can" is radical in a progressive sense) but those who venture out to engage with concrete others.

A concrete embodiment of refusals demands that Western middle-class revolts be rooted in the struggles waged by the wretched of the earth.[3] Frantz Fanon brings forth what Marcuse understood: if emancipatory claims are not in coalition (striving for solidarity) with the "struggle . . . waged outside," then liberation will not come for the White European Man.[4]

The term *Great Refusal* is inspired by André Breton's surrealist dissent against alienated reality. Marcuse identifies the term, throughout his corpus, with the positionality of nonintegrated outsiders.[5] He depicts the "outsiders" living on the urban outskirts of the West as genuine resources of liberation. They often stage their clowning and refusal within an increasingly nihilistic world. These kinds of rebellion, by mirroring the nihilism of an established order, project hope in another than this hopeless world. The refusals are thus decentered by multiple non-European foci of struggle and cannot be identified with philistine bourgeois individualism. The clowns and *refuse-niki* preserve and imagine revolutionary possibilities as much within the hegemony of one-dimensional mentality as in confrontation politics or in an age of nihilism.

For Marcuse, then, the Great Refusal offers to be a "real spectre of liberation" that subverts the rhetorical and really existing specters of one-dimensional orders. Effective refusals cannot but ironize and subvert such orders existentially and sociopolitically. The one-dimensionality of the inner and the outer is undone by an obstinate thought, a counterhegemonic gesture, or communicative, sociopolitical, and economic action. Without opposing one-dimensionality as at once inner-outer, we get abstract either-or; opt either for margins or for institutions. Each option is projected

---

3. Marcuse, *An Essay on Liberation*, 6–7, 76; Herbert Marcuse, "Repressive Tolerance" in *A Critique of Pure Tolerance*, by Herbert Marcuse, Robert Paul Wolff, and Barrington Moore Jr. (Boston: Beacon, 1965), 110, 116; Frantz Fanon, *The Wretched of the Earth*, trans. Constance Farrington (New York: Grove, 1963).

4. Marcuse, *An Essay on Liberation*, 7; Frantz Fanon, *Black Skin, White Masks*, trans. Charles Lam Markmann (New York: Grove, 1967), 92, 224.

5. Herbert Marcuse, *Reason and Revolution: Hegel and the Rise of Social Theory* (New York: Oxford University Press, 1941); see also Marcuse, "Preface: A Note on Dialectic," in *Reason and Revolution* (Boston: Beacon, 1960), vii–xiv; Marcuse, *One-Dimensional Man*, 63; Marcuse, *An Essay on Liberation*, 35; and Douglas Kellner, *Herbert Marcuse and the Crisis of Marxism* (Berkeley: University of California Press, 1984).

undialectically. Abstractly celebrated margins and formal delimitations of institutional democracy—both can lead to dead ends.[6]

Those on the margins are anything but unnameable tokens for radicality. They do not seek a decentering via anonymous others. They do not long for intertextuality without a human face. In the margins of the West lie the voices of those to be heard in oppositional speech, the faces and hands to be made visible in ironical grimace and clenched fist, the persons to affect us as agents of personal and institutional change. Are the marginalized served when they remain the perpetual margins—that is, postponed texts, undecidable gestures, sporadic transgressions? An economically secure romantic or academic might think so. The aporias of marginality and institutions are not set in stone. They disappear when the struggle for justice becomes informed by the concrete material analyses about it and the plight of the marginalized, as in the works of Marcuse.

One had better stop babbling about margins as something that makes *us*, theoreticians in the Eurocenters of the West, decentered and posttheoretically radical. If projects of liberation aim at radically multicultural democracies with human faces, these must admit an existential dimension. This existentiality issues in a reconstructed historical materialism, not in the wasteland haunted by spiritual ghosts. Democracy concerns the entirety of human existence, or it is abstract. Revolution concerns the entirety of human existence, or it is abstract. Dissent and democracy concern the entirety of human existence, or they are abstract.

Fanon's Great Existential Refusal

Alongside Marcuse stands Frantz Fanon, whose work can be enlisted in the liberation project of radical multicultural and existential democracy. Marcuse's existentially material critical social theory should be read along with Fanon:

> The colonized . . . who [write] for . . . [colonized] people ought to use the past with the intention of opening the future, as an invitation to action and a basis for hope. But to ensure that hope and to give it form, . . . [one] must take part in action and throw . . . [one]self body and soul into the national struggle. You may speak about everything under the sun; but when you decide to speak of that unique thing in . . . [human] life that is represented by the fact of opening up new horizons, by bringing light to your own country, and by raising

---

6. Marcuse, *One-Dimensional Man*, 52; see also 68–83, 123, 132, 134, 140–143, 167, 225–246.

yourself and your people to their feet, then you must collaborate on the physical plane.[7]

Great Refusals must provide bridges for coalitions and solidarity of the middle-class revolts with the struggles by the immiserated (both in affluent cities and at the world margins). To be sure, Fanon speaks about Western intellectual alienation with a definitive and understandable disdain. Some students of existential despair, particularly those coming from an economically secure background, might resort to quietist inaction or even self-distancing nihilism as responses to their anomic and fragmented worlds. Herein lies a key to Marcuse's notion of refusals read through a Fanonian perspective: existential rebellions within the colonial empires to the material struggles of the colonized. The latter struggles, pace Fanon and Jean-Paul Sartre, would not be antinomical to existentially positioned critical social theory and practice. This opening has come to be obvious in works of existential theorists of the African American and Caribbean experience. For example, Lewis R. Gordon shows that European existentialist texts about anguish and bad faith may not wake one to gender and race apartheid. For this, one must confront sexism and racism in its embodied forms of self-evasion. Cornel West provides many descriptions of inner-city nihilism. With this background, one can better grasp Marcuse's claim that it is often the outsiders who genuinely raise the specters of Great Refusals.[8]

Fanon and Marcuse grasp that decolonization means the death of Man. Insurgent literature portrays "Man" as a patriarchal and epidermically challenged colonial desire of masters. One may distinguish from Man's death other antihumanist celebrations—the death of the last man and the end of the subject. To wit, those who celebrate an empty set may still live in a bad faith of anti-Black racism or Man's hypermasculinity.

As an existential activist and revolutionary, Fanon does not throw out the human baby with the dirty water of Europe's inhuman humanism. European antihumanism has a racist underside. Why else would the "Europe" after the death of European Man prescind from *all* humanism? Since when does historical Europe—an antihuman humanist monster of Columbus, Auschwitz, gulag, Hiroshima—define humanity? After the colonial

7. Fanon, *Wretched of the Earth*, 232.
8. Lewis R. Gordon, *Bad Faith and Antiblack Racism* (Atlantic Highlands, NJ: Humanities, 1995); Lewis R. Gordon, *Fanon and the Crisis of European Man: An Essay on Philosophy and the Human Sciences* (London: Routledge, 1995); Lewis R. Gordon, ed., *Existence in Black: An Anthology of Black Existential Philosophy* (London: Routledge, 1996); Lewis R. Gordon, *What Fanon Said: A Philosophical Introduction to His Life and Thought* (New York: Fordham University Press, 2015); Cornel West, *Race Matters* (Boston: Beacon, 1993); Marcuse, *An Essay on Liberation*, ix–x, 6, 35n8, 47, 61.

conquests by Western moderns, who gains from relegating the human face to antihumanist postmodern textuality?

> Decolonization never takes place unnoticed, for it influences individuals and modifies them fundamentally. It transforms spectators crushed with their inessentiality into privileged actors. . . . It brings a natural rhythm into existence, introduced by new men, and with it *a new language and a new humanity. Decolonization is the veritable creation of new men.*[9]

As if cowriting Fanon's text, Marcuse sounds rare hope for "a human universe without exploitation and toil."[10] The rarity of such hope makes it ring hollow in the oligopolies of the West. It echoes the exhausted, at best liberal, imagination of some postmodern and critical social theorists. Yet it empowers those imaginative escapists and democratic *refuseniki* who speak today, for example, from the Lacandon Jungle. Mentioning hope threatens rupture, "the historical break in the continuum of domination—as expressive of the needs of a new type of man."[11] A postracist, postpatriarchal, postcolonial solidarity—it would sustain democracy as an imagined, invented, embodied new *social-natural kind*—requires dissent from "a conservative continuum of needs,"[12] from the very socialized "biological foundation" of exclusionary and commodity relations.[13]

A Marcusean performative *body politics* dissents from socialized racist, sexist, commodified sensitivity, "but such rupture itself can be envisaged only in a revolution . . . which, by virtue of this 'biological' foundation, would have the chance of turning quantitative technical progress into qualitatively different ways of life."[14] Marcuse's transgressive agency raises a specter of "a type of man with a different sensitivity as well as consciousness: men who would speak a different language, have different gestures, follow different impulses; men who have developed an instinctual barrier against cruelty, brutality, ugliness."[15]

Like Fanon, Marcuse gropes for a new sensibility, "a new *language* to define and communicate the new 'values' (language in the wider sense which includes words, images, gestures, tones)."[16] There is no guarantee now for the future career of uttered and written words, even those written on this page.

---

9. Fanon, *Wretched of the Earth*, 36 (emphasis added).
10. Marcuse, *An Essay on Liberation*, 19.
11. Ibid.
12. Ibid., 18.
13. Ibid., 7–22.
14. Ibid., 18–19.
15. Ibid., 21; see also 10n1, 32–36.
16. Ibid., 33 (emphasis in original).

No symbol of achieved liberation (e.g., red flag or institutionalized languages of inclusion or pierced body) succeeds to carry liberation to others on its own without renewed alliances with the wretched of the earth, still among us, who communicate their pain today.

Envision Fanon's radical positionality: "the real *leap* consists in introducing invention into existence."[17] Marcuse's category of the Great Refusal bespeaks a kinship with this sociopolitical reading of leap. When Marcuse invokes the wretched of the earth, this allies him with Fanon's at once existential and Marxian senses of the leap. One need not privilege one category—race, gender, sex, class—over the rest. Marcuse engages regional and political liberation struggles. He begins to thematize racism and patriarchy as distinct forms of oppression, and he envisions democracy beyond formal liberal terms as radically political, multicultural, and economic. With Fanon, his refusals engender the personal and social aspects of liberation within the entire existence of the marginalized. The entirety of human existence in need of transformation joins the personal with the institutional.[18]

If one refigures Marcuse's refusals through Fanon's existential inventions, leaps can serve to link transgressive singularities with personal and global agencies of liberation. Existentially material leaps proffer historical inventions. Such leaps live without historical teleologies or determined essences. Leapers learn to refuse; they dance, in a body politics—that is, they refuse performatively. Performatives that matter raise the real "spectre of a world which could be free."[19] The "real spectre of liberation" is the "Enemy . . . of all doing and undoing."[20] Hope's refusals raise the "specter which haunts not only the bourgeoisie but all exploitative bureaucracies."[21]

A concrete critical theory of liberation today gathers refusing voices from multiple margins. This thought can deliver on an earlier promissory note that democracy-to-come must become morally and sociopolitically anticolonial and ethically postcolonial.

Habermas's Great Refusal

In a 1985 *New Left Review* interview, Habermas records an "affinity with the existentialist, i.e. the Marcusean, variant of Critical Theory."[22] He recalls receiving from Marcuse a personally "dedicated" copy of *One-Dimensional*

---

17. Fanon, *Black Skin, White Masks*, 229 (emphasis in original).

18. Marcuse, "Repressive Tolerance," 110, 116; Marcuse, *An Essay on Liberation*, 6.

19. Herbert Marcuse, *Eros and Civilization: A Philosophical Inquiry into Freud* (Boston: Beacon, 1974), 93.

20. Marcuse, *One-Dimensional Man*, 52.

21. Marcuse, *An Essay on Liberation*, ix.

22. Jürgen Habermas, "A Philosophico-Political Profile," *New Left Review*, no. 151 (May–June 1985): 78.

Man with "a flattering quote from Benjamin—'to the hope of those without hope.'"[23] This book is one of Marcuse's darkest (aligned with Max Horkheimer and Theodor Adorno's *Dialectic of Enlightenment*), yet it has been a source of hope for a more just world. "Rebellious subjectivity," "a new sensibility," and "the Great Refusal" are at the heart of "the existentialist, i.e., the Marcusean, variant of Critical Theory" with which Habermas feels intellectual kinship.[24]

Habermas's friendship with Marcuse began in the 1960s. These were years marked by the student revolts and attempts at reconciling existential phenomenology with Marxian social theory. Habermas does not claim that Marcuse develops an existential variant of Critical Theory for the first time upon publishing *One-Dimensional Man* (1964). One could get this impression about Marcuse's line of thought, since in 1948 he opposed critical social theory to what he deems to be Sartre's problematic individualism;[25] he revalued Sartre's existentialism more positively only in 1965. At this time, he linked Sartre's existential philosophy to a liberation struggle—primarily on behalf of Fanon's *Wretched of the Earth* (for which Sartre wrote the preface). It is more interesting to witness how Habermas reminds Marcuse[26] of a different genealogy leading to an existential variant of critical social theory:

> Marcuse's early works which appear before his emigration . . . represent the first original attempt at a *phenomenologically* oriented *Marxism*. . . . Sartre comes upon this path much later [1948] when Marcuse has already abandoned it for a long time. The left Existentialists in Paris and the Praxis philosophers in Prague and Zagreb could after the War replace Heidegger's *Daseinsanalysis* with lifeworld analyses of late Husserl, but both "schools" rely on the phenomenological

---

23. Ibid. Recall that the quotation from Walter Benjamin that Marcuse used as the last words of *One-Dimensional Man* reads as follows: "It is only for the sake of those without hope that hope is given to us." Walter Benjamin, quoted in Marcuse, *One-Dimensional Man*, 257.

24. Jürgen Habermas, "Psychic Thermidor and the Rebirth of Rebellious Subjectivity," in *Habermas and Modernity*, ed. Richard J. Bernstein (Cambridge, MA: MIT Press, 1985), 67–77, 218n; see also Jürgen Habermas, *Autonomy and Solidarity: Interviews with Jürgen Habermas*, ed. Peter Dews (London: Verso, 1992), 234.

25. Herbert Marcuse, "Sartre's Existentialism," in *From Luther to Popper*, trans. Joris de Bres (London: Verso, 1972). This piece was originally published in 1948 as Herbert Marcuse, "Existentialism: Remarks on Jean-Paul Sartre's *L'Être et le Néant*," *Philosophy and Phenomenological Research* 7, no. 3 (1948): 309–336. See also Herbert Marcuse, *Schriften*, vol. 1 (Frankfurt, Germany: Suhrkamp, 1978).

26. Jürgen Habermas, "Theorie und Politik" [Theory and Politics], in *Gespräche mit Herbert Marcuse* [Conversations with Herbert Marcuse] (Frankfurt, Germany: Suhrkamp, 1978), 22.

groundwork of a Marxism which has been anticipated characteristi-
cally by Herbert Marcuse.[27]

Habermas insists that Marcuse precedes (1928–1932), even if he subsequently abandons (1933), what became Sartre's later parallel though unin-
fluenced effort at forging existential Marxism (1950s). Yet Habermas insists
that "the existentialist moment remains alive in Marcuse's theory."[28] Indeed,
this moment forms the forefront of Marcuse's work and political engagement
at the time when Sartre and dialectical phenomenologists on both sides of
the Iron Curtain elaborated a Marxian reception of existential philosophy.[29]
Habermas can, thus, trace an existential variant of Critical Theory to Marcuse's Freiburg years, interrupted in the 1930s by the rise of Nazi political existentialism and National Socialism along with Marcuse's exile to the
United States (1933), and follow it in the United States until about 1964. The
period of the 1960s retains a Marcusean existential-revolutionary hope for
a more just world; it spearheads complex movements of refusal within late
industrial societies.[30]

Much more could be said about Habermas's polemics with Marcuse concerning the normative basis of critical social theory, but I restrict myself to a
capsule of their conversation before Marcuse's eightieth birthday. Habermas
argues that the site of rationality and democracy lies in exercising one's communicative competencies. Performative employment of these competencies
enables an intersubjective formation of common meaning and will. Marcuse
situates rationality in coming to a mutual self-understanding and recognition of human desire (Eros) and needs.[31] Habermas appears suspicious of any
recourse to an uncritical (irrational) anthropology[32] or naturalist (ahistorical) human biology. He finds residues of both at the core of Marcuse's (however otherwise historical and material) foundations for liberated (socialist)
existence.[33] Conversely, Marcuse grows suspicious of existential blind spots
(abstractness) at the very heart of any strictly formal analysis of rational and
democratic society.[34] Starting from either side, the objection is that, in matters of rationality, the other thinker lacks critical concretion—that is, each
is placing a cart before the horse: Marcuse's access to needs and desire seems

27. Jürgen Habermas, "Zum Geleit" [Introductory Comments], in *Antworten auf Herbert Marcuse* [Responses to Herbert Marcuse], ed. Jürgen Habermas (Frankfurt, Germany:
Suhrkamp, 1968), 1 (emphasis in original; my translation).

28. Ibid., 12 (my translation).

29. Ibid., 11.

30. Habermas, *Autonomy and Solidarity*, 234–236.

31. Habermas, "Theorie und Politik," 32–38.

32. Ibid., 26–28.

33. Ibid., 29–30.

34. Ibid., 30–38.

precritical, while Habermas's communications model seems to abstract from what motivates human interaction in the first place.

The core of Habermas's objection to Marcuse's or any other existential-ist variant of liberation is that "it cannot consistently account for its own possibility."[35] Habermas's inquiry into performative consistency has the character of Meno's paradox:[36] If existential refusals were to emerge from below or beyond rational recognition by individuals-in-communities (e.g., from desire), how could one discover a liberation one did not know? And if one encountered a liberation possibility one did not know, how could one even recognize it and then rationally defend it? Habermas, however, distin-guishes Marcuse from a subjectivist or popularized existentialist who would "evoke the pathos of emancipation" and "the vital needs of freedom" without doing the hard labor of critical social theory to "ground action in reason."[37] Possibilities of resistance and rebellion are concretely historical, not an irrationalist's whim or one's private, amoral, or premoral affair. Refusals have cognitive and critical value and represent the basis for historically rec-ognized needs for a more just world, Marcuse would argue. Their "basic value judgments are rooted in compassion, in our sense for the suffering of others."[38] (Habermas cites this quotation, Marcuse's last words to him before dying, to mark their basic agreement.)

Even if Habermas suspects Marcuse for merely shifting from uncritical ontology (Heidegger) to a precritical anthropology (Freud's theory of in-stincts), he values him as a concrete thinker and a responsible activist. And that continued valuation has marked Marcuse's and Habermas's earlier part-ing with Heidegger's transcendental and ahistorical history and politics of Being. Habermas records this succinctly: "You may understand better what it meant for me, as someone who has been a thoroughgoing Heideggerian for three or four years, to read Marcuse for the first time. It was while I was working on the concept of ideology [Frankfurt, 1956] that I came across Marcuse's early articles."[39]

Marcuse's essays (1928–1932)[40] serve the young Habermas to become more concrete in a twofold sense: to move away from abstract historicity and to move closer to historical and material analysis with practical intent (i.e., the problematics of the Great Refusal). Habermas himself states that he "always felt" close "to the idea that the life of theory is a project of practical reason, or conducted in its name."[41]

---

35. Habermas, "Psychic Thermidor and the Rebirth of Rebellious Subjectivity," 75.
36. Plato, *Meno* 80d–80e.
37. Habermas, "Psychic Thermidor and the Rebirth of Rebellious Subjectivity," 76.
38. Ibid., 77.
39. Habermas, *Autonomy and Solidarity*, 189–192.
40. Marcuse, *Schriften*.
41. Habermas, *Autonomy and Solidarity*, 190.

During 1968, the radical student activism in Germany conjured up for Habermas "a rhetoric of violence"—a nightmare left over from the Nazi period. He even begins to worry, albeit hypothetically, about the possible dangers of "left fascism."[42] It is Marcuse's moral and democratic responsibility as a voice within the student movement (in the United States and Germany alike) that provides Habermas with a practical bridge to an existential variant of Critical Theory. Remember that this path is barred for Habermas just as much as for Marcuse by Heidegger's elusive and undemocratic stance on the political realities of the present age.[43] A theoretical bridge is erected in the 1980s when Habermas expands existential categories into a communicative competence for posttraditional and postnational identity.[44]

These posttraditional and postnational types of individual and group identity formations emerge, says Habermas,[45] under the pressures of modern nationalism. On the one hand, there are the universalist ideals of moral autonomy and political democracy of 1789;[46] on the other hand, there exist the particularized ethics of individual and group authenticity.

While cultures strive for genuine recognition,[47] no tradition or history is innocent—consider the Holocaust, anti-Black slavery, ethnic cleansing,

---

42. Jürgen Habermas, *Die nachholende Revolution: Kleine politische Schriften* [Reclaiming Revolution: Brief Political Commentaries], vol. 7 (Frankfurt, Germany: Suhrkamp, 1990), 25 (my translation); Habermas, *Autonomy and Solidarity*, 233; Jürgen Habermas, "Die Scheinrevolution und ihre Kinder: Sechs Thesen über Taktik, Ziele und Situationsanalysen der oppositionellen Jugend" [The Illusory Revolution and Its Progeny: Six Theses on Tactics, Goals and Contextual Analysis of Youth in Opposition], in *Die Linke antwortet Jürgen Habermas* [The Left Replies to Jürgen Habermas] (Frankfurt, Germany: Europäische Verlagsanstalt, 1968), 34–47.

43. Habermas, "Psychic Thermidor and the Rebirth of Rebellious Subjectivity," 76–77.

44. For more on this theoretical bridge, see Martin J. Matuštík, *Postnational Identity: Critical Theory and Existential Philosophy in Habermas, Kierkegaard, and Havel* (New York: Guilford, 1993); and Martin J. Matuštík, *Jürgen Habermas: A Philosophical-Political Profile* (Lanham, MD: Rowman and Littlefield, 2001).

45. Habermas, *Die nachholende Revolution*, 25–26; Habermas, *Autonomy and Solidarity*, 233–236; Jürgen Habermas, "Historical Consciousness and Post-traditional Identity: The Federal Republic's Orientation to the West," in *The New Conservatism: Cultural Criticism and the Historians' Debate*, ed. and trans. Shierry Weber Nicholsen, (Cambridge, MA: MIT Press, 1989), 249–267; Jürgen Habermas, "Citizenship and National Identity," in *Between Facts and Norms: Contributions to a Discourse Theory of Law and Democracy*, trans. William Rehg (Cambridge, MA: MIT Press, 1996), 491–515.

46. Jürgen Habermas, "Popular Sovereignty as Procedure," in *Between Facts and Norms: Contributions to a Discourse Theory of Law and Democracy*, trans. William Rehg (Cambridge, MA: MIT Press, 1996), 463–490.

47. Jürgen Habermas, "Struggles for Recognition in the Democratic Constitutional State," trans. Shierry Weber Nicholsen, in *Multiculturalism: Examining the Politics of Recognition*, by Charles Taylor, with K. Anthony Appiah, Jürgen Habermas, Steven C. Rockefeller, Michael Walzer, and Susan Wolf, ed. Amy Gutmann (Princeton, NJ: Princeton University Press, 1994), 107–148.

patriarchy. Rebellious subjectivity and existential individualism, combined in the practice of the Great Refusal, thus offer legitimate vehicles in which problematized cultures undergo critical evaluation. When received traditions become reflexively decentered, new forms of autonomous publics are then likely to emerge through existential refusals and revolt. For Habermas, the key significance of the 1968 student revolt in Germany is that it brought out in the open the loss of national innocence with a new intensity. In comparison, constitutional reforms after 1945 barely scratch the surface of entrenched fascist culture.[48] The generation of 1968 shook up its parents by critically evaluating the core of German identity. To be sure, this is as much true of the antiwar protests in the United States and of "Prague Spring" in relation to the Cold War era after 1948. I propose that the student revolts of 1968 mark historically that existential dimension of social analysis, which immigrates later into Habermas's critical democratic and constitutional theory. The need for this latter critical democratic theory, Habermas's major lifetime contribution, emerges historically from his own adolescent experience during the post-1945 years. Nonetheless, his mature intimation of a plausible complementarity between existential and communicative categories integrates the vital needs of two postwar generations: 1945 and 1968.

If one radically democratized the postmetaphysical promise of existential freedom, then all elitist figures of identity formation, decisionist ethics and morality, and an exception-seeking political authoritarian could be criticized or rendered normatively invalid. A democratic equivalent of existential self-choice is a community of choice.[49] An intersubjectivist moral point of view replaces the morality of private conviction or decision by asking me to commensurate my radical freedom with that of all affected by my deliberations and choices.

By engaging one another in public deliberations, radically self-choosing existential individuals become socially integrated. With a democratically oriented freedom and self-choice, existential issues—*How shall I be a self that I am always already through individualization via socialization?*—become a matter for public conversation. This existential question turns on the Hegelian ethical problem of received identities and the Kantian search for the moral point of view: Which tradition are we to embrace and which to jettison? Which are life-giving and which disastrous?

Habermas's sociopolitical version of the either-or self-choice, influenced by his intense intellectual engagement with Marcuse's works, thus

48. Habermas, *Die nachholende Revolution*, 22–24, 26, 28; Habermas, *Autonomy and Solidarity*, 231, 234, 236.

49. For more on the concept of "a community of choice," see Marilyn Friedman, "Feminism and Modern Friendship: Dislocating the Community," *Ethics* 99 (January 1989): 275–290.

retains its radical existential character but within the Hegelian struggle for recognition and the Kantian moral discourse: in both, the existential self-choice is projected into a communicatively structured deliberative democracy.

Habermas projects both noncalculative, communicative reason and radically democratized existential individuals into public spheres of complex modern societies, which procures a sorely needed existential-communicative dialectics. Marcuse's concepts of radical subjectivity, new sensibility, and the Great Refusal immigrate into Habermas's ethical, moral, and democratic deliberations about our inherited traditions—about the canons of truth, history, beauty, gender, race, and general culture—and make the antipatriarchal, antiracist, and anticolonial potential of Habermas's communicative theory sufficiently concrete and critical.

Envisioning Existential-Communicative Variants of Critical Theory

A Marcusean variant of Critical Theory deploys "existential" categories from the vantage point of social movements rooted in dissensus. Existence or existential claims need not be and should not be conceived of as communitarian value claims or moral validity claims. Rather, one's total claim to existing affects how one can embody traditions (communitarian domains) and deliberative procedures (liberal domains) alike. Existence is that concrete category in virtue of which claims to good or evil and those to procedural right can be raised and communicated in the first place. In communicating existence, one expresses that in virtue of which one asks, how am I (are we) to be who I (we) always already become in the process of individualization through socialization? This way of posing the question begins with a linguistic turn (i.e., that none of us is born with a private self-relation, private language, or private norms). Existential questions address both the received goods and the formal procedures, without thereby implying monologism (private language) or decisionism (conflating value decisions with existing). Existence raises neither liberal nor communitarian claims; it affects how one embodies communicative competencies, whether as an individual or a member of a group.

While validity claims can be communicated directly, existence cannot. Trying to do the latter would violate communicative ethics as existentially understood. An existential-communicative dialectic comprises direct and indirect modes of communicative action. A dissident life in the totalitarian state; a Marcusean Great Refusal, new sensibility and rebellious subjectivity in one-dimensional democracies; or a Sartrean philosophy of freedom: these very possibilities hinge on an existential or indirect style of communication. If there were nothing in one's existing in virtue of which one could take a distance from (become incommensurable with) received traditions or skewed procedural debates, then the worrisome prospects of a totally administered society would be more real than fictitious. Philosophies of existence can harness a Marcusean two-dimensionality (i.e., a competence for incommensurability with or critique of the received points of view). That one's "existential" competence must be won performatively and communicatively—even though not by a direct validation—saves it from drawing on precritical anthropologies or ontologies of existence.

Moreover, by integrating the possibility of existential dissensus into communications theory, one need not follow the line of acommunicative transgressive thought. Elitist, authoritarian, or exceptional transgressions put aside, there is a legitimate place for democratic dissent, communities in resistance, and the struggles of the wretched of the earth. One may have critical—historical and material—reasons for not conforming to the nation-state, for dodging the military draft, for refusing the authority of an abusive police force, for trespassing borders of the rich out of hunger and immiseration, or for revolutionary activity against colonial powers that be. This is a far cry from the German political existentialists of the 1930s who confused responsibility for existing with the choice of a *Führer*.

A radically democratic existential variant of Critical Theory opens up upon leaving "European" debates on existentialism and social theory behind—particularly when putting aside the Heideggerian *Existenzphilosophie*, which, as the young Marcuse discovered in 1932, abstracts from concrete existing. There is a different crisis of humanism than the one chiseled out of the fascist political aesthetics for a new White Man. The late Marcuse and Sartre anticipate another path for an existential critical theory: they demand that the middle-class European existential revolts join with the wretched of the earth. From within their marginal existence, the wretched of the earth can place little hope in Europe's second chance.

This is prima facie verifiable by those who communicate their struggles for existing from the margins. Their existence matters for sustaining communicative competencies concretely and critically, and this situation traces a rather different genealogy toward a critical theory of existence than the received debate on existentialism and social theory offers. One may even speak today of a marked renaissance in existential thought—in critical race and gender theory. Fanon's work in key regards stands as a midpoint between social analyses of the 1960s in the West (works by Marcuse and Sartre) and in eastern European dissent (from Karel Kosík to the Yugoslav Praxis philosophers to the Czechoslovak Charter 77 and Václav Havel's "Power of the Powerless"). From Husserl's *The Crisis of European Sciences*, a path can be traced to a renewed Fanonian crisis of the European Man.[50] After the revolutionary events of 1989, this was minimally a triple crisis of patriarchy, racism, and colonialism—of the New World Order. A second chance for an existential variant of Critical Theory cannot be found in "European Man."[51]

I claim, first, that existence matters to forming concrete and critical communicative competencies. Second, from the positionalities of marginal existence, only antipatriarchal, antiracist, and anticolonial attitudes can be sufficiently critical—that is, communicatively competent in ways that existential variants of Critical Theory regulatively demand. Third, only that critical theory which also articulates the communicative competencies in terms of antipatriarchal, antiracist, and anticolonial attitudes in practical discourse is sufficiently concrete and critical. The Great Refusal with a democratic intent presupposes such attitudes. But it is only an existential critique of motivated deception—of racist, patriarchal, and colonial bad faith—that likewise shows how to embody undeceptive communication in concretion.

---

50. Edmund Husserl, *The Crisis of European Sciences and Transcendental Phenomenology*, trans. David Carr (Evanston, IL: Northwestern University Press, 1970). Husserl's "Crisis" lectures were given in 1935 in Prague at the invitation of Jan Patočka after Husserl, as a Jew, was forced to leave Freiburg. Lewis Gordon's lecture in Prague (1994) links Husserl's *Crisis* to Fanon and a crisis of Europe today; see Gordon, *Fanon and the Crisis of European Man*, 2, 7–8, 17, 46, 52, 62. See also Václav Havel, "The Power of the Powerless," trans. P. Wilson, in *Living in Truth: Twenty-Two Essays Published on the Occasion of the Award of the Erasmus Prize to Václav Havel*, ed. Jan Ladislav (London: Faber and Faber, 1986); and Karel Kosík, *Dialectics of the Concrete: A Study on Problems of Man and World*, trans. Karel Kovanda with James Schmidt (Boston: D. Reidel, 1970).

51. Jacques Derrida, *The Other Heading: Reflections on Today's Europe*, trans. Pascale-Anne Brault and Michael B. Naas (Bloomington: Indiana University Press, 1992), 21, 69. By the idea of "Europe," I mean its crisis in the senses articulated by Husserl, Fanon, Derrida, and Gordon. I am not saying that European persons have no second chance; to be sure, these come increasingly also from many continents.

19

A Critical Praxis from the Americas

Thinking about the Zapatistas in Chiapas
with Herbert Marcuse, Bolívar Echeverría,
and Adolfo Sánchez Vázquez

STEFAN GANDLER

The radical theorists Herbert Marcuse[1] and Bolívar Echeverría[2] have in common their challenge to orthodox Marxism and their working through and beyond a Heideggerian Marxism to articulate a more open and generative Marxism that theorizes in close relation with existing social movements and that challenges capitalism and other forms of domination. They are both searching for a postcapitalist alternative, thinking that inside the existing reality is already the germ for this other, new society. In contrast with a brand of dogmatic Marxism, Marcuse and Echeverría are convinced that this liberation from the capitalist form of reproduction would be a social and civilizational rupture, not merely an economical one. Though Marcuse and Echeverría understand such a break as a concrete negation of

I express my appreciation to Andrew Lamas for his collaboration and editorial contributions to this chapter.

1. Herbert Marcuse (1898–1979) has been considered "the first 'Heideggerian Marxist.'" Alfred Schmidt, "Herrschaft des Subjekts: Über Heideggers Marx-Interpretation" [Dominion of the Subject: On Heidegger's Marx Interpretation], in *Martin Heidegger: Fragen an sein Werk; Ein Symposion* [Martin Heidegger: Questions to His Oeuvre; A Symposium], ed. Jürgen Busche (Stuttgart, Germany: P. Reclam, 1977), 59.

2. Bolívar Echeverría (1941–2010) began his serious intellectual development through readings and discussions in high school and college in Quito, Ecuador. In a reading circle, together with Ulises Estrella, Fernando Tinajero Villamar, Iván Carvajal, Luis Corral, and occasionally Agustín Cueva Dávila, he discussed Miguel de Unamuno, Albert Camus, and Jean-Paul Sartre. "When we began to read Heidegger we saw that, yes, Heidegger's thought was much more radical than that of Sartre. We liked Sartre for his connection to concrete politics, with concrete history, and Heidegger because he was a great philosopher." Bolívar Echeverría, interview by the author, Mexico City, Mexico, July 10, 1996.

the existing ways of producing, consuming, communicating, and living together, they nonetheless believe that in certain—even presently existing—
forms of sociality and humanity are to be found material that could, should,
and would be the basis for a postcapitalist society. Marcuse finds such evidence, for example, in new understandings and practices of "femininity" and
"humanity" inspired by the radical feminist and antiracist movements of the
1960s and 1970s; meanwhile, Echeverría finds support in ways of living together, which still exist—for example, in some places of Latin America—and
which he called in a short period of his writing "natural nations."[3]

In both cases, the danger of falling into a certain ontologizing Heidegger-
ianism, which looks for a Being untouched by the destructive forces of capitalism, is overcome. Marcuse—cutting off his personal relationship with Martin
Heidegger because of his Nazi past and his unwillingness to make a clear rupture with it—reads Marx, Hegel, and György Lukács in a way that enables him
to discard Heidegger's ahistorical and antidialectical way of understanding
human society and history. The nonontological concepts of femininity and
humanity that are developed by radicals in the feminist and antiracist movements of his time further contribute to Marcuse's critical theory.

Echeverría, too, distanced himself from the temptation to search for *authentic* precapitalist forms of living together, and his resistance was fed by
two sources. The first source is his long-standing, critical engagement with
Marx and Marxist theory, which began in earnest in Lukács- and Marcuse-
inspired semiclandestine lecture circles in West Berlin in the early 1960s
(alongside Rudi Dutschke, Bernd Rabehl, Horst Kurnitzky, and others).
Echeverría explains:

> Regarding what you ask me about the importance of my time in Ber-
> lin . . . it is the following: I began in Berlin to roll out—you could

---

3. Echeverría speaks elsewhere of "a subjective-objective being, provided with a particular historic-cultural identity . . . , the historico-concrete existence of the productive and con-
sumptive forces, that is, . . . the substance of the nation." Bolívar Echeverría, "El problema de
la nación desde la 'Crítica de la economía política'" [The problem of the nation viewed from
the "Critique of political economy"], in *El discurso crítico de Marx* [Marx's critical discourse]
(Mexico City: Era, 1986), 192. With this line of thought, Echeverría could be speaking of
the subsystems of a society in which, in each case, codes predominate that are more or less
unified; however, since this concept of the "substance of the nation" (transformed elsewhere
into that of the "natural nation") is problematic to us, we do not want to use it here without a
critical introduction. Here a problem emerges that is generally present in Echeverría's theory.
On the one hand, it is suitable for indicating the internal differences within a society and
within the social system today, which is organized on a global level, and to make these the
objects of investigation; however, it could appear to move in the direction of a return to highly
dubious conceptualizations, like that of the "substance of the nation," which falls short of a
critical theory of society. The "nation" is a product of history, of the bourgeois period, and
corresponds to it. So, then, Echeverría's theory is arguably problematic to us if and when the
"natural nation" suggests an ahistorical essentialism.

say—all of my functions: vital, intellectual, corporeal. So there I connected a lot with Rudi Dutschke, but in a kind of dialogue between the Third World and the European center or something of the sort. So we, some Latin American *compañeros* and I, started the Association of Latin American Students in Germany, the AELA. I was at one time president of the AELA. We had meetings where we read literature, like, for example, Frantz Fanon's *The Wretched of the Earth* or works by Marcuse presented by Rudi Dutschke or Bernd Rabehl, who was also in the group. So it was a sort of internal seminar.[4]

The second source is a constellation of theoretical and activist spaces in Mexico (that generated political and intellectual positions critical of capitalism), such as the Mexican journal *Cuadernos Políticos* and certain social movements in Latin America, especially the Zapatistas from the Ejército Zapatista de Liberación Nacional (Zapatista Army of National Liberation—EZLN), who helped him avoid falling into an ontologizing theoretical position. Discussions among the members of the editorial board of *Cuadernos Políticos*—to which many of the most significant of Mexico's leftist authors (including exiled Latin American authors living at the time in Mexico) belonged—were, for Echeverría over the years, the only place for the continuous analysis of "more political, social, and economic approaches" without which, he says, he "would be lost in . . . objects of pure theory."[5] On this matter, here is an excerpt of my 1996 interview with Echeverría.

> GANDLER: Was this participation important for your own political-theoretical development?
>
> ECHEVERRÍA: In *Cuadernos Políticos*, yes, because it was the only place that I had a connection to more political discussions and all that. For me it was very important, because if not for that, I would be lost in my purely theoretical things. But there [it was] good: I discussed and read all sorts of articles, because we read all the articles; we discussed article by article. It was a very serious journal. The articles were distributed to everyone, and we had a session discussing every article. This was very good. So I read all kinds of things there. It was very important for me, because it kept me tied a bit to more political, social, and economic themes. . . .
>
> GANDLER: So this allowed you to avoid falling into the same situation as Heidegger? [This question alludes to a previous passage in the interview, in which Echeverría explains Heidegger's participation

---

4. Bolívar Echeverría, interview by the author, San Ángel, Mexico, April 26, 1994.
5. Echeverría, interview by the author, July 10, 1996.

in National Socialism with, among other reasons, the fact that
Heidegger left aside the real world in his studies and analysis.]
ECHEVERRÍA: The antidote. [*Laughs.*]
GANDLER: And what do you do these days?
ECHEVERRÍA: [*Laughs.*] Now we have the Zapatistas; now we have the
Subcomandante [Marcos's] communiqués.[6]

On January 1, 1994, the day that the North American Free Trade Agreement (NAFTA)—the momentous, neoliberal trade agreement between
Canada, the United States, and Mexico—entered into force, an armed indigenous rebellion broke out in Mexico's southernmost state of Chiapas—in
the Lacandon Jungle and the Los Altos region. The EZLN, which became
known throughout Mexico and then the world through its praxis and its
declarations,[7] broke down the wall of silence and forgetting[8] that had been
built around indigenous peoples and their (generally extreme) poverty.[9] In
early July 1996, in San Cristóbal de las Casas, Chiapas, the Ecuadorian Mexican philosopher Echeverría participated (as an advisor to the EZLN) in the
Foro Especial sobre la Reforma del Estado (Special Forum on State Reform)

---

6. Ibid.

7. See, for example, Subcomandante Marcos, "War! First Declaration of the Lacandón
Jungle," in *Our Word Is Our Weapon: Selected Writings*, ed. Juana Ponce De Leon (New York:
Seven Stories, 2001), 13–16. Additional declarations have been issued by the EZLN since this
first declaration (written in December 1993) was publicly issued in January 1994.

8. The (formerly) best-known member of the EZLN, Subcomandante Marcos, understands their war as a struggle against oblivion. "The government's position [is] that it wants
to eliminate the causes that made us an oppositional force so that we can become part of
the government. We say that this is a lie, because they aren't going to be able to solve the
causes or resolve the demands of the communities for health, land, work, housing, [and]
food because they don't have money, they are in a crisis and aren't willing to invest. They
only put money where they will get more, with the mentality of businessmen. The governors
cease to govern and set themselves to the administration of a business. Mexico ceases to be
a country and becomes a business with parts that are profitable and others that don't yield a
profit. The indigenous people are the ones who don't produce a profit. If you don't produce
a profit you're fired, but since they can't fire them from the country, they need to annihilate
them with bullets, with oblivion. They simply begin to make decisions as though they didn't
exist. This is the fundamental origin of the Zapatista uprising. It is a war against oblivion."
Subcomandante Marcos, quoted in Francoise Escarpit, "El gobierno, sin una línea clara de
negociación, asegura Marcos [The government, without a clear negotiation agenda, declares
Marcos], *La Jornada* [The Working Day] (Mexico City), December 27, 1995 (my translation).

9. For background information and details on the Zapatista rebellion, see Etienne Lar-
gend, "Was gibt die Bestie im Tausch für das, was sie nimmt? Zum Kräfteverhältnis zwischen
EZLN und dem mexikanischen Regime" [What Does the Beast Give in Exchange for What
It Is Taking? On the Relations of Forces between the EZLN and the Mexican Regime], *Die
Beute: Politik und Verbrechen* [The Booty: Politics and Crime] 6 (1995): 7–18; and Ejército
Zapatista de Liberación Nacional (México), *EZLN: Documentos y comunicados* [EZLN: Docu-
ments and communiqués], 5 vols. (Mexico City: Ediciones Era, 1994–2003).

called by the Zapatistas; he gave a presentation in the session titled "Transición a la democracia en México" (Transition to Democracy in Mexico).[10]

This forum was, with regard to domestic Mexican discussions with the Zapatistas, the most important event since the great leftist assembly called by the EZLN at the first "Aguascalientes"[11] constructed beside the village of Guadalupe Tepeyac, in Chiapas, in the summer of 1994. Formally, Echeverría was an integral part of the EZLN's negotiations with the Mexican government, and the outcome of the final resolutions was sent to the Mexican Congress for debate. The Mexican government maintained (with the support not only of its own partisans) that the "democratization" of the state was intimately related to the "modernization" of the country. This official stance has been confusing and requires critical scrutiny. It certainly suggests modernization in the technical-industrial sense; however, in reality, this has not been the case, since the neoliberal (or laissez-faire) policies applied since the 1980s have resulted in a tendency toward the deindustrialization of the country. "Modernization," praised by many, has in reality meant, above all, the unshakable validity of capitalist mechanisms, which up to this point had still coexisted with regulative state intervention, practiced in part according to the model of actually existing socialism. "Modernization," as practiced by the Mexican state, has meant, among other things, the shrinking of the state in certain respects. We can see as part of this actually existing "modernization" the de facto suspension of Article 27 of the Mexican Constitution, which originated during the revolution and prohibits the sale of large portions of arable agricultural lands (especially that of the *ejidos*, which are communally cultivated). Large sectors of the population and even many of those critical of the government understood the promise of "modernization" as a means of putting an end to state corruption and curbing the old power elites—with hopes that if Mexico "looked like" the First World, "modern political culture" would make its appearance in Mexico, thereby resolving old problems. It is in the context of these prevalent debates, one on democracy

---

10. The basis of this speech is Echeverría's essay, "Postmodernidad y cinismo" [Postmodernity and cynicism] (or, alternatively, "Postmodernismo y cinismo" [Postmodernism and cynicism]). Bolívar Echeverría, interview by the author, Mexico City, June 9, 1996. See also Bolívar Echeverría, "Postmodernidad y cinismo," *Viento del sur* 1 (1994): 55–61. The same essay appears under the title "Postmodernidad y cinismo" in Bolívar Echeverría, *Las ilusiones de la modernidad* [The illusion of modernity] (Mexico City: UNAM/El Equilibrista, 1995), 39–54.

11. "Aguascalientes" is what the Zapatistas call the meeting places they have established on various occasions in the Lacandon Jungle, where thousands of people with meager means are housed. The name refers to the capital of the Mexican state of Aguascalientes, where the "Aguascalientes Convention" was held during the Mexican Revolution; it was there that foundations were laid for a new, postrevolutionary constitution, with the participation of the two most radical Mexican revolutionaries, Emiliano Zapata and Pancho Villa.

and the other on modernization, that Echeverría's theoretical position can be located.

The concept of revolution, similarly subjected to general critical analysis by Echeverría in his theory, is, in the majority of political contexts in Mexico, much more frequently used than is the case in Germany. Something similar occurs with the concept of the nation, which is also on everyone's tongue and often refers to national independence vis-à-vis the United States. In general, the need for "national unity" is thus elevated, so goes the argument, in order to stand strong against attempts at foreign intervention. Internal differences—for example, those of a linguistic nature—are seen by practically all political currents as a danger to "national unity," and, as a result, the more than fifty existing languages in Mexico aside from Spanish are understood as an unavoidable evil. And this situation was not transformed much either by the EZLN's armed rebellion or the countless rounds of conversation, assemblies, and so on with the (mostly urban) Spanish-speaking Left, who lack interest in the problems created by ignoring the de facto existence of a multilingual Mexico. Up to the present, most Mexicans act as though this were a problem that will be resolved by the purported gradual disappearance of the other languages.

Echeverría's theory is one of the few to emerge in Mexico that—without redefining the question as though it were ethnological—enters into these contradictions. Echeverría advocates, then, a concept of history that does not crush the powerful dynamic proper to tradition and which, as a result, is conscious of the importance of the sturdiness of those forms of everyday praxis that similarly are not *automatically* modified by the transformation of the political, social, and economic constitution.

> This is the reason for the critique of the myth of revolution—the myth of revolution, which is the myth of this omnipotence of the human being: "The human being is able to change whatever, whenever he wants." So, for example, with regard to his own traditions, his own cultural forms, the modern human being believes that these have no density and that he can make and unmake [with ease] the social substance, the historical-social substance.[12]

But this should not be understood in the sense of throwing overboard the idea of a fundamental transformation of social relations; rather, Echeverría means quite the opposite. He is interested in saving the *concept* of revolution through a radical critique of the *myth* of revolution—in other words, a totally wrongheaded understanding of revolution that simultaneously glorifies

---

12. Echeverría, interview by the author, July 10, 1996. When Echeverría speaks of the "myth" of revolution, as a general rule, he is *not* referring to Marx's theories.

it.[13] Giving concrete character to the concept of praxis requires that we pass through a demonstration of the difficulties of a possible revolutionary transformation while at the same time revealing its true possibilities, which up to this point have been hidden. In the current sociopolitical context of Mexico, apparent submission to the government turns out to be against a background of rebellion,[14] which is expressed as follows in Echeverría's 1996 interview with me:

GANDLER: Is this a critique of a concept of praxis, which is emptied of its historical content?

ECHEVERRÍA: Yes, exactly.

GANDLER: So we could say, simplifying, that while [Adolfo] Sánchez Vázquez is constantly looking forward, you want to look back as well?

ECHEVERRÍA: Yes, yes, or he only looks upward and in general terms, and I, on the other hand, tend to look downward at the whole swamp [*laughs*] that we're trying to swim through.

GANDLER: Could we say then that . . . , on the theoretical level, you are a pre-1994 Zapatista?

ECHEVERRÍA: Yes, this is why I like very much what the Zapatistas say, because they realize that the question is not purely one of the political game—that is to say, "Let's replace the politicians, and with that we have already decided that history goes that way."

---

13. This banality of sticking the concept of revolution in the same sack as the myth of revolution is something that certain leftist circles—and above all, the dogmatic ones—share with conservative circles. Echeverría criticizes this elsewhere on the basis of certain political statements by the deceased organic intellectual of recent Mexican governments, Octavio Paz. Alongside these two positions, which equate the myth with the concept of revolution in order to no longer need to hear anything more of the latter, there can still exist those other positions—as residues—that Echeverría himself in certain moments upheld; they are present in groups that occasionally place extreme trust in their fantastic imaginations in order to not become discouraged too early on and thus to bring the concept of revolution closer to realization. Despite similarities to the former position in terms of the equation of the concept of revolution with the myth, we should not forget that this latter orientation is diametrically opposed to the former. Echeverría himself, in the 1996 interview with me, agreed that a certain degree of self-stimulation via fantastic and exaggerated elements is necessary in order to bear the load of a revolutionary action. Echeverría, interview by the author, July 10, 1996.

14. Already during the Mexican Revolution, which began in 1910, a peculiar contradiction was present in the country: even in everyday life, it was only an invisible line that separated a calm bordering on apathy from violent forms of expression, with intermediate forms less present than in, for example, in Frankfurt in the 1980s. Under the dictatorship of Porfirio Díaz, Mexico was considered to be one of the most stable countries on Earth, when the Revolution suddenly exploded. In a similar way, almost no one foresaw the Zapatista rebellion that began on January 1, 1994; moreover, it was launched in a region in which the governing PRI (Institutional Revolutionary Party) always registered certain electoral victory.

They say, "No, it's not that easy; the problems are much older, much heavier. How are we going to change all of this . . . just because we simply take Los Pinos [the seat of the presidency] or the Government Palace and decide that beginning tomorrow, Mexico is no longer this but that?" Like they say, "No, no, that's not how it is. That isn't possible. There is a knot of historical conflicts here that needs to be awakened first, so that it itself can begin to generate its own solutions," and not, "We came from the mountains of Chiapas, and we say that this is the solution."

They are revolutionaries who are relativizing very much their own power, to such a degree that the only thing that they say is "We don't even struggle to survive because they are killing us. That is a fact; we are dying, and all we are doing is dying in a way that seems more elegant to us," they say, don't they? In reality, the Zapatistas' most profound message is this. It is a very terrible message, because it isn't optimistic; it isn't luminous like the October Revolution: the upward gaze and the horizon of the rising sun and such things, no. Instead it's a terrible view, because they say, "We are corpses. They are killing us. Our people are dying. While I am here speaking, my people are dying, and I myself am dying as well."

So "our movement exists only to affirm" what they call "our dignity, to die with dignity." . . . We don't care about [Porfirio] Muñoz Ledo or [Manuel] Camacho. If they get rid of Salinas and replace him with someone else, it is not worth a bean. It is a murderous machinery that is killing us—and a bit in the way of thinking of [Max] Horkheimer and [Theodor W.] Adorno [*laughs*], "It would be good if things were different. Hopefully it wouldn't be like this."

Here we do indeed find . . . these rare connections between the apparently elitist discourse of Horkheimer and Adorno and that of the Indians of Chiapas. Because what they say is a little like this. You aren't going to find historical optimism, but to the contrary, they see a machine and say, "If only it weren't like this."[15]

---

15. Echeverría, interview by the author, July 10, 1996. Note that shortly before the interview, Echeverría participated as an advisor to the Zapatistas in the Special Forum on State Reform that the rebels organized and that included various discussion tables, each presided over by a Zapatista representative. The cited phrases were obviously stated by Echeverría as he recalled what the rebel representatives from the Mexican southeast had said. Also note that in this interview excerpt, Echeverría remarks briefly on the Spanish-born Mexican philosopher, Adolfo Sánchez Vázquez (1915–2011), who arrived in Mexico in 1939 in the wake of the defeat of the Republic in the Spanish Civil War. Sánchez Vázquez developed a nondogmatic

These commentaries from Echeverría about the Zapatistas are strongly related to his way of understanding the contemporary, multiple, existing forms of capitalist modernity—the four modern ethe (of the contemporary historical ethos) that Echeverría describes as the *realist ethos*, the *romantic ethos*, the *classic ethos*, and the *baroque ethos*.[16] While Marcuse investigates forms of domination and subordination and theorizes the Great Refusal as a political and elemental refusal of repression and injustice, Echeverría—who joins with Marcuse in a nondogmatic Marxist project of anticapitalism— would understand Marcuse's Great Refusal as linked to rebellion against the dominating realist ethos (the ethos that Echeverría understands as dominant in the First World's capitalist modernity). Echeverría focuses less on Europe and the United States and places greater focus on the Americas, particularly Latin America, where he sees capitalist modernity's dominating ethos as the baroque ethos; we see, then, that Marcuse and Echeverría understand their respective projects in different yet compatible and somewhat overlapping ways. Echeverría seeks to lay the foundations for a materialist theory of culture.[17] If in Latin America the baroque ethos prevails with its "paradoxical combination of sobriety and rebellion,"[18] the freedom struggle in Latin America is formulated on a different terrain. For Echeverría, one must ask what forms of subordination and what forms of rebellion are typical for each historical ethos? Echeverría's theory tries to understand the specific and apparently absurd combination of *conservatism and rebellion* in one moment, one person, one group, one movement—a combination that occurs *at the same time* as well as *in the same perspective*. It is this strange combination that is central to his description of the baroque ethos, and, very interestingly, it is something that can be found in the praxis (and, in some ways, also in the texts) of the Zapatistas. Some of them wear clothing that might seem to

---

Marxism that is consistent with tendencies in Marcuse's Critical Theory. For additional historical context regarding Echeverría's 1996 interview, see Stefan Gandler, "Life and Work of Bolívar Echeverría," *Critical Marxism in Mexico: Adolfo Sánchez Vázquez and Bolívar Echeverría* (Leiden, Netherlands: Brill, 2015), 42–83. Porfirio Muñoz Ledo was the leader of the Left-reformist PRD (Party of the Democratic Revolution), the only party in Mexico with parliamentary relevance that was not situated to the right of the governing PRI (Institutional Revolutionary Party). Manuel Camacho Solís was the representative of the Mexican federal government during the first peace negotiations with the Zapatistas and, in that period (1994), was a close confidant of the then president, Carlos Salinas de Gortari. In 1996, Camacho Solís abandoned the PRI and stood with the PCD (Party of the Democratic Center) and then with the PRD on the reformist Left.

16. Bolívar Echeverría, "El *ethos* barroco" [The baroque *ethos*], in *Modernidad, mestizaje cultural,* ethos *barroco* [Modernity, cultural mestizaje, baroque *ethos*], ed. Bolívar Echeverría (Mexico City: UNAM, 1994), 19. For a description and analysis of Echeverría's concepts and his theory of capitalist modernity, see Gandler, *Critical Marxism in Mexico,* 295–310.

17. Gandler, *Critical Marxism in Mexico,* 281.

18. Ibid., 300.

be from the distant past, many speak languages that have been assumed to be dead or disappearing, and they use ways of undertaking collective decision making that they claim have been in continuous use for hundreds and hundreds of years; yet, at the same time, they have excited many worldwide by the sophisticated use of digital media to broadcast their declarations, and they are one of the few leftist groups in the world that openly uses arms to advance their territorial demands and their openly anticapitalist political agenda.

Fascination with this strange combination is likely one of the reasons why the Zapatistas are so excitedly discussed in leftist and antiracist circles across the Americas and the whole world. The tension captures—in a way similar to the theoretical proclamation of the Great Refusal by Marcuse—a liberatory defiance that seems impossible and wholly necessary. At the same time, the Zapatistas' way of making politics, of theorizing, of organizing themselves—in different circumstances than those facing revolutionaries in Marcuse's time and place—may be understood, with Echeverría's theory of multiple modern ethe, not as expressions of a "more or less developed" modernity but as expressions of *different* but parallel developments of capitalist modernities as well as ways of fighting against capitalism and its destructive logics.

Alongside Echeverría's contributions, Marcuse's concept of the Great Refusal can and should be applied—with great usefulness—to the analysis of contemporary uprisings in Mexico and across Latin America, but, moreover, these conceptual resources enable us to see our way to politics. That is the point of critical praxis. These rebellions become understandable, and we see how—on a political level—it could be necessary and possible to be in solidarity with such rebellions, without presumption and condescension, without falling into the typical First World mind-set that wrongly misunderstands all *other* movements as underdeveloped. Starting from this new theoretical point of departure, what might be called *a critical praxis from the Americas*, a new way of international solidarity, could be founded; that is to say, a new way of organizing the anticapitalist struggle on a worldwide scale that proceeds without overprivileging the United States (including its particular forms of popular struggle) as an analytical category and without glorifying Subcomandante Marcos and the Zapatistas, as both moves, at the end of the day, represent obscuring forms of Eurocentric analysis.

Such reflections lead to a consideration of a theoretical problem that arises when analyzing the Zapatistas from a traditional leftist viewpoint: Are the Zapatistas' politics reformist or revolutionary? Echeverría can be helpful here, as he—and not only in his concept of baroque ethos—tries to unfold a social theory beyond this duality of reform and revolution.

It is true that there is no continuity between the revolutionary resort and the reformist solution. As Rosa Luxemburg liked to say, revolution is not an accelerated accumulation of reforms, and reform is not a revolution in small doses. . . . However, while these are totally different from one another—and even hostilely counterposed— revolutionary and reformist perspectives are mutually necessary within the political horizon of the Left.[19]

In the essay "Postmodernidad y cinismo" (Postmodernity and Cynicism), Echeverría thinks about where the "reformist search" meets the "revolutionary search" by reflecting on the condition of alienation.

If a political theory that starts from the concept of "reification" accepts that there exists the possibility of a politics *within* alienation, that society—while deprived of the possibilities of its sovereignty— is neither politically demobilized nor paralyzed nor condemned to await the messianic moment in which its political liberty will be returned to it. The problem that is posed consists in establishing points of contact at which the reformist search for an appropriate democratic game for the conversion of civil interests into the citizens' will comes into contact with the revolutionary search for a substantial broadening of the scale according to which society is capable of making decisions with regard to its own history.[20]

Such affirmations could appear reformist, but in the current Mexican context they are quite the contrary and have been confirmed as such—at least for now—by the Zapatista rebellion, which is not suffering the full military violence of the Mexican federal army, in part because of the fact that reformist forces protest and act against the institutions of the Mexican state with their own specific (reformist) methods.[21] This is one more reason why the philosophical reflections from Echeverría, inspired by Hegel, Marx, and

---

19. Echeverría, *Las ilusiones de la modernidad*, 36 (my translation).

20. Ibid., 94 (emphasis in original).

21. As a practical tool for more easily discovering the "points of contact" between reformist and revolutionary politics, Echeverría proposes the capacity for self-irony and a more critical attitude toward the "spirit of seriousness" (meaning the lack of a sense of humor), since the latter leads to dogmatism and censorship. "There is something that could be learned from the *brother enemies* of the Left: there is little that is healthier than dumping a bit of *irony* on one's own certainty. The same spirit of seriousness that leads to absolutizing and dogmatizing, whether for revolutionary or reformist truths, leads also to the need for censorship, discrimination, and the oppression of the one by the other." Echeverría, *Las ilusiones de la modernidad*, 37 (my translation).

the Critical Theory tradition, can be very helpful for understanding the rebellion of the EZLN. The Zapatista rebellion must be understood without
reducing it to its moral impulse and, at the same time, without reducing it to
its revolutionary aspects—meaning its radical nature should not be obscured
by critiquing it for not being in every moment and in every situation "fully
revolutionary."

Finally, no such discussion of Echeverría and Marcuse would be complete without a consideration of the important philosopher Adolfo Sánchez
Vázquez, particularly given his theoretical and political relationship with the
Zapatistas. Sánchez Vázquez was invited as an advisor to the Special Forum
on State Reform, held in July 1996 by the EZLN, and he participated by sending a contribution discussing the question of human rights in Mexico, as a
way of considering the Zapatista rebellion and its causes.[22] Sánchez Vázquez,
as a veteran of the Spanish Civil War and an antidogmatic Marxist, does not
stand at a distance from the Zapatistas, but probably he would nevertheless
need to make certain theoretical leaps in order to conceptually approach the
Zapatista praxis and doctrine. At first glance, the combination of radical and
reformist leftist elements with apparently "premodern" ideas and traditions
is highly unusual—and not only, perhaps, to Sánchez Vázquez. However,
using Echeverría's theoretical conception of the baroque ethos, this strange
combination is made more understandable, since Echeverría makes an effort
to follow the tracks of the survival of ancient traditions and those conflicts
that are aggravated under the capitalist modernity that is presently dominant in Latin America. Hence, Sánchez Vázquez, in the document prepared
for the Special Forum on State Reform, does, of course, enter into questions
of democracy and human rights (which are of extreme importance for the
Zapatistas), but he stops short of engaging in the arguably necessary analysis
of *different* forms of democracy (for example, the parliamentary form on one
hand, and, on the other hand, the communal form that is practiced in many
parts of Chiapas under Zapatista control) and of *different* understandings
of what human dignity is or ought to be. Here, Sánchez Vázquez remains
framed, in some ways, within the classic Western ideals inherited from the
French Revolution.

Playing a role in Latin America since the 1980s similar to the role Marcuse played in the United States in the 1960s and 1970s, Sánchez Vázquez
was one of the first Marxists in Mexico who underlined the necessity of
opening critical theory toward other rebellious subjects—beyond proletarian mass organizations. In so doing, Sánchez Vázquez prepared the theoretical scaffolding in Mexico and Latin America with which a movement such

22. Adolfo Sánchez Vázquez, interview by the author, Mexico City, August 1996 (less
than one month following the presentation of Sánchez Vázquez's document to the Special
Forum on State Reform).

as the Zapatistas from Chiapas could be understood—in Marxist and leftist circles—not only intellectually, but also politically.

The wide public recognition in Mexico of Sánchez Vázquez as an important intellectual bestowed a great significance—and not only in leftist circles—on his open defense of the moral impulse of the Zapatistas, particularly under the prevailing conditions in which important sections of Mexican intellectual circles and leftist political forces had long declared the revolutionary use of arms as something completely anachronistic. The impact of his defense was felt beyond the Left, and resistance followed. On October 25, 2007, Sánchez Vázquez's book *Ética y política*[23] was presented in a public event at the Librería del Fondo de Cultura Económica Octavio Paz (the bookstore of the major Mexican editorial house). One of the book reviewers, José Woldenberg, the former president of the Instituto Federal Electoral (Federal Institute for Elections), whom Sánchez Vázquez had invited, expressed on that occasion, "By the way, following the logic of professor Sánchez Vázquez himself, I just cannot understand his condescension with the EZLN."[24] Woldenberg continued, "Precisely because in our country the paths of public and peaceful politics are not . . . closed, [I consider as] absolutely unjustifiable . . . the option of armed struggle."[25]

By framing his critique in this way, Woldenberg reveals (likely without realizing it) what makes Sánchez Vázquez such a remarkable figure: the philosopher's radicality is expressed not only through his theories but through his politics—an expression that, in the public homages delivered by the philosopher's own followers, too often disappears from view. Let us recall just a few significant highlights: his membership in the Spanish Communist Party; his directorship, at the young age of twenty-one, of the newspaper *Ahora* of the Spanish Juventudes Socialistas Unificadas (Unified Socialist Youth) and its more than two hundred thousand members; and his military service, including his editorship of the journal *Acero* for Enrique Líster's Fifth Army Corps, during the Spanish Civil War in the fight against Francisco Franco's fascist dictatorship. For Sánchez Vázquez, the commitment to radical transformation toward a world without exploitation and repression was honored in the relationship between theory and practice in a philosophical and political life.

Even though Sánchez Vázquez never openly recognizes a direct relationship with Marcuse, in his turn to the concept of *praxis* (distancing him from

---

23. Adolfo Sánchez Vázquez, *Ética y política* [Ethics and politics] (Mexico City: Fondo de Cultura Económica, 2007).

24. José Woldenberg, "Ética y política" [Ethics and politics], *Nueva Época* [New Era], no. 46 (December 2007), available at http://www.revistadelauniversidad.unam.mx/4607/woldenberg/46woldenberg.html.

25. Ibid.

dogmatic Marxism),[26] to Marx's *Economic and Philosophical Manuscripts of 1844* (for which he did the first Spanish translation), and to the 1968 student movement (noting also the significance of his texts for the movement) it is clear, not only philosophically but also politically, that there exists an important proximity between the lives and work of Sánchez Vázquez and Marcuse. Both look for alternative ways of theorizing anticapitalist struggle beyond the dogmatic reduction to the struggle of proletarian mass organizations. Marcuse finds this new—not hierarchical—way of struggle in the Great Refusal. Sánchez Vázquez finds it in his critical concept of *praxis*, as the union—in every struggling individual—between critical, theoretical reflection and political and material activity. The political and philosophical presence of Sánchez Vázquez in Mexico—including his famous classes at the Universidad Nacional Autónoma de México, to which not only Che Guevara but also one who later became famous as Subcomandante Marcos contributed—has been, and still is, one of the elements that created the situation in which the Zapatistas could surge and, in some way, win.

---

26. See Adolfo Sánchez Vázquez, *Filosofía de la praxis* (Mexico City: Editorial Grijalbo, 1967). For the English-language version, see Adolfo Sánchez Vázquez, *The Philosophy of Praxis* (New York: Humanities, 1977).

20

Where Is the Outrage?

The State, Subjectivity, and
Our Collective Future

Stanley Aronowitz

The Collapse of the American Dream in the United States

We are in the midst of a multiyear depression, the deepest since the early 1930s. By official measures, economic growth has slowed to a near standstill; because of union weakness and a ferocious employer campaign, wages are declining, and so are living standards. Equally grim is the social wage: the panoply of state benefits such as jobless payments, Medicare, and Social Security are sagging because of budget cuts or, in the case of Social Security, an artificial cap on maximum taxable income. The attack on the social wage extends far and wide: cuts to school lunch programs and to school operating budgets that result in increased class sizes, the termination of income support for the chronically unemployed, layoffs of workers in the public sector (for years, until recently, together with health, the only real growth sector of the labor market), and slashed food-stamp and housing subsidies. And the recent right-wing offensive against women's health, particularly abortion rights, has had tragic consequences. The American dream of having a job and owning a house is fundamentally finished for many. With structural unemployment, high debt levels (in 2013, the size of student debt even exceeded credit card debt), mass incarceration (disproportionately of Blacks and Latinos), and four million households having recently suffered foreclosure, the bleak prospect is that this economic downturn will last much longer; one might speculate that it signifies chronic stagnation. As the U.S.

This chapter is a much revised and expanded version of Stanley Aronowitz, "Where's the Outrage?," *Situations: Project of the Radical Imagination* 5, no. 2 (2014): 19–48.

population grows, jobless levels will also likely grow or at least fail to shrink, even when the economy adds paid work.[1]

We are now in the fourth decade of unrelieved retreat for the working and living conditions of the great majority of those living in the United States. The unions, once the bulwark of the U.S. standard of living, are in free fall; the few instances in which they were moved to resistance yielded only a sprinkle of victories.[2] But the 1980s and 1990s were marked by a string of lost strikes over employer demands for wage, benefits, and work rules concessions. In many instances, union members and their leaders were willing to give ground without a fight. They believed that resistance would lead to either certain defeat or the disappearance of their jobs. These were decades when the hallowed labor slogan "solidarity" was either forgotten or brazenly violated by terrified workers and their unions. The desperate desire for security overwhelmed nearly all other considerations. It was also the era when "replacement" workers undermined strikes. Union members were advised by their leaders not to thwart replacements and certainly to maintain peaceful picket lines. The results were invariably disastrous. In sum, public- and private-sector workers have endured steady wage deterioration, onerous working conditions, and threats of plant or business removal or layoffs that have proven to be permanent, even if the company stays afloat.

Black people and Latinos have suffered the worst. Blacks had made significant gains in goods-producing industries during and after World War II. But 1970s and 1980s deindustrialization left millions destitute. Even when they found alternative employment, these "jobs" typically paid half or less the wages they earned in production industries, came with few or no benefits, and were absent protections against arbitrary firings, unilateral employer changes in work rules and work schedules, and decent safety conditions. It is true that federal government policies, especially the expansion of public-sector jobs, and especially in the post office and local and state administrations, created a layer of stable working and middle class in their communities. But as many as 80 percent experienced growing economic instability. Private employers sensed the weakness of the workers' organizations and boldly went on a permanent offensive, and public officials were not far behind. Today, the heavily Black cities like Detroit, Newark, Cleveland,

---

1. I will not dignify most of the growth of paid labor with the term *job*. A job is employment offered at a living wage substantially above the poverty line. It usually carries health, pension, and paid vacation benefits, and the worker expects to be recalled, if laid off temporarily; there is almost no instance of wage theft. Apart from major institutions in the health, social-media, and electronic computing sectors, most employment is now offered on the basis of temporary contracts.

2. The most notable victory was the 1997 United Parcel strike of 180,000 workers. The Teamsters union, led by a reform administration, fought for more full-time jobs and wage parity for part-timers and won most of its demands.

and Flint are destitute. Others like New York, Philadelphia, and Chicago are segregated both in terms of racial and ethnic composition and economic inequality. Gentrification has decimated traditional Black and Latino communities, and it is barely different in historically White working-class neighborhoods. New York's Harlem and Brooklyn's Bedford-Stuyvesant neighborhoods have become sites of White, young, middle-class settlement as rents have skyrocketed and brownstones are for sale at exorbitant prices. San Francisco, once a racially and ethnically diverse city, is now largely white-ified. These developments are symptoms of the changed economy, but they raise the question: *Where will the service workers live?*

Margaret Somers has argued that differential treatment of class and racial formations in our societies raises the stakes of what we mean by "citizenship."[3] One of her prime examples is the response to Hurricane Katrina by federal and state governments. The predominantly Black community of the Lower Ninth Ward of New Orleans has not been significantly restored, more than ten years after the disastrous destruction of entire neighborhoods in 2005. Somers's claim that the right to vote, however important, merely scratches the surface of genuine citizenship may be one of the most salient ideas in social and political theory. If the state ignores fundamental economic and social needs of its constituents, they are effectively excluded from participating in the decisions that affect their lives. In the storm's wake, tens of thousands of Black residents were forced to migrate elsewhere, principally to Texas, Oklahoma, and California, and many have no prospect of return. Poor, working-class residents are thus in a state of exception. Of course, the crumbling of the lifeblood of much of Detroit and similar industrially vacated cities and towns elevates this condition to a major national class and racial crisis. We are heirs to a time when elementary democratic participation, let alone genuine democracy, for a clear minority of the population has become normative and in time may no longer be the exception as growing legions of the younger generations confront their own economic and political disenfranchisement.[4] The bankruptcy filing by the city of Detroit on July 18, 2013, is merely a symptom of the extent of disenfranchisement.

---

3. Margaret R. Somers, *Genealogies of Citizenship: Markets, Statelessness, and the Right to Have Rights* (Cambridge: Cambridge University Press, 2008). This argument is elaborated in Fred L. Block and Margaret R. Somers, *The Power of Market Fundamentalism: Karl Polanyi's Critique* (Cambridge, MA: Harvard University Press, 2014), 211–213.

4. My comments on New Orleans do not rely on Somers's evaluation, although her formulation of the citizenship question is superb. I toured New Orleans block by block, in 2007 and again in 2013, and observed the dereliction of city, state, and federal governments. The levees have been rebuilt under the supervision of the U.S. Army Corps of Engineers, according to specifications that duplicate the inadequate standards of the previous barriers, even as independent engineering recommendations argued, among other things, for erecting higher walls between the water and the land.

Signs without Organization

The disenfranchised have not been completely silent. The public employees' uprising in early 2011 in Madison, Wisconsin, was the first shot in a season of discontent. When Governor Scott Walker and his Republican allies were poised to outlaw collective bargaining for public workers, thousands occupied the state capitol, and as many as one hundred thousand protesters took to the streets.[5] Madison-area labor unions threatened a general strike but retreated before the Democratic Party's proposal to recall four state senators and the governor. The recall failed to change the balance of legislative power, or to recall Walker, but the most telling result was that the direct-action movement was dispersed and the old progressives' electoral strategy reemerged. The nation's unions fell into line behind U.S. president Barack Obama's 2012 reelection campaign, donating $400 million to the Democrats—a gift that remains unrewarded. But neither labor nor progressives have been moved into the opposition. Most cling to the forlorn hope that somehow the center-right formation, which controls the Democratic Party, will rise to the occasion and lead us to the promised land. The union leaders grouse but can be counted on to stay the course because they cannot imagine going into the opposition.

Fall 2011 was even more inspiring. A few hundred, mostly youthful protesters occupied Zuccotti Park, a privately owned park near New York's Wall Street. Their sole demand was that the 1 percent of the population that had accumulated 45 percent of the country's wealth be held accountable, in various ways, for the relative deprivation of the remaining 99 percent. New York's municipal powers hesitated to drive them from the site, but when the Occupy Wall Street movement ventured to block Brooklyn Bridge, the police came out swinging and arrested more than seven hundred demonstrators. The arrests provoked elements of the local unions to mount a demonstration at a downtown courthouse, but, more significantly, the Occupy Wall Street movement caught fire. In hundreds of cities and towns in the United States and around the globe, activists of all ages established encampments in city parks, business districts, and city halls. Protesters occupied public space in a largely spontaneous demonstration of the will to resist. The progressives greeted direct action with sympathy but were determined, following Madison, to steer the protest into acceptable channels. The Occupy movement was inundated with liberal entreaties to craft a list of demands that could be presented to the local and federal governments and to the leading financial institutions. This strategy would have provided the liberal center, including

5. Steve Contorno, Dan Benson, and Ben Jones, "Police: Wisconsin Protest Saturday 'One of Largest,'" *USA Today*, February 27, 2011, available at http://usatoday30.usatoday.com/news/nation/2011-02-26-wisconsin-saturday-rally_N.htm.

the Obama administration, with leverage to negotiate a settlement, thwart further direct action, and enlist some of the organizers in the 2012 national electoral campaign. The organizers spurned these efforts, and their refusal was rewarded by a coordinated action by the administrations of eighteen cities, most of which were Democratic strongholds, to clear the spaces that had been occupied. The coordination was probably the work of the U.S. Department of Justice and succeeded by the use of police force.[6]

In April 2013, civil-rights activists in North Carolina spearheaded a project called Moral Mondays. They have demonstrated against the state legislature's frontal assault on voting rights and in opposition to its severe restrictions on abortion, the most onerous in the country. Hundreds have been arrested in acts of civil disobedience. The largest demonstration in the South since 1965 took place in the state's capital city of Raleigh, on February 8, 2014.[7] The revival of such direct action, however, is still defensive. Like the Madison uprising, the religious-led coalition that stages these protests seeks to preserve the status quo, but—like Madison and Occupy—the movement has no discernible strategy to form a permanent organization that is able to stay alive after the initial flow of activity is spent and to engage the flagrant attack against the Black poor on a number of fronts. Similarly, students occupied the governor's office in Florida against the cruel acquittal of George Zimmerman for his murder of Trayvon Martin on February 26, 2012. In protest against solitary confinement and other abusive policies, approximately thirty thousand California prisoners went on a hunger strike beginning on July 8, 2013, that lasted sixty days. Beginning on November 29, 2012, with a small strike by fast-food workers in New York City, fast-food workers in numerous cities, in a series of one-day strikes, demanded a minimum wage of fifteen dollars an hour, about double what the leading corporations offer their nonunion workers. In response to this pressure, some legislatures and city councils have voted for increases but typically with long implementation periods; for example, the "phase-in" means that Los Angeles workers will

---

6. A few years now after Occupy's demise, small Occupy units are still active. In some places, amid the ongoing economic crisis, Occupiers have assisted the evicted to reclaim their homes after foreclosure. In 2012, in the aftermath of Hurricane Sandy (one of the most devastating hurricanes in U.S. history), Occupy committees rendered exemplary service to the homeless and displaced residents of Staten Island and other lowland areas. Organizers promise a comeback and claim that the movement is not dead; however, what remains can hardly be called a movement.

7. "The North Carolina NAACP estimated that upward of 80,000 people attended; the police said they'd granted a permit for up to 30,000. Either way, it was the largest civil rights rally in the South since the legendary Selma-to-Montgomery march in support of the Voting Rights Act in 1965." Ari Berman, "What's Next for the Moral Monday Movement?" *The Nation*, February 19, 2014, available at http://www.thenation.com/article/whats-next-moral-monday-movement/. The state chapter of the National Association for the Advancement of Colored People (NAACP) provides leadership for Moral Mondays in North Carolina.

not have a fifteen-dollar minimum wage until July 2020. Meanwhile, income and wealth inequality increase without legislative limitation, and still these minimum-wage workers may have only employment—not a job (see note 1).

The rash of protests in recent years are *signs without organization*. The unions and the established civil-rights organizations that support many of these protests are still tied to the legacies of the New Deal and Great Society. They cannot (yet) conceive of calling into question the limitations of the liberal center that, in the main, has revealed itself to be a reliable ally of (or at least unwilling to challenge) finance capital, a fact that was made all too apparent during the depth of the 2008 financial meltdown when Obama, as much as his predecessor George W. Bush, lost no time in bailing out the banks, insurance companies, and troubled auto corporations by a massive transfer of working-class and middle-class tax money. We have heard almost no dissent against Medicare cuts, Obama's willingness to entertain proposals to reduce Social Security, and counterproductive efforts to address escalating student debt.

We are at a moment when unease characterizes the response of large sections of the people, but there is little evidence that, with few exceptions, there is sustained, multifaceted organized opposition to the prevailing austerity. The intellectuals are mostly bystanders, and the activists have returned to largely uncoordinated local protests. In fact, the most impressive movement of this period, Occupy Wall Street, explicitly rejected forming a national organization, developing a set of priorities to give flesh to its imaginative slogan, suggesting a large alternative vision to the status quo, and spelling out a strategy to achieve it. Some of Occupy's organizers and supporters argued that to fulfill these goals would inevitably "split the movement."

But the lessons of history cannot be ignored or dismissed. All great insurgencies entail splits. The American Revolution left fairly substantial groups of British loyalists behind. The Civil War witnessed debates between those wishing only to limit slave expansion and the abolitionists who wanted to abolish it. Radical Republicans pushed through Reconstruction, which empowered Blacks, against those whose desire to preserve the Union prompted their proposal to restore elements of the old order. As for social movements, populists broke from the Democratic Party in the 1880s, only to be reintegrated within it through the presidential candidacy of William Jennings Bryan, and the labor movement endured a half century of struggle between its craft and industrial contingents. Syndicalists who spurned electoral activity and advocated sabotage as a strike tactic bolted the American Federation of Labor (AFL). They formed the Industrial Workers of the World (IWW), a revolutionary industrial union, and were expelled from the Socialist Party, which in the early 1900s was committed to participating in liberal democratic institutions and eschewed all forms of violence, even in self-defense.

Students for a Democratic Society (SDS) and the anti–Vietnam War movement that it helped inaugurate were estranged from liberal Democrats who, until 1967, steadfastly insisted that U.S. president Lyndon Johnson would end the war and that militant opposition to his administration would aid the Right. Only when Johnson escalated U.S. intervention in Southeast Asia did some prominent liberals, like U.S. senator Eugene McCarthy, United Auto Workers (UAW) president Walter Reuther, the Black freedom leader Martin Luther King Jr., and Michael Harrington, the leading socialist intellectual of his generation, openly criticize the administration's war policy. It must be remembered that the short but powerful career of the Black Panthers was propelled by the conviction that Black oppression could not be effectively countered by peaceful means. Their advocacy and practice of armed—always defensive—struggle, internationalism instead of Black nationalism, and revolutionary dialectical materialism represented a sharp departure from the mainstream of the civil-rights movement and evinced hostility among Black cultural nationalists, although the Panthers worked with others to oppose police violence against Black communities and their own members.

Divisions do not necessarily weaken the movement. But without a strong organization, a vision, and a strategy for change as well as a commitment to openly debate controversial questions within and without the organization, the initial impetus for the expansion of the movement will likely peter out. SDS, which took on its initial older sponsors on questions of anticommunism and the Vietnam War and, after 1967, was often allied with the Panthers, ultimately failed because it refused to become a more coherent political formation. "Coherence" would not have meant strict discipline and ideological unanimity, as was the tendency of communist parties. But it would have recognized the importance of vigorous debate about larger ideological questions, crafted an organizing program that assisted fledgling chapters to prosper, and honed its relationships with other, like-minded organizations and movements. Instead, it remained a loose federation of autonomous groups and did not organize regionally with offices, regular conferences, and organizers. It maintained a publications program, mainly with the occasional periodical *New Left Notes* and some pamphlets, which did provide members with news and opportunities for presenting their views. When challenged to adopt Marxist-Leninist politics, its leadership was largely unarmed; it had no alternative perspective to offer its sixty thousand members and dozens of chapters and thus fragmented into Leninist fractions—most of which were Maoist or neo-Trotskyist or veered toward the Communist Party—and a small anarchist group. The radical democrats who had founded the organization had mostly moved on: some joined the liberal Democrats and ran for public office, some became union functionaries, and some earned their graduate degrees and entered higher-education teaching. But some of the most talented SDS leaders of the late 1960s became Weather Underground activists or affiliated with various revolutionary communist organizations. Two efforts toward New Left regroupment followed: the Movement for a Democratic Society (MDS) was all but stillborn, and a few years after the demise of SDS in 1969, the New American Movement (NAM) was formed in 1971 and lasted until it merged with Harrington's Democratic Socialist Organizing Committee (DSOC) to form Democratic Socialists of America (DSA) in 1982.[8]

The State: Ideology, Syndrome, and the Media

There are two problems that inform the history of the U.S. Left and the social movements that have, periodically, electrified a significant fraction of the underlying population. The first and the most ubiquitous is the enormous weight of the state. The second is that of subjectivity.

In contrast to Europe with its centralized political structures, the American state, historically, was decentralized. Although the national government controlled international affairs, domestic politics were left, largely, to state and local governments where, at different times, the Left and Left-liberals exercised some influence. Some held electoral office, especially at the level of cities and towns; however, beginning in the 1920s and through the 1930s, the populists controlled rural state governments in the North and South, notably Minnesota's Farmer-Labor Party and populist governments in the Dakotas, the city of Cleveland, and Pennsylvania, as well as California governors who were confirmed populists. Left Democrats were serious contenders for municipal power in Detroit as late as the 1970s, controlling the city council and electing a mayor, Coleman Young, who had been part of the Communist Left in the UAW. Socialist administrations governed the cities of Milwaukee, Wisconsin; Reading, Pennsylvania; and Bridgeport and Norwalk, Connecticut, into the 1950s.

However, by the late 1970s and the 1980s, the Left faded from the electoral scene as, in an era of fiscal crisis, the dominance of the federal government over state and local jurisdictions was tightened. Capital flight and tax concessions to the rich and to corporations left many communities flat broke; in fact, in an effort to preserve industry, local governments granted tax and infrastructure concessions to keep plants in town, further reducing

---

8. In the interest of full disclosure, I was close to SDS. I joined the NAM in 1976 and became active in its Los Angeles chapter, taught in its Socialist School, and helped with the Gramsci School that preceded its annual national convention. I became a member of its national executive committee and was on the negotiating committee that effected the merger with DSOC in 1982. I have apologized in print for my support of that merger.

their tax base. Federal education grants, construction funds, and straight cash grants to bolster local employment meant that the resources for local communities were more dependent on the federal and state governments. These were years of gradual surrender of home rule. In New York, for example, the 1976 fiscal crisis resulted in measures that deprived the city of the ability to control its own finances; local autonomy was confined largely to nonfiscal matters. The city could propose a budget, but it had to be approved by the state. Since Wall Street had gone on a virtual capital strike to provoke the crisis, New York and many other cities were condemned to permanent servitude. Tragically, state and municipal public unions gave their consent to fiscal austerity and showed their loyalty by agreeing to mass layoffs, wage freezes, and relaxation of work rules and job security. The strike weapon, which had been the hallmark of the organizing phase earlier in the century, was systematically surrendered through the enactment of state laws prohibiting them. Unions were now willing to enter into a Faustian bargain: in return for surrendering the strike, state and local governments reversed decades of refusal to recognize unions for the purpose of collective bargaining.

But some rank-and-file movements since the turn of the twenty-first century have succeeded in taking union power at the local level. In 2010, the Chicago teachers union, an affiliate of the American Federation of Teachers (AFT), was won by the insurgent rank-and-file slate; in 2012, the union conducted a strike that, for the first time in decades, demanded that teachers be involved in curriculum decisions and that high-stakes test results be removed from the list of criteria for teacher evaluations.[9] The strike was settled when the city administration offered a salary increase and agreed to limit the role of student performance in teacher evaluation. The union did not win a new voice in determining the content of what is learned and what is taught, but union members built strong alliances with parents and community organizations—a step that prepared teachers to fight another day and that emboldened teacher unions across the country. In March 2014, in Los Angeles, an insurgent teacher slate captured the second-largest local chapter of the AFT. Teacher insurgencies in Massachusetts, Washington, Oregon, Minnesota, New York, and elsewhere have registered impressive gains. Outside of the education arena, other public-sector unions, such as the fabled Local 100 of the Transport Workers Union in New York, have also seen the rise of insurgent leadership.

---

9. I was part of the insurgent movement of the Professional Staff Congress (PSC), the union that represents more than twenty-five thousand faculty and staff at the City University of New York (CUNY) and the CUNY Research Foundation, which took office in 2000. I served on the executive council and negotiating team for nine years. Like other public workers' unions, without the strike weapon we could only nibble at the edges of urgent issues such as adjunct equity pay, shared governance, and salary demands.

Despite signs of protest from below, Big Labor remains committed to the preservation of the status quo, as evidenced most recently by its shunning of U.S. senator Bernie Sanders and embrace of former U.S. secretary of state Hillary Clinton in the contest for the Democratic Party's nomination for the U.S. presidency. Randi Weingarten, who annually makes $540,000 as AFT's national president, serves on the board of Clinton's largest super PAC (enabling unlimited political contributions from corporate and wealthy donors). In July 2015, AFT's national board voted unanimously to endorse Clinton. Weingarten offered this comment in response to a question about the Sanders campaign:

> Both in terms of Sanders and Trump, people are pissed with the way that life has treated them, that the economy has treated them, and I totally understand that passion. But there's a difference between a message and actually having a plan to win.[10]

By the end of 2015, eleven national unions had endorsed Clinton, including not only AFT but also the National Education Association (NEA), the American Federation of State, County and Municipal Employees (AFSCME), the Service Employees International Union (SEIU), and the International Association of Machinists and Aerospace Workers (IAMAW), while only three—National Nurses United (NNU), the American Postal Workers Union (APWU), and the small National Union of Healthcare Workers (NUHW)— had endorsed Sanders. Meanwhile, a number of locals and insurgent groups within the pro-Clinton national unions actually campaigned for Sanders. NNU executive director RoseAnn DeMoro explained: "I always expect the unions to fall in line with the DNC [Democratic National Committee]. There's the unions, and then there's the workers."[11]

Like the Teamsters and Mineworkers before them, public workers' insurgencies could capture union offices and restore a degree of democratic unionism. What they cannot do is change the nature of collective bargaining without repealing the laws that imprison negotiators and subject unions to punitive controls. That the Chicago teachers can strike without penalty, except by the courts, accounts for their relative success in limiting the power of city authorities to break their strike—power seen recently when transport workers in New York City suffered fines, deprivation of their rights, and other forms of humiliation. The history of labor insurgency is replete with

10. Josh Eidelson, "Why Unions Aren't Uniting behind Hillary Clinton or Bernie Sanders," *Bloomberg Politics*, August 3, 2015, available at http://www.bloomberg.com/politics/articles/2015-08-03/why-unions-aren-t-uniting-behind-hillary-clinton-or-bernie-sanders.

11. Josh Eidelson, "Labor for Bernie Means Headaches for Hillary," *Bloomberg Politics*, November 12, 2015, available at http://www.bloomberg.com/politics/articles/2015-11-12/labor-for-bernie-means-headaches-for-hillary.

instances in which, rather than being liberating, the law and the state's enforcement of it have proven to be barriers to workers' autonomy.

The collapse of the Soviet empire, beginning in 1989 with the tearing down of the Berlin Wall, plunged the battalions of the global Left into crisis. The Soviet Union may not have been admired by the independent Left (remember Herbert Marcuse's early critique in the 1950s[12]), but its demise realigned world politics: the developing world (Third World) found itself without a powerful defender; capitalist countries were now free to pursue austerity policies even during economic slumps; and capital's triumphalism infected the morale of a Left that, against its will, had to admit that its fate had been, even unwillingly, tied to the fate of the really existing socialist world. Western communist parties, already battered since 1956 by the revelations of Stalin's crimes, began to lose militants and chunks of their once considerable periphery. More to the point, suddenly capitalism's new regime of accumulation was the only realistic game in town. The idea that social movements could function outside the liberal or social democratic consensus, that capitalism was the given within which social struggles occurred, became a utopian fantasy and all but disappeared. Revolutionaries became parliamentarians, and those parties with a long history in parliament abandoned their radical education programs and became, in effect, center-left formations. This pattern was duplicated in the United States on a much smaller scale.

It was almost a decade before signs of a movement revival appeared. The 1999 anti–World Trade Organization (WTO) demonstrations in Seattle, follow-up mass gatherings and protests in Quebec and elsewhere, and the formation of the World Social Forum in Brazil promised a new beginning for the Left. The Seattle demonstrations were notable for the coalition of students, feminists, United Steelworkers (USW), the International Longshore and Warehouse Union (ILWU), and others who participated. The ILWU shut down all West Coast ports in support of the protest, although the Steelworkers confined themselves to a peaceful march. The direct-action wing of the movement briefly shut down the downtown Seattle area as city officials were caught napping.

But the attacks on the World Trade Center in New York and the Pentagon in Washington, D.C., on September 11, 2001, brought a resounding halt to the new movement's promising beginnings. In reaction to allegations that the terrorist attacks were perpetrated by Al-Qaeda, the United States became an avowed National Security State, which, through the Patriot Act and other

---

12. Marcuse, a severe critic of Stalinism, began researching and writing his powerful account, and deconstruction, of Soviet Marxism in 1952–1953 while at Columbia University, and the resulting book may be the most insightful study of the subject. See Herbert Marcuse, *Soviet Marxism: A Critical Analysis* (New York: Columbia University Press, 1958).

measures—under U.S. presidents George W. Bush and Obama—has openly violated constitutional guarantees and international law. That both Democratic and Republican leaders in the U.S. Congress support the program of indiscriminate surveillance on the entire population is no longer an emergency measure prompted by flagrant and violent attacks. It has little to do with security; instead, the state is now engaged in arbitrary population control that, conceivably, could extend to any form of protest and resistance, as it did against the Occupy movement in 2011. In the United States, restrictions on liberty have become a permanent feature of political and social rule. Some congressional libertarians have opposed the continued surveillance by the National Security Agency (NSA), and public opinion polls in 2013 showed that two-thirds of Americans oppose the broad-scale surveillance program. But lacking a genuine public debate, state intervention into private lives will likely expand, and its response to forms of direct action by social movements will become even harsher.

Sixty years ago, the social theorist C. Wright Mills concluded that, at the national level, there was no democracy in America.[13] Contrary to constitutional limits to executive powers, he argued that Congress had been relegated to the middle levels of power, at best, and that the U.S. Supreme Court usually ratified the executive's unilateral initiatives. The National Security State, an executive combination of multinational corporations, the military, and the top layer of the political directorate, had virtually no limits to its exercise of authority in a time when the business of government was focused chiefly on foreign policy, particularly on securing U.S. military and economic interests. Today, Mills's judgment, sadly, seems vindicated. The widely publicized congressional gridlock applies chiefly to how much the social wage should be trimmed, but as for the operation of war, war preparation, and domestic population controls, the consensus at the top is all but complete.

Beyond description, this explanation requires a review of the consolidation of power at the top of the political and economic systems, through the historical materialist theory of the state. Under liberal or democratic and authoritarian systems, the state is constituted by three related but distinctive domains. Chief among them are the *repressive* apparatuses of army, police, courts, and prisons. For most of the industrialization era of the eighteenth and nineteenth centuries, repression was the main feature of rule. Workers' efforts to organize unions were usually met by a combination of army and police violence against strikes, prison terms for activists, or state terrorism in the form of assassination.

---

13. C. Wright Mills, *The Power Elite* (New York: Oxford University Press, 1956). For further analysis, see Stanley Aronowitz, "The Structure of Power in American Society," in *Taking It Big: C. Wright Mills and the Making of Political Intellectuals* (New York: Columbia University Press, 2012), 167–186.

But the rise of workers' movements modified the forms of state rule, leading to the state's second domain: what Jürgen Habermas has termed its "legitimation" functions[14]—or, in Louis Althusser's parallel formulation, "ideological state apparatuses."[15] The rise of the state's ideological function in the twentieth century was forced by the spread of social wage demands by insurgent labor movements and the Left. Althusser suggested that the ideological apparatuses of the state now include the trade unions, civil-society organizations, religious institutions, and certainly the public schools. These apparatuses were first initiated by the German government under Otto von Bismarck but greatly extended in the United States by the New Deal in the 1930s, when the right of workers to organize and bargain with their employers was guaranteed by law, social security (old-age pensions) and unemployment compensation was enacted, and limited public housing was built for working-class tenants. After World War II, European governments added universal health-care services financed by taxes, and all advanced industrial societies vastly expanded access to higher education, a measure of the overlap between legitimation (and ideology) and the third major function of the state, its historic investment in the stability and expansion of the economy.

The third key function of the state is its *support of the capitalist economy and its expansion*. Karl Polanyi insisted that the state has played a vital economic role in the development of capitalism for centuries by providing transportation and communications systems (e.g., roads, railways, postal services), imperialist adventures abroad aimed at securing raw materials (e.g., cotton, iron ore, minerals, oil) for industrial production.[16] The state's support of colonies, subsidies to settlers, and support of exploration and research in natural resources are, alongside repression, intrinsic to its character—as are the U.S. state's serial military interventions, its permanent state-funded war economy, and its massive bailout of Wall Street banks in 2008.

The present role of the state in promoting empire dates from the prerevolutionary period in the service of geographic and commercial expansion. British troops conducted unrelenting wars against Native Americans. This program pervaded U.S. policy throughout the nineteenth century. State legalization of various forms of labor exploitation and racial rule, including indentured servitude, slavery, sharecropping, convict labor, and Jim Crow, are of defining significance. But since the early decades of the twentieth century, the ideological or legitimation function has taken on increasing political importance. Of course, the great impetus was the uprisings that

---

14. Jürgen Habermas, *Legitimation Crisis*, trans. Thomas McCarthy (Boston: Beacon, 1975).

15. Louis Althusser, "Ideology and Ideological State Apparatuses (Notes towards an Investigation)," in *Lenin and Philosophy and Other Essays* (New York: Monthly Review Press, 1971).

16. Karl Polanyi, *The Great Transformation* (Boston: Beacon, 1944).

finally responded to the brutality of the Great Depression, especially the indifference of the giant monopolies and the federal government to mass suffering. In the post–New Deal era, the rising social wage, along with war and war preparation, became central themes of government, with the important exception of the never-ending state repression of Black and Brown people, radicals, and the Southern labor movement.

The liberal center insists that racial discrimination and the repression of political expression are gradually alleviated by laws such as the Civil Rights Act and Voting Rights Act and a succession of Supreme Court decisions supporting political freedoms, racial integration, and abortion rights. The liberal center, including the unions, has supported, with varying degrees of enthusiasm, the main direction of U.S. foreign policy, which, despite the breach of Vietnam War protest, has been received with either indifference or only rhetorical opposition. For example, after the mass multicity demonstrations against the U.S. invasion of Iraq in winter 2003, with few exceptions, there has been no popular protest for the past decade. America's eyes are diverted. We are experiencing a moment of what might be called the September 11 syndrome. Vietnam no longer lingers as a brake on the popular support for war; although the Iraq War was never popular, the specter of terror has effectively overwhelmed our willingness to contest, by direct action, American imperial interventions. Many have lost sight of the radical transformation that has occurred since September 11.

The state's legitimation or ideological domain has not disappeared; it still lives in the fading institutions that support the social wage and the popular imagination. We still want a state that will address popular needs in the fragile economy that emerged from the post–Cold War era. We want to be secure in our retirement years, we do not want to starve when our jobs disappear, and we want our schools to educate our children, not keep their noses to the grindstone in order to produce what Marcuse termed their "systematic moronization."[17] Despite the general view that education is a key to prosperity for the many, our schools continue to deteriorate, their budgets slashed and classrooms overcrowded. In many areas of the country, access to health care is severely resisted by similar budget reductions. But state power has turned its attention away. In fact, it is engaged in dismantling many of the social institutions that were built throughout the twentieth century, except, of course, the prison system that now holds two million people (quadrupled since 1980), more than half of them Blacks and Latinos. But the unions, as well as rights and advocacy organizations representing racial and ethnic minorities and women, have born witness to the dismantling, even as they

---

17. Herbert Marcuse, "Repressive Tolerance," in *A Critique of Pure Tolerance*, by Robert Paul Wolff, Barrington Moore Jr., and Herbert Marcuse (Boston: Beacon, 1965), 83.

loyally support the purveyors of demolition. In short, the repressive apparatuses and their functions have taken command.

We can observe the often hidden fact that at this moment the United
States has been engaged in permanent war for a hundred years. Further, the
local police, schools, and urban streets have been militarized. "Law and order," once the leading edge of Republican national administrations but often
contested by the Democrats, has now become a consensual perspective as
two recent Democratic presidents have fostered deep reductions in the social
wage, even as they pursue aggressive wars and police repression to counter
domestic protest. Thus, we can no longer declare the equivalence of the three
historic state functions. *Repression is now dominant.*

Toward the end of his life, in 1960, Mills called the "cultural apparatus"
a relatively autonomous domain of the state. The cultural apparatus—newspapers, television, film, and, recently, the Internet and social media—may
not be subsumed under ideology, although they perform a major ideological function; beyond political economy, the cultural apparatus has become
the crucial determinant of the system's reproduction. Mills was among
the earliest proponents of this position. In his unfinished exploration of the
cultural apparatus, the originality of his discovery was that electronic media were not merely an industry but formed a new mass sensibility, a new
condition for the widespread acceptance of the capitalist system and even the
general belief in its eternity. Our social character has become entwined with
communications technology. He linked the institutions of culture with what
he termed the Fourth Epoch—what is now commonly called postmodernism. This intricate interlock between cultural institutions, political power,
and everyday life constitutes a new moment of history. It has become the
primary machinery of domination. A central aspect of domination is the
abrogation of our ability to know the totality; instead, we are condemned
to understand the division of the world as a series of specializations. Thus,
the well-known fragmentation of social life is a result of the rearrangement
of both social space and the modes by which knowledge is produced, disseminated, and ingested. The cultural apparatus is largely responsible for the
intellectual darkness that has enveloped us.

Since the development of the mass-circulation newspaper, critics on the
Left have referred to commercial publications as the "bought" press. Newspapers were regarded as tools of capital, subordinated through advertising,
their life-blood, and punctuated only by a handful of independents like the
St. Louis Post-Dispatch, the *Chicago Sun-Times*, the *New York Herald*, and,
briefly, the *New York Post* and *PM*. Accordingly, the *New York Times* has
been viewed as the establishment's organ, barely reliable in its coverage of
foreign affairs and rarely fair to labor and other social movements. The emergence of radio and television as leading sources of news and commentary did
not basically alter this evaluation because these media followed the game

plan of the newspapers. Most stations were run by profit-seeking corporations. Consequently, until the late 1970s, which witnessed, via the computer, the beginnings of electronic, consumer-based media, reporters—save for a few genuinely independent journalists—were employees rather than critical or independent writers and, in the main, took orders from editors and publishers.

But what is the contemporary role of the news media? Is it a state cultural apparatus? Does it have an independent or subordinate role and spirit? The media have been assigned to the state's legitimation or ideological spheres by most theorists. But Mills, Paul Baran, and Paul Sweezy are among those who place what Mills calls the "cultural apparatus" as a fourth major domain that cannot be reduced to political economy, even though they overlap in both the corporate and state spheres. In his recent book *Digital Disconnect*, Robert McChesney has decisively shown that media are now a powerful part of monopoly capital.[18] The collective influence of its hardware, electronic, and communications sectors extends to the state as well as to the composition of the capitalist division of labor. However important media may be for the assessment of the social and technical division of labor, for our purposes, we will concentrate on the significance of the cultural apparatus for the constitution of subjectivity.

Digital Disconnect brings the complex story of corporate domination of the media, which shattered the democratic dreams of inventors for a noncommercial communications technology, up to date. It is perhaps the most comprehensive narrative and analysis of the political economy of the Internet, which is today the leading edge of mass communications. In addition to providing a detailed account of the structures of corporate hegemony over the media and the Internet in particular, McChesney argues that our politics are ineluctably shaped by media corporations, that freedom of the press has been crippled by corporate intrusion, and that journalism itself has lost its stature as a public good. Journalism is now an adjunct of corporate domination of news and other forms of public knowledge.

Digital Disconnect differs from both celebrations and critiques of the older technologies in two principal respects. McChesney is interested in stressing the importance of a political economy of communication rather than updating the social and cultural critiques of previous writers. And while Lewis Mumford, the Frankfurt School, Mills, and philosophers like Martin Heidegger and Hans Jonas link, in various ways, the relation of technology to nature and its consequences for the relations among human beings, McChesney not only focuses almost exclusively on the power of the leading media corporations over every aspect of the industry—from the production

---

18. Robert McChesney, *Digital Disconnect: How Capitalism Is Turning the Internet against Democracy* (New York: New Press, 2013).

of hardware to the production of knowledge and its dissemination—but also claims that knowledge and information is fully controlled. Since knowledge, including the news, is now the main productive force and source of political wisdom, corporate control of the most advanced digital media as well as conventional broadcasting endangers democracy itself. Beyond the field of communication, according to McChesney, this power has extended to all levels of government, including the executive branch's regulatory agencies, such as the Federal Communications Commission, and Congress, which are so successfully influenced by corporate lobbies and campaign contributions that independent journalism is collapsing: as governmental institutions have become "soft" on media moguls, news gathering is now largely a function of public relations. McChesney writes:

> The dirty secret of journalism is that a significant percentage of our news stories, in the 40 to 50 percent range, even at the most prestigious papers in the glory days of the 1970s, was based upon press releases. Even then, a surprising amount of the time, these press releases were only loosely investigated before publication.[19]

Journalism has, in the main, become an institutional apparatus of the state.

McChesney notes one of the limitations of American-style professional journalism, by quoting Christopher Lasch:

> What Democracy requires is vigorous public debate, not information. . . . We do not know what we need to know until we ask the right questions, and we can identify the right questions only by subjecting our own ideas about the world to the test of public controversy.[20]

What is missing is public controversy about the most important questions. For McChesney, this absence is primarily due to dominant media cartels and monopolies. Entailed in this formulation is the claim that the political directorate, its regulatory agencies, and the media monopolies together conspire to stifle public debate. He argues that the Internet, many features of which have by now been privatized, has "done much more damage to news media than it has done to entertainment media."[21] Since news is for most people their main source of political knowledge, when journalism is not a source of debate, knowledge is reduced to "information" bereft of controversy because its origin is almost always an official source. Democracy becomes the loser because the public has been blocked from participating in an informed

---

19. Ibid., 90.
20. Ibid.
21. Ibid., 91.

manner in the processes that determine political decisions. These decisions remain in few hands, largely hidden from public view. But, lest we believe that private ownership of the news media is solely at issue, public broadcasting is subject to some of the same constraints as the commercial media. According to McChesney, "paltry budgets" and "spotty performance" are largely to blame, though the public media have higher public approval than their commercial counterparts. Public media's paltry budgets are significantly supplemented by corporate sponsors, among which are oil companies, big agricultural-product corporations such as Monsanto and Archer Daniels Midland (ADM), and major banks. The administration of public broadcasting is occasionally constrained by these sponsors, not necessarily by their direct intervention but, more typically, by self-censorship, a tendency that spans commercial and noncommercial media.

Marx's subtitle for the first volume of *Capital* was "a Critique of Political Economy." The term "critique" connotes his intention to interrogate the categories of classical political economy to show their partial but incomplete adequacy. Elsewhere, in the thesis on Feuerbach, he criticizes traditional materialism for its failure to address "subjectivity," a criticism that can be directed to the tendency prevalent among Marxists to engage in "objective" analysis at the expense of asking the question: *What is the relation between forms of economic power, the state's complicity with capitalist hegemony, and the forms of social and political reception and participation of the underlying population?* Marxism has honed a finely tuned political economy of capitalism and its state and, according to McChesney's work, a powerful extension of political economy to communications, especially the media and its corporate powers. But political economy tends to treat *the people* as objects of largely autonomous corporate actors. The problem of subjectivity, which Marx found lacking in materialism, remains in the twenty-first century. Marxists have followed the script, written by the theorists of the Second and Third Internationals, which, in the main, regard capital and its personifications as the subjects of history and the people as objects who become agents when they perceive that their economic interests are violated. The workers, no less than other social formations, are interpellated by the system but have no genuine subjectivity.

What emerges from the changing focus of the state toward repression and foreign intervention, and away from meeting the fundamental needs of the underlying population, depends on how ordinary people act, not on a presumed breakdown of the capitalist system. The current crisis has not been met by sustained widespread resistance or by alternatives to the conclusive orientation of the state toward financial capital, the very rich, and their own emphasis on building the U.S. empire at the expense of advancing the social wage. Nor can the putative public rely on the media. The fundamental question is subjectivity. How have the people introjected or resisted domination?

What are the fundamental influences on how they become social and political actors?

What Is Subjectivity and Its Role in Determining Our Collective Future?

I deploy the term *subjectivity* to connote both the collective disposition and its capacity to resist capital's encroachments on popular autonomy, especially the barriers to democratic practices that, beyond voting, empower ordinary people to make the crucial decisions that affect their lives. Subjectivity is conditioned but not determined solely by economic conditions. The cultural apparatus, institutions of everyday practice, especially the workplace, organized religion, schools, and the media, are immensely influential on perceptions of social reality, but social formations also have predispositions that are situated in biographies, biological needs—fulfilled and unfulfilled—and social relations, both of production and of everyday life. Thus, subjectivity is not merely based on "consciousness" but involves the will to act. It is not enough for individuals and social formations to recognize their oppression by external powers over which they have little or no control. It is true that many Americans are in thrall of the rich and famous and devoutly aspire themselves to those heights. But throughout the histories of the United States and other capitalist countries, many people of the subaltern classes and social formations recognize that the game of politics and economic power is rigged and understand that they are the objects—not the subjects—of power. The question is, why, in the United States, is protest and resistance sporadic and episodic? Why do we lack workers' movements and Black freedom, feminist, and environmental movements that define themselves as ideologically and politically counterhegemonic to the domination by capital and the repressive state? The overwhelming majority of the U.S. population seems unable to craft a viable alternative to overdeveloped capitalism.

With some exceptions, the small but growing entourage of radical journalists and political commentators in the United States is prone to the view that Americans lack the knowledge—as a function of the mendacity of its leaders, secret and not-so-secret deals with corporate capital, nefarious foreign dictators, and instances of outright robbery of the public till. The assumption is that if we knew the truth and could link it with our "interests," we would act to free ourselves and the country of the yoke of corruption and greed. Left-liberals like Bill Moyers and Amy Goodman are constant sources of revelations about the sorry state of democracy at home and abroad. The coverage of the injustices that plague the world are rays of enlightenment in a cloud-filled sky; mainstream news is a cover for the misdeeds of the wealthy and otherwise powerful, while sports and other entertainments are distractions produced by a complicit culture industry. Accordingly, exposure is the work of journalism and committed scholarship.

The invocation to rational discourse, however necessary, is insufficient. What is lacking is an explanation for the absence of a struggle for genuine alternatives to the prevailing set-up, including a debate on why protest and resistance, even when it grips the popular imagination, does not lead to a genuine challenge to power. The answer to these questions goes beyond the thesis of mass ignorance. It requires an exploration of subjectivity, a journey that embraces, to be sure, a historical, geographic, and political economic analysis but also requires plumbing the dimensions of depth psychology to the regions of the political and cultural unconscious.

We began this analysis by arguing that we have entered an era of the authoritarian, repressive state. This means that for the most part, the state is increasingly unresponsive to the traditional manifestations of protest and resistance, and if the resistance becomes too dangerous, it is perfectly willing to use force to disperse any uprising. For example, as long as North Carolina's Moral Mondays or Black Lives Matter actions remain peaceful and its legions fairly contained, the police will arrest demonstrators, but the legislatures will continue to enact onerous laws. However, when Oakland's Occupy movement called on longshore workers to shut down the port and asked for a general strike, the police came in, batons swinging, shooting pellets.

In the United States, there is no political formation capable of generating sustained movement against capital or, indeed, proposing a comprehensive, systemic alternative to the cotemporary capitalist system. This absence reflects the fragmentation of the Left into small groups and the lack of a vigorous theoretical debate on the Left about almost anything but also the lack of Left media that reaches a large fraction of the politically active population, let alone Left-liberals.[22] The small grouplets that pretend they are some kind of vanguard often publish periodicals. But these are mostly unreadable, even by their own adherents. They rarely offer news and commentary about health and schooling and are cursorily involved, if at all, in ecological questions. They offer rants that regularly proclaim a new upsurge on the basis of isolated evidence.

The geography of the American landscape has radically changed since the 1940s. Although suburbs already dotted the metropolitan landscape in the 1920s, the rapid displacement of farmland by suburbs became a central

---

22. It is true that there are several Left-liberal online magazines and news services. For example, *CounterPunch* (http://www.counterpunch.org), *Truthout* (http://www.truth-out .org), *Truthdig* (http://www.truthdig.com), the *Nation* (http://www.thenation.com), and *Alternet* (http://www.alternet.org) offer news that counters the mainstream, but mostly they fall into the category of exposure rather than critical reflection. None regularly rehearse controversies within the Left, let alone provide in-depth analysis of the outrages they report. The assumption is that their audience has a ready explanation—a conceit that is incomplete.

factor for solving the chronic housing crisis and accompanied the deindustrialization of our cities. What has been described as sprawl on the basis
of one-household homes resulted in the dispersal of a large fraction of the
working and salaried middle class and contributed to the emergence of consumer society. The suburbanization and ex-urbanization of America meant
that politics and culture were bifurcated. The city was the heart of civil engagement, the concentration of industrial unions, progressive legislators,
and cultural communities, in both senses of the term—ethnic and racial
enclaves and the arts. The relative dispersal into the suburbs changed the
political culture. Individualism replaced collective action to address social
grievances, families were relatively isolated as neighborhoods disappeared,
and the suburbs and their middle-class composition became the social basis
of many forms of mass culture.

Underlying fragmentation and submission is what Wilhelm Reich
termed the "emotional plague." One of its key components is fear of taking
power, a trait that is endemic to the contemporary European Left. If there is
a will to power, it is confined to action within the liberal-democratic parliamentary system and rarely raises the question of systemic transformation.
Decades of frustration have led to mass despair. In Europe, no less than in
the United States, many who understand, broadly, that the prevailing system
is against them cannot envision taking power. Reich traced mass despair
about the chance of social change to dammed up sexuality and, connected
to it, mass subordination to authority, whose personification is the father.
In his study *The Mass Psychology of Fascism*,[23] Reich disputed the common
Left analysis that ascribed the Nazi victory, either to the unstoppable power
of "the most reactionary section of the capitalist class" (the Communists) or
the capture by the Nazis of the middle class (the Socialists). Exempt in both
was the participation of a significant fraction of the working class in the
Nazi orbit. Reviewing the election results of 1932, he demonstrated that the
Nazis won a sizeable vote in working-class precincts and asked the question,
why? He answered with an exploration of the economic and social crisis that
proved disastrous for working people. While the Communists and Socialists wrangled, the Nazis offered hope in the personification of a leader who
could lead the nation to glory. Nazism was more than a regime of state terror,
although it was that. It also adroitly combined the promise of socialism, German racial superiority, global conquest, revenge for the humiliation visited
on Germany by the Treaty of Versailles and the Dawes Plan that mandated
German reparations, mysticism, and a revival of the family as a haven in the
heartless world. In sum, the fascists promised pleasure in redemption as well

---

23. Wilhelm Reich, *The Mass Psychology of Fascism* (New York: Farrar, Straus and Gi-
roux, 1980). Originally published in 1933.

as revenge, tapping into the collective libido while the Left tarried, equipped with only its old slogans and programs.

It is important to remember that U.S. president Ronald Reagan, perhaps the most important contemporary figure corresponding to the authoritarian father, who, in contrast to the grim prognoses of both U.S. president Jimmy Carter and the Left, proclaimed "morning in America." Surely, Reaganism was a regime of falsification, international duplicity, and relentless neoliberal policies that did not sit well even with many of his supporters. But the blue-collar "Reagan Democrats" did not vote their pocketbook. They voted their hopes and for a figure who exuded optimism. Reagan was a product of the cultural apparatus, who understood that politics is, at the bottom, about symbols. Taking a page from Franklin Roosevelt's playbook, he scorned fear, even as he promised nothing. That the Left has no conception of the cultural unconscious is among the reasons for its malaise. The Right may be dangerous, not only for its policies but for its rhetorical talent and its command of imagery.

Marcuse expands Reich's exploration of the political and cultural unconscious by addressing the dialectical relation of alienated labor to the advent of consumer society. He notes that workers do not fulfill themselves through their labor. For Marcuse, alienated labor would provoke revolt unless the system of domination offered a way to satisfy the innate drive for pleasure. Since the pleasure principle cannot be satisfied within the systems of capitalist rationality that reduce labor to a series of repetitive tasks, mainly by technologies that increase the quantity of goods at the expense of extending the destructive domination of nature, capital offers a series of satisfactions to an otherwise alienated labor force. Marcuse was among the Critical Theorists who focused on the emergence, in the 1930s and 1940s, of consumer society, which provided a credit line—to anyone who had a full-time job—to purchase a car and one or two homes, to make tuition payments, and to buy other pleasurable items. He called attention to "repressive de-sublimation"— that is, sexual practices without emotional ties. The old regime repressed premarital sex, consigning it to the cultural underground. Late capitalism opens the doors, via mass cultural images, to sex as a compensation for the general lack of genuine erotic experience in work and love. For Marcuse, the condition of reproducing the relations of production is that the system has penetrated the soma to human character structure.

Of course, television and film, the main sites of entertainment, crucially evoke images that become models for how we understand the social world. Series like *The Simpsons* and, more recently, *24* accomplish more than assisting exhausted people to pass the time; they offer interpretations of the world. *The Simpsons* is a salve for viewers who know that the world is suffused with cynicism and receive confirmation. With *24*, we are reminded that this is a dangerous world, that death and dying, violence and mayhem are now considered the new normal. For subscribers of HBO, Showtime, and other premium channels, series such as *The Sopranos*, *The Wire*, and *The Newsroom* reassure them that the media are capable of producing art and providing critique of aspects of the social world, which, taken together, reinforce the idea that all is not conformity. These series are, at least on the surface, departures from the 1950s, when programs such as *Father Knows Best* and *Marcus Welby, M.D.* were veritable adverts for the system. Perhaps the long-running multivariant *Law and Order* is a complex but ultimately conformist reminder that the rule of law remains part of the dominant discourse. Its popularity can be read as a vindication of the proposition that we still need reassurance that, despite all, the social order is still secure.

Althusser argues that we are always already interpellated by the ideological state apparatuses, especially the cultural institutions of schools and the media. Our character, values, beliefs, and experiential orientations are not individually acquired but inhere in these apparatuses to which we are subordinate. The "reproduction of the relations of production," a phrase Althusser borrows from Henri Lefebvre, is accomplished by what Lefebvre terms the "bureaucratic society of controlled consumption," by habitual practices of everyday life: shopping as a colonization of free time, the routinization of household tasks.[24] We are enslaved by the routines of labor whose elements are reproduced in the time away from paid work. Lefebvre argues that the achievement of social ownership of the means of production, the traditional goal of the socialist movements, is undercut by family obligations, consumption, and everyday life. He insists that if there is no revolution of everyday life, the old system is bound to creep back, as it did in the Soviet Union.

Thus, the capitalist system and the state require an underlying population that participates in its own subjugation, a theme repeated in Michel Foucault's notion of "discursive formation," which ascribes, chiefly, our subordination to a language. In this modality, we may grasp state surveillance of its citizens (the Panopticon effect), concepts such as the rule of law that neutralizes domination in favor of scripture, and the requirement that we yield to established authority as constituents of social reproduction, not as extraordinary creations of policy.[25] If this is true, authoritarianism is by no means aberrant in liberal democratic regimes. It is normative and, as Reich shows, is ever present in the structure of human biological constitution as well as in the drive for cooperation and love.

---

24. Henri Lefebvre, "The Bureaucratic Society of Controlled Consumption," *Everyday Life in the Modern World*, trans. Sacha Rabinovitch (London: Continuum, 2002), 68–109.

25. For discussion of the Panopticon effect, see Michel Foucault, *Discipline and Punish: The Birth of the Prison*, trans. Alan Sheridan (London: Penguin, 1977); for discussion of discursive formation, see Michel Foucault, *The Archaeology of Knowledge*, trans. Alan Sheridan (New York: Pantheon, 1972).

When the Left refuses to debate issues of the cultural and political unconscious and restricts its critique to the categories of political economy, it disarms itself. For the present, it is not imperative that we accept any of these specific readings; what is imperative, however, is that we are prepared to entertain the habituation engendered in everyday life and in the unconscious as sites of reproduction and as possible explanations for why the radical imagination seems to have fallen into barren fields.

Where is the outrage? It has turned inward by blaming itself for outrageous fortune, on the one hand, and outward in the form of rage against the poor and indigent on the other. It seeks respite in sports and money-making and money-losing schemes like the lottery, gambling, and undercapitalized small businesses that are almost never brought to fruition. For most people to rage against the system requires, among other remedies, addressing unconscious desire and its vicissitudes and coming to terms with the distractions that detain them. A viable Left must continue to analyze the political economy of capitalism but also critique economic determinism by coming to terms with the critique of everyday life, the institutions that engulf us, and the cultural apparatus that penetrates our imagination. To revive a radical imagination requires serious attention to psychoanalysis as much as to politics and economics.

21

From Great Refusals
to Wars of Position

Marcuse, Gramsci, and Social Mobilization

LAUREN LANGMAN

The progressive social movements of 2011, followed by the rise of Left parties such as Syriza in Greece and Podemos in Spain, can be best understood as examples of what Herbert Marcuse called the Great Refusal: the rejection and contestation of domination reflecting a variety of grievances stemming from the multiple legitimation crises of contemporary capitalism. As Jürgen Habermas argued, the multiple legitimation crises of the capitalist system migrate to "lifeworlds," the realms of subjectivity and motivation that evoke strong emotions such as anger, anxiety, and indignation that dispose social mobilizations.[1] What is especially evident as a goal of these movements is the quest for dignity as rooted in an emancipatory, philosophical, anthropological critique of alienation, domination, and suffering pioneered by the Frankfurt School—quite cogently argued in Marcuse's analysis of Marx's *Economic and Philosophical Manuscripts of 1844*.[2] But grievances and emotions alone do not lead to sustained social movements; there must also be recruitment, organizing and organization building, leadership, strategy, tactics, and vision. The Frankfurt School's critique of domination can be complemented by Antonio Gramsci's theory of hegemony, in which "organic intellectuals" understand how the system operates (with due

---

1. See Jürgen Habermas, *Legitimation Crisis* (Boston: Beacon, 1975); and Jürgen Habermas, *The Theory of Communicative Action: Lifeworld and System* (Boston: Beacon, 1985).
2. Herbert Marcuse, "The Foundations of Historical Materialism," in *The Essential Marcuse: Selected Writings of Philosopher and Social Critic Herbert Marcuse*, ed. Andrew Feenberg and William Leiss (Boston: Beacon, 2007). Essay originally published in 1932. See also Karl Marx, *Economic and Philosophic Manuscripts of 1844*, ed. Dick J. Struik, trans. Martin Milligan (New York: International, 1964).

attention to the salience of the cultural barriers to change), while also proffering counterhegemonic narratives, organizing subalterns, and initiating "wars of position."[3] A critical perspective on contemporary social movements provides a politically informed critique with visions of utopian possibility in which membership in democratic, egalitarian, identity-granting and identity-recognizing communities of meaning allows for, and indeed fosters, community, agency, creative self-realization, and the dignity of all.

Ideology, Hegemony, and Domination

Why do the vast majority of people "willingly assent" to the domination by the few, despite vast economic inequalities, growing hardships, and the thwarting of the self? This has long been one of the central questions for the Frankfurt School's critique of ideology and character structure in which authority becomes embedded within the self, making possible uncritical acceptance and conformity. These insights provide a rich understanding of the conditions of our age, especially of those that enable (or thwart) emancipatory social movements.

The grievances that result from the contradictions and adversities of neoliberal capitalism need to be articulated by intellectually informed, radical activists. Quite independently of the Frankfurt School, a parallel line of analysis and critique was developed by Antonio Gramsci, the Italian communist theoretician and organizer who conceptualized "hegemony" as the ideological control of culture, which produces the "willing assent" to the domination of the "historic bloc" (the capitalists) and through which the "naturalization" of the historically arbitrary is presented as normal, natural, and in the best interests of all.[4] For Gramsci, the critique of hegemony and the development of counterhegemonic ideologies and organizational practices are the tasks of "organic intellectuals" who understand the role of culture in sustaining domination. They understand the ways in which the dominant culture thwarts political and social change, which, in turn, necessitates a cultural rebellion, mediated through the "wars of position" in which counterhegemonic discourses would overcome cultural barriers and the "normality" of social existing arrangements in order to achieve social transformation. One of the major tactics for such organization is so-called popular education, which enables people to understand how ruling class privileges are based on the exploitation of the masses. Gramsci's analysis

---

3. Antonio Gramsci, "The Intellectuals," in *Selections from the Prison Notebooks*, ed. and trans. Quintin Hoare and Geoffrey Nowell Smith (New York: International, 1971), 3–23; Antonio Gramsci, "The Transition from the War of Manoeuvre (Front Attack) to the War of Position," in Gramsci, *Selections from the Prison Notebooks*, 238–239.

4. Gramsci, *Selections from the Prison Notebooks*.

complements the Frankfurt School's critiques, while his experiences as an activist provide insights and tools to envision and, indeed, make possible an alternative kind of society.

Critical Theory

The Psychological Foundations of Politics

The Frankfurt School brought psychoanalysis into the critique of domination. Wilhelm Reich and Erich Fromm subsequently developed a political psychology in which authoritarianism, an aspect of character acquired in childhood, made possible the embrace of conservative and, indeed, reactionary politics.[5] The understanding of the superego as internalized authority showed that people would passionately submit to "powerful," authoritative leaders in order to gain their love and assuage feelings of anxiety, loneliness, powerlessness, and meaninglessness.[6] Thus, authoritarians are psychologically disposed to embrace the elite's political agendas that stress toughness, determination, and power. Authoritarianism is typically coupled with a sadomasochistic need to dominate, denigrate, and feel contempt toward the weak and the helpless, and authoritarians typically project aggression toward the out-groups (paranoia).

The early Frankfurt School studies of authoritarianism showed how these authoritarian character structures resonated with fascist propaganda and ideology. In a number of books, papers, and empirical studies of working-class Germans, and in a large postwar study of Americans, authoritarianism was shown to be highly correlated with the conservative-to-reactionary political positions that glorified authority, denigrated subordinates, and projected anger and aggression toward the out-groups, especially racial minorities and Jews. Authoritarians are thus generally patriarchal, homophobic, and racist, in addition to being highly conventional and conformist and maintaining a rigid, black-white, either-or cognitive stance. The enduring significance of these studies can be seen in the contemporary work of Robert Altemeyer.[7] We might also note that, in many ways, these studies of authoritarianism anticipated some of the recent approaches in cognitive psychology and emotion research.

Nevertheless, while being a crucial aspect of political beliefs and actions, authoritarianism is only a part of the story of the internalization of various ideologies. *It is absolutely essential to underline the fact that people's*

---

5. While lacking a theory of developmental psychology, Gramsci did note the importance of early childhood as the period in which cultural values were learned.

6. Erich Fromm, *Escape from Freedom* (New York: Holt, Rinehart and Winston, 1941).

7. Robert Altemeyer, "The Authoritarians" (unpublished manuscript, 2006), available at http://members.shaw.ca/jeanaltemeyer/drbob/TheAuthoritarians.pdf.

political beliefs are not shaped by rational considerations, logic, or evidence. Rather, the character structure and the patterning of various needs and desires shape the ways in which people perceive the world, evaluate events, and choose actions. For Gramsci, the ideological control of culture shaped the production of ideology to produce the "willing assent" to domination. But without a theory of psychodynamics, he could not explain the motivation of people to assent to their own subordination. In 1930, Sigmund Freud provides the first hint, claiming that the values, norms, and laws of society that demand sexual repression and obedience to social dictates are mediated through identification with parents and become sedimented within the superego.[8] People subsequently develop identities that have been ideologically crafted, but not under the circumstances of their own choosing. The identities of prior generations, shaped by earlier authority relationships, weigh down on the individual to colonize his or her consciousness and desires in the way that the values of the ruling classes or hegemonic blocs become internalized as essential parts of the individual's identity and values.[9] That this is not a rational process is also made evident by the studies of authoritarianism and anti-Semitism mentioned earlier in the chapter.

One function of ideologies is to alleviate anxieties over uncertainties in this world and, perhaps, over getting into the next world. Moreover, the maintenance of group ties through conformity to group norms and values can be a source of powerful attachments as well as a basis for self-esteem, but this, in turn, leads to conformity, "groupthink," and what Marcuse called "one-dimensional thought." Thus, ideologies are not simply explanations of social reality or misrepresentations of social reality that both mystify and sustain the power of the ruling classes. Rather, ideologies and values are essential components of one's identity, which has both conscious and unconscious components that are closely intertwined with powerful feelings and emotions. *Assent to hegemonic ideologies and social arrangements rests upon emotional configurations.* As Fromm put it:

> The fact that ideas have an emotional matrix is of the utmost importance because it is the key to the understanding of the spirit of a culture. Different societies or classes within a society have a specific character, and on its basis different ideas develop and become powerful.[10]

---

8. Sigmund Freud, *Civilization and Its Discontents*, trans. James Strachey (New York: W. W. Norton, 2005). Originally published in 1930.

9. The superego and authority relations were central in the work of Erich Fromm, Herbert Marcuse, Max Horkheimer, and Theodor Adorno.

10. Fromm, *Escape from Freedom*, 277–278.

Fromm continues:

> Our analysis of Protestant and Calvinist doctrines has shown that those ideas were powerful forces within the adherents of the new religion, because they appealed to needs and anxieties that were present in the character structure of the people to whom they were addressed. In other words, *ideas can become powerful forces, but only to the extent to which they are answers to specific human needs prominent in a given social character.*
>
> Not only thinking and feeling are determined by man's character structure but also his actions. . . . The actions of a normal person appear to be determined only by rational considerations and the necessities of reality. However, with the new tools of observation that psychoanalysis offers, we can recognize that so-called rational behavior is largely determined by the character structure.[11]

Within Marx's critique of alienation, there is an implicit social-psychological theory of emotions and desire. More specifically, alienated labor estranges workers from their work and the products of that work, rendering people powerless, their lives meaningless, objectified, dehumanized, and estranged from others as well as from their own potential creative self-realization (the inherent tendencies of what Marx called a "species being").

In more modern parlance, alienation frustrates fundamental needs for (1) attachments to others and communal belonging, (2) a sense of agency and empowerment, (3) social recognition, and (4) fulfillment of one's potentials as a human being—awareness of one's capacity as a being that can anticipate and shape one's own future. The various frustrations and deprivations of capitalism thwart fundamental human needs for respect, recognition, and dignity.[12] Alienated labor creates warped expressions of selfhood. The fundamental moral imperative of Marx revealed how capitalism truncated human capacities for community, freedom, and self-realization and how a postcapitalist social order could enable the self-realization and dignity of all.[13]

Political values, beliefs, and understandings are based not on evidence, logic, or rationality but on emotions, feelings, and identities. This important insight, part and parcel of the Frankfurt School's understandings of fascism, xenophobia, and anti-Semitism, has been rediscovered by various academic psychologists. People embrace various ideologies because such ideologies,

---

11. Ibid., 279–280 (emphasis in original).
12. Lauren Langman, "Political Economy and the Normative: Marx on Human Nature and the Quest for Dignity," in *Constructing Marxist Ethics*, ed. Michael Thompson (Leiden, Netherlands: Brill, 2015), 43–65.; Richard Sennett and Jonathan Cobb, *Hidden Injuries of Class* (New York: Knopf, 1972).
13. Langman, "Political Economy and the Normative."

much as Émile Durkheim claims about religion, provide people with a sense of solidarity and connection. Ideologies provide people with a sense of agency and empowerment. By incorporating a person into a valorized group, ideologies provide individuals with a sense of dignity and purpose. Thus, the legacy of Marx's critique of alienation, refracted through a critical psychodynamic prism pioneered by the Frankfurt School, provides us with an understanding of the affinity between the character structure and the embrace of an ideology.

The recent work of George Lakoff has shown how different political orientations rest on the notions of morality, which reflect the values, role models, and child-rearing practices of one's early family life (which is seen as a model for society).[14] The "strict father" pattern fosters a morality based on a competitive orientation and, in turn, the necessity for strength, toughness, and independence in order to survive in a tough, dangerous world. There is an intolerant, if not punitive, orientation to those who appear to be weak or dependent. Conversely, the "nurturant parent" orientation fosters caring, sharing, compassion, and empathy, while creative self-fulfillment is its most important value. But political ideologies rest on more than the gratification of particular desires; perhaps equally important is that *ideologies depend on restricting contradictory information and barring arguments, facts, evidence, and data that might undermine the given ideology.* Insofar as an ideology is an essential part of one's identity, people actively ward off challenges to it. Ideologies provide a variety of gratifications, not the least of which is to minimize anxiety by organizing reality and providing a sense of meaning to one's life. Various defense mechanisms protect one's identity and enable one to function in everyday life.

The first line of defense is denial, the flat-out rejection of evidence or values contrary to one's ideology. Whether the issue is the single-payer healthcare system, global warming, racial or gender superiority, or heteronormativity, the denial of contravening evidence serves to protect one's self-esteem and dignity, which, in turn, leads the person to reject and discredit any information inconsistent with one's ideology and identity. Closely tied to denial is displacement—deflecting a challenge or directing it toward an unworthy target. Finally, cognitive dissonance works to eliminate challenges to or inconsistencies in one's beliefs and values. Collectively, such defenses reinforce "one-dimensional thought" and reproduce subjugation to the status quo.

Consumer Society: One-Dimensional Thought, New Sensibilities, and Great Refusals

In 1964, writing at a time of growing affluence, Marcuse noted that the working classes, especially better-paid skilled workers, had internalized the

---

14. George Lakoff, *The All New Don't Think of an Elephant! Know Your Values and Frame the Debate* (White River Junction, VT: Charles Green, 2014).

"artificial needs" fostered by capitalism and satisfied through consumerism and were thereby incorporated into the consumer society, anchored through consumption-based identities and enjoying mass-mediated escapism provided by the culture industries, while embracing "one-dimensional thought" devoid of critical reflection. Marcuse's *One-Dimensional Man* offers a comprehensive analysis of the postwar growth of the consumer society, which was aided and abetted by the promises of growing material abundance as providing the "good life," which included good sex and promises of ever more prosperity.[15] For Marcuse, behind the goods and goodies of mass consumption are alienation, shallowness, and the thwarting of creativity and self-fulfillment. No longer was alienation simply the product of wage labor; it was an intrinsic aspect of consumer capitalism. While the writers and poets of the beat generation of the 1950s critiqued the complacency, conformity, banality, and superficiality of the dominant culture, Marcuse moved beyond that observation to locate the problem in the intertwining of consumer capitalism and "one-dimensional thought." Moreover, he claims that understanding the role of dialectics, contradiction, and negation—amid conditions of oppression—fosters a "new sensibility" critical of capitalism in general and its many forms of domination, including its production of "artificial needs" that could never be satisfied.

Marcuse's critique resonated with and informed (and was informed by) young college students and marginalized youth activists in or from the ghettos of racialized minorities. The times called for the Great Refusal—rejections of the system of capitalist domination, White supremacy, patriarchy, inequality, and social injustice that characterized the 1960s. Marcuse's formulations connected with the civil-rights and antiwar movements, feminism, and anticolonialism, as well as struggles for sexual freedom, environmental protection, and gay liberation. Meanwhile, hippie movements rejected repressive asceticism and publicly articulated their critique by extolling drugs, sex, and rock and roll. Marcuse was deemed the guru of these movements and considered especially dangerous by the reactionary forces. Like Socrates, he was accused of corrupting youth, but instead of taking hemlock, he became the intellectual inspiration for progressive scholars and young activists—an influence that endures to the present.

Legitimation Crises

How do we move from the critique of the present and the visions of the possible to social mobilizations? Habermas offered a systematic theory of legitimation crises that occur when there are failures in the objective "steering

---

15. Herbert Marcuse, *One-Dimensional Man: Studies in the Ideology of Advanced Industrial Society* (Boston: Beacon, 1964).

mechanisms" of the systems of advanced capitalist societies.[16] There may be crises of (1) the economy that produces and distributes goods and services, (2) the political system that sustains the legitimacy of the whole, or (3) social integration secured by ideology and the state. System integration depends on the mechanisms of domination (e.g., the state and the mass media). Social integration and solidarity, as parts of the lifeworld, depend on normative structures—value systems that express norms and identity as well as secure loyalty and cohesion. Each form of integration possesses distinct logics and, in turn, a different kind of rationality. Social integration comes through socialization and the creation of meaningful lifeworlds—namely, a culture and ideology that legitimates the social system and provides individuals with personal meaning. In contemporary societies, the logic of the state and the market has "migrated" into the subjective and "colonized the lifeworld." Thus, legitimation has subjective consequences in the lifeworlds where social and political identities are experienced and performed.

Social movements emerge at the intersections of the system and the lifeworld. Demands for justice and emotional reactions, often in the form of moral shocks, are responses to crises; anger, anxiety, and indignation become the triggers that impel and propel social movements.[17] But emotional reactions do not lead to social movements per se. *The crisis-engendered collective emotions must be interpreted within the existing frames, or the emergent new frames, that resonate with the actor's social location, networks, identity, character structure, and values to impel joining or creating the organizations of actors in which alternative understandings, visions, and even identities can be negotiated whilst actors engage in collective struggles toward social change.* This engagement can be seen as an attempt to retain or recreate meaningful, gratifying identities and lifestyles at the level of social integration rather than redistribution.

The Economic Aspect. *The recent crises must be understood as structural crises in which the "steering mechanisms" of capitalism failed.* Neoliberalism, with its disdain for state controls and regulations and celebration of the "freedom of the marketplace," led to the 2007–2008 collapse of financial markets. The dreams of short-term profits based on speculation turned into nightmares. When the subprime mortgage crisis hit, the financial bubble burst, and the stock market plummeted. This was followed by a wave of bankruptcies and devastating layoffs and unemployment for many workers, especially the vulnerable "precariat." The monetary value of many pension funds evaporated. Economic stagnation followed. The meltdown led many

---

16. Jürgen Habermas, *Legitimation Crisis* (Boston: Beacon, 1975).
17. James Jasper, *The Art of Moral Protest: Culture, Biography, and Creativity in Social Movements* (Chicago: University of Chicago Press, 1999).

ordinary people to question the very legitimacy of neoliberal capitalism. Although, according to many statistical measures, the economy has "recovered," stock markets are up, and construction as well as new car sales are up, a closer inspection reveals that income growth has been stagnant and that the majority of new jobs are at lower levels of skill and pay. With affordable housing on the decline and student loans escalating, approximately one-third of college students now live at home with their parents.[18]

The Political Aspect. The political system attempts to regulate the economic system in order to make possible the profit-making of the elites and the legitimacy of global capital while minimizing the negative trends that may lead to discontent, protest, and domestic disturbances or upheavals. Capitalist states face a twofold problem of maintaining the profitability of the monopoly sector and the low-wage competitive sector while sustaining the legitimacy of the system by providing citizens with infrastructure and entitlements that maintain both economic growth (profits) and promote social peace and harmony. These two main functions are often contradictory insofar as the state must appear "neutral."[19] The modern state serves to control markets in such a way as to minimize volatility and secure the general conditions of capital accumulation, but, at the same time, it needs to tax the citizenry to provide functioning infrastructure and social benefits. Moreover, in the time of financial crisis, the state is the only institution with the resources to deal with its consequences.

The legitimacy of the U.S. state, and many others across the world, was challenged by the meltdown and subsequent bailouts that helped the elites who had rigged the system. In 2011, the Occupy Wall Street protesters chanted, "The banks got bailed out, we got sold out." While the economy was stabilized at great cost to the vast majority of people, the result was

---

18. "In 2012, 36% of the nation's young adults ages 18 to 31—the so-called Millennial generation—were living in their parents' home, according to a new Pew Research Center analysis of U.S. Census Bureau data. This is the highest share in at least four decades and represents a slow but steady increase over the 32% of their same-aged counterparts who were living at home prior to the Great Recession in 2007 and the 34% doing so when it officially ended in 2009. A record total of 21.6 million Millennials lived in their parents' home in 2012, up from 18.5 million of their same aged counterparts in 2007." Richard Fry, "A Rising Share of Young Adults Live in Their Parents' Home: A Record 21.6 Million in 2012," Pew Research Center, August 1, 2013, available at http://www.pewsocialtrends.org/2013/08/01/a-rising-share-of-young-adults-live-in-their-parents-home/. "In fact, the nation's 18- to 34-year-olds are less likely to be living independently of their families and establishing their own households today than they were in the depths of the Great Recession." Richard Fry, "More Millennials Living with Family Despite Improved Job Market," Pew Research Center, July 29, 2015, available at http://www.pewsocialtrends.org/2015/07/29/more-millennials-living-with-family-despite-improved-job-market/.

19. James O'Connor, *The Fiscal Crisis of the State* (New York: Palgrave Macmillan, 1973).

a "global slump," with high unemployment, especially for the young. The state was seen as boosting the profits of "the 1 percent"—the Occupy Wall Street epithet for the wealthy elite and powerful. The protests in the squares, streets, and other public sites were directed against the governments and challenged their legitimacy. More often than not, they were met with ruthless violence that quelled the protests for the time being but, at the same time, also inspired future mobilizations. Nevertheless, it should be noted that in some cases, as evidenced, for example, in the rise of Syriza in Greece and Podemos in Spain, organic intellectuals can organize discontent, fashion political movements, and gain political power.[20] Perhaps the same discontent, progressive mobilization, and hope have found their expression in the strong support for Bernie Sanders's presidential campaign in the United States, notwithstanding the very low historical odds for a left-wing outsider to get a presidential nomination, let alone win the election.

The Cultural Aspect. The cultural system of meanings, values, norms, and interpretations of reality express the identity of the society, regulate conduct, and maintain cohesion and integration. The values of every society are shaped by the ruling classes to sustain their power. But today we see questions about the cultural values that underpin enormous wealth for the elites. Today, large numbers of youth, perhaps as many as 50 percent, have become much more sympathetic to socialism, especially since the equation of socialism with the long-past eras of Stalin and Mao falls on deaf ears. The protests and mobilizations seek more than economic redress; millions of youth seek a major social-cultural transformation informed by the visions of an alternative system based on human needs, democratic communities, and careers that provide individual self-realization, creativity, and dignity.

The Utopian Aspect. Movements depend on the shared interpretations of reality and the frameworks that explain the causes and consequences of adversities as well as the goals to be attained and the strategies to attain them. Marx generally rejected utopian socialism as such, but emancipatory possibilities came with the transcendence of private property—namely, the cultivation of artistry, caring, creativity, curiosity, empathy, faith, honor, humor, love, sensitivity, and other virtues celebrated by healthy, life-appreciating people everywhere. Utopian values contain the critique of the contradictions of capitalism, which thwarts their realization, since promoting human good would cut profits. As Russell Jacoby pointed out, there is a vital legacy of "messianic" utopianism in Critical Theory that envisions more than a just, egalitarian,

---

20. The question of how effective Syriza has been and will be remains open, as the terms of the Greek bailout are still dictated by the Troika (the European Commission, the European Central Bank, and the International Monetary Fund), and the long-run consequences are impossible to predict from this vantage point.

democratic version of contemporary society but also a radical transformation of society into the postcapitalist forms in which private property is no longer the defining feature.[21] The utopianism found in Martin Buber, Ernst Bloch, Walter Benjamin, Erich Fromm, and Herbert Marcuse is imperative for understanding contemporary movements. But this utopia is not so much spelled out; rather, it is a critique of domination, anchored within the character structure, embodied within the state institutions, and valorized by hegemonic ideologies. When moving from necessity to freedom, human fulfillment can take place in various forms, which cannot be specified or predicted in advance. Utopian goals require locating the desirable within the dialectic of the undesirable—namely, within the conditions created by existing political and hegemonic ideologies that entail their own negation. The overcoming of alienation and domination would transform work from the necessity for bare survival to the expression of human creativity and fulfillment that would enable the free development of each and the free development of all.

Hegemony

Following Marcuse's notions of one-dimensional thought, new sensibilities, and the Great Refusal and Habermas's theory of legitimation crises, Gramsci's theory of hegemony complements the Critical Theory tradition in explaining how hegemony, as the ideological control of culture, fosters the willing assent to the power and domination of the given historic bloc. Today, neoliberalism as an ideology valorizes and celebrates the financial, political, and intellectual elites. Hegemony normalizes that which is historically arbitrary; renders domination natural, normal, and in the "best interests of all"; and thereby sustains the political and economic power of particular historic blocs. Hegemony is just "common sense," as opposed to that which, for Gramsci, is the "folklore" of philosophy and may assume countless different forms but, for the most part, is fragmentary, incoherent, and inconsequential. On the other hand, hegemonic ideologies serve to buttress power, prevent critical thought and action, and thereby sustain domination.

Intellectuals, teachers, professors, journalists, novelists, artists, religious leaders, and others, drawn from the coalitions of groups that share a common interest in holding onto power, generally collude in creating and articulating a more or less integrated hegemonic ideology. This begins with the "expert" advice over child-rearing values and practices, school curricula, religion, and mass media, especially the news and popular culture, as well as the high culture that collectively and systematically produces worldviews and understandings that legitimate existing class relations and political

---

21. Russell Jacoby, *Picture Imperfect: Utopian Thought for an Anti-Utopian Age* (New York: Columbia University Press, 2005), 127.

leadership. "National themes" in collective celebrations and rituals affirm and augment the current society, glorifying its governance and its leaders past and present. Dissenters are marginalized as traitors and pathological characters, as deviant and bizarre. Gramsci's analysis enables us to bridge critique and alternative visions with praxis as philosophically informed political activity. This is why he called his work "the philosophy of praxis."[22]

But how and why do people assent to values, worldviews, and understandings that are the basis of their domination and subjugation? While Gramsci was a communist organizer, he was, however, quite critical of the economism of the party. He placed more emphasis on the subjectivity of the worker and the collective will of the masses, which unfortunately had been colonized and corrupted by hegemonic ideologies. These ideologies affected the structures and processes of socialization to produce general worldviews, values, and understandings that masked the ways in which the system operates. To illuminate the *willing* part of the "willing assent," the Frankfurt School provided a critical social psychology of emotions, explaining how ideologies were actively internalized and incorporated within the individual character, self, and identity. They provided the motivational basis for (1) the "willing assent" to domination based on the colonized feelings, emotions, and desires that became the intrinsic components of character structure and (2) the cognitive processes that led to the active denial of the validity of alternative claims and the denigration of the claimants.

In other words, people employ what has been called "motivated reasoning" to accept certain "information" or "evidence" that is consistent with their own values and colonized identities, while rejecting and denying what is inconsistent with their beliefs and self-images. Thus, identity acts as either a facilitator or a barrier to particular worldviews, cognitive frameworks, and understandings, which in turn motivate both reasoning and action. The shaping of the character structure generally serves the political and economic interests of the elites, but it also engenders human suffering, which in turn may foster resistance and contestation. Capitalist domination alienates and frustrates basic human needs for community, agency, recognition, and self-fulfillment. *This contradiction between the demands of the system and the thwarting of human fulfillment, experienced in the times of crises, becomes the opening for counterhegemonic mobilization.*

Counterhegemony

How do we mediate between critique and action? Domination fosters resistance, but how does resistance get organized and channeled to foster social

---

22. Antonio Gramsci, "Some Problems in the Study of the Philosophy of Praxis," in Gramsci, *Selections from the Prison Notebooks*, 381–419.

change? Organic intellectuals from subordinated classes, often themselves the victims of the adversities of capital, find themselves in strategically significant positions for organizing resistance. By bent of character, experience, and formal or informal education or training, they become aware of the contradictions in the system, particularly the chasm between the hegemonic ideology crafted by the elites and the actual life conditions for the subalterns who "willingly assent" to being dominated.

According to Gramsci, the "organic intellectual" acquires the type of critical education typically reserved for the elites. Moreover, having roots and ties to the subordinate classes, these individuals are aware of the experienced, if not articulated, ambivalence of subaltern classes and, in turn, the extent to which they may be open to, or resistant toward, counterhegemonic discourses. As Chris Hedges puts it:

> No revolt can succeed without professional revolutionists . . . [who] live outside the formal structures of society. They are financially insecure. . . . They dedicate their lives to fomenting radical change. They do not invest energy in appealing to power to reform. They are prepared to break the law. They, more than others, recognize the fragility of the structures of authority. They are embraced by a vision that makes compromise impossible. Revolution is their full-time occupation. And no revolution is possible without them. . . . Largely unseen by the wider society, they have severed themselves from the formal structures of power. They have formed collectives and nascent organizations dedicated to overthrowing the corporate state. . . . All revolutionary upheavals are built by these entities.[23]

Few academics have the background and the required experience, organizational skills, and available time for the nitty-gritty of social organization and mobilization. Nevertheless, the analyses and critiques of political and economic domination, along with the deconstruction of hegemonic ideologies, are extremely important tasks and absolutely necessary antecedents for developing counterhegemonic narratives. Theorists as varied as Georg Simmel, W.E.B. Du Bois, and Frantz Fanon have talked about "dual consciousness," the ability to navigate between different, often contradictory, worldviews and social networks. The realms of critique and political activism come together in fashioning counterhegemonic discourses, alternative visions, and the critical understandings of the nature of social reality as well

---

23. Chris Hedges, "Why We Need Professional Revolutionists," *Truthdig*, November 24, 2014, available at http://www.truthdig.com/report/item/why_we_need_professional _revolutionists_20141123.

as engaging in the ideological struggles that make actual political transformation possible.

Typically, intellectuals, especially those trained formally or informally in critical theorizing, understand the world in far more complex ways than many ordinary people. The organic intellectual, coming from the subaltern classes, is in a different position to influence subalterns than is the elite scholar. He or she better understands the lifeworld of the workers and knows how to encourage them to comprehend their situation and envision the alternatives. He or she also has a legitimacy in their eyes that an outsider would have to work hard to earn. For Gramsci, every person is an implicit intellectual, a "naive" philosopher, who tries to make sense out of his or her world. Moreover, at some level, most people become aware of the gap between the dominant culture (ideology) and the actual conditions of their lives. That dissonance creates openings for contestation, especially when crises render the legitimacy of the system problematic. Organic intellectuals understand that the political struggles must begin with the demystification of the dominant ideology. This is why the most significant part of their work consists of organizing so-called wars of position in which hegemonic ideologies are challenged through "popular education" that offers not only critique but also a counterhegemonic discourse. Organic intellectuals, as the bearers of counterhegemonic visions, illuminate the contradictions of class, power, and dominant ideologies and articulate alternatives that have the potential to transform mass consciousness deadened by the siren song of capitalist consumerism.

Contradictions are especially evident during times of crisis when people become more receptive to critique and alternative visions. During crises, people may withdraw their loyalty from the existing social order, creating spaces for alternative views, values, understandings, and even identities. They may become more receptive to organic intellectuals who enable people to see through the contradictions, illusions, and distortions of hegemonic ideologies and better understand their own circumstances.

As Gramsci found out, because of the passivity and fatalism of the Italian workers and their embrace of Catholicism, there were major cultural barriers to the embrace of communism. As Fabio de Nardis and Loris Caruso explain, "Social transformation is a function of the creative role of the masses and of the political ability to articulate a revolutionary consciousness."[24] From this point of view, the role of organic intellectuals becomes crucial, as the subjective barriers for the development of radical subjectivity among the mass of workers are immense. As Gramsci writes, "Every revolution

---

24. Fabio de Nardis and Loris Caruso, "Political Crisis and Social Transformation in Antonio Gramsci: Elements for a Sociology of Political Praxis," *International Journal of Humanities and Social Science* 1, no. 6 (2011): 14.

has been preceded by an intense labor of criticism, by the diffusion of culture and the spread of ideas amongst masses of men."[25] As de Nardis and Caruso well summarize, "The basic themes of his writings, therefore, concern the clear rejection of mechanistic and economistic interpretations of Marx's doctrine and the adherence to a fully historicist and humanist form of Marxism. Marxism is for Gramsci not only an economic science, but first and foremost a worldview that points to an intellectual and moral reform of society."[26]

Social transformation then depends on a prior cultural transformation of consciousness that overcomes the existing ideology of the status quo in order to enable a different kind of political economy and social organization.

> If the revolution is primarily a process of cultural reform, then both intellectuals and the party, interacting with the popular masses, must work toward the development of a political consciousness and a collective will, corresponding to the elaboration of a historically rooted ideology of transformation. If the aim is the revolutionary seizure of power, it is also true that the subaltern classes, in order to be successful, must work towards creating the conditions for transformation, aiming to be an ideologically hegemonic class well before becoming the dominant social group.[27]

According to Gramsci, culture is the terrain for revolutionary struggle, where "wars of position" are necessary before "wars of maneuver." A "war of position" is a process that "slowly builds up the strength of the social foundations of a new state" by "creating alternative institutions or alternative intellectual resources within existing society."[28] Organic intellectuals, understanding the salience of the dominant culture, are essential for organizing workers, and organic intellectuals must be in a dialectical relationship with the mass of workers. "How classes live" determines how people view their worlds and act within them and, perhaps most importantly, "shapes their ability to imagine how [the world] can be changed, and whether they can see such changes as feasible or desirable."[29]

Thus, instead of offering workers economics or history lessons, organic intellectuals provide alternative cultural understandings that undermine

---

25. Antonio Gramsci, *Selections from Political Writings, 1910–1920*, ed. Quintin Hoare, trans. John Mathews (New York: International, 1977), 12.

26. de Nardis and Caruso, "Political Crisis and Social Transformation in Antonio Gramsci," 14.

27. Ibid.

28. Robert Cox, "Gramsci, Hegemony and International Relations: An Essay in Method," *Millennium: Journal of International Studies* 12, no. 2 (1983): 162–175.

29. Kate Crehan, *Gramsci, Culture and Anthropology* (London: Pluto, 2002), 71.

and erode the received understandings (e.g., "common sense") that sustains the system. They open possibilities for imagining alternatives by showing what people's lives might be like in a more equitable, democratic, and just society and contrasting that with the existing society in which everyday life is a struggle and is without the possibilities of genuine freedom, transcendence, and self-fulfillment, in addition to being torn asunder by episodic crises.

Organic intellectuals understand the underlying resentment that workers may have about the system but that they are reluctant to articulate because of the fear of being ostracized by others and the anxiety that might come from an uncertain future. The key repressive strength of religion qua hegemonic ideology is that it sustains solidarity, assuages anxiety, and hence acts as a barrier against social change. This is why the initial task of organic intellectuals is the formulation of counterhegemonic discourses that not only critique the existing hegemonic frameworks but also suggest other, more fulfilling alternatives. Organizing successful resistance requires a long and difficult struggle because the struggle is focused on centuries-old cultural frameworks.

Much of Gramsci's work refers to workers, trade unions, and factory councils at the time when production was predominantly Fordist. Conditions changed. For Marcuse, writing three decades later, the stimulating agents of progressive change are more likely to be the young people, students, and marginalized minorities. Today, another fifty years later, it appears that the growing precariat, which includes the same marginalized groups mentioned by Marcuse, can spearhead social and political change. By their very existence, the members of the precariat question the legitimacy of the system as well as the legitimacy of political leaders who are either indifferent to popular concerns or openly hostile, repressive, and violent.

During the recent mobilizations, some activist groups called themselves the "indignant ones." This is why some scholars claimed that the quest and demand for recognition and dignity is more significant for the occupiers or activists than material gain.[30] The struggles in the cultural and ideological realm are more salient for the rebels of today than the purely material issues.

Contesting Domination

From Grievances to Action

Hierarchical societies generate dissatisfaction and discontent. One of the functions of hegemonic ideologies is to suppress, normalize, and mollify

---

30. Benjamín Tejerina, Ignacia Perugorría, Tova Benski, and Lauren Langman, "From Indignation to Occupation: A New Wave of Global Mobilization," *Current Sociology* 61, no. 4 (2013): 377–392; Manuel Castells, *Networks of Outrage and Hope* (Malden, MA: Polity, 2012).

the alienated masses. This has been seen in the functioning of religion as an "opiate." Unlike the premodern modes of production, capitalism, as Marx has shown, requires a constant change, the so-called creative destruction to gain ever greater profits; however, the constant change in production, transportation, communication, finance, entertainment, and leisure generates dysfunctions and crises. The Fordist mode of production created vast wealth, and, eventually, organized resistance articulated by trade union movements brought into existence the relatively affluent working class. However, as Marcuse noted in *One-Dimensional Man*, the working class was increasingly diverted from radicalism by the consumerist ideology of mass culture, which eroded its class consciousness and revolutionary potential.

Because of the processes of globalization and the emergence of digital technologies, with post-Fordist flexible production based on the "just in time" arrival of components, automation, and import substitution, many jobs—on the basis of which the working class built its affluence—disappeared. At the same time, the antiunion campaigns were successful, leading to the erosion of living standards for most workers who either became unemployed or were forced to take low-paying jobs. This generated a great deal of anger and resentment, and dominant, hegemonic intellectuals attempted to shift the blame onto the victims of the system, such as racial minorities and undocumented workers, as well as onto supposedly liberal government policies. This was soon followed by the financial crisis of 2007–2008 and the wave of repressive austerity and retrenchment policies, which gave rise to the 2011 progressive mobilizations across the world. Millions took to the streets and protested, but there has been very little immediate structural change of significance, though change may come.[31]

The Party: Organize or Perish

In the 1930s, when Gramsci wrote his major works, the Communist Party was the only significant political organization dedicated to the fundamental transformation of capitalism. While communist or socialist parties were *not* the major actors in the various uprisings in recent years, in some cases they did play important roles, especially in the 2010–2011 Tunisian uprising and

---

31. In Tunisia, there was democratization of governance but not the economy. In Chile and Quebec, tuition hikes were rescinded without any fundamental changes in the nature of governance. Syriza, as we note earlier in this chapter, came to power in Greece in January 2015, when its party chairman Alexis Tsipras became prime minister, but Syriza has not radically changed economic policies. Its Spanish cousin, Podemos, formed in 2014 in the aftermath of the radical 2011 Movimiento 15-M (15-M Movement) or Indignados (Indignants) movement, quickly grew into Spain's second largest political party and in May 2016 formed the electoral alliance Unidos Podemos with other parties. To date, Podemos, like Syriza, uses anti-austerity rhetoric but pursues rather mainstream Left reformist policy proposals.

the election of a secular government in December 2014. Why was that the case? Tunisia, a former French colony, was a relatively secular country and had a vibrant civil society with a number of progressive nongovernmental organizations (NGOs) and social-movement organizations (SMOs), especially labor unions and women's organizations. Its universities were secular and included extensive liberal-arts programs, quite unlike the universities of many other countries in the Middle East and North Africa, in which education is largely either technical or, more often, religious.[32]

Thus, in Tunisia, after many years of stagnation, ever growing inequality, hardships, and dissatisfaction with the government, compounded by the WikiLeaks revelations of corruption of the ruling Ben Ali family, the self-immolation of a fruit peddler became the catalyst for massive demonstrations in Tunisia and then elsewhere. The bulk of the demonstrators were young people. Broad coalitions quickly formed, thanks in large part to the existing networks of progressive organizations and the widespread use of the Internet. From this example, we can conclude that a social movement requires not only organic intellectuals and counterhegemonic discourses but also social organizations with dedicated, professional revolutionaries fully committed to long-term struggles to achieve social and political change. Absent such organizations and leadership, we have the passions of Occupy as well as its brief history.

Virtual Public Spheres

Organizing social movements today is both more difficult and easier than in the past. The potential actors of today—college students, minorities, and certain members of the precariat—have much more diverse class positions and are generally more geographically dispersed. Today's college students who take liberal-arts and social-science classes are likely to be exposed to a variety of critical perspectives, even in those cases when the professors are not especially radical.

Moreover, the importance of the Internet should be stressed, especially insofar as the Internet enables the proliferation of a number of "virtual public spheres," providing a great deal of critical, up-to-date information as well as the space for various debates.[33] The Internet made possible the formation of the variety of transnational activist networks and "internetworked social movements."[34] In the 2011 uprisings, for instance, computers, cell phones,

---

32. Neither the United States nor the European Union will intervene to defend freedom and democracy in any country unless that country possesses geopolitically important raw materials and resources. Tunisia is the case in point.

33. Lauren Langman, "From Virtual Public Spheres to Global Justice: A Critical Theory of Internetworked Social Movements," *Sociological Theory* 23, no. 1 (2005): 42–74.

34. Ibid.

tablets, and social media played important roles in organizing and directing the mobilizations and occupations in real time: activists received information about where to gather and what routes to avoid, and they were able to act in concert even if they numbered in the tens of thousands. While it is true that the movements in each country had some unique features, the Internet was able to keep millions informed and connected around the globe.

Digital Memory

Even though the uprisings of 2010–2011 have waned and receded from public attention, it is evident that these mobilizations are far from being forgotten. There now exist thousands of blogs, websites, and YouTube videos in which the critiques and analyses by various progressive and radical intellectuals remain accessible. There are also many websites that present well-informed, cogent, radical critiques of the capitalist status quo.[35] Moreover, the ongoing critical analyses provided by radical public intellectuals such as Noam Chomsky, Cornel West, Chris Hedges, Richard Wolff, and Naomi Klein are only a mouse click or app button away. These analyses and critiques, unlike the mass-media reports of the civil-rights, feminist, and antiwar movements of the 1960s, are relatively free of corporate control and censorship.

Cohort Flow

As one surveys the political landscape of the United States and beyond, the conditions for a sustained political rebellion from the Left appear almost nonexistent. As Gramsci said, these are times that bring the "pessimism of the intellect" but demand the "optimism of the will."[36] The reactionary forces of the populist Right, coupled with the fundamentalist evangelicals and neoliberal technocratic elites, seem formidable. Throughout the European Union, various right-wing, if not openly fascist, organizations are growing. Where the Left has gained strength, for example in Latin America and in southern Europe, it is presently being challenged and disciplined by austerity and reaction.

The wealth and seeming influence of global capital and the near invisibility of strong radical organizations can no doubt give rise to pessimism. Because such pessimism itself precludes the possibilities of change, current conditions require a more critical examination. For Gramsci, the old system

---

35. See, for example, *Alternet* (http://www.alternet.org), *Democracy Now!* (http://www.democracynow.org), Occupy Wall Street (http://occupy.org), *Popular Resistance* (https://www.popularresistance.org), the *Real News Network* (http://therealnews.com/t2), *Truthdig* (http://www.truthdig.com), and *Truthout* (http://www.truth-out.org).

36. Gramsci, *Selections from the Prison Notebooks*, 175.

is dying, but the new cannot yet be born. This is why we have to move beyond the prevailing pessimism to envision utopian alternatives in the tradition of Marx, Fromm, and Marcuse. The growing inequality and the rising precariat, together with the speculative essence of finance capital, are the harbingers of further crises. Young people and minority communities have borne the brunt of the adverse consequences of neoliberalism in general and the subsequent economic implosion during and in the aftermath of the 2007–2008 crisis. In many European countries, unemployment among young adults remains very high, with rates of 52.4 percent in Greece and 53.2 percent in Spain in 2014.[37] In the United States, approximately 30 percent of college students move back home after finishing their studies, unable to afford rent, college loans, and the essentials of what is considered a "normal" lifestyle.[38] As has been noted by scholars such as Marcuse and Habermas, such youth are the primary agents for social and political change.

What is to be done? The critique of domination is the essential task for organic intellectuals who mediate between critical theories and political praxis. They critique the cultural realms such as religion, education, liberal-democratic ideology, and media, which mask the domination of capital and sustain hegemony. They organize and wage "wars of position" where an emancipatory critique articulates hope and the vision of a society where caring and sharing displace greed and indifference; where love and community trump anger, hatred, and exclusion; where creative self-fulfillment displaces banal conformity; and where people find dignity, instead of humiliation.

But how does this happen? We should consider the importance of generational change, observed by Karl Mannheim almost a century ago.[39] The social, political, and economic context of every generation shapes its worldview and endures as each cohort ages, matures, and becomes the mainstream of society. While each generation may itself be exposed to very different conditions, what is especially evident today is how the younger generations seem to be notably more progressive as evidenced by their support for government intervention into the economy. Half of American youth support socialism. Contemporary youth have become racially tolerant, open to differences of gender and sexual orientation, and embrace diverse lifestyles ranging from gay marriage to cohabitation to puffing weed.

Moreover, some of these values are responses to the fundamental changes in the character structure fostered by new social realities. Growing numbers

---

37. "Unemployment Statistics," *Eurostat*, May 31, 2016, available at http://ec.europa.eu/eurostat/statistics-explained/index.php/Unemployment_statistics.

38. Fry, "A Rising Share of Young Adults Live in Their Parents' Home"; Fry, "More Millennials Living with Family."

39. Karl Mannheim, "The Problem of Generations," in *Essays in the Sociology of Knowledge* (London: Routledge, 1952), 276–322.

of young people are not simply aware of the adverse conditions of their lives, but they are especially receptive to the arguments and analyses of various progressive organic intellectuals. Many have given up on the existing political system in favor of an amorphous but democratic anarchism.[40] This is a good starting point, because it exposes youth to counterhegemonic critiques and alternatives and encourages them to enter various activist communities.

Conclusion: Whither Mobilization?

As Marx revealed, capitalism rests on inherent contradictions of ownership and ever changing market factors resulting in inevitable crises. Yet class reproduction over time, notwithstanding crises, is maintained by the combination of ideological justifications, character structures, and emotional dispositions to consent. Nevertheless, amid crises, we often see various kinds of resistance, from sabotage to retreatist forms of cultural escapism; moreover, long-standing grievances may erupt, fostering from below progressive social movements that seek ameliorative social changes ranging from reforms to uprisings and revolutions.

The recent cycle of mobilizations—generated in the wake of the 2007–2008 financial crisis—confirms the historical pattern: (1) when existing class relationships and elite leadership prove dysfunctional, corrupt, or both and/or (2) when their legitimating ideologies (promising inclusion and a "glorious" future) are in conflict with actual realities of fragmentation, conflict, or declining wealth and power, mobilizations may ensue.

Current conditions (e.g., rising inequality, austerity, bleak job prospects for youth) are fostering fundamental changes in the character structure, subjective values, and aspirations. Much like in the 1960s, many of today's young people feel alienated from the capitalist system and its dehumanizing culture of competition, shallow consumerism, endless war, and inordinate waste. Unlike in the 1960s, however, we now face economic stagnation and, for

---

40. Those who are engaged in electoral politics are increasingly moved to support progressive candidates, such as, in the United States, Jill Stein (Green Party) and Bernie Sanders (the democratic socialist senator from Vermont)—both of whom attracted many youth and young adults to their campaigns during the 2016 U.S. presidential election season. Senator Sanders was more highly regarded by the U.S. public than the eventual nominees of the two major parties—the Republican Party's Donald J. Trump and the Democratic Party's Hillary Rodham Clinton. Frank Newport and Andrew Dugan, "Clinton Still Has More Negatives among Dems than Sanders," *Gallup*, June 16, 2016, http://www.gallup.com/opinion/polling-matters/192362/clinton-negatives-among-dems-sanders.aspx. Sanders's critiques of the injustices of the capitalist system seem to have hit some very responsive chords, and his rallies attracted tens of thousands of people. The enthusiasm generated by his campaign suggests that more and more people in the United States support fundamental political and social changes; however, whether such transformation can be achieved through the Democratic Party remains very questionable.

most people, the first genuine encounter with "inverted totalitarianism."[41] These factors give rise to widespread anger and indignation, which, in turn, may lead to openness to change and receptivity for the traditions of dialectical critique, including the critical insights of Marx and Marcuse.

The primary task for contemporary organic intellectuals is to keep the critical tradition alive and adapt it to our times. Progressive change must begin with the multidimensional critique that is as much concerned with the critique of the prevailing domination as with offering imaginative visions of alternative futures. Such a change will require many dedicated organic intellectuals to organize and mobilize the "wars of position" in order to transform the capitalist culture of greed, selfish profit-making, blatant inequality, discrimination, and environmental destruction. The winds of change are blowing, although, admittedly, progressive mobilizations are still weak relative to the power of economic and political opposition. What is certain, however, is that the Frankfurt School's critical approach to capitalist hegemony, focusing on the cultural and psychological aspects as well as on the political and economic, as elaborated in the works of Fromm and Marcuse, and brought together with the activist counterhegemonic analysis and strategies of Gramsci, provide us with the needed "optimism of the will."

---

41. The basic contradiction of capitalism is the class-based ownership of private property and competing interests between labor and capital; however, there are also other contradictions: ideologies of freedom, equality, and brotherhood mask domination, inequality, and antagonisms between classes. Capital extolls democracy while actual power is wielded by the financial elites that control the state—what Sheldon Wolin has called "inverted totalitarianism." Sheldon Wolin, *Democracy Incorporated: Managed Democracy and the Specter of Inverted Totalitarianism* (Princeton, NJ: Princeton University Press, 2008).

Afterword

The Great Refusal in a One-Dimensional Society

Arnold L. Farr and Andrew T. Lamas

"A comfortable, smooth, reasonable, democratic unfreedom prevails in advanced civilization, a token of technical progress."[1] This opening line in Herbert Marcuse's famous book, *One-Dimensional Man*, is constituted by a series of words that seem incompatible. How can *comfortable*, *smooth*, *reasonable*, and *democratic* be used to describe *unfreedom*? On first reading, the sentence itself appears contradictory; however, Marcuse's assertion merely reflects contradictions he observes in advanced technocapitalism.[2] Capitalist society places human subjectivity and freedom under erasure as it whittles down the possibility of critical consciousness by encouraging conformity and positive thinking amid the oppressive order of things. Thus, unfreedom may appear democratic in the sense that individuals seem to comply freely with their domination and exploitation. In *One-Dimensional Man*, Marcuse explores various social mechanisms that work to diminish critical subjectivity in such a way that people submit or give support to the economic, political, and social systems by which they are damaged and oppressed.

---

1. Herbert Marcuse, *One-Dimensional Man: Studies in the Ideology of Advanced Industrial Society* (Boston: Beacon, 1964), 1.

2. The concept of "technocapitalism"—the matrix of capital and technology—was introduced in Douglas Kellner, "Techno-capitalism," in *Critical Theory, Marxism, and Modernity* (Cambridge: Polity, 1989), 176–203. See also Andrew Feenberg, *Critical Theory of Technology* (New York: Oxford University Press, 1991); and Stephen Best and Douglas Kellner, *The Postmodern Adventure: Science, Technology, and Cultural Studies at the Third Millennium* (New York: Guilford, 2001).

But, historically, the erasure has never been complete. Popular struggles of resistance rise and rise again. The Great Refusal is Marcuse's concept for resistance—for freedom dreams and the struggle for liberation in and against a one-dimensional society.

The Great Refusal—"the protest against that which is"[3] and "the protest against unnecessary repression, the struggle for the ultimate form of freedom"[4]—is arguably Marcuse's most potent concept because of its *radically democratic* nature. "The Great Refusal takes a variety of forms."[5] It is accessible to all by their reason and emotion. It is intuitively understood by all who have not turned their backs on humanity. It is a shield and a sword for all who choose to resist oppression, injustice, and humiliation. The Great Refusal is the instinctual and philosophical *No!* that generates the revolutionary *Yes!* It is the soul force of the fight back. Its praxis can be at once restorative amid dehumanization and a political force that generates solidarities for confronting structures of domination. It is the ground of revolutionary subjectivity. It is the foundation of the blues and the general strike.[6]

As Douglas Kellner writes in his introduction to the second edition of *One-Dimensional Man*, "The legacy of the 1960s, of which Marcuse was a vital part, lives on, and the Great Refusal is still practiced by oppositional groups and individuals who refuse to conform to existing oppression and domination."[7] Elsewhere, Kellner suggests that the Great Refusal may even be "the starting point for political activism in the contemporary era."[8]

Substantial evidence exists for the contemporary resurgence of the Great Refusal—not only as a concept for critical theoretical analysis but also for the popular articulation of resistance and political solidarity. In opposition to austerity measures in Europe in the wake of the global financial crisis of 2007–2008, common bonds of solidarity were formed within and among countries by use of the language of refusal: *¡Basta!* (Enough!) in Spain and Όχι! (No!) in Greece became the slogans for massive demonstrations, occupations, and new political formations of the Left. Mohamed Bouazizi, the Tunisian street vendor who set himself on fire on December 17, 2010, in response to state-sponsored humiliation and harassment, became a catalyst for

3. Marcuse, *One-Dimensional Man*, 66.

4. Herbert Marcuse, *Eros and Civilization: A Philosophical Inquiry into Freud* (Boston: Beacon, 1966), 149. Originally published in 1955.

5. Herbert Marcuse, *An Essay on Liberation* (Boston: Beacon, 1969), vii.

6. Andrew T. Lamas, "Accumulation of Crises, Abundance of Refusals," *Radical Philosophy Review* 19, no. 1 (2016): 3.

7. Douglas Kellner, "Introduction to the Second Edition," in *One-Dimensional Man: Studies in the Ideology of Advanced Industrial Society*, 2nd ed., by Herbert Marcuse (Boston: Beacon, 1991), xxxix.

8. Douglas Kellner, "From *1984* to *One-Dimensional Man*: Reflections on Orwell and Marcuse," *Current Perspectives in Social Theory* 10 (1990): 248.

the Tunisian Revolution, the Arab Spring, and occupations around the world in 2011. Suicides and protests by farmers in India's villages, by rural migrant workers in China's cities, and by miners in South Africa have catalyzed resistance movements to government policies that are facilitating corporate land grabs, debt servitude, labor exploitation, environmental destruction, and other measures of capital accumulation by repression and dispossession.

So the one-dimensional nature of our society is not the whole story. The system that creates mechanisms for domination also creates the means for liberatory struggle. Capitalism creates "its own grave-diggers,"[9] who dig in the name of the specter of liberation that hovers over them, waiting to materialize in our social world. The historical fact that domination is never total makes possible what Marcuse calls the Great Refusal. Dismantling a system of domination requires a refusal of that system. Liberation movements—as well as their liberation philosophies and theologies—are born of struggle. In the fight for abolition, as Frederick Douglass says, "If there is no struggle there is no progress. . . . Power concedes nothing without a demand. It never did and it never will."[10]

Marcuse's project of critical social theory is a two-pronged form of analysis or, we may say, a dialectical approach to social phenomena by which he studies the social, political, economic, and psychological mechanisms that produce one-dimensional thinking as well as the possibilities of refusal and liberation. In Marcusean theory, forms of resistance develop alongside mechanisms of oppression. The Great Refusal is like a specter that is present even if it is not completely visible. But what is present, even if only as a specter, is the social, political, economic, and psychological unrest that an oppressive society produces. This unrest may be manifest in many different forms. Radical subjectivity is not just one thing. It is not just expressed in one way. "The Great Refusal takes a variety of forms."[11] Marcuse's version of critical theory is unique insofar as he never tired of looking for new forms of revolutionary subjectivity. *He never abandoned the working class as the subject of revolution*; rather, he expanded the notion of class—or the understanding of oppression—beyond the orthodox interpretation of Marx's theory in order to include a variety of disenfranchised, alienated, exploited, and marginalized groups, to whom he referred as "potential catalysts of

9. Karl Marx and Frederick Engels, *The Communist Manifesto* (London: Verso, 1998), 50. Originally published in 1848.

10. Frederick Douglass, "West India Emancipation," in *Two Speeches by Frederick Douglass: One on West India Emancipation, Delivered at Canandaigua, Aug. 4th, and the Other on the Dred Scott Decision, Delivered in New York, on the Occasion of the Anniversary of the American Abolition Society, May 1857*, by Frederick Douglass (Rochester, NY: C. P. Dewey, 1857), 22, available at https://www.loc.gov/resource/mfd.21039/?sp=22.

11. Marcuse, *An Essay on Liberation*, vii.

rebellion."[12] These various groups were socially situated in such a way that they were oppressed in the one-dimensional society and had every reason to resist the present order of things.

Marcuse's awareness of the struggles of multiple social groups influenced his theorizing.[13] Many claim that Marcuse was a "guru of the student rebels" in the 1960s.[14] Rejecting this title, Marcuse argues that he was not a guru, father figure, or grandfather figure for the student activists of the 1960s. Their activism was inspired by their own experiences of repression, alienation, waste, violence, and dehumanization. Their refusals were a demand for a qualitatively different and better form of life. Thus, the Great Refusal was, for them, the critical negation of the present reality principle. Kellner notes that "even at the height of his militant enthusiasm, Marcuse never said that the counterculture and new sensibility was a *revolutionary* force."[15] Marcuse welcomes the uprising because it signals a break with repression, reveals "cracks in the system," and constitutes "a catalyst for change which may play a revolutionary role in connection with other forces, as it is contagious and may spread throughout society."[16] Kellner concludes, "Hence Marcuse's position is that the new sensibility could contribute to producing a new revolutionary movement but is not itself *the* revolutionary subject."[17]

Although Marcuse's work is Marxist in nature, his main concepts, such as the Great Refusal, tend to expand Marx's concepts. Marcuse's notion of the Great Refusal is an expansion of the Marxist concept of revolution insofar as it extends beyond revolution at the economic, and even political, level. More than just capitalism must be overthrown by revolutionary action; the grip of one-dimensional thinking, which maintains and protects capitalism, must be overthrown. The Great Refusal is not only a refusal of capitalism and its forms of exploitation and alienation but also a refusal of the social, political, cultural, psychological, and other mechanisms that reproduce and protect capitalism.

One is reminded here of Friedrich Nietzsche's theory of the transvaluation of values.[18] Nietzsche maintains that western society is permeated with values that actually work against the individual. We must always question the function of values that are handed down to us. Quite often these values are designed to benefit a particular group at the expense of others. We often

---

12. Ibid., 51.

13. Arnold L. Farr, *Critical Democratic Theory and Democratic Vision: Herbert Marcuse and Recent Liberation Philosophies* (Lanham, MD: Lexington, 2009).

14. See, for example, "One-Dimensional Philosopher," *Time* 91, no. 2 (1968): 38.

15. Douglas Kellner, *Herbert Marcuse and the Crisis of Marxism* (Berkeley: University of California Press, 1984), 286 (emphasis in original).

16. Ibid.

17. Ibid. (emphasis in original).

18. Friedrich Nietzsche, "The Antichrist," in *The Portable Nietzsche*, ed. and trans. Walter Kaufmann (1954; repr., New York: Penguin, 1982), 565–656. Essay originally written in 1888.

internalize values that devalue our own need for autonomy. The transvaluation of values does not mean that we become value free. It simply means that values are human creations and that values serve certain human purposes. There are times when certain values become obsolete or oppressive. Freedom is the ability to transcend useless or harmful values and construct new, more useful or liberating values. This position occurs again in the work of Michel Foucault.[19] Foucault's method of genealogy is Nietzschean. For Foucault, contemporary values and institutions are products and producers of relations of power. Although Marcuse uses different conceptual language, the same idea is present in his work. For example, in *An Essay on Liberation*, he writes:

> Obscenity is a moral concept in the verbal arsenal of the Establishment, which abuses the term by applying it, not to expressions of its own morality but to those of another. Obscene is not the picture of a naked woman who exposes her pubic hair but that of a fully clad general who exposes his medals rewarded in a war of aggression; obscene is not the ritual of the Hippies but the declaration of a high dignitary of the Church that war is necessary for peace.[20]

In this passage, Marcuse demonstrates the way in which morality can be ideological. What we take to be moral values may merely be ideological tools that dupe individuals into conforming to the system by which they are oppressed. In *One-Dimensional Man*, Marcuse argues that individuals tend to identify with their masters; they internalize the values of their masters. This view is consistent with the claim Marx makes in *The German Ideology*:

> The ideas of the ruling class are in every epoch the ruling ideas, i.e. the class which is the ruling material force of society, is at the same time its ruling intellectual force. The class which has the means of material production at its disposal, has control at the same time over the means of mental production, so that thereby, generally speaking, the ideas of those who lack the means of mental production are subject to it. The ruling ideas are nothing more than the ideal expression of the dominant material relationships, the dominant material relationships grasped as ideas; hence of the relationships which make the one class the ruling one, therefore, the ideas of its dominance.[21]

19. Michel Foucault, *The Archaeology of Knowledge* (New York: Routledge, 2002); Michel Foucault, *Discipline and Punish: The Birth of the Prison* (New York: Vintage, 1995); and Michel Foucault, *The History of Sexuality*, 3 vols. (New York: Pantheon, 1978–1988).

20. Marcuse, *An Essay on Liberation*, 8.

21. Karl Marx and Friedrich Engels, *The German Ideology*, in *Collected Works of Karl Marx and Friedrich Engels, 1845–47*, vol. 5, "Theses on Feuerbach," "The German Ideology"

Hence, human consciousness often develops in a way that confirms the will of the establishment. However, this is not the end of the story. In *An Essay on Liberation*, Marcuse goes on to say:

> Similarly, the sociological and political vocabulary must be radically reshaped: it must be stripped of its false neutrality; it must be methodically and provocatively "moralized" in terms of the Refusal. Morality is not necessarily and not primarily ideological. In the face of an amoral society, it becomes a political weapon, an effective force which drives people to burn their draft cards, to ridicule national leaders, to demonstrate in the streets, and to unfold signs saying, "Thou shalt not kill," in the nation's churches.[22]

No one preaches this message—the radical revolution of values—better than Martin Luther King Jr., who, on April 4, 1967, at Riverside Church in New York City, eloquently delivered these theoretically critical and radically prophetic words in an address titled "Beyond Vietnam":

> I am convinced that if we are to get on the right side of the world revolution, we as a nation must undergo a radical revolution of values. . . . [W]e must rapidly begin the shift from a thing-oriented society to a person-oriented society. When machines and computers, profit motives and property rights, are considered more important than people, the giant triplets of racism, extreme materialism, and militarism are incapable of being conquered.[23]

In rejecting Nietzsche's claim in *The Antichrist* that love for one's enemies is a sign of weakness and cowardice,[24] King—in a brilliant move of critical irony—adopts Nietzsche's formulation of the "transvaluation" or "revaluation" of values but repurposes it for the creation of a "radical love" that has the power to challenge power and change the world.

and Related Manuscripts, by Karl Marx and Friedrich Engels (New York: International, 1976), 59.

22. Marcuse, *An Essay on Liberation*, 8.

23. Martin Luther King Jr., "Beyond Vietnam," in *A Call to Conscience: The Landmark Speeches of Martin Luther King, Jr.*, ed. Clayborne Carson and Kris Shepard (New York: Warner, 2001), 157–158.

24. Friedrich Nietzsche wrote *Der Antichrist* in 1888, and it was first published in 1895. In the English translation by H. L. Mencken, the German phrase "*Umwertung aller Werte*" is translated as "the transvaluation of all values"; see Friedrich Nietzsche, *The Antichrist* (New York: Knopf, 1920). In the English translation by Walter Kaufmann, the phrase is translated as "the revaluation of all values"; see Kaufmann's preface to Nietzsche, "The Antichrist," in *The Portable Nietzsche*, ed. and trans. Walter Kaufmann (New York: Penguin, 1977), 568.

In his Riverside Church remarks, King continues to introduce critique after critique with the phrase "revolution of values." Channeling the Jewish prophets and Maimonides's critique of charity, King critically turns on charity—as it is evidence of an unjust economy. In other words, the measure of a society is how the least of its members are treated. A society requiring charity is one that is producing beggars. A restructuring of the capitalist edifice itself is required.

> A true revolution of values will soon cause us to question the fairness and justice of many of our past and present policies. On the one hand, we are called to play the Good Samaritan on life's roadside, but that will be only an initial act. One day we must come to see that the whole Jericho Road must be transformed so that men and women will not be constantly beaten and robbed as they make their journey on life's highway. True compassion is more than flinging a coin to a beggar. It comes to see that an edifice which produces beggars needs restructuring.[25]

The critique of unjust economy is then extended to the hubristic materialism of capitalist imperialism. In other words, the measure of a global society is how the least of its member countries is treated. Again, King links the production of wealth with the production of poverty:

> A true revolution of values will soon look uneasily on the glaring contrast of poverty and wealth. With righteous indignation, it will look across the seas and see individual capitalists of the West investing huge sums of money in Asia, Africa, and South America, only to take the profits out with no concern for the social betterment of the countries, and say, "This is not just." It will look at our alliance with the landed gentry of South America and say, "This is not just." The Western arrogance of feeling that it has everything to teach others and nothing to learn from them is not just.[26]

Finally, like George Orwell and Marcuse, King challenges the twisted and established conception of a world "order" that is based on violence, militarism, and war.

> A true revolution of values will lay hand on the world order and say of war, "This way of settling differences is not just." This business of burning human beings with napalm, of filling our nation's homes

---

25. King, "Beyond Vietnam," 158.
26. Ibid.

with orphans and widows, of injecting poisonous drugs of hate into the veins of peoples normally humane, of sending men home from dark and bloody battlefields physically handicapped and psychologically deranged, cannot be reconciled with wisdom, justice, and love. A nation that continues year after year to spend more money on military defense than on programs of social uplift is approaching spiritual death.[27]

This is the language of the Great Refusal—in King's words, "Somehow this madness must cease. We must stop now."[28]

The Great Refusal requires the reshaping of our vocabulary, a new sensibility, a transvaluation of values, and a reshaping of consciousness as well as the unconscious. It is a total revolution—"a true revolution of values"—that definitely requires but goes well beyond revolution at the economic level. The Great Refusal gives birth to a new morality that is no longer ideological. It is a morality that is in the interest of all members of a society. It is the negation of a false morality that encourages people to submit to oppressive forces, and it bears the promise of what King called "the beloved community."[29]

The ideas, values, and forms of human relations that have produced and maintain society in its present oppressive, repressive, wasteful, and violent state must be dismantled altogether. The old sensibility must be replaced by a new sensibility. The development of a new sensibility leads to the ascension of the life instincts (Eros) over the aggressive instincts (Thanatos). This requires the cultivation of new forms of subjectivity. It requires new forms of production, organization, and governance. It requires new relations between humanity and the larger natural ecology of which it is a part.[30] As presently constituted, human subjectivity is a product of established power relations

---

27. Ibid., 158–159.

28. Ibid., 153.

29. The philosopher and theologian Josiah Royce, who founded the Fellowship of Reconciliation, is generally credited with originating the term "the beloved community," which was then further developed and popularized by King, who was also a member of the Fellowship of Reconciliation.

30. "So, why be concerned about ecology? Because the violation of the Earth is a vital aspect of the counterrevolution. . . . [Through its resistance,] the ecological movement is attacking the 'living space' of capitalism, the expansion of the realm of profit, of waste production. However, the fight against pollution is easily co-opted. . . . In the last analysis, the struggle for the expansion of the world of beauty, nonviolence and serenity is a political struggle. The emphasis on these values, on the restoration of the Earth as a human environment, is not just a romantic, aesthetic, poetic idea which is a matter of concern only to the privileged; today, it is a question of survival. . . . Authentic ecology flows into a militant struggle for a socialist politics which must attack the system at its roots, both in the process of production and in the mutilated consciousness of individuals." Herbert Marcuse, "Ecology and Revolution," in *Collected Papers of Herbert Marcuse*, vol. 3, *The New Left and the 1960s*, ed. Douglas Kellner (New York: Routledge, 2005), 173, 175–176.

and systems of domination. We can rid society of its systems of domination only by ridding it of the forms of subjectivity produced by such systems and replacing them with new forms of subjectivity.

Marcuse sees the possibility for this kind of change in what he calls catalyst groups. Here he includes the radical currents within the Black liberation movement, the civil-rights movement, the feminist movement, the antiwar movement, the environmental movement, student activism, and other formations. With respect to these new militant and progressive groups, who might, under certain social and economic circumstances, be positioned to catalyze a broader mass resistance, Marcuse writes:

> In proclaiming the "permanent challenge" (*la contestation permanente*), the "permanent education," the Great Refusal, they recognized the mark of social repression, even in the most sublime manifestation of traditional culture, even in the most spectacular manifestations of technical progress. They have again raised a specter (and this time a specter which haunts not only the bourgeoisie but all exploitative bureaucracies): the specter of a revolution which subordinates the development of productive forces and higher standards of living to the requirements of creating solidarity for the human species, for abolishing poverty and misery beyond all national frontiers and spheres of interest, for the attainment of peace.[31]

This passage indicates that the standard for radical social movements is the demand for a total transformation of society. The specter of liberation haunts not only the bourgeoisie but "all exploitative bureaucracies"—that is, forces of domination. Hence, in some ways, the Great Refusal is perhaps more radical than the Marxist revolution. It has to be. Within the orthodox Marxist tradition, the focus is on economic exploitation, with the assumption that the working class would naturally become self-conscious and throw off its chains. But if capital—and the working class itself—is in part constituted and facilitated by White supremacy, patriarchy, and caste, among other things, then clearly oppression has multiple forms—and so, too, must resistance.

The evidence is all around us: we live at a time of an "accumulation of crises" and an "abundance of refusals."[32] In this epoch when economic and ecological crises are intensifying, existence itself seems at stake—if not for all of us now, perhaps for all future generations. As sea levels rise along with profits of the most wealthy, threatening natural and social systems of life, we also see the rise of a continuous, resistant wave of peoples' movements from below. From the Zapatistas, Seattle, and Porto Alegre to the global uprisings

---

31. Marcuse, *An Essay on Liberation*, ix–x.
32. Lamas, "Accumulation of Crises, Abundance of Refusals," 1.

of 2011 and the more recent mobilizations against austerity, global warming, mass incarceration, police brutality, White supremacy, militarization and war, land grabs, debt slavery, and more, the movements from below keep coming, but their victories and accomplishments, though sometimes mighty and impressive, find a destructive system of racialized capitalist hegemony intact—though perhaps not so *comfortable, smooth, reasonable,* and *democratic.* The neoliberal counterrevolution that began in the final years of Marcuse's life remains ascendant today, but the future remains open.

As Marcuse indicates, one-dimensional society produces various mechanisms that prohibit the development of a critical revolutionary consciousness. But the limitations of domination do not totally overwhelm the possibilities for critique and change. The contradictory, crisis-ridden nature of capitalist society produces opportunities for personal resistance and social unrest that may give birth to the broader demand for transformative social change. In the words of King, "We are confronted with the fierce urgency of now. Now let us begin. Now let us rededicate ourselves to the long and bitter, but beautiful, struggle for a new world."[33] The one-dimensional society is pregnant with its own oppositional force, the Great Refusal. There is no due date for the birth of the total transformation that the Great Refusal demands. There is only an indefinite period of labor that makes it impossible for the oppressive forces of a one-dimensional society to rest at night.

---

33. King, "Beyond Vietnam," 150.

Contributors

Kevin B. Anderson is professor of sociology, political science, and feminist studies at the University of California, Santa Barbara. His research and teaching interests are in social and political theory and especially the works of Marx and Hegel, Marxist Humanism, the Frankfurt School, Foucault, and the Orientalism debate. Writing from a dialectical and humanist perspective, he has concentrated on Marxist, Critical Theory, poststructuralist, and postcolonial traditions and on the intersections of class, race, gender, and sexuality with social theory. He has also written on critical criminological theory. He recently published an expanded edition of *Marx at the Margins: On Nationalism, Ethnicity, and Non-Western Societies* (2016). He coedited, with Russell Rockwell, *The Dunayevskaya-Marcuse-Fromm Correspondence, 1954–1978: Dialogues on Hegel, Marx, and Critical Theory* (2012).

Stanley Aronowitz teaches social theory at the City University of New York (CUNY) Graduate Center. He is coeditor of *Situations*, a journal of the Project for the Radical Imagination. He is author or editor of more than twenty-five books, most recently *Against Orthodoxy: Social Theory and Its Discontents* (2015) and *Taking It Big: C. Wright Mills and the Making of Political Intellectuals* (2012). He also wrote *Against Schooling* (2008), *Left Turn* (2006), *How Class Works* (2003), *Crisis in Historical Materialism* (1981), and *False Promises* (1973). His books and articles have been translated into French, German, Italian, Spanish, Chinese, Japanese, and Serbo-Croatian. He previously worked as a steelworker, union organizer, antipoverty administrator, and high-school planner. He taught at Staten Island Community College, Columbia University, and the University of California–Irvine.

Joan Braune is lecturer of philosophy at Gonzaga University in Spokane, Washington, and the author of the book *Erich Fromm's Revolutionary Hope: Prophetic Messianism as a Critical Theory of the Future* (2014). She has also contributed to the books *Reclaiming the Sane Society: Essays on Erich Fromm's Thought* and *We Saved the Best for You: Letters* *of Hope, Imagination, and Wisdom for 21st Century Educators* as well as to the journals *Radical Philosophy Review, Fromm Forum, Marx and Philosophy Review of Books*, and *American Catholic Philosophical Quarterly*. She is an activist in antiwar, immigration rights, and similar causes.

Jenny Chan is assistant professor of sociology at the Hong Kong Polytechnic University. Previously, she was lecturer of sociology and contemporary China studies at the School of Interdisciplinary Area Studies and a Junior Research Fellow of Kellogg College, University of Oxford. Educated at the Chinese University of Hong Kong and the University of Hong Kong, she was a Reid Research Scholar while studying at the University of London, where she received her Ph.D. in 2014. She received a Great Britain–China Educational Award for 2013–2014. Currently, she serves on the board of the International Sociological Association's Research Committee on Labor Movements. Her recent articles have appeared in *Current Sociology, Modern China, Human Relations, Critical Asian Studies, Global Labor Journal*, the *Asia-Pacific Journal*, the *South Atlantic Quarterly, New Labor Forum*, and *New Technology, Work and Employment*. She coauthored, with Yang and Xu Lizhi, *La machine est ton seigneur et ton maître*, translated by Célia Izoard (2015). Her forthcoming book from Rowman and Littlefield, coauthored with Ngai Pun and Mark Selden, is *Dying for an iPhone*.

Angela Y. Davis is the Distinguished Professor Emerita in the History of Consciousness and Feminist Studies Departments at the University of California–Santa Cruz. A former student of Herbert Marcuse, she is the author of many articles and books, including *Angela Davis: An Autobiography* (1974), *Women, Race and Class* (1981), *Blues Legacies and Black Feminism: Gertrude "Ma" Rainey, Bessie Smith, and Billie Holiday* (1998), *Are Prisons Obsolete?* (2003), *Abolition Democracy: Beyond Empire, Prisons, and Torture* (2005), *The Meaning of Freedom* (2012), and *Freedom is a Constant Struggle: Ferguson, Palestine, and the Foundations of a Movement* (2016). She is a founding member of Critical Resistance, which is dedicated to the dismantling of the prison industrial complex. She is the subject of the acclaimed documentary *Free Angela and All Political Prisoners* (2012).

Arnold L. Farr is professor of philosophy at the University of Kentucky. His research interests are German idealism, Critical Theory, Marxism, Africana philosophy, psychoanalysis, postmodernism, and liberation philosophy. He is coeditor and coauthor of *Marginal Groups and Mainstream American Culture* (2002) and author of *Critical Theory and Democratic Vision: Herbert Marcuse and Recent Liberation Philosophies* (2009). He is coeditor of "Critical Refusals," a double special issue of the *Radical Philosophy Review* (2013). He is the founder and serves on the board of the International Herbert Marcuse Society.

Andrew Feenberg is the Canada Research Chair in philosophy of technology in the School of Communication, Simon Fraser University, where he directs the Applied Communication and Technology Lab. He was a student of Herbert Marcuse. His books include *Between Reason and Experience: Essays in Technology and Modernity* (2010), *Democratizing Technology* (2006), *Heidegger and Marcuse: The Catastrophe and Redemption of History* (2005), *Transforming Technology: A Critical Theory Revisited* (2002), and *Questioning Technology* (1999). He coedited with William Leiss *The Essential Marcuse: Selected Writings of Philosopher and Social Critic Herbert Marcuse* (2007). His most recent book is *The Philosophy of Praxis: Marx, Lukács and the Frankfurt School* (2014).

Michael Forman is associate professor and member of the politics, philosophy, and economics faculty at the University of Washington–Tacoma, where he teaches social and political theory. He is author of *Nationalism and International Labor Movement: The Idea of the Nation in Socialist and Anarchist Theory* (1998). His work focuses on Critical Theory, the Enlightenment, human-rights and working-class movements, and normative innovation and global protest movements in the context of capitalist crisis. His current research aims to assess the emancipatory viability of human-rights and cosmopolitan discourses in the contemporary context.

Christian Fuchs is professor of media and communication studies at the University of Westminster. He is editor of the journal *tripleC: Communication, Capitalism and Critique* (http://www.triple-c.at) and author of more than two hundred publications, including *Emanzipation! Technik und Politik bei Herbert Marcuse* (2005), *Herbert Marcuse interkulturell gelesen* (2005), *Internet and Society: Social Theory in the Information Age* (2008), *Foundations of Critical Media and Information Studies* (2011), *Digital Labour and Karl Marx* (2014), *Social Media: A Critical Introduction* (2014), *OccupyMedia! The Occupy Movement and Social Media in Crisis Capitalism* (2014), and *Culture and Economy in the Age of Social Media* (2015).

Peter N. Funke is associate professor of politics in the School of Interdisciplinary Global Studies at the University of South Florida. He received his Ph.D. from the University of Pennsylvania and his *Vordiplom* from the Freie Universität Berlin. His research focuses on social movements and contentious politics, capitalism and class, and media and technology. He has published in various journals, including *Studies in Social Justice, Globalizations, Social Movement Studies,* and *New Media and Society.* He coedited, with Harry E. Vanden and Gary Prevost, *The New Global Politics: Social Movements in the 21st Century,* which is currently under review at Routledge. More information is available at http://www.peterfunke.net.

Stefan Gandler is professor of social theory and philosophy at Universidad Autónoma de Querétaro and Universidad Nacional Autónoma de México and has been visiting professor at the Goethe Universität Frankfurt (2001–2002), the University of California–Santa Cruz (2009–2010), and Tulane University (2015–2016). He is author of *El discreto encanto de la modernidad: Ideologías contemporáneas y su crítica* (2013), *Frankfurter Fragmente* (2013), *Fragmentos de Frankfurt* (2009), *Materialismus und Messianismus* (2008), and *Marxismo crítico en México* (2007), and he is editor of *Modernidad y diferencia* (2010). His research project *Critical Theory from the Americas* (Council for Science and Technology, CONACYT, México) analyzes the possibility of overcoming the Eurocentric limitations of the Frankfurt School, confronting its Critical Theory with contemporary sociotheoretical debates in Latin America.

Christian Garland writes and publishes in the broad tradition of Critical Theory (Frankfurt School) and focuses on the changing terms of material existence and social subjectivity as well as recent manifestations of class struggle. With degrees in philosophy and politics (B.A., University of East Anglia) and social and political thought (M.A., University of Sussex), he is working on a Ph.D. at the University of Manchester. His thesis title is "Flexible Subjects: Precarious Labour in the Contemporary UK," and it aims to critically examine the nature of social reproduction in the form of precarious work— paid and unpaid, "voluntary" and involuntary—in the contemporary United Kingdom.

His publications include "An Explosive Catalyst in the Material Base: Technology, Precarity, and the Obsolescence of Labor—One Dimensional Society, 2015" in *Radical Philosophy Review* (2016) and "Inveterate Antagonism, Recurrent Opposition: Power from Above Meeting Power from Below" in the *Heathwood Journal of Critical Theory* (2015).

Toorjo Ghose is associate professor at the School of Social Policy and Practice at the University of Pennsylvania. His work focuses on structural interventions in the areas of substance abuse, homelessness, and HIV—both at the domestic and international levels. His research examines the manner in which contextual factors such as housing, community mobilization, and organizational characteristics influence substance use and HIV risk. He is currently working with community-based agencies in New York City to study the effectiveness of providing housing as an intervention for substance-using women with HIV who have been released from prisons and jails. A second project involves a collaboration with scholars at the Treatment Research Institute in Philadelphia, state substance abuse agencies in the United States, and addiction treatment centers to examine the effects of facility-level financial interventions in treatment effectiveness. Finally, Ghose works with collectives of sex workers and transgendered people with HIV in India, New York, and Philadelphia to examine the effectiveness of social-movement mobilization in reducing HIV risk.

Imaculada Kangussu is professor of philosophy at Universidade Federal de Ouro Preto in Brazil. She was a postdoctoral fellow at the School of Arts and Science at New York University with a scholarship from Coordenação e Aperfeiçoamento de Pessoal de Nível Superior (CAPES). She is a member of the art and knowledge research group at Conselho Nacional de Pesquisa (CNPq). She works primarily in the areas of Critical Theory, aesthetics, and philosophy of art. She has published articles in numerous books and journals, including *Theoria Aesthetica* (2005), *The Comic and the Tragic* (2008), *Aesthetic Displacement* (2008), and *Fantasia and Criticism* (2012). Her books include *About Eros* (2007) and *Laws of Freedom* (2008). Her current research is on the juncture between phantasy and reality. She serves on the board of the International Herbert Marcuse Society.

George Katsiaficas was a member of Rosa Luxemburg Students for a Democratic Society (SDS) at the Massachusetts Institute of Technology (MIT) in 1969 and has been active in social movements ever since. His book *The Subversion of Politics: European Autonomous Social Movements and the Decolonization of Everyday Life* (1997) was co-winner of the 1998 Michael Harrington Book Award. Among his edited volumes are *Liberation, Imagination, and the Black Panther Party* (with Kathleen Cleaver, 2001) and *Vietnam Documents: American and Vietnamese Views of the War* (1992). With R. George Kirkpatrick, he coauthored *Introduction to Critical Sociology* (1987). A student of Herbert Marcuse, he recently authored two volumes about East Asian uprisings in the 1980s and 1990s, *Asia's Unknown Uprisings* (2012 and 2013). His website is http://www.eroseffect.com.

Douglas Kellner is the George F. Kneller Philosophy of Education Chair at the University of California–Los Angeles. He is the author of many books on social theory, politics, history, and culture, including *Herbert Marcuse and the Crisis of Marxism* (1984) and *Cinema Wars: Hollywood Film and Politics in the Bush-Cheney Era* (2010). He is the editor of the six-volume *Collected Papers of Herbert Marcuse* (1998–2014). With Tyson Lewis, Clayton Pierce, and K. Daniel Cho, he coedited *Marcuse's Challenge to Education*

(2009). His most recent book is *Media Spectacle and Insurrection 2011: From the Arab Uprisings to Occupy Everywhere* (2012). He serves on the board of the International Herbert Marcuse Society.

Sarah Lynn Kleeb has a Ph.D. in religion from the University of Toronto, where she also teaches. Her doctoral thesis, "Gustavo Gutiérrez's Notion of 'Liberation' and the Legacy of Marx's 'Ruthless Criticism,'" examines connections between religious belief and dissent as well as potential limits of discourse within particular structures of religious authority. As a critical analysis, this work raises questions regarding the ability of faith-based emancipatory movements to freely engage all possible avenues of thought or (social, political, economic, and theological) resistance while working within predefined, orthodoxical, and ideological constructs. Consideration of these issues is grounded in the works of Frankfurt School Critical Theorists and is directed primarily toward the trajectory of Gustavo Gutiérrez's liberation theology prior to and following the 1984 and 1986 Vatican condemnations of this movement. Her current research interests include the recent rise of Pope Francis, who frequently uses liberationist language and economic critique in interviews and encyclicals and yet has long distanced himself from liberation theology.

Filip Kovacevic is a Montenegrin author, global justice activist, and university professor with a Ph.D. in political science from the University of Missouri. He has taught and lectured across Europe and the United States. He is the author of several books, including *Liberating Oedipus? Psychoanalysis as Critical Theory* (2007), and dozens of academic articles and newspaper columns on contemporary Critical Theory and geopolitics. Currently, he is on leave from the University of Montenegro and teaches at the University of San Francisco.

Andrew T. Lamas teaches a broad range of critical theories—with a focus on radical political economy, economic democracy, religion, art, and critical pedagogy—at the University of Pennsylvania, where he organized the 2011 "Critical Refusals" conference of the International Herbert Marcuse Society, on whose board he serves. He is a long-standing board member of the Bread and Roses Community Fund in Philadelphia, and he is on the editorial advisory board of the *Radical Philosophy Review*. He founded and directed Penn's Social Justice Research Academy (2012–2015). He is the editor of four special issues of *Radical Philosophy Review*: he is coeditor, with Douglas Kellner, Charles Reitz, and Arnold Farr, and general editor on two issues titled "Critical Refusals" (2013), and he is editor of two issues titled "Refusing One-Dimensionality" (2016, forthcoming 2017). He served on the organizing committee for the 2016 "Black Radical Tradition in Our Time: Reclaiming Our Future" conference at Temple University, and he co-organized the 2016 "Critical Theories from the Americas" symposium at the University of Pennsylvania.

Lauren Langman is professor of sociology at Loyola University, Chicago. He has long worked in the tradition of the Frankfurt School, writing on social movements, culture, identity, and political movements. He was president of the Alienation Research Committee of the International Sociological Association and of the Marxist section of the American Sociological Association. Recent publications cover globalization, alienation, global-justice movements, the body, nationalism, and national character. His books include *The Evolution of Alienation: Trauma, Promise, and the Millennium* (2005), coedited with Devorah Kalekin-Fishman; *Alienation and the Carnivalization of Society* (2013), coedited with Jerome Braun; and *Gods, Guns, Gold and Glory: American Character and Its Discontents* (2016), coauthored with George Lundskow. He serves on the board of the International Herbert Marcuse Society.

Heather Love is the Jean R. Brownlee Term Associate Professor at the University of Pennsylvania. Her research interests include gender studies and queer theory, modernism and modernity, affect studies, disability studies, film and visual culture, psychoanalysis, sociology and literature, and Critical Theory. She is the author of *Feeling Backward: Loss and the Politics of Queer History* (2007); editor of "Rethinking Sex," a 2011 special issue of *GLQ: A Journal of Lesbian and Gay Studies* on the scholarship and legacy of Gayle Rubin; and coeditor of a 2000 special issue of *New Literary History*, "Is There Life after Identity Politics?" A book of her essays, *Queer Affect Politics: Selected Essays by Heather Love*, edited by Liu Jen-Peng, has been published in Taiwan (2012).

Peter Marcuse (born in 1928 in Berlin) is a lawyer and professor emeritus of urban planning at Columbia University. He holds a J.D. from Yale Law School (1952) and a Ph.D. from the University of California–Berkeley, in City and Regional Planning (1972). He was a professor of urban planning at the University of California–Los Angeles from 1972 until 1975 and at Columbia University from 1975 to 2003. In recent years, he has written extensively on the Right to the City, Occupy, and critical planning issues. He is the son of Herbert Marcuse. His many books and articles include *Missing Marx: A Personal and Political Journal of a Year in East Germany, 1989–1990* (1991); *Of States and Cities: The Partitioning of Urban Space*, coedited with Ronald van Kempen (2002); *Cities for People, Not for Profit: Critical Urban Theory and the Right to the City*, coedited with Neil Brenner and Margit Mayer (2011); and "Occupy Consciousness: Reading the 1960s and Occupy Wall Street with Herbert Marcuse," in *Radical Philosophy Review* (2013). He serves on the board of the International Herbert Marcuse Society.

Martin Beck Matuštík is the Lincoln Professor of Ethics and Religion, professor of philosophy and religious studies, and director of the Center for Critical Inquiry and Cultural Studies at Arizona State University. While a first-year student at Charles University, at nineteen, Matuštík signed "Charta 77," the Czechoslovak manifesto for human rights, issued in January 1977 by Václav Havel, Jan Patočka, and Jiří Hájek. He became a political refugee in August of that year. As a Fulbright student of Jürgen Habermas in Frankfurt in 1989, he witnessed the historic November fall of the Berlin Wall and the Velvet Revolution in Czechoslovakia. He has authored six books, edited two collections, and coedited New Critical Theory, a series at Rowman and Littlefield. Among his publications are *Postnational Identity: Critical Theory and Existential Philosophy in Habermas, Kierkegaard, and Havel* (1993); *Kierkegaard in Post/Modernity* (1995), coedited with Merold Westphal; *Specters of Liberation: Great Refusals in the New World Order* (1998); *Jürgen Habermas: A Philosophical-Political Profile* (2001); and *Radical Evil and the Scarcity of Hope: Postsecular Meditations* (2008).

Russell Rockwell coedited, with Kevin B. Anderson, *The Dunayevskaya-Marcuse-Fromm Correspondence, 1954–1978: Dialogues on Hegel, Marx, and Critical Theory* (2012). He has taught sociology at Fordham University and St. John's University in New York, and he has published articles on Marxist Humanism and Critical Theory in sociology and philosophy journals; many of his papers and talks presented at forums in the United States, the Philippines, the Czech Republic, and elsewhere can be accessed at http://marxist-humanistdialectics.blogspot.com.

AK Thompson got kicked out of high school for publishing an underground newspaper called the *Agitator* and has been an activist, writer, and social theorist ever since. Between 2005 and 2011, he served on the editorial committee of *Upping the Anti: A Journal of Theory and Action*. He is the author of *Black Bloc, White Riot: Anti-globalization and the Genealogy of Dissent* (2010). He coedited, with Caelie Frampton, Gary Kinsman, and Kate Tilleczek, *Sociology for Changing the World: Social Movements/Social Research* (2006), and, with Kelly Fritsch and Clare O'Connor, *Keywords for Radicals: The Contested Vocabulary of Late-Capitalist Struggle* (2016).

Marcelo Vieta is assistant professor in workplace and organizational learning for social change at the Ontario Institute for Studies in Education at University of Toronto. He has served on the board of directors of the Association for Nonprofit and Social Economy Research, the Canadian Association for Studies in Co-operation, and the Toronto School of Creativity and Inquiry. His areas of research and teaching include sociology of work; alternative work organizations; workers' control, participation, ownership, and self-management/*autogestión*; political economy of labor; social economy studies; economic democracy; critical community development; philosophy of technology; Critical Theory, with a focus on the Frankfurt School; class-struggle Marxism; anarchist theory and economics; social movements; and communication studies. His publications include the forthcoming book from Brill Academic and Haymarket *There's No Stopping the Workers: Crisis, Autogestión, and Argentina's Worker-Recuperated Enterprises*.

Todd Wolfson is associate professor in the Department of Journalism and Media Studies at Rutgers University. Trained as a sociocultural anthropologist, his research focuses on the convergence of new media and social movements, and he is author of *Digital Rebellion: The Birth of the Cyber Left* (2014). He is also cofounder of the Media Mobilizing Project (MMP; http://www.mediamobilizing.org), which uses media as a tool for building a movement of poor and working people in Philadelphia and beyond. MMP is recognized as a national leader in harnessing media as an organizing tool and advocating at the intersection of poverty and technology.

Index

abolitionist movements, viii, 72n13, 348, 391

Abu-Jamal, Mumia, viii

ACFTU (All-China Federation of Trade Unions), 105, 107, 112

Adam and Eve, 291

Adbusters, 43, 72n14, 221

administered society, xi, 19, 33, 52, 98n1, 129, 135, 286

administration, language of, 33

Adorno, Theodor: on authority relations, 370n9; *Dialectic of Enlightenment*, 229, 291, 310, 321; Echeverría on, 336; on emancipation, 61; freedom as living without anxiety, 262; and Marcuse, 229, 258n2, 261–262; and ontology of negativity, 55

The Aesthetic Dimension (Marcuse), 296

aesthetic dimension, ix, 33, 144; and fascist politics, 327; of Great Refusal and negation, 59, 126–127, 143n59, 259, 261; and mic check (Occupy), 147; and new sensibilities, 11

"aesthetic *Lebenswelt*," 233

affirmationism, 57

Afghanistan, 38, 252

AFU (Anarchist Free University), 272

alienated labor: Marcuse on, 76–77, 243, 262, 265, 364; Johnson-Forest Tendency on, 301; Marx on, 300–301, 303, 371–372. *See also* labor movement

Al Jazeera, 213, 216, 218, 222

allies, need for, 71, 167

Altemeyer, Robert, 369

alterglobalization movement, 5, 41, 46, 48, 85, 87–88, 144, 263n31, 279. *See also* global justice movement

alternative socioeconomic practices, 260, 263, 265, 266–280

Althusser, Louis, 355, 365

American dream, collapse of, 46, 343–345

American Muslim, 172

anarchism in Occupy movement, 47

anarchists, identifcation of protestors as, 170, 197

Andalib-Goortani, Babak, 187

"Another world is possible" slogan, 13, 138, 278

anti-austerity protests, 2, 6, 42–43, 59, 65, 155, 213, 348, 383, 398

The Antichrist (Nietzsche), 392, 394

anticolonialism, 75, 315, 326, 328, 373

anti-identity platform, 121–122

antinormativity, 118–122, 128

antiracist movements, 330. *See also* Black struggle

Arab Awakening/Arab Spring: effects of, 214, 218–219, 226–228, 390–391; as media spectacle, 212–217, 225–226, 228; nature of, 29, 70, 73, 215, 221, 313–316; and other mobilizations, 6, 51, 54, 83–84, 86–87, 91, 211; and social media, 88, 222, 253

Aramark, 199
Argentina: *clubes de trueque* in, 267–268,
271; community education experiments
in, 273; Marcusean interpretations on
resistance in, 268, 269; Universidad Trashumante in, 273; worker-recuperated enterprises (ERTs) in, 13, 47, 268, 274–278
Aristotle, 142, 231
art as radical protest, ix, x, 11, 12, 75, 94,
126, 140–147, 291. *See also* clowning;
humor
artificial "needs," 68, 133, 372–373
asambleas barriales (neighborhood assemblies), 268
Asian Wave (1986–1992), 83–84, 91–93,
96–97
assimilation: Black liberation in resistance
to, viii; liquidation of queer culture
through, 128; and occupational stratification, 32
Austin, John Langshaw, 148
authenticity, 238–239, 324
authoritarianism, 83, 99, 135, 179–180, 219,
301, 325, 354, 362–372
automation, 40, 258, 262, 265, 304, 311–312,
383
autonomia operaismo, 59
autonomist Marxism, 264, 268
autonomous act, 150–151, 243
autonomous formations: alternative media,
subaltern, and grassroots, 88; as secularism, 92; in communist Eastern Europe,
94; in politics, 96, 349; as alternative to
trade unions in China, 101, 111, 115; in
alternative society, 133, 270; for direct
action, 153, 226; as prefigurative, 263n31;
as refusal, 325

Baader-Meinhof Group, 72n15, 292
Badiou, Alain, 150, 155
Baeck, Leo, 287
Bangladesh, 83, 88, 93
banking and finance: and bailouts, 43,
138n32, 223, 348, 355, 375; and crisis,
383, 386; history and rise of, 35, 50;
protests against, 87, 144, 196; and social
media, 248
Bank of America, 224
Baran, Paul, 301, 358
barter clubs (*clubes de trueque*), 267–268,
271
Baudelaire, Charles, 162

Beck, Ulrich, 235
Being and Time (Heidegger), 231, 238
"Bellamy Clubs," 292
beloved community, 147, 154, 396
Benhabib, Seyla, 302
Benjamin, Walter: on documents of civili-
zation and barbarism, 58; on hope, 321;
and Marcuse, 261, 296, 320–321; mes-
sianism of, 284, 288, 290, 293n45; on
nostalgia, 161; utopianism of, 377; on
violence and moral choice, 185
Berlin Wall collapse as media spectacle,
216–217
"Beyond Vietnam" (King), 394
Billionaires for Bush, 145
"biopolitics," 33–34n14
bipolar strategy against protestors, 197–198
Bismarck, Otto von, 355
black bloc actions, 72n14, 167–175
Black Bloc, White Riot (Thompson), 168
Black Marxism (Robinson), viii
Black struggle: Black Feminism, ix–x; Black
Lives Matter, x, 6, 141, 166n30, 178n5,
189, 362; and Black music, ix, 161n10;
Black Panther Party, viiin5, 349; Black
radical imagination, ix; Black Radical
Tradition, viii, ix–x; and Black women,
x; Black Youth Project 100, x; Combahee
River Collective, x; and deindustrializa-
tion and gentrification, 344–345; Dream
Defenders, x; and Haitian constitution
(1805), ix–x; and Johnson-Forest Ten-
dency, 301; and labor movement, 46; and
liberation movements, 9, 36, 75, 140, 361;
Long Black Freedom Movement, viii;
and Marcuse, 9, 17, 32, 312, 397; and
Moral Mondays, 347, 362; and the Oc-
cupy movement, 48, 147; and state vio-
lence, 2, 44, 167, 178n5, 347, 356. *See also*
King, Martin Luther, Jr.
Blackstone, John, 171
Blair, Bill, 188, 190
Blanquism, 293
Bloch, Ernst, 284, 377
"Bloody Sunday," 155n101
Boggs, Grace Lee, 300
Bolivia, 219, 256, 275
bottom-up resistance, 263, 267–270, 274,
279
Bouazizi, Mohamed, 1–2, 29, 226, 390–391
Brat, David, 138n32
Brazil, 77, 138, 180, 219, 270, 275, 353

Breines, Wini, 16n48
Breton, André, 143–144n59, 154n97, 261, 316
Bryan, William Jennings, 348
Buber, Martin, 284, 377
Bukharin, Nikolai, 304
Burma, 83, 93
Bush, George W., 215, 224–225, 348, 354
Butler, Judith, 121

Cage, John, 163
Camacho Solís, Manuel, 336, 336–337n15
Câmara, Dom Hélder, 180–184, 189, 192
Canadian Dimension (Davidson-Harden), 169
Can Masdeu intentional community (Barcelona), 270
Cantor, Eric, 138n32
Capital (Marx), 64n20, 174, 305–309, 312, 360
capitalism: being-in-the-world as not recognized by, 56; capitalist crisis as negating moment, 242–243; in crisis, 64; invisibility of, 33; Marcuse's analysis of, 14–15, 31–34, 133, 239, 243; Occupy Wall Street focus on, 222; as racial capitalism, ix, 15, 398; stability versus durability of, 14; as technocapitalism, 389; working class integration into, 3, 9, 35. *See also* neoliberalism
Carney, Jay, 195
Carter, Jimmy, 364
Caruso, Loris, 380–381
caste, 94, 397
Castells, Manuel, 5, 45
catastrophic messianism, 283–284; emergence of, 288, 292; in *Eros and Civilization*, 288–293; Fromm on, 286–287, 289; in *One-Dimensional Man*, 288, 290–291, 293–294; Scholem and, 288, 291–292
Catastrophism (Lilley et al.), 293
Centri Sociali Autogestiti (Italy), 270
Chan, Anita, 107
charismatic Latin American leaders, 219
chemical weapons use on protestors, 44–45, 197
Cheney, Dick, 215
child care, undervaluation of, 77
China, 251; accession of, to WTO, 102; agricultural land tenure in, 102; class in, 99–100; "incomplete proletarianization" in, 102; labor movement in, 105–114; Marcuse and, 99, 106, 251; "People

Power" in, 83; "repressive modernization" in, 99; resistance from the margins in, 98; rural migrant workers within, 101–105; shifting demographics of, 116; "socialist modernization" in, 99; strikes in, 105–110; suicides in, 104, 106–107, 111, 115; women's rights in, 113; as world's largest economy, 100
Chinese dream, 99, 117
Chomsky, Noam, 385
Chun Doo-hwan, 83
citizens' media check, 256–257
"civic culture," 32, 36, 93
civil rights, 174, 220, 356; attorneys for, 207; civil-rights movement, 76, 155n101, 347–349, 373, 385, 397
civil society: in Asia, 84, 88, 91; and Eurocentrism, 84, 90–95; and Foucault's Orientalism, 92n19; and Left mobilization, 252; and Marcuse's concept of "repressive tolerance," 194; and 3M strategy, 205
class struggle, x, 10, 31, 33–34n14, 58–61, 64, 99–100, 138, 149, 247–248
Clinton, Hillary, 352
clowning, 94, 144–146, 313–314, 316. *See also* art as radical protest; humor
clubes de trueque (barter clubs), 267–268, 271
Cohen, Cathy J., 128
Cohen, Hermann, 287–288, 289
Cold War, 94, 132, 315, 325, 356
commoning praxis, 146, 275
communism: as fulfillment of history, 284; and Internet, 256; Marcuse on, 309–310; Marx on, 284; and migrant labor, 103; and Nazism, 363; as permanent enemy, 33, 38; SDS and, 349–350; uprisings against, 216–217; in the West, 353. *See also* Gramsci, Antonio
community economies, 266–271
complex unity, 130
Confucius, 93
consciousness: class, 10n30, 239, 244, 383; liberation of, 79; mutilated, 396n29; of servitude, 133
"conscious spontaneity" of global protests, 84, 95
consensus decision making, 4, 48
conspiracy theories, 50
consumerism, 7, 9, 53, 57, 58, 104, 135–136, 267, 372–373, 380, 383, 387

cooperatives, 264, 270, 274–277
Copenhagen Squatters' Movement, 269
counterculture of 1960s, 161–162, 392
Counterrevolution and Revolt (Marcuse),
265; on accessing "existential truths,"
233; advocating independent schools,
free universities, 272; on Argentina,
269; on Black music, ix, 161n10; endors-
ing "long march through the institutions," 239, 252; and exploitation beyond
blue-collar class, 64–65; as foreseeing
neoliberalism, 34–35, 37; as foreseeing
"qualitatively different" revolution, 63;
on freedom as rooted in human sensibility, 62, 86, 161n10; on global destruction
of resources, 57; on "gut hatred" and gestures of love, 175; on high modernist art,
163–164; on "internal contradictions"
of status quo, 263–264; on refusal and
"radical consciousness," 259
Crack Capitalism (Holloway), 60
credit and debt, 36
crime as permanent enemy, 38
CrimethInc., 153, 166
crisis: of accumulation, 29, 34, 41; in
Argentina, 47, 267; of capitalism and
neoliberalism, 50, 51–54, 213, 242, 248; of
Europe, 328nn50–51; Fanon on, 328; and
financialization, 247; of humanism, 327;
Husserl on, 327, 328n50; of Internet economy, 248; of Marxism, 8; Marx on dialectics and, 242–243; in 1970s, 35; as opportunity, 263–265; of patriarchy, racism,
and colonialism, 328; preparation for, 70,
74; of profitability, 59; of queer studies,
121; of the system, 70, 263; of 2007–2009,
2, 6, 41, 108, 374, 383, 386–387, 390
*The Crisis of European Sciences and Tran-
scendental Phenomenology* (Husserl),
327–328
critical race and gender theory, 327
"Critical Refusals" conference, vii, xiii, 130,
131, 193
Critical Theory, 142, 304–312, 320–328,
369–377
Critical U, 273
CSA (community-sustained agricultural)
movement, 271
Cuba, 2, 99, 251, 271
"cultural apparatus," 357–360, 364, 366
cultural revolution, 37, 99, 175

Cuomo, Andrew, 224
CUPE (Canadian Union of Public Employees), 170

Davidson-Harden, Adam, 169
Davies, James, 91
Davis, Angela Y., 17, 130, 193
de Blasio, Bill, 138n32
Debord, Guy, 212, 223
decolonization and death of Man, 318–319
Deconstructionist Institute for Surreal
Topology, 145
degrowth movement, 271
deindustrialization, 344–345
Deleuze, Gilles, 220
demands and dreams, 152–156, 390
Democratic Party, 42, 46, 78, 138n32, 346,
348, 352, 387n40
"democratic threshold," 91
democratic unfreedom, 8, 132, 167, 389
DeMoro, RoseAnn, 352
de Nardis, Fabio, 380–381
Denby, Charles, 311
Deng Xiaoping, 99, 102
de Peuter, Greig, 273n84, 275
deprived, Marcuse on the, 15, 68–69,
70–71, 74
determinate negation, 233, 243–246, 248,
259–260
Dialectic of Enlightenment (Horkheimer
and Adorno), 229–230, 291, 310, 321
dialectics: active and passive, 242; of
chance and necessity, 248; conscious
human activity and, 245–246; of desirable and undesirable, 377; dialectical
materialism, 304; and Dunayevskaya,
304; of enlightenment, 229; of essence
and existence, 249–250; existential-
communicative, 326; of freedom and
necessity, 244; and Fromm, 294; Great
Refusal and, 251–252; of Hegel, 152,
246, 249, 254–255, 305; and Horkheimer
and Adorno, 291, 321; imagination in,
12; of individual and society, 247, 314;
Kellner on, 12; Marcuse on Hegel and,
246; Marcuse on Marx and, 242–246;
Marcuse's contribution to, 12–13, 55,
254–257, 309–310, 312, 373, 391; of
necessity and freedom, 305, 307, 309; in
One-Dimensional Man, 40, 49, 52, 241,
245; of organic intellectuals and workers,

381; and power of the negative, 60, 65; as practical force, 250; of reification versus dereification, 230, 237, 238; of social media, 253–257; of subject and object, 242, 244, 246–248

Díaz, Porfirio, 335n14

Digital Disconnect (McChesney), 358

Dignity Revolution, 2

Dilworth Park Plaza, 193–201, 203, 204–207. *See also* 3M strategy

direct democracy, 90, 95–96, 147, 268, 279

dissatisfaction versus deprivation, 68–69, 77–78

"divine violence," 290

DIY (do-it-yourself) movement, 271, 272

Douglass, Frederick, 17, 72, 154, 391

Dream Defenders, x

"dropping out," 238

"dual consciousness," 379

Du Bois, W.E.B., 15, 379

Duggan, Lisa, 118–119

Dunayevskaya, Raya, 299–312

Duncombe, Stephen, 136–137, 155

Durkheim, Émile, 372

Dutschke, Rudi, 78, 252, 330–331

Dwyer, John, 305

Dyer-Witheford, Nick, 275

Echeverría, Bolívar, 329–335, 336n15, 337–340

"Ecology and Revolution" (Marcuse), 396n29

Economic and Philosophical Manuscripts of 1844 (Marx). *See Paris Manuscripts*

ecovillages movement, 270

education, radical initiatives in, 140, 261, 266, 272–274, 279, 353, 379; popular education, 277, 368, 380

"education through history," 134

Egypt, 2, 5, 51, 213–215, 218. *See also* North African Arab uprisings; Tahrir Square protests

elite versus nonracial democracy, ix

"end of history," 12, 217n8

"The End of Utopia" (Marcuse), 67, 69–70n8

Eng, David, 119–121

Engels, Friedrich, 151, 309

entrepreneur as folk hero, 37

environmental (ecological) movement, 17, 49, 227–228n26, 235–236, 361, 396n29, 397

Eros and Civilization (Marcuse), 11–12; catastrophic messianism in, 288–293; and conditions for unrest, 32; and destruction of present order, 297; Dunayevskaya on, 305; on freedom, 62, 86, 151; on Freud and phantasy making, 141–143, 151, 259–260; on Fromm, 286; on Great Refusal, 86, 98n1, 124, 262, 390; on internal antagonism, 62; on material leaps, 320; and "a new sensibility," 156; and 1960s social movements, 7; on Orpheus and Narcissus, 123, 126–127; on the performance principle, 39, 265; on the political fight, x–xi, 19; "Political Preface" to, 19; present and future in, 296; on psychoanalysis, 124n23; on repression of feelings, 67n5; on romantic love, 62; on sexuality, 123–124, 126; on "surplus repression," 123; on work and freedom, 277, 278n107; on youth and protest, x–xi, 53

eros effect, 84–89, 91, 96

ERTs (worker-recuperated enterprises), 13, 47, 268, 274–278

Escobar, Arturo, 5

An Essay on Liberation (Marcuse): on "aesthetic *Lebenswelt*," 233; on "areas of withdrawal," 272; on catalyst groups, 397; on consciousness and imagination, 151; on "crisis of the system," 263–264; and eros effect, 85; on false morality, 394; Fromm on, 296; on Great Refusal, 2–3, 34, 98n1, 118, 124, 251, 390–391; and hope for future, 319; on joy of freedom preceding liberation, 261; on new rebels, 144–146; on "new sensibility," 156; and 1960s social movements, 7, 47; on obscenity, 393; and prefiguration, 263n31, 265; on resistance, 268–269; as search for critical theory, 315; on "second nature of man," 33; on technological rationality, 258–260

essence: concept of, 231–232; Hegel on, 249; life as, 235; Marcuse on, 233, 249; public-service media as, 250

Ética y política (Sánchez Vázquez), 341

Eurocentrism, 90–95

European antihumanism, 318–319

existentialist-communicative critical social theory, 326–328

existentialist critical social theory, 320–326

existentialist rebellions/refusal, 315–320

experience and "existential truths," 233

EZLN (Zapatista Army of National Liberation), 331–342

la fábrica abierta (the open factory), 276

Facebook, 39, 88, 197, 216, 223, 241–242, 247–248

"The Failure of the New Left?" (Marcuse), 16

Fanon, Frantz, 316, 317–321, 327, 331, 379

fantasy: and art, 11; and phantasy, 141n46; and play, 143, 259, 265; protest demands as, 141; utopian, 353. See also phantasy

fascist resurgence, 77

Father Knows Best (TV series), 365

Federal Reserve System, U.S., 50

Feeling Backward (Love), 126

Feenberg, Andrew, 252–255

femininity and humanity, 125, 330

feminism: and Asian uprisings, 88; Black feminism, ix–x; feminist socialism, 125; and intersectionality, 118–119; Marcuse and, ix, 124–126, 330, 397; social movements and, 353, 361, 385; and queer politics, 118; and Robin Kelley, ix

Fenton, David Mark, 187–188

Ferguson, Missouri, protests, 2, 178n5

Ferguson, Roderick, 119

feudal inheritance, 159–160, 163

finance. See banking and finance

financialization of the Internet, 247–248

First Nations, 53

Fisher, William, 200

Floyd, Kevin, 119, 123–125

forced tolerance, 194

"forcing" the revolution, 292–293

Fordist production, 31, 382, 383

Foucault, Michel, 33–34n14, 92n19, 124, 126, 365, 393

Foxconn, 105–107

Frankfurt School, viii, 7, 229–230, 258n2, 302, 358; and critique of existing society, 294, 303, 367; and critique of ideology, hegemony, and domination, 368–388; and Gramsci's critique of hegemony, 368–369; influence of Judaism on, 284; influence of Lukács on, 230; influence of messianism on, 283; on toxic work, 77; on "willing assent," 378

The Frankfurt School, Jewish Lives, and Antisemitism (Jacobs), 284–285

"freeconomy," 250, 268

freedom, instinctual need for, 85

Freedom Dreams (Kelley), ix

"freedom from the economy," 30

"freedom wills freedom," 134

"free election of masters," 134

free enterprise, Cold War ideology of, 132–133

free schools, 268, 292

Freies Jüdisches Lehrhaus, 285

Freud, Sigmund, viii, 141–143, 151, 220, 261, 313, 370

The Freudian Left (Robinson), 122

Friedman, Milton, 35

Fromm, Erich: on authoritarianism and religion, 369–371; and critique of "forcing the Messiah," 288–298; influence of Judaism on, 285; on life under capitalism, 295; on love under capitalism, 295; on Marcuse's embrace of destruction, 283–284, 286, 293–298; on Marx, 288; and positive goals, 294, 377, 386; on prophetic and catastrophic messianism, 284–288; The Revolution of Hope, 284, 286, 289, 292–294; on Scholem, 292; on young activists, 292

FTAA (Free Trade Area of the Americas), 145, 168n33

Fukuyama, Francis, 217n8

Gaddafi, Muammar, 214

Galbraith, John Kenneth, 31, 135

Galileo, 139

Gallagher, Mary, 114

Gandhi, Mohandas, 226

Gaynor, Shawn, 196

gender and race apartheid, 318

gender diversity, x

gentrification, 344–345

Georgetti, Ken, 170

Gerbaudo, Paolo, 5

The German Ideology (Marx and Engels), 393

Germany: Echeverría and his theory in, 331, 334; Marcuse in, 77, 302; Nazism in, 77, 233, 330–332, 363; radical student activism in, 78, 292, 324–325

Gibson-Graham, J. K., 266

Gini index, 105n26

Gitlin, Todd, 5, 138n32

Glass, Philip, 226

global grammar of insurgency, 96

globalization, 35, 37, 121, 383
global justice movement, 4, 5, 6, 72, 146–147, 155, 169. *See also* alterglobalization movement
global media ecology, 218
Global North and South, 35–38, 45, 266, 272
global slums movement, 269
Goldman Sachs, 226
good American, being a, 314
Goodman, Amy, 195, 361
Goodwin, Jeff, 11
Google, 227, 247, 248
Gorbachev, Mikhail, 84
Gordon, Lewis R., 318, 328n50
Gou, Terry, 106
Graeber, David, 144
Gramsci, Antonio, 70, 367–368, 370, 377–383, 385, 388
Gray, Freddie, 177n1
Great Recession, 41–42, 138n32, 155, 374–376, 383
Great Refusal concept, 86, 316; acts of refusal, 59, 110, 264n40; in advanced industrial society, 259; advocacy for, 8; art and, 11, 126, 291; as ceasing to make capitalism, 58; concrete existential thought in, 314–316, 328; *Eros and Civilization* on, 86, 98n1, 124, 262, 390; germs of in our times, 265–278; as an ideal, 262; from 1950s–1970s perspective, 76, 78; and North African Arab uprisings, 220–221; and Occupy movements, 221; *One-Dimensional Man* on, 86, 129–130, 259–262, 316–317, 390–391; politics of refusal, 55–56, 59, 65, 259–265, 272–274; relying on excluded peoples, 34; reworking of, viii, xi, 2–3, 262, 264, 316, 397; transgressive strategies of, 313; and transvaluation of values, 396; and violence, 173, 175
Greece, 42, 212–213, 251, 376, 383n31, 386, 390
Greenberg, Michael, 224, 226
"groupthink," 370
Grundrisse (Marx), 299, 305–309, 311–312
G20 Toronto protests, 167–170, 178n5, 186–191
Guantanamo Bay detention facility, 178n3
Guattari, Félix, 220
Guevara, Che, 342
Guo Jun, 107

guru of the New Left, Marcuse as, 3, 67, 373, 392
"gut hatred," 175
Gutiérrez, Gustavo, 182–183
Gwangju People's Uprising, 83, 86, 87, 88–90, 92, 94, 140

Habermas, Jürgen: on "genuine" civil society, 92; on "legitimation," 355, 373–374; and Marcuse, 321–324, 326; on messianism, 283; and 1968 student revolts, 325; on subjectivity, 321, 325–326, 367
Hahn, Fred, 170
Haiti, ix–x
Halberstam, Judith (Jack), 120–121
Hampton, Fred, 9n30
Hardt, Michael, 56–57n5, 211, 218–220, 221
Harrington, Michael, 349–350
Harvey, David, 155, 193, 204
Haug, Wolfgang Fritz, 244–245
Havel, Václav, 217n7, 327
Hayek, Friedrich von, 35
Hedges, Chris, 171, 379, 385
Hegel, Georg Wilhelm Friedrich: on determinate negation, 244; and dialectic of necessity and freedom, 305; Dunayevskaya on, 305; Echeverría as inspired by, 339; on essence, 249; Feenberg and, 254–255; on freedom, 134; Freud and, 141; Marcuse on, 17, 241, 246, 255; and owl of Minerva, 294; *Philosophy of Right*, 134; Pippin on, 150; on received identities, 325–326; Žižek on, 149, 150–151
Hegel's Ontology and the Theory of Historicity (Marcuse), 302–303
hegemony and counterhegemony, 140, 316, 361, 368, 377–382
Heidegger, Martin: and authenticity, 238–239; Echeverría on, 329n2, 331–332; *Existenzphilosophie*, 327; and Habermas, 323–324; Marcuse and ideas of, 7, 230–233, 238–240, 258, 302, 329n1, 330; as Marcuse's doctoral supervisor, 238, 258n2, 285; and technology, 233–238
Hennessy, Rosemary, 119
Heschel, Abraham Joshua, 285
History and Class Consciousness (Lukács), 230, 304, 306
The History of Sexuality (Foucault), 124
Hitler, Adolf, 7
Hollibaugh, Amber, 119
Holloway, John, 15, 58–60, 62–63

Holz, Hans Heinz, 244
Homeland Security measures, 196
homeless youth in Occupy movement, 48
homonormativity and homonationalism,
    119–120
homosexuality, Marcuse on, 122–123
Honda strike, 112
Hong, Grace Kyungwon, 119
horizontalism (*horizontalidad*), 47–48, 147,
    277
Horkheimer, Max, 229, 291, 310, 321, 336
How to Do Things with Words (Austin), 148
Hua Guofeng, 99
Hudson, Hosea, x
humanist Marxism, viii, 133
human life as site of investment, 14–15n43
human nature, 86, 132, 287, 290, 297, 306
human rights, 38, 49, 121, 183, 340
Human Rights Watch, 89
humor, 144, 200, 223, 313, 314, 316, 339n21,
    376. *See also* clowning
Huntington, Samuel, 90–91
Hurricane Katrina, 212, 345
Hurston, Zora Neale, x
Husserl, Edmund, 7, 327

ICE (Immigration and Customs Enforce-
    ment), 203–204
Iceland, 42
"ideal speech situations," 92
identity formation, 10–11
Ignatieff, Michael, 38
"I Have a Dream" speech (King), 154
Ilnyckyj, Milan, 171
imagination, 143
IMF (International Monetary Fund), 88–
    89, 95, 96, 144
income inequality, 36, 100, 105, 375; and
    wealth inequality, 138, 348
"incomplete proletarianization" in China,
    102
India, 93–94, 194, 199, 391
Indignados (15-M Movement), 29, 43, 47,
    49n52, 53, 54, 251, 383n31
Indignant Heart (Denby), 311
individualism, 37, 47, 253, 266, 279, 316,
    321, 325, 363
individualization through socialization,
    314, 325, 326
information technology, 236
innocence, 160, 290–291

instrumental rationality, 14–15n43, 34, 63
insurrection(s): as media spectacle, 212–
    221, 226, 228; 2011 as year of, 211, 214;
    use of term, 214
intentional community movements, 269–
    270
Internet: political economy of, 358; and
    privatization, 359. *See also* social media/
    new media
invention, 320
"inverted totalitarianism," 388
Iran, 316
Iraq, 38, 178n3, 196, 215, 225, 356
"iron rice bowl," 103
is and ought to be, 137
ISIS, 214
Israel, pinkwashing in, 120
Italy, 32, 59, 212–213, 222, 270, 274

Jackson, George, 9n30
Jackson, Jesse, 193
Jacobs, Jack, 284–285
Jacoby, Russell, 376
Jainism, 94
James, C.L.R., 300
Jameson, Fredric, 143, 161, 163, 164
Jasper, James M., 11
Jay, Martin, 143n52
"J-curve," 91
Jewish messianism, 283, 284, 287
Johnson, Lyndon, 349
Johnson-Forest Tendency, 300–301, 303
Jonas, Hans, 358
Jones, Claudia, x
Joseph, Miranda, 119
JPMorgan Chase, 224
Judaism, 284–285, 287; and Marcuse, 285
Juris, Jeffrey, 4

Kangussu, Imaculada, 141n46
Kant, Immanuel, 17, 136–137, 139, 142,
    325–326
Kasich, John, 224
Katsiaficas, George, 11
Keane, John, 91
Kelley, Robin, ix, 153
Kellner, Douglas, 8, 12, 14–15n43, 86, 136,
    303, 390, 392
"kettling," 186n24, 188
Keynesianism, 34
Keystone XL pipeline, 227

"KFC Clinic," 140
Kierkegaard, Søren, 138
Kim Dae Jung, 93
King, Martin Luther, Jr., 9n30, 48, 154, 349, 394–396, 398
KKK (Ku Klux Klan), 185–186n22
Klein, Naomi, 298, 385
Kleist, Heinrich von, 290
Koch brothers, 224
Kong Xianghong, 112
Korean civil society, 83, 87–90, 94
Kosík, Karel, 327
Kosovo, 252
Kraus, Karl, 289
Krugman, Paul, 42
Kuhn, Thomas, 137
Kürnberger, Ferdinand, 61n13
Kurnitzky, Horst, 330

labor: child care as, 77; and consumerism, 58; "creative work" as, 77; and nature, 132; oversupply of, 64; privileging play over, 265; and radical subjectivity, 15, 67, 113, 361; reducing time spent on, 262; reorganization of life and work, 264, 265–271; two kinds of, 60; worker cooperatives, 274–278
labor movement: and anti-WTO protests, 46; in China, 105–114; and decline of unions, 36, 64, 344, 346; merge of, with management, 39–40; Scott Walker's attack on, 42; and signs without organization, 348; and support of Occupy, 46–47; in the United States, 36, 64, 344, 346, 350–353. See also alienated labor
Lacan, Jacques, 149
Lakoff, George, 372
Landauer, Gustav, 286
Lao-tzu, 93
Lasch, Christopher, 359
Latinos, 197, 343–345, 356
Law and Order (TV series), 365
Lee, Ching Kwan, 99, 107
Lee Kuan Yew, 93
Lefebvre, Henri, 365
"left fascism," 324
legitimation crises, 373–374
Lenin, Vladimir, 90, 211, 301
Lewis, Ray, 193
LGBT politics, 120–128
"liberation of consciousness," 79

Libya, 214. See also North African Arab uprisings
Liebknecht, Karl, 7
Lipset, Seymour Martin, 91
Líster, Enrique, 341
"long march through the institutions," xvi, 78, 239, 252, 256–257
Lorde, Audre, x
Lot's Wife, 126
Lower Ninth Ward (New Orleans), 345
Löwith, Karl, 302
Löwy, Michael, 288
Lukács, György, 90, 149, 230, 237, 255, 304, 306, 330
Luxemburg, Rosa, 7, 87n6, 253, 286, 288, 339

Madison, Wisconsin, protests, 14, 42–43, 212, 213, 228, 346, 347
Mahathir bin Mohamad, 93
Maimonides, 395
Malcolm X, 9n30
managerial knowledge, 39
Manhattan 1987 blackout, 162n12
Mannheim, Karl, 386
Manning, Bradley, 226
Mao Zedong, 99, 376
Marcos, Ferdinand, 83, 87
Marcos, Subcomandante, 145, 332, 338, 342
Marcus Welby, M.D. (TV series), 365
market feudalism, 37
Márquez, Gabriel García, 145
Martin, Trayvon, 347
martyrs' funerals, 216
Marx, Karl, and Marxism, 255, 261, 313, 386, 391, 393; on acts of refusal and exodus, 264n40; on alienated labor, 300–301, 303, 371–372; and "atheist" prophetic messianism, 285; on automation, 311; autonomist Marxism, 264, 268; Badiou on Saint Paul and, 150n80; Black Marxism (Robinson), viii; on bourgeois revolution, 164–165; Capital, 64n20, 174, 306–309, 312, 360; on capitalist crisis as negating moment, 242–243; on changing, not interpreting, world, xvi, 182n15; on creative destruction, 383; on creative human essence, 64n20; "crisis of Marxism," 8; on deprived groups, 71; on developed countries as image of the future, 94–95; on distinguishing humans

Marx, Karl, and Marxism (*continued*)
from other animals, 60; on free time as "real wealth," 272–273; and Fromm, 288, 297; on *Gattungswesen* (species-being), 60, 297, 371; Gramsci on, 381; *Grundrisse*, 299, 306–309, 311–312; and Hegel, 249; Hermann Cohen on, 287; humanist Marxism, 133; as lacking concept of revolutionary identity, 239; on law of value and surplus value, 300; Lukács and, 230–231; Marcuse advocating revision of, 30, 58, 151; Marcuse as early Marxist, 64, 301–302; Marcuse-Dunayevskaya debate on, 299, 303–307, 310, 312; Marcuse fusing Freud and, viii, 313; Marcuse on automation and "humanization of labor," 311; Marcuse on dialectic and praxis, 243–244, 250; Marcuse on *Grundrisse*, 309, 311, 312; Marcuse on *Paris Manuscripts*, viii, 302–303, 306, 367; Marcuse on wage labor, 243, 308; Marcuse's existential Marxism, 238–239, 320; Marcuse's Great Refusal and, 262, 392–393; Marcuse's Hegelianized version of, 303–304; Marxist feminism, 118, 124–126; McChesney on, 360; *Paris Manuscripts*, 284, 291, 302–303, 306, 342, 367; on philosophers, xvi, 182n15; rejection of utopian socialism by, 376; relevance of, to current conditions, 387–388; and role of historical agent, 233; on role of imagination, 174; Sánchez Vázquez on, 336–337, 340; SDS and, 349; on subjectivity and materialism, 360; theory of emotions and desire, 371–372; theses on Feuerbach, xvi, 182n15, 360; on violence, 72. *See also* class struggle; revolution
"Marxism and Feminism" (Marcuse), 124–126
Marxism and Freedom (Dunayevskaya), 299, 300–301n7, 304–308, 310
Marxist Humanism, 304–312
Mason, Paul, 5
The Mass Psychology of Fascism (Reich), 363
McCarthy, Eugene, 349
McChesney, Robert, 358–360
McDonald, CeCe, x
McRuer, Robert, 119
media and entertainment, Marcuse on, 296–297
media spectacle(s), 228; Bush-Cheney Iraq intervention as, 215; as central events of

an era, 212; defined, 212; do-it-yourself, 212; effect of, on other countries, 216–217; Occupy movement as, 221–228; political insurrection as, 211–221. *See also* news coverage; social media/new media; television coverage
meditation. *See* 3M strategy
Mencius, 93
messianism: Adorno on, 55; "forcing the Messiah," 289; of Fromm, 284–288; Habermas on, 283; Jewish, 283, 284; of Marcuse, 284–286, 288–294; of Walter Benjamin, 288, 290, 293n45
Mexico: and civic-culture thesis, 32; contributions of Echeverría and Marcuse to uprisings in, 338; Dunayevskaya and Trotsky in, 300; early Marxism in, 340; Mexican Revolution, 335n14; recognition of Sánchez Vázquez in, 341, 342; theoretical praxis in, 331; worker takeovers of firms in, 275; Zapatistas in, 140, 145, 332–335, 338, 340–341
mic check/people's mic, 138, 146–149, 151–152, 204
militarism and militarization, 6, 394, 398. *See also* 3M strategy
military-industrial complex, 38
Mills, C. Wright, 354, 357–358
Mitchell, John Cameron, 161
Monsanto, 360
Moyers, Bill, 361
Mumford, Lewis, 358
Muñoz, José Esteban, 120–121
Muñoz Ledo, Porfirio, 336
Musaji, Sheila, 172
music, power of, ix, 161n10
Muslim Brotherhood, 214
Muslim society, 84, 91n17

NAFTA (North American Free Trade Agreement), 332
Narcissus, 123, 126–127
National Security State, 353–354
"natural nations," 330
Nazism, 185–186n22, 233, 301, 322, 324, 330–332, 363
negativity: defined, 56–57; in Great Refusal, 126, 139, 174; and Marcuse's dialectics, 245; and Marxist conception of the proletariat, 58; "negation of the negation," 55, 57, 60–65, 129, 243, 256, 294; ontology of, 55–56; political resources of,

127; in queer history, 128, 131; and social contradictions, 52

Negri, Antonio, 56–57n5, 211, 218–220, 221, 268

neoliberalism: and alterglobalization movement, 5; Argentine resistance to, 268–269; in Asia, 87; as causing economic uncertainty, inequality, 30, 374–375; as causing insecurity and fear, 40–41; as counterrevolution, 34–41; as hegemonic ideology, 377; as linked to global protests, 213, 251; Marcusean analysis of, 14, 51–54, 261, 263; Obama and, 42; as technological rationality, 259; and Tunisian uprising, 1–2, 213; and U.S. labor movement, 46; as utilizing protest waves, 87; weak popular resistance to, 45; youth and minorities as damaged by, 45–46, 386

Nepal, 83, 88, 93, 94

Neruda, Pablo, 132

Netherlands, 120

New Left: as addressing dissatisfaction, not deprivation, 68–71; limited progress of, 9; Marcuse on, 3, 10–11, 16, 50, 67, 123, 233–239, 252, 261, 291; opposition of U.S. labor movement to, 46; politics within, 350; of the twenty-first century, 211, 256

news coverage: of Occupy, 171, 222; of police actions, 200; role of dominant media, 357–362. *See also* media spectacle(s); social media/new media; television coverage

The Newsroom (TV series), 365

Nietzsche, Friedrich, 138, 261, 392–394

"99 percent," 2, 10, 131, 138, 155, 221, 223, 346

Nobody, Adam, 187

nonnormative sexuality, 122, 123, 128

nonviolent demonstrations, 44, 140–141, 144, 188–190, 197; in Egypt and Tunisia, 43, 140, 218; Gandhi's method of, 226; historical roots of, 48; Marcuse on, 174, 396n29; as neutrality, 176; and Occupy, 44, 48, 49, 207; rhetoric of, 176, 186. *See also* violence

North African Arab uprisings, 212–217, 228. *See also* Arab Awakening/Arab Spring

nostalgia in postmodernism, 161

"A Note on Dialectic" (Marcuse), 310–311

Noys, Benjamin, 57

Nuit Debout, 14, 59

NYABC (New Yorkers against Budget Cuts), 42–43

Obama, Barack: and Keystone XL pipeline, 227; and labor unions, 346; national security actions of, 353–354; and neoliberalism, 42, 348; and Occupy Movement, 225, 347; and 2008 election, 212

OccupyMedia!, 253

Occupy movement: anti-intellectualism of, 50–51, 53; authenticity of, 59; bottom-up structure of, 224; and choice of term "occupy," 44, 71, 228; and class identity (99 percent), 10, 131; commitment of, to nonviolence, 48; compared to 1960s New Left, 3–4, 59, 68, 75; and documentation of police actions, 225–226; and general assembly model, 47, 95; as global movement, 2, 72, 228, 346; hypothetical Marcusean statement regarding, 74–75; labor movement solidarity with, 46; lack of organization within, 51; Left critique of, 16, 346–348; media coverage of, 138; and Obama, 225, 347; Occupy Berkeley, 205; Occupy Central, 41n35; Occupy Davis, 205; Occupy Everywhere, 211, 221, 223, 226; Occupy Los Angeles, 198, 200, 205; Occupy Oakland, 167, 171–172, 205, 362; Occupy Philadelphia, vii, 193–201, 204–207; Occupy Seattle, 41n36, 47–50; and other mobilizations, 6, 13, 76, 86–87; police overreaction to, 44–45; position and demands of, 49; public support for, 224–225; as radically inclusive, 130; successful containment of, 45, 345; targeting of politicians by, 227; timeline and structure of, 221–226; use of flash mobs by, 225–226; weaknesses of, 16, 50–51. *See also* mic check/people's mic; Occupy Wall Street

Occupy Wall Street: and changing political climate, 224–225; CrimethInc. letter to, 153; as first Occupy action, 2; focus of, against financial capitalism, 222; and general assembly model, 47; Marcuse on movements similar to, 70; police response to, 346; position and demands of, 49, 223, 346–347; public support for, 224, 346; and realizable utopia, 67; rejection of going national by, 348; results of, 348; role of Adbusters in, 72n14, 221; slogans of, 221, 223, 375–376; start of,

Occupy Wall Street (*continued*)
43–44, 346; use of flash mobs by, 225;
use of new media, social networking by,
222–225. *See also* mic check/people's mic;
Occupy movement
Olsen, Scott, 225
One-Dimensional Man (Marcuse), 7, 35, 37,
41, 166, 238, 389; on absence of representative institutions, 135; on "absolute
refusal," 129; on "aggressiveness," 164;
on art, 144; on capitalism and "one-
dimensional society," 31–33; catastrophic
messianism in, 288, 290–291, 293–294;
on comfortable "unfreedom," 167, 389; on
consumerism, 373, 383; on determined
negation, 244; on dialectical theory, 40,
49, 52, 241, 245; Dunayevskaya correspondence and, 310–312; on false realism and concreteness, 40, 49, 52, 314; on
freedom and consciousness, 139, 259; on
freedom *from* the economy, 30; Fromm
on, 293–294; on the Great Refusal, 86,
129–130, 259–262, 316–317, 390–391;
Heidegger's influence on, 230, 231; historical setting of, 64, 250; on internalization of masters' values, 393; on "is" and
"ought," 10, 12, 34, 137, 159, 174; Kellner
on, 390; on loss of catastrophic power,
296; on "obscenity," 163; on "outcasts
and outsiders," 140, 220; on "positive
thinking," 39; on "post-technological
rationality," 258; on prerequisites for
negating capitalism, 245; quoting Walter
Benjamin, 321n23; on "real spectre of
liberation," 134, 316, 320, 316–317; on
"refusing to play the game," 154; on
"repressive desublimation," 104, 123, 173;
speculating on loss of television, 296–
297; on survival of feudal society, 160; on
theoretical and practical reason, 232; on
validation of truth, 150; on values, 235
"On the Marionette Theater" (Kleist), 290
ontology of negativity, 55–56
Orpheus and Narcissus, 123, 126–127
Orwell, George, 296n51, 395
Osceola, x
"outcasts and outsiders," Marcuse on, 129,
140, 220
ownership, 103, 239, 266, 269, 271, 360,
365, 387

Paris Commune (1871), 47, 89–90, 140, 155

Paris Manuscripts (*Economic and Philosophical Manuscripts of 1844*) (Marx): on alienated labor, 300; on humanity, 291; Marcuse and, viii, 302–303, 306, 367; messianism in, 284; Sánchez Vázquez and, 342
Parsons, Lucy Gonzalez, x
participatory media fee, 256–257
passive tolerance, 184
past, recovering the, 288–289
Patch, Rashid, 172
Paul (Apostle), 150n80
Paz, Octavio, 335n13
Peng, Chen, 106
"people power" movements, 83, 87, 88, 218
People's Climate March, 156
PERF (Police Executive Research Forum),
195–198, 205
performance principle, 37, 39, 125–126, 247,
259, 260, 265, 295n50
phantasy, 141–143. *See also* fantasy
Philippines, 83, 87, 88, 93
"Philosophy and Critical Theory"
(Marcuse), 142
Philosophy of Mind (Hegel), 305, 307
Philosophy of Right (Hegel), 134
Pierce, Clayton, 14–15n43
Piketty, Thomas, 30n3, 36n24, 138n32
Pink Block, 144–145
pink tide, 274
pinkwashing, 120
PIPA (Preventing Real Online Threats
to Economic Creativity and Theft of
Intellectual Property Act), 227
Pippin, Robert, 150
piquetero road blockages, 267–268
Piven, Frances Fox, 193
play, 142–143, 152, 202, 253, 259, 265–266,
277, 280, 308
pleasure principle, 61, 260
Pleyers, Geoffrey, 5
Poland, Solidarity demonstrations in, 216
Polanyi, Karl, 355
police action against demonstrations:
compared to action against murderer,
73; Occupy Oakland, 225; Occupy
Philadelphia, 193–195, 197–205; police
"bipolar" strategy, 197–198; police brutality, 2, 141, 176, 186–189, 196, 223, 398;
unconstitutional arrests, 188, 196, 205,
206–207; use of bicycles, 199–201, 207;
use of horses, 201; use of pepper spray,
44–45; use of school buses, 199

political economy: alternative, 381; of capitalism, 5, 7, 360, 366; Chinese, 101; and cultural apparatus and communications, 357–360; Marcuse's Marxian, 30; and sexuality, 118–119

"political eros"/eros effect, 84–89

"Political Preface" (Marcuse), 19

politics of refusal, 55–56, 59, 65, 259–265, 272–274. *See also* Great Refusal concept

Polletta, Francesca, 12

Popkin, Jeremy, 285

populism, 46

"positing of presuppositions," 149

"positive thinking" in one-dimensional society, 39

postcapitalist society, 262, 300, 305, 329–330, 371, 377

Postmodernism (Jameson), 161, 163

"post-technological rationality," 258, 265

posttraditional and postnational identity formations, 324

poverty: abolishment of, 57, 397; and Chinese migration policy, 102; escalation of, 2; "heritage" of, 181–182; of indigenous people, 332; as intersectional, 118; and living wage, 344n1; and misery, 69; overcoming, 76; racialized, 141; as related to wealth production, 395; and social movements, 7; and stability, 76; and violence, 180

power and struggle, Frederick Douglass on, 72n13, 154, 391

precariat, 36, 42, 46, 53, 374, 382, 384, 386

Pringle, Tim, 113

prisons: and mass incarceration of Blacks and Latinos, 356; privatization of, 37

production process under civic culture, 32–33

professional revolutionists, 379, 384

prophetic messianism, 284–287, 289

Proudhon, Pierre-Joseph, 47

psychological theories of politics, 369–372

Puar, Jasbir, 119

"Punks, Bulldaggers, and Welfare Queens" (Cohen), 128

Pye, Lucian, 93

Quan, Jean, 195

Quechua, 270

Queers for Economic Justice, 118

queer theory and refusal, 118–130

"The Question Concerning Technology" (Heidegger), 231

Rabehl, Bernd, 330–331

Rabinbach, Anson, 288

Rabinkov, Salman, 285

race: and Haiti, ix–x; Marcuse and Fanon on, 320; Marcusean-influenced antiracist potential in Habermas, 326; multiracial democracy, 315; nonracial democracy, ix; racial bias in community economies, 266; racial capitalism, ix, 15, 398; racial domination, exclusion, and hierarchies, 36, 120, 122n12, 128, 129, 140, 185–186n22, 220, 355, 356, 369, 383; racial inequality, 7, 141; racial justice, 119; racial segregation, 10, 194, 345, 363, 373; racial superiority, 363, 372; racial toleration, 386; racial violence, 175, 184; and queer theory, 118, 120, 128; and species-being, 95; tokenism, 315. *See also* critical race and gender theory; gender and race apartheid; White supremacy

radicalism: diversion of working class from, 383; Fromm on Marcuse's radicalism, 293; *how* of radical change, 72; of left or right, 74; meaning of, 316; "misplaced radicalism," 37; and politics of refusal, 259; radical simplicity movement, 271; radical subjectivity, viii, 6, 10–11, 15, 67–71, 136, 301, 380, 391; and spontaneity, 261. *See also* subjectivity

Raleigh, North Carolina, demonstration, 347

Ramsey, Charles, 196–197, 200, 206

Reagan, Ronald, 364

"reality principle," 39, 141–142, 143, 265, 278, 292

Reason and Revolution (Marcuse), 296; on capitalism as dialectical, 243; on communicative reflection-into-another, 255–256; on determinate negation, 245, 256; on "essence," 151–152; on freedom, 134, 151; on Hegel, 241, 255, 303; influence of, on Dunayevskaya, 303; on the laboring classes, 310–311; on Marx/Marxism, 244, 303, 309n43; on nonintegrated outsiders, 316; preface to, 310–311

"Reclaiming Our Future" conference, vii

recuperating spaces of production, 274–278

Reddy, Chandan, 119

"redemption through sin," 289, 291

refusal, language(s) of, 2, 49, 144, 319, 390, 396

refusal and exodus, acts of, 264n40

refusal of nonexistence, 58, 140
Reich, Wilhelm, 124, 363–365, 369
reification versus dereification, 123, 230, 237, 238
Reitz, Charles, 151–152
religion: and "Asian" values, 93–94; and character structure, 371; as cultural apparatus, 361; and ideology, 371–372, 382–383, 386; and intersectionality, 119; and species-being, 95
The Religion of Reason (Cohen), 287
Rennick, Candace, 170–171
repression within discourse of tolerance, 206
repressive desublimation, 14, 61–62, 104, 123, 160, 164–167, 172–175
"repressive hypothesis," 124
"repressive modernization" in China, 99
"Repressive Tolerance" (Marcuse), 159, 173, 176, 193; on exercise of political rights, 173; and "radical right" strategies, 206; on state's use of tolerance, 201; on tolerance as serving oppressors, 188–189; on tolerating the intolerable, 176–179; on violence, 183–185
Republican Party, 42, 71, 78, 138n32, 224, 228n27, 348
rerationalizations of life, 269
restructuring, 12, 34, 63, 64, 395
Reuther, Walter, 349
revolution: in Arab world, 29, 43, 51, 54; Bernie Sanders and, 78; and Black art, ix; bourgeois, 164–165; Chris Hedges on, 379; cultural, 37, 99, 162, 175; in Eastern Europe, 84; Echeverría on, 334–336, 338–339; and existentialism, 317; French, 288, 340; Fromm on, 283, 286, 289, 291, 292, 293–294, 295, 297; global, 96; Gramsci on, 380–381; Haitian, ix–x; in Latin America, 13; Lukács on socialist, 230; and Marcuse's Great Refusal, 3, 5, 68, 78, 86, 95, 252, 261; Marxist, 239, 299, 307, 397; media coverage of, 211–228; Mexican, 333, 335n14; from 1960s perspective, 78; and queer politics, 118, 119, 123, 126; reform and, 338–339; "soil for revolution," 151; in Tunisia (Dignity Revolution), 1–2; use of term, 213–214n3; of values, 394–396; violence of, 181, 183–184, 191. *See also specific movements; works by Marcuse*
Revolutionary Anarchist Clown Bloc, 145

The Revolution of Hope (Fromm), 284, 286, 289, 292–294
Right, resurgence of the, 77
Right to the City Alliance, 71
Roach, Max, x
Robeson, Paul, x
Robinson, Cedric, viii
Robinson, Paul A., 122
robotic technologies, 40. *See also* automation
Romney, Mitt, 71
Rosenzweig, Franz, 284, 285
"Roundhouse" police station, Philadelphia, 202–204
Roy, Arundhati, 68
Royce, Josiah, 396n28
Ryan, Sid, 169–170

Saddam Hussein, 215
Sánchez Vázquez, Adolfo, 335, 336–337n15, 340–342
Sanders, Bernie, 74n22, 78, 352, 376, 387n40
San Francisco Bay Guardian, 195–196
Sargeson, Sally, 101
Sartre, Jean-Paul, 162, 318, 321–322, 327, 329n2
Schmitt, Carl, 173n47, 290
scholarship on contemporary social movements, 4–5
Scholem, Gershom, 284, 285, 288, 291–292
school buses, police use of, 199
schools, radical initiatives of, 268, 272–274, 292
scientific-technical rationality, 231
SDS (Students for a Democratic Society), 349
Seattle protests against the WTO (1999), 47, 87, 171, 353, 397–398
senses, emancipation of the, 62
September 11, 2001, attacks, 353–354, 356
sex, gender, and sexuality, 118–120
sexuality studies, 121–122
sexual repression, 62
Shen, Yuan, 99
The Shock Doctrine (Klein), 298
Shortbus (film), 161, 162n12
signs without organization, 346–348
Simmel, Georg, 379
Simmons, Karen, 205
Simone, Nina, x
The Simpsons (TV series), 364
singing in dark times, 156

Situationist International, 221, 223
16 Beaver Group, 272–273
slavery, 48, 152, 161n10, 285, 324, 348, 355;
    economic and social enslavement, 58,
    134, 151, 181–182, 244, 365, 398
Smaller Logic (Hegel), 309
social democracy, 252–253
Social Democratic Party (Germany), 252,
    286, 287, 288
socialism: betrayals in 1914 of, 286; bureau-
    cratic, 3; democratic, 256; as determinate
    negation of capitalism, 233; feminist, 125;
    and genuine revolution, 95; humanist,
    8; and LGBT rights, 118–119; Marcuse
    on feminism and, 125; Marx's critique
    of utopian, 376; and messianism, 287;
    and modernization, 99, 333; Nazism
    and promise of, 363; and Occupy, 50;
    potential for, 239, 244, 249; Soviet theory
    of, 300; state, 29, 31; and technology,
    234; youth support for, 376, 386. *See also*
    Sanders, Bernie
social media/new media, 197–198, 218,
    247; commodity and community of, 253;
    communicative reflection in, 255–256;
    coverage of police actions, 44, 199;
    defined, 241–242; dialectics of, 246–250,
    255–256; and Great Refusal, 250–257;
    Internet-based community projects, 268;
    Internet-based movements, 88, 111, 221–
    224, 384–385; Internet blackout against
    SOPA/PIPA, 227; and use of flash mobs,
    225. *See also* Internet; media spectacle(s)
social-natural democracy, 319
"social pact" between state, capital, and
    working class, 31
social wage cuts, 343–344
Society of the Spectacle (Debord), 212
solidarity: and alternative economy, 271;
    and Argentinian worker networks, 277;
    barriers to, 35, 38, 40; of Chinese work-
    ers, 113; and cooperation, 96; and a
    critical theory from the Americas, 338;
    demands for, 153; Dunayevskaya on
    how White racism undermines, 304; of
    Egyptians with protestors in Madison,
    Wisconsin, 212–213; and eros, 11, 96;
    Fanon on Marcuse's understanding of,
    316, 318; global, 156, 390; and Gwangju
    People's Uprising in South Korea (1980),
    89; as hallowed labor slogan, 344; and
    ideologies, 371–372; Marcuse on, 259–

260, 263n31, 265, 269, 276, 279, 397; be-
    tween movements, 212–213; and Occupy,
    45, 46, 49, 146, 151, 152, 199, 207; of po-
    lice, 188n35; postracist, postpatriarchal,
    postcolonial, 319; and religion, 372, 382;
    and resistance, 140, 390; and social inte-
    gration, 374
Solidarność (Solidarity) movement, 94, 216
Solnit, Rebecca, 48
Somers, Margaret, 345
"Some Social Implications of Modern
    Technology" (Marcuse), 303
SOPA (Stop Online Piracy Act), 227
The Sopranos (TV series), 365
Sorel, Georges, 289
South Korea, 83, 87, 88, 89–90, 94
South of the Border (film), 219
Soviet Marxism (Marcuse), 242, 305, 309–
    310, 353n12
Soviet Union: collapse of, 216–217, 353; as
    state-capitalist society, 300
Spade, Dean, 119
Spain: resistance in, 5, 29, 212–213, 222,
    270, 274, 386, 390; Podemos in, 251, 367,
    376, 383n31. *See also* Indignados (15-M
    Movement)
Spartacist uprising, viii, 7
species-being (*Gattungswesen*), 60, 95–97,
    287
spectacle. *See* media spectacle(s)
Spinoza, Baruch, 285
Spiral of Violence (Câmara), 181–182
"spirit," defined, 150
spontaneity, 14, 15, 16, 47, 85, 259, 261. *See
    also* "conscious spontaneity" of global
    protests
SP-SDF (Socialist Party–Social Democratic
    Federation), 291, 292
Squat!net autonomous infrastructures ini-
    tiative, 270
squatter community movements, 269–270
Stamper, Norm, 196–197
"state of exception," 290, 345
Stiglitz, Joseph, 42
Stone, Oliver, 219
stress epidemic, 77
strike(s): by capital, 351; in China, 110–114;
    general, 85, 225, 289, 362, 390; hunger,
    347; and resistance, 1, 7, 59, 88, 344n2,
    347; as sabotage, 348; violence against,
    354; wildcat, 35, 268, 301
student opposition, 67, 70, 71, 325

"subaltern communities" versus "sexual subcultures," 121
Subcomandante Marcos, 145, 332, 338
subjectivity, 361–366; and Chinese labor, 113–116; Gramsci on, 378, 380–381; and the Great Refusal, 389–391; Habermas on, 321, 325–326, 367; Holloway on, 60; Marcuse on, 57, 61–62, 74–75, 134–136, 220, 238, 243–246, 247–248, 396–397; Marx on, 360; negative, resistant, 56, 57, 60; in queer studies, 121; radical, revolutionary, viii, 6, 10–11, 15, 67–71, 136, 301, 391; rebellious, 238–240, 321, 325, 326; technological domination of, 39
suicides: in China, 104, 106–107, 111, 115; Marcuse on establishment framing of, 106; in India, 391; of queer youth, 122
sumak kawsay (buen vivir, good living), 270
Sumerian republican government, 93
surveillance, 2, 10, 38–40, 135, 354, 365
Sweezy, Paul, 358
Sylvia Rivera Law Project, 118
Syriza (Greece), 251, 256, 367, 376, 383n31

tactical frivolity, 144
Tahrir Square protests, 42–43, 51, 95, 140, 163, 213
Taiwan, 83, 87, 88, 93
Taksim Square, 95, 163
Tarnac Nine, 165n27
Tea Party, 43, 74, 224, 228
technē, 231–234
technology: as enabling utopia, 67; as functional and meaningful, 236–237; Heidegger on, 238–239; Marcuse on technological rationality, 234–235, 258–260; and Marcuse's "aesthetic Lebenswelt," 233; Marcuse's critique of, 229–238; negatives of, 51–52, 229, 235–236; positives of, 236; reappropriation of, 268–278
Tel Aviv, Israel, tent city, 213
television coverage: of arrests of demonstrators, 200; as cultural apparatus, 357; in Eastern bloc in 1980s, 216–217; Fox News, 224; of government statements, 202; hypothetical loss of, 296–297; as interpreting the world, 364–365; of political insurrection, 212–221. See also media spectacle(s)
terrorism as permanent enemy, 38
Thailand, 83, 88, 93

Thanatos (Freud), 220
Thatcher, Margaret, 12
A Theology of Liberation (Gutiérrez), 182–183
theory preceding knowledge, 139
Third World, 58; and collapse of Soviet empire, 353; and feminism, 118–119; Marcuse and, 8, 17, 75–76, 291; United States as part of, 95; uprisings against IMF in, 88–89
Thoreau, Henry David, 48
3M strategy, 195, 205–206; lessons learned from, 206–208; management, 195–198; meditation, 202–204; militarization, 198–201
Tibet, 83
time: "disposable," 273; prolongation of labor, 39; as vanquished by revolution, 288
Timoney, John, 168n33, 196
Tiqqun, 165
tolerance, 177–180, 189–190. See also "Repressive Tolerance" (Marcuse)
Toronto Freeskool, 272
Toronto G20 summit, 180, 186–191. See also G20 Toronto protests
total administration, 40, 45–52. See also administered society
totality, 60, 63, 220, 249, 255, 357
Touraine, Alain, 5
"A Toxic Work World," 76–77
tree of knowledge, eating from, 290
Troika (European Commission, European Central Bank, International Monetary Fund), 376n20
Trotsky, Leon, 300, 303
Trudeau, Justin, 190
Trump, Donald, 77–78, 352
truth: essence as truth of being, 151; existential, 233; and freedom, 361; as revealed in dreams, 154; speaking truth to power, 144, 153; versus success, 139, 150; true versus false consciousness, 137; Whitehead on, 143n59
TSCI (Toronto School of Creativity and Inquiry), 272–273
Tsipras, Alexis, 383n31
Tumblr, 221, 241
Tunisia: Bouazizi's self-immolation in, 1–2, 29, 226, 390–391; communist/socialist role in, 383–384; demonstra-

tions for democracy in, 1, 218, 383n31, 384; uprising and aftermath in, 43, 51, 213–214, 219. *See also* North African Arab uprisings

24 (TV series), 364–365

Twitter, 88, 216, 223, 247

UK Uncut, 42

unconstitutional arrests, 196, 205, 206–207

underdog, politics of the, 129

underprivileged. *See* deprived, Marcuse on the

unions. *See* labor movement

United States, 385–386; labor movement in, 36, 64, 344, 346, 350–353; permanent war status of, 357; Reagan's symbolism and neoliberalism in, 364; September 11 attacks and aftermath in, 353–354, 356; as Third World country, 95; TV and film narratives in, 364–365. *See also* Obama, Barack; Occupy movement

Universidad Trashumante (Argentina), 273

Uprising 2.0, 88

utopianism, 67, 273, 376–377

value, question of, 132

values, transvaluation of, 34, 392–396

Vancouver, 273

Velvet Revolution, 217

Venezuela, 256

Vietnam: and the Great Refusal, 2–3, 251; movements against war in, 7, 12, 59, 69–70n8, 88, 349, 356

Villaraigosa, Antonio, 197

violence: Câmara's First, Second, and Third Violence, 181–182, 188–189; Marcuse on, 72–74; by the oppressed, 160–161, 164–167; and the reproduction of labor, 164; of the state, 1, 2, 40, 44–45, 216; status quo as reproduced by, 175

voluntarism, 4, 13, 14, 15, 16, 91, 254. *See also* "conscious spontaneity" of global protests; spontaneity

Walker, Scott, 42–43, 212, 228, 346

Wallerstein, Immanuel, 96

Walmart, 105, 107

war: and catastrophe, 296; and media spectacle, 212, 215; Mills on, 354; nuclear, 31, 40; privatization of, 37–38; and prosperity, 87; as state policy, 356; utopia instead of, 67; welfare/warfare state, 33; and world "order," 395

wars of position and maneuver, Gramsci's concept of, 368, 381, 386, 388

waste, 7, 238, 387, 392, 396

waves of insurgency, 83–84, 86–87, 96, 115, 352–353. *See also* Asian Wave (1986–1992)

wealth: accumulation of, 109, 148, 155; and class conflict and integration, 383, 397; and culture, 93, 249, 272, 276, 376; and impoverishment, 2, 179, 243, 250, 395; inequality of, 30, 138, 148, 348; and the "1 percent," 2, 10, 36, 46, 148, 346, 376; and power, 76, 352, 387; and queer theory, 118; social, 69, 96, 148, 266, 307

Weather Underground, 292, 350

Weimar messianism, 284

Weingarten, Randi, 352

welfare state, 31–32, 35

Wells, Ida B., x

Wells Fargo, 224

West, Cornel, 318, 385

Wexler, Chuck, 195–198

White European Man, 316, 327–328

Whitehead, Alfred North, 143, 143n59, 261

White supremacy, 141, 373, 397, 398

Whitman, Walt, 160

WikiLeaks, 226, 384

Wikipedia, 227, 250

Williams, Eric, viii

Winston, Henry, x

The Wire (TV series), 365

Wittgenstein, Ludwig, 138

Woldenberg, José, 341

Wolf, Tom, viii

Wolff, Richard, 385

Wolin, Sheldon, 388n41

women: Black Feminism, ix–x; femininity and humanity, 125, 330; feminist socialism, 125; from Global South, 35; Marcuse on women's movement, 125; in Middle East and Latin America, 53; women's rights in China, 113. *See also* feminism

worker cooperatives, 274–278

Workers Battle Automation, 311

working class: Filipina domestic worker, 58; Marcuse on catalysts for, 9; as integrated into capitalism, 3, 9, 35; Keynesian "social pact" with, 31; in South Korea, 87; suicide among, in China, 107, 111,

working class (*continued*)
115; technicians, engineers as new, 71;
workplace takeovers, 274; "workspaces
without bosses," 277
World Bank, 96, 144, 196, 222
worldhood, 231
World War I, 30, 284, 286–287, 292
World War II, 7, 76, 245, 300, 344; post–
World War II era, 29, 31, 36, 46, 85, 303,
355
wretched of the earth, 314, 315, 316, 320,
327
Wretched of the Earth (Fanon), 321, 331
WTO (World Trade Organization), 45,
46, 96, 102, 196–197, 222, 353. *See also*
Seattle protests against the WTO (1999)

Young, Coleman, 350
young intellectuals and Marcuse, x–xi,
16–17, 67–71, 373, 386

You Shall Be as Gods (Fromm), 289
YouTube, 216, 247
Yue Yuen Industrial (Holdings) Ltd., 111–
112
Yugoslavia, 316

Zapatistas: and Echeverría, 332–337;
EZLN, 331, 333; horizontally controlled
economic systems of, 270; and paper
airplane letters, 145; resistance of, 140,
154, 332n8; and Sánchez Vázquez, 340–341.
See also Subcomandante Marcos
"zero-hours contracts," 64
Zevi, Sabbatai, 289, 291–292
Zhao Ziyang, 99
Zimmerman, George, 347
Žižek, Slavoj, 134, 137–138, 149, 150,
218–220
Zuccotti Park, 44, 49. *See also* Occupy Wall
Street

www.ingramcontent.com/pod-product-compliance
Lightning Source LLC
Chambersburg PA
CBHW021806270326
41932CB00007B/76